Microsoft®

PROGRAMMING MICROSOFT® .NET XML WEB SERVICES

Damien Foggon, Daniel Maharry,
Chris Ullman, and Karli Watson

PUBLISHED BY
Microsoft Press
A Division of Microsoft Corporation
One Microsoft Way
Redmond, Washington 98052-6399

Foggon, Damien.
Programming Microsoft .NET XML Web Services / Damien Foggon, Daniel Maharry, Chris Ullman, and Karli Watson.
p. cm.
Includes index.
ISBN 0-7356-1912-3
1. Microsoft .NET. 2. XML (Document markup language) 3. Internet Programming. I. Maharry, Daniel. II. Ullman, Chris. III. Title.

QA76.76.H94F65 2003
005.2'76--dc21 2003048711

Printed and bound in the United States of America.

1 2 3 4 5 6 7 8 9 QWT 8 7 6 5 4 3

Distributed in Canada by H.B. Fenn and Company Ltd.

A CIP catalogue record for this book is available from the British Library.

Microsoft Press books are available through booksellers and distributors worldwide. For further information about international editions, contact your local Microsoft Corporation office or contact Microsoft Press International directly at fax (425) 936-7329. Visit our Web site at www.microsoft.com/mspress. Send comments to *mspinput@microsoft.com*.

Acquisitions Editor: Anne Hamilton
Project Editor: Kathleen Atkins
Technical Editor: Donnie Cameron
Copyeditor: Ina Chang
Principal Compositor: Dan Latimer
Interior Graphic Designer: James D. Kramer
Interior Artist: Michael Kloepfer
Proofreader: nSight, Inc.
Indexer: Bill Meyers
Cover Designer: Methodologie, Inc.

Body Part No. X09-45920

Table of Contents

Acknowledgments

Damien Foggon

So many people and so little space.

Thanks to Dan for bringing this up—even if he was wearing a very loud Hawaiian shirt at the time—and to Chris for having a computer that breaks down more than mine does. Thanks to Anne and Kathleen for giving us this opportunity to write a book and for not screaming and shouting too much when we missed deadlines.

Thanks to Mum who asked for nothing but gave everything. To Granddad. To Jill, even if she did get to see New Kids on the Block before I got to see Iron Maiden. To the lads for being around when I needed to let off steam. And finally to Gran—for love and support in everything I ever did. Always missed.

Dan Maharry

Thanks to Chris and Damien for keeping up, Anne and Kathleen for trusting three guys who hadn't a clue when they started, James and Niels for their wisdom, Karli for bailing Chris out, Aaron and Simon for their knowledge, DaveB for saying no, DaveS for saying yes, the house for putting up with me, and finally, the makers of Red Bull.

Big hugs to Jane and my family.

All chapters were planned and written at an altitude of about 20 feet. To understand the panic inherent in writing a book on a subject you know nothing about to begin with, check out *http://www.hmobius.com/blog*. The second edition will be even better. Contact Dan at danm@hmobius.com.

Chris Ullman

Thanks to Dan and Damien for making this happen, to Anne and Kathleen for still believing it would happen even when nothing was appearing weeks after we said it would, to Karli for picking up the slack I left, to Donnie for making this consumable by fellow developers and other human beings, and last to my wife, Kate, for keeping me calm, rational, and focused enough to complete it.

Karli Watson

Thanks, always, to Donna.

Introduction

In the film *Tron*, an evil force called the Master Control Program gains strength by systematically assimilating other programs across the worldwide networks. The *Terminator* depicts the same sort of hostile takeover mentality: the Terminator's creator, Skynet, gains consciousness as scientists hook together systems around the world and these systems begin to work together. While we all hope that such scenarios won't prove to be prescient, in the spirit of mutual trust and cooperation we're still trying to open up the terabytes of legacy data and the functionality of current systems to a worldwide network. The obstacles we face in this effort might not have indestructible exoskeletons like Arnie's, but we still haven't solved the problem of how to connect the dozens of incompatible operating systems, protocols, and file systems.

One possible solution lies with XML Web services. The idea of augmenting your applications, whether desktop or Web-based, with online information has long since been put into practice. From news sites that share daily headlines with each other as RSS feeds to more interesting ideas like Philip Greenspun's Wealth Clock (*http://philip.greenspun.com/WealthClock*), developers have been propagating and using online resources since 1995.

Resource sharing and system interoperability have gained tremendous importance over the last few years, but the basic ideas for achieving those goals have remained the same during that time. Those goals are just a bit easier to achieve today. Amazon.com, for example, provides a set of Web services to retrieve book information directly from its databases so we don't have to scrape it off book pages with regular expressions. Requesting data from Amazon.com is still a matter of sending text over the wire, but the text now means more than "Give me the following page."

The beauty of keeping this more meaningful interaction between online applications spelled out in simple text is in its inclusiveness. Any system—current or legacy—can send text over the wire, and as long as the meaning of the text is understood, we have the basis for universal system interoperation. The potential of this approach is so great that Microsoft has thrown its weight behind the advancement, making Web services a focal point of the Microsoft .NET Framework. Together with companies such as IBM and Sun Microsystems and the open source community, Microsoft is pushing us toward a Web services utopia.

Who Should Read This Book

The .NET Framework has been in use for a good two years already, and a great many people are now comfortable developing with it in Microsoft Visual C# or Microsoft Visual Basic .NET. This book is designed for those developers, and in particular those who've worked with Web services. This book is not for those who want to learn about Web services completely from scratch, although everything you need to know is contained herein. The only tutorial is in Chapter 1. The rest of the book, as the title suggests, is a programming reference for those who are already familiar with .NET and Web services. The book has three main parts. (A fourth part is devoted to appendixes.)

- Part I looks at the standards that make up the Web service base platform and the classes that provide the functionality of the Microsoft ASP.NET Web service framework.
- Part II explains how to build .asmx services on these core technologies and how to tailor clients to fit any given scenario. It then looks at the functionality available in the .NET Framework that allows you to extend services to be stateful, scalable, transactable, and secure. You'll also learn why you might want the extra flexibility of writing raw services rather than .asmx services in certain circumstances.
- Part III examines the new developments from Microsoft in the form of Web Services Enhancements (WSE) and the Global XML Web Services Architecture (GXA) and looks at what the future is bringing to the world of Web services.

In the interest of keeping this book slightly smaller than the Bible, we're aiming it squarely at .NET developers. The examples will be mostly in C#. As a brief nod to the world of COM, we'll look at building a COM-based client for a .NET Web service with the SOAP Toolkit in Chapter 8. If you're building Web services with Visual C++ and ATL Server, let this book encourage you to start working with .NET.

Sample Code

Because the book is aimed at intermediate to advanced developers, it's a complete reference to the standards and .NET classes at the heart of Web service development. However, for the sake of readability, it doesn't contain many complete code listings for the examples. We'll focus on illustrating on how a specific feature works, and you can find the complete code and working examples on the companion Web site. For example, we won't look more than once at the code that Microsoft Visual Studio .NET autogenerates when you build a Web service project.

You'll find the book's companion Web site, including the complete code listings for the examples, at *http://www.microsoft.com/mspress/books/6707.asp*. See the instructions on that site for how to install the samples on your own PC. Check the site for corrections and updates to the book as well.

Future Developments

Of course, a printed book can only present information that's accurate at a certain point in time. C# and .NET won't change often, but the open standards that enable them will change from time to time, as will the WSE, UDDI Server SDK, and GXA standards, to name but a few. Don't forget to supplement what you read here with up-to-date information from the MSDN Web services home page (*http://msdn.microsoft.com/webservices*), GotDotNet (*http://www.gotdotnet.com*), and other Web service reference sites.

System Requirements

To use the sample applications available for download, you'll need to have Visual Studio .NET Professional Edition. You can get a 60-day trial version from Microsoft at *http://msdn.microsoft.com/vstudio/productinfo/trial/default.asp*. We use the .NET Framework version 1.1 and Visual Studio .NET 2003 in this book.

You also need a computer capable of running Visual Studio .NET. The Visual Studio .NET Web site at *http://msdn.microsoft.com/vstudio* specifies the following minimum configuration:

- PC with a Pentium II–class processor, 450 MHz
- Microsoft Windows 2000 Professional or Advanced Server with Service Pack 3, Windows XP Professional with Service Pack 1, or Windows Server 2003
- Minimum RAM requirements:
  - Windows Server 2003: 256 MB
  - Windows XP Professional: 160 MB
  - Windows 2000 Professional: 96 MB
  - Windows 2000 Server: 192 MB

- Hard disk with 3.5 GB free on installation drive, which includes 500 MB on system drive
- CD-ROM or DVD-ROM drive
- Super VGA (800 x 600) or higher-resolution monitor with 256 colors
- Microsoft Mouse or compatible pointing device

Please note that Visual Studio .NET is our recommended integrated development environment (IDE) for this book, but if you haven't got the resources to run it, Microsoft also provides a free tool called Web Matrix that will do the job just fine and will run on anything that can cope with .NET. You can download Web Matrix from *http://www.asp.net*.

Corrections, Comments, and Help

Every effort has been made to ensure the accuracy of this book and the contents of the companion Web site. Microsoft Press provides corrections for books through the World Wide Web at the following address:

http://www.microsoft.com/mspress/support

To connect directly to the Microsoft Press Knowledge Base and enter a query regarding a question or an issue that might have, go to

http://www.microsoft.com/mspress/support/search.asp

If you have comments, questions, or ideas regarding this book or the companion content, or questions that aren't answered by querying the Knowledge Base, please send them to Microsoft Press by e-mail to

mspinput@microsoft.com

or by postal mail to

Microsoft Press
Attn: *Programming Microsoft .NET XML Web Services* Editor
One Microsoft Way
Redmond, WA 98052-6399

Please note that product support is not offered through the preceding mail address. For product support information, please visit the Microsoft Support Web site at

http://support.microsoft.com.

Part I

The Core

1 Web Services 101

The Microsoft .NET Framework has provoked divergent opinions since its beta release at the Microsoft Professional Developers Conference (PDC) in July 2000. Microsoft developers consider it a breath of fresh air and a great foundation on which to program. To open source and Java developers, it's simply Microsoft's attempt to catch up with Java, although many in this group admit a grudging respect for its standards-based core. Managers, who see it as just another toy for developers to play with, are wondering, "Why can't we stick to the old way? There's nothing tangible that distinguishes a .NET application from a COM-based one anyway, is there?"

As a .NET developer reading this book, you already know the answer to the managers' questions. The .NET Framework improves on Microsoft's COM architecture for applications and compares favorably with every other development platform in use. We could spend the next 10 pages listing its benefits and disadvantages, but rather than repeat what's been said several hundred times by others, we'll spend the next 15 chapters looking at just one big plus—Web services.

Web services have been sufficiently misunderstood that their uptake has been slower than might have been expected. However, they represent the next step in a lot of efforts—distributed computing, interoperability, Internet-based applications, access to legacy data…the list goes on. But, like the main character in *Rocky* at the beginning of the movie, the technology has yet to prove itself the world-beater that it is. For the past few years, rather than creating the killer Web service application, the developers and standards bodies have focused their efforts on strengthening the underlying technologies on which Web services work. As the plumbing nears completion and we wait for the eBay of the Web services world to appear, now is the time to start learning about this maturing technology.

Our view is perhaps better explained by a look at the evolution of the Web services architecture, the technologies it has been designed to reinvigorate and the problems it has been created to solve, and the questions the architecture itself has asked. You'll see why Web services had to be invented and what role they play in today's systems.

From Past to Present Platform

In the beginning, the universe was created. This has made a lot of people very angry and been widely regarded as a bad move.
—Douglas Adams

Like all things (even the universe), the Internet and the World Wide Web were not created perfect. When Tim Berners-Lee invented HTML and HTTP in 1990, he did it to make academic papers and other texts easily available to those who wanted to read them. This humble aim is hardly recognizable in the powerful, glitzy, customized, interactive sites of today, as companies sell their wares and plumb the depths of their corporate data for thousands of clients at a time. Still, the goal of data dissemination holds true. Needless to say, HTML 1.0 wasn't designed with online markets in mind. Only in its sixth incarnation—XHTML 2.0—which came into being while this book was being written (*http://www.w3c.org/TR/xhtml2*)—does it cater to the current and future needs of the Web development community. The same is true of HTTP 1.0. HTTP 1.1 plus authentication digest and cookies, along with HTTPS, provide the backbone of today's online community.

A great deal has happened to HTML since its inception. Central to that development has been a change of thinking. In 1993, a Web site was thought of as a collection of associated pages, much like a book or a thesis. Today, a Web site is thought of as a Web-based application.

Web Applications

Faster than the adoption of the Web by users was the adoption of server-side programming for the Web by developers. Client-side scripting let us give users the impression of some personalized interaction when they visited a site, when in truth there was little, if any. The Common Gateway Interface (CGI) gave developers control over what users saw, but it was difficult to learn and left everything beyond the basic input/output connection between client and server to the programmer. It was only in 1996 when Philip Carmichael designed and implemented version 1.0 of Active Server Pages (ASP) that we had something to sink our teeth into. Then version 2.0 arrived the following year as part of the Windows NT Option Pack, and we realized just how much we could actually do.

What ASP and its contemporaries—JavaServer Pages (JSP), PHP, and Cold-Fusion—offered developers was the ability to glue all the resources they had for traditional server-based applications to a Web-based front end. Web sites were no longer simple collections of single pages. They had become individual applications whose appearance and content could be tailored to the user. Developers had a quick and reliable way of maintaining the state of a user's session across the stateless HTTP protocol and could dynamically generate content tailored to that user by asking for and reacting to the user's input. They could make use of information stored in databases and create compiled business components on the server side, leading to faster reactions to a user's clicks and requests. They could design these components *just like any other three-tier application*. (See Figure 1-1.)

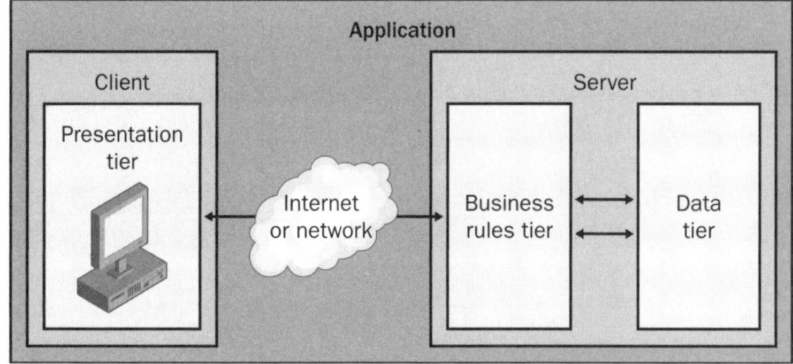

Figure 1-1 A Web application as a three-tier application

That we could approach Web development much as we did a windowed application was a revelation. Very quickly, huge sites (and not just e-commerce ones) appeared on the Web, enabled by server-side technology. They kick-started the dot-com boom.

XML

Soon after he published HTML 1.0, Tim Berners-Lee realized that the Web was becoming a digital Wild West with different lawmen (browsers, companies) making their own laws and developers struggling to provide the same sites to users under different jurisdictions. In 1994, he and Michael Dertouzos founded the World Wide Web Consortium (W3C) with the purpose of creating open standards for the Web that everyone should adhere to instead of building and using their own technologies. HTML was one of the first Web technologies they published as a standard (with HTML 3.2 coming in 1997), and a little over a year later, in February 1998, they released version 1.0 of the XML specification.

XML has been a cornerstone in the development of the programmable Internet, thanks to what it does and what it doesn't do. Instead of being designed for a specific purpose, like HTML, which is designed to identify and mark up the various elements in a Web page, XML is designed as a metalanguage. That is, it provides the foundation for marking up anything we want—record collections, books, mathematical equations, chemical formulas, the contents of our databases, and so on—in plain text. By using XML to mark up data, we can make that data available in a platform-neutral format that can be shared online regardless of the operating system, database, and firewalls the host platform uses. All that's required of the receiving system is the ability to parse the XML data and act on it. The parsing implies a slight performance hit, of course, but the gains of universally acceptable data far outweigh the hit.

A few other problems needed getting around, of course. The first was simply that two XML grammars might define a tag with the same name. How would parsers translate the tag? Namespaces were introduced to solve that problem, offering ways to define an unambiguous context within which to place tags. Together, XML and namespaces form the basis of all XML standards.

Even text itself presented developers with a few obstacles. Base64 encoding offered one solution for sharing pictures and sounds, but what about the encoding of the text itself? Every machine running Windows presented at least two encoding schemes—MS-DOS codepages and ANSI encoding—and many localized character sets. The solution was to base XML on the then-current version of Unicode (2.0) and have XML documents declare what character set and language their text was written in. XML parsers are required to understand Unicode and its most important encodings, so data can be safely exchanged between platforms. Now that Unicode 3.1 is stable, XML also needs to be updated, and sure enough, XML 1.1 is being prepared accordingly.

XML Schemas

The biggest issue with XML is making sure that both sender and recipient agree on the grammar of the XML so they know how to mark it up at one end and parse it back into text at the other. XML itself has a few rules—for example, a document is well-formed only if no elements overlap—but only a few. The rest of the grammar was initially laid down in Document Type Definitions (DTDs), an idea inherited from XML's parent language, Standard Generalized Markup Language (SGML). By creating a DTD, you specified the order in which data elements would appear in your document, the attributes they could be given, and the child elements they could have. An XML document could then be checked and validated against the DTD while being parsed.

Like every other standard we've mentioned in this chapter, however, DTDs were only the first step toward the ideal and were far from perfect. They allowed us only to define content in terms of parsed or unparsed text, and, more important, they didn't give us a means to map content to programming language data types such as integer or Boolean. Unless the systems on each end of a data exchange use the same means to convert numbers, dates, or Boolean values to text, we can't guarantee how well, if at all, they will interoperate.

In 2001, the W3C released a successor to DTDs called XML Schemas that addressed the limitations in their predecessor (*http://www.w3.org/XML/Schema*). The ability of XML Schemas to strongly type the data being passed as XML is very good. There are 44 base types (known as *XSD types* from the abbreviation for XML Schema Definition language) from which you can define any complex type for a piece of data and convert the data to and from text in a standardized manner. Indeed, as you read this, many W3C XML standards are being rewritten to make use of the strong typing made possible by XML Schemas.

Distributed Applications

Parallel to the development of Web-based applications, the industry also made inroads into the construction of distributed applications. *Distributed* in this case meant applications splitting their workload privately and securely over more than one machine using their system's own Remote Procedure Call (RPC) protocol to call methods and send information from machine to machine to machine as if they were all the same machine.

However, not for want of trying, the architectures and frameworks on which distributed applications were built—DCOM, CORBA, Java RMI—worked exclusively with themselves. The machines were tightly coupled together, and each architecture had its own RPC protocol, message format, and message description language. That is, an application written in CORBA would not cooperate with—or, indeed, understand—the same application written in DCOM or Java RMI on another machine, and vice-versa.

More important, your machines' setups had to be almost identical to get a distributed application to work at all. Not only did all three architectures exist on several operating systems, but you also faced an uphill struggle to reconcile different data types, security systems, and debugging environments. For Java users, this was slightly less of a problem, but in general, such applications weren't as distributable as you might have wished.

Building the Platform

Rather than trying to build a replacement for distributed application frameworks and protocols, those working to evolve the Web application beyond *n*-tier applications realized they could take the idea of a distributed application's binary calls across machine boundaries and turn them into platform-neutral calls—matching a Web application's indifference to platform and operating system. By 1998, the term *Web services* had been coined by either Andrew Layman or John Montgomery of Microsoft (they both think the other guy did it) to characterize this Web-based framework, and the model for the platform that enabled this ability was given some serious thought. Like any other distributed application framework, it needed the following:

- A platform-independent format language for structured data exchange
- A way of describing the structure of the data being exchanged
- A standard method of packaging the data for transmission over the Internet
- A way for Web services to describe their public interface to clients
- A framework for programmatically locating Web services via their capabilities or description

The model was sound, but of course large pieces of it didn't exist yet. Developers already had XML and XML Schemas for the transmission and description of data, and they had HTTP as a transport protocol. All of these were common to all systems, but how could they transform RPC calls over a proprietary protocol into something any system could receive and understand?

SOAP

The answer once again was to use XML, and in 1999 version 0.1 of the Simple Object Access Protocol (SOAP) was released by Don Box, Tim Ewald, and a few others. Now in version 1.2, SOAP describes a message framework for a function call and answer from one machine to another in the manner of RPC but formatted as an XML text stream rather than as a binary call. A SOAP message, be it a request or a response, is written in plain XML text and adheres to the SOAP standard, so any system can understand what it says and act accordingly. SOAP 1.2 even caters to the serialization of complex objects into text-based XSD-typed collections of their properties. Thus you can make calls in SOAP to any remote method regardless of the complexity of the method's parameters or return type.

SOAP has developed rapidly since its inception, but it has stuck to one of its goals—to keep things simple. You'll see how simple a little later on.

WSDL and UDDI

With a way for client and service to converse and exchange data, the next question was how to describe the interface between the two and the required resources: the type and structure of the calls, required parameters, return values, protocol bindings, and so on. Another XML grammar called Web Services Description Language (WSDL) was developed for this task. However, unlike SOAP, WSDL is not so simple that you can write a WSDL document in a text editor. Instead, most Web service toolkits contain a tool that generates the WSDL description of a service and its methods for you. WSDL does perform the task it was designed for, but it is still evolving and becoming (we hope) more straightforward to use. We'll look at it in detail in Chapter 3.

With WSDL able to describe the service details to potential clients, all that was needed was a way to discover that description once the service was published. In other words, Web search engines tailored specifically to locating services and their WSDL were required. The means to build them arrived in the form of Universal Description, Discovery, and Integration (UDDI).

UDDI is the standard for Web service cataloging. Much like a business directory, a UDDI server lets you store the contact locations of your Web service, a broad description of the Web service's purpose, and the location of the service's WSDL documents. For example, you can create a Web service to return shipping costs for DVDs, return a weather report, or return the string *'Hello World'*. Then you can create an entry on a UDDI server to let the world know about your Web service.

Developers looking for a service with certain functionality can also use UDDI servers to help them find what they seek. For these clients, the servers act as an open directory supporting idle browsing and directed searches by name, business type, or binding template. If the developer finds a matching service, he can follow the link to the service's WSDL document for more information.

So Where Are We Now?

Every platform and development language now has some effort ongoing toward the use of Web services. It wasn't difficult to see that Web services could affect a great many systems, be they Internet, intranet, or extranet connected. The applications are not limited to returning simple information or performing simple functions, as you can see in Figure 1-2.

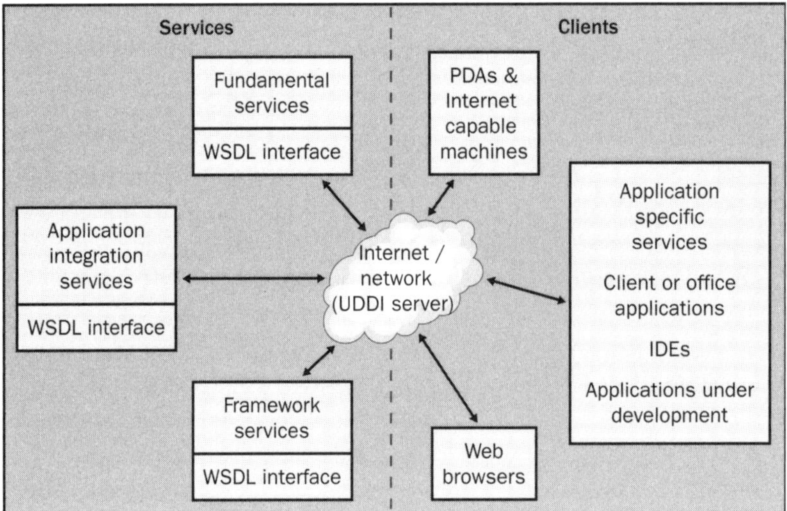

Figure 1-2 Web services can be at the heart of everything.

The continuing growth of available bandwidth and network communication speed across LANs, WANs, and the Internet means that calls to such services will not take very long. Legacy data systems can be integrated into enterprise LANs at much less cost than having their data ported to a more contemporary setup. Businesses can expose their information and expert systems to the public and other companies, and they can expose additional functionality as Web services as well. Employees working off site can use their company's system through a Web service interface. When a company updates its system, those consuming its services can make use of the updates automatically. Unlike components in DCOM applications, which talk to each other over the wire and nothing else, these Web services have taken the concepts of application service providers, distributed applications, open standards, and platform agnosticism and rolled them all into one grand scheme. In short, they have the potential to alter the way we think about and develop applications.

With the plumbing (XML, SOAP, WSDL, UDDI, HTTP) more or less complete, the universal adoption of Web services is assured as long as those developing the applications keep to the following three tenets:

- Systems are only loosely coupled together by nothing more than SOAP messages transmitted over HTTP or another open transport protocol (such as TCP or SMTP).
- A service must be described in a widely supported open interface definition language (such as WSDL).

- If service and client need to exchange data, the exchange must be done in a universal data format with agreement on how data types are serialized (using XML and XML Schemas, for example).

With Web service toolkits appearing for most development platforms, programmers now have the option of either working with the plumbing directly or using the APIs for boilerplate code. It's an interesting time, and nowhere more so than in the Microsoft camp. First they gave us the SOAP Toolkit for COM developers, and now we have .NET.

.NET

When Microsoft announced .NET as the replacement for COM and DCOM, one new feature it placed front and center was its intrinsic support for Web services. Whereas the SOAP Toolkit gave COM developers the ability to create and consume Web services, the .NET Framework and Visual Studio .NET made it considerably easier to do both. The creation and transmission of a request to a Web service was reduced to a single method call if you chose to leave it as such. The .NET Web service classes are also open enough that you can alter almost any aspect of a call or XML if you want.

Web services are not just a part of the .NET Framework; they're at the heart of Microsoft's strategy for future application development. Microsoft's *n*-tier design for enterprise applications hasn't changed the division between data, business logic, and presentation logic, but it has refined the categorization of that logic into seven service layers. Figure 1-3 shows the .NET model for a distributed enterprise application.

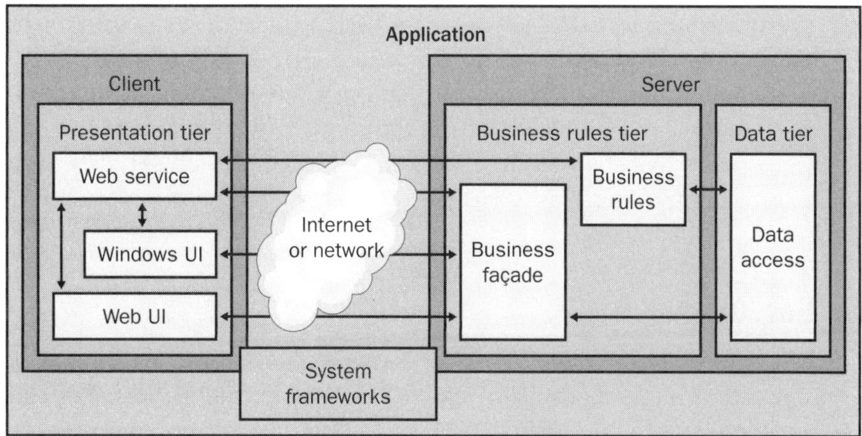

Figure 1-3 The model for a .NET distributed enterprise application

In this model, the Web services layer acts as an intermediary between the presentation and business rules tiers, receiving and returning input and data from clients and acting accordingly. Of course, this assumes that the presentation and business rules tiers are on different machines that are connectable over some type of network. If they're both on the same machine, the Business façade layer takes on this middleman role.

One of the first products Microsoft tried to bring out under the .NET banner was a set of consumer-oriented Web services that replaced and enhanced the Microsoft Passport and Wallet products. However, .NET My Services, as it was known, was rejected by potential users, who were not convinced that Microsoft could provide and be trusted with a secure central data store on which the services would run.

Public trust aside, the protracted rollout of .NET-based servers and applications means that the Microsoft world will be a place where almost every document is in XML and every server can expose some of its functionality as a Web service that applications can make use of remotely. As far as Microsoft is concerned, interoperability is the key to the future.

Web Service Scenarios

Everyone has an answer to the question "What is a Web service?" but at least you can now see where Web services fit into the grand scheme of things and can settle on a definition of your own. Here, we define a Web service as *a remotely accessible application component that listens for certain text-based requests, usually made over HTTP, and reacts to them*. Web services might not return results in the same way, and what the request is for is irrelevant. Similarly, a service might be used internally by a single application or exposed externally over the Internet for use by any number of applications. What matters is the agnostic nature of the request and its handling.

In practice, there are three general types of Web services: simple services, application integration services, and framework services. We'll look at each in turn.

Simple Services

The most basic premise for Web services is to provide a simple piece of functionality to the client: data retrieval or simple calculations. For example, an e-commerce site might allow a client to query the shipping cost for a given number of items or query for further details about an item. The workings behind the service might be complex, but its purpose is quite straightforward. We'll look at a few very simple services later in this chapter.

Application Integration Services

As networks and Internet connections get faster, companies are taking advantage of the increased bandwidth by spreading out their applications and resources over networks and locales. Several servers can talk to each other autonomously and to other applications as well. This integration is fine within a company that uses the same kind of systems, but what if companies want to share their resources with other companies? Common sense would say that their systems would not be instantly compatible.

One fundamental point about the Web service platform is that any machine can expose Web services to and consume Web services from various other platforms—something that cannot be said for any other technology that enables distributed applications. Application integration, or middlemen, services work as intermediaries between applications that wouldn't normally be able to talk with each other because they were written for different platforms, use different component architectures, and so on. Their functionality or data can be exposed through a set of Web services. Composite applications can then be created on one central system that knows the calls to make to the services to get the information they need from the various systems.

Framework Services

The idea of Web services as application add-ins probably shouldn't surprise anyone. The concept of a bolt-on component that provides additional functionality to an application isn't new, but it fits the way Web services work to a tee. Consider for a moment the general characteristics of Web services—loosely coupled, omnipresent thanks to permanent Internet connections—and you can see how they could be used in the same way as add-ins but on the hosting server rather than on the client.

These characteristics of Web services, along with their platform-agnosticism, means that a developer need only write one plug-in for the application regardless of the platform it runs on as long as the Web service interface fits in with the framework laid down by the application. And because the code for the add-in is centralized on the server rather than on the client, deploying an update to the code is a matter of making it live on the server rather than giving it to all clients.

The Microsoft BizTalk Framework already supports this kind of "plug-in" solution. The workflow solutions that a developer creates against BizTalk allow for the inclusion of Web service plug-ins to mirror the addition of new decisions and expansions to already established processes.

This concept also mirrors neatly the continuing development of XML grammars for various vertical markets—finance, bioinformatics, chemistry, and so on. Consider the use of service plug-ins in a situation where a finance package is given information formatted using a schema other than its default. A service plug-in can be called on to transform the information from one markup language to another (using XSLT, for example).

Web Services vs .NET Remoting

This book is very pro–Web services, as it should be, but it's worth reiterating that Web services are not a substitute for a full-fledged distributed application built using DCOM, RMI, or the .NET equivalent, .NET remoting. There are very good reasons why one might use remoting or an equivalent model over Web services as the basis for a solution:

- **Performance** Web services work over open standards, which take a lot of work to adhere to. For example, converting messages to and from XML on each side of the network takes a lot of work. Likewise, using HTTP as the transport protocol is relatively slow, even on a LAN.
- **Security** Web services are not very secure yet. Even though calls might be made over HTTPS and new ideas for secure communication appear quite frequently, there is no security standard and little help to fall back on if things go wrong.
- **Control** Not having to adhere to standards means you have greater control over your application and can play to the framework's strengths. In .NET, for example, you can use data types that don't serialize faithfully into XSD types and back, customize the communications infrastructure, and optimize the application as you see fit.

If the various endpoints of a distributed application are running on the same platform, there's no need to worry about the agnostic advantages of Web services. You can instead take advantage of the native RPC calls that remoting makes without having to worry about prior parsing and reparsing, and you can make some useful performance improvements. Likewise, you can lock down a remoted application with Windows-based and code-based security measures more tightly than you can a Web services–based application.

Developing a Web Service

Now to the nitty-gritty of Web services: how do you create one and then get an application to make use of it? What tools do you use?

Truth be told, although we work with trivial code for demo purposes, a basic text editor such as Notepad can do the job. Likewise, you can use any tool you'd usually use for .NET development to work with services—Emacs, Dreamweaver MX, CodeWarrior. However, we'll use Visual Studio .NET throughout the book for examples of larger projects that favor the creation and consumption of Web services. As you'd expect, Visual Studio .NET helps a great deal in the creation of boilerplate code and easy-to-manage projects, and it provides a lot of help in packaging up code for deployment elsewhere. We'll look at the Web service–specific features of Visual Studio .NET as we go.

A Simple Example in Notepad

We'll start with a quick example in Notepad to prove that, as with ASP.NET pages, we don't have to have a huge IDE to develop a Web service. A quick trawl of the UDDI servers out there reveals well over 200 Web services named Hello World or Test; rather than follow the trend, we'll build something just as simple but a bit more fun. So fire up Notepad and type the following:

```
<%@ WebService Language="C#" Class="SimpleServices" %>

using System;
using System.Web.Services;

[WebService(Namespace="http://www.notashop.com/wscr",
            Description="SimpleService1")]

public class SimpleServices : System.Web.Services.WebService
{
    [WebMethod(Description="A first warning")]
    public string WakeUp(string yourName)
    {
        return "Wake up " + yourName + ". The Matrix has you";
    }
}
```

Or, in Visual Basic .NET, type this:

```
<%@ WebService Language="VB" Class="SimpleServices" %>

Imports System
Imports System.Web.Services
```

```
<WebService(Namespace:="http://www.notashop.com/wscr", _
            Description:="SimpleService1")> _
Public Class SimpleServices
    Inherits System.Web.Services.WebService

    <WebMethod(Description:="A first warning")> _
    Public Function WakeUp(ByVal yourName As String) As String
        Return "Wake up " + yourName + ". The Matrix has you"
    End Function
End Class
```

Create the directory structure wscr\01 under the root folder of your Web server, and save the code as simple1.asmx in the 01 folder. Now start your browser and navigate to your new file at *http://localhost/wscr/01/simple1.asmx*. You'll find that Microsoft Internet Information Services (IIS) has generated a test page for the service, as shown in Figure 1-4.

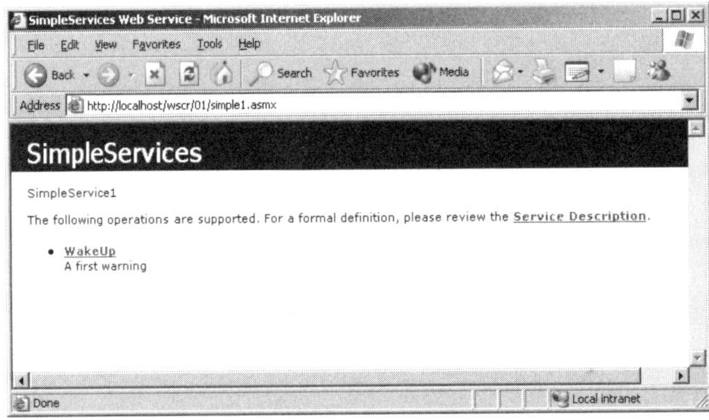

Figure 1-4 The test page for our simple1.asmx service

The test page holds entries for each method the service makes public, so in this case, there's just a single entry for the *WakeUp* method we've defined. Click it, and you'll see a form in which you can set the value of the *WakeUp* method's *yourName* parameter and an Invoke button to send your request to the service. The response we receive is in XML, as shown in Figure 1-5.

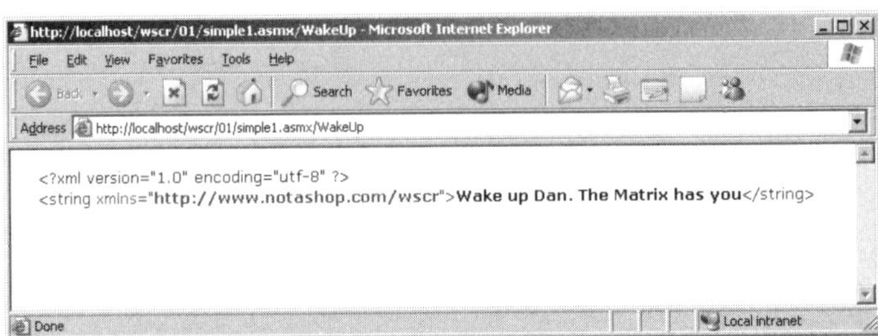

Figure 1-5 Our service returns a response in raw XML.

Congratulations. You've just successfully written and tested your first Web service. That wasn't too hard, was it? Let's see what went on behind the scenes.

> **Note** If you're not using Microsoft Internet Explorer for your browser, the response might differ slightly according to how the browser deals with unformatted XML. It is the same XML, however.

The Life Cycle of a Web Service Request

So exactly how do Web services work? What makes them tick? How do client and server interact when Web services are involved? Perhaps the best way to answer these questions is to look at how a client holds a conversation with a service.

Figure 1-6 shows the interaction between a client and a server as we call the *WakeUp* method on the service we just created. In this case, it starts when we click Invoke on the test page:

1. The client (in our previous example, the service's test page) makes a call to the service. It collects the parameters needed for the call by having you enter their values in a form, and it translates them into the desired format for transmission over the Web in a process known as *serialization*.

2. In our simple example, the test page form sends the parameters and the name of the method to the server in the URL. As you'll see in the rest of the book, calls are more frequently serialized into SOAP request messages stored in the body of the HTTP message. However, the service test page doesn't cater to this.

3. The SOAP request message is deserialized (in our case, the URL is followed), and the call is executed on the server. If the conversation is one-way, the cycle ends here. An acknowledgment that the work has been done is returned to the client (and nothing else).

   If the client expects a value or values to be returned, the server serializes the return values and out parameters into a given format and transmits them back. (Note that the response might be an error message if things go wrong.)

   Again, the norm here is for the values to be serialized into a SOAP response message to be sent over HTTP, but the results of our simple example are returned as an HTTP response instead. The

WakeUp test page shows the different response messages that it can produce depending on how the method call was originally sent to the server.

4. The client receives the response from the server and acts accordingly. In our example, the browser had no instructions about what to do with the returned XML, so it just displayed it. The client actually has two options: work with the XML as it was returned or deserialize it into .NET objects and work with them. In .NET, the latter is the default.

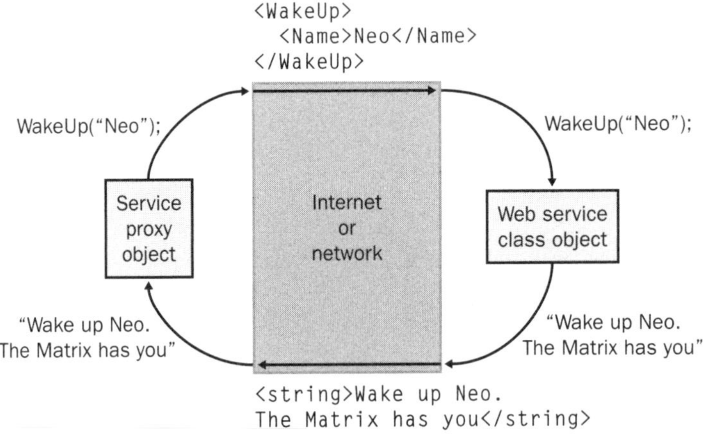

Figure 1-6 The life cycle of a Web service request

Note that like a request for a Web page, our Web service and its test page were accessed via a URL. This use of HTTP as the transport protocol for requests is the most common possibility but not the only one. Web services have been set up and run over Simple Mail Transfer Protocol (SMTP), Microsoft Message Queue (MSMQ), and IBM's WebSphere MQ, but because the SOAP standard defines a binding only to HTTP, HTTP will continue to be the most popular choice. Of course, you still have to work around its weaknesses. For example, a SOAP request working over HTTP (or HTTPS) doesn't carry any notion of state from client to server or vice-versa unless it has been programmed to do so. By default, the standard state mechanism over HTTP—cookies—is not supported for Web services.

From a developer's perspective, Web services are quite straightforward to develop and their clients are simpler still. Web services enforce and enable a high level of abstraction between client and server. When a client is built, it uses the WSDL document that unambiguously describes the service's interface (or behavior) to generate the proxy class. (See *http://localhost/wscr/01/simple1.asmx?wsdl* for our example service's WSDL.) Depending on whether a Web method is one-way or two-way, the WSDL document also defines the format to be expected for the return message. It's up to the client how it uses the methods presented in that interface and how objects are serialized, how queries are generated, and how responses are interpreted. In this way, the Web service client and provider are freed from needing any knowledge of each other beyond the contract of inputs and outputs laid down by the interface and the location of the Web service provider.

Message Formats

Have another look at the page where you can invoke the *WakeUp* method on our simple service. If you closed the browser already, you should find it at *http://localhost/wscr/01/simple1.asmx?op=WakeUp*. Underneath the form to query the service, you'll find templates for both request and response messages to and from the service in three formats—HTTP-GET, HTTP-POST, and HTTP-SOAP. As an experienced Web developer, you'll already be familiar with the first two formats, but what exactly does a SOAP message consist of anyway?

SOAP The schema for SOAP is actually stricter than XML in an effort to keep things simple. (The *S* in SOAP does stand for *simple*, after all.) It prevents the use of DTDs and XML processing instructions in a message, for example. There's nothing to stop the client or the server from validating the structure of the message against a DTD or a schema, but you can't include the DTD or the schema in the message for the recipient of the message to use.

The SOAP specification defines a SOAP message as an XML document consisting of up to three main elements.

- The *<Envelope>* element is the top-level element of a SOAP message and encompasses the actual contents of the message and any processing information that might need to be followed for its successful delivery.
- The *<Header>* element contains the delivery instructions for the message and any other information that isn't the message itself—for example, any transactional information, cryptography keys, delivery routes, and so on. Adding a SOAP header to your message is optional.
- The *<Body>* element contains the actual message from the sender, be it a request, a response, or a SOAP *<fault>* element containing an error message.

Figure 1-7 illustrates the hierarchy of these elements.

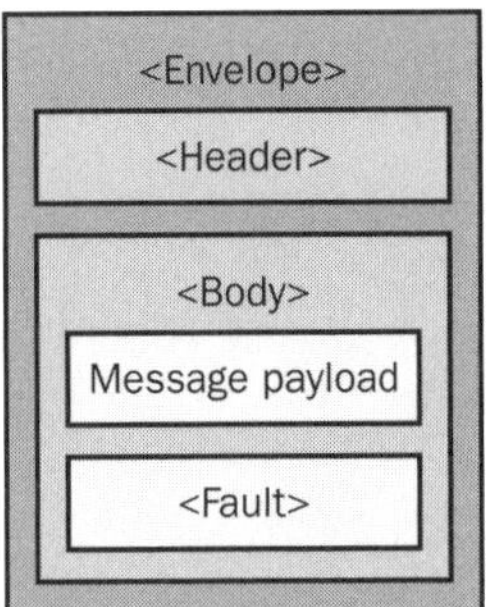

Figure 1-7 A SOAP message has an Envelope that encompasses <Header> and <Body> elements.

For example, if we had sent our simple service a SOAP request, it would have looked like this:

```
<soap:Envelope xmlns:xsi="http://www.w3.org/2001/XMLSchema-instance"
               xmlns:xsd="http://www.w3.org/2001/XMLSchema"
               xmlns:soap="http://schemas.xmlsoap.org/soap/envelope/">

  <soap:Body>
    <WakeUp xmlns="http://www.notashop.com/wscr">
      <yourName>Dan</yourName>
    </WakeUp>
  </soap:Body>

</soap:Envelope>
```

Note that we defined four XML namespaces for our reference in the message:

- *http://schema.xmlsoap.org/soap/envelope* is the namespace for SOAP 1.1 elements.
- *http://www.w3.org/2001/XMLSchema* and *http://www.w3.org/2001/XMLSchema-instance* let us define any custom types and strongly type the variables inside the SOAP envelope. (We don't actually need these in our simple example, but they're handy to know.)
- *http://www.notashop.com/wscr* is the service's namespace. We used this to differentiate the message payload from the SOAP protocol elements.

You can also define an optional attribute in the *<Envelope>* element called *encodingStyle* that allows you to set the serialization rules used in the SOAP message. The actual custom serialization routines are defined in the code behind the service and its client. The .NET serializers were designed to make this process very simple, and the simple and complex types defined by .NET all correspond to XSD types as defined in XML schemas, making the actual serialization process faster to perform.

A Simple Example in Web Matrix

For those of you who would rather not work with raw text but who don't want a copy of Visual Studio .NET, the Web Matrix project, available for download at *http://www.asp.net*, is well worth looking into. A cut-down version of Visual Studio .NET purely for ASP.NET (and therefore Web service) development, Web Matrix crosses the feel and RAD capabilities of a proper IDE with the absolute control of a text editor. Like Visual Studio .NET, it also has its own Web service wizard.

Start Web Matrix, and when you're asked to create a new file, select XML Web Service from the panel on the right, as shown in Figure 1-8. You'll be asked to give a location, a filename, a class, and namespace for your code. We'll call this service simple2.asmx. Enter **C:\Inetpub\wwwroot\wscr\01** for the location (adjusting the path according to the location of your IIS wwwroot folder), **simple2.asmx** for the filename, **SimpleServices** for the class, and **notashop.wscr** for the namespace. Also, select C# or Visual Basic .NET from the Language drop-down list.

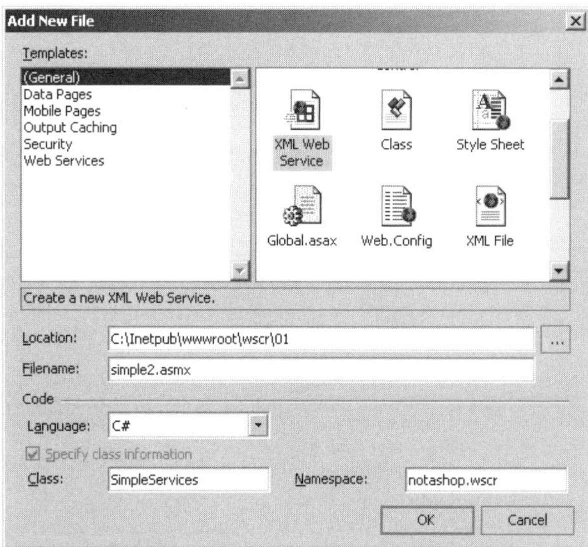

Figure 1-8 Web Matrix has a Web service wizard.

As you'll see, Web Matrix adds some demonstration code to our file before we get started. In this case, it asks for two numbers and returns their sum. Replace this demo code so simple2.asmx looks like this in Visual C#:

```
<%@ WebService language="C#" class="SimpleServices" %>

using System;
using System.Web.Services;
using System.Xml.Serialization;

public class SimpleServices {

    [WebMethod]
    public string BioVolts(int age) {
        int volts = age * 240000;

        return "You have generated " + volts
            + " biovolts in your lifetime.";
    }
}
```

Or, in Visual Basic .NET:

```
<%@ WebService language="VB" class="SimpleServices" %>

Imports System
Imports System.Web.Services
Imports System.Xml.Serialization

Public Class SimpleServices

    <WebMethod> Public Function BioVolts(age As Integer) As String
        Dim volts As Integer = age * 240000
        Return "You have generated " & volts _
            & " biovolts in your lifetime."
    End Function

End Class
```

The structure of the code surrounding the new method isn't exactly the same as simple1.asmx, and some of that difference is reflected when we browse to our new service (as shown in Figure 1-9).

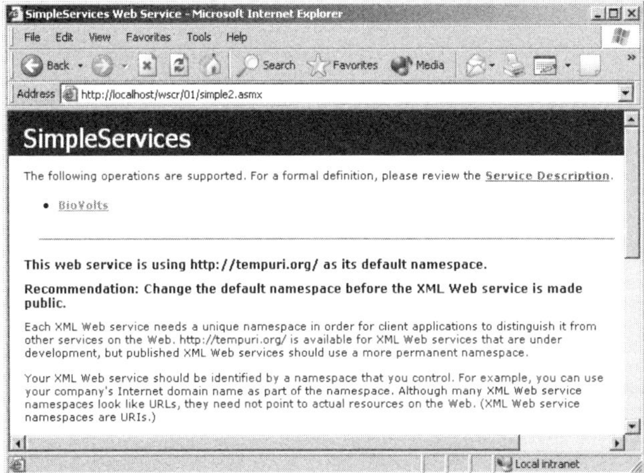

Figure 1-9 A new service, but this time with a warning

The initial test page at *http://localhost/wscr/01/simple2.asmx* now warns us to change the Web service's namespace before we make it public. You'll see how to do this in our next example, and you'll see the difference it makes when our Web service class inherits from the .NET service base class, *System.Web.Services.WebService*, as it did in our first example. For the time being, the service works exactly as we'd expect it to.

A Simple Example in Visual Studio .NET

As you'd expect from Microsoft's development environment of choice, you get a great deal more assistance with your Web service development in Visual Studio .NET than you do Notepad or Web Matrix. Visual Studio .NET sets up projects, creates files and virtual directories, and makes your Web service publicly available to those who can see it.

To add a new C# Web service project to your current Visual Studio .NET solution, follow these steps:

1. Choose New Project from the File menu, and in the New Project dialog box, select Visual C# Projects from the left pane and ASP.NET Web Service from the right.

2. In the Location box, type in the URL through which your Web service will be accessible. The folder name there will also be the name of the project. For example, *http://localhost/hello* or *http://www.not-ashop.com/wscr/hello* in the location box both mean that the project's name is hello. We'll put ours at *http://localhost/wscr/01/simple3*.

   Note that Visual Studio .NET expects the remote location you give for the Web service's home to be available; if it can't contact the Web server in question, an error appears reminding you to get it started. The same is true when you need to reopen a Web service project.

3. Click OK, and Visual Studio .NET generates a new virtual directory for the service and creates several new files, including the .asmx file we're starting to know.

Project Files

When Visual Studio .NET initially sets up a Web service project, it generates several files, as shown in Figure 1-10. If you don't see all of them, select the Show All Files option from the set of icons in the Solution Explorer window.

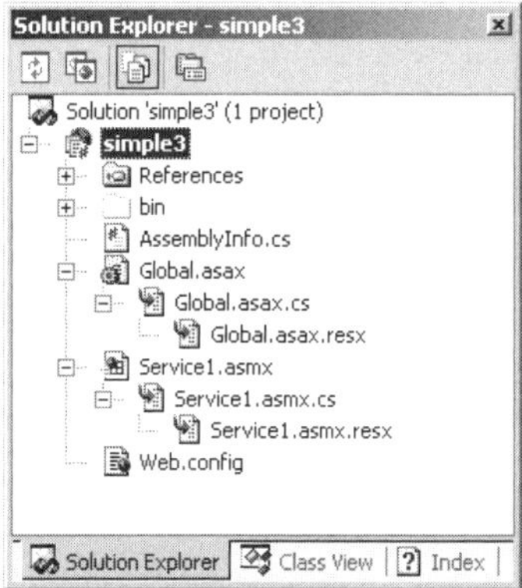

Figure 1-10 Solution Explorer shows the files in our Web service project.

AssemblyInfo.cs, Global.asax, Global.asax.cs, Global.asax.resx, and Web.config work in exactly the same way as for a standard Web Forms project. It's the .asmx files we need to investigate.

The .asmx file is the focus of your Web services. As you've seen, this is the file that contains the Web service and that, together with its associated .asmx.cs or .asmx.vb code-behind file, implements its functionality. By default, Visual Studio .NET opens the .asmx file in design view. As you'll see in Chapter 7, it is possible to incorporate .NET components into your service by dragging them onto the canvas from the Toolbox window, but for now switch to code view (right-click in the design view and choose View Code) to open a copy of the .asmx.cs code-behind file.

Let's look at the code generated (minus the comments). We'll start off with a set of references to pieces of the .NET Framework. Only *System.Web.Services* and *System.ComponentModel* are really needed for the code included, so you can remove the others if you want.

```
using System;
using System.Collections;
using System.ComponentModel;
using System.Data;
using System.Diagnostics;
using System.Web;
using System.Web.Services;

namespace Simple3
{
```

Like any other .NET application, a Web service is written as a class, so it might be instantiated as an object by your application. Although it's not necessary for services as trivial as the ones demonstrated so far, you can choose to derive your class from *System.Web.Services.WebService*, the .NET base class for Web services. In doing so, you gain access to the common ASP.NET objects, such as *Application*, *Session*, *User*, and *Context*, which will come in handy when you need to manage session state and identify your service's users.

```
    public class Service1 : System.Web.Services.WebService
    {
        public Service1()
        {
            InitializeComponent();
        }
```

The constructor for this class calls only the usual *InitializeComponent* method that Visual Studio .NET autogenerates to initialize the components that are to be used by the service. This, along with a *Dispose* method to allow for a clean exit from the service, should be left to the IDE to update as necessary.

```
        #region Component Designer generated code
        private IContainer components = null;

        private void InitializeComponent()
        {
        }

        protected override void Dispose( bool disposing )
        {
```

```
            if(disposing && components != null)
            {
                components.Dispose();
            }
            base.Dispose(disposing);
        }
        #endregion
```

Finally, to demonstrate the basic mechanics of a Web service, Visual Studio .NET also includes a commented out "Hello World" example:

```
        // WEB SERVICE EXAMPLE
        // The HelloWorld() example service returns the string Hello World
        // To build, uncomment the following lines then save and build the
        // project. To test this web service, press F5

//          [WebMethod]
//          public string HelloWorld()
//          {
//              return "Hello World";
//          }
    }
}
```

Like the Web Matrix code, Visual Studio's dummy code works straight away. All you need to do is uncomment the *HelloWorld* method or delete it and replace it with the following and then press F5. A test page will appear as normal.

```
        [WebMethod]
        public string TakeAPill(string color)
        {
            string response;
            switch(color)
            {
                case "red":
                    response = "Welcome to Wonderland Alice";
                    break;
                case "blue":
                    response = "The Matrix still has you";
                    break;
                default:
                    response = "Red or blue to leave this crossroads";
                    break;
            }
            return response;
        }
```

How Does It Work?

The code in an .asmx or code-behind file is written in a language supported by .NET and contains the usual class and function definitions, so why do we get a Web service and not an ASP.NET page or something else when we browse to an .asmx file? What transformed the simple function into a public method exposed by a Web service?

Declaring a Web Service

When you create an .asmx file, you first need to declare that it's a Web service. In our first two examples, we did this manually by adding the *@WebService* directive at the top of our .asmx file. This tells ASP.NET how the Web service has been implemented.

```
<%@ WebService language="C#" class="SimpleServices" %>
```

The directive has four attributes that allow us to specify the language the code is written in, the class (and assembly) implementing the Web service, the location of the code-behind page, and whether the service should be compiled with debug symbols.

If you're wondering about the Visual Studio .NET example and why there's no sign of this directive in the default code, just open the .asmx file in Notepad. Sure enough, you find the following.

```
<%@ WebService Language="C#" Codebehind="Service1.asmx.cs"
    Class="Simple3.Service1" %>
```

Visual Studio .NET tries to keep you from looking at the actual .asmx page code. Instead, you either work in design view or edit the code-behind file.

The *WebService* Attribute

You might have noticed in our last two examples that the test pages warned about using the *http://tempuri.org/* namespace URI in a live environment. This is the temporary default namespace that any .asmx service uses unless one is explicitly assigned. As the test page notes, you make this assignment with the *WebService* attribute.

Not to be confused with the class of the same name, the *WebService* attribute is used just in front of the class declaration for your Web service. In C#, this looks like the following:

```
[WebService(Namespace="http://www.notashop.com/wscr",
            Description="SimpleService1",
            Name="Try This Out")]

public class SimpleServices : System.Web.Services.WebService
{
    ⋮
```

Here is the Visual Basic .NET equivalent:

```
<WebService(Namespace:="http://www.notashop.com/wscr", _
            Description:="SimpleService1", _
            Name:="Try This Out")> _
Public Class SimpleServices
    ⋮
```

The *WebService* attribute allows you to declare your own namespace for your Web service, its name, and a brief description of what it does. Its use is optional, as are the items you can define, but it's recommended if you want to distinguish your Web service when you put it live on a production server.

The *WebMethod* Attribute

Now that our file is recognized as a unique Web service, we're left to declare which methods in our class will be made public under the service and be included as an operation in the service's WSDL document. This we do with the *WebMethod* attribute, in much the same way that we used the *WebService* attribute, as in the example:

```
[WebMethod]
public string WakeUp(string myName)
{
    return "Wake up " + myName + ". The Matrix has you";
}
```

Here's the Visual Basic .NET version:

```
<WebMethod()> _
Public Function TakeAPill(ByVal color As String) As String
    ⋮
End Function
```

The *WebMethod* attribute also has a collection of qualifiers that you can use to establish how the method works within the context of a Web application. For example, you can set the following:

- Whether the response from the method is buffered (*BufferResponse*)
- Whether the method can handle state information (*EnableSession*)
- How long the method's response is kept in the server's cache (*CacheDuration*)
- Whether the method supports transactions (*TransactionOption*)
- An alias for the client to call the method by instead of its actual name (*MessageName*)
- A brief description of the method's use (*Description*)

We'll revisit these qualifiers later in the book.

People often make a few erroneous assumptions about using the *WebMethod* attribute. Let's look at some examples. *MethodOne* works exactly as you'd expect:

```
public class SimpleServices : System.Web.Services.WebService
{
    [WebMethod(Description="Example method")]
    public string MethodOne()
    {
        ⋮
    }
```

However, *MethodTwo* doesn't. A function must be declared public for the *WebMethod* attribute to make sense. Private and protected methods will not be made public even if they're tagged with the attribute.

```
    [WebMethod]
    private string MethodTwo()
    {
        // Private class methods can't be Web methods
    }
```

A common false assumption is that classes implementing Web services need to declare every method as a *WebMethod*. This is wrong. *MethodThree()*, for example, will not be exposed as a Web method but will remain public to other .NET classes as usual:

```
    public string MethodThree()
    {
        // Methods can remain private to the class implementation
    }
```

Last but not least, it's worth reiterating that Web methods do not need to return values. It's perfectly feasible for Web service communications to be one-way only:

```
    [WebMethod]
    public void MethodFour()
    {
        // WebMethods don't have to return anything
    }
}
```

Code-Behind Files

Our three examples have demonstrated that like any other page or form, the class that gives a Web service its functionality doesn't have to be stored in the .asmx file itself. You have two other options. You can store it in a code-behind

(.asmx.cs or .asmx.vb) file, or you can place it in a precompiled assembly. It's just a matter of using the *@WebService* directive to tell the .NET runtime where the code is.

You've already seen how to declare the class when it's located in the .asmx file or its code-behind .asmx.cs or .asmx.vb file:

```
<%@ WebService Language="C#" Class="LocalClassName" %>
```

or

```
<%@ WebService Language="VB" Class="LocalClassName" %>
```

To point the service at a class inside a precompiled assembly, you give the directive the class's full name and the name of its assembly, as in this example:

```
<%@ WebService Language="C#" Class="Wscr.SimpleServices, WscrAssembly" %>
```

and this example:

```
<%@ WebService Language="VB" Class="Wscr.SimpleServices, WscrAssembly" %>
```

Note that the assembly you nominate in the directive must be located in the bin directory of the Web application hosting the XML Web service. If you don't give an assembly name, ASP.NET will search through all the assemblies in the bin directory until it finds the correct one or it runs out of assemblies. Needless to say, it's in your interest to provide it.

At its simplest, producing a Web service is a matter of taking some code you've already written, adding the *WebMethod* attribute to the methods you want to expose, and referencing the code from an .asmx file.

Developing a Web Service Client

Now that we've developed a few simple Web services, it's time to write a client that makes use of it. Almost any part of an application, be it desktop-based or Web-based, can consume a Web service. A Windows Forms client can present the user with a user interface affected by a Web service, and a interfaceless client, such as a .NET component or even another Web service, can exercise some sort of autonomous operation that doesn't require a human user to see the results.

As you've seen, the .NET Framework has a great deal of support for Web service development, and developing a client can be even easier than writing the service! It's just a matter of implementing two tasks—finding the service you want to use and referencing it.

A Simple Windows Forms Client

Let's whip up a simple Windows Forms client for the three Web services we've created. Each of these Web services exposes a single method that takes a user-defined value as a parameter and returns a string, so for each service we'll provide a text box, a Submit button, and a label for the service to populate.

Start up a new C# Windows Forms Application project in Visual Studio .NET and call it SimpleClient. Add a text box, a button, and a label for each of the simple Web services we created earlier—simple1.asmx, simple2.asmx, and simple3.asmx (as shown in Figure 1-11). For simple1.asmx, the text box, the button, and the label should be called SvcInput1, Submit1, and SvcOutput1, respectively.

Figure 1-11 A simple Windows Forms client for our Web services

With the basic framework set up, we'll add in our calls to the Web services. But first we need to find them.

Finding Your Service

If you can access a Web page on a server by using an HTTP request, you can work with a Web service on the same server. Only problem is, with millions of Web servers out there, how do you find the service you want to use? We've already touched on UDDI—at this point, we need to make use of it.

Externally with UDDI

As mentioned earlier, UDDI is an open XML-based standard that allows companies to disseminate information about the Web services they have deployed to potential clients on the Web.

Four root UDDI servers (currently known as *business registries*) maintain and mirror a complete directory of available Web services to sites such as *http://uddi.microsoft.com*, which developers can browse and search to find a desired service. Their goal is to provide the location of the WSDL file for the service, which unambiguously defines the public interface (behavior) of an XML Web service and tells potential clients how to interact with it. We need to reference this information to make our client.

We'll look more at UDDI in Chapter 4, but for now, it's worth noting that UDDI isn't just something you get at in your browser:

- Windows Server 2003 contains a UDDI server for companies who want to publicize services available internally but not publicly on the Internet.
- Visual Studio .NET has a link to the UDDI registries built into the Start Page it displays each time it boots up. Just click on the XML Web Services tab, and if you're on line, you'll get the home page for Microsoft's UDDI server. Visual Studio .NET also has an upload feature that we'll look at later in the chapter that helps you register your service.

Locally with DISCO

The alternative to using the business-centric UDDI directory is to use .disco and .vsdisco DISCO files for Web service discovery. DISCO is a Microsoft protocol that isn't a standard, so its use tends to be restricted to Microsoft-centric environments, usually local servers on a LAN. If that's not a problem and if you already know the server's location, DISCO can offer you a more straightforward listing of the services available at that location, either generated automatically using .vsdisco files or manually with .disco files.

So, for example, you can advertise a top-level directory on your development server for your team to discover the services to code against without needing to formally register them on a UDDI server. With Dynamic Discovery switched on (it's off by default), all you need to do is query the list of local discovery files kept in a file called default.vsdisco in the server's root directory.

If you want to keep a tighter rein on what services are visible on your servers, you can manually create a default.disco file to do the same job, leaving out the undesirables that Dynamic Discovery includes. Each Web service has an autogenerated .disco file that can be found by appending *?disco* to the address for the service's .asmx file, in the same way that you append *?wsdl* to the service's address to generate the service's WSDL file.

You'll learn more about both dynamic and static discovery files in Chapter 4.

Adding a Reference

Back to our SimpleClient project in Visual Studio .NET. The upshot of our discussion about finding a service is that to locate our Web services' WSDL files, we use Visual Studio to locate first their DISCO files and then their description files. Of course, we already know how to get to their WSDL files, but that might not always be the case. Likewise, UDDI entries might point to a service's .disco or WSDL file—normally the latter.

In Visual Studio, right-click on the SimpleClient project entry in Solution Explorer and choose Add Web Reference from the shortcut menu. A rather large dialog box appears (as shown in Figure 1-12), offering you five choices:

- Specify the location of a .disco or WSDL file directly
- Browse Web services on the local machine
- Browse UDDI servers on the local network
- Search the UDDI directory of live Web services
- Search the UDDI directory of Web services still in development

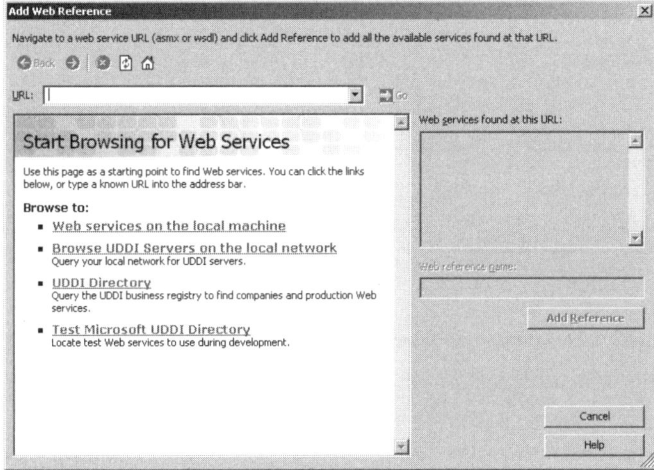

Figure 1-12 The Add Web Reference dialog box

We'll have to give the address of the .disco file directly in the dialog box's Address text box. The addresses of the .disco files for the three simple Web services we created earlier are

- *http://localhost/wscr/01/simple1.asmx?disco*
- *http://localhost/wscr/01/simple2.asmx?disco*
- *http://localhost/wscr/01/simple3/service1.asmx?disco*

Type the first address listed above and click Go. The dialog box will show the contents of the DISCO file, the WSDL file you can reference for the service, and other related material that developers might want to read.

Enter **simple1** in the Web Reference Name text box and click the Add Reference button. After a small delay, the reference will have been added into the project (as shown in Figure 1-13), incorporating the service's .disco and WSDL files and another file called Reference.map that details where the other two were found on the Web. Remember to click Solution Explorer's Show All Files button if you can't see these files.

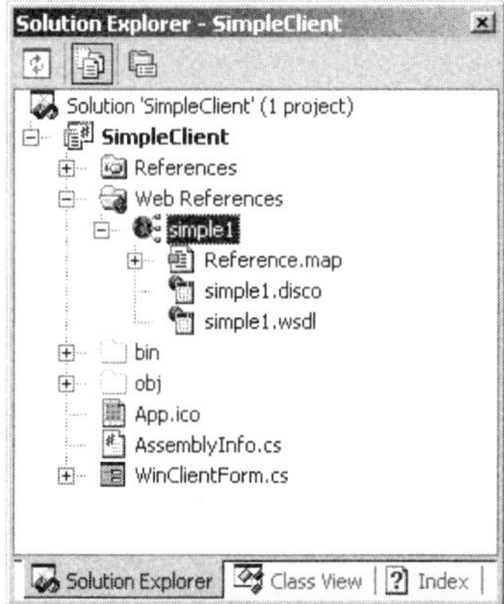

Figure 1-13 Solution Explorer offers easy access to our Web service's information.

Behind the scenes, Visual Studio .NET generates a proxy class for the service from the WSDL file that allows you to call Web methods as you would any other call. If you switch to the class view pane, you'll see that the name of the class is derived from the names of the server and service, as shown in Figure 1-14.

The new class contains both synchronous and asynchronous versions of calls to each of the exposed Web methods that you can call directly. The serialization of the calls and their binding to the transport protocol nominated in the WSDL file is transparent. With the proxy class available to our Visual Studio .NET project, all we have to do is incorporate calls to the service into the client application.

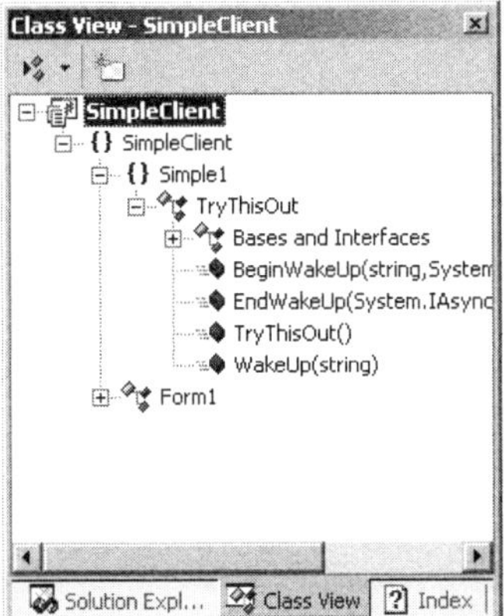

Figure 1-14 Class view provides the name of the service proxy class and method signatures.

If you're wondering why the service is called *TryThisOut* and not *SimpleServices*, it's because we used the *WebService* attribute to give Simple1.asmx the name *TryThisOut*. For our client, all we need to do is instantiate an object of type *Simple1.TryThisOut* and call its *WakeUp* method when the Submit button is clicked, as follows:

```
private void Submit1_Click(object sender, System.EventArgs e)
{
    Simple1.TryThisOut svc1 = new Simple1.TryThisOut();
    SvcOutput1.Text = svc1.WakeUp(SvcInput1.Text);
}
```

The last line of code serializes a call to *WakeUp* using the contents of the *SvcInput1* text box as the parameter, sends the request to the service, receives the string result back as a SOAP response, deserializes it, and then sends it to the *SvcOutput1* label. As we noted earlier, .NET really does abstract a lot of the conversation with Web services unless you want to get involved. The idea of services as application plug-ins works really well here. As long as the signature of the method calls to the service's proxy class remains the same, an application can call any plug-in without any need for changes to the code.

Save our simple client application and press F5 to try it out. As an exercise, you can add references to the remaining two services and tie calls to them into the click event of their respective buttons. If you get stuck, you'll find the solution in the book's sample files.

Adding a Reference Manually

If you don't have a copy of Visual Studio .NET, you can achieve what adding a Web reference does in Visual Studio .NET by using a pair of command-line tools in the .NET Framework SDK (in the bin directory). Because the tools are command-line-based, you of course have more control over what they do and how they do it. As an example, we'll use Web Matrix to build a Web Forms client for simple1.asmx. We'll call it SimpleWebClient and add a text box, a button, and a label to the form, just as we did with the Windows Forms client. (See Figure 1-15.)

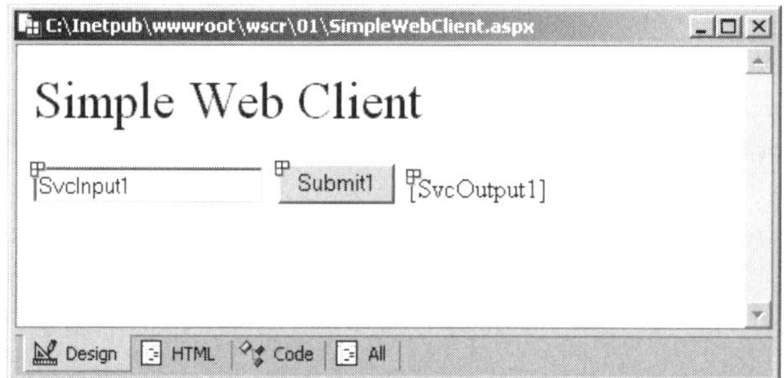

Figure 1-15 A simple Web client

Disco.exe

We know where the WSDL file for simple1.asmx is, but we'll use its .disco file to download it to our local drive instead. The first tool, disco.exe, downloads the resource files for a Web service to a place of your choosing, given the .disco file of the service on the network. The basic syntax for the call is

```
disco /out:directory_to_save_files url
```

where *url* points to the location of the service's .disco file. The */out* flag is optional but handy when the default is to save the files in the directory that you make the call from. If the .disco file requires authentication before it allows access, disco.exe has */password*, */username*, and */domain* flags to let you set the relevant information. For a full list of flags, search for disco.exe in the .NET SDK or type **disco /?** at the command prompt.

For our example, open a command prompt, navigate to the SDK bin directory, and at the prompt, type the following:

```
disco /out:WebClient_directory http://localhost/wscr/01/simple1.asmx?disco
```

We get the following response and downloaded files:

```
Disco found documents at the following URLs:
http://localhost/wscr/01/simple1.asmx?disco
http://localhost/wscr/01/simple1.asmx?wsdl
```

```
The following files hold the content found at the corresponding URLs:
WebClient_directory\simple1.disco <- ↴
    http://localhost/wscr/01/simple1.asmx?DISCO
WebClient_directory\simple1.wsdl <- ↴
    http://localhost/wscr/01/simple1.asmx?wsdl

The file WebClient_directory\results.discomap holds links ↴
    to each of these files.
```

Wsdl.exe

Now that we have local copies of the discovery files for the simple1.asmx Web service, we need to generate a proxy class for the Web service. We do this with wsdl.exe, which takes the WSDL file and returns a standard .cs file containing the proxy class:

```
Wsdl /out:name_of_file_to_contain_proxy_class  /language:language  url
```

Again, wsdl.exe uses the */out*, */password*, */domain*, and */username* flags for the same purpose as disco.exe. Three other useful flags are the */language* flag, which lets you set the language the class is written in (the default is C#); the */namespace* flag, which lets you set the namespace for the generated proxy class; and the */protocol* flag, which lets you set the transport protocol the proxy will use to send to and receive from the Web service. The default protocol is SOAP. Again, a complete list of flags can be found in the .NET SDK or by typing **wsdl /?** at the command prompt.

> **Note** In some cases, you have to alter the WSDL file for a service before you can run wsdl.exe on it or add the reference in Visual Studio .NET. You'll learn why in Chapter 3.

To generate the proxy class for simple1.asmx, we make one of the following calls, depending on whether we want the class in C# or in Visual Basic .NET:

```
Wsdl /out:Simple1Proxy.cs simple1.wsdl
```

or

```
Wsdl /out:Simple1Proxy.vb /language:VB simple1.wsdl
```

With the proxy class file available, we need to compile it into an assembly and then make a reference to the assembly. Again, depending on the language of choice, the call to make is

```
csc /out:Simple1Proxy.dll /t:library /r:System.XML.dll /
r:System.Web.Services.dll Simple1Proxy.cs
```

or

```
vbc /out:Simple1Proxy.dll /t:library /r:System.XML.dll /
r:System.Web.Services.dll Simple1Proxy.cs
```

Manual References

Now we have the proxy assembly ready, and all we need to do is create an instance of the class and call a method on it, as we did with the Windows Forms client. Again, we attach our call to the click event of the Submit button:

```
void Submit1_Click(Object sender, EventArgs e) {
    TryThisOut svc1 = new TryThisOut();
    SvcOutput1.Text = svc1.WakeUp(SvcInput1.Text);
}
```

Or, in Visual Basic .NET:

```
Sub Submit1_Click(sender As Object, e As EventArgs)
   Dim svc1 As New TryThisOut()
   SvcOutput1.Text = svc1.WakeUp(SvcInput1.Text)
End Sub
```

With the code ready, all that's left is to deploy our Web form to a Web application and the proxy assembly to the bin directory for that application. We simply call up SimpleWebClient.aspx (as you see in Figure 1-16) to prove it.

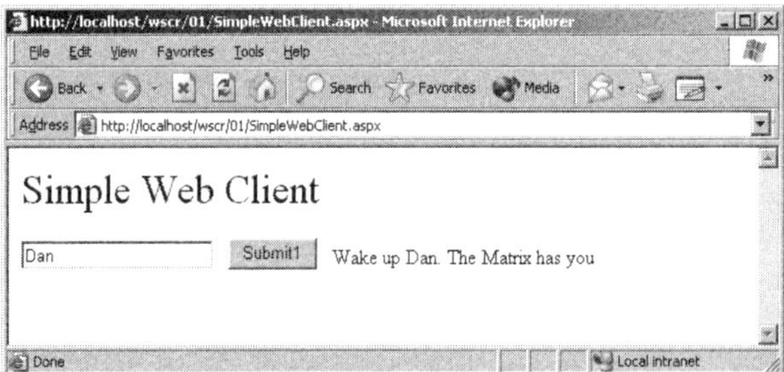

Figure 1-16 A simple Web Forms client is just as effective as a Windows Forms client.

That's it for building simple services and clients that use them. The basics aren't that hard to grasp, but as you can imagine, building on the foundation we've just covered can get tricky quite quickly. Indeed, we'll spend the rest of this book exploring exactly how far we can go from here. But first, let's get our services out on the Web.

Deploying Web Services

Once you're happy with the state of your service, you need to move it off the development server onto a public, live server and then register it.

Manual Deployment

If you have access to your own Web server running .NET or have a .NET-enabled account with an Internet service provider (ISP), you can deploy your Web service by copying the following files from one server to another using an ftp client or some other file upload utility:

- The .asmx Web service files
- The .vsdisco and .disco files for your services, if you created them
- The web.config file for the project
- The bin directory and its contents

Visual Studio .NET also has the capacity to deploy these files for you. Simply select the project to deploy in Solution Explorer and click the Copy Project button (just above the solution tree, the second button from the left). This calls up the Copy Project dialog box (shown in Figure 1-17), which uploads the files mentioned above and more if required.

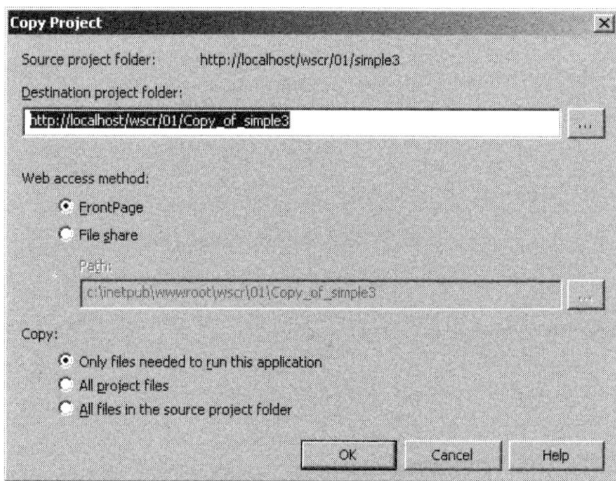

Figure 1-17 The Copy Project dialog box

In this dialog box, you can specify whether the files should be handled by Microsoft FrontPage Server Extensions or placed in the file share you specify. Clicking OK starts the transfer process.

One-Click Hosting

If you don't fancy copying the files to a server because you don't have one or you don't have an account with an ISP, you can use a solution built into the Visual Studio .NET Start Page:

1. Bring up the Start Page, select Online Resource, click on the Web Hosting tab, and you'll be given the choice of several hosting providers offering free Web space to users.
2. Select and sign up with a provider, and then return to the Web Hosting tab.
3. Click on the Upload To Your Account link that's appropriate to your new provider, and sign in with your username and password.
4. A dialog box appears with a list of Web-based projects on your local server on the left side and a list of any projects and files currently on our providers server on the right. Select the project you want to upload to the provider, and click Upload. This is quite literally one-click hosting.

Whichever way you deploy the files for your service to your live server, you still need to declare it to a UDDI registry before the general public can find the service and make use of it. Visual Studio .NET users can click on the Start Page's XML Web Services tab to go straight to Microsoft's online UDDI server. Those without Visual Studio .NET should just browse to *http://uddi.microsoft.com* or *http://uddi.ibm.com* and register there instead.

The registration process itself is quite straightforward:

1. Specify whether the service should be registered as a test service or one of production quality.
2. Identify yourself either by logging in to a previously established account on the UDDI server or by creating an account and then using it.
3. Fill in details about your service and, most important of all, the location of the service's WSDL file.

As with a DNS entry, it takes a little time for your completed entry to be propagated to the other three root UDDI servers (IBM, SAP, and NTT-Docomo), but overnight your new service will be available for all to discover and use over the Web.

Building on the Foundation

If Web services were limited to the kind of simple operations we've used to demonstrate how to create a service and client, there would be no need for a book like this. Using .NET to build your services means you have complete access to the .NET Framework and the functionality it offers—data access, directory services, window management services, and so on. There are few aspects of the Windows operating system and the applications running on it that Web services cannot access. Indeed, Microsoft has already integrated Web services into its Office application, MapPoint, SQL Server, and several more of its server applications. This should give you an idea of the ways in which Web services will soon be a part of everyday applications.

Aside from the functionality that a service and its methods can provide, it's worth noting the way in which they can be integrated into a larger application. Indeed, the possibilities mirror those for standard ASP.NET pages.

State Management

By deriving your Web service's class from the .NET base class for Web services, *System.Web.Services.WebService*, you have access to the *HttpContext* class's *Application* and *Session* properties in the same way an ASP.NET application's *Page* object does. That is, you can use, maintain, and update session-level and application-level variables for the Web application as a whole inside a Web method. All you do is set the *WebMethod* attribute's *EnableSession* property to *true* and make sure your class inherits from the *WebService* class. Here's an example in C#:

```
<%@ WebService Language="C#" Class="OneArmBandit" %>
⋮
public class OneArmBandit : System.Web.Services.WebService
{
    [ WebMethod(EnableSession=true) ]
    public prizemoney Gamble()
    {
        ⋮
        Session["Kitty"] = 25;
```

```
        Application["Jackpot"] = ((int)Application["Jackpot"]) + 10;
        ⋮
    }
}
```

And here's one in Visual Basic .NET:

```
<%@ WebService Language="VB" Class="OneArmBandit" %>
⋮
Public Class OneArmBandit : Inherits System.Web.Services.WebService

    < WebMethod(EnableSession:=True) > _
    Public Function Gamble() As prizemoney
        ⋮
        Session["Kitty"] = 25;
        Application["Jackpot"] = CInt(Application["Jackpot"]) + 10;
        ⋮
    End Function

End Class
```

We'll look more at maintaining state within Web methods in Chapter 7.

Incorporating Transactions

You can also make use of .NET support for transactions to ensure that a Web method completes its task either completely or not at all. That is, you can treat the Web method as a transaction. All you do is add a reference to and then import *System.EnterpriseServices*, which holds the transactional support in .NET, and set the *WebMethod* attribute's *TransactionOption* property to the appropriate level. Here's an example in C#:

```
<%@ WebService Language="C#" Class="OneArmBandit" %>
<%@ Assembly name="System.EnterpriseServices" %>
⋮
using System.EnterpriseServices;
⋮
public class OneArmBandit
{
    [ WebMethod(TransactionOption=TransactionOption.RequiresNew) ]
    public CashInChips(prizemoney Winnings)
    {
        ⋮
    }
}
```

And here's one in Visual Basic .NET:

```
<%@ WebService Language="VB" Class="OneArmBandit" %>
<%@ Assembly name="System.EnterpriseServices" %>
:VE>
using System.EnterpriseServices;
⋮
Public Class OneArmBandit

    < WebMethod(TransactionOption:=TransactionOption.RequiresNew) > _
    Public Sub CashInChips(Winnings As prizemoney)
        ⋮
    End Sub

End Class
```

There are a couple of things to note here, even with this cursory glance:

- Your service class does not need to inherit from the .NET *WebService* base class to support transactions.
- There is no need for your method's code to explicitly commit or roll back the transaction if it succeeds or fails. If an exception is thrown while the method is running, the transaction is automatically aborted. If no exceptions are thrown, the transaction is automatically committed.
- Because HTTP is a stateless protocol, Web methods can take part in a transaction only as the root of a new transaction. If one transactional Web method calls another, they each take part in their own transaction. This is true whether the *TransactionOption* property is set to *RequiresNew* or *Required*.

Asynchronous Services

Our examples have thus far used HTTP as the go-between protocol, as will be the case most of the time. As we've noted, however, HTTP isn't the only protocol you can use to send a SOAP message. SOAP defines a binding to HTTP where the call and its response are sent asynchronously. Indeed, SOAP messages have also been carried over SMTP (e-mail) and several message queuing systems such as MSMQ and even floppy disk. (Carrier pigeons, as proposed in RFC 1149, have yet to be tested.)

The curious will have already noticed that the service proxy class you generate by creating a Web reference in a Visual Studio .NET project or by calling WSDL contains a pair of asynchronous methods for each Web method. These functions, *BeginMethodName* and *EndMethodName*, are called to send a message to the service and to process the results of the service's response, respectively. Barring the additional method to call, however, the building of both service and client remain essentially the same as when you use HTTP or other synchronous protocols.

The structure of the SOAP message remains the same, and the only extra consideration is how the application will know when to call the *End* method for the call to the Web service. You have two choices:

- Send the *Begin* method a callback function that will be triggered when the method has finished.
- Have the client use a member of the *WaitHandle* class to listen for the *Begin* method to finish running.

The SOAP request to a service is dealt with by a different thread than the one looking after the SOAP response, so there's no performance hit.

You'll see more on client-server synchronicity in Chapter 8.

Security

Consumers and developers are both worried about holes through which malicious code can harm our systems and our data. This concern applies to Web services as well, and several efforts are ongoing to secure the contents of SOAP messages as they're sent over the Web and make sure they're from who they say they're from.

Here are the three most common ways to secure your Web services communications:

- Send all the requests and responses between client and service over HTTPS rather than HTTP.
- Use Windows authentication to validate the identities of both client and service before reading and acting on the content of the SOAP message. Optionally, you can strengthen this authentication by using client certificates or Secure Sockets Layer (SSL).
- Incorporate additional information into the SOAP message headers to provide a custom authentication solution. A couple of extensions to the SOAP standard are designed for just this purpose.

- Set up a file/IP/URL authorization policy on your server that restricts access to clients based on the files they're requesting or the IP/URL the request came from.

Microsoft's .NET My Services was going to use a Kerberos-enabled version of Passport to identify users and establish which set of records their requests would read from and write to. Ironically, this was probably the nicest feature of .NET My Services. The point is that you can easily come up with your own security solution, as you can an XML grammar, or you can use a tried and trusted solution. The whole of Chapter 11 deals with this issue.

Summary

This chapter offered a fairly quick overview of Web services and clients and the fundamental techniques needed to start creating them in .NET. We also covered how to deploy these services and register them for public consumption.

In the remainder of Part I, we'll look in depth at the standards that make up the Web services platform and the .NET classes and attributes that immediately enable you to work with those standards. Part II will make a more detailed case for building services and their clients before we go on to extend them into traditional Web realms and beyond. Part III will look at what Web services might evolve into and the changes being made in that direction.

2

Web Services and SOAP

Having started in the opening chapter with an overview of how Web services expose functionality via the Web, we'll focus over the next few chapters on the building blocks that allow Web services to be called remotely. One of the vital processes involved in the invocation of Web services is the provision of data to and from the Web service. Messages carrying the necessary data can be parceled in a variety of different formats, but a popular and effective way of invoking Web services, and one that is governed by a set of standards, is to pass messages within a SOAP wrapper.

SOAP is an XML-based message format that allows two applications to exchange data over the Web. Web services use SOAP to carry method calls from a client to a remote server; a SOAP message is sent containing data that the Web service will need to act on. The Web service can also return a response to a method call, again placing information within the format of a SOAP message. The vast majority of Web services will use SOAP whether the user physically creates a SOAP message or leaves it to the application to parcel up the message in XML and send it.

Using SOAP is preferable to just wrapping up your messages in XML because SOAP is tailored to the needs of carrying method calls and provides the minimum format required to send a message from one application to another. Information in SOAP messages is stored within a simple header and body structure within an envelope. The information can be stored either as a straight XML document or as a remote procedure call (RPC), together with information about accompanying data types. The information in a SOAP message is spread between header and body—information about the Web service (metadata) is kept in the header, and the data itself is stored in the body. The metadata in the header is easily retrievable by applications other than those that need to receive the data. The SOAP message structure also makes it easier to uniquely identify elements within the message body because they can be defined in the envelope using XML namespaces.

Although it's possible to hide from the internals of SOAP, SOAP really isn't difficult to master. And if you understand how SOAP works, tasks such as debugging and testing your Web services become much simpler. Because SOAP closely couples with the other Web service technologies, most notably Web Services Description Language (WSDL), understanding SOAP also makes it easier to understand those technologies.

We'll start with a quick overview of what SOAP is and then discuss the current state of the standards. Next, we'll break down SOAP into its constituent parts, examine the format of a SOAP message, and look at what kind of information can be sent in a SOAP message. We'll then invoke a simple Web service using SOAP to send the necessary information the Web service needs. We'll also take a close look at SOAP headers and the kind of information that can be sent in them, the XML payload contained in the SOAP body, and how other applications might act on that payload. We'll look at how to use SOAP messages to send fault information and what the recipient of the fault message can do with this information. Last, we'll embark on a brief introduction to the SOAP extensibility model, which will lead to a subject explored more fully in Chapter 12.

What Is SOAP?

The original objective behind the design of SOAP was reflected in its name, Simple Object Access Protocol. (As of the latest version, 1.2, SOAP is no longer considered an acronym but is a word in its own right.) The word *simple* encapsulates everything SOAP was meant to stand for. A SOAP message was intended to be a well-formed XML document—in other words, pure text. SOAP has outgrown its original name because it is now considered not a protocol but a framework for exchanging messages between a Web client and a Web service.

You can see the difference between a protocol and a framework by considering the HTTP protocol, which revolutionized the exchange of data between browsers and Web servers. HTTP keeps millions of people connected to the Web via browsers, but it doesn't provide a platform for the free exchange of data. SOAP addresses this problem by leveraging existing protocols to allow SOAP messages to be sent as part of a message in an existing protocol.

The hitches involved in exchanging data between applications over the Web are well documented. For starters, because of HTTP's omnipresence, many business networks have geared up with a multitude of firewalls, proxies, and other assorted security paraphernalia to exclude anything other than HTTP data.

SOAP solves this problem by sending the SOAP message as part of the HTTP data in a process known as *layering* SOAP over HTTP. HTTP can send instructions such as "get me this resource," "get me this resource if it hasn't expired yet," "get me this bit of this resource," "tell me about this resource," "process this data with this resource," and so on. All SOAP needs to do is provide a way of using the "process this data with this resource" instruction in HTTP. With other protocols, SOAP uses other message types. For example, over SMTP, SOAP uses the SMTP "send this data to this entity" message.

SOAP data packets, once they've reached their destination via SMTP or HTTP or whatever, contain messages that normally say things along the lines of "give me the result of running this procedure with this data as an input," but they might say something like "process this data and forward the results to this entity."

SOAP adds a new vocabulary to HTTP, allowing an HTTP message to contain more instructions than it typically could otherwise. The interesting thing is that you can render most common types of SOAP messages (such as "give me the result of running this procedure with this data as an input") using simple HTTP messages ("process this data with this resource").

As we've mentioned, SOAP can be combined with HTTP or SMTP, but it doesn't stop there: SOAP can also be combined with File Transfer Protocol (FTP) and Microsoft Message Queuing (MSMQ) technology to send its data, as well as countless other more esoteric formats. However, these latter solutions don't have as much to do with Web services, so we'll concentrate on binding SOAP to HTTP.

SOAP's *raison d'etre* was far removed from Web services. Tim Ewald, the program manager for XML Web services at Microsoft, said in a conference speech that an original aim of SOAP was "to usher Java or CORBA messages through firewalls to do remote method calls." So although SOAP mirrors RPCs, it doesn't always provide all the functionality you might imagine. However, the process of sending XML documents rather than RPCs has proven to dovetail naturally with SOAP's abilities.

In fact, SOAP is concerned totally with the process of sending messages from the client to the Web service. It assumes that the applications involved will deal with how to interpret any accompanying metadata and how to check the validity of the XML that houses the SOAP message (although this isn't always true with Web services). Because the route from client to Web service might require the intervention of other applications, it is possible to transfer SOAP between other applications or portals on the route, such as security portals. These points are known as *intermediaries*, and they are distinguished simply by their ability to receive and forward SOAP messages, possibly acting on information contained in the header of the SOAP message. SOAP is made easily extensible by this process.

To ensure that this message exchange process is standardized across platforms and applications, the W3C consortium is presiding over the standardization of SOAP. Unlike other standards (such as HTML), the most recent draft version of the SOAP standard is intended to be the final revision. In a recent keynote speech, the architect on the Microsoft XML Web services team, Don Box, said he envisaged SOAP 1.2 as the end of the line because the development team is very happy with it.

SOAP and WSDL

SOAP's links to WSDL are important, too, because a SOAP message means nothing on its own to the Web service that receives it. To make sense of it, the Web service requires a document in WSDL that describes the function of the Web service. The WSDL document describes the parameters the Web service expects—in other words, what data the Web service should receive. The WSDL document also completely describes the contents of the SOAP message. Many of the data type representations come straight from this, and these can be tied into the XML Schema specification. WSDL doesn't apply only to SOAP—it can also be used with many other protocols. In fact, the WSDL document specifies a binding that details how each operation described in the document can be accessed in a protocol-specific way.

We'll look at WSDL in the next chapter and describe SOAP's relationship to it more fully, but bear in mind that SOAP is concerned only with carrying the message to and from the Web service. The content of SOAP messages is an application-level concern, and you'll see more about how this content is structured in Chapter 6.

Now that we've discussed SOAP at a fairly abstract level, let's look at the elements that comprise a SOAP message.

The SOAP Message Structure

A SOAP message is composed of two required sections—the *<Envelope>* section and the *<Body>* section—and an optional *<Header>* section. The *<Envelope>* section contains both the *<Body>* section and the optional *<Header>* section. Both the *<Envelope>* and *<Body>* elements belong to the SOAP envelope namespace, which is found at *http://schemas.xmlsoap.org/soap/envelope* (in SOAP 1.1) or *http://www.w3.org/2002/12/soap-envelope* (in SOAP 1.2). A traditional SOAP message conforming to both the 1.1 and 1.2 versions of the standard has the structure shown in Figure 2-1.

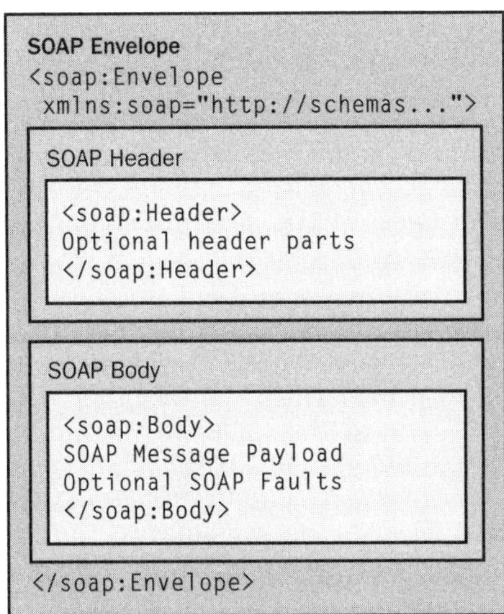

Figure 2-1 The traditional SOAP message structure

The first thing to note about the diagram is that although it is far from being a fully formed SOAP message, each element in the message is prefixed by the *soap:* namespace. This namespace is defined in the *<Envelope>* element and applies to all elements contained in the SOAP namespace. We've chosen to call the SOAP namespace *soap* because this is the default namespace that Microsoft Visual Studio .NET uses when it automatically creates SOAP messages. All elements prefixed with *soap:* belong within the *envelope* namespace.

Also note that the SOAP body can contain two sections. One section contains the details of the method call or response and the name of the XML payload. Another section contains fault information. SOAP parcels up the message (the document or the RPC) in an XML document within the *<Envelope>* element using namespaces to identify parts of the body.

Namespaces

Namespaces play a big part in SOAP. They are used to combat the problems of ambiguity between two or more XML documents by preventing clashes in element and attribute names. This is done by prefixing the element or attribute name with additional identifying text, such as the *soap:* prefix we just used (for example, *<soap:body>*). The namespaces themselves are arbitrary URIs that must be specified when a prefix mapping for the namespace is defined, as in our SOAP 1.1 envelope namespace, *xmlns:soap="http://schemas.xmlsoap.org/soap/envelope"*.

Namespaces are pervasive in SOAP: there are namespaces for the SOAP envelope, the elements in the SOAP body, the method's request and response, and even the Web service itself. There are also namespaces that define the schema documents that apply to the SOAP message. We won't digress into a full-blown explanation of how they work—see Appendix A for a refresher on XML Schema definition language (XSD) if you need reminding. Instead, we'll concentrate on the namespaces that apply to SOAP.

The SOAP 1.1 standard defines two namespaces, the SOAP envelope namespace (*http://schemas.xmlsoap.org/soap/envelope/*) and the SOAP serialization namespace (*http://schemas.xmlsoap.org/soap/encoding/*). We'll use the *soap:* prefix to identify the contents of the SOAP envelope throughout this chapter. To validate our SOAP messages and XML documents, we'll also use the common *xsd:* prefix to specify a namespace for our schema document and we'll use the *xsi:* prefix for the schema instance documents. The XML Schema belongs to the *http://www.w3.org/2001/XMLSchema* namespace, and the XML Schema instance belongs to the *http://www.w3.org/2001/XMLSchema-instance* namespace. These namespaces contain elements defined in the XML Schema standard; you should specify them in the SOAP envelope whenever prefix name mappings are defined.

Namespaces in SOAP 1.2

SOAP's use of namespaces has been improved in SOAP 1.2; version 1.1 left room for ambiguity between elements. For instance, when developing an application, I tested the SOAP returned, which used a *<title>* element, and wrote it straight to the screen along with the HTML. The browser immediately assumed that this was the HTML *<title>* element and wrote it to the title bar. Namespace qualification would have resolved this. In SOAP 1.2, all subelements within the namespace body should be qualified. The namespaces all have new URIs in SOAP 1.2 as well. (The URI for the envelope is *http://www.w3.org/2002/12/soap-envelope*.) Apart from these two points, nothing else has changed. The namespaces can be relative or absolute URIs, just as before. For more information about namespaces, we suggest you check out *http://www.w3.org/TR/REC-xml-names/*.

The namespace differences aren't the only differences between the two versions of the SOAP standard. In fact, it's worth a brief digression to consider the current state of the standard because we'll discuss it again during the course of the chapter.

The Current State of the SOAP Standard

The SOAP standard has rattled around for a few years now. When SOAP originally came into being in early 1998, it was called XML-RPC. Several developers worked on it, including Dave Winer and Don Box, in collaboration with a small team at Microsoft that wanted to create a method of sending RPCs via XML. However, SOAP's structure changed early on with the addition of items such as structs and arrays, and according to "Dave's History of SOAP," an article that Dave Winer published on *www.xmlrpc.com*, the SOAP specification soon looked like it couldn't even have come from the original XML-RPC specification. This necessitated a name change, and XML-RPC was removed from the specification as a separate adjunct to SOAP. The first version of the specification was released separately by Dave Winer to keep things rolling with the specification and to ensure that Microsoft made it "more than just a press release." The SOAP 1.0 standard was ready by 1999, and version 1.1 included contributions from other major companies such as IBM, Sun, and Oracle. SOAP 1.1 was to be the final release of the standard, but pressure from developers who wanted to improve some of the features led to work on SOAP 1.2 in late 2001.

The most up-to-date final recommendation is still only SOAP 1.1, although SOAP 1.2 is in a pretty complete state and is due to be released soon. In this chapter, we'll consider both the "old" standard and the new one, but bear in mind that much of the 1.2 standard has yet to be implemented in .NET Web services.

SOAP 1.1

You can find the SOAP 1.1 specification at *http://www.w3.org/TR/SOAP/*. SOAP 1.1 is based on the XML specification and has four parts:

- The envelope for encapsulating data
- Optional data rules for encoding data types defined within the application
- A message exchange pattern
- An optional part for binding SOAP to HTTP

Some aspects of SOAP 1.1 have yet to be implemented, but the specification does outline the general format for the *<Envelope>*, *<Header>*, and *<Body>* elements that make up a SOAP message.

The two main design goals are stated clearly in the standard: simplicity and extensibility. If you're familiar with the often esoteric terminology of W3C, the standard can make for fairly swift reading. If you're not, however, lines such as "using SOAP for RPC is orthogonal to the SOAP protocol binding" can make for heavy going. The document is intended more for implementers than developers, but it's still worth summarizing the main points.

Apart from descriptions of the general structure of a SOAP message and the fundamentals of one-way message exchange, you'll find that over half the standard is taken up by a discussion of SOAP encoding and how simple types (such as strings and enumerations) and compound types (such as arrays and structs) can be serialized. We'll touch on the subject of encoding later in the chapter, but it isn't of much interest to us here because it's already supported by .NET. Rather than let SOAP handle the encoding, .NET performs the task of serializing data into different data types. We'll look at this further in Chapter 6. The marshaling of arguments is the one thing that can cause problems for any RPC mechanism, not just SOAP—hence the standard's preoccupation with it. XML is a perfect format for sending data, but because of its limitations it's preferable to handle the serialization separately.

SOAP 1.2

The latest version of the SOAP standard, 1.2, is no more than a last-call working draft on the W3C site as of this writing. It's quite a bit longer than the 1.1 standard, in part because it's based on the XML Information Set (Infoset), which makes for more precise and formal reading but is also more painfully drawn out. SOAP 1.2 can be found at *http://www.w3.org/2000/xp/Group/#soap12*.

> **Note** The XML Infoset is a consistent set of definitions for use in other specifications that need to reference XML documents. It is managed by W3C. The current standard can be found at *http://www.w3.org/TR/xml-infoset/*.

Even though the 1.2 standard is incomplete as of this writing, its status as a proposed recommendation document indicates that not much should change before final ratification.

SOAP 1.2 introduces some new features into the standard and removes one or two as well. Of particular interest is the fact that SOAP's most notable features are described more fully in this version of the specification. They include

- **Nodes** Nodes are the processing logic needed to send and receive information. Nodes can be broken down into senders and receivers. The initial sender is the SOAP node that started the correspondence, and the ultimate receiver is the intended destination of the message.
- **Roles** Roles replace actors from the 1.1 standard. A role or an actor is the intermediary that receives a SOAP header.
- **Features** Features are abstract pieces of functionality associated with the passing of SOAP messages. Examples include "reliability" and "security."
- **Modules** A module is a feature expressed as a SOAP header.
- **Message Exchange Patterns** These are templates for the exchange of SOAP messages between SOAP nodes. They were present in the SOAP 1.1 standard but take on a greater significance in the newer standard.

The standard hasn't changed dramatically, but the alterations include corrections to problems in SOAP 1.0 and SOAP 1.1. SOAP 1.2 also addresses the XML Schema specification, which didn't exist when SOAP first came into being. The standard is also now split into two main sections, one describing the messaging framework and one describing a set of adjuncts to the framework. No fundamental changes have been made to the structure of the SOAP message, though, so in this chapter we'll mainly talk about SOAP 1.1 because the .NET Framework version 1.1 supports it. We'll refer to SOAP 1.2 where the changes are likely to make a difference in the future.

Elements Defined in the SOAP Standard

We'll now talk about each of the main elements generically and point out any differences between SOAP 1.1 (which you'll be using if you're using the .NET Framework version 1.0 or 1.1) and SOAP 1.2 where they crop up. We'll start with the topmost element of a SOAP message, the SOAP envelope.

The SOAP Envelope

The SOAP envelope must always be the top-level element in a SOAP message. It must also contain a fully qualified namespace. A typical SOAP envelope element, prefixed by the *soap* namespace (the envelope namespace in the 1.1 standard), looks like this:

```
<soap:Envelope xmlns:soap="http://schemas.xmlsoap.org/soap/envelope">
.... SOAP Header and Body here ...
</soap:Envelope>
```

In either version of the SOAP standard, the SOAP header (if there is one) must come before the SOAP body. The SOAP header is optional and contains extra information about the message being sent. The SOAP body contains the XML payload—the information that is intended for the Web service or that is sent back by the service. We'll look at it first.

The SOAP Body

We've pointed out that SOAP is used to convey method calls to a Web service and method responses from the Web service. Indeed, the SOAP body is typically used to transmit the name of the method to be called, along with associated parameters and a response from the receiving application. The body can contain the information requested by the calling application if the response was successful or a fault message if a problem occurred.

The SOAP body request is the request document that is sent to the server. Here's a quick example Web method in C#, which, given a percentage value and a number, calculates what value is a percentage of the number and returns that to the client. The Web method to provide the functionality might look like this:

```
[WebMethod(Description="Calculates the percentage value "
    + "given a percentage and a number")]
public double CalcPercent(int Percent, double Number)
{
    double Value = Number / 100 * Percent;
    return Value;
}
```

SOAP Body Request

The SOAP message generated by a client of the Web service is as follows:

```
<?xml version="1.0" encoding="utf-8" ?>
<soap:Envelope xmlns:soap="http://schemas.xmlsoap.org/soap/envelope/"
    xmlns:xsi="http://www.w3.org/2001/XMLSchema-instance"
    xmlns:xsd="http://www.w3.org/2001/XMLSchema">
    <soap:Body>
        <CalcPercent xmlns="http://www.notashop.com/wscr">
            <Percent>25</Percent>
            <Number>4</Number>
        </CalcPercent>
    </soap:Body>
</soap:Envelope>
```

You can see in the SOAP body that the *<Envelope>* element is prefixed by the *soap:* namespace. This is the default used by .NET. The *<Envelope>* element contains the *<Body>* element, and inside the body is our CalculatePercent document. The document contains three elements, two of which represent the parameters supplied in the Web method, *<Percent>* and *<Number>*. These are both enclosed by the *<CalcPercent>* element, which represents our method. The document also has two autogenerated namespaces that aren't actually used: *xsi* and *xsd*. For the time being, just ignore them; they'll be used in later examples.

Note that both *Percent* and *Number* are actually strings in the SOAP. This string data is translated from the XML document into method parameters, which map to particular data types. Nothing in the SOAP provided here can stop textual data being passed, but the code would of course break when it got to the Web method. This translation is handled transparently by the code.

SOAP Body Response

A successful response document to our previous request looks like the following. (We won't consider faults until later in this chapter.)

```
<?xml version="1.0" encoding="utf-8" ?>
<soap:Envelope xmlns:soap="http://schemas.xmlsoap.org/soap/envelope/"
    xmlns:xsi="http://www.w3.org/2001/XMLSchema-instance"
    xmlns:xsd="http://www.w3.org/2001/XMLSchema">
    <soap:Body>
        <CalcPercentResponse xmlns="http://www.notashop.com/wscr">
            <CalcPercentResult>1</CalcPercentResult>
        </CalcPercentResponse>
    </soap:Body>
</soap:Envelope>
```

Just as our Web method returns only one value as a response, the SOAP body now has only one element to contain the response. This element, *<CalcPercentResult>*, contains the corresponding response to our request (What is 25 percent of 4?).

Capturing SOAP Messages

The SOAP messages are transmitted between the client and the Web service, so if you want to capture and view them, you can choose between a couple of approaches. One is to use the SOAP extensions to create a log and write the SOAP messages to a log. (We'll cover SOAP extensions in Chapter 10.) The second approach is to use the SOAP trace utility provided in the Microsoft SOAP Toolkit (whose latest version is 3.0). This toolkit allows developers to add XML Web service functionality to their existing COM applications, but it also contains the useful utility mssoapt3.exe, which allows you to listen to a port for incoming and outgoing messages and displays whatever is sent to the port. To get the utility to work, you need to set it up to listen on a port and get it to forward all requests it receives on that port to a specified server address.

> **Note** Trace utilities aren't unique to SOAP; you can also use them to listen to HTTP requests and responses. Indeed, if you don't want to use the SOAP Toolkit, you can find equally effective monitors such as TcpTrace (found at *http://www.pocketsoap.com/tcptrace/*).

We suggest pointing the utility at port 8080 of the server and then sending traffic to destination port 80. Responses returned from the server are then forwarded back to the client that made the original request. All requests and responses that go through the monitor are displayed on the trace utility screen. This works because to the client the monitor looks exactly like the server and to the server the monitor looks exactly like the client. The only thing is that you have to tell the client to talk to the monitor. This means you can no longer call your own server (for example, *http://localhost*) directly; instead, you must append the suffix *:8080* to wherever the Web service is called.

Once you've done this, you need to ensure that your application sends the messages via SOAP and not via HTTP *GET*, which is what it does by default if you use a browser to view the Web service. You must set up a Windows application using Visual Studio .NET to act as a client to call the Web method. The Windows application then has to interact with a client proxy class (that you've generated) to exchange details with the Web service.

You can autogenerate a proxy class from the WSDL created by the Web service by using wsdl.exe, a tool provided with the .NET Framework SDK. Here's the syntax you need. (A full discussion of how this tool works can be found in Chapter 1.)

```
wsdl /l:language /o:nameOfProxyClass http://urlOfWSDL /n:serviceName
```

For this example, you can use the following to generate a proxy class for our previous Web method in C#:

```
wsdl /l:cs /o:PercentProxy.cs ➘
    http://localhost/Percent1/service1.asmx?WSDL /n:PercentService
```

or in Visual Basic .NET:

```
wsdl /l:vb /o:PercentProxy.vb ↵
    http://localhost/Percent1/service1.asmx?WSDL /n:PercentService
```

Next you need to open the proxy class and alter the reference *this.url* (or *me.url* in Visual Basic .NET) to point from *http://localhost* to *http://localhost:8080*:

```
this.Url = "http://localhost:8080/wscr/02/Percent1/service1.asmx";
```

You then need to compile the class created by wsdl.exe into a DLL using the C# compiler and include a reference to that DLL in your Windows application. You can then make calls to the Web service and the Web method via the names you supplied to wsdl.exe.

Last, you need to create the Windows application to interact with the Web service via the proxy.

Simple Types in a SOAP Body

Now that you have an idea of how to use a monitor to view the SOAP messages passed by the Web method, let's look at how to pass simple types, such as an integer and a double, to a Web service and in what format the answer is returned.

Start by creating a Windows application with a form containing a single button and two text box controls for the input and a label control for the answer, as shown in Figure 2-2. Call the application CalcPercentClient.

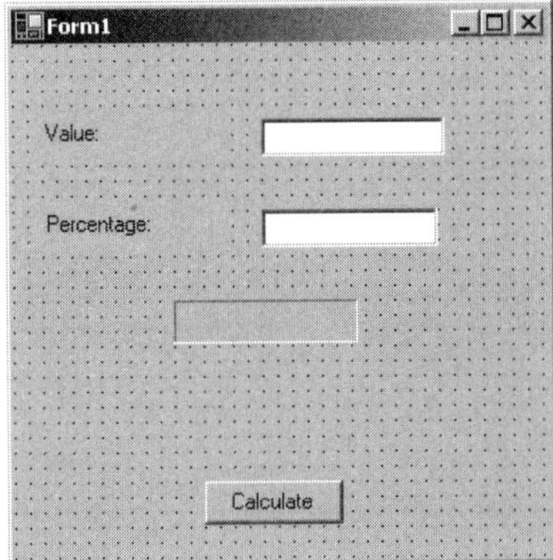

Figure 2-2 Form for sample Windows application that uses the CalcPercent Web service

Add references to *System.Web.Services* and to the WebPercentProxy.dll assembly you created in the previous section. Then add the following event handler code to return information from our CalcPercent Web service:

```
private void button1_Click(object sender, System.EventArgs e)
{
    PercentService.Service1 wsp = new PercentService.Service1();
    double Total = wsp.CalcPercent(Convert.ToInt32(textBox1.Text),
       Convert.ToDouble(textBox2.Text));
    label1.Text = Total.ToString();
}
```

If you have the SOAP trace utility turned on, you can view the same SOAP messages between your application and Web service that we looked at earlier.

How .NET Handles Structs in the SOAP Body

The first example passed only simple types in our Web method, but if we alter our Web method to use a structure (the C# type *struct*), we can see how more complex types are treated in the SOAP body. The main difference here is that .NET looks after the serialization of the data types. This is not specified in the SOAP standard.

Here's a struct containing three data types:

```
public struct DataTypes
{
    public Boolean Smoking;
    public String Name;
    public Int32 Age;
}
```

We can assign values to each of these fields within the body of our Web method:

```
[WebMethod(Description="sends structs")]
public DataTypes ReturnValues()
{
    DataTypes MyStruct = new DataTypes();
    MyStruct.Smoking = true;
    MyStruct.Name = "Shane DeSeranno";
    MyStruct.Age = 56;

    return MyStruct;
}
```

If we create a small Windows application to fetch this data much as we did in the previous application, the SOAP response we can receive in the SOAP trace utility looks like this:

```
<?xml version="1.0" encoding="utf-8" ?>
<soap:Envelope xmlns:soap=http://schemas.xmlsoap.org/soap/envelope/
    xmlns:xsi="http://www.w3.org/2001/XMLSchema-instance"
    xmlns:xsd="http://www.w3.org/2001/XMLSchema">
    <soap:Body>
        <ReturnValuesResponse xmlns="http://www.notashop.com/wscr">
            <ReturnValuesResult>
                <Smoking>true</Smoking>
                <Name>Shane DeSeranno</Name>
                <Age>56</Age>
            </ReturnValuesResult>
        </ReturnValuesResponse>
    </soap:Body>
</soap:Envelope>
```

The difference between this structure and the simple types we looked at previously is that an extra set of elements has been added within the SOAP body. The *<ReturnValuesResult>* element contains three elements that contain our values. The elements correspond to the three types we passed as part of the struct and are treated just like separate data types, with an element for the *Boolean*, *String*, and *Int32* variables, respectively. Apart from the extra elements, there are no other differences in the body of the message.

How .NET Handles Arrays in the SOAP Body

Structures are sequences made up of different types; you can use them to collect these types in one structure. You use arrays, on the other hand, when you need to represent several instances of the same data type. You can create an array of structures and then read data into them using a Web method.

Start by declaring a struct, this one containing one string and two integers:

```
public struct Order
{
    public String Name;
    public Int32 OrderNum;
    public Int32 Price;
}
```

The Web method creates an array of structs and then uses a loop to read a string and two integers into each struct. Here's the code:

```
[WebMethod(Description="sends arrays")]
public Order[] ReturnValues()
{
    Order [] Array = new Order[3];
    for (int i=0; i<=2; i++)
    {
        Order Field = new Order();
        Field.Name = "Shane DeSeranno";
```

```
        Field.OrderNum = i+1;
        Field.Price = 10;
        Array[i] = Field;
    }
    return Array;
}
```

The SOAP message that this method creates looks like this:

```
<?xml version="1.0" encoding="utf-8" ?>
<soap:Envelope xmlns:soap="http://schemas.xmlsoap.org/soap/envelope/"
    xmlns:xsi="http://www.w3.org/2001/XMLSchema-instance"
    xmlns:xsd="http://www.w3.org/2001/XMLSchema">
    <soap:Body>
        <ReturnValuesResponse xmlns="http://www.notashop.com/wscr">
            <ReturnValuesResult>
                <Order>
                    <Name>Shane DeSeranno</Name>
                    <OrderNum>1</OrderNum>
                    <Price>10</Price>
                </Order>
                <Order>
                    <Name>Shane DeSeranno</Name>
                    <OrderNum>2</OrderNum>
                    <Price>10</Price>
                </Order>
                <Order>
                    <Name>Shane DeSeranno</Name>
                    <OrderNum>3</OrderNum>
                    <Price>10</Price>
                </Order>
            </ReturnValuesResult>
        </ReturnValuesResponse>
    </soap:Body>
</soap:Envelope>
```

The SOAP body created by the array differs from the one created for the structure. We've created an array of structures, and inside the containing *<ReturnValuesResponse>* and *<ReturnValuesResult>* elements, the struct is repeated three times, one for each index number. However, the SOAP message makes no effort to distinguish between the different structures in the array, other than to represent their data. So each structure is represented by an identical *<DataType>* element, which in turn contains elements for the string and two integers. The element names are identical, and the only reason you'd notice that the information isn't just being repeated is that we read the loop counter from the array into one of the numbers. Even if the same element were included 3000 times, this wouldn't just mean the information was repeated; it would mean that the content was an array of 300 identical values. The important thing to notice here is that XML treats the order of elements as a part of the infoset, and it preserves the infoset.

This is straightforward enough, but we'll start to look behind the scenes at what's actually going on. For starters, there is no indication of any data types being retained by the SOAP. This isn't the job of SOAP; instead, it is defined by the WSDL that accompanies the SOAP and the Web service. However, we've only looked at one type of SOAP message formatting; a second type provides data type information in the message body as well.

SOAP Message Validation

Before you process a message sent to your Web service, you might want to validate it against some kind of definition. XML provides validation against a DTD or a schema, so this should be easy, shouldn't it? As it turns out, it's not: references to a schema or a DTD are not allowed inside the *<Body>* element. But you can define the message schema outside of SOAP—for example, in a WSDL file. This approach is called the *document-literal style*, or *doc-lit*, after the corresponding names in WSDL.

You won't find these names in the SOAP specification. Using doc-lit means using SOAP as a trusted postman to deliver the message, and SOAP won't look inside. This is the default approach taken by the .NET Framework Web service implementation.

SOAP 1.1 was designed before the advent of WSDL and the XML Schema, so it offers its own serialization standard, known today as *SOAP encoding* or *section 5 encoding*. In this case, a message is valid only if it uses the constructs and type names offered by the SOAP encoding specification.

For special kinds of applications, the SOAP standard has some extra validity rules. If you're using SOAP in a remote method invocation or RPC scenario, you can use so-called RPC representation. RPC representation makes the use of encoding mandatory and defines additional structural requirements for when you use .NET Remoting. However, you don't have to use SOAP in RPC mode to be able to make RPC-like method calls. This is an important point—you can do this just as easily in the document format.

Most of the time, you'll find yourself using the document format because the RPC format is a bit of a throwback to the early days of SOAP. The document format, despite its name, can handle both XML documents and RPC calls, and in .NET it does just about everything that the RPC format can. The main thing the RPC format does is handle the different XML data types. With the document format, you can leave it up to .NET to handle the process of serializing each data type correctly. As a result, strong signs are emerging that the RPC style might be on its way out. The Web Services Interoperability organization (WS-I) has removed RPC-encoded format from its first draft. One reason for this is the document format's better interoperability; the SOAP section 5 encoding poses some insurmountable problems. Also, you can do more in the document format. For example, the RPC style doesn't work well with asynchronous services and can't be validated against an XML schema.

We'll take a look at both programming models, but we'll primarily concentrate on the document format.

Document Format

In the document format, the message structure inside the *Body* element is not defined by SOAP—it's simply not the SOAP protocol stack's business. As you saw in our example, the document format is preferable; it is described in WSDL files instead by Web services and is the default type in most development kits. It is also the default in .NET.

The document format is meant to deal only with one-way transactions, but it is also possible to use it to model two-way request-response messages. You've already seen an example of how the document format parcels up the SOAP body of our *CalcPercent* Web method:

```
⋮
<soap:Body>
    <CalculatePercent xmlns="http://www.notashop.com/wscr">
        <Percent>25</Percent>
        <Number>4</Number>
    </CalculatePercent>
</soap:Body>
⋮
```

Each subelement is known as a *part*, and it must be contained within the SOAP body. The part corresponds to a part element within the WSDL document. Other than the SOAP document being well formed, the structure has no other restrictions.

In .NET, you can specify that you want to use the document format by using the *SoapDocumentMethod* attribute, which you can specify after the *WebMethod* attribute in the .NET class as follows, if you include the *Systems.Web.Services.Protocols* namespace:

```
using System.Web.Services.Protocols
⋮
[WebMethod(Description="Calculates the percentage value "
    + "given a percentage and a number")]
[SoapDocumentMethod]
public double CalcPercent(int Percent, double Number)
{
    ⋮
}
```

This is already the default format, so it makes no difference to the SOAP messages that are produced unless you set the accompanying attributes.

The *SoapDocumentMethod* attribute also has a set of properties, all but one of which can be set by using the *[SoapDocumentMethod]* specifier:

- ***Action*** Sets the SOAP Action header. (More about this later.)
- ***Binding*** Sets the SOAP binding.
- ***OneWay*** Specifies whether the client should wait for the server to finish processing the method.
- ***ParameterStyle*** Specifies how the parameters are formatted in a SOAP message. Can be set to either *Wrapped* (sent in a single XML element in the body) or *Bare* (sent in several XML elements in the body). By default, in ASP.NET it is set to wrapped. *ParameterStyle* can apply only to document-literal style messages.
- ***RequestElementName*** Specifies the XML element for an XML service method that is used in the SOAP request.
- ***RequestNamespace*** Specifies the namespace for the SOAP request.
- ***ResponseElementName*** Specifies the XML element for an XML service method that is used in the SOAP response.
- ***ResponseNamespace*** Specifies the namespace for the SOAP response.
- ***TypeId*** Gets a unique identifier for the attribute.
- ***Use*** Determines whether literal or encoded serialization style is used.

These properties are passed as initialization parameters of the attribute. In C#, they are set in the *[SoapDocumentMethod]* body within separate parentheses, for example:

```
[SoapDocumentMethod(
    RequestNamespace="http://www.notashop.com/wscr"
    ResponseNamespace="http://www.notashop.com/wscr"
    Use=SoapBindingUse.Encoded)]
```

RPC Representation

In the RPC representation, each message part is a parameter of the operation being called. Each message part is placed inside an element that shares the name of the operation being called. This element is contained within the SOAP body. In practice, the first difference you'll see is that this adds an extra element to the SOAP message for the method name. This is closer to the HTTP-GET/HTTP-POST format because it also uses a similar request/response-type structure. Unlike the document format, it's possible with RPC to include type information for each argument of the call. The RPC format uses the encoding style, which means it uses SOAP encoding to serialize the information according to the different data types.

If we change the previous CalcPercent Web service example to read as follows:

```
[WebMethod(Description="Calculates the percentage value "
    + "given a percentage and a number")]
[SoapRpcMethod]
public double CalcPercent(int Percent, double Number)
{
    ⋮
}
```

and then re-create the WSDL, compile the client and service, and run the service while listening on SOAP trace, we get back the following SOAP message for the request:

```
<?xml version="1.0" encoding="utf-8" ?>
<soap:Envelope xmlns:soap="http://schemas.xmlsoap.org/soap/envelope/"
    xmlns:soapenc="http://schemas.xmlsoap.org/soap/encoding/"
    xmlns:tns="http://www.notashop/wscr"
    xmlns:types="http://www.notashop/wscr/encodedTypes"
    xmlns:xsi="http://www.w3.org/2001/XMLSchema-instance"
    xmlns:xsd="http://www.w3.org/2001/XMLSchema">
    <soap:Body
        soap:encodingStyle="http://schemas.xmlsoap.org/soap/encoding/">
        <tns:CalcPercent>
            <Percent xsi:type="xsd:int">3</Percent>
            <Number xsi:type="xsd:double">52</Number>
        </tns:CalcPercent>
    </soap:Body>
  </soap:Envelope>
```

and the following SOAP message for the response:

```
<?xml version="1.0" encoding="utf-8" ?>
<soap:Envelope xmlns:soap="http://schemas.xmlsoap.org/soap/envelope/"
    xmlns:soapenc="http://schemas.xmlsoap.org/soap/encoding/"
    xmlns:tns="http://www.notashop.com/wscr"
    xmlns:types="http://www.notashop.com/wscr/encodedTypes"
    xmlns:xsi="http://www.w3.org/2001/XMLSchema-instance"
    xmlns:xsd="http://www.w3.org/2001/XMLSchema">
    <soap:Body soap:encodingStyle="http://schemas.xmlsoap.org/soap/encoding/">
```

```
        <tns:CalcPercentResponse>
            <CalcPercentResult xsi:type="xsd:double">1.56
            </CalcPercentResult>
        </tns:CalcPercentResponse>
    </soap:Body>
</soap:Envelope>
```

There are several important points to note. The first is the addition of some extra namespace definitions to the *<Envelope>* element. The *tns* namespace is defined and it applies to your own target namespace. The second is the addition of types to the SOAP body. This information isn't actually omitted in the document format; it's included separately inside the WSDL document. The type information is specified according to the rules of the XML Schema types rather than the .NET types. This means the *Percent* variable has the type *int* rather than *Int32*. The type name belongs to the XML *schema* namespace, and the type attribute belongs to the XML *schema instance* namespace. This information is used in the serializing of the different types. The third and final point is the inclusion of an *encodingStyle* attribute in the SOAP body. This attribute specifies what encoding rules should be used to serialize a SOAP message. By default, the method marked *[SoapRpcMethod]* can use only the encoding style (as opposed to the literal style).

The *SoapRpcMethod* attribute has all the same properties as its *SoapDocumentMethod* relative, with a couple of notable exceptions. The first is that the *ParameterStyle* and *Use* properties are missing. *ParameterStyle* can apply only to the document format and is therefore missing; also, as we discussed earlier, only the encoding style can be specified for the RPC style, so there is no need to have a property that explicitly sets this.

Overall, the document format is preferable for sending SOAP messages. You have more control over the contents of the XML payload, and you can also make it conform to a schema. RPC/encoding style can be useful, in theory, for more specialized situations, such as when you serialize items that need to use RPC (object graphs, for example). Before we move on, let's investigate SOAP encoding a bit more.

SOAP Encoding

SOAP encoding, also known as section 5 encoding, is a hot topic of debate. It is seen in some quarters as a "shadow from the past"—a legacy of the original SOAP specification, when SOAP was seen as a better way to integrate with object technologies such as DCOM and CORBA rather than as a means of calling functionality of other applications remotely. Because SOAP is now interlinked with WSDL, which describes the behavior that a Web service supports and is, along with UDDI, an essential building block of Web services, problems can occur when you try to serialize data to XML and apply it to XML Schema definitions. In fact, the WS-I considers these problems insurmountable in some places.

The SOAP encoding rules contain details on serializing application data into arrays and objects, but they don't specify any particular interpretation of the data. This is left up to the receiving application, which itself doesn't always specify a particular interpretation. We'll take a brief look at how the different types are treated in SOAP encoding.

Simple Types

The simple types are types such as strings and enumerations. You saw in the previous section how integers and doubles are encoded—with a type attribute that .NET includes (although not all SOAP implementations include this attribute):

```
<soap:Body
    soap:encodingStyle="http://schemas.xmlsoap.org/soap/encoding/">
    <tns:CalcPercent>
        <Percent xsi:type="xsd:int">3</Percent>
        <Number xsi:type="xsd:double">52</Number>
    </tns:CalcPercent>
</soap:Body>
```

SOAP encoding allows you to use all of the XSD data types that are contained in the XML Schema specification. Little changes in the process when you encode other simple types, such as strings. For example, if we change our *Percent* variable to a string as follows, information specified in the type attribute actually changes:

```
<Percent xsi:type="xsd:string">Three</Percent>
```

Compound Types

The compound types are arrays and structures (C# *struct*). We've looked at how both of these types are handled by .NET serialization in the document format, so now let's see how they can be encoded according to the SOAP 1.1 specification.

Structures

Structures consist of a collection of independent types, so it makes sense that each type specified within a struct should be serialized according to the rules of its own particular type. For example, if we amend our previous example of a struct as follows

```
[WebMethod(Description="sends structs")]
[SoapRpcMethod]
```

```
public DataTypes ReturnValues()
{
    DataTypes MyStruct = new DataTypes();
    MyStruct.Smoking = true;
    MyStruct.Name = "Shane DeSeranno";
    MyStruct.Age = 56;

    return MyStruct;
}
```

and then we send the SOAP message, the following is returned:

```
<?xml version="1.0" encoding="utf-8" ?>
<soap:Envelope xmlns:soap="http://schemas.xmlsoap.org/soap/envelope/"
    xmlns:soapenc="http://schemas.xmlsoap.org/soap/encoding/"
    xmlns:tns="http://www.notashop.com/wscr"
    xmlns:types="http://www.notashop.com/wscr/encodedTypes"
    xmlns:xsi="http://www.w3.org/2001/XMLSchema-instance"
    xmlns:xsd="http://www.w3.org/2001/XMLSchema">
    <soap:Body
        soap:encodingStyle="http://schemas.xmlsoap.org/soap/encoding/">
        <tns:ReturnValuesResponse>
            <ReturnValuesResult href="#id1" />
        </tns:ReturnValuesResponse>
        <types:DataTypes id="id1" xsi:type="types:DataTypes">
            <Smoking xsi:type="xsd:boolean">true</Smoking>
            <Name xsi:type="xsd:string">Shane DeSeranno</Name>
            <Age xsi:type="xsd:int">56</Age>
        </types:DataTypes>
    </soap:Body>
</soap:Envelope>
```

You can see that each type within the struct has its own type attribute, but each type is also collected in a *DataTypes* element. As before, there is also a separate *Response* element for *ReturnValues*.

Array Handling

SOAP RPC-style messages also allow for encoding of arrays. We can't change our previous array example to use *[SoapRpcMethod]* because an array of structs cannot be serialized using RPC-encoded SOAP. Instead, here's a simplified example of an array that just defines the integers 1 to 5:

```
[WebMethod(Description="sends array")]
[SoapRpcMethod]
public int [] ReturnArray()
{
    int [] Numbers = {1, 2, 3, 4, 5};
    return Numbers;
}
```

When sent, this yields the following SOAP response:

```
<?xml version="1.0" encoding="utf-8" ?>
<soap:Envelope xmlns:soap="http://schemas.xmlsoap.org/soap/envelope/"
    xmlns:soapenc="http://schemas.xmlsoap.org/soap/encoding/"
    xmlns:tns="http://www.notashop.com/wscr"
    xmlns:types="http://www.notashop.com/wscr/encodedTypes"
    xmlns:xsi="http://www.w3.org/2001/XMLSchema-instance"
    xmlns:xsd="http://www.w3.org/2001/XMLSchema">
    <soap:Body
        soap:encodingStyle="http://schemas.xmlsoap.org/soap/encoding/">
        <tns:ReturnArrayResponse>
            <ReturnArrayResult href="#id1" />
        </tns:ReturnArrayResponse>
        <soapenc:Array id="id1" soapenc:arrayType="xsd:int[5]">
            <Item>1</Item>
            <Item>2</Item>
            <Item>3</Item>
            <Item>4</Item>
            <Item>5</Item>
        </soapenc:Array>
    </soap:Body>
</soap:Envelope>
```

The array is serialized with five parts, which all share the name *<Item>*. These parts are contained within a *soapenc:Array* element, which has an attribute specifying the array type, in this case *int*, and also the number of elements within the type. There is also still the issue of mapping our data types to XML, but this is dealt with in the WSDL document, so we'll leave that discussion until the next chapter.

Because SOAP encoding seems to be an endangered species these days and the most you'll use it for will probably be debugging and troubleshooting, this coverage should be enough.

Sending SOAP over HTTP

One major advantage of SOAP is that it isn't tightly coupled to any protocol. SOAP messages are just XML documents, so you can bind SOAP to many other protocols—in fact, any protocol capable of transporting XML. However, with ASP.NET Web services, SOAP by default can be bound only to the HTTP protocol. If you call a Web service using an ASP.NET client, you get SOAP bound to HTTP.

So far, we've discussed only the contents of the SOAP message, but that's not all that's contained in the SOAP request and SOAP response when you send messages. When you use HTTP to send SOAP, the SOAP message is sent as part of an HTTP request or response; also included in the SOAP message are the HTTP headers.

Sending Information via HTTP-POST

The HTTP protocol commonly uses two formats to send information, but when you send SOAP envelopes via HTTP, you'll find that in .NET 1.0, according to the SOAP 1.1 standard, this information is sent via HTTP-POST. The protocol binding allows for extensions that allow SOAP messages bound to HTTP to pass through firewalls.

When you test a Web service using a browser, an example version of the HTTP header information is automatically generated:

```
POST /recordstore1/service1.asmx HTTP/1.1
Host: chrisuhome
Content-Type: text/xml; charset=utf-8
Content-Length: length
SOAPAction: "http://chrisuhome:8080/GetRecord"
```

Five headers are typically sent when you test a Web service method using the browser (although potentially far more can be used). HTTP itself has a similar structure to SOAP in that it, too, breaks down into a header and a body. The HTTP header contains details about the client's request, such as the length of the content in the request, the type of content, its intended destination, and the method of its carriage. The POST method indicates that the data of the request is transported in the message body.

SOAP Content Type

When you send SOAP over HTTP, some rules always apply. First, you must set the Content-type header. This is commonly set to type *text/xml,* although the SOAP 1.2 standard suggests that this should be *application/soap+xml* in the future. Also, in SOAP 1.1 you can send a SOAPAction header along with the request; this header can indicate the intent of the SOAP HTTP request, which contains an endpoint. The SOAP action does not need to be the address of the endpoint or any other resolvable address. It can even be empty. However, not setting the SOAPAction header in .NET might cause problems.

SOAPAction Header

The idea of the SOAPAction header is that it can define richer types of messages, such as those with multiple actions. The firewall that deals with the message can then use the SOAPAction header to help discern the message's content and decide whether to let it through. As we've mentioned, a SOAPAction header must be present to make the message valid, and indeed we'll look at what happens in the SOAP fault section if we don't send one. It's possible, however, to specify a blank SOAP header, as in the following:

```
POST /wscr/02/RecordFinder/service1.asmx HTTP/1.1
Host: www.notashop.com
Content-Type: text/xml; charset=utf-8
Content-Length: length
SOAPAction:
```

Indeed, no strict rules govern the format of the SOAPAction header; it is set to whatever the Web service wants it to be. As a result, meaningful use of it has been minimal and its usefulness is questionable; it has been removed in version 1.2 of the standard. The problem is that even if you do get to send a message and communicate its intent via a SOAPAction header, it is possible to mask its intentions, so as a security check it becomes fairly useless.

Changes to Bindings in SOAP 1.2

As we've discussed, in SOAP 1.1 when you bind SOAP across HTTP you're by default using HTTP-POST; the SOAP envelope is the payload to the request, and the body of the response is the response SOAP envelope. To complicate matters, SOAP 1.2 defines both HTTP-GET and HTTP-POST as being allowed for the underlying transport.

HTTP-GET

The HTTP-GET method is used exclusively with the SOAP Response Message Exchange Pattern. This message pattern describes a SOAP-formatted response that is returned in reply to a non-SOAP request. This abstract definition simply means

- No HTTP-GET request can carry a SOAP-formatted message. The GET request uses normal *url* encoding, and only the response is SOAP.
- Any HTTP-GET request without a reply is outside the scope of the SOAP standard. There simply is nothing on the wire to check against the standard.
- An ordinary HTTP-GET request that returns a SOAP-formatted message is covered by the SOAP 1.2 standard.

HTTP-POST

The HTTP-POST method is used exclusively with the SOAP Request-Response Message Exchange Pattern. This pattern mirrors the default (and only) pattern that exists in SOAP 1.1.

Binding to Other Protocols

You can also bind SOAP over a number of other protocols and formats: SMTP, FTP, and even floppy disk, to name a few. But because Web services work over HTTP, we won't consider how SOAP is bound to these other protocols.

Sending Datasets via an Application

We've examined the basic contents of the SOAP message and the HTTP header that accompanies it when it's sent over HTTP, and we've demonstrated how SOAP can encode basic and compound types, but you'll find that even the simplest applications need to send more complex types, such as datasets. We'll take this opportunity to not only show how datasets are sent, processed, and received in SOAP, but also to build a small Web client that uses ASP.NET to send the SOAP message and return a SOAP message back to the page rather than requiring us to use SOAP trace to snoop on it.

This application provides a search on a hypothetical music store with a simple query interface (by artist or by record title), and then it returns either a single album or multiple albums in the form of a SOAP message. Because the ASP.NET ISAPI filters ensure that you can send messages only via HTTP and not via SOAP, we've had to circumvent the automatically generated proxy client that wsdl.exe builds and build one ourselves to be able to send a SOAP message. If you were to view the message with a monitor such as the one provided in the SOAP Toolkit, you wouldn't get a SOAP message because there wouldn't be one to view. You'd only get to see the HTTP message. Instead, we'll have to construct and send the SOAP message manually.

To do this, we'll create a proxy client that physically constructs the SOAP request and sends it as a stream of bytes and then receives the results back from the database in the same way. We won't spend a lot of time discussing how the code does this; we'll keep it to a brief overview and focus on just the SOAP part of the service.

Our example is in ASP.NET C#, and the hypothetical music store uses Microsoft SQL Server to keep its stock details. The SQL database is then exposed to the Web via a couple of Web methods. This sample database and the code are available with this book's sample files. Our example takes a query from a user in HTML form and creates a SOAP request that the user doesn't get to see. Then the example's code loads the user-supplied data from the form into the request. This request is then sent to a server, which runs the contents of the query/SOAP request against an SQL database and returns a response to the user as a SOAP message. Our application has four separate pieces of logic—the example database (which has already been created), the Web service, the communication layer, and the ASP.NET client. We'll create them in that order.

The Web Service

The Web service is called RecordFinder, which is the name of our namespace; the service itself is called Service1. Here's our code for the two Web methods in the RecordFinder Web service:

```
⋮
using System.Web.Services.Protocols;
using System.Data.OleDb;
⋮

[WebMethod(Description="Service that gets the records "
    + "using the artist name", MessageName="GetArtist")]
[SoapDocumentMethod (Action="/GetArtist")]
public DataSet GetArtistRecords(string Artist)
{
    OleDbConnection objConnection;
    OleDbDataAdapter objCommand;
    string strConnect;
    string strCommand;
    DataSet DataSet1 = new DataSet();

    strConnect = "Provider=SQLOLEDB.1;Password=a12s;"
        + "Persist Security Info=True;User ID=ASPNET;"
        + "Initial Catalog=dansrecordsSQL;Data Source=(local)";
    strCommand = "SELECT Title From Records WHERE Artist='"
        + Artist + "'";
    objConnection = new OleDbConnection(strConnect);
    objCommand = new OleDbDataAdapter(strCommand, objConnection);
    objCommand.Fill(DataSet1,"Records");

    return DataSet1;
}

[WebMethod(BufferResponse=true, CacheDuration=20,
        Description="Service that get a record "
    + "using the title name", MessageName="GetTitle")]
[SoapDocumentMethod (Action="/GetTitle")]
public DataSet GetTitleDetails(string Title)
{
    OleDbConnection objConnection;
    OleDbDataAdapter objCommand;
    string strConnect;
    string strCommand;
    DataSet DataSet1 = new DataSet();
```

```
    strConnect = "Provider=SQLOLEDB.1;Password=a12s;"
        + "Persist Security Info=True;User ID=ASPNET;"
        + "Initial Catalog=dansrecordsSQL;Data Source=(local)";
    strCommand = "SELECT Artist From Records WHERE Title='"
        + Title + "'";
    objConnection = new OleDbConnection(strConnect);
    objCommand = new OleDbDataAdapter(strCommand, objConnection);
    objCommand.Fill(DataSet1,"Records");

    return DataSet1;
}
```

The two Web methods are nearly identical in terms of code. Both open connections to a SQL database and create a dataset. The only difference is the SQL used to create the dataset. The *GetArtist* method uses SQL to extract the relevant titles from the database, and the *GetTitle* method uses SQL to extract the relevant artists. Ideally, a full application would return more than just the title or the artist name, but the SOAP generated would be quite extensive and we don't want to further complicate the example. We're more interested in the SOAP that's generated.

The Web Service Communication Class

Wsdl.exe is of course capable of autogenerating the code needed for the proxy class, but because we're creating the SOAP messages as strings in the Web page, we need to construct a communication class that's capable of picking up the SOAP message string and sending it to the Web service properly packaged and also receiving the response in the *DataSet* format. We can add a class *ASPNETclient.cs* to our project as follows:

```
⋮
using System.IO;
using System.Text;
using System.Net;
⋮
public class ASPNETclient
{
    public string soapResult= "Empty";
    public string serviceURL =
        "http://localhost/wscr/02/RecordFinder/Service1.asmx";
    public string serviceNamespace = "http://www.notashop.com/wscr";

    public string SOAPResult
    {
        get
        {
            return soapResult;
        }
    }
```

```
public void SendSOAPRequest(string actionName, string soapBody)
{
    WebRequest servRequest;
    servRequest = WebRequest.Create(serviceURL);
    servRequest.Headers.Add("SOAPAction",actionName);
    HttpWebRequest serviceRequest = (HttpWebRequest)servRequest;
    serviceRequest.ContentType = "text/xml";
    AddSOAP(serviceRequest, soapBody);
    _soapResult = ReturnSOAPResponse(serviceRequest);
}

private void AddSOAP(HttpWebRequest serviceRequest, string body)
{
    serviceRequest.Method = "POST";
    UTF8Encoding encoding = new UTF8Encoding();
    byte[] bodyBytes = encoding.GetBytes(body);
    serviceRequest.ContentLength = bodyBytes.Length;
    Stream serviceRequestBodyStream =
        serviceRequest.GetRequestStream();
    serviceRequestBodyStream.Write(bodyBytes, 0, bodyBytes.Length);
    serviceRequestBodyStream.Close();
}

private string ReturnSOAPResponse(HttpWebRequest serviceRequest)
{
    StreamReader serviceResponseStream;
    try
    {
        WebResponse servResponse;
        servResponse = serviceRequest.GetResponse();
        HttpWebResponse serviceResponse =
            (HttpWebResponse)servResponse;
        serviceResponseStream = new StreamReader(
            serviceResponse.GetResponseStream(),
            System.Text.Encoding.ASCII);
    }
    catch (WebException e)
    {
        serviceResponseStream = new StreamReader(
            e.Response.GetResponseStream(),
            System.Text.Encoding.ASCII);
    }
    catch (Exception e)
    {
        return e.Message.ToString();
    }
    string serviceResponseBody;
    serviceResponseBody = serviceResponseStream.ReadToEnd();
```

```
        serviceResponseStream.Close();
        return (serviceResponseBody);
    }
}
```

The *ASPNETClient.cs* class is composed of three functions and a single read-only property. The first function, *SendSOAPRequest*, creates the HTTP header that is necessary for the binding to take place. It starts by creating a Web request for our Web service URL and then takes the header that is generated and adds a SOAPAction header and a Content-type header. It then calls the section function *AddSOAP* from within its body, supplying the HTTP header details and the SOAP body (which is supplied by our ASP.NET client). *AddSOAP* then writes our complete SOAP request (HTTP header and SOAP body) to a stream that's received by the Web service implemented by the Web methods defined above. We then use *ReturnSOAPResponse* to get the response returned by the Web service.

The ASP.NET Client

Next we can create the ASP.NET Web form, which we've named SOAPSender.aspx. This Web form can call the communication class to access our Web methods with one drop-down list containing the entries Artist and Title (corresponding to the two searches we can do), one text box for the search, and a button to instigate it:

```
<%@ Page language="c#" Codebehind="SOAPSender.aspx.cs"
    AutoEventWireup="false" Inherits="RecordFinder.SOAPSender" %>
⋮
    <body MS_POSITIONING="GridLayout">
        <form id="RecordStoreQuery1" method="post" runat="server">
            <asp:ListBox ID="listBox1"
                Runat=server SelectionMode=Single Rows=1>
            <asp:ListItem>Artist</asp:ListItem>
            <asp:ListItem>Title</asp:ListItem>
            </asp:ListBox>
            <asp:Label ID="label1" Runat="server">
                Type artist to find here:
            </asp:Label>
            <asp:TextBox id="txtUserInput" runat="server"></asp:TextBox><br>
            <br>
            <asp:Button ID="button1" Runat="server"
                Text="Click here to search" OnClick="RetrieveRecords">
            </asp:Button>
        </form>
    </body>
</HTML>
```

The code-behind is as follows:

```
using System.Xml;
using System.Data.OleDb;
using System.Data;
⋮
public void RetrieveRecords(object sender, EventArgs e)
{
    string lbs = listBox1.SelectedItem.Text;
    string actionName = "/Get" + lbs;
    string soapBody = "<?xml version = \"1.0\" "
        + "encoding = \"utf-8\" ?>"
        + "<soap:Envelope "
        + "xmlns:soap=\"http://schemas.xmlsoap.org/soap/envelope/\""
        + " xmlns:xsi=\"http://www.w3.org/2001/XMLSchema-instance\" "
        + "xmlns:xsd=\"http://www.w3.org/2001/XMLSchema\">"
        + "<soap:Body><Get" + lbs + "  xmlns=\"http://tempuri.org/\">"
        + "<"+lbs+">" + txtUserInput.Text + "</" + lbs + "></Get"
        + lbs + ">" + "</soap:Body></soap:Envelope>";
    RecordFinder.ASPNETclient wsp = new RecordFinder.ASPNETclient();
    wsp.SendSOAPRequest(actionName, soapBody);
    XmlDocument doc = new XmlDocument();
    doc.LoadXml(wsp.SOAPResult);
    doc.Save("C:\\inetpub\\wwwroot\\wscr\\02\\RecordFinder\\SOAPResponse.xml");
    Response.Redirect("SOAPResponse.xml");
}
```

The ASP.NET client creates a SOAPAction header based on the method name to be called. The client determines the method to be called by deriving it from the drop-down list. The SOAPAction is important because if you don't supply a SOAPAction header that matches up with the one specified in the Web service, the .NET Framework generates a "SOAP did not recognize the value of the HTTP Header: SOAPAction" error. If you omit the SOAPAction header completely, you generate a "Request format not recognized" error because in SOAP 1.1 a SOAPAction header is mandatory for a SOAP message.

The ASP.NET client also creates the SOAP envelope and a body for a request, and it substitutes the elements in the SOAP body depending on whether the client wants the artist name or the artist's titles. We then create an instance of the ASPNETClient class called *wsp* and call the *SendSOAPRequest* method with a value for the SOAPAction header and the SOAP message text. We load the result as an XML document object model (DOM) object to avoid problems such as an error being generated because the URI of the different namespace is not recognized. Finally, we take the slightly clumsy action of saving this XML document and redirecting the browser to the saved document.

When we run the query shown in Figure 2-3 against the database, the SOAP in Figure 2-4 is returned.

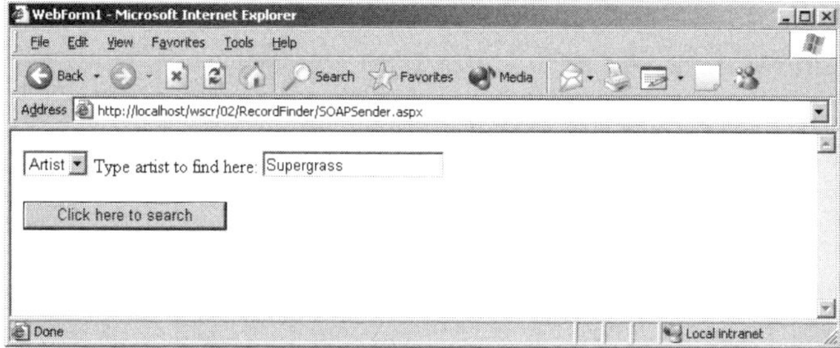

Figure 2-3 Using the SOAPSender ASP.NET application to search for an artist

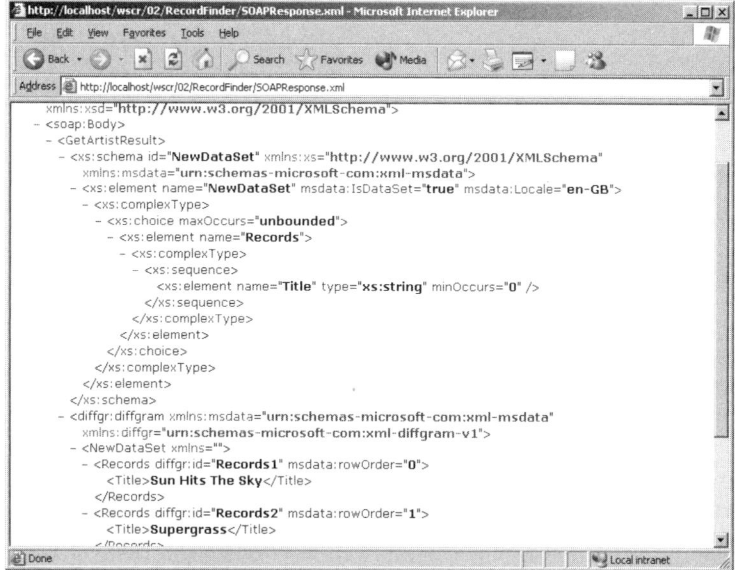

Figure 2-4 The SOAP document that the SOAPSender application returns

The SOAP that is returned is quite lengthy. It divides roughly into two sections: the XSD schema information, which denotes the correct format for the XML data, and a dataset that contains the data returned by the SQL database. We won't go into much detail here, but it's interesting to note that because we're using the document format, the SOAP message doesn't contain type information. However, the SOAP message contains a schema because a *DataSet* object needs a set of type information to be reconstituted correctly.

The *DataSet* object is returned in the *<NewDataSet>* element, which contains a repeating set of records. The *<NewDataSet>* element is itself contained within a *<diffgr>* element. Diffgrams are the .NET Framework way to transport dataset updates as XML. This is the default format the .NET Framework uses when sending database information via SOAP. (We'll consider this in greater detail in Chapter 9.)

If we dig within the *<NewDataSet>* element, we'll see that we've actually returned three records that match our query "Supergrass" in the record store database. Each record is returned as a *<title>* element contained within a *<Records>* element, along with an identifying *rowOrder* attribute that reflects the order in which they were found in the database (unsorted). The diffgrams are of type *Insert* because the client—not knowing anything yet—has to insert the data returned from the server into whatever local representation is required.

The SOAP Header

Having considered the major data types that can be returned in the SOAP body, it's time to turn our attention to a less used, but still very important, part of the SOAP message: the header. The SOAP header is used to extend the message by adding metadata outside the data in the SOAP body. As mentioned earlier, SOAP information isn't always sent straight from client to server—it can also pass through a set of intermediate points. Moving tasks to specialized systems makes the overall system more scalable and flexible. SOAP headers can be used to convey information such as security keys and digital signatures that might be dealt with by a security service. Other headers might be used to route the SOAP message to other intermediaries or to declare the message as part of a distributed transaction.

SOAP headers are analogous to proxy headers in the HTTP protocol, but they are much more flexible because the SOAP specification provides only the general header mechanism and doesn't limit the type or number of headers.

In our record store example, each customer who has registered and bought an item from the store will be allocated a separate account. However, to get details about the user's account, the application asks the user to supply a login ID and password. To be able to return the account details, some sort of authentication must be performed, and for security and scalability reasons we might want to perform authentication as a separate service on a separate machine.

To provide this functionality for our example, we can specify the user ID in a *<loginid>* element, which is passed in the SOAP header along with the user password:

```
<soap:Header>
    <loginid>CPU01</loginid>
    <password>raz0rf!sh</password>
</soap:Header>
```

A security portal could use this header for authentication and return a fault to the client if the credentials are not valid. In this case, our database Web service would not even see the request because the message would not reach its intended destination.

Soap Header Block

If a SOAP header is present, the SOAP header block must be namespace qualified. In our example, say that we need to submit our identifier every time we query the database. An example SOAP message complete with header block might look like this:

```
<?xml version="1.0" encoding="utf-8" ?>
<soap:Envelope xmlns:soap="http://schemas.xmlsoap.org/soap/envelope/"
    xmlns:xsi="http://www.w3.org/2001/XMLSchema-instance"
    xmlns:xsd="http://www.w3.org/2001/XMLSchema">
    <soap:Header>
        <Credentials xmlns="http://testserver/">
            <loginid>CPU01</loginid>
            <password>raz0rf!sh</password>
     </Credentials>
    </soap:Header>
    <soap:Body>
        <GetArtist xmlns="http://www.notashop.com/wscr">
            <Artist>Nine Inch Nails</Artist>
        </GetArtist>
    </soap:Body>
</soap:Envelope>
```

In addition to containing text, the SOAP header can also take a couple of attributes, *mustUnderstand* and *Role*.

SOAP *mustUnderstand* Attribute

The SOAP *mustUnderstand* attribute is used to indicate whether the SOAP header must be processed. If it is set to 1, the header must be processed or the message must fail. By default it is set to 0. The *mustUnderstand* attribute conveys the importance and, implicitly, the type of information contained in the SOAP header. If the attribute is set to 0 (optional), this means the information contained is advisory. If the attribute is set to 1, this means the header contains critical information that must be understood by the endpoint.

```
<SOAPHeader1 xmlns="http://testserver/"
    soap:mustUnderstand="1">
    <loginid>CPU01</loginid>
    <password>raz0rf!sh</password>
</SOAPHeader1>
```

SOAP *actor* or *role* Attribute

The *actor* attribute was present in the SOAP 1.1 standard and was used to target the header to a specific type of endpoint. It didn't really apply to Web services, where the endpoint was the Web service being targeted, and it came into use only when the Web service went via intermediaries. In SOAP 1.2, it has been replaced by the *role* attribute, which broadly fulfills the same purpose.

When processing a message, a SOAP node is said to act in one or more roles. The roles defined in the standard are

- ***next*** Each SOAP intermediary and the final receiver must act on the role.
- ***none*** SOAP nodes must not act on this role.
- ***ultimateReceiver*** Only the ultimate receiver should act on this role; intermediaries must not.

By default, all headers are targeted at the *ultimateReceiver* node. The SOAP *role* attribute is used to determine a specific node or the first node to receive the message and act on this header. It does this by specifying a URI indicating the node a SOAP header has been targeted at. The *role* attribute helps divide the application protocols from the data-encoding and binding sections of the protocol—something that plays a big part in the Microsoft Global XML Web Services Architecture (GXA).

The *role* attribute then prefixes our SOAP elements as follows:

```
<soap:Header>
    <rs:Credentials xmlns="http://testserver/"
        xmlns:rs="http://testserver/profiles"
        soap:role="http://testserver/profiles"
        soap:mustUnderstand="1">
        <loginid>CPU01</loginid>
        <password>raz0rf!sh</password>
    </rs:Credentials>
</soap:Header>
```

Processing and Building a SOAP Header with .NET

Thus far we've talked about SOAP headers only in an abstract, non-platform-specific way. Now it's time to use some of the classes provided with .NET to access this functionality.

You can create a custom SOAP header by deriving a class from the *SoapHeader* class (*System.Web.Services.Protocols.SoapHeader*). This class can be associated with the *WebService* method. The *SoapHeader* class can be defined in a Web service .asmx file. In our record store example, we can create a custom *SoapHeader* class to define our login ID as follows:

```
public class Credentials : System.Web.Services.Protocols.SoapHeader
{
    public string loginid;
    public string password;
}
```

We then need to create a corresponding field in the Web service to store the instance of the SOAP header:

```
public class Service1: System.Web.Services.WebService
{
    ⋮
    public Credentials UserEntryIn;
    ⋮
}
```

The Web service can now receive any method call within this SOAP header.

The next step is to apply a *SoapHeader* attribute to each Web service method that will need to process the SOAP header. This attribute should share a name with the field created earlier in the Web service.

Our Web method needs to have the following attribute specified:

```
[WebMethod]
[SoapHeader("UserEntryIn")]
⋮
```

If our Web method receives a request with this SOAP header set, the *UserEntryIn* variable will contain a *Credentials* object that matches the provided header.

The *SoapHeader* Attribute's Attributes

The *SoapHeader* attribute has several other properties of interest. We'll consider only two in this chapter. The first, *Direction*, can be set to *SoapHeaderDirection.In*, *SoapHeaderDirection.Out*, or *SoapHeaderDirection.InOut*, depending on whether you want the header to convey information to the Web service, from the Web service, or to and from the Web service, respectively. By default, it is set to *InOut*.

The second attribute, *Required*, can be set to *true* or *false*, depending on whether the header should receive or send any information within the SOAP header, respectively.

Sending Information via SOAP Headers

Let's augment our record store example so it requires a user to log in with an ID and a password before accessing the functionality of our Web service. The user supplies credentials, which are then passed in the SOAP header. The login is checked against the database, and if a match is found, the corresponding account number is returned as a SOAP header. If no match is found, the information is still returned as a SOAP header and the user is denied access.

We start by creating our SOAP header classes, both derived from *SoapHeader*. One class will have two members, one for the login name and password the user will send, and the other class will have one member for the login ID (proof of authentication) that will be returned by our Web service:

```
public class Credentials1: System.Web.Services.Protocols.SoapHeader
{
    public string loginname;
    public string password;
}
public class Credentials2: System.Web.Services.Protocols.SoapHeader
{
    public int loginid;
}
```

Next we add two member variables that implement the types created in our SOAP header classes:

```
public class Service1 : System.Web.Services.WebService
{
    public Credentials1 userEntryIn;
    public Credentials2 userEntryOut;
    ⋮
```

We then add two Web methods to our service1.asmx file to define our inbound and outbound SOAP headers:

```
[WebMethod(Description="Service that returns the login id")]
[SoapHeader("userEntryIn")]
public int GetLoginID()
{
    int userIdent;
```

```
    int numberOfMatches;
    string strConnect = "Provider=SQLOLEDB;"
        + "Persist Security Info=False;User ID=ASPNET;"
        + "Initial Catalog=dansrecordsSQL;Data Source=CHRISUHOME";
    OleDbConnection dataConn = new OleDbConnection(strConnect);
    string dataComm1 = "SELECT Count(*) AS NumberOfMatches "
        + "From Users WHERE UserName='" + userEntryIn.loginname
        + "' AND Password = '" + userEntryIn.password + "'";
    string dataComm2 = "SELECT UserId FROM Users WHERE UserName='"
        + userEntryIn.loginname + "'";
    OleDbCommand cmd1 = new OleDbCommand(dataComm1,dataConn);
    OleDbCommand cmd2 = new OleDbCommand(dataComm2,dataConn);

    dataConn.Open();
    numberOfMatches = (int)cmd1.ExecuteScalar();
    if (numberOfMatches != 0)
    {
        userIdent = (int)cmd2.ExecuteScalar();
    }
    else
    {
        userIdent=0;
    }
    dataConn.Close();
    return userIdent;
}

[WebMethod(Description="Service that returns the login id")]
[SoapHeader("userEntryOut")]
[SoapDocumentMethod (Action="/GetLoginReturn")]
public void GetLoginReturn(int UserId)
{
    userEntryOut = new Credentials2();
    userEntryOut.loginid = UserId;
}
```

The first method takes a name and a password, checks them against the database via a SQL query, and returns the corresponding ID. To prevent an empty set being returned if there is no result, we first run a SQL query that counts the number of records that match. If this is zero, we know to assign a value of 0 to our user identifier. Our ASP.NET client will reject entry if access is denied (if 0 is returned). Our second method just returns the login ID in the *loginid* member of our *UserEntryOut SoapHeader* class.

We also need to add references in our Web service to the following namespaces:

```
using System.Web.Services.Protocols;
using System.Data.OleDb;
```

We then autogenerate our proxy class using wsdl.exe because the SOAP headers that travel back and forth from the client are pretty straightforward and we don't want to get into the physical details of specifying them ourselves.

The ASP.NET client changes slightly in that we now have two buttons and two sets of event handling code, and we use two panels to display the login ID and then hide it and display the Web service functionality instead:

```
<body MS_POSITIONING="GridLayout">
    <form id="RecordStoreQuery1" method="post" runat="server">
        <asp:Label ID="label1" Runat="server"></asp:Label>
        <asp:Panel ID="PanelLogin" Runat="server" Visible="True">
            Enter Login Id:
            <asp:TextBox id="UserLogin" Runat="server"></asp:TextBox>
            <BR><BR>Password:
            <asp:TextBox id="Passwording" Runat="server"></asp:TextBox>
            <BR><BR>
            <asp:Button id="button1" onclick="RetrieveRecords"
                Runat="server" Text="Click here to search"></asp:Button>
        </asp:Panel>
        <asp:Panel ID="PanelMusic" Runat="server" Visible="False">
            <asp:ListBox id="listBox1" Runat="server" Rows="1"
                SelectionMode="Single">
            <asp:ListItem>Artist</asp:ListItem>
            <asp:ListItem>Title</asp:ListItem>
            </asp:ListBox>Type artist to find here:
            <asp:TextBox id="txtUserInput" runat="server"></asp:TextBox>
            <BR><BR><BR>
            <asp:Button id="button2" onclick="SendSoap" Runat="server"
                Text="Click here to search"></asp:Button>
        </asp:Panel>
    </form>
</body>
```

The bit that looks after the login process is as follows:

```
public void RetrieveRecords(object sender, EventArgs e)
{
    SOAPCredentials.Credentials1 header1 = new SOAPCredentials.Credentials1();
    header1.loginname = UserLogin.Text;
    header1.password = Passwording.Text;
```

```
    SOAPCredentials.Service1 chk = new SOAPCredentials.Service1();
    chk.userEntryIn = header1;
    chk.GetLoginReturn(chk.GetLoginID());
    int Result = chk.userEntryOut.loginid;

    if (Result != 0)
    {
        label1.Text = "Welcome Account No: " + Result.ToString();
        PanelLogin.Visible = false;
        PanelMusic.Visible = true;
    }
    else
    {
        label1.Text = "Login Denied - Details Incorrect";
    }
}
```

This code creates an instance of our header and assigns it the contents of the text box in which the user supplied login information. It then reads the whole header into our *SoapHeader* class and calls our two Web methods, supplying one as a parameter of the other. In other words, we take the ID returned by the *GetLoginID* method and supply it to the *GetLoginReturn* method. We could of course achieve the functionality within only one Web method, but then we'd have to send both an ID and a name to our SOAP header class and return both an ID and a name from it. This way is cleaner, with just the string containing the name being sent in and the integer containing the ID being sent out.

If we run the program, it works as follows. We have two logins in our database, one for Chris and one for DeSeranno. Figure 2-5 shows what happens if we log in as Chris.

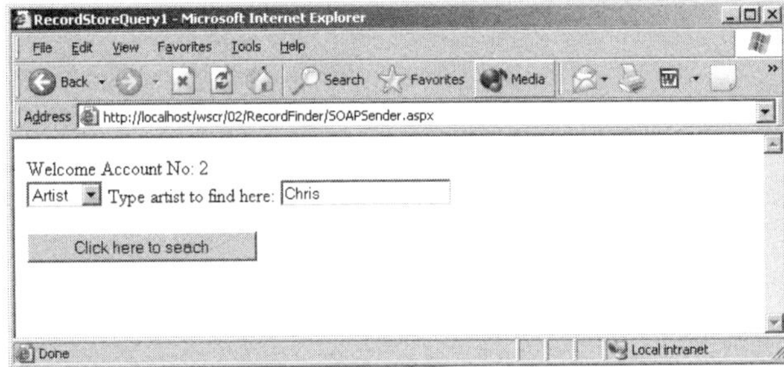

Figure 2-5 Using the SOAPSender ASP.NET form to log in as Chris

There's no direct way of viewing the SOAP sent here except with the monitor again, but if you quickly view the service (.asmx file) directly, it generates an example version of the SOAP that's used. For the header used to supply our *GetLoginID* method, the SOAP is as follows:

```
<soap:Header>
    <SoapHeader1 xmlns="http://www.notashop.com/wscr">
        <loginname>string</loginname>
    </SoapHeader1>
</soap:Header>
```

For the header returned by our *GetLoginReturn* method, the SOAP is as follows:

```
<soap:Header>
    <SoapHeader2 xmlns="http://www.notashop.com/wscr">
        <loginid>int</loginid>
    </SoapHeader2>
</soap:Header>
```

Our ASP.NET client can now act on the information it has sent and has had returned in the form of SOAP headers.

Note that using your own SOAP headers to perform authentication tasks probably isn't the most desirable approach. You should consider using the new WS-Security standard instead. We've taken the SOAP header approach here because it provides a simple and quick demonstration of how SOAP headers can be sent and acted on by an endpoint.

Unknown Headers

Web service clients can also send headers to the service that haven't been defined and that the Web service is not expecting to receive. The Web service will probably ignore these headers, but if you process them, you can use them to call Web services and potentially set up a chain of Web services.

SOAP 1.2 Relay Header

In SOAP 1.2, a SOAP header can carry a relay attribute that can be set to *false* or *true*. When it's set to *true*, you can forward the SOAP message to a SOAP node other than the one that received it for processing, although it must follow the same set of rules for processing.

SOAP Exceptions and Errors

The SOAP body can also contain error information. You can send this error information as XML elements. Web method exceptions returned to a .NET application are automatically packaged as SOAP faults. .NET proxy classes package SOAP faults as exceptions, which makes them easier to handle. A SOAP fault can be parceled up either as a *System.Web.Services.Protocols.SoapException* object or a *System.Web.Services.Protocols.SoapHeaderException* object. The *SoapException* and *SoapHeaderException* objects function as a wrapper to the fault message. However, before we look at how to deal with SOAP faults in .NET, we'll look at the structure of the *<fault>* element that SOAP provides.

The *<fault>* Element

In the SOAP 1.1 standard, the *<fault>* element is specified as having four parts: *<faultcode>*, *<faultstring>*, *<faultactor>*, and *<detail>*. A typical SOAP fault element is enclosed inside the SOAP body and might look like this:

```
<soap:Body>
    <soap:Fault>
        <faultcode>rs:application:database</faultcode>
        <faultstring>Could not add record to
            database</faultstring>
        <faultactor></faultactor>
        <detail></detail>
    </soap:Fault>
</soap:Body>
```

The SOAP body can contain only one fault, even if there are several. To see an example of a SOAP fault element generated by an application, we can go back to our record store Web service and generate one. All we need to do is amend the code in our ASP.NET client SOAPsender.aspx to send something via the SOAP request that isn't strictly legal. If we remove the closing *<GetArtist>* or *<GetTitle>* element as follows, a SOAP fault is duly returned, informing us of our omission (as shown in Figure 2-6).

```
⋮
string lbs = listBox1.SelectedItem.Text;
string actionName = "/Get" + lbs;
string soapBody = "<?xml version = \"1.0\" encoding = \"utf-8\" "
    + "?><soap:Envelope "
    + "xmlns:soap=\"http://schemas.xmlsoap.org/soap/envelope/\" "
    + "xmlns:xsi=\"http://www.w3.org/2001/XMLSchema-instance\" "
    + "xmlns:xsd=\"http://www.w3.org/2001/XMLSchema\">"
    + "<soap:Body><Get" + lbs
    + "  xmlns=\"http://tempuri.org/\"><"+lbs+">"
    + txtUserInput.Text + "</" + lbs + "></soap:Body>"
    + "</soap:Envelope>";
RecordFinder5.ASPNETclient wsp = new RecordFinder5.ASPNETclient();
⋮
```

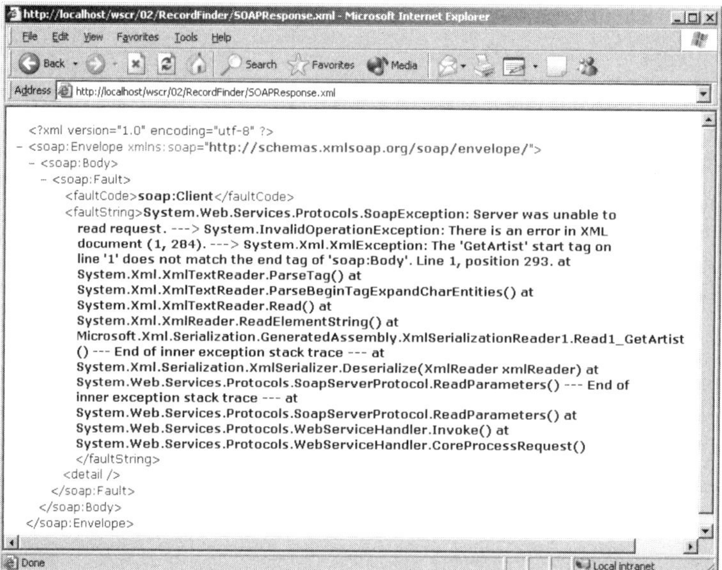

Figure 2-6 SOAP fault indicating that the closing *<GetArtist>* element was not found

Four separate elements are within *<soap:Fault>*, but in this example only two of them are returned containing any information. Of the others, one is empty and one is absent. Let's take a look at what each of the subelements does.

<faultcode>

The *<faultcode>* element can contain any fully qualified application name to indicate where an error might have occurred. In our example, it just specifies *soap:Client*. The two possible entries by default are *soap:Client* and *soap:Server*, which simply indicate who's responsible for the error. In our example, because the message created and sent by the client is ill formed, the faultcode returned is *soap:Client*. Had we shut down the SQL server instead, the service would have returned a *soap:Server* fault code.

The SOAP 1.2 standard mentions five possible fault codes:

- ***DataEncodingUnknown*** The type of encoding used within some or all of the SOAP elements isn't recognized by the endpoint.
- ***MustUnderstand*** An element marked with a *mustUnderstand* attribute wasn't processed.

- ***Receiver*** An endpoint has generated an error that has nothing to do with the content of the SOAP message. This is the SOAP 1.2 name for the SOAP 1.1 fault code *Server*.
- ***Sender*** An endpoint has generated an error caused by information or the format not conforming to the endpoints specifications. This is the SOAP 1.2 name for the SOAP 1.1 fault code *Client*.
- ***VersionMismatch*** The Web service expected a SOAP 1.2 message but received a message qualified with the SOAP 1.1 namespace.

Note that in SOAP 1.2 the fault code here is represented by an element named *Code*, as opposed to *<faultcode>* in SOAP 1.1.

<faultstring>

The *<faultstring>* element provides a text message to the user describing why the fault happened. This message can be presented via a text box, dialog box, or something similar. In our example, it provides extensive information about what caused the fault (the missing closing tag) and where the opening tag is located. SOAP 1.2 calls this element *<Reason>*.

<detail>

The optional *<detail>* element describes something that happened when the SOAP body was being processed; it can be used to bundle up extended error information. In SOAP 1.2, the element name is *<Detail>*.

<faultactor>

The *<faultactor>* element is also optional and is used to specify the endpoint that caused the fault. By default, this is *ultimateReceiver*. SOAP 1.2 refines this approach and allows you to return the URI of the Web service sending the fault (the actor) in a *Node* element and the role the actor is currently playing in the new *Role* element.

The *SoapException* Object

The elements we just described map almost directly to the properties provided by the .NET *SoapException* object. This object can take an array of XML elements that it can forward back to the client. It has the following properties:

- ***Code*** An object containing details about the source of the exception
- ***Detail*** Application-specific details that relate to the SOAP body
- ***Actor*** The endpoint that threw the exception

The *SoapException* object also inherits the following properties from the *Exception* class:

- ***HelpLink*** The link to the help file associated with the exception
- ***InnerException*** The inner exception containing more details about the fault that generated the exception
- ***Message*** The message describing the exception
- ***Source*** The application that caused the exception
- ***StrackTrace*** A string of the frames on the call stack when the exception was thrown
- ***TargetSite*** The method that threw the exception

You can use the *SoapException* object to throw a SOAP exception within a Web method and then query the properties. Throwing a SOAP exception is as simple as the following code, which manually generates an exception:

```
throw new SoapException("This will cause an error",
    SoapException.ServerFaultCode);
```

You can take the details created and read them into a *XMLDocument* object, as described shortly. First we'll consider the code object.

The *Code* Object

The *Code* object can be set to one of a number of constants that map partially to the errors generated in the *<faultcode>* element. The fault code constants are as follows in .NET:

- ***VersionMismatchFaultCode*** An invalid namespace was sent.
- ***MustUnderstandFaultCode*** An element marked "must process" wasn't processed.
- ***ClientFaultCode*** The content of the message caused a processing error.
- ***ServerFaultCode*** A processing error occurred that wasn't caused by the content of the message.

These constants help add to detail to the error generated. There is also a name property of the code object that supplies more details about the constant that created the error.

Example of Passing a Fault

You can see in the following example how the *SoapException* class works and what information is passed in SOAP messages. If we augment our previous example by adding a new Web method to cause an error, we can throw an exception that causes a SOAP fault as follows:

```
[WebMethod]
public void SOAPFault()
{
    XmlDocument faultdoc = new XmlDocument();
    XmlNode[] faultnodes = new XmlNode[1];
    faultnodes[0] = faultdoc.CreateNode(XmlNodeType.Element,
        "SOAPFaultException","http://testserver/");
    faultnodes[0].InnerText = "This is a SOAP error";
    throw new SoapException("This will cause an error",
        SoapException.ServerFaultCode,
        Context.Request.Url.AbsoluteUri, faultnodes[0], null);
}
```

We can handle the SOAP fault by adding the following code to our client:

```
⋮
RecordFinder5.SoapHeader1 header1 = new RecordFinder5.SoapHeader1();
header1.loginname = UserLogin.Text;

RecordFinder5.Service1 chk = new RecordFinder5.Service1();
try
{
    chk.SOAPFault();
}
catch(System.Web.Services.Protocols.SoapException SoapExcep)
{
    Response.Write("Error Message: " + SoapExcep.Message);
    Response.Write("<br>Role: " + SoapExcep.Actor);
    Response.Write("<br> Fault Code: " + SoapExcep.Code.Name);
}
⋮
```

This error is parceled up in the *SoapException* object, and we return information to the screen by querying the *SoapException* object's *Message* and *Actor* properties, and the *Name* property of the *Code* object, as shown in Figure 2-7.

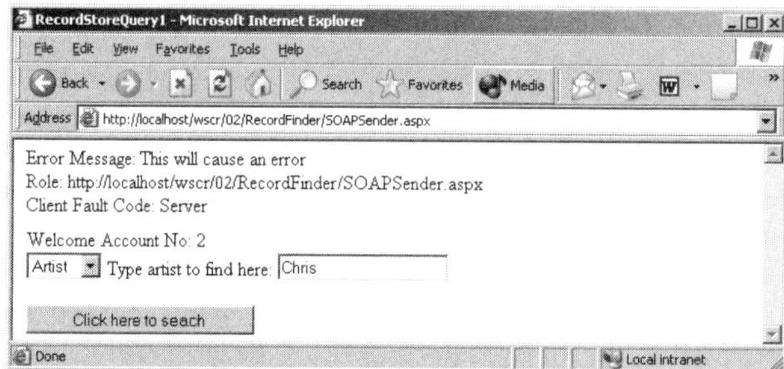

Figure 2-7 Client application displaying details of a *SoapException* object to the user

The details are displayed to the user in a more user-friendly format; it is up to you whether you continue with the execution or end it there.

Extending SOAP

SOAP 1.2 defines how new features should be introduced into SOAP. This part of the specification targets the authors of additional specifications. Unless you're an active participant in the W3C Web service activity, you don't need to read this section of the spec. An extensible standard calls for an extensible implementation. Therefore, the .NET Framework SOAP implementation can also be extended. You can create custom extensions by deriving them from a SOAP extension class; you can then use your extensions for logging, encryption and decryption of Web service calls, or compression or decompression of SOAP messages before they're processed. However, custom extensions are a separate subject, which we'll cover in Chapter 10.

Summary

We've covered a lot of ground in this chapter. We started by defining SOAP and looking at the standards—the current 1.1 and the soon-to-be-ratified 1.2. We noted that 1.1 is the existing standard that current .NET SOAP implementations adhere to, and that 1.2 is just around the corner and should prove to be the final version of the standard. We then looked at the structure of a SOAP message, which is entirely contained within a root *<Envelope>* element and splits up broadly into a header and a body. We looked at how information is transmitted within the SOAP body and the kinds of formatting and encoding that are provided. We looked at how SOAP is bound by default to the HTTP-POST protocol and the extra information required on this layer.

We created a small application that uses ASP.NET to send and receive SOAP messages. We looked at the purpose of the SOAP header and how it can be used to convey information for other endpoints to act on. Last, we looked at how SOAP error messages are transmitted and the facilities that .NET possesses for handling them. We briefly touched on the subject of SOAP extensions, which we'll cover in detail in later chapters.

3

Describing Web Services

In the last two chapters, we briefly went through the process of building and using Web services, and we looked at all the facets of SOAP messaging. We also discussed the SOAP interaction between the client and Web service. However, we still haven't fully explored how the client knows what the interface to the Web service actually is. This is where Web Services Description Language (WSDL) comes in.

WSDL is an XML-based language that's used to define Web services and describe the mechanisms that must be employed to access those Web services. One advantage of WSDL is that it was designed from the ground up to be extensible and, like SOAP, doesn't force the use of a specific transmission protocol nor does it force the use of a specific type schema to describe the types used.

Although Microsoft .NET provides a framework for using Web services without having to understand WSDL, an understanding of WSDL lets you modify the autogenerated files and troubleshoot any problems that occur. Most of the time, you won't need to look at the WSDL files you use, and .NET doesn't generate the most elegant or readable WSDL description of a Web service anyway. However, it can sometimes be beneficial to modify the WSDL file that .NET generates. When we look at Universal Description, Discovery, and Integration (UDDI) in the next chapter, you'll see that to fully use the Microsoft UDDI Business Registry you must manually write some of the WSDL.

Note WSDL is specified in a W3C Note under the auspices of the Web Services Description Working Group at *http://www.w3.org/2002/ws/desc/*, and the latest released version of the specification is always at *http://www.w3.org/TR/wsdl*. The current released version is version 1.1 and the next version, version 1.2, is currently a working draft. Because version 1.1 of the WSDL specification is the released version and the version that .NET implements, this chapter will concentrate on that version. The reader is directed to the Web Services Description Working Group Web site for details regarding later versions of the specification.

We'll start by looking at WSDL in relation to a simple Web service. Once you have an understanding of WSDL, we can look at how .NET handles WSDL and some of the complexities that are added to what is a simple concept.

The Anatomy of WSDL

WSDL defines a Web service in two parts. The *abstract definition* contains a description of the Web service that is independent of the platform and language, with no mention of how messages are transported between the client and the server. The abstract definition specifies the interface to the service but not how to access that interface. The *concrete definition* adds the details describing how to access the Web service.

In theory, this separation into abstract and concrete definitions allows you to reuse the abstract definition to create several concrete definitions and therefore several different implementations of a given service. Or, to put it more succinctly, you can access the same Web service across different protocols.

However, as you'll see as we move through the chapter, the abstract definition of a Web service is not truly abstract; it contains some implementation-specific details. You'll also see when we look at UDDI in the next chapter that we don't split the WSDL along these lines and that we consider the definition of the Web service to be the entire WSDL description of the service except its address.

It would be easy to simply rehash the WSDL specification as the bulk of this chapter. But instead we're going to introduce WSDL in relation to a simple Web service similar to the one in Chapter 2. In that chapter, we looked at several examples that showed how to do complex things with the SOAP messages passed between the client and the server. The end result would be an application that's too complex for our purposes, so here we'll work with a simple Web service that implements only enough functionality for our purposes.

You can find the complete Web service for this chapter, RecordFinder, at *http://localhost/wscr/03/RecordFinder.asmx*; it contains all of the code that is introduced in this chapter but uses only the SOAP transport protocol. The complete Web service is rather complex and, because it uses only SOAP, doesn't provide an ideal starting point to discuss WSDL. Instead, as a starting point we'll take one of the methods, *GetAlbumsForArtist*, from the complete Web service and create a new service, SimpleRecordFinder, that exposes only this method. To show the use of various protocols with WSDL, this service has all three transport protocols enabled and can be found at *http://localhost/wscr/03/simple/SimpleRecordFinder.asmx*.

> **Note** As you saw in Chapter 2, you can encode a SOAP message in five ways. Not surprisingly, the WSDL that's generated depends on the way in which the SOAP message is encoded. In this chapter, we'll introduce WSDL using the SimpleRecordFinder service, which has the default options for Web services in .NET that give us a message format that is document-oriented, nonencoded (literal), with wrapped parameters. You'll see when we change the message formatting options in the "SOAP Message Formats" section that you can change the WSDL quite substantially.

As with all Web services created in .NET, you can look at the WSDL by appending *?wsdl* to the URL. Rather than present the complete WSDL in one block, we'll look at each part of the WSDL in turn. The WSDL for the SimpleRecordFinder service, and indeed all Web services, has several elements, as shown in Figure 3-1.

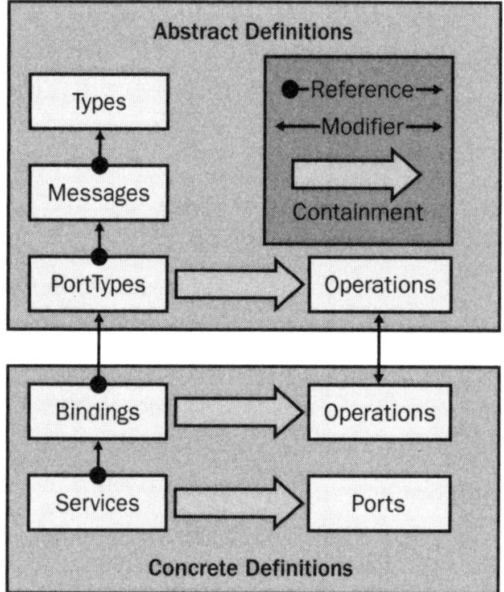

Figure 3-1 Major elements of WSDL and their relationships

The abstract definition of the Web service defines the service as a *portType*, and each *portType* has a series of operation elements. Within an *operation* you might have input, output, and fault messages that are defined to either the XSD schema or to type definitions in the WSDL file. When related to a .NET Web service, the *portType* is the class and an *operation* corresponds to an exposed method of that class.

The concrete definition of the service builds on the abstract definition and adds protocol-specific details to the *portType* to provide a *binding*. The binding also has *operation* elements, which correspond directly to the *operation* elements in the *portType* but are protocol-specific. The bindings are combined into a protocol-specific *port*, and the ports are combined to create the *service*.

We'll cover the elements of the WSDL document in detail later in the chapter, but a brief introduction to the elements here will give you a good grounding and avoid a lot of needless "read-ahead" to the sections that follow:

- **Types** The data type definitions used by the messages to be exchanged. These can be any typing scheme that the creator of the Web service wants to use, but WSDL assumes that the XSD definitions are used.
- **Message** The definitions of the data that is to be transmitted. Each message is associated with one of the types defined or an XSD type. Messages can have multiple parts that allow different types to be combined into a single message.

- **PortType** The abstract definition of the Web service. Each *portType* has a set of operations. An operation is the abstract definition of a method exposed by the service. Depending on the type of the operation, it might have input, output, and fault elements that map back to the defined messages.
- **Binding** The concrete definition of the *portType*. Within the binding, you specify what protocol the binding uses. Each binding has a set of operations. In this case, an operation is the concrete definition of a method exposed by the service. Each binding operation maps back to a *portType* operation. Depending on the protocol being used, the operation might define the encoding used, the ordering of the messages within the operation, and so forth.
- **Service** The concrete definition of the Web service, which is used to group together a set of ports. A port specifies the address of the Web service and ties that address to a specific binding.

The grammar used by WSDL to build a service definition file covers both the abstract and concrete definitions of the service. The core framework defines the overall service, and binding extensions are used to add the protocol-specific details to the service.

The WSDL specification supports three binding extensions (as discussed later in the chapter): HTTP, MIME, and SOAP. However, nothing precludes the addition of further binding extensions.

Document Structure

At the root of a WSDL document is a *<definitions>* element that contains all the other elements that describe the Web service. For our SimpleRecordFinder service, the *<definitions>* element is as follows:

```
<definitions
    xmlns:http="http://schemas.xmlsoap.org/wsdl/http/"
    xmlns:soap="http://schemas.xmlsoap.org/wsdl/soap/"
    xmlns:s="http://www.w3.org/2001/XMLSchema"
    xmlns:s0="http://www.notashop.com/wscr"
    xmlns:soapenc="http://schemas.xmlsoap.org/soap/encoding/"
    xmlns:tm="http://microsoft.com/wsdl/mime/textMatching/"
    xmlns:mime="http://schemas.xmlsoap.org/wsdl/mime/"
    targetNamespace="http://www.notashop.com/wscr"
    xmlns="http://schemas.xmlsoap.org/wsdl/">
    ⋮
</definitions>
```

As you can see, several namespaces are defined as part of the *<definitions>* element. The most important namespace is the one defined by the *xmlns* attribute. This is the root namespace for the *<definitions>* element; all child elements that aren't prefixed are assumed to be in this namespace.

When you use the automatic facilities of Web services in .NET to generate the WSDL, you automatically have six namespaces defined and added to the WSDL, as shown in Table 3-1.

Table 3-1 Namespaces that .NET Defines When Generating WSDL

Prefix	Namespace URI	Definition
http	*http://schemas.xmlsoap.org/wsdl/http*	HTTP binding extensions
mime	*http://schemas.xmlsoap.org/wsdl/mime*	MIME binding extensions
s	*http://www.w3.org/2001/XMLSchema*	XSD schema
soap	*http://schemas.xmlsoap.org/wsdl/soap*	SOAP binding extensions
soapenc	*http://schemasxmlsoap.org.soap/encoding*	SOAP encoding namespace
tm	*http://microsoft.com/wsdl/mime/textMatching*	Text matching namespace

These six namespaces are added to the WSDL document regardless of whether they're used. If you build a Web service that uses only the SOAP protocol, the HTTP binding extension prefix is still declared and added to the automatically generated WSDL.

> **Note** As you'll see shortly, several of the element names in different namespaces clash, so you must be clear which namespace you're referring to. In the remainder of this chapter, all elements that are referred to outside of code fragments will be prefixed with the namespace to which they belong. The exceptions are the elements that are part of the WSDL specification; these are used without any prefix.

The SimpleRecordFinder service also defines two namespaces that are specific to the service. The *s0* prefix and the *targetNamespace* attribute for the *<definitions>* element both point at *http://www.notashop.com/wscr*, which is the namespace we've used throughout the book. These in combination allow us to place the elements that we define in the correct namespace and allow us to use the *s0* prefix to reference those elements.

The *<import>* Element

The autogenerated WSDL for a Web service provides a complete description of the Web service, with everything in one file. It tells you everything you need to know, but it doesn't make for the most readable of documents.

The WSDL specification defines the *<import>* element for importing other documents into the current file. The format of the element is as follows:

```
<import namespace="NamespaceURI" location="LocationURL" />
```

You specify the location of the document you want to import and the namespace you want the document to be imported as. Specifying the namespace for the imported document allows you to use elements defined in a namespace other than the namespace for the overall WSDL document. This might not be overly important when you're writing the entire WSDL document, but if you need to use type definitions from other developers, for instance, you'll soon run into naming conflicts.

From the brief description of the WSDL document so far, it should be obvious that you can split the document neatly into two parts. If you create an abstract definition document, and you import it into the concrete definition document, you can potentially reuse the same abstract definition in multiple concrete definitions. You can go even further and split the type definitions that are required into a separate document and import these into the abstract definition document.

Simply using the *<import>* element (without having to make any additional changes to a WSDL document) makes the reuse and maintenance of documents easier.

The *<documentation>* Element

Within each WSDL element you can add a *<documentation>* element to provide human-readable documentation. This documentation can contain both text and valid XML elements because it is not processed as part of the WSDL.

The simple case of a string of text

```
<documentation>NotAShop.com record store</documentation>
```

is as valid as:

```
<documentation>
  <author>Mr. Smith</author>
  <date>20th March 2002</date>
  <version>1.0.24.3112</version>
</documentation>
```

The Core Framework

In the *<definitions>* element you define the entire Web service using a series of elements that match ones shown earlier in Figure 3-1. As you can see by pointing your browser to *http://localhost/wscr/03/simple/SimpleRecordFinder.asmx?wsdl*, the WSDL for the SimpleRecordFinder service is quite a long document. However, the overall structure is relatively simple. If you take a WSDL document and strip out any details specific to a particular service, you're left with a WSDL shell:

```
<?xml version="1.0" encoding="utf-8" ?>
<definitions xmlns="http://schemas.xmlsoap.org/wsdl/"
  xmlns:s="http://www.w3.org/2001/XMLSchema">
  <types>
    <s:schema>
      ⋮
    </s:schema>
    <-- extensibility element -->
  </types>

  <message>
    <part />
    ⋮
    <part />
  </message>
  ⋮
  <message>
    <part />
    ⋮
    <part />
  </message>

  <portType>
    <operation>
      <input />
      <output />
      <fault />
    </operation>
    ⋮
    <operation />
  </portType>
  ⋮
  <portType />

  <binding>
    <!--- binding extension element -->
    <operation>
      <!--- binding extension element -->
```

```
      <input>
        <!--- binding extension element -->
      </input>
      <output>
        <!--- binding extension element -->
      </output>
      <fault>
        <!--- binding extension element -->
      </fault>
    </operation>
    ⋮
    <operation />
  </binding>
  ⋮
  <binding />

  <service>
    <port>
      <!--- binding extension element -->
    </port>
    ⋮
    <port />
  </service>
</definitions>
```

Although the WSDL document is written with the abstract details at the top of the document and the concrete details at the end, you can more easily understand what's going on if you consider the elements in the other direction.

In a WSDL document, only one *<service>* element is defined; it contains a *<port>* element for each protocol supported by the Web service. A *<port>* is mapped to a *<binding>*, so it follows that there is also a *<binding>* element for each protocol. Within each *<binding>* element is an *<operation>* element that corresponds to the *<operation>* element defined in the *<portType>*. All of the elements that make up the concrete definition of the service have extensibility elements within them that specify the physical implementation of the service—you can see these in a WSDL document by looking for the elements prefixed with *http*, *mime*, and *soap*.

The abstract definition of the Web service is described by the *<portType>* element. Within this element is a series of *<operation>* elements that correspond to the exposed methods of the Web service. Each *<operation>* element can contain *<input>*, *<output>*, and *<header>* elements that specify messages that are used in accessing the Web service. The messages themselves are defined in *<message>* elements, and these point at elements and types defined in the *<types>* section of the WSDL document.

> **Note** In an ideal world, we'd have one *<portType>* element describing the Web service and multiple *<binding>* elements that build on it to provide concrete implementations of the service. This was the original vision of the authors of the WSDL specification. As you can see by looking at the WSDL for SimpleRecordFinder, this is not the case in the real world; we have a complete set of definitions for each of the protocols that the service supports.

The *<service>* Element

The *<service>* element is the concrete definition of the service. It contains a *<port>* element for each binding that the service supports. If you look at the WSDL for the SimpleRecordFinder service, you can see that it follows that basic structure and that we have a *<port>* element for each protocol that the service supports:

```
<service name="SimpleRecordFinder">
  <port name="SimpleRecordFinderSoap"
   binding="s0:SimpleRecordFinderSoap">
    ⋮
  </port>
  <port name="SimpleRecordFinderHttpGet"
   binding="s0:SimpleRecordFinderHttpGet">
    ⋮
  </port>
  <port name="SimpleRecordFinderHttpPost"
   binding="s0:SimpleRecordFinderHttpPost">
    ⋮
  </port>
</service>
```

The naming rules for the *<service>* and *<port>* elements require that they be unique within the WSDL file. In .NET, the names are generated based on the class name of the Web service and the protocol used. As you can see for the SimpleRecordFinder service, the *<service>* is named SimpleRecordFinder and the *<port>* elements are suffixed with the protocol used by that particular port.

If you look at the *<port>* elements, you'll see that they each have a *binding* attribute that points at a given *<binding>* element in the WSDL file.

The *<binding>* Element

The *<binding>* element is the element in the WSDL file that ties together the concrete definition and the abstract definition. As you've seen from the details for the *<port>* elements, we have a *<binding>* element for each of the protocols that the Web service supports. Looking at the WSDL for the SimpleRecordFinder service, you can see that this is indeed the case:

```
<binding name="SimpleRecordFinderSoap" type="s0:SimpleRecordFinderSoap">
  ⋮
  <operation name="GetAlbumsForArtist">
    ⋮
    <input>
      ⋮
    </input>
    <output>
      ⋮
    </output>
  </operation>
</binding>
<binding name="SimpleRecordFinderHttpGet"
 type="s0:SimpleRecordFinderHttpGet">
  ⋮
  <operation name="GetAlbumsForArtist">
    ⋮
    <input>
      ⋮
    </input>
    <output>
      ⋮
    </output>
  </operation>
</binding>
<binding name="SimpleRecordFinderHttpPost"
 type="s0:SimpleRecordFinderHttpPost">
  ⋮
  <operation name="GetAlbumsForArtist">
    ⋮
    <input>
      ⋮
    </input>
    <output>
      ⋮
    </output>
  </operation>
</binding>
```

You can see that the *<binding>* elements have the same naming scheme as the *<port>* elements we looked at previously. The elements must have unique names, and in the autogenerated WSDL they're named after the class name and the protocol they use. Within the *<binding>* element is one *<operation>* element for each method exposed by the Web service; not surprisingly, these have the same names as the methods. An *<operation>* element might contain one *<input>* and one *<output>* element or any combination, and there's an element here if there's an element within the corresponding *<portType>* element.

> **Note** The WSDL specification defines a *<fault>* element that can also exist within the *<operation>* element. As you saw in the previous chapter, SOAP faults are generated by exceptions within the Web service, and these are handled automatically by the .NET runtime at both the client and the server. Nothing is added to the autogenerated WSDL to handle SOAP faults. Full details of the *<fault>* element are not discussed here; see the WSDL specification for more details.

You can also see that if we take away the details from the extensibility elements, the three *<binding>* elements are identical. It's the details we add via the extensibility elements—the encoding used, the location of the operations, and so forth—that make the *<binding>* elements useful.

Finally, note that each *<binding>* element has a *<type>* attribute, which is used to bind a particular *<binding>* to a *<portType>*.

The *<portType>* Element

The *<portType>* element is the abstract definition of the service. You can use it to build the basic interface of the service. Within the *<portType>* element are a series of *<operation>* elements, which correspond to the *<operation>* elements within the *<binding>* element.

The basic structure of the *<portType>* element is quite simple, as you can see in the WSDL for the SimpleRecordFinder service:

```
<portType name="SimpleRecordFinderSoap">
  <operation name="GetAlbumsForArtist">
    <input message="s0:GetAlbumsForArtistSoapIn" />
    <output message="s0:GetAlbumsForArtistSoapOut" />
  </operation>
</portType>
<portType name="SimpleRecordFinderHttpGet">
  <operation name="GetAlbumsForArtist">
    <input message="s0:GetAlbumsForArtistHttpGetIn" />
    <output message="s0:GetAlbumsForArtistHttpGetOut" />
  </operation>
</portType>
```

```
<portType name="SimpleRecordFinderHttpPost">
  <operation name="GetAlbumsForArtist">
    <input message="s0:GetAlbumsForArtistHttpPostIn" />
    <output message="s0:GetAlbumsForArtistHttpPostOut" />
  </operation>
</portType>
```

The *<portType>* element follows the same naming scheme as the *<binding>* and *<port>* elements, and the *<operation>* element has the same name as its counterpart within the *<binding>* element.

Within each *<operation>* element is a series of elements that correspond to the messages that are required to communicate with the Web service. The elements allowed within the *<operation>* element need not always be present, but if they are, there can be only one *<input>* element and one *<output>* element. Because there is only one of each element, it is not necessary to name these elements. The *<input>* and *<output>* elements each possess a message attribute that references a *<message>* element defined elsewhere in the WSDL document.

> **Note** As with the *<binding>* element, we'd also have a corresponding *<fault>* element here if one existed in the *<binding>*. See the WSDL specification for more details.

For the SimpleRecordFinder service, we have a simple request-response scenario, and we have an *<input>* and an *<output>* element that correspond to parameters and return values required by the exposed method. Although request-response is the nearly ubiquitous format for accessing a remote method, the WSDL specification supports three other scenarios for accessing a method within a Web service:

- **One-way** The client sends a request to the Web service and requires no reply.
- **Solicit-response** The Web service sends a message and receives a response from the client.
- **Notification** The Web service sends a message and requires no reply.

The operation type is not specified directly within the WSDL file; rather, it is inferred from the presence and ordering of the child elements of the *<operation>* element. A request-response operation has an *<input>* element and then an *<output>* element. The opposite operation, solicit-response, has the *<output>* element followed by the *<input>* element. For one-way and notification operations, you simply have the *<input>* or the *<output>* element. The notification operation has only the *<output>* element, and the one-way operation has only the *<input>* element.

Although the base WSDL structure specifies all four scenarios, only the one-way and request-response operations are defined as bindings by WSDL.

The *<message>* Element

The *<message>* element defines a message that will pass between the client and the server. Things start to get a little tricky here. As we discussed briefly, implementation-specific details are embedded in the abstract definition of the service, and these details depend on the protocol in use. This is further complicated by the various options available for encoding SOAP messages.

If you look at the autogenerated *<message>* elements for the SimpleRecordFinder service, you can see these complications and that we have a set of messages for each protocol:

```
<message name="GetAlbumsForArtistSoapIn">
  <part name="parameters" element="s0:GetAlbumsForArtist" />
</message>
<message name="GetAlbumsForArtistSoapOut">
  <part name="parameters" element="s0:GetAlbumsForArtistResponse" />
</message>
<message name="GetAlbumsForArtistHttpGetIn">
  <part name="strArtist" type="s:string" />
</message>
<message name="GetAlbumsForArtistHttpGetOut">
  <part name="Body" element="s0:ArrayOfString" />
</message>
<message name="GetAlbumsForArtistHttpPostIn">
  <part name="strArtist" type="s:string" />
</message>
<message name="GetAlbumsForArtistHttpPostOut">
  <part name="Body" element="s0:ArrayOfString" />
</message>
```

Within each *<message>* element is a *<part>* element that corresponds to a piece of data that must be passed. For the SimpleRecordFinder service, we have only one part per message, but it is quite possible to have multiple parts, and these are accommodated by simply having multiple *<part>* elements within a *<message>*, the ordering of the *<part>* elements reflecting the order expected by the method.

A *<part>* element can reference any of the types defined or imported into the WSDL document. For the XSD typing system, WSDL defines two attributes that can be used on *<part>* elements, only one of which can be used in a given *<part>* element:

- ***element*** References an *<s:element>* defined in the types section
- ***type*** References an *<s:simpleType>* or an *<s:complexType>* defined in the types section

Each *<message>* must have a unique name within the WSDL document. .NET gives it the default name constructed from the method name, the protocol, and the direction of the message. The naming of the *<part>* elements is slightly more complex; it depends on the protocol and, for SOAP, the message format being used. You can name the *<part>* elements in three ways, as described in Table 3-2.

Table 3-2 Naming of *<part>* Elements

Protocol	"In" Message	"Out" Message
HTTP	Parameter name in code	Always *Body*
Wrapped SOAP	Always *parameters*	Always *parameters*
Bare SOAP	Parameter name in code	*Result* appended to method name

As you can see from the table, for the HTTP protocol the naming rules are quite simple. These also translate to the types and elements used, and if you think about how the message is passed from the client to the server, this makes sense. You can't encode messages sent via HTTP in the same manner that you can encode messages sent via the SOAP protocol. WSDL for HTTP is simple; it's SOAP that causes the complexities.

For the default SOAP message format, which we're using with SimpleRecordFinder, you always bind the *<part>* elements to a defined *<s:element>* in the *<types>* section. For the other SOAP message formats, this is not always the case, as you'll see in the "SOAP Message Formats" section later in the chapter.

The *<types>* Element

The *<types>* element defines the data that the network service uses in the message transfer. Although WSDL allows any type system to be used, it assumes that XSD is being used, and .NET uses this type schema exclusively.

A complete discussion of XSD is beyond the scope of this book, and the intricacies of XSD are best left to other books such as *Definitive XML Schema* by Priscilla Walmsley (Prentice Hall, 2001). We will, however, talk about how the SOAP message format affects the types that are defined.

For the default SOAP message format that we're using with SimpleRecordFinder, you always define *<s:element>* elements that wrap complex types that ultimately refer to either an XSD complex or intrinsic type. For the other SOAP message formats, this is not always the case, as you'll see in the "SOAP Message Formats" section later in the chapter.

The Binding Extensions

We already discussed why you need binding extensions, and we briefly looked at what they allow you to do. Before we dive into the specifics of the three extensions defined by WSDL, it is worthwhile to discuss what's missing from the WSDL file as it stands.

You saw earlier that in the *<service>* and *<binding>* elements we laid the foundation for the protocol-specific information to be added. We have a service that has a series of ports, and each port has a binding that details the operations that are possible on each port. Did you notice that we're missing the addressing details? Nowhere in the core framework does it mention the address of a service—it's up to the binding extensions to define this address.

We also barely discussed how the messages are to be transmitted across the wire. We have an abstract definition of the messages provided by the *<message>* elements, but how does this get across the wire? Do we send it as XML? What if it's an image? How do we specify that we want to send an image across the wire? Again, the binding extensions come to the rescue.

As noted earlier, WSDL defines binding extensions for HTTP, MIME, and SOAP. We'll start with a look at the HTTP binding extensions because these are the least complex and have the fewest options.

The MIME binding extensions are the odd man out of the three binding extensions described in the WSDL specification. Rather than relating to a protocol that allows the Web service to be accessed, the MIME binding extensions provide a means of encoding arbitrary data into a format that can be transported as part of a request to the Web service using the HTTP or SOAP protocol.

SOAP is the most complex binding extension defined in the WSDL specification. As you saw in Chapter 2, SOAP has options for the encoding used, the type of call, whether the messages are wrapped or bare, and so forth. We'll cover each of these options and see how they affect the WSDL that is generated.

HTTP Binding Extensions

The HTTP binding extensions describe the interface provided by the Web service to users of the HTTP protocol. Although HTTP 1.1 defines eight methods of access across HTTP, only the GET and POST methods have bindings defined by WSDL 1.1.

The schema for the HTTP binding extensions can be found at *http://schemas.xmlsoap.org/wsdl/http*. As you've seen, .NET adds this schema to the WSDL document with a namespace prefix of *http*.

Data returned from a Web service accessed using HTTP is returned as an XML document, with the names of the types returned used as the XML tags. The same document is returned regardless of whether you access the Web service using the GET method or the POST method.

The differences between the two methods become apparent when you look at how to send data to the Web service—that is, how to pass the parameters to the service. You can pass the parameters to the Web service in three ways—two ways that use HTTP-GET and one that uses HTTP-POST:

- HTTP-GET with the payload replacing the URL, as in */service.asmx/34/45/56*.
- HTTP-GET with the payload as a query string, as in */service.asmx?a=34&b=45&c=56*.
- HTTP-POST with the payload in the body of the request. For example, the body of the request would be *a=34&b=45&c=56*.

If you look at the WSDL generated for the two versions of the HTTP protocol for the SimpleRecordFinder service, you'll see that they differ only in the HTTP binding extension used in the *<input>* element and the *verb* attribute of the *<http:binding>* element. Rather than show both versions, we'll simply show the HTTP-GET version here:

```
<binding name="SimpleRecordFinderHttpGet"
 type="s0:SimpleRecordFinderHttpGet">
  <http:binding verb="GET" />
  <operation name="GetAlbumsForArtist">
    <http:operation location="/GetAlbumsForArtist" />
    <input>
```

```
      <http:urlEncoded />
    </input>
    <output>
      <mime:mimeXml part="Body" />
    </output>
  </operation>
</binding>
<service name="SimpleRecordFinder">
  <port name="SimpleRecordFinderHttpGet"
   binding="s0:SimpleRecordFinderHttpGet">
    <http:address
     location="http://localhost/wscr/03/simple/SimpleRecordFinder.asmx"
    />
  </port>
</service>
```

Although not part of the HTTP binding extensions, the MIME extension bindings are shown in the HTTP outline because it is not possible to return data from an HTTP operation without reference to the MIME extensions.

> **Note** Although we'll discuss both *<http:urlEncoded>* and *<http:urlReplacement>* in the sections that follow, .NET always uses *<http:urlEncoded>* when accessing a Web service using the HTTP-GET protocol and always uses the *<mime:content>* element when accessing using the HTTP-POST protocol. .NET has no facilities to change this.

The *<http:binding>* element The *<http:binding>* element indicates that the binding uses the HTTP protocol and specifies which method the protocol uses. The basic format of the element is as follows:

```
<http:binding verb="Method">
```

The *verb* attribute specifies which method of the HTTP protocol the binding is using—GET or POST. Note that the attribute is case sensitive.

The *<http:operation>* element The *<http:operation>* element specifies the location of an operation relative to the address given in the *<http:address>* element. The basic format of the element is as follows:

```
<http:operation location="OperationURL">
```

The *location* attribute must be a relative URL; it is combined with the location specified in the *<http:address>* element to generate the complete URL for the operation.

For the GET method of accessing the Web service, you have two options for passing parameters to the Web service. Depending on the option you choose, you might have something slightly different than a simple relative URL. Specifying *<http:urlReplacement>* for an *<input>* operation requires the *location* attribute of the *<http:operation>* to be modified. We'll explain this in more detail shortly.

The *<http:urlEncoded>* element The *<http:urlEncoded>* element indicates that the input parameters to the Web service are to be encoded using the standard URL encoding rules. The element has no attributes, and it can simply be added as a child of the *<input>* element.

The names of the parameters correspond to the names of the message parts, and parameters are separated with the *&* character. For the GET method, the parameter list is simply appended to the end of the URL after the *?* character has been added. This is equivalent to the query string method of passing parameters to pages. For the POST method, the query string is still used but is passed as the content of the message rather than appended to the URL.

The *<http:urlReplacement>* element The *<http:urlReplacement>* element is valid only for the GET method of accessing the Web service. With URL replacement, all the parameters to the Web service are encoded into the URL.

The replacement follows quite a simple algorithm and relies on the location attribute of the *<http:operation>* element containing the parameters to be replaced.

Within the *location* attribute of the *<http:operation>*, you enclose each parameter you want to pass within parentheses; the name within the parentheses is the name of the message part you want to replace. Each message part is then replaced with the value that's expected when the method call is made. So if we want to access a Web service at */service.asmx/34/45/56* and the parameters to our call are *a*, *b* and *c*, the *<http:operation>* element becomes

```
<http:operation location="/service.asmx/(a)/(b)/(c)" />
```

The *<http:address>* element The *<http:address>* element specifies the base URL for the port. There can be only one address element for each port. It is combined with the *<http:operation>* element to give the complete URL for the Web service. The basic format of the *<http:address>* element is as follows:

```
<http:address location="LocationURL">
```

The *location* attribute must be a fully qualified URL; it is automatically updated by .NET to be the current location of the Web service. If you use WSDL files that are not generated automatically, you obviously need to change this to the correct location.

MIME Binding Extensions

The MIME binding extensions allow arbitrary data to be encoded and passed to and from Web services. They allow any type of data that can be MIME-encoded to be used as a parameter to or a return value from a Web service.

The schema for the MIME binding extensions can be found at *http://schemas.xmlsoap.org/wsdl/mime*; .NET adds this to the WSDL document with a namespace prefix of *mime*.

Unlike the HTTP and SOAP binding extensions, the MIME binding extensions are added to the WSDL file as children of the *<input>* or *<output>* element and cannot be used without one of the other two binding extensions.

.NET does not natively support the MIME extensions—we cannot, for instance, pass images as parameters to and from Web services. If we want to do this we are moving into the realm of the Web Service Enhancements (WSE) that are covered in Chapter 13.

> **Note** .NET always defines the HTTP bindings to use *<mime:content>* for the input to a HTTP-POST method and always uses *<mime:mimeXml>* as the return from both HTTP-GET and HTTP-POST methods. The MIME binding extensions are never used in combination with the SOAP protocol.

The *<mime:content>* element The simplest MIME binding extension you can use is the *<mime:content>* element, whose basic format is as follows:

```
<mime:content part="MessageName" type="MimeType">
```

The *part* attribute specifies which part of the message the binding applies to. If the message has only one part, you don't need to specify this attribute.

The *type* attribute specifies the MIME type. If you don't specify it, all MIME types are assumed to be acceptable. A MIME type has two sections, separated by a slash; you can use the wildcard (*) character to specify that you want to allow an entire family of MIME types.

For example, if you want to allow only the *"text/xml"* MIME type, you can specify the *<mime:content>* element as follows:

```
<mime:content type="text/xml">
```

If you want to allow the entire *text* MIME type family, you can specify the element as follows:

```
<mime:content type="text/*">
```

The *<mime:mimeXML>* element The *<mime:mimeXML>* element indicates that the data you're expecting to receive is an XML document—that is, a *"text/xml"* document that adheres to the schema of the referenced message part. The basic syntax for the *<mime:mimeXml>* element is as follows:

```
<mime:mimeXml part="MessageName">
```

As with the *<mime:content>* element, the *part* attribute specifies which part of the message the binding applies to. If the message has only one part, you don't need to specify this attribute.

The *<mime:multipartRelated>* element The *<mime:multipartRelated>* element is used to combine several MIME elements into one message using the *multipart/related* MIME type. The basic syntax for the *<mime:multipartRelated>* element is as follows:

```
<mime:multipartRelated>
  <mime:part>
    <mime:content> or <mime:mimeXml> or <mime:multipartRelated>
  </mime:part>
  ⋮
  <mime:part />
</mime:multipartRelated>
```

A *<mime:multipartRelated>* element must have at least one *<mime:part>* element within it. Within the *<mime:part>* element, you specify the individual MIME binding extensions that make up the parts of the message. If more than one MIME binding extension is within a *<mime:part>*, they indicate alternatives; only one of them can be present in the transmitted message.

SOAP Binding Extensions

By now you should be wondering about the role of SOAP in Web services. We've discussed how to describe a SOAP-free Web service in WSDL, how to accept HTTP-GET and HTTP-POST requests, and how to return data formatted as some arbitrary MIME type. WSDL is certainly not limited to SOAP. But as the only transport-independent Web service protocol, SOAP is important and is the basis for the majority of the work occurring in the Web services arena. In the previous chapter, we walked through all the options for using the SOAP protocol as the transport mechanism for Web services.

The schema for the SOAP binding extensions is at *http://schemas.xmlsoap.org/wsdl/soap*; .NET adds this to the WSDL document with a namespace prefix of *soap*.

You add the SOAP binding extensions to the WSDL in the same way that you add the HTTP binding extensions, as you can see in the WSDL for the SimpleRecordFinder service at the top of the next page.

```
<binding name="SimpleRecordFinderSoap" type="s0:SimpleRecordFinderSoap">
  <soap:binding transport="http://schemas.xmlsoap.org/soap/http"
   style="document" />
  <operation name="GetAlbumsForArtist">
    <soap:operation
     soapAction="http://www.notashop.com/wscr/GetAlbumsForArtist"
     style="document" />
    <input>
      <soap:body use="literal" />
    </input>
    <output>
      <soap:body use="literal" />
    </output>
  </operation>
</binding>
<service name="SimpleRecordFinder">
  <port name="SimpleRecordFinderSoap"
   binding="s0:SimpleRecordFinderSoap">
    <soap:address
     location="http://localhost/wscr/03/simple/SimpleRecordFinder.asmx"
    />
  </port>
</service>
```

In addition to the four elements in the WSDL above, there are another two that aren't used in this Web service. The *<soap:fault>* element sits inside a *<fault>* element, and the *<soap:header>* element sits inside the *<input>* or *<output>* element if you're using SOAP headers.

> **Note** .NET does not use the *<fault>* element, so it doesn't use the *<soap:fault>* element, either. See the WSDL specification for more details.

The *<soap:binding>* element The *<soap:binding>* element is used in the same way as the *<http:binding>* element; it indicates that the SOAP protocol is being used. The basic format of the *<soap:binding>* element is as follows:

```
<soap:binding transport="TransportSchema" style="rpc|document">
```

The value for the *style* attribute specifies whether the operations in the binding are RPC-oriented or document-oriented; if a value isn't specified, the *style* attribute defaults to *document*.

The *transport* attribute specifies the underlying transport that the binding is using. SOAP currently defines only the HTTP transport; its schema is at *http://schemas.xmlsoap.org/soap/http*. You can use other transports (such as FTP and SMTP), but the details for these have not been defined yet, and as far as we know, no Web services have been built that use protocols other than HTTP.

The *<soap:operation>* element The *<soap:operation>* element is used in the same way as the *<http:operation>* element; it provides settings that affect the operation as a whole. Unlike the HTTP version, the SOAP version doesn't have a *location* attribute because the details about the method we're trying to access is contained in the SOAP envelope. The basic format of the *<soap:operation>* element is as follows:

```
<soap:operation soapAction="ActionURL" style="rpc|document">
```

The *style* attribute indicates whether the operation is RPC-oriented or document-oriented. If the attribute is not specified, the value specified for the *<soap:binding>* element is used.

The *soapAction* attribute specifies the value of the SOAPAction header for the operation. For the HTTP transport this value is required, and it has no default value. In .NET, it defaults to the operation name appended to the namespace of the service.

The *<soap:body>* element The *<soap:body>* element defines the *Body* element of the SOAP envelope. The basic format is as follows:

```
<soap:body parts="PartsList" use="literal|encoded"
    encodingStyle="StlyeURL" namespace="NamespaceURL" />
```

The *parts* attribute indicates which parts of the message are contained within the SOAP body, with the message determined from the *<portType>* element that the *<binding>* element references. If you don't specify a *parts* attribute, all parts of the message are assumed to be contained in the SOAP body.

The *use* attribute indicates whether the message parts are literal or encoded. If the method expects literal parameters, the *encodingStyle* and *namespace* attributes are not present; if the method expects encoded parameters, the *encodingStyle* attribute lists the encodings used by the message and the *namespace* attribute is used to point at the namespace of the message.

The *<soap:header>* element Although not used by the SimpleRecordFinder service, the *<soap:header>* element defines the *Header* element of the SOAP envelope and has a syntax similar to that of the *<soap:body>* element:

```
<soap:header message="MessageName" part="PartName" use="literal|encoded"
 encodingStyle="StlyeURL" namespace="NamespaceURL" />
</soap:header>
```

The *use*, *encodingStyle*, and *namespace* attributes are used in the same way as the *<soap:body>* element.

The *message* and *part* attributes reference the *<message>* element and the part of the enclosed message that defines the header type. You must specify which message you're referring to because the SOAP headers are specific to the SOAP binding extensions and therefore have no intrinsic referencing within WSDL, as the *<soap:body>* element does.

> **Note** The WSDL specification also specifies a *<soap:headerfault>* element that allows problems with the header to be communicated back to the client. As with the handling of faults in the SOAP body, the handling of errors in the SOAP header is automatic. See the WSDL specification for more details.

The *<soap:address>* element The *<soap:address>* element is used in the same way as the *<http:address>* element. It indicates the address of the Web service. It is the only element in the SOAP binding extensions that indicates the address of the Web service because the details about the method called are contained in the SOAP envelope.

The basic format of the *<soap:address>* element is as follows:

```
<soap:address location="LocationURL">
```

The location attribute must be a fully qualified URL.

.NET and WSDL

Now that you've had a brief introduction to WSDL via the SimpleRecordFinder service, it's time to talk about the options in .NET for modifying the WSDL that's automatically generated for a Web service. All of the options that we're going to look at here are implemented in the complete Web service, RecordFinder, for this chapter at *http://localhost/wscr/03/recordfinder.asmx*.

We'll start by looking at how to control what protocols a Web service supports and then look at the different SOAP message formats, one-way methods, and method overloading, among other topics.

Supported Protocols

The SimpleRecordFinder service supports the three protocols you'd expect—SOAP, HTTP-GET, and HTTP-POST. This is not always ideal. On production servers, we tend to turn off HTTP-GET and HTTP-POST and allow only SOAP to access the Web service. Indeed, the tools provided with .NET and Microsoft Visual Studio .NET use only the SOAP protocol when constructing their proxies, so disabling the HTTP-GET and HTTP-POST protocols makes sense.

You can do this easily by adding a few entries to the web.config file for the application hosting the Web service, as we have done for the RecordFinder service:

```
<configuration>
  <system.web>
    <webServices>
      <protocols>
        <remove name="HttpGet" />
        <remove name="HttpPost" />
      </protocols>
    </webServices>
  </system.web>
</configuration>
```

If you look at the WSDL for the RecordFinder service, you'll see that it does indeed support only the SOAP protocol and that all the details for HTTP-GET and HTTP-POST have been removed.

You can also turn off the use of the SOAP protocol. However, although we've shown the use of the HTTP-GET and HTTP-POST protocols, the remainder of the book will assume the use of only the SOAP protocol when accessing Web services because higher-level features such as WS-Security require the use of the SOAP protocol.

You can also turn off the automatic documentation of Web services by specifying *<remove name="Documentation"/>*. In practice this might seem like a good idea, but that's not necessarily so—if you turn off the documentation, you also turn off the Web service's ability to generate its own WSDL. You can get around this limitation by viewing the WSDL for the Web service before you turn off the documentation feature and then saving it as a static WSDL file. This file will contain the correct WSDL for the Web service, and the *<soap:address>* element will point at the correct .asmx file on the server. Once you turn off the documentation feature, you can still access the Web service by using the static WSDL file.

> **Note** One notable feature of .NET is that if you're accessing a Web service that's hosted on the same machine as the client, you can still test the Web service using the HTTP-POST protocol even if you've turned off support for that protocol in the configuration file. The WSDL for the protocol isn't created, but you can test the Web service to see that it's working correctly. If you access the same service using a different machine, the ability to test the Web service disappears.

SOAP Message Formats

As we pointed out earlier, you have five options for the message format you use with the SOAP protocol. So far we've only looked at the default options in .NET for the message format—document-oriented, no encoding, with wrapped parameters—and this is the WSDL we've looked at so far. However, four other message formats are available:

- Document-oriented, no encoding, with bare parameters
- Document-oriented, encoded, with wrapped parameters
- Document-oriented, encoded, with bare parameters
- RPC-oriented (which is encoded, with bare parameters)

To show the changes that are made to the WSDL that's generated for these different formats, we've created five new Web services on the server. These all implement exactly the same code as SimpleRecordFinder and differ only in the message format that they require. The first of these, RecordFinder1, is a simple copy of the SimpleRecordFinder service that we've already looked at and has the default options for the message format. We'll introduce the remaining four services, RecordFinder2 through RecordFinder5, as we look at the options that follow.

You can change the format of SOAP messages quite easily in .NET with the use of attributes. For example, you can control whether an entire Web service is RPC-oriented or document-oriented by applying the *SoapRpcService* or *SoapDocumentService* attribute, respectively, to the class. Within a service, you can control whether an individual method is RPC-oriented or document-oriented by using the *SoapRpcMethod* or *SoapDocumentMethod* attribute, respectively. If you apply an attribute to the method, it overwrites the attribute applied to the class; you can use message formats for a method different from the one that applies to the class as a whole.

As you'll soon see, the choice of SOAP message format greatly affects the WSDL that's generated for a Web service. Note that the message format changes only the details in the *<message>* and *<types>* sections of the WSDL document. The values of attributes in the other WSDL elements, such as the *style* attribute of the *<soap:binding>* element, change to illustrate the options you've chosen but the structure of those elements doesn't change.

Document-Oriented Messages and Types

Once you specify a document-oriented service or method, you have two further options for how to construct the SOAP messages. The *SoapDocumentService* and *SoapDocumentMethod* attributes both support the *Use* and *ParameterStyle* parameters.

The *Use* parameter controls whether the Web service expects encoded messages. It can take one of two values, *Encoded* or *Literal*. The default in .NET is literal messaging, but you can easily change this:

```
[SoapDocumentMethod(Use=SoapBindingUse.Encoded)]
```

The *ParameterStyle* parameter controls whether the Web service expects bare or wrapped messages. It can take one of two values, which are, not surprisingly, *Bare* and *Wrapped*. As you saw in the previous chapter, with wrapped messaging each element you use is described as an XSD complex type that contains various sequence details, whereas bare messaging maps to an XSD simple type. The default in .NET is wrapped messages, but you can easily change this:

```
[SoapDocumentMethod(ParameterStyle=SoapParameterStyle.Bare)]
```

Literal messages and types With a literal message, the message parts use the *element* attribute to point at an element defined in the *<types>* section of the document. They cannot point directly at an XSD type.

The RecordFinder1 service (which is at *http://localhost/wscr/03/soap/recordfinder1.asmx*) uses the document-literal-wrapped message format. The RecordFinder2 service (which is at *http://localhost/wscr/03/soap/recordfinder2.asmx*) uses bare parameters rather than the wrapped parameters used by RecordFinder1.

As we saw when we looked at SimpleRecordFinder, the *<part>* elements in RecordFinder1 are all created with the name *parameters* and point at an *<s:element>* defined in the *<types>* section. The naming of the elements in the *<types>* section for the document-literal-wrapped message format is as follows:

- The *<s:element>* element that wraps the complex type is named after the *<operation>* it's being used in, with *Response* appended if it's the response from the method.

- Each wrapper *<s:element>* eventually contains an *<s:element>* that defines the data type. The name for incoming types is the name of the parameter; for outgoing types, it's the name of the *<operation>*, with *Result* appended.

RecordFinder2 uses bare parameters, so there's no need to wrap the elements we're using inside a complex type. The *<part>* elements now follow the naming scheme introduced earlier in Table 3-2, and they still reference an *<s:element>* defined in the *<types>* section. The element we reference can now reference defined XSD types directly—we do away with the wrapping in a complex type. The *<part>* element and the *<s:element>* it references share the same name:

- For incoming messages, the elements have the same name as the parameter name in code.
- For outgoing messages, the elements have the same name as the method, with *Result* appended.

Encoded messages and types With an encoded message, the message parts use the *type* attribute to point at a complex type defined in the *<types>* section of the document or at an intrinsic XSD type. As with literal messaging, what the *<part>* elements contain depends on whether you're using wrapped or bare messaging.

As you've probably gathered, we now have two new versions of the Web service on the server that show the options we've discussed. RecordFinder3 (at *http://localhost/wscr/03/soap/RecordFinder3.asmx*) uses wrapped parameters; RecordFinder4 (at *http://localhost/wscr/03/soap/RecordFinder4.asmx*), uses bare parameters.

If you look at the WSDL for RecordFinder3, you'll see that the *<part>* elements are all created with a name of *parameters* and use the *type* attribute to point at an *<xsd:complexType>* defined in the *<types>* section. A complex type is created even if the message part is actually an intrinsic type. The rules used to name the types are the same as those for wrapped parameters when you use the literal message format:

- The *<s:complexType>* elements are named after the *<operation>* they're being used in, with *Response* appended if they're the return from the method.
- Each *<s:complexType>* eventually contains an *<s:element>*. The name, for incoming types, is the name of the parameter; for outgoing types, it's the name of the *<operation>*, with *Result* appended.

If you look at WSDL for RecordFinder4, which uses bare parameters, you can see that it behaves similarly for encoded messages and for literal messages. As with literal messaging, you do away with the need for the containing element, but when you use encoding you can go one step further. Whereas with literal messaging you have to point to an element, with encoded messaging you can point straight to an intrinsic type rather than a defined complex type if you want. You'll see this if you compare the *GetAlbumsForArtistSoapIn* message across all four versions of the service.

The naming rules are the same for bare parameters regardless of whether you're using literal or encoded messaging, but for the encoded message format you no longer have XSD elements that must be named:

- For incoming messages, the *<part>* element has the same name as the parameter name in code.
- For outgoing messages, the *<part>* element has the name of the method, with *Result* appended.

RPC-Oriented Messages and Types

The last option for the SOAP message format is to use RPC-oriented messaging. As you saw in Chapter 2, this forces the use of encoding and bare parameters.

The quick-thinking among you will realize that using RPC-oriented messaging is nearly the same as using document-oriented messaging when you encode the message and use bare parameters. If you compare the WSDL generated for the RecordFinder4 service with the WSDL generated for RecordFinder5 (at *http://localhost/wscr/03/soap/RecordFinder5.asmx*), you'll see that the WSDL is the same except for the *style* attributes of the *<soap:binding>* and *<soap:operation>* elements.

Other Configuration Options

Now that we've covered the options specific to RPC-oriented and document-oriented messages, we'll look at seven other options that are common to the *SoapRpcMethod* and *SoapDocumentMethod* attributes.

Rather than creating a new Web service for every example, as we've done so far, we'll simply add the code to the complete version of the RecordFinder service (which is at *http://localhost/wscr/03/RecordFinder.asmx*). To avoid any confusion, this service uses the default options in .NET for the message format.

One-Way Methods

As we mentioned, WSDL allows two operation types to be used for exposed methods: request-response and one-way. In .NET, the default operation type is request-response, but you can override this behavior on a method and change it to one-way by using the *OneWay* parameter and setting its value to *true*.

Contrary to what you might assume, specifying a method as *void* is not the same as implementing a one-way method. If you expose a *void* method as a method of a Web service, you don't actually create a one-way method—you simply create a method that has a type containing a return parameter that is ultimately defined as not containing any data.

To correctly declare a method as one-way, you must specify the method as one-way in the attribute, and you must also declare the method as *void*. If you declare it as anything other than *void*, the code will build correctly but when you attempt to access the Web service, you'll generate an exception, as shown in Figure 3-2.

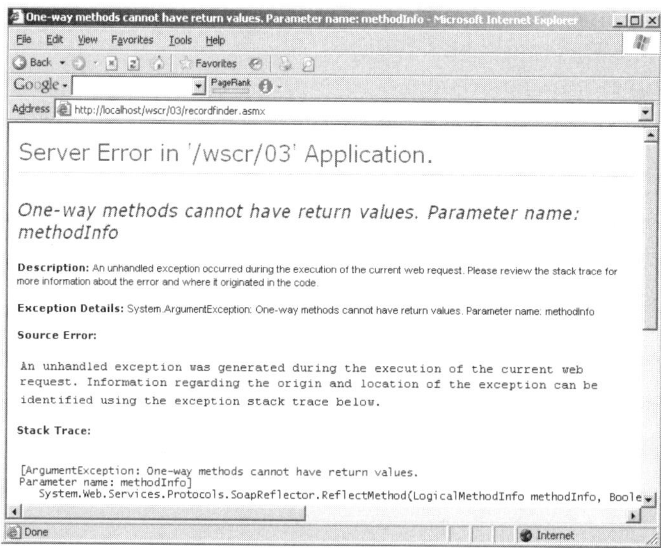

Figure 3-2 Error returned when a one-way method returns a value

If you look at the RecordFinder service, you'll see that it has a one-way method called *UpdateAlbum*. Although it functionally does nothing in this example, in the real world it would be used to update details in the database for a particular album. The signature for the method is as follows:

```
[WebMethod,SoapDocumentMethod(OneWay=true)]
public void UpdateAlbum(string strTitle, string strArtist)
```

If you now look at the WSDL for the service, you can see that there is no *<output>* element for either the *<portType>* or the *<binding>* elements for the *UpdateAlbum* method. You can see this by looking at the *<portType>* details for the service:

```
<portType name="RecordFinderSoap">
  <operation name="UpdateAlbum">
    <input message="s0:UpdateAlbumSoapIn" />
  </operation>
</portType>
```

Similarly, if you look at the WSDL for the service, you can see that the *<binding>* element also has only an *<input>* element.

Changing the SOAP Action

As you saw in the previous chapter, you must provide the SOAP action value when you use the SOAP protocol across HTTP. You've already seen that the default value is the operation name appended to the namespace of the Web service. This is certainly adequate for most Web services, but if you need to change it, you can do so by using the *action* parameter of the *SoapDocumentMethod* or *SoapRpcMethod* attribute.

You can add this value to the *UpdateAlbum* method for RecordFinder service as follows:

```
[WebMethod,SoapDocumentMethod(OneWay=true, Action="UpdateAlbum")]
public void UpdateAlbum(string strTitle, string strArtist)
```

If you now look at the *<operation>* element within the *<binding>* element, you can see that the *soapAction* attribute has changed:

```
<operation name="UpdateAlbum">
  <soap:operation soapAction="UpdateAlbum" style="document" />
  ⋮
</operation>
```

Note, however, that as we've shown here, .NET allows any string to be used as the value of the SOAP action. This is not strictly correct; the SOAP specification states that this value must be a URI.

Changing the Request and Response Namespaces

Although we declared our Web service to be in a given namespace using the *Namespace* parameter of the *WebService* attribute, sometimes you might want the request and responses to individual methods to be in different namespaces. .NET allows you to do this by using the *RequestNamespace* and *ResponseNamespace* parameters of the *SoapRpcMethod* and *SoapDocumentMethod* attributes.

You can add request and response namespaces to your methods quite easily; the format is the same whether you use the RPC or document version of the attribute, as you'll see with the new *GetArtistForAlbum* method that we've added to our RecordFinder service:

```
[WebMethod,
    SoapDocumentMethod(
        RequestNamespace="http://www.notashop.com/wscr/request",
        ResponseNamespace="http://www.notashop.com/wscr/response")]
public string GetArtistForAlbum()
```

This affects the WSDL that's generated for the service in several ways. As soon as we use different namespaces with the Web service, we immediately have new prefixes added to the *<definitions>* element. These are all in the same format as the prefix we declared for the namespace for the overall service. Because we added two new namespaces, we now have an *s1* and *s2* prefix as well as the "standard" *s0* prefix. Additional namespaces would be named along the same lines: *s3*, *s4*, and so on.

The actual type definitions within the *<types>* section are also moved into their own schema sections:

```
<s:schema elementFormDefault="qualified"
  targetNamespace="http://www.notashop.com/wscr">
  ⋮
</s:schema>
<s:schema elementFormDefault="qualified"
  targetNamespace="http://www.notashop.com/wscr/request">
  ⋮
</s:schema>
<s:schema elementFormDefault="qualified"
  targetNamespace="http://www.notashop.com/wscr/response">
  ⋮
</s:schema>
```

The actual definitions of the types used by the Web service do not change at all. We simply refer to the types in the *<part>* elements using their new prefix rather than the old prefix.

For encoded messages, you also add the namespace to the *<soap:body>* elements in the *namespace* attribute of the respective *<input>* and *<output>* messages for the *<binding>*.

Changing the Request and Response Element Names

Having changed the namespace of the requests and responses to a method, we can, if we're using wrapped parameters, change the name of an element or complex type that's defined in the *<types>* section by using the *RequestElementName* and *ResponseElementName* parameters.

Even if we change a name in the *<types>* section, this action has no effect on the proxy that .NET generates because the names of the parameters are actually the names of the *<s:element>* elements that specify the data types and not the names of the elements or complex types referenced by the *<part>* element.

If you're using bare parameters, you can't change the name of the element or complex type in the *<types>* section because the names in this case contain the information used to generate the proxy at the client. If you try to change the names in this case, the values are ignored and the types are created with the default names.

We can change easily the element names for our *GetArtistForAlbum* method:

```
[WebMethod,
    SoapDocumentMethod(
      RequestNamespace="http://www.notashop.com/wscr/request",
      ResponseNamespace="http://www.notashop.com/wscr/response"
      RequestElementName="GAFA_Request",
      ResponseElementName="GAFA_Response")]
public string GetArtistForAlbum(string strAlbum)
```

If you now look at the types that are generated, you'll see that they use the names we specified and that the *<part>* elements point to the correct element:

```
<message name="GetArtistForAlbumSoapIn">
    <part name="parameters" element="s1:GAFA_Request" />
</message>
<message name="GetArtistForAlbumSoapOut">
    <part name="parameters" element="s2:GAFA_Response" />
</message>
```

Specifying Documentation Elements

One of the first things we looked at in the WSDL specification was the ability to add basic documentation to all elements within a WSDL file. You can add documentation in .NET, but only to methods and classes, which in WSDL equate to the *<portType>* and *<service>* elements, respectively.

To add a *<documentation>* element, you simply specify a string as the value of the *Description* parameter to the *WebService* or *WebMethod* attribute:

```
[WebService(Namespace="http://www.notashop.com/wscr",
    Description="RecordFinder service")]
public class RecordFinder : System.Web.Services.WebService

[WebMethod(Description="Search for albums by a given artist")]
public string[] GetAlbumsForArtist(string strArtist)
```

We've similarly added the *Description* parameter to the three methods that we've looked at so far. If you now look at the WSDL that is generated, you'll see the added *<documentation>* elements:

```
<portType name="RecordFinderSoap">
  <operation name="UpdateAlbum">
    <documentation>Update the artist for a given album</documentation>
    ⋮
  </operation>
  <operation name="GetArtistForAlbum">
    <documentation>Get the artist for a given album</documentation>
    ⋮
  </operation>
  <operation name="GetAlbumsForArtist">
    <documentation>Search for albums by a given artist</documentation>
    ⋮
  </operation>
</portType>
⋮
<service name="RecordFinder">
  <documentation>RecordFinder service</documentation>
  ⋮
</service>
```

If you look at the service in Microsoft Internet Explorer, you'll see that the *<documentation>* elements are also picked up by .NET. (We'll shortly look at the *LogMessage* and *LogMessageWithName* methods.) This process is shown in Figure 3-3.

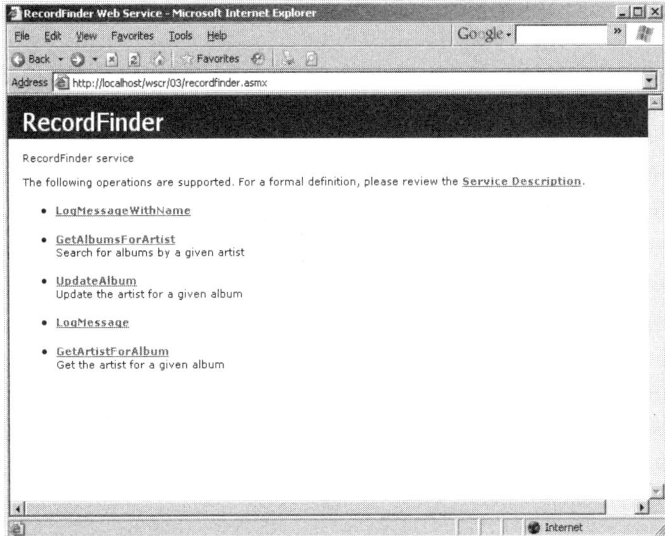

Figure 3-3 Documentation elements are pulled from the WSDL file.

SOAP Headers

As you saw in Chapter 2, you can quite easily add SOAP headers to a Web service you've created. We briefly mentioned how the WSDL is altered when you use SOAP headers. We'll now explain this further.

We've added a SOAP header to the *UpdateAlbum* method of the RecordFinder service, and we'll pass security information in this header. This is very insecure because we're sending username and password details in the open. We'll see in Chapter 15 that there are infinitely better ways to validate users. But for our purposes here, it's fine.

As you know, to add a SOAP header you need a class to pass as the header and a public instance of that class. You must also add an attribute to tell the method that it needs a header. Here's the code we've added to the RecordFinder service:

```
public class UserHeader : SoapHeader
{
    public string username;
    public string password;
}

public UserHeader authHeader;

[WebMethod(Description="Update the artist for a given album"),
    SoapDocumentMethod(OneWay=true,Action="UpdateAlbum"),
    SoapHeader("authHeader",Direction=SoapHeaderDirection.In)]
```

Chapter 2 discussed how to pass this to the Web service, the serialization that takes place, and everything else that occurs when you use SOAP headers, so we won't repeat all that here. What we're interested in here is the WSDL that's generated.

As you've seen, .NET serializes classes correctly and creates an *<s:element>* or an *<s:complexType>* for the class, depending on whether you're using wrapped or bare parameters. RecordFinder uses wrapped parameters, so the *UserHeader* class becomes an element and a complex type in the *<types>* section:

```
<s:element name="UserHeader" type="s0:UserHeader">
<s:complexType name="UserHeader">
  <s:sequence>
    <s:element minOccurs="0" maxOccurs="1" name="username"
      type="s:string" />
    <s:element minOccurs="0" maxOccurs="1" name="password"
      type="s:string" />
  </s:sequence>
</s:complexType>
```

We now have the necessary type defined for the header, so it's time to look at the WSDL that's actually generated for the *<soap:header>* element, as well as the required *<message>* element that maps to the element we created for the SOAP header class.

Because this header is specified with a direction of *SoapHeaderDirection.In*, the *<soap:header>* element is added to the *<input>* element of the *UpdateAlbum* operation. The *<soap:header>* element maps to the correct *<message>* and *<part>* elements by using the *message* and *part* attributes, as you can see for the RecordFinder service:

```
<soap:header
  message="s0:UpdateAlbumUserHeader"
  part="UserHeader"
  use="literal" />
```

From the *<soap:header>* element you can see that we're referring to a specific *<message>* element and a specific *<part>* element within it. There's nothing special about the *<message>* element we use with a SOAP header. It's identical to the *<message>* elements we've been looking at:

```
<message name="UpdateAlbumUserHeader">
 <part name="UserHeader" element="s0:UserHeader" />
</message>
```

That's it. We've specified that we require a SOAP header for the *UpdateAlbum* method, and .NET generates all of the required WSDL. This is not the end of the story, however. We have two more issues to explore.

Although the *UpdateAlbum* method has a header, it is defined as being an "in" header only, so the *<soap:header>* element is added to the *<input>* element. As you'll remember, you can also specify *out* and *inout* as directions for the header, and this changes where the *<soap:header>* element is added. For a direction of *out*, the header is added to the *<output>* element; for a direction of *inout*, the header is added to both the *<input>* and *<output>* elements and both *<soap:header>* elements point at the same *<message>* element and *<part>* element.

The second issue is that when you use SOAP headers, they follow the same message format rules as everything else concerned with the SOAP protocol. If you use encoding, the *<soap:header>* element shows the encoding details. If you use bare parameters instead of wrapped parameters, you use *<s:complexType>* elements instead of *<s:element>* elements.

Method Overloading

One topic that's inadequately defined in the current version of the WSDL specification is method overloading. This is being looked at in the next draft of the specification. In fact, the current specification neither allows overloading nor outlaws it. All of the languages supported by .NET allow method overloading, so it follows that Web services developed in .NET allow overloaded methods to be exposed.

To overload methods in .NET, you simply define two methods with the same name and a different parameter list. We'll add two overloaded methods to our RecordFinder service:

```
[WebMethod(), SoapDocumentMethod(OneWay=true)]
public void LogMessage(string strMessage)
{
    // logging code would go here
}

[WebMethod(), SoapDocumentMethod(OneWay=true)]
public void LogMessage(string strMessage, string strUserName)
{
    // logging code would go here
}
```

This isn't all. This code builds correctly if you try to browse to the Web service, but an *InvalidOperationException* is generated, as you can see in Figure 3-4.

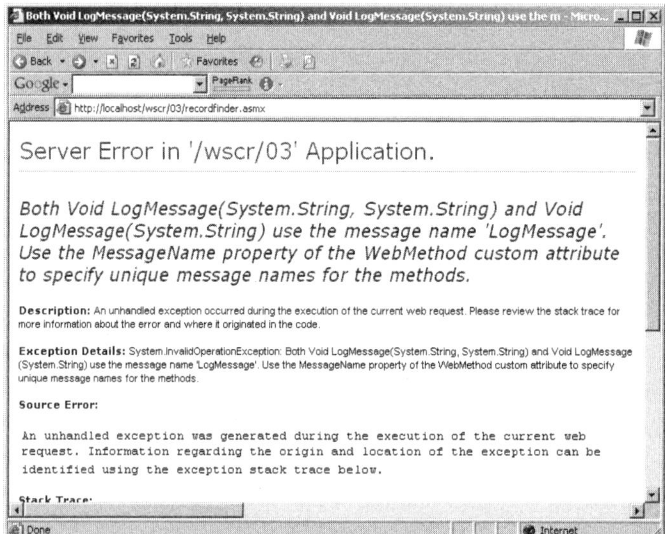

Figure 3-4 Overloading methods isn't as simple as it could be.

The error message we received provides a clue about what went wrong. WSDL *<message>* elements must have unique names and must follow the naming rules we've talked about. .NET is trying to create two *<message>* elements with the same name.

For overloading to work correctly, you need to specify a different message name for each of the overloaded methods exposed to the Web service. The error we received offers a clue to the solution. We must use the *MessageName* parameter of the *WebMethod* attribute to change the message name used for one of the overloaded methods:

```
[WebMethod(MessageName="LogMessageWithName"),
    SoapDocumentMethod(OneWay=true)
]
public void LogMessage(string strMessage, string strUserName)
```

If you now browse to the Web service, you'll see that the value we specified for the *MessageName* is used in place of the method name. We now have *LogMessage* and *LogMessageWithName* methods, as you can see in Figure 3-5.

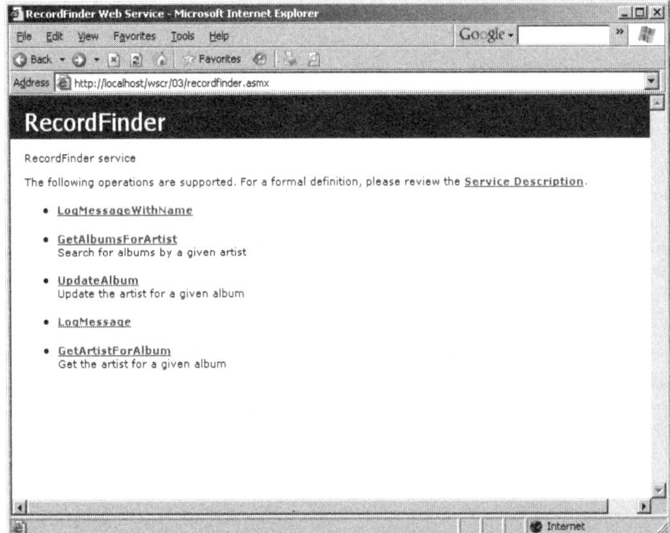

Figure 3-5 Overloaded methods take the wrong name.

When you first look at this, you might think we have a problem. Until now, the name displayed on this page has been the name of the method we have in code. Our use of the *MessageName* parameter has changed this. The methods are overloaded correctly, as you'll see shortly, but the *MessageName* is used rather than the method name so a distinction can be made between the overloaded methods when you look at the Web service in this manner.

To prove that the methods are overloaded correctly, you can look at the WSDL that's generated. The *<operation>* elements of both the *<binding>* and *<portType>* elements have the name *LogMessage*, and the *<input>* elements take the value of the *MessageName* parameter, as you can see from the *<operation>* elements for the *<portType>* element:

```
<operation name="LogMessage">
  <input message="s0:LogMessageSoapIn" />
</operation>
<operation name="LogMessage">
  <input name="LogMessageWithName"
   message="s0:LogMessageWithNameSoapIn" />
</operation>
```

If you still don't believe that the overloaded message names have been used, you can add the Web service to a Visual Studio .NET project and look in the Object Browser; you'll see that the correct method names have indeed been retained, as shown in Figure 3-6.

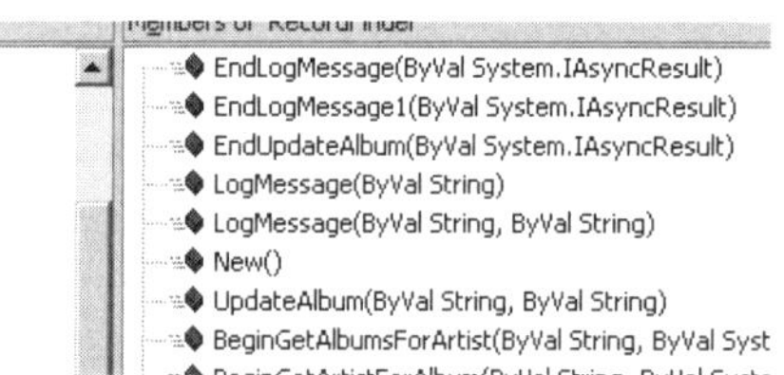

Figure 3-6 Overloaded methods in the Object Browser

Using the WSDL Files

You should now have a thorough understanding of WSDL. You've seen how .NET creates the WSDL file for a Web service and the options available for modifying the WSDL that's produced. We'll now take a look at the ways you can use WSDL.

Wsdl.exe

Wsdl.exe is a command-line tool provided with the .NET Framework SDK that generates the proxies for a specified WSDL file. Here's the basic format for using this command:

```
wsdl.exe http://localhost/HelloWorld.asmx
```

This command generates a proxy in C# for the given URL and saves the file at the current location with the same name as the service we created the proxy for.

A plethora of options are available for the wsdl.exe tool—16 in the current release of the SDK. You'll probably never use most of the options, but as you'll see in Chapter 4, you might need some of them. One important option allows you to specify the language you want the proxy built in.

By specifying the */l:* flag, you can specify whether you want the proxy to be built in C# (cs), Visual Basic .NET (vb), or JScript .NET (js). C# is the default language, so you need not specify it. JScript .NET doesn't support attributes, so for most purposes it is impossible to use it to build a proxy for a Web service; JScript. NET is therefore best ignored.

Once you have the proxy built, you can include it in any project you want because it's simply a normal code file. We've already talked endlessly about Web services being language agnostic, but as you can see in Figure 3-7, it makes no difference what language the developer wants to use. We've created a Visual Basic. NET proxy from a C# Web service.

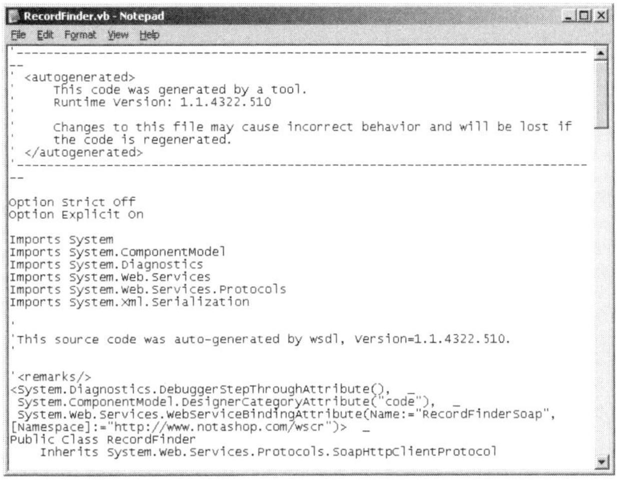

RecordFinder.vb - Notepad

```
'------------------------------------------------------------------------------
--
' <autogenerated>
'     This code was generated by a tool.
'     Runtime Version: 1.1.4322.510
'
'     Changes to this file may cause incorrect behavior and will be lost if
'     the code is regenerated.
' </autogenerated>
'------------------------------------------------------------------------------
--

Option Strict Off
Option Explicit On

Imports System
Imports System.ComponentModel
Imports System.Diagnostics
Imports System.Web.Services
Imports System.Web.Services.Protocols
Imports System.Xml.Serialization

'
'This source code was auto-generated by wsdl, Version=1.1.4322.510.
'

'<remarks/>
<System.Diagnostics.DebuggerStepThroughAttribute(),  _
 System.ComponentModel.DesignerCategoryAttribute("code"),  _
 System.Web.Services.WebServiceBindingAttribute(Name:="RecordFinderSoap",
[Namespace]:="http://www.notashop.com/wscr")>  _
Public Class RecordFinder
    Inherits System.Web.Services.Protocols.SoapHttpClientProtocol
```

Figure 3-7 Proxy code created by wsdl.exe

It's fine to create proxies for Web services in this way, but Visual Studio .NET offers a graphical interface to perform the same operation and also offers a few maintenance advantages along the way.

Visual Studio .NET

Visual Studio .NET provides a graphical tool for performing the same task that wsdl.exe performs—creating the proxies for Web services. It also provides a few other helpful features.

Adding a Web Reference

To add a reference to a Web service to a .NET application, you can simply choose the Add Web Reference command from the shortcut menu for the project or from the Project menu. A dialog box appears that contains a built-in Web browser, as shown in Figure 3-8.

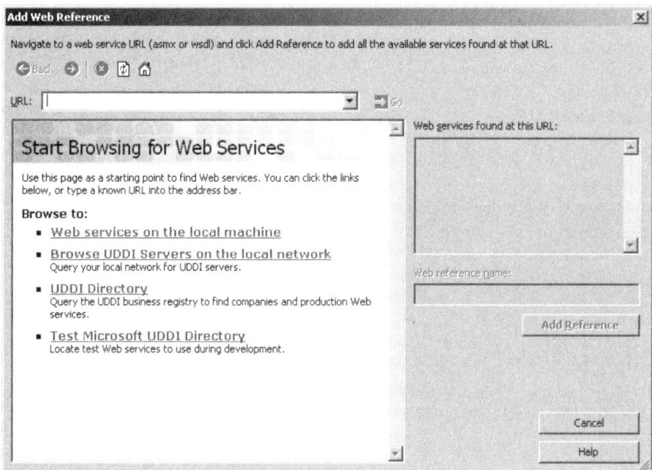

Figure 3-8 The Add Web Reference dialog box

You're immediately presented with several options for finding Web services. We'll deal with discovering Web services and UDDI in Chapter 4, so we'll ignore these options for now.

At the top of the dialog box is a URL text box. You can use the browser pane of the dialog box to navigate the Internet to find the appropriate Web service. As you know, this kind of search can be tedious, so the text box also allows you to type a URL to get to the Web service. If we enter the URL for the RecordFinder service, it appears in the left pane, as shown in Figure 3-9.

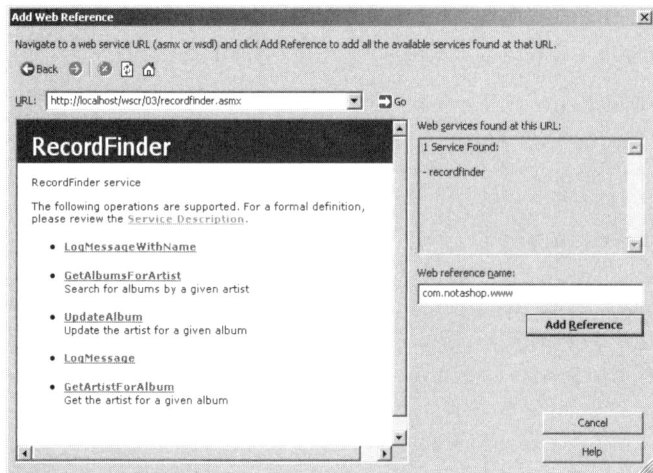

Figure 3-9 Finding the RecordFinder service

We now have the view of the Web service we know and love. However, we're more interested in the right pane, which has some details in it plus an Add Reference button. When the dialog box finds a page with the necessary details to allow the creation of a proxy, the right pane displays the details of the services that are available and the Add Reference button is enabled.

We can click the Add Reference button to create the proxy for the RecordFinder service and add it to the project.

Viewing the Proxy Code

When we add a reference to the Web service to our project, Visual Studio .NET does the job of wsdl.exe in the background and creates the proxy for the Web service. However, in the default setup of Visual Studio .NET this process is not visible. To view the proxy that has been created, you must show all files for the project by clicking the Show All Files button when an item in the project is selected. This displays all the files that are part of the project. If you take a close look at the Reference.map file, you can see that it has a child, as shown in Figure 3-10.

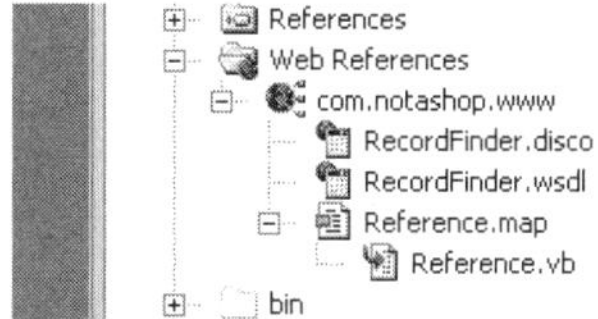

Figure 3-10 Viewing the proxy code

We happened to add the Web service to a Visual Basic .NET project, so the proxy was built in Visual Basic .NET. If we had added the Web service project to a C# project, the proxy would have been built in C# and would have had a .cs extension. If we open the Reference.vb file, as shown in Figure 3-11, we can see that it bears a remarkable resemblance to the proxy code we created with wsdl.exe.

```
'------------------------------------------------------------------------------
' <autogenerated>
'     This code was generated by a tool.
'     Runtime Version: 1.1.4322.510
'
'     Changes to this file may cause incorrect behavior and will be lost if
'     the code is regenerated.
' </autogenerated>
'------------------------------------------------------------------------------

Option Strict Off
Option Explicit On

Imports System
Imports System.ComponentModel
Imports System.Diagnostics
Imports System.Web.Services
Imports System.Web.Services.Protocols
Imports System.Xml.Serialization

'
'This source code was auto-generated by Microsoft.VSDesigner, Version 1.1.4322.510.
'
Namespace com.notashop.www

    '<remarks/>
    <System.Diagnostics.DebuggerStepThroughAttribute(),  _
     System.ComponentModel.DesignerCategoryAttribute("code"),  _
     System.Web.Services.WebServiceBindingAttribute(Name:="RecordFinderSoap", [Namespac
    Public Class RecordFinder
        Inherits System.Web.Services.Protocols.SoapHttpClientProtocol
```

Figure 3-11 Proxy code created by Visual Studio .NET

Updating the Web Service

One problem with using wsdl.exe occurs when a Web service is updated. We created a proxy locally, and any changes are not reflected in the proxy we have. Using wsdl.exe, we'd need to rerun the command line and replace the proxy in our project with the new one we generated. As with most things, Visual Studio .NET provides a quick and easy way to update the proxy to match the new version.

We can select the relevant reference and choose Update Web Reference from the shortcut menu, as shown in Figure 3-12, to update the proxy to match the version currently on the server. It's as simple as that!

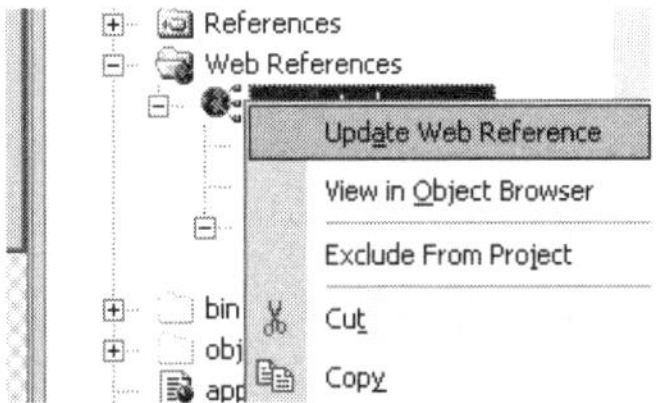

Figure 3-12 Updating a Web reference

Summary

In this chapter, we started by looking at why we need a language such as WSDL and then briefly discussed the grammar of the WSDL 1.1 language in the context of a simple Web service. We then looked at how to programmatically change the WSDL that's generated automatically for a Web service.

It should now be apparent that although WSDL is relatively simple, once you start adding protocol-specific details, it becomes complex very quickly—so much so that in most (if not 99.999 percent) of the cases where you need to use WSDL, you'll do so without ever looking at a single line of WSDL.

You should now have a thorough understanding of SOAP, the transport protocol used by our Web services, and WSDL, the language used to describe those Web services. But a huge piece is still missing—namely, how to find the Web service in the first place. This is where Microsoft's DISCO protocol and the standardized UDDI come into play. We'll cover these topics in the next chapter.

4

Discovering Web Services

In the previous two chapters, we looked at two-thirds of the infrastructure that makes Web services possible. You now know how to communicate with Web services, and you know how to describe Web services. The piece of the puzzle that's missing is how to actually find the Web services you want to use.

Most Web services are still discovered by traditional means—you're told the address of the service by e-mail or on a Web page, and you navigate to it directly, creating the proxy class as required. Nothing is wrong with this method of discovering Web services, and indeed both Amazon (*http://www.amazon.com/webservices*) and Google (*http://www.google.com/apis*) use it to promote the use of their Web services.

However, what we really need is a method that standardizes the process of discovering Web services and allows searches for Web services that perform particular tasks. For example, we might want to find a Web service that performs Internet searches; without such a standard, we might not know that Google provides such a service.

Two technologies currently allow this method of searching: Microsoft Discovery (DISCO) and Universal Description, Discovery, and Integration (UDDI). We'll look at both of these in turn. A third possibility, WS-Inspection, is on the horizon; it sits on top of the UDDI infrastructure and allows Web services to be described in a more technology-agnostic way. At the moment, this specification has no real implementation. We'll look at WS-Inspection in more detail when we cover Global XML Web Services Architecture (GXA) in Chapter 12.

Microsoft Discovery (DISCO)

DISCO is a Microsoft-defined specification for discovering Web services that are available on a server. However, its scope extends only to individual servers and to providing the client with a WSDL document. If you need to publish more details of available Web services on a larger scale, you must use UDDI instead.

> **Note** Rather than write new Web services to show the facilities that DISCO offers, we'll use the seven Web services that we created in Chapter 3. You can find them at *http://localhost/wscr/04*, using the same directory structure as in Chapter 3.

The DISCO Specification

The basis of the entire DISCO process is the *discovery document*, which contains the information that enables a client to find the physical address of the Web service on the server. The discovery document can also provide links to other discovery documents and to schema documents that describe the Web service.

The basic outline of the discovery document is as follows:

```
<?xml version="1.0"?>
<discovery xmlns="http://schemas.xmlsoap.org/disco/">
  <contractRef />
  ⋮
  <contractRef />
  <discoveryRef />
  ⋮
  <discoveryRef />
  <schemaRef />
  ⋮
  <schemaRef />
</discovery>
```

Within the *<discovery>* element, we defined three child elements that can appear multiple times. These elements are used to link to different documents on the server:

- ***<contractRef>*** This is the most important element in a discovery document because it provides the link to the actual Web service. The *ref* attribute points to the WSDL file for the Web service, and the *docRef* attribute provides details of any accompanying documentation for the Web service. For ASP.NET Web services, the *docRef* attribute points to the actual .asmx file, and the *ref* attribute points to the .asmx file with the *?wsdl* query string.

- ***<discoveryRef>*** This element provides a link, via the *ref* attribute, to another discovery document.
- ***<schemaRef>*** This element provides a link, via the *ref* attribute, to an XML Schema (XSD) file that details the Web service. This element is not used in version 1.1 of the Microsoft .NET Framework.

Discovery Document Types

You can write a discovery document using the format we've discussed, give it a .disco extension, and place it on a Web server. Discovery-enabled browsers such as the Add Web Reference dialog box in Visual Studio .NET will correctly parse this document. Writing a discovery document manually and using it to discover the available Web services is known as *static discovery*, and in most cases this is the best way to use discovery because it provides the most control. However, .NET offers two other methods for generating discovery documents: dynamic discovery and .asmx file discovery.

A dynamic discovery document, which has a .vsdisco extension, automatically searches the server's directory structure to gather references to all of the available Web services and other discovery documents. With .asmx file discovery, any Web service you write can also be used as a discovery document; you specify the *?disco* query string when you view a Web service via HTTP.

We'll look at each type of discovery document in turn.

Static Discovery

Static discovery is the simplest approach to implement and involves manually creating a file with a .disco extension and adding the required *<discovery>* element to it. Within the document, you add a *<contractRef>* element for each Web service you want to make available; if you want a reference to only one Web service, add only one *<contractRef>* element.

As you can see if you look at the static discovery document at *http://localhost/wscr/04/default.disco*, adding a reference to a Web service is simple. This discovery document has a single reference to the *RecordFinder* Web service:

```
<?xml version="1.0"?>
<discovery xmlns="http://schemas.xmlsoap.org/disco/">
  <contractRef
   ref=" http://localhost/wscr/04/recordfinder.asmx?wsdl"
   docRef=" http://localhost/wscr/04/recordfinder.asmx"
   xmlns="http://schemas.xmlsoap.org/disco/scl/" />
```

You can add as many *<contractRef>* elements as are required, and you can also add links to other discovery documents by adding *<discoveryRef>* elements:

```
  <discoveryRef
   ref="http://localhost/wscr/04/simple/default.disco" />
  <discoveryRef
   ref="http://localhost/wscr/04/soap/default.vsdisco" />
</discovery>
```

As you can see, we added links to two other discovery documents—one static and one dynamic. You're free to mix and match types of discovery documents that you're linking to.

Dynamic Discovery

Dynamic discovery lets you forget about the discovery document and have .NET generate it. This might seem like an ideal scenario, but it comes with several security problems. Microsoft has deemed the problems so severe that dynamic discovery is disabled in .NET; before you can use dynamic discovery, you must enable it on the server.

.NET integration with IIS has two parts, and only one of these is actually disabled. As with all files that you want IIS to handle, you need a mapping for the extension to the correct handler. When .NET is installed, this mapping is already in place, and files with the .vsdisco extension are mapped to the aspnet_isapi.dll handler. It is within the .NET configuration itself that the handling of the .vsdisco files has been disabled.

To enable handling of the .vsdisco files, you must modify the configuration files, at either the machine level (in machine.config) or the application level (in a web.config file). At either level, you must add the following to the *<httpHandlers>* element:

```
<configuration>
  <system.web>
    <httpHandlers>
      <add verb="*"
           path="*.vsdisco"
           type="System.Web.Services.Discovery.DiscoveryRequestHandler,→
             System.Web.Services, Version=1.0.3300.0,→
             Culture=neutral, PublicKeyToken=b03f5f7f11d50a3a"
           validate="false" />
    </httpHandlers>
  </system.web>
</configuration>
```

After you enable dynamic discovery on your server, you can use it by creating a file with a .vsdisco extension, and instead of adding a *<discovery>* element, you can add a *<dynamicDiscovery>* element. In the dynamic discovery document at *http://localhost/wscr/04/soap/default.vsdisco*, we added this *<dynamicDiscovery>* element and also specified several directories to exclude from the search:

```
<?xml version="1.0" encoding="utf-8" ?>
<dynamicDiscovery xmlns="urn:schemas-dynamicdiscovery:disco.2000-03-17">
  <exclude path="_vti_cnf" />
  <exclude path="_vti_pvt" />
  <exclude path="_vti_log" />
  <exclude path="_vti_script" />
  <exclude path="_vti_txt" />
  <exclude path="Web References" />
</dynamicDiscovery>
```

We told the parser to exclude the various Microsoft FrontPage directories, as well as the Web References directory; if you specify a directory that doesn't exist, the entry is simply ignored.

Barring the excluded directories, the parser searches all the directories from the location of default.vsdisco downward in the directory tree, looking in any real directories that it finds (ignoring virtual directories). Within each directory, the parser looks for any files with the extensions .vsdisco, .disco, and .asmx, in that order. One word of warning: the parser looks first for files with the extension .vsdisco, and if it finds one, it stops searching that part of the directory tree; it ignores all other files in that directory and all its subdirectories.

After searching the directory tree as described, the parser constructs a *<discovery>* element that contains a *<contractRef>* element for each .asmx file it found and a *<discoveryRef>* element for each .vsdisco or .disco file it found.

The *http://localhost/wscr/04/soap/default.vsdisco* discovery document in Internet Explorer returns five Web services, as shown in Figure 4-1.

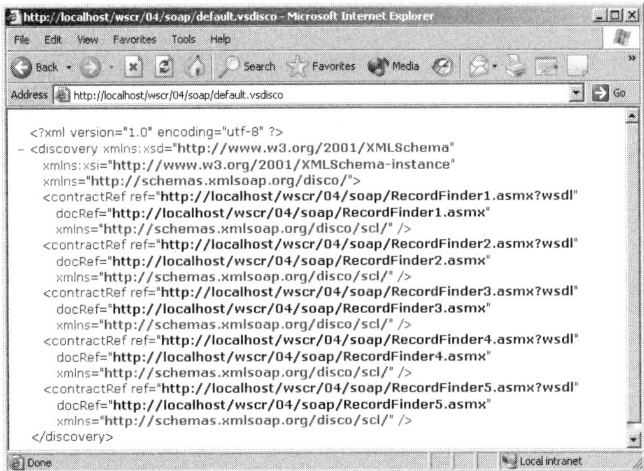

Figure 4-1 A dynamically generated discovery document

As you can see, we returned the correct five Web services, which, as you might recall, show the different SOAP message formats. You'll also see two extra namespaces mapped to the *<discovery>* element—one with the prefix *xsd* and the other with the prefix *xsi*. You'll probably gather from the prefixes and the addresses they map to that the namespaces are concerned with XSD documents. Even though we don't have any *<schemaRef>* elements in our discovery document, the parser still adds the namespaces to our document.

.asmx File Discovery

In addition to the two physical discovery documents that you can create for static or dynamic discovery, the .asmx files that contain your Web services can also generate an .asmx discovery file.

In much the same way that you can interrogate an .asmx file to provide the correct WSDL for the Web service by using the *?wsdl* query string, you can use the *?disco* query string to force an .asmx file to give you the discovery document for itself.

The RecordFinder Web service that we mentioned in the static discovery document shown earlier generates a discovery document for itself, as shown in Figure 4-2.

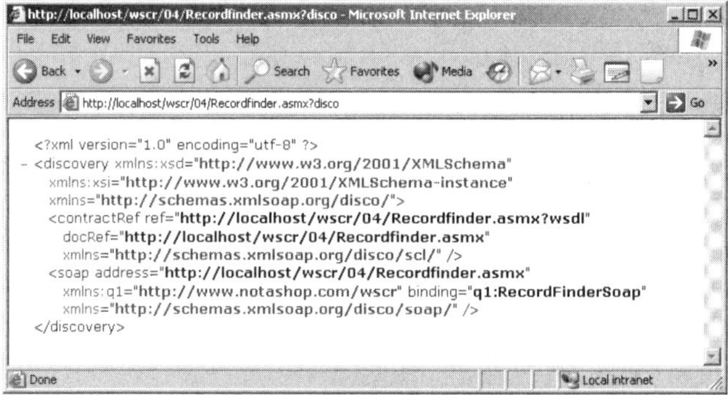

Figure 4-2 A discovery document from an .asmx file

Like the dynamically generated discovery document described previously, the .asmx discovery document includes two extraneous namespaces and a *<soap>* element that you can safely ignore. The *address* and *binding* attributes of the *<soap>* element map to the details contained in the .wsdl file, but they are never used, so you can ignore the entire element.

Visual Studio .NET and DISCO Files

Now that we've looked at the DISCO specification and the three types of discovery documents, it's time to see how Visual Studio .NET actually deals with discovery. We'll use the Web services from Chapter 3 and the two discovery documents we just looked at.

In Visual Studio, selecting Add Web Reference from the Project menu launches the Add Web Reference dialog box, where you can navigate to the discovery document you're interested in or enter the document's URL and then click Go.

If we navigate to *http://localhost/wscr/04/default.disco*, the static discovery document we looked at earlier, Visual Studio .NET will display the returned document in the browser window, as shown in Figure 4-3.

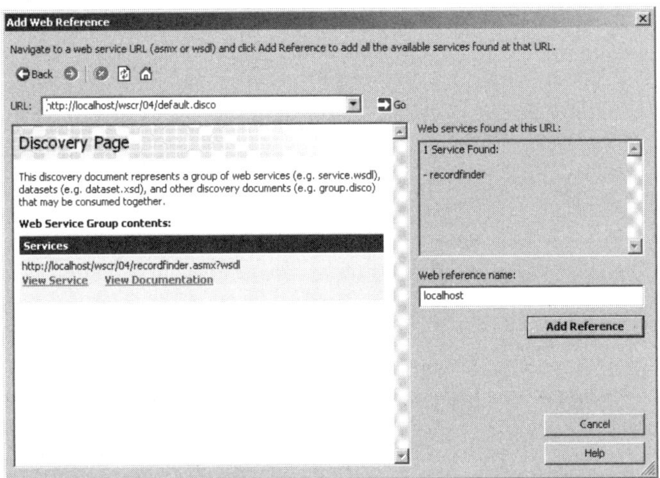

Figure 4-3 Adding a reference using a discovery document in Visual Studio .NET 2003

The Web server returns the discovery document we created earlier to the dialog box, and the dialog box does some processing on this returned file to present the user-friendly version of the document shown in Figure 4-3.

Clicking the View Service link takes us to the URL that is specified as the *docRef* attribute of the *<contractRef>* element. Similarly, the View Documentation link takes us to the URL specified in the *ref* attribute.

If you look again at Figure 4-3, you'll notice that some of the information we described in the discovery file is missing. We specified two links to other discovery documents that are missing from the details shown in the Add Web Reference dialog box in Visual Studio .NET 2003. As shown in Figure 4-4, the previous version of Visual Studio .NET, Visual Studio .NET 2002, displays these links when we navigate to a discovery document.

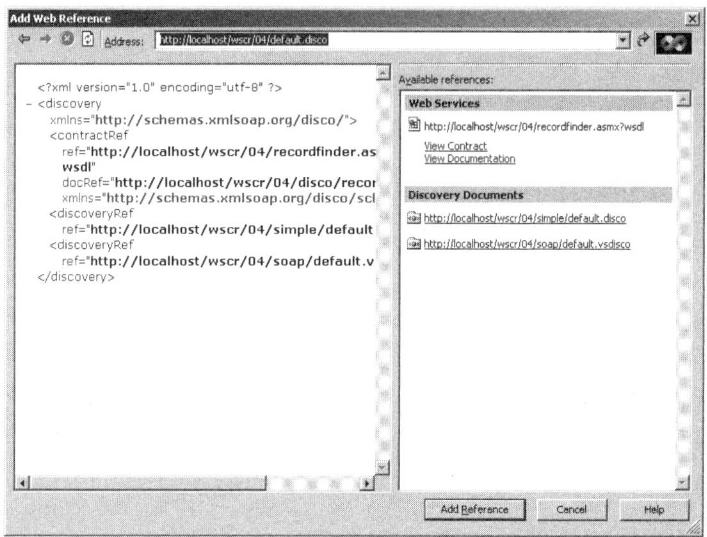

Figure 4-4 Adding a reference using a discovery document in Visual Studio .NET 2002

In Visual Studio .NET 2002, we can use the links to other discovery documents to navigate to those documents without needing to know the address of the discovery document. Without this feature in Visual Studio .NET 2003, we need to know the addresses of the individual discovery documents.

Adding a Web Reference from a Discovery Document

When you view a discovery document, as you saw in Figure 4-3, you have the option of adding the reference directly from the discovery file. If only one Web service is referenced in the discovery document, this isn't a problem—the correct reference to the Web service is added to the project. But problems occur when you try to add references from a discovery document that contains multiple Web service definitions. If you look at the discovery document at *http://localhost/wscr/04/soap/default.vsdisco*, you'll see five Web services defined, as shown in Figure 4-5.

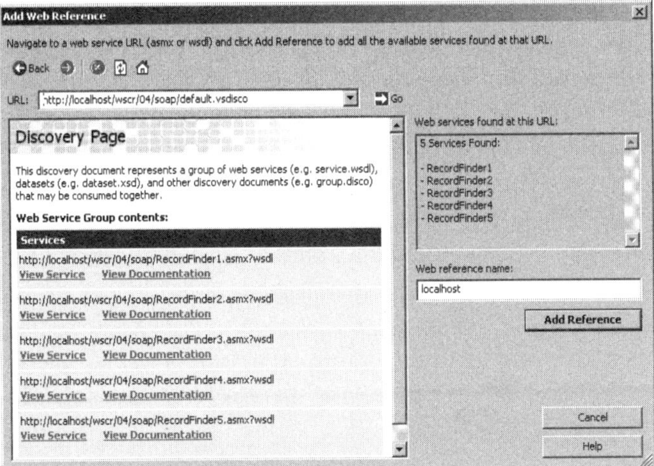

Figure 4-5 Adding a reference from a discovery document with multiple Web services

You might think that clicking the Add Reference button will add references to all five Web services to the project. Instead, although all five referenced WSDL documents are downloaded and added to the reference, a proxy class is created only for the last Web service referenced in the file—in this case, RecordFinder5.

Because of the behavior that Visual Studio .NET exhibits when you add references from a discovery document that contains multiple Web service definitions, you should always add a reference to the Web service from the .asmx file itself, not from a discovery document. You can thereby avoid problems that might occur with the ordering of the Web services within the discovery document.

Adding a Web Reference from a Web Service

In the previous chapter, we looked at adding references to Web services from the .asmx file itself and also from the .asmx file with the *?wsdl* query string added. You just learned how to get to these references from the discovery document, and we recommended this approach as the best way to add references to Web services.

As you saw in Chapter 3, when you add a reference to a Web service, Visual Studio .NET in some cases automatically queries the Web service for a discovery document for itself. We said then that we'd leave the discussion of the .disco file until this chapter; we'll address that subject now.

When you view an .asmx file and add it as a reference, Visual Studio .NET has no idea what the .wsdl definition of that document is. To retrieve the WSDL definition of the Web service, Visual Studio .NET queries the .asmx file with the *?disco* query string to return the discovery document for the Web service. Because this discovery document contains the contract details for the Web service, Visual Studio .NET can locate the WSDL for the Web service, download it, and create the proxy, as you'd expect. Visual Studio .NET keeps a copy of the discovery document and the WSDL file, and if you look at those two files you'll see that the two cached files are the same as those we'd see if we were to query the Web service by using the *?wsdl* and *?disco* query strings.

When you view an .asmx file with the *?wsdl* query string, you see the WSDL definition of the document. When you add a reference to a Visual Studio .NET project by using a WSDL document, Visual Studio .NET adds the WSDL file to the reference and creates the proxy class from it—it doesn't need to query for a discovery document because it already has the WSDL definition of the Web service.

Universal Description, Discovery, and Integration (UDDI)

DISCO does a good job of allowing Web services on a particular server to be detailed and used, but it has one major problem: you have to know the server that the Web service sits on and, in most cases, also the exact address of the Web service.

To address this shortcoming, Microsoft and IBM teamed up to produce the UDDI specification, which allows Web services to be added to an online "yellow pages" of Web services. The specification has since been passed to OASIS (a not-for-profit, global consortium) and now has the backing of most of the major players in the industry—Sun, VeriSign, SAP, and Compaq, to name just a few.

> **Note** The UDDI Web site is at *http://www.uddi.org*, and the OASIS Web site is at *http://www.oasis-open.org*. The latest release of the UDDI specification can always be found at *http://www.uddi.org/specification.html*. Although the current release of the specification is version 3.0, version 2.0 of the specification is the latest version to be ratified by OASIS. The Microsoft tools support only up to version 2.0, and the UDDI Enterprise Services in Windows 2003 Server are compliant only up to this version. Therefore, we'll concentrate on version 2.0 of the specification in this chapter.

UDDI is not a specification for describing Web services. As you'll see, the actual description of Web services is accomplished using WSDL—UDDI is simply used as a yellow pages of Web services. Within the definition of a Web service in UDDI, you point at the WSDL document that describes the Web service.

UDDI is also not simply a specification. Microsoft, IBM, SAP, and NTT Communications have also implemented what might be described as root UDDI Business Registries (UBRs), which you can use to store the details of the Web services you create.

We'll go into detail about UDDI in upcoming sections. First you need a basic understanding of how a Web service and its ancillary details are described within UDDI. Figure 4-6 shows the elements that the UDDI specification defines for storing information in the UBRs.

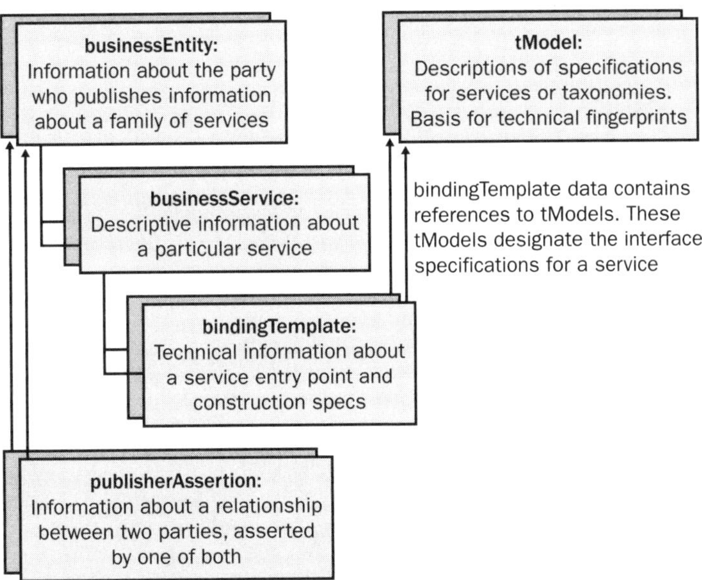

Figure 4-6 Overview of the data structures used by UDDI

The entire point of UDDI is to allow access to information about Web services. In UDDI parlance, we're looking for information about a businessService. The businessService structure represents the service you access (a high-level description of the Web service) and is the structure in UDDI that you're likely to see most often.

As you can see in Figure 4-6, a businessService is a child of the businessEntity structure. The businessEntity structure represents the publisher of the Web service. A publisher can publish many different Web services. Closely related to the businessEntity structure is the publisherAssertion. A publisherAssertion structure allows the relationship between businessEntity objects to be quantified. For example, the different divisions within a company might be registered as separate businessEntity objects, but can show the relationship among the divisions with a publisherAssertion structure.

The businessService structure on its own doesn't tell the full story, however. As Figure 4-6 shows, a tModel structure, which is ultimately related to the businessService structure, gives UDDI much of its strength.

You can think of a tModel as the interface of the Web service. It describes the methods that a businessService exposes, as well as the way in which the tModel must be accessed.

A businessService can expose multiple interfaces, and as such it can be related to multiple tModel structures. The relationship between the businessService and the tModel structures is handled via a bindingTemplate structure. The bindingTemplate structure also contains, among other things, the address of the businessService.

The relationships between the structures are constrained using Universally Unique Identifiers (UUIDs). Each instance of a structure has a UUID that identifies that structure. When a structure references another structure, it simply holds a pointer to the UUID of the referenced structure. For example, a businessService object that's related to a businessEntity object contains a reference to the UUID for the businessEntity object.

The UDDI Business Registries

As mentioned earlier, UDDI is not simply a specification. A rather large specification document details the data structures and the API that UDDI exposes, but without the UBRs, the API is useless.

Four UBRs are currently available (as well as three test registries):

- *http://uddi.microsoft.com* (and *http://test.uddi.microsoft.com*)
- *https://uddi.ibm.com/ubr/registry.html* (and *https://uddi.ibm.com/testregistry/registry.html*)
- *http://uddi.sap.com* (and *http://udditest.sap.com*)
- *http://www.ntt.com/uddi*

As you can see from the list, Microsoft, IBM, and SAP all provide test registries as well as live registries. The live registries are used to advertise Web services that are, well, live. You should use the test registries for all development and testing work and move the details across to the live registry only when you go live with the Web service.

All of these UBRs store the information required by the UDDI specification, but they differ slightly in how they allow the information to be interrogated and amended. We'll concentrate on the Microsoft test UBR, *http://test.uddi.microsoft.com*.

Both the live and test UBRs have exactly the same functionality. The only difference is in the URL of the calls to the UBR.

> **Note** Both of the Microsoft UBRs use Microsoft Passport as the authentication mechanism for accessing the sites. We'll assume in this chapter that you already have a Passport account.

UBR Concurrency

You might assume that each of the four UBRs contains unique data. This is not the case; the data between the live registries is synchronized on a daily basis. Details entered on the Microsoft UBR will be available on the IBM and SAP UBRs after a day or two.

Although the data is synchronized on all the UBRs, only the UBR that originated the data can modify the data. Only it knows which account the details belong to.

Categorization and Identification

The mainstay of the yellow pages is the categories that contain the entries. We can do a similar thing with UDDI entries by applying categories to businessEntity objects, businessService objects, and tModel objects. We'll now look briefly at the categorization and identification of Web services; keep in mind that this is far from an exhaustive discussion.

The UDDI Category System

It is perfectly possible to search for a Web service by name, but this is not always practical. If you have a simple Web service that adds two numbers, it might be called AddTwoNumbers, SumNumbers, NumberAdd, or one of other names that you can no doubt think of. It would be better in this case to classify the Web service by category. Adding it to a Mathematics category would be a start, and adding it to an Addition subcategory would be even better. Users looking for the Web service can then narrow their search as appropriate.

We can add categorization data to businessEntity, businessService, and tModel objects. Three taxonomies that have been defined thus far, and they are a core part of UDDI. These are shown in Table 4-1.

Table 4-1 Taxonomies Defined in the UDDI Specification

Taxonomy	tModel Name
North American Industry Classification Scheme (NAICS)	ntis-gov:naics:1997
Universal Standard Products and Services Classification (UNSPSC)	unspsc-org:unspsc
ISO 3166	uddi-org:iso-ch:3166:1999

The first two taxonomies are used to categorize the Web service into functions; ISO 3166 is used to provide geographical categorization. A deprecated version of the UNSPSC category is also defined in the specification; because it is deprecated, it is wise to use the latest version, which is listed in the table.

Each UBR can also define its own category taxonomies. Microsoft has added, among others, the VS Web Service Search Categorization taxonomy, which allows easier searching from within Visual Studio .NET, and microsoft-com:geoweb:2000, a geographical taxonomy.

> **Note** Categorization helps immensely, but it is not a perfect solution. Not everyone will correctly categorize a Web service in minute detail. Suppose we're using the UNSPSC taxonomy and I register my Web service in the Janitorial Equipment category, which is a subcategory of Cleaning Equipment And Supplies. Nothing can stop a direct competitor from registering its Web service in the far more general Cleaning Equipment And Supplies category and potentially getting more searches that find its Web service. Someone searching for Janitorial Equipment and someone searching for Cleaning Equipment And Supplies will see a completely different set of results because UDDI does not support the searching of hierarchies within categories.

The UDDI Identifier System

Although you can use the category system to document your Web services, sometimes you'll want to store data that doesn't fit into any of the existing categorization schemas. In addition to a category system, UDDI implements an identifier system that allows you to add arbitrary identifiers to businessEntity structures and tModel structures. The UDDI specification defines two identifier taxonomies—Dun & Bradstreet Numbers (see *http://www.dnb.com*) and Thomas Register Supplier Codes (see *http://thomasregister.com*). If your business has a Dun & Bradstreet Number or a Thomas Register Supplier Code, you might want to allow your customers to search for your business in this manner.

When you add an identifier, you must select a tModel that the identifier you're entering belongs to. Each UBR can define its own identifier taxonomies. Also, you can define your own tModel structures for this purpose. The UDDI specification provides two tModel structures that relate to the identifier taxonomies we've already seen, as shown in Table 4-2.

Table 4-2 Identifiers Defined in the UDDI Specification

Identifier	tModel Name
Dun & Bradstreet	dnb-com:D-U-N-S
Thomas Register	thomasregister-com:supplierID

Searching for Web Services

As you'll see later in the chapter when we cover the UDDI API and the Microsoft SDK, you can access the data stored in a UBR in several ways. For now, we'll look at using the Microsoft UBR to search for Web services.

The Microsoft UBR allows you to search for available Web services in a number of ways, depending on your requirements. You can navigate to the main search screen by choosing Search from the toolbar of the Microsoft UBR Web page or from the Tools menu on the left of the page. The search page is shown in Figure 4-7.

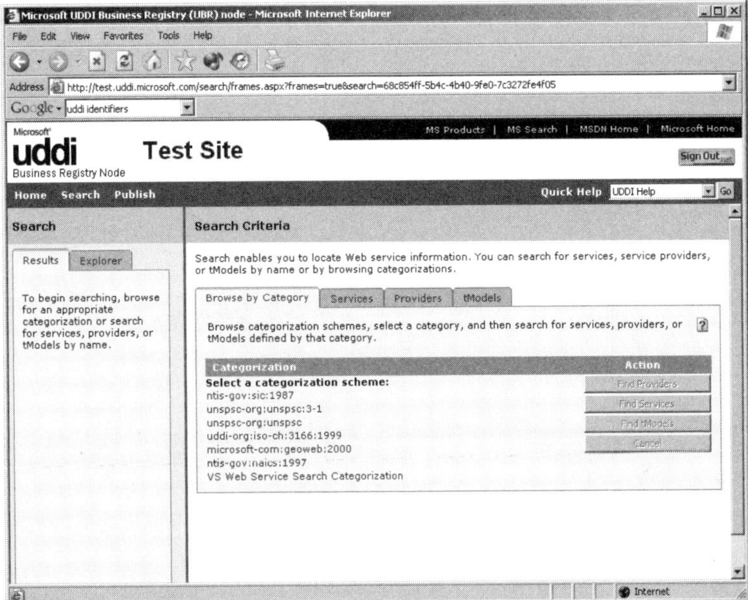

Figure 4-7 Searching the Microsoft UBR

> **Note** The Microsoft UBR uses slightly different terminology from that used by the UDDI specification and the other UBRs. In the Microsoft UBR, businessEntity structures are called *providers* and businessService structures are called *services*. These might make more sense to a user of the UBRs, but as you'll soon see, the Microsoft SDK uses the names given by the UDDI specification. The terms can be used interchangeably, which is worth bearing in mind when you use UDDI.

As you can see in Figure 4-7, four tabs allow you to query the UBR in different ways. The default option is to specify a categorization scheme, select a category to query, and then search by provider, service, or tModel.

You also have the option of querying the UBR for providers, services, or tModel structures by using one of the other tabs. You can immediately limit your search and be more specific about the item you're searching for. On the Services tab, for example, you can specify two criteria instead of the one on the Browse By Category tab. As shown in Figure 4-8, you can specify the category or a tModel to limit the search.

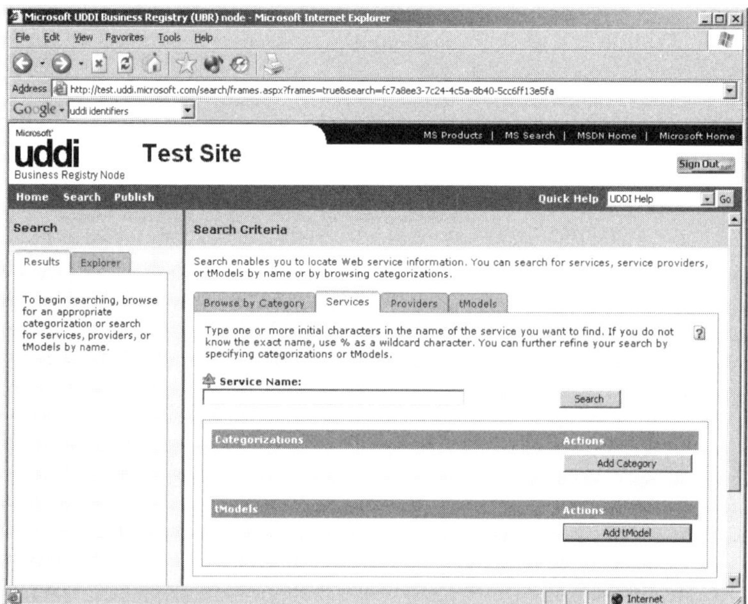

Figure 4-8 Specifying the query type to further refine a search

Searching for services allows you to specify search criteria based on the category or the tModel; searching for providers or tModels allows you to specify different search criteria. If you search for a tModel, you obviously can't specify a tModel as a search criterion; you're limited to specifying categories and identifiers. When you search for providers, you can specify criteria based on categories, identifiers, and tModels.

When you perform a query using the Microsoft UBR, you are presented with a summary of the results in the left pane. You can select one of the results to see its complete details.

Later in the chapter, we'll implement some Web services and add them to UDDI. If we perform a search for one of these services, NOSBasicServiceA, and then click on its name in the results pane, we'll see the details of the service, as shown in Figure 4-9.

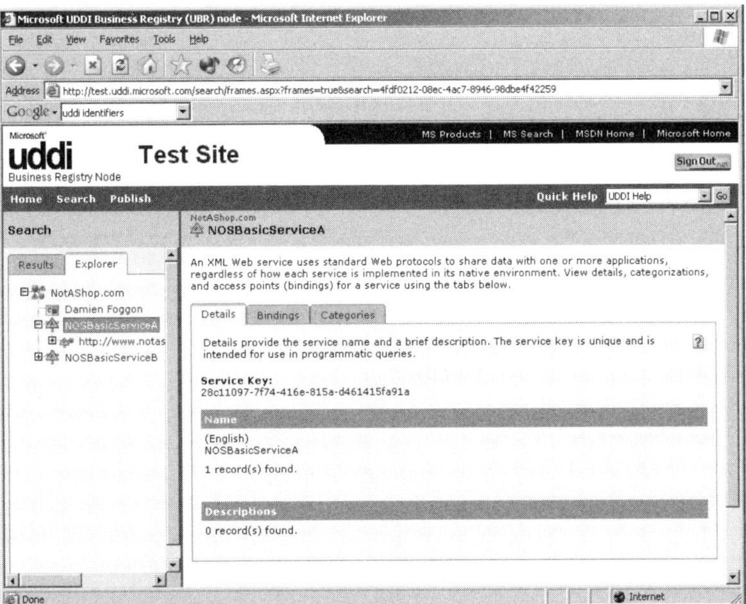

Figure 4-9 Viewing service details

As you can see, we've obtained the full details of the service. However, if you look at the Explorer tab of the left pane, you'll see that we've also obtained the provider for the service (NotAShop.com) and a sibling service (NOSBasicServiceB). The Explorer tab allows you to navigate the results that are returned.

The UDDI API

We mentioned that you can query the data stored in the UBRs using the UDDI API. In this section, we'll briefly talk about how to do this. What we won't do is use the UDDI API to access the UBRs. Not only would this be extremely tedious, but better tools are available for querying the UBRs programmatically. Here we'll simply give a high-level overview of the UDDI API so you can get an idea of what is possible. The Microsoft UDDI SDK is an excellent wrapper for the complexities of the UDDI API and is the preferred method for programmatically accessing the data stored in the UBRs.

The UDDI API has two parts, the Inquiry API and the Publishing API. The Inquiry API provides all the searching functionality of the UBRs, and the Publishing API provides all of the details about the management of the information within the UBRs.

The Inquiry API

The Inquiry API, which contains methods for interrogating the UBRs, supports two methods of searching—one traditional method and one in which you specify exactly what you require using a UUID. These methods are differentiated by the *find_* and *get_* prefixes, respectively.

The methods with a *find_* prefix, shown in Table 4-3, are used to query the UBR based on search criteria.

Table 4-3 The *find_* Inquiry API Methods

API Method	Description
find_binding	Returns a bindingTemplate message with details for a given service UUID and tModel UUID.
find_business	Returns the list of businessEntity UUIDs that meet the optional search criteria (name, tModel, categories, and identifiers).
find_relatedBusinesses	Returns a list of businessEntity UUIDs of businesses that are related to the given business UUID.
find_service	Returns a list of businessService UUIDs that meet the search criteria (name, tModel, and categories). You can also limit this search to a given businessEntity.
find_tModel	Returns a list of tModel UUIDs that meet the search criteria (name, categories, and identifiers).

Each of these methods, with the exception of the *find_binding* method, returns a list of UUIDs. The *find_binding* method is different because it is the lowest-level method you can use. Rather than returning a list of UUIDs that meet the search criteria, *find_binding* returns details of a specific bindingTemplate.

Table 4-4 lists the *get_* methods, which return details of a given item when you know its UUID.

Table 4-4 The *get_* Inquiry API Methods

API Method	Description
get_bindingDetail	Returns bindingTemplate details for a given bindingTemplate UUID.
get_businessDetail	Returns businessEntity details for a given businessEntity UUID.
get_businessDetailExt	Functionally equivalent to the *get_businessDetail* method. This method is meant to be extended for nonroot UBRs and allows extra data to be returned.
get_serviceDetail	Returns businessService details for a given businessService UUID.
get_tModelDetail	Returns tModel details for a given tModel UUID.

The Publishing API

The Publishing API allows you to modify the data within a UBR and is considerably more complex than the Inquiry API.

The first group of methods we need to look at are the methods that control access to the UBR, as described in Table 4-5. Before you can use any of the methods available in the Publishing API, you must retrieve an authentication token from the UBR that can be passed whenever you make a call to a Publishing API method.

Table 4-5 Publishing API Authentication Methods

API Method	Description
discard_authToken	Releases the authentication token specified in the call.
get_authToken	Requests an authentication token using the details provided.
get_registeredInfo	Returns the complete businessEntity and tModel data stored in the UBR for the authenticated user.

The second group of methods are for modifying the data in the UBR. This group includes methods to delete objects from the UBR and methods to save objects to the UBR, as described in Table 4-6.

Table 4-6 Publishing API Data Modification Methods

API Method	Description
delete_binding	Deletes the bindingTemplate specified by the given binding-Template UUID.
delete_business	Deletes the businessEntity specified by the given businessEntity UUID.
delete_service	Deletes the businessService specified by the given businessService UUID.
delete_tModel	Deletes the tModel specified by the given tModel UUID.
save_binding	Saves the bindingTemplate specified to the UBR.
save_business	Saves the businessEntity specified to the UBR.
save_service	Saves the businessService specified to the UBR.
save_tModel	Saves the tModel specified to the UBR.

The *delete_* methods take a UUID and simply delete the object in question. The *save_* methods are used in two situations. If you want to modify an object in the UBR, you call the *save_* method with the UUID specified; the data in the UBR will be overwritten with the new data that you pass as part of the method. To add a new object to the UBR, you call the *save_* method without a UUID specified, and a new entry will be created within the UBR.

When you attempt to modify an item in the UBR, a check is made to ensure that the details you provided when you were authenticated allow you to perform that action. You can delete only items that you created, and you can save an item only if you created the item's parent. (For example, you can't save a businessService to a businessEntity that you didn't create.)

The final group of methods, described in Table 4-7, deal with relationships.

Table 4-7 Publishing API Data Modification Methods

API Method	Description
add_publisherAssertions	Allows publisherAssertion information to be added.
delete_publisherAssertions	Deletes existing publisherAssertion information.
get_assertionStatusReport	Returns the status of the publisherAssertions for the authenticated user.

Table 4-7 Publishing API Data Modification Methods

API Method	Description
get_publisherAssertions	Returns the complete set of publisherAssertions for the authenticated user.
set_publisherAssertions	Replaces the publisherAssertions with those specified in the call.

The UDDI SDK

As we mentioned, the Microsoft UDDI SDK provides a wrapper around the methods that are available in the UDDI API. Every method in the API has a corresponding class with a *Send* method that allows you to query and modify the details in a UBR. You simply populate the necessary properties of the class that you instantiated and call the *Send* method to make the call to the specified UBR.

> **Note** The latest version of the UDDI SDK for .NET is part of the February 2003 Platform SDK, which can be downloaded from *http://www.microsoft.com/msdownload/platformsdk/sdkupdate/update.htm*. You need to download the Windows Server 2003 Core SDK. To correctly install the UDDI SDK, follow the instructions in the uddireadme.htm file contained in the bin directory.

It would take an awfully long time to walk through every property and method of every class that is available in the UDDI SDK. Because of the similarities in how the underlying data is structured, the same methodology is applied to the four groups of methods (*find_*, *get_*, *save_* and *delete_*). We won't look at the portions of the UDDI SDK that deal with the relationships between providers, but once you have an understanding of the way the rest of the UDDI SDK works, you can quickly learn to use those portions.

Connecting to the UBR

The UDDI SDK controls access to a UBR through the use of a *UddiConnection* object. In addition to allowing you to specify which UBR you want to use this, class also wraps the implementation of the UDDI API authentication classes.

As you saw in Table 4-5, three methods in the UDDI API deal with authentication. Using these methods to retrieve authentication information is tricky; thankfully, the UDDI SDK handles all of the details of retrieving the *AuthInfo* token from the UBR and attaching it to requests to the Publishing API, as you'll soon see.

To connect to the UBR, you simply create a new *UddiConnection* object and pass in the necessary details to the constructor. The *UddiConnection* class provides seven constructors, but in most cases you'll deal with only two of them.

If you want only to query the UBR, you can create the *UddiConnection* object and simply pass in the URL of the Inquire API that you want to access. This will create a connection object that can query the UBR but nothing more. You'll see this type of connection in use in the Query application, which we'll build shortly.

If you want to publish to the UBR, you must create the *UddiConnection* object and pass it a few more details. In addition to passing the URL of the Inquire API, you must also pass the URL of the Publishing API and the username and password that you want to use as the authentication details. In our second application, the Browser application, you'll see this type of connection in use; this application allows you to modify the information contained in the UBR.

As you'll see shortly, all the classes that interact with the UBR have a *Send* method. You must pass a valid *UddiConnection* object to this method for the call to the UBR to be made.

When you're finished with a *UddiConnection* object, you can close the connection using the *Close* method.

The *Find* Classes

The first methods we'll look at are the *find_* methods: *find_binding*, *find_business*, *find_service*, and *find_tModel*. As you saw in Table 4-3, these methods allow you to set various search criteria and then query the data in the UBR. The four API methods are wrapped by classes with names that start with *Find*. These classes expose properties (such as the *Names* property and the *CategoryBag* property) that allow you to set the search criteria before you call the *Send* method to interrogate the UBR.

For three of the classes—*FindBusiness*, *FindService*, and *FindTModel*—the *Send* method interrogates the UBR and returns an object of the corresponding class: *BusinessList*, *ServiceList*, or *TModelList*. The fourth class, *FindBinding*, doesn't return a list of bindings; it returns the details of a specific binding, *BindingDetail*, which we'll look at shortly when we deal with the *Get* classes.

The three lists—*BusinessList*, *ServiceList*, and *TModelList*—each contain a collection of objects that represent the individual items returned. The *BusinessList* class exposes a collection of *BusinessInfo* objects through the *BusinessInfos* property; the *ServiceList* class has a *ServiceInfos* property, which is a collection of *ServiceInfo* classes; and the *TModelList* class exposes a collection of *TModelInfo* classes via the *TModelInfos* property. The *BusinessInfo*, *ServiceInfo*, and *TModelInfo* classes each expose properties for the object's UUID and for its name.

The *BusinessInfo* class also contains the *ServiceInfos* collection, which contains a *ServiceInfo* class for each of the services that the business owns.

When you have a list of items, you still don't have any real information about the item—just the names of the items and their UUID. You must use the *Get* classes to obtain the full details.

The *Get* Classes

You use the *Find* classes to search the UBR; you use the *Get* classes to return complete details about one or more items within the UBR. Like the *Find* classes, the *get_* API methods are wrapped in a class of the same name. They each require a collection of UUIDs to be specified and return the full details for the given UUIDs.

Each call to the *Send* method of a *Get* class returns an object that contains the collection of items requested. *GetBusinessDetail* returns an object of class *BusinessDetail*, *GetServiceDetail* returns a *ServiceDetail* object, *GetBindingDetail* returns a *BindingDetail* object, and *GetTModelDetail* returns a *TModelDetail* object.

Unfortunately, the common name scheme that we've followed thus far breaks down when we look at the collections of objects that these detail classes expose. The *BusinessDetail* class exposes the *BusinessEntities* property, which is a collection of *BusinessEntity* objects. The *ServiceDetail* class has the *BusinessServices* property, which is a collection of *BusinessService* objects. The *BindingDetail* class exposes the *BindingTemplates* property. And the *TModelDetail* class has the *TModels* property.

As you know, the data stored in the UBR is hierarchical—a binding is related to a service, which is related to a business. The information returned by the *Get* classes maintains this relationship. Each *BusinessEntity* object that the *Get* classes return contains a *BusinessServices* property that exposes a collection of all the services that the business owns. The *BusinessService* class, in turn, has a *BindingTemplates* property, which exposes a collection that contains all of the bindings for the service.

The *Save* Classes

The four *save_* methods of the API allow you to both add and update information in the UBR, and the wrapper classes follow the naming scheme that we've come to expect—*SaveBusiness*, *SaveService*, *SaveBinding*, and *SaveTModel*. To save an item in the UBR, you must create a collection of the correct type and then add this collection to the appropriate *Save* class before calling the *Send* method.

Not surprisingly, the collections you must create are the same as the collections that the *Get* classes return. To save a service to the UBR, you create a

BusinessService object representing the service and add the object to the *BusinessServices* collection of the *SaveService* class.

Forcing the use of the same collections for the *Get* and *Save* classes allows modifications to the UBR to be made easily, by reusing the collections that are returned. You can query for the item you want, modify the returned collection, and save the collection back to the UBR.

One point to consider is the difference between adding data to the UBR and modifying data that is already in the UBR. You perform either action in the same way—the only difference is in the data that you pass to the appropriate *Save* class. If you're adding an item to the UBR, the item will not have a UUID; if you're modifying an item, it will.

The *Delete* Classes

The five delete API methods are wrapped within five *Delete* classes (*DeleteBinding*, *DeleteBusiness*, and so on) and require you to specify the UUIDs of the items you want to delete. As with the *Get* classes, you can specify as many UUIDs as you require, and they will all be deleted in the same call to the UBR.

Using the UDDI SDK

The possibilities for what you can do with UDDI and the SDK are vast, and in many cases can simplify processes that you already have in place. We'll introduce the SDK by building two applications.

The first application uses the SDK to query the Microsoft UBR for Web services that fit a particular tModel. This scenario allows us to call Web services at run time without any prior knowledge of them. Any new services that reference our tModel will be available to us whenever we run the application.

The second application is a simple UDDI browser that allows us to search and modify the information we've entered into the UBR. This is a substantially more complex application and introduces the concept of modifying data contained in the UBR.

The sample code for this chapter includes both of these applications.

The Query Application

Imagine a company with several offices around the world that has grown sporadically through planned growth and mergers. Because of the way the company has grown, the information technology systems at the different locations are not the same. However, the company needs to be able to produce management reports that are consistent across the company.

Using UDDI and the tModel concept, we can allow the developers at the various branch offices to build their own proprietary solutions against an interface that is easily propagated. We can publish our tModel and then inform the branch offices that it is available. The branch offices can then develop their solutions and register them as Web services in the UBR.

When we run the monthly reports, we can query the UBR for any services that implement the correct tModel. This query will return a list of services that we can call to generate the report. When new branch offices come online, no changes will need to be made to the head office application because the new Web service will be returned automatically by UDDI.

> **Note** Our example uses the Microsoft test UBR at *http://test.uddi.microsoft.com* to share the tModels and the details of the available services. In the real world, we wouldn't want to use a public UBR because it would make the details available to the world at large. Furthermore, if we were building services on an intranet, we wouldn't be able to use the public UBRs. The solution to the problem of building UBRs for the intranet is UDDI Enterprise Services, which is available in Windows Server 2003. We're using the public UBR here so we can show the facilities available without requiring a server that's running Windows Server 2003.

Building the Web Services

We've presented a real-world situation in which you would want to use the UDDI SDK to query a UDDI registry for Web services that meet your requirements, but we won't actually build any Web services that are this complex. For the purposes of this example, we'll simply use Web services that implement a simple interface. We have three methods—*GetDate*, *GetURL*, and *Echo*—that return strings to the user; the first two return the information that their name implies, and the third returns whatever string has been passed to it, with a prefix added.

Because we're dealing with the possibility of accessing multiple Web services at run time, we'll build two Web services with the same methods. We could simply write the code for these two Web services from scratch, with the interface that we require; doing so would no doubt provide us with two Web services that meet our requirements. However, we can greatly improve on this method by providing an interface, or more correctly a tModel, that can be used as the basis for the Web services that we're going to build.

The two services we're going to build are called NOSBasicServiceA and NOSBasicServiceB. They can be found at *http://www.notashop.com/wscr/04/servicea.asmx* and *http://www.notashop.com/wscr/04/serviceb.asmx*, respectively.

> **Note** Because the tModel we're using is available on the Microsoft UBR (in a test version), it is available to anyone. Feel free to build on this example and register your own Web services that relate to this tModel. As long as the Web services exist on a Web server that is available on the Internet, they will be available when you query the UBR using our sample application.

Creating a tModel from a Web service When you build multiple Web services that expose the same interface, you build one version of the Web service as the master. The Web service you select as the master is usually the one you've worked with the most, throughout the entire design process. Once the service has been tested and meets your design criteria, you can use it to define the tModel structure for all of the other Web services you plan to implement.

Thanks to the tools provided by the .NET Framework, viewing the WSDL that is generated for a Web service is easy. You simply specify the *?wsdl* query string when we view the Web service in a browser. We could use this dynamically generated WSDL file as the tModel, but this approach isn't advisable—any changes to the Web service will result in the WSDL changing. Any services that are built after the change will no longer meet the requirements that we originally defined. To that end, we'll create a static WSDL file that we can use for the tModel. We're less likely to change this WSDL file accidentally, and it gives us a means of fixing the interface for our tModel.

To create the tModel for this service, however, we will start with a dynamically generated WSDL file. If we view the WSDL file, we can save it and use it as the basis for our tModel. We can then modify the file to meet the necessary criteria for a tModel definition in UDDI.

To create a tModel from the WSDL for a real Web service, we must first remove the *<wsdl:service>* element. We now have a correct WSDL document that can be used as a tModel.

> **Note** As they stand, neither the WSDL specification nor the UDDI specification explicitly defines how the two specifications should interact. This task is left to a UDDI.org best-practice document titled "Using WSDL in a UDDI Registry" (available at *http://www.oasis-open.org/committees/uddi-spec/bps.shtml*). The crux of this document concerns the definition of tModels that use WSDL, and it describes what is required in the tModel definition. Thankfully, the WSDL required for a tModel is the same WSDL that you'd expect for a Web service, minus the *<wsdl:service>* element.

We could stop here and use the WSDL document that we now have as our tModel, but normally we further modify the WSDL for the tModel so it is not specific to the master Web service. The item we must change is the *<wsdl:binding>* element; this is the name used when we generate the proxy classes, and the default ServiceASoap name is specific to the Web service that we used to create the initial WSDL document. In this case, we've replaced ServiceASoap with NOSBasic; the WSDL for the tModel can be found at *http://www.notashop.com/wscr/04/nosbasic.wsdl*.

Generating a Web service from a tModel Now that we have a tModel, we'll use it to build the rest of the Web services in this example. We know the full URL for the tModel, so we don't have to use a UBR to find details about the tModel.

To build a Web service according to a tModel definition, we can use wsdl.exe, the tool we used in Chapter 1 to create proxies to existing Web services. One of the parameters to wsdl.exe is the */server* switch, which makes the tool generate an abstract class rather than a proxy. (As you saw in Chapter 1, we can also control the language that the class is generated in as well as a whole host of other parameters.)

To build the abstract class for the tModel that we registered earlier in the chapter, we execute the following command line:

```
wsdl.exe /server http://www.notashop.com/wscr/04/nosbasic.wsdl
```

This creates a C# file called output.cs in the current directory that contains an abstract class called *NOSBasic*. If we add this class to our project, we can inherit from it as we would any other class. We don't even need to worry about any *WebService* or *WebMethod* attributes because they're all already part of the base class.

Although the subsequent service, serviceb.asmx, was created from this abstract class, we've also modified servicea.asmx, the service we used to create the abstract class, so that it, too, inherits from the abstract class.

> **Note** Be sure to apply the correct namespace for the *WebService* attribute to your derived classes. Even though we have a namespace specified in the tModel WSDL file, it is not used when we generate an abstract class. If we don't specify this namespace correctly, we cannot make calls to the Web services because the SOAPAction header will be incorrect and will be rejected automatically by .NET.

Managing Web Services

So far we've created three Web services with a consistent interface. We mentioned that we used a tModel when creating the classes, but we haven't yet used any of the UDDI facilities available.

We'll start by using the test UBR at *http://test.uddi.microsoft.com* to register the interface that we defined at *http://www.notashop.com/wscr/04/nosbasic.wsdl* as a tModel. We can then register the Web services we've built and relate them to the correct tModel. This procedure allows us to search for Web services based on the tModel and search for new Web services at run time.

Until now, we've used the UBR without actually logging in. Earlier, when we searched in the Microsoft UBR, the Passport Sign In option was present, indicating that we were not logged in. Before we can actually manage our services, we must log in to Passport and then register with the UBR.

Once we've logged in using a valid Passport account, we must also create an account in the Microsoft UBR. This is easy; all we need to provide is an e-mail address (which can be the Passport address we're using) and, at a minimum, our name and phone number. Clicking Save takes us to the Terms And Conditions page. Accepting the conditions causes the UBR to send us an activation e-mail. Within the activation e-mail is a link that we must click to activate our account within the UBR. Once we've activated our account, we're free to publish to the Microsoft UBR.

The main page when we're publishing in the UBR is a standard two-pane Web page, with the left pane showing a tree view that has a My UDDI entry—the parent for everything we'll add to our account. The My UDDI entry currently has empty Providers and tModels folders.

We'll now walk through the steps for adding the details to allow our service to be used by other developers.

Providers As you'll recall from Figure 4-6, the businessEntity (or in Microsoft parlance, the provider) is the root of the data that we store in the UBR. Before we can add any tModels or services, we must enter the details for a provider in the UBR. Within the UBR, we're normally allowed only one provider per login, but it's possible to have more providers per login by contacting Microsoft directly.

To add a provider, click on the Providers folder and click the Add Provider button in the right pane or choose Add from the shortcut menu for the folder.

> **Note** Throughout the Microsoft UBR, a shortcut menu is available in the left pane that performs the same operations as the buttons in the right pane. For clarity, we'll refer only to the buttons in the right pane.

When we click Add, the Microsoft UBR adds a provider with default values. The name, <New Provider Name>, is not particularly helpful. We can click the Edit button to change the name; as you can see in Figure 4-10, we've specified a much more meaningful name.

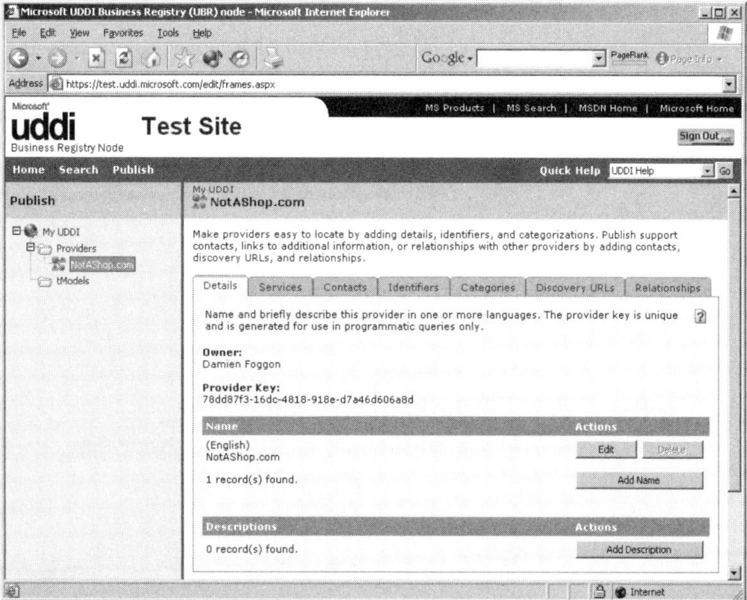

Figure 4-10 A provider added to the Microsoft UBR

The Add Description and Add Name buttons on the page allow us to add a description and another name. If you're wondering what's the point of adding a second name to the provider, you should look closely at the English text above the provider name in Figure 4-10. UDDI is language neutral, but it defaults to U.S. English when you add new entries.

The page also has a series of tabs along the top that allow you to add lots of other information about the provider. We'll cover the Services tab shortly (after we've added the tModel details); the other five tabs allow you to add ancillary details to the provider entry:

- **Contacts** For adding contacts to providers with full addressing details (both online and offline) as well as the person's role, as shown in Figure 4-11.
- **Identifiers** For adding free-form data to the provider.
- **Categories** For placing the provider into any of the categorization schemes we've previously discussed.
- **Discovery URLs** For adding further technical details for the provider as separate documents. We automatically have an entry to the provider details at the Microsoft UBR that we can't modify, but we can add further details if required.
- **Relationships** For adding details about any relationships that apply to this provider and to authorize relationships that have been requested with this provider.

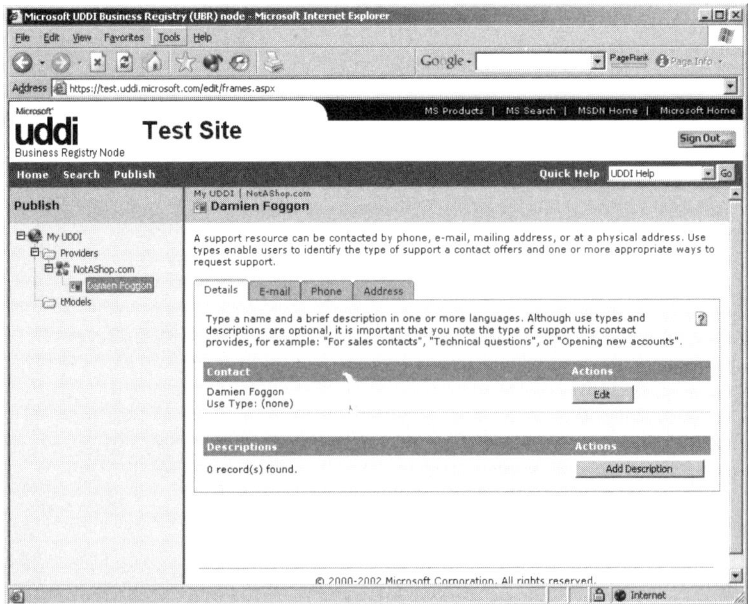

Figure 4-11 A contact added to a provider

tModels Although we can add services to the UBR without any reference to a tModel, we don't want to do this in our scenario. We're relying on the services referencing the tModel, so we'll add the tModel before we add the service.

Adding a tModel is similar to adding a provider. You click on the tModels folder and click the Add tModel button. Once the tModel has been added and its name has been changed to the more meaningful NOSBasic, it appears in the My UDDI tree, as shown in Figure 4-12.

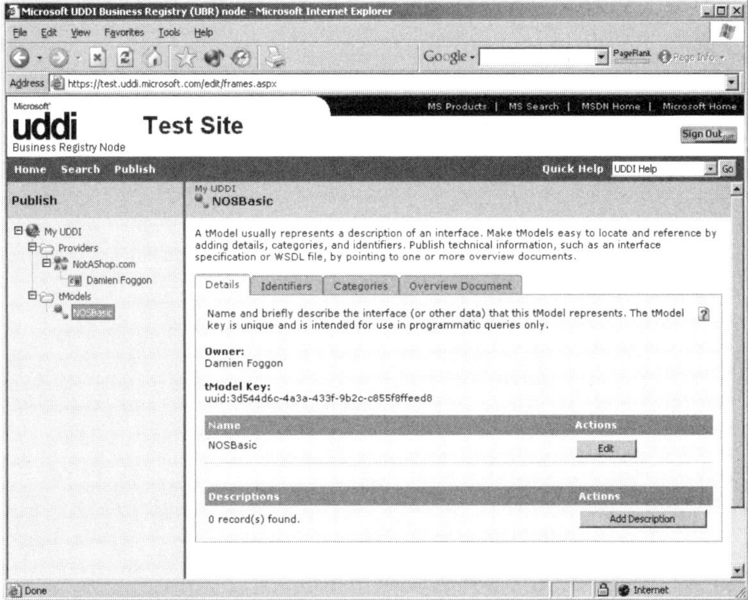

Figure 4-12 A tModel added

Unlike the provider, however, a tModel can have only one name that is language neutral. We can add multiple descriptions to the tModel, and these can have a culture specified. (The default is en-US.) As with the provider, we can also add identifiers and categories, which perform the same functions as with the provider.

The point of interest for a tModel is the Overview Document tab. On this tab, we can add the WSDL details for the document by clicking Edit and adding the full URL to the WSDL for the Web service. Figure 4-13 shows the tab after we've added the full URL for the Web service.

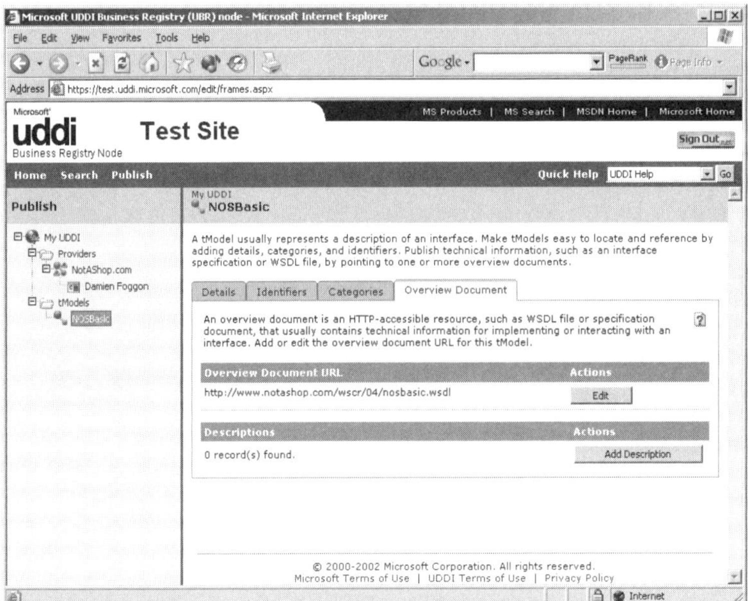

Figure 4-13 A WSDL document added to the tModel

As you can see in the figure, we can also add a description to the overview document and specify the language for this description (which is in the en-US culture by default).

Services Now that we have a provider and a tModel added to the UBR, we can add our Web service and correctly relate it to the tModel. This procedure, again, is as simple as navigating to the provider we added earlier and clicking on the Services tab. We can then click the Add Service button to add the new service, and once we've changed the default name, <New Service Name>, to a more sensible name, we'll see the Web service added as a child of the provider, as shown in Figure 4-14.

As with the provider, we can add multiple names and descriptions in different languages, the only proviso being that we must have at least one name.

The Categories tab behaves in the same way as for providers and tModels; the Bindings tab allows us to give the service we've added a presence in the real world by giving it an address.

On the Bindings tab, we can click the Add Binding button to add a binding as a child of the service in the left pane, and we can add the URL of the Web service as the access point, as shown in Figure 4-15.

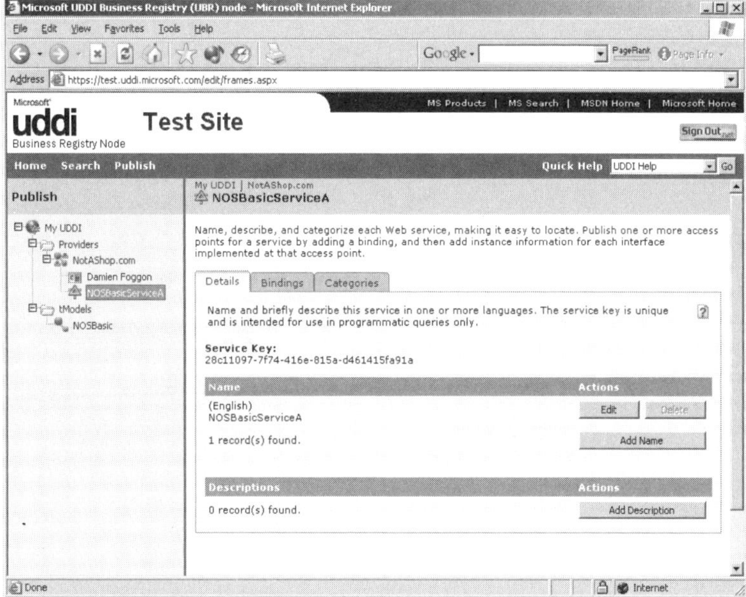

Figure 4-14 A service added to the provider

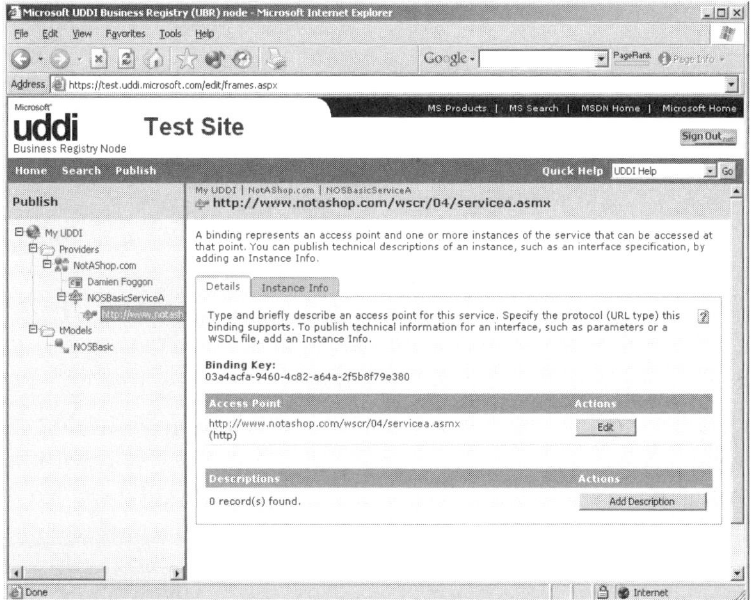

Figure 4-15 An access point added to the service

Again, we can add multiple descriptions in different languages to the binding we just added.

Although we have a fully working Web service that we can use as is, we still haven't associated it with a tModel, so we still can't use it in our application. We can associate a binding with a tModel by clicking the Instance Info tab and entering the name of the tModel that we want to reference, as shown in Figure 4-16.

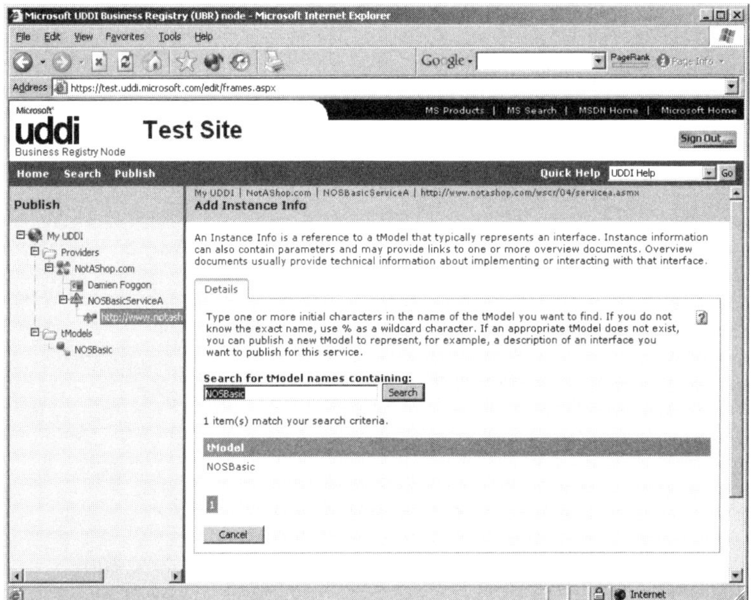

Figure 4-16 Searching for a tModel to add to a service

Once we specify the tModel, the UDDI site adds it to the left pane as a child of the binding, as shown in Figure 4-17.

As with everything else we've added, we can add multiple descriptions to the tModel reference and also add any parameters that are required and an overview document that we can use to store more information.

Category Information Although we've stayed away from adding categories to objects that we've created within the UBR, we pointed out that it is possible to add categories to providers, tModels, and services. For the service, we've added two categories—one that puts the Web service in England (using the ISO 3166 categorization schema) and one that adds us to the Internet Business Services category (in the SIC categorization schema). If we click on the Categories tab for the service, we'll see the categories for the service listed, as shown in Figure 4-18.

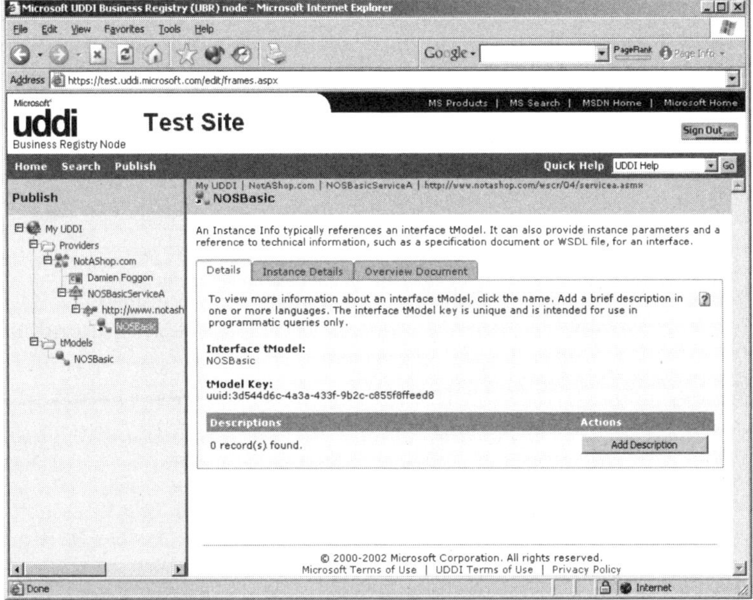

Figure 4-17 Category details added to a service

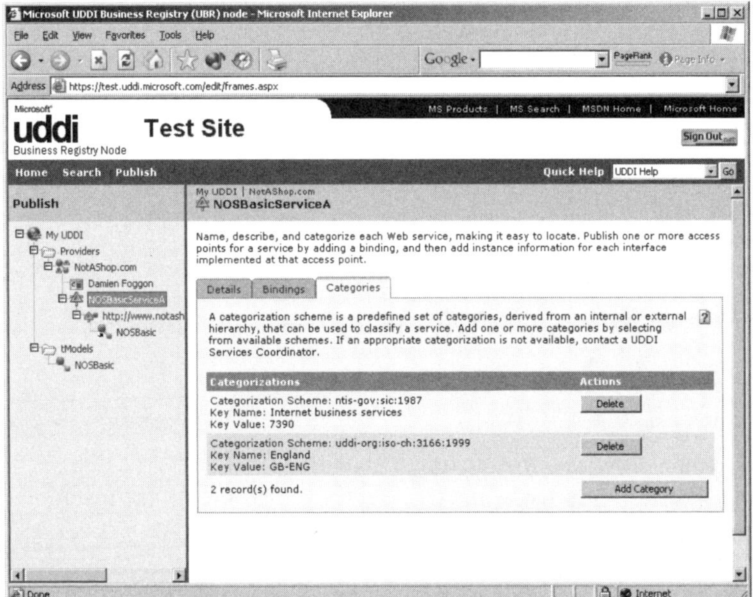

Figure 4-18 A tModel added to a service binding

The Client

After all that pointing and clicking, we're in a position to actually use the UDDI SDK to access the details in the UBR. Included with this book's sample files is a simply Query application that allows us to query the UBR for Web services that relate to our tModel.

We won't go through all of the code for the application. A lot of it doesn't deal with UDDI, anyway—we'll just discuss the code that is directly related to accessing the UDDI SDK.

Searching for Web services The first thing we need to do is search for the Web services that implement our tModel. As you'll recall, all the entities we add to the UBR are referenced using UUIDs. Figure 4-12 showed that when we added the tModel to the UBR, a UUID was automatically generated. To find Web services that implement this tModel, we can use this UUID, 3d544d6c-4a3a-433f-9b2c-c855f8ffeed8, as the search criterion.

Before we use the SDK, we must add a reference to the correct assembly, *Microsoft.Uddi*, to our project. We must also add references to the namespaces within the SDK that we're using. In this case, we need to add the base namespace, *Microsoft.Uddi*, as well as one of its child namespaces, *Microsoft.Uddi.Services*:

```
using Microsoft.Uddi;
using Microsoft.Uddi.Services;
```

Now that we've created the necessary references, we can start writing code to access the UBR. The first thing we need to do is create the *UddiConnection* object that we'll use, specifying the URL that we're calling—in this case, the Inquire API of the test UBR. The results are added to a list box control, so we'll also clear that before we start querying the UBR:

```
// Create the connection to the UBR
UddiConnection m_Connection = new
    UddiConnection("http://test.uddi.microsoft.com/inquire");

// Clear the listbox
lstResults.Items.Clear();
```

From Table 4-3 you'll recall that the *find_service* method allows us to specify the tModels we want to search for. We create an instance of the *FindService* class and add the tModel details to the *TModelBag* collection before calling the *Send* method:

```
// Create the find object and set the tModel we want to find
FindService findService = new FindService();
findService.TModelBag.Add("uuid:3d544d6c-4a3a-433f-9b2c-c855f8ffeed8");

// Make the call and return a ServiceList
ServiceList serviceList = findService.Send(m_Connection);
```

The *Send* method returns a collection of *ServiceInfo* entities. We can simply iterate through this collection, extracting the information we need. We'll use the first entry in the *Names* collection of the *ServiceInfo* class to retrieve the name of the service. We'll call this service, so we need to know its UUID to find its address; we can use the *ServiceKey* property for this purpose:

```
// Iterate through the returned collection
foreach (ServiceInfo serviceInfo in serviceList.ServiceInfos)
{
    lstResults.Items.Add(serviceInfo.Names[0] + " - "
        + serviceInfo.ServiceKey);
}
```

This code populates the list box control with the list of Web services that relate to the tModel we specified, as shown in Figure 4-19. As you can see, not only do we have the name of the service, but we also have its UUID.

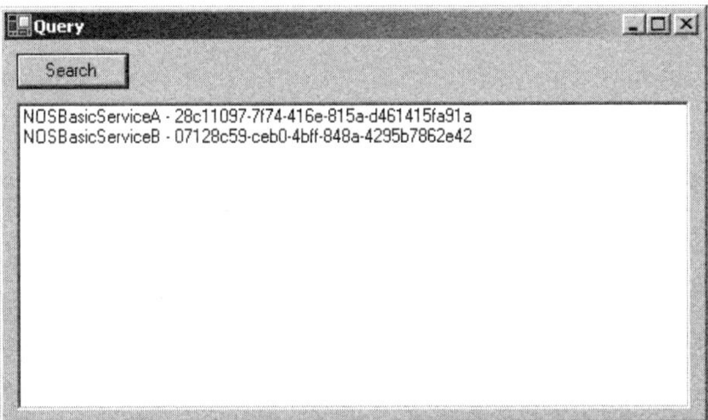

Figure 4-19 Web services that match the tModel

The list box responds to double-click events, and double-clicking on a Web service launches a dialog box that calls the service.

Calling the Web service Calling a Web service is a little trickier than simply querying for the details of the service. We search for the details necessary to call the service in a way that is similar to how we get the list of services. However, we must perform a little more work first.

When we call a Web service, we need a proxy class so we can call methods on that class to execute the methods on the Web service. However, we're discovering Web services dynamically. We don't have the luxury of being able to create a proxy class because we don't know the location of the Web service at design time.

The way to overcome this problem is to create a Web reference to the tModel that we based our Web service on, *http://www.notashop.com/wscr/04/nosbasic.wsdl*. This file has the complete structure of the Web service and allows a proxy class to be generated. What is missing from this .wsdl file is the address of the service; if we try to call the proxy generated from the tModel, we'll receive an error telling us that no address to call has been set. We must set this address before we call any methods on the proxy. Confused? All will become clear shortly.

As with any call to the UDDI SDK, we must reference the correct namespaces. We must also reference the proxy we generated from the tModel:

```
using Microsoft.Uddi;
using Microsoft.Uddi.Services;
using com.notashop.www;
```

Again, we set the URL of the UBR that we're calling. We also create a proxy class so we can call it when required:

```
// Create the connection to the UBR
UddiConnection m_Connection = new
    UddiConnection("http://test.uddi.microsoft.com/inquire");
// Create the proxy that we're going to use
NOSBasic proxy = new NOSBasic();
```

Before we can call the service, we must know its address; we need to tell the proxy where to call. You'll recall that the address of the service is contained as a child of a binding to the service. We must retrieve the details of the relevant binding before we can access the address of the service.

Because we don't actually have the UUID that will allow us direct access to the binding details, we must use the details we know to obtain the correct binding. We know the UUIDs for both the service and tModel, so we can specify these when we make a call to the UBR using the *FindBinding* class. As you'll see, the process for querying for bindings is the same as the process for querying for services.

Note that when we search for bindings we don't return a list of bindings that meet our criteria—we return a specific binding, a *BindingDetail* object. We must provide enough information when we make a call to allow us to find an individual binding. If we don't, the UBR will throw an exception.

```
// Use the service key to get the binding detail
FindBinding findBinding = new FindBinding();
findBinding.ServiceKey = m_key;
findBinding.TModelKeys.Add("uuid:3d544d6c-4a3a-433f-9b2c-c855f8ffeed8");

// Make the call and return a BindingDetail
BindingDetail bindingDetail = findBinding.Send(m_Connection);
```

Now that we've retrieved the binding from the server, it should be a simple matter to retrieve the URL of the service. When we added the details of the service to the UBR, we added the URL with the binding and then simply added pointers to the tModels. The UDDI SDK doesn't follow this pattern, however. The URL of the service is within the pointer to the tModel rather than the binding. This deviation isn't a big deal—just something to be aware of.

We can have multiple tModels related to this binding, but the URL will be the same across all of them, so we can simply pick one of them at random. The only one we're sure will be present is the first item in the collection—we can only return results that have a reference to our tModel, so we know for sure that we have at least one reference.

The *BindingDetail* object that we've returned contains a *BindingTemplates* collection that contains the references to the tModels. We use the first item in this collection and retrieve the *Text* property of its *AccessPoint* object, which is the URL of the service. We use this value to set the title of the form as well as the URL of the proxy:

```
// Set the details correctly
this.Text = bindingDetail.BindingTemplates[0].AccessPoint.Text;
proxy.Url = bindingDetail.BindingTemplates[0].AccessPoint.Text;
```

Once the proxy has a URL, we can call the methods on that proxy, safe in the knowledge that the call will be made to the correct location. As you'll recall, the Web services expose three methods. We call these and place the returned strings into text box controls in the dialog box:

```
// Call the remote service
txtDate.Text = proxy.GetDate();
txtUrl.Text = proxy.GetUrl();
txtEcho.Text = proxy.Echo(Environment.MachineName);
```

If we select NOSBasicServiceA from the list of services retrieved, we'll see that a call has been made to the Web service and the results are displayed in the dialog box, as shown in Figure 4-20.

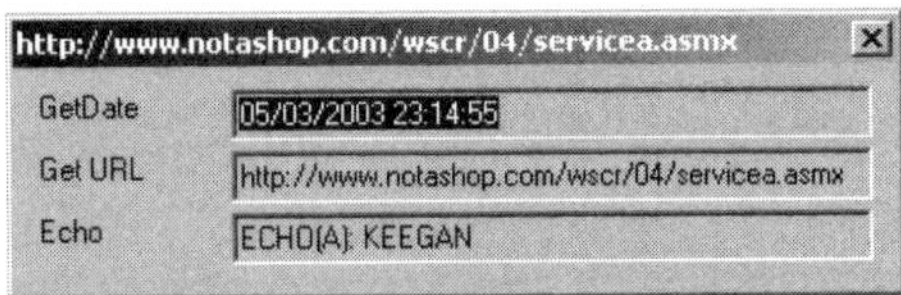

Figure 4-20 The results from a dynamically referenced Web service

The UDDI Browser

We'll now move on to a much more exciting application to show off the power of the UDDI SDK. We'll build a UDDI browser that allows us to add Web services to the Microsoft UBR.

The UDDI browser will allow us to add services as well as details of the tModels that those services are related to. The application is not designed as a replacement for using the UBRs, and it doesn't implement the complete UDDI feature list. It's intended only as an introduction to the more complex features of the UDDI SDK. As we mentioned earlier, trying to completely describe every feature of the UDDI SDK would require an awfully large chapter. For reasons of clarity, we'll present only the code that is directly related to our interaction with the UDDI SDK. Of course, nothing can stop you from writing a complete UBR replacement, if you want.

The *Helper* Class

Rather than have code that interacts with the UBR littered throughout the application, as we did in the Query application, we'll place all the code that interacts with the UBR in a *Helper* class, contained in the helper.cs file. This class contains static methods that we can call to interact with the UBR. For instance, we have a *GetService* method that accepts the UUID for a service and returns a *BusinessService* object representing the requested service and a *DeleteService* method that accepts the UUID for a service and deletes the service from the UBR.

Rather than detail all of the methods that the *Helper* class exposes, we'll look at the methods as we walk through the Browser application.

Connecting to the UBR and Logging In

On launching the application, the first thing we have to do is to log in to the UBR that we're using. In fact, the Browser application is designed so that if we don't provide correct authentication details, execution of the application will halt.

Connecting to the UBR to use both the Inquire API and Publishing API is not much more complex than simply connecting to the Inquire API. We simply need to create an instance of the *UddiConnection* object and specify the correct details.

Within the *Helper* class is a *Connect* method that accepts a username and password and creates the correct *UddiConnection* object, which it then stores as the *m_Connection* static variable. The complete code for this method is shown here:

```
internal static void Connect (string strUsername, string strPassword)
{
    // Connect to the server
    m_Connection = new UddiConnection(
        "http://test.uddi.microsoft.com/inquire",
        "https://test.uddi.microsoft.com/publish",
        "",
```

```
        strUsername,
        strPassword);
}
```

Even though we created the *UddiConnection* and passed in a username and password, these are not validated with the UBR at this time. Only when we make a call to the Publishing API will the details be validated.

Whenever we make a call to a method of the Publishing API, we must attach an *AuthInfo* token to the method call. As we pointed out, the UDDI SDK takes care of retrieving the *AuthInfo* token and adding it to the request to the Publishing API.

On the first call to the Publishing API, the UDDI SDK first makes a call to the *get_AuthToken* method to retrieve the *AuthInfo* token. The token is cached and added to all future requests to the Publishing API.

> **Note** If you don't want the *AuthInfo* token to be automatically retrieved and added to requests to the Publishing API, you can set the *AutoGetAuthToken* property of the *UddiConnection* object to *false*. This approach requires an *AuthInfo* token to be populated manually and added to the *AuthInfo* property of the class that we're using.

Editing Business Details

The first thing we need to do when we log in to the UBR is retrieve a list of items that the user has permission to modify. When we looked at searching using the UDDI SDK in the previous example, we found that we can use API methods to search for specific items, such as businesses. However, we can't use these methods now because all we know is the user who is logged into the UBR, and the API has no facility for searching by the owner of an item.

The API provides a solution to this problem—the *get_registeredInfo* method, which returns a list of the businesses and tModels that the user has permission to modify. As with the other API calls, this method is wrapped in its own class, *GetRegisteredInfo*, and this is wrapped in the *GetForUser* method of the *Helper* class.

```
internal static BusinessInfo GetForUser()
{
    // Create the GetRegisteredInfo class
    GetRegisteredInfo getRegisteredInfo = new GetRegisteredInfo();

    // Make the call
    return(getRegisteredInfo.Send(m_Connection).BusinessInfos[0]);
}
```

We don't need to set any properties of this class because the method requires only a valid *AuthToken* to be added, and the UDDI SDK handles this automatically.

The business details returned from the call to the UBR are a collection of *BusinessInfo* objects. Although the UDDI specification allows more than one provider per user, the specification requires only one provider per user. The Microsoft UBRs allow only one provider to be managed, so we simply return the first item in the collection. The business details returned are then used to populate the main form, as shown in Figure 4-21.

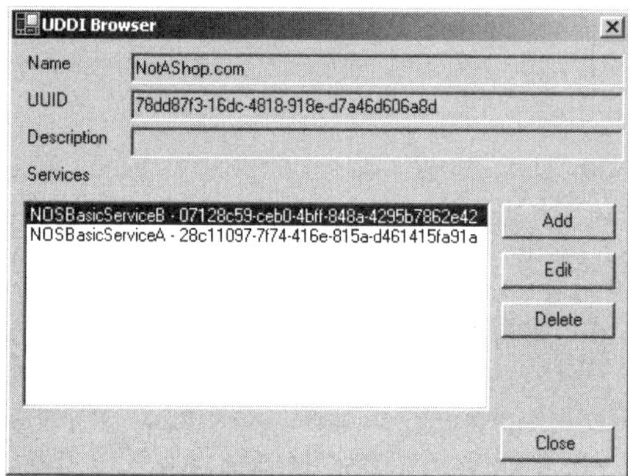

Figure 4-21 Editing the business details

We populate the main form of the application by first making a call to the *Helper.GetForUser* static method. This call returns a *BusinessInfo* object that we store in the *l_Business* local variable:

```
// Return the details for the user
BusinessInfo l_Business = Helper.GetForUser();
```

After checking to be sure that we have obtained a *BusinessInfo* object, we use the cached local variable to populate the details on the form. The *Names* collection contains the names for the business and, because the business must always have at least one name, we extract only the first name from the collection. The business has only one UUID, and we can extract it from the *BusinessKey* property. As you'll recall, the description of the service can be added in multiple languages, and all of the descriptions for the business are returned in the *Descriptions* collection. The description of a service is not mandatory, so we check that we have a description before attempting to populate the form with the first description in the collection:

```
// Populate the form
txtName.Text = m_Business.Names[0].Text;
txtUUID.Text = m_Business.BusinessKey;
if (m_Business.Descriptions.Count>0)
{
    txtDescription.Text = m_Business.Descriptions[0].Text;
}
```

We then iterate through the collection of services that are registered for the business. The *ServiceInfos* collection is a collection of *ServiceInfo* objects, and we can use the first entry in the *Names* collection and the *ServiceKey* property for each of the members of the collection. These are simply added to the list box on the form:

```
// Iterate through the services
lstServices.Items.Clear();
foreach(ServiceInfo serviceInfo in m_Business.ServiceInfos)
{
    lstServices.Items.Add(serviceInfo.Names[0].Text + " - "
        + serviceInfo.ServiceKey);
}
```

Now that the form has been populated, we can add new services, edit the bindings for an existing service, or delete an existing service from the UBR. We can click Add at any time, but the Delete and Edit buttons become enabled only when we have a service selected in the list box.

Adding and Deleting Services

You add and delete services by clicking the respective buttons on the main form, as shown earlier in Figure 4-21.

Adding a service Clicking the Add button launches a dialog box in which we can specify a name and a description for the service we want to add. We must provide a name for the service, but the description is optional.

As we pointed out in the discussion of the UDDI SDK, the *Save* methods require a collection of objects of the correct type to be passed to them. These objects are then used to populate the details in the call to the API.

To save a service, we must create a *BusinessService* object and populate it with the necessary details. First, we associate the *BusinessService* object with a business that we have permission to modify. We already have the UUID for the business (which was passed as part of the dialog box creation process and stored as the *m_BusinessKey* variable), and we simply add this to the *BusinessKey* property.

Next we add the name and the description of our service to the necessary collections; as you'll recall, a service can have names and descriptions in multiple languages, so we have to add the details using the *Add* method of the underlying *CollectionBase* class:

```
// Create the object and set the values
BusinessService l_Service = new BusinessService();
l_Service.BusinessKey = m_BusinessKey;
l_Service.Names.Add (txtName.Text);
l_Service.Descriptions.Add (txtDescription.Text);
```

Once we create the *BusinessService* object, we can call the static method on the *Helper* class, *SaveService*, passing in the *BusinessService* object we've populated.

The *Helper.SaveService* static method creates a new instance of the *SaveService* class and adds the received *BusinessService* object to the *BusinessServices* collection. Then *SaveService* calls the *Send* method to make the call to the UBR:

```
internal static bool SaveService(BusinessService businessService)
{
    // Do the save
    SaveService saveService = new SaveService();
    saveService.BusinessServices.Add (businessService);
    saveService.Send(m_Connection);

    return(true);
}
```

The *Send* method returns a *ServiceDetail* object that contains the details we've added to the UBR, along with the new UUID for the service. We could write code to extract the name and the service key from the returned object and add these details to the list of services that the business supports, but in this simple application we won't do this.

Whenever we add, delete, or edit a service, we force a complete repopulation of the business details. This involves an extra call to the UBR, but it does remove a lot of code from the application and allows us to concentrate on the parts of the application that are specific to the UDDI SDK.

Deleting a service Deleting a service from the UBR is as simple as specifying the UUID of the service and making a call to the UBR. We retrieve the key from the populated list box with a little bit of string manipulation. We know that the UUIDs that we're using are 36 characters long, so we simply take the last 36 characters and assign these to a string variable:

```
string strKey = lstServices.Text.Substring(lstServices.Text.Length - 36);
```

We then make a call to the static *Helper.DeleteService* method, passing in the UUID of the service that we want to delete.

The *Helper.DeleteService* method creates a new instance of the *DeleteService* class and adds the key that was passed in to the *ServiceKeys* collection. We then call the *Send* method of the *DeleteService* instance:

```
internal static bool DeleteService(string strServiceKey)
{
    // Do the delete
    DeleteService deleteService = new DeleteService();
    DeleteService.ServiceKeys.Add(strServiceKey);
    deleteService.Send(m_Connection);

    return(true);
}
```

The *Send* method here also returns a class that we can use to determine the outcome of the delete request. We're not going to use these details, so we'll rely on a complete repopulation of the business details form.

Editing a Service

We can select a service and click the Edit button to edit the binding details for the selected service. Although we're dealing with services, the process is similar to the process for editing the business details, which we've already seen. As you can see in Figure 4-22, the form for editing a service is similar to the form for editing the business details.

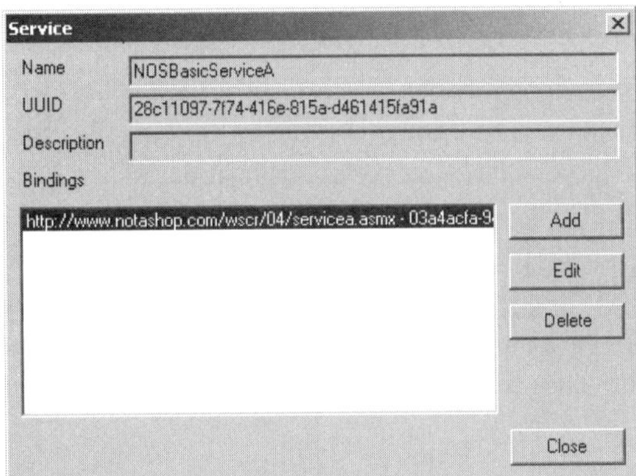

Figure 4-22 Editing the service details

The code that sits behind this form is similar to the code we wrote for the business details screen; we're simply working with a set of classes that are one step lower down the chain—services instead of businesses.

To open this form, we selected an existing service with a known UUID key (which is passed to the form as part of the form constructor and stored as the *m_ServiceKey* local variable). In the Query application, we searched for services that met our search criteria and used the *find_service* API method; because we know the UUID for the service we're looking for, we can use the *get_serviceDetail* method in the UDDI API to return the complete details of the service. We've wrapped this call in the static *GetService* method of the *Helper* class.

The complete code for the *Helper.GetService* method is shown here. If you compare this code to the code for the *Helper.GetForUser* method shown earlier, you'll see that they are remarkably similar. We're using the *GetServiceDetail* class, and we add the key of the service that we want to find to the *ServiceKeys* collection. We can call the *Send* method and make the call to the UBR.

```
internal static BusinessService GetService(string strServiceKey)
    // Create the GetServiceDetail class
    GetServiceDetail getServiceDetail = new GetServiceDetail();
    getServiceDetail.ServiceKeys.Add(strServiceKey);

    // Make the call
    return (getServiceDetail.Send(m_Connection).BusinessServices[0]);
}
```

The *Send* method actually returns a *ServiceDetail* object that has a *BusinessServices* collection of *BusinessService* objects. If we were to add multiple keys to the *ServiceKeys* collection before making the call to the *Send* method, the method would return multiple items in the *BusinessServices* collection. Because we've specified only one key, the *Send* method returns a *ServiceDetail* object with only one *BusinessService* object in its *BusinessServices* collection.

We save the *BusinessService* object that the *Helper.GetService* method returns to the *l_Service* local variable and use this variable to populate the form. Given that a service can have names in different languages, we simply use the first name in the *Names* collection. We don't perform any checks to ensure that a name is present in the *Names* collection because a service must always have at least one name. The *ServiceKey* value is extracted from the *BusinessService* object. We check that the *Descriptions* collection has at least one description before displaying the first item in the collection on the form.

```
// Return the details for the service
BusinessService l_Service = Helper.GetService(m_ServiceKey);

// Populate the page
txtName.Text = l_Service.Names[0].Text;
txtUUID.Text = l_Service.ServiceKey;
```

```
if (l_Service.Descriptions.Count>0)
{
    txtDescription.Text = l_Service.Descriptions[0].Text;
}
```

We then iterate through the *BindingTemplates* collection to retrieve each of the bindings that the service supports. For the services we used the name of the service, but a binding doesn't have a name; we can use the *AccessPoint* object exposed by the *BindingTemplate* object to identify the binding. We display the contents of the *AccessPoint.Text* property as well as the UUID of the binding, which is accessible via the *BindingKey* property, in the list box on the form.

```
// Iterate through the bindings
lstBindings.Items.Clear();
foreach (BindingTemplate bindingTemplate in l_Service.BindingTemplates)
{
    lstBindings.Items.Add(bindingTemplate.AccessPoint.Text + " - " +
        bindingTemplate.BindingKey);
}
```

Now that we've populated the form, we can add new bindings, delete existing bindings, or edit the details for the bindings that already exist.

Adding and Deleting Bindings

The process for adding and deleting bindings is the same as for adding and deleting services; we just use a different set of objects.

Adding bindings As with adding services, we first gather the information we need from the user; in this case, we need the URL of the service as well as an optional description. We use this information to populate *l_Binding*, a *BindingTemplate* object. We must first specify the UUID of the service that we want to add the binding to, and this is retrieved from the *m_ServiceKey* variable (which was populated as part of the construction process for the form). We must then provide the URL details of the *AccessPoint* object and the URL's type; in this case, we default to *UrlType.Http*, but several other values are possible.

```
BindingTemplate l_Binding = new BindingTemplate();
l_Binding.ServiceKey = m_ServiceKey;
l_Binding.AccessPoint.Text = txtURL.Text;
l_Binding.AccessPoint.UrlType = UrlType.Http;
```

Once the *l_Binding* object has been populated correctly, we call the *Helper.SaveBinding* method, passing it the *BindingTemplate* object.

The *Helper.SaveBinding* method is functionally the same as the *Helper.SaveService* method. We create a *SaveBinding* object, add the *BindingTemplate* we received to the *BindingTemplates* collection, and call the *Send* method:

```
internal static bool SaveBinding(BindingTemplate bindingTemplate)
{
    // Do the save
    SaveBinding saveBinding= new SaveBinding();
    saveBinding.BindingTemplates.Add(bindingTemplate);
    saveBinding.Send(m_Connection);

    return(true);
}
```

When we save the binding, we are returned a *BindingDetail* object that contains the complete details of what we've added to the UBR. Rather than use this object, we'll again rely on the form being completely repopulated from the UBR. We could write code to use the returned object to keep the form and the UBR synchronized, but we've used the repopulation of the form to accomplish the same task.

Deleting bindings Deleting a binding is also remarkably similar to deleting a service. We can retrieve the key of the binding we want to delete from the list box by retrieving the last 36 characters from the entry:

```
string strKey = lstBindings.Text.Substring(lstBindings.Text.Length - 36);
```

We pass this key as the sole parameter to the *Helper.DeleteBinding* method. The helper method creates an instance of the *DeleteBinding* class, adds the key of the binding we want to delete to the *BindingKeys* collection, and calls the *Send* method:

```
internal static bool DeleteBinding(string strBindingKey)
{
    // Do the delete
    DeleteBinding deleteBinding = new DeleteBinding();
    deleteBinding.BindingKeys.Add(strBindingKey);
    deleteBinding.Send(m_Connection);

   return(true);
}
```

Editing a Binding

Selecting a binding and clicking the Edit button brings up a form, shown in Figure 4-23, that allows us to modify the details for the binding we've selected.

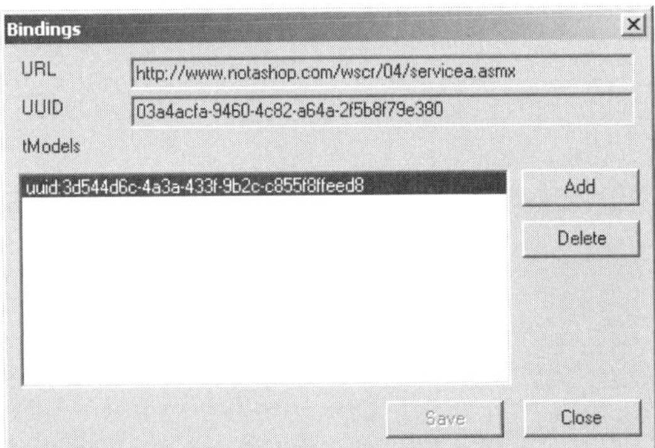

Figure 4-23 Editing the binding details

Based on Figure 4-23 and the information about modifying businesses and services, you're probably expecting the process of editing a binding to be roughly the same. Unfortunately, this isn't the case. The business and the service have child objects, and we have API methods to deal with these children, but the binding is the lowest level in the hierarchy and doesn't have any children. It simply contains pointers to tModels. The API has no methods to save these references independent of the binding to which they belong. We have to follow a different paradigm for modifying the bindings.

The clue to the new paradigm lies in the addition of the Save button that is now present on the form. When we added or deleted a new service, we made changes directly to the UBR, but we won't actually save the changes to the references to the tModels until we're finished with all the modifications to the binding.

When we add or delete a reference to a tModel, we update the list box that contains the UUIDs for the tModels. Only when we choose to save the changes will the details be sent to the UBR.

Populating the form The method by which we initially populate the form is the same one you've seen for both the business and service details. We call a wrapped method in the helper class, *Helper.GetBinding*, that accepts the UUID for a binding and returns a *BindingTemplate* that contains the details for the specified binding.

To retrieve the details for a specified binding, we use the *get_bindingDetail* API call, which is wrapped by the *GetBinding* helper method. We simply add the UUID of the binding we want to find to the *BindingKeys* collection of the class and call the class's *Send* method.

```
internal static BindingTemplate GetBinding(string strBindingKey)
{
    // Create the GetServiceDetail class
    GetBindingDetail getBindingDetail = new GetBindingDetail();
    getBindingDetail.BindingKeys.Add(strBindingKey);

    // Make the call
    return (getBindingDetail.Send(m_Connection).BindingTemplates[0]);
}
```

If we'd added multiple UUIDs to the *BindingKeys* collection, we might have returned multiple bindings in the *BindingTemplates* collection of the *BindingDetail* object that is returned from the *Send* method. We specified only one UUID, however, so we return only one binding—the first item in the *BindingTemplates* collection.

Now that we've retrieved the binding details, we can use them to populate the form. We first populate the static page details using the *AccessPoint.Text* and *BindingKey* properties. Then we iterate through the *TModelInstanceInfo* objects in the *TModelInstanceInfos* collection and add the *TModelKey* values to the list box:

```
BindingTemplate l_Binding = Helper.GetBinding(m_BindingKey);

// Populate the page
txtURL.Text = l_Binding.AccessPoint.Text;
txtUUID.Text = l_Binding.BindingKey;

// Iterate through the bindings
lstTModels.Items.Clear();
foreach (TModelInstanceInfo tModelInstanceInfo in
    l_Binding.TModelInstanceInfos)
{
    lstTModels.Items.Add(tModelInstanceInfo.TModelKey);
}
```

Adding a reference to a tModel To add a reference to a tModel to the binding, we must provide some way of specifying the UUID of the tModel that we want to reference. We could allow the user to type the UUID in manually, but this is far from user-friendly. As shown in Figure 4-24, we'll allow the user to specify a name or a partial name for the tModel and perform a search for a tModel with that name.

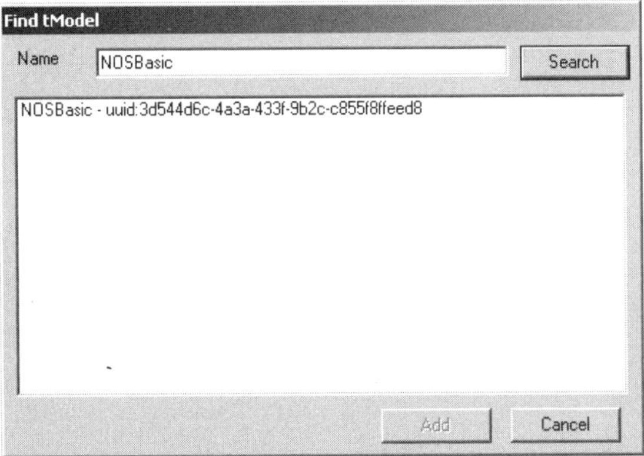

Figure 4-24 Searching for tModels

Clicking the Search button calls *FindTModels*, another static method on the *Helper* class. We pass in the text we entered in the text box and use the *FindTModel* class to return a *TModelList* object that contains all of the matches for the name we entered:

```
internal static TModelList FindTModels(string strName)
{
    // Create the FindTModel class
    FindTModel findTModel = new FindTModel();
    findTModel.Name = new Name(strName);

    // Make the call
    return (findTModel.Send(m_Connection));
}
```

The *TModelList* object has a collection of *TModelInfo* objects that represent the matches for the search. The list box is simply populated with the contents of the *Name* and *TModelKey* properties of the *TModelInfo* objects for the list we retrieved from the UBR:

```
// Get the results
TModelList tModelList = Helper.FindTModels(txtName.Text);

// Iterate and populate the results
foreach (TModelInfo tModelInfo in tModelList.TModelInfos)
{
    lstResults.Items.Add(tModelInfo.Name.Text + " - "
        + tModelInfo.TModelKey);
}
```

Selecting the tModel that we want to add a reference to and clicking the Add button closes the screen and adds the selected tModel to the list box. We simply take the UUID of the selected item and add this to the list box that contains the tModel references. The actual addition of the details to the UBR will take place when we save the details for the binding.

Deleting a reference to a tModel Deleting a reference to a tModel is simplicity itself: we remove the selected item from the list box. The item will actually be deleted from the UBR when we save the details for the binding.

Saving the binding To save the details of the binding, we can use one of the methods of the helper class that we've already discussed: the *Helper.SaveBinding* method. We used this method to add the details of a new binding to the UBR, and we can now use it to save the updated binding.

As you'll recall, the *Helper.SaveBinding* method accepts an instance of the *BindingTemplate* class, which we simply need to populate with the correct details and pass to the method. We specify values for the *BindingKey* and *ServiceKey* properties for the *BindingTemplate* object (which are passed to the form when it is first created and are stored as local variables), and then we specify the *Text* and *UrlType* properties for the *BindingTemplate* object's *AccessPoint* property:

```
BindingTemplate l_Binding = new BindingTemplate();

// populate the binding template
l_Binding.BindingKey = m_BindingKey;
l_Binding.ServiceKey = m_ServiceKey;
l_Binding.AccessPoint.Text = txtURL.Text;
l_Binding.AccessPoint.UrlType = UrlType.Http;
```

We now iterate through the items in the list box and add these to the *BindingTemplate* object. When we populated the form earlier, we iterated through the *TModelInstanceInfos* collection to retrieve the existing references; now we simply add a new *TModelInstanceInfo* to that collection for every entry in the list box:

```
// Iterate through the list box and
foreach (string l_strKey in lstTModels.Items)
{
    // Add to the object
    TModelInstanceInfo tModel = new TModelInstanceInfo();
    tModel.TModelKey = l_strKey;
    l_Binding. TModelInstanceInfos.Add(tModel);
}
```

We then make the call to *Helper.SaveBinding*, and the details we specified for the binding overwrite the details in the UBR.

Extending the UDDI Browser

As we pointed out earlier, the UDDI Browser application is by no means a complete application. We've taken a lot of shortcuts that we'd never take in a real-world application. We've also ignored some of the facilities that UDDI provides, such as the use of multiple languages when adding names and descriptions to items.

A fully functioning UDDI browser can be developed—the application we've provided here can serve as a starting point for a more complete implementation.

Visual Studio .NET and UDDI

So far, we've looked at using the UBRs online and using the UDDI SDK to access the data stored at the UBR directly. Although these are perfectly acceptable ways to use the UBRs, you can also do everything from within Visual Studio .NET.

Searching for Web Services

You can search for a Web service within Visual Studio .NET in two ways—each with its own slight peculiarities.

The easiest way to search for a Web service is from the Start Page, by clicking on the Online Resources tab and then selecting the XML Web Services option. This will immediately present the option to search for Web services. You'll see at the top of the Web page that you also have the option to register Web services. We'll explore that option shortly.

You can search in the production environment or in the test environment. These environments are equivalent to the live and test registries that we used earlier. You can also specify the category that you're searching. These are not the same as the categories we looked at earlier—they are specific to Visual Studio .NET. These categories are defined in the VS Web Service Search Categorization and the microsoft-com:geoweb:2000 taxonomies.

We're not likely to map our Web services to any of the categories in these taxonomies, so selecting any of the categories in the drop-down list or selecting (All Built-In Categories) will not return any results. We need to select (All Of UDDI) to get any results. This option doesn't add any category information to the search criteria—it allows only the name to be used as the search criteria.

We can select the test environment, select the (All Of UDDI) option in the Category drop-down list, type **NOSBasic** in the Search For text box, and click the Go button to return the two services we registered earlier, as shown in Figure 4-25.

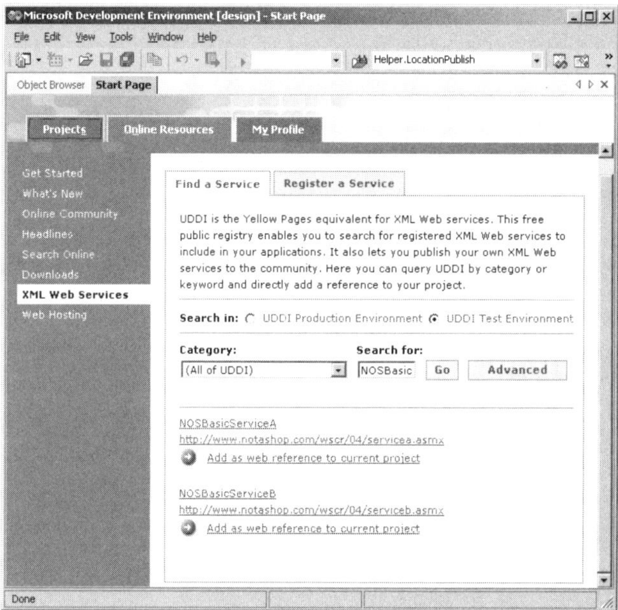

Figure 4-25 Searching for Web services in Visual Studio .NET

As you can see, we've found the two Web services we registered, and we can view the details of a service by clicking on its name (which will take us to the Microsoft UBR) or by clicking on the URL that is presented (which will show us the binding details for the service).

We also have the option of adding a reference to the Web service by clicking the Add As Web Reference To Current Project link. This will add the reference to the currently selected project in Solution Explorer. If we don't have a project open, we'll get a dialog box informing us that we must have an open project to add a Web reference.

> **Note** If the reference we're adding already exists in Visual Studio .NET, it will be updated; a new reference will not be created.

We can also perform an advanced search by clicking the Advanced button. This launches a new browser window within Visual Studio .NET and takes us to the UBR Web interface that we described earlier.

The other way to add a Web reference is to use the Add Web Reference dialog box. We can choose to search either the UDDI directory or the test UDDI directory. Clicking on either link will launch a Visual Studio–specific section of the Microsoft UBR, as shown in Figure 4-26.

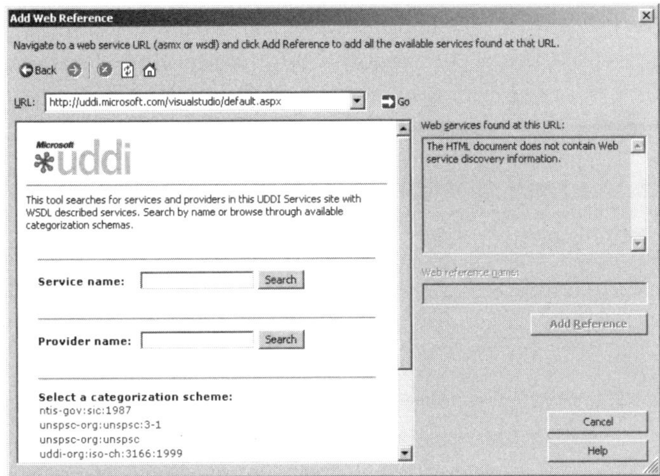

Figure 4-26 Using the Add Web Reference dialog box to search for Web services

We have what appear to be the standard options for searching for both services and providers, as well as options to navigate through the categories and search for services that fit into those categories.

By specifying the name of a service, we can obtain details of any matching Web services as well as a link to the WSDL file for the service. Opening the WSDL file for the service will enable the Add Reference button, which you can click to add a reference to the Web service.

Registering Web Services

Although the searching functionality in Visual Studio .NET is similar to the functionality available in the UBRs, the management side of the equation is not the same. In Visual Studio .NET we can create a new Microsoft UBR account and add providers and services to that account, but we cannot modify any details once they have been added to the UBR.

If we launch the Start Page within Visual Studio .NET and again navigate to the XML Web Services option on the Online Resources tab, you'll see a Register A Service tab that we haven't discussed yet. We can click this tab and the subsequent Register Your XML Web Service Today link to launch a new browser window within Visual Studio .NET where we can specify whether to use the test or production environment.

Selecting the registry that we require will force us to log in using a Passport account that has already been registered with the UBR. If the Passport account we're trying to use hasn't been registered with the UBR, we'll get an error message with a link to the registration page on the selected UBR.

If we haven't registered a business with the UBR, we're asked for a name and a description for our business, as shown in Figure 4-27.

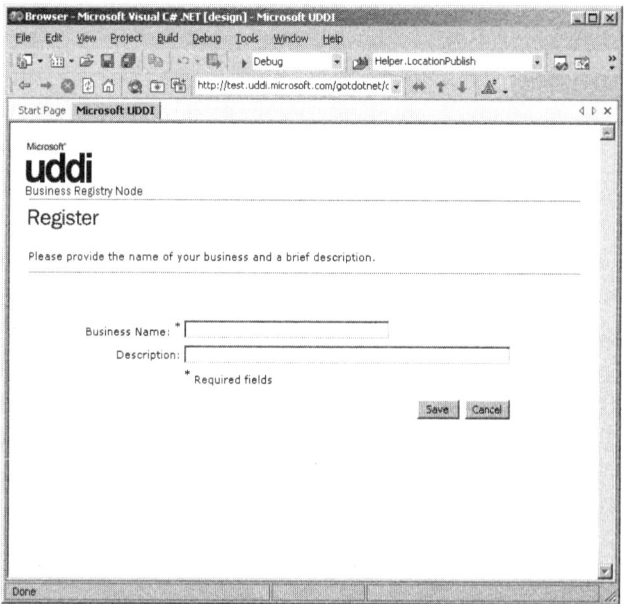

Figure 4-27 Adding a business to the Microsoft UBR in Visual Studio .NET

Once we enter the name and description, we can click the Save button to add the new business to the UBR. We must again select the UBR we want to use before we can move on to the next step.

After we registered a business to our UBR account, we must select it (or another business already registered to our UBR account) before we can add the details of the a Web service. We can add the details for the Web service using the form shown in Figure 4-28.

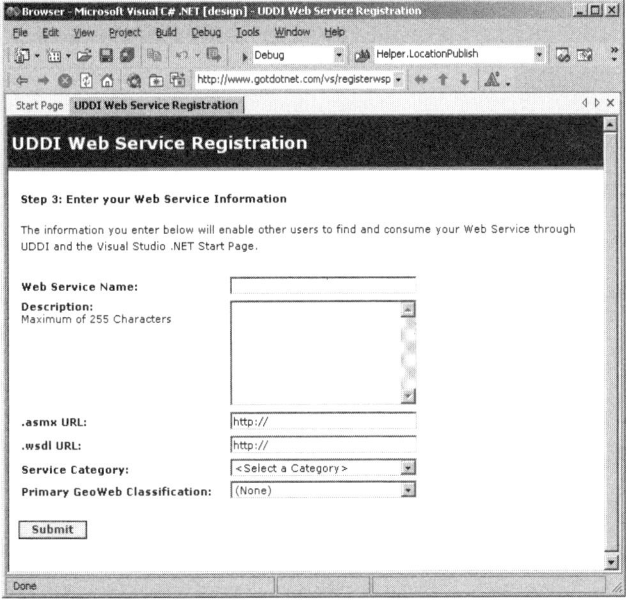

Figure 4-28 Adding a service to the Microsoft UBR in Visual Studio .NET

As you can see, we can register the service by specifying, at a minimum, a name, a description, an address for the Web service, and an address for the service's WSDL file.

If we want to use the VS Web Service Search Categorization and the microsoft-com:geoweb:2000 taxonomies to categorize our Web services, we can select entries from the Service Category and Primary GeoWeb Classification drop-down lists as required.

UDDI Enterprise Services in Windows 2003 Server

So far, we've looked at using the public UBRs that are available to every user of the Internet. Earlier in the chapter, we pointed out that it's not a good idea to use the public UBRs in certain cases and that you can't use the public UBRs for Web services that are running on an intranet.

Thankfully, there is a solution to this problem: UDDI Enterprise Services, an optional component that is available in the Standard, Enterprise, and Datacenter editions of Windows Server 2003. UDDI Enterprise Services provides a completely functional UBR that implements the requirements of version 2 of the UDDI specification.

Using the local UBR provided by UDDI Enterprise Services is virtually identical to using any of the public UBRs, so we can use all the knowledge we've gained so far in the chapter.

> **Note** When you use UDDI Enterprise Services, you don't have the limits imposed on the providers, services, and tModels that you have when you use the public UBRs. With the public UBR, you can only have one provider per account, but the local UBR allows you to have as many providers per account as you want. The same also applies to services and tModels.

A few little details are slightly different between the public and private UBRs, as detailed in the upcoming sections.

Authentication

UDDI Enterprise Services installs with two versions of the local UBRs, which by default are at *http://localhost/uddi/* and *http://localhost/uddipublic/*. If you inspect how these are configured within IIS, you can see that they are virtual directories that point at the same physical directory on the server. The difference between the two directories is that the first requires a valid Windows account for access and the second allows anonymous access.

Forcing users to have a valid Windows account before they can access the UBR allows us to determine, as you'll shortly see, what role the user has and what he is allowed to accomplish on the server. The anonymous access allowed by the second UBR allows the user only to search the UBR; we have no means of determining who the user is, so we cannot give the user a higher level of access.

Roles in UDDI Enterprise Services As we mentioned briefly, access to *http://localhost/uddi/* is controlled using Windows authentication, and the user must have a valid Windows account to access the UBR. The permissions within the UBR are determined by the role the user has been granted.

There are four roles within UDDI Enterprise Services, each with different permissions within the UBR. The roles and their permissions are listed in Table 4-8.

Table 4-8 Roles Defined in UDDI Enterprise Services

Role	Permissions
User	Can search the UBR
Publisher	The preceding permissions, plus permission to publish information in the UBR
Coordinator	All of the preceding permissions, plus ■ Can modify information belonging to other users and can change the ownership of existing information ■ Can view UBR statistics ■ Can modify and delete existing category taxonomies
Administrator	All of the preceding permissions, plus permission to import data, including category taxonomies, from other sources

To determine which role a Windows account belongs to, UDDI Enterprise Services allows a Windows group to be assigned to each of the roles. By default, the BUILTIN/Administrators group maps to the Publisher, Coordinator, and Administrator roles, and the BUILTIN/Users group maps to the Users role. As shown in Figure 4-29, you can change these mappings in the Properties dialog box for a UBR instance within Management Console.

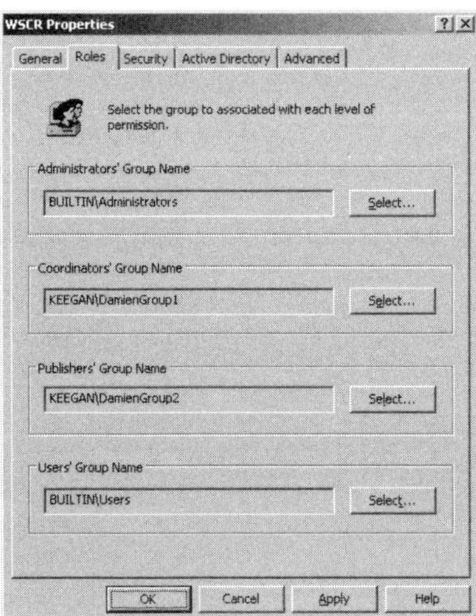

Figure 4-29 Managing roles with UDDI Enterprise Services

You can specify any of the Windows groups that are valid on the server, whether they are local (as we've used here) or controlled across a domain. When a user matches a role, that user will be given the permissions appropriate to that role. If the user belongs to a group that doesn't have a mapping to a role, he will be placed in the *Users* role.

UDDI Enterprise Services and the UDDI SDK

We can use a local UBR with the UDDI SDK with minimal change to the code that we wrote for accessing a public UBR. The only change needed is in the way that we create the *UddiConnection* object that we use to talk to the UBR.

When we created the *UddiConnection* object earlier, we used UDDI Authentication and passed in the username and password that we wanted to use. If we use a different version of the *UddiConnection* constructor, we can set it to use Windows Authentication instead.

We can replace the code in the *Helper.Connect* method with the following to access the UBR running on the local machine using Windows Authentication:

```
m_Connection = new UddiConnection(
    "http://localhost/uddi/inquire.asmx",
    "http://localhost/uddi/publish.asmx"
);
```

We don't need to make any other changes to the Browser application to use the local instance of the UBR. The request for the *AuthToken* from the UBR as well as adding it to any requests to the Publishing API is handled by the UDDI SDK automatically.

Summary

We've spent many pages looking at DISCO and UDDI and what they currently allow us to do. But the specifications have moved past that point, even though the development tools we have access to are still geared toward an earlier specification.

The use of DISCO has pretty much reached the point where it can go no further. Because it is limited to a single server, it was never going to take over the world—we still need some way of telling the world that a discovery document exists. Microsoft's participation in the creation of UDDI shows that Microsoft realized this quite early on. UDDI allows us to publicize our Web services in a "yellow pages" type of directory and allow anyone to search for those Web services.

But UDDI is still not the end of the story. Yet another specification has been released that allows you to discover Web service—WS-Inspection. As you'll see in Chapter 12, this specification allows you to create documents that correspond to your Web services and link to descriptions of those Web services in a UBR or directly to the WSDL definition of the Web service.

5

Raw Handlers and Clients

So far in this book, we've looked at the netwide standards that comprise the Web services base platform. Indeed, we have one more standard—XML Schema—to look at in the next chapter before we complete this section on core technologies. But first we'll take a step into the Microsoft .NET camp and look at the constructs that underlie .asmx Web service pages and their clients.

"Excuse me? I seem to have a bit of a dirty fork."

—Monty Python

Take a look at something you've worked hard on and you'll always find some reason to tweak it some more. There's always that speck of dirt on your nice clean fork. The same is true of the .NET team and the Web method abstraction they created over the workings of Web services. It works fine a lot of the time, but there are plenty of situations in which you'll want to bypass it and work at a lower level.

If you've used ASP.NET fairly extensively, you've probably come across the ASP.NET handler—the piece of code that takes in all the requests to your Web application, processes them, and builds a response to send back to the client. You might even have needed to write a custom handler for requests to one of your Web applications. The .NET Framework provides a standard handler for Web services that translates (deserializes) SOAP messages into objects and method calls that the service can understand. This is the dirty fork we need to clean, and we can do that by creating our own handler to field SOAP requests as they appear. In a similar fashion, we can choose not to use the proxy class that Microsoft Visual Studio .NET generates for us and go it alone on the client as well.

In this chapter, we'll look at the following topics:

- Why you sometimes need to build your own handlers
- How handlers fit into the HTTP pipeline modeled by the .NET Framework
- How the default Web service handler works and where you can make changes to your own client to add functionality
- How to implement your own proxy class on the client side

The actual code isn't that difficult, but the theory is important. Knowing how Web service requests are processed will provide a cornerstone for Part III of this book.

HTTP Handlers

So what is an HTTP handler? Put simply, it's an object that processes requests for individual URLs or URLs with certain file extensions (such as .asmx or .aspx). It's the endpoint for an HTTP request. Thus far, the examples in this book have all used the default handler for .asmx files to handle the communication between client and service. You might want to replace this handler for a number of reasons.

Between them, the client-side proxy class and server-side handler perform eight tasks you can take for granted when you use the Web method abstraction (as shown in Figure 5-1). But you might want to skip these steps or change how they're accomplished, such as in the following situations:

- The server or client or both are already working with raw XML rather than .NET objects. They therefore have the option of skipping some or all of the four serialization steps and building and parsing SOAP requests directly.
- The serializer used automatically by the built-in Web handler doesn't do all that you need it to do. For example, in both version 1.0 and version 1.1 of the .NET Framework, the serializer supports only SOAP 1.1 messages. If you want to use SOAP 1.2, you must augment the serializer's abilities or write your own serializer.
- The server needs to preprocess or postprocess the request before the contents can be translated into a call on the Web service. For example, the server might need to decrypt or decompress the contents of the payload. You can't do this with Web methods as they stand.

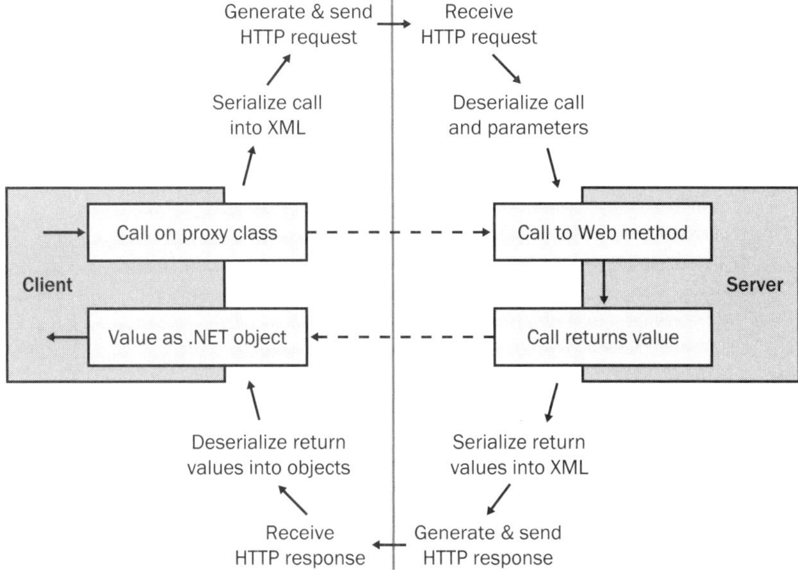

Figure 5-1 The steps beneath the Web method abstraction

You shouldn't be afraid of working at this lower level. As long as you adhere to the standards that Web services are built on, your handlers will work happily with other systems. If it helps, you can think of a custom handler as a Web service that parses and builds its own SOAP messages.

Building a custom handler doesn't mean you need a custom client. If you write a valid WSDL document for the service that the handler implements, developers can generate a proxy class against it in the normal way. Likewise, you can create a custom client over any Web service. As long as you know the shape of the SOAP request it requires and the response it will return, it doesn't matter how those messages are built or parsed.

Approximating the Default Handler

Let's get to it and start coding. Our first task is to determine how a handler works and then build on it so it can mirror the functionality of the default .asmx handler.

The *IHttpHandler* Interface

We'll start by building the simplest kind of handler—one that responds in exactly the same way whenever it's used. Open a new file in Notepad and write the following code:

```
<%@ WebHandler language="C#" class="SimpleHandler1" %>
```

```
using System;
using System.Web;

public class SimpleHandler1 : IHttpHandler {

    public void ProcessRequest(HttpContext context) {
        context.Response.Write("<b>I only return this message</b>");
    }

    public bool IsReusable {
        get {
            return true;
        }
    }
}
```

Create a new folder called wscr\05 under your Web server's root folder, and save the file there as SimpleHandler1.ashx. The extension .ashx identifies your file as an ASP.NET handler to be dealt with by—you guessed it—another handler. Now open up a browser and access the handler at *http://localhost/wscr/05/SimpleHandler1.ashx*. The handler returns a simple response (as shown in Figure 5-2).

Figure 5-2 A simple response from a simple handler

As you can see from the code, building your own handler is ultimately a matter of writing a class that inherits from and implements a single interface—*IHttpHandler*. As you'll see later in the chapter, if you want to implement an asynchronous HTTP service handler, you should implement *IHttpAsyncHandler* instead, but we'll leave that to one side for now. The first line of the handler file identifies the file as a *WebHandler* listing and identifies the class that implements the interface. If the class isn't in the handler file or its code-behind file, you must place the DLL that contains it in the bin directory of the Web application containing the handler or in the global assembly cache (GAC).

```
<%@ WebHandler language="C#" class="SimpleHandler1" %>
:
public class SimpleHandler1 : IHttpHandler {
```

The class inherits a property and a method from *IHttpHandler* that you must implement:

- *IsReusable*, a property that indicates whether the single handler object should be reused to field all incoming requests.
- *ProcessRequest*, a method that is called when a request is received; this is where you implement the code that constructs the response and sends it back. It takes one argument—the *HttpContext* object for this request.

The *ProcessRequest* method is the key to building a handler. By telling the handler how to deal with each type of request (GET, POST), you effectively implement the same functionality as the default Web service handler but retain complete control over what happens and what doesn't.

In this example, for instance, *ProcessMessage* just returns a message, regardless of how the request to the handler was made, using the context object to write to the response stream:

```
public void ProcessRequest(HttpContext context) {
    context.Response.Write("<b>I only return this message</b>");
}
```

> **Note** Visual Studio. NET does not support the editing of ASHX files, but Web Matrix does. In fact, Web Matrix practically writes this simple handler for you as example code.

Accounting for Request Types

The first task our replacement default handler has to undertake is to identify which type of request has been sent and then execute the appropriate code. As you learned in Chapter 1, ASP.NET Web services respond to four types of request binding:

- Requests for user-readable service documentation, which are sent as HTTP-GET requests to the service with no additional information attached to the URL
- HTTP-GET requests, which supply the method to be called and any parameters required in the call as part of the query string attached to the URL

- HTTP-POST requests, which identify the method to be called in the URL being requested but store any parameters needed in the body of the HTTP request
- HTTP-SOAP requests, which identify the service to be used in the URL, the method to be called in the HTTP SOAPAction header, and both method and parameters in the SOAP message stored in the body of the request

Our handlers should be able to deal with some or all of these types of requests and return the appropriate response. The second piece of code, SimpleHandler2.ashx, illustrates how to achieve this. We start as before with the *WebHandler* directive. Note that if the handler's implementation class has been defined in a namespace, the directive must include the complete class name:

```
<%@ WebHandler language="C#" class="notashop.wscr.C5.SimpleHandler2" %>

using System;
using System.Web;

namespace notashop.wscr.C5
{
    public class SimpleHandler2 : IHttpHandler {
```

Inside *ProcessRequest*, we can determine what type of HTTP request was sent to the handler using the *Request* object's *HttpMethod* property:

```
public void ProcessRequest(HttpContext context) {
    try
    {
        switch (context.Request.HttpMethod)
        {
```

If the request type is GET, the client is either looking for a documentation page or has sent an HTTP-GET request. If the former is true, the query string is empty and we can redirect the browser to the help page. If the latter is true, we must retrieve the method name and its parameters from the query string and act on them:

```
            case "GET":
                if (context.Request.QueryString.Count==0)
                    context.Response.Write
                        ("A documentation request has been made");
                else
                {
                    context.Response.Write
                        ("An HttpGet request has been made");
                }
                break;
```

If we detect a POST request type, we can distinguish between HTTP-POST and HTTP-SOAP according to the content type of the request body. If the type is plain text or the contents of a HTML form, it's an HTTP-POST request:

```
case "POST":
    switch (context.Request.ContentType)
    {
        case "text/plain":
        case "application/x-www-form-urlencoded":
            context.Response.Write
                ("An HttpPost request has been made");
            break;
```

If the body of the request contains XML, the request is probably an HTTP-SOAP request. If it is, the SOAPAction header will be present, so we can retrieve the method being called from the SOAPAction header, and we'll know the format of the SOAP request we have to parse or deserialize. If the SOAPAction header is not present or contains an unknown method, we need to return a SOAP fault message:

```
        case "text/xml":
            switch (context.Request.Headers["SOAPAction"])
            {
                case "method_one":
                    context.Response.Write("An HttpSoap "
                        + "request for Method One "
                        + "has been made");
                    break;
                case "method_two":
                    context.Response.Write("An HttpSoap "
                        + "request for Method Two "
                        + "has been made");
                    break;
                default:
                    context.Response.Write("A bad HttpSoap "
                        + "request has been made");
                    break;
            }
            break;
```

Finally, we need to account for the requests we cannot accommodate and return errors appropriately. Note that if the request wasn't in XML, we need use only regular error messages and not return SOAP faults.

```
        //Content-type not text, form or XML
        default:
            throw new Exception("Your request must be either"
                    + "written plain text "
                    + "or as a SOAP message.");
    }
```

```
                break;
            default:
                throw new Exception("This service accepts only "
                    + "GET and POST requests");
        }
    }
    catch(Exception e)
    {
        context.Response.Write(String.Format("error: {0}", e.Message));
    }
}
```

We've created only a skeleton for our handler here. The actual determination of the method being called and the parsing or deserializing of the parameters of that method has been left blank to keep things clear. However, a question arises: does the method being called have to be a part of the handler? No—it can be any part of an application and shouldn't have to be grouped with the handler. So there are two possible relationships between the handler and the method the client is calling:

- Like a Web service, the handler is requested directly by the client and contains the method being called.
- Like the default Web service handler, our custom handler looks after requests to several different Web services and passes on the deserialized request to the appropriate method in a separate file or assembly, or in a class that inherits from the handler's class.

Our first two examples demonstrate the first scenario neatly, so we'll look next at how to associate a handler with a set of requests using the same file extension.

Mapping a Handler to a File Extension

If you need to handle the processing of files with a certain file extension, you must first compile your class into an assembly and then place that assembly in either the GAC or, preferably, your Web application's bin directory. You cannot associate a class inside a handler or code-behind file to a file extension.

In this example, we'll associate requests for .wbsvc files with the following class, which has been compiled using Visual Studio .NET (you can also compile it from the command line) into an assembly called notashop.wscr.c5.wbsvc.dll.

```
using System.Web;

public class wbsvcHandler : IHttpHandler
{
    public void ProcessRequest(HttpContext context)
    {
```

```
        context.Response.Write("You asked for a .wbsvc file");
    }

    public bool IsReusable
    {
        get
        {
            return true;
        }
    }
}
```

We must notify two processes of our new mapping before our handler is properly set up. The first is Microsoft Internet Information Services (IIS). We must specify the virtual application within which the association of requests and handler is valid. We can restrict this association to requests within the wscr\05 directory by making the directory a virtual application and working within it, or we can make the association valid across the whole Web site by working on the root application in IIS. Either way, you first bring up the Properties dialog box for your virtual application in the IIS Administration tool and click the Configuration button in the Application Settings section of the Directory tab. The Mappings tab of the Application Configuration dialog box shows you all the current associations between file extensions and the DLLs hosting the processing pipeline that the request goes through. We need to send .wbsvc to ASP.NET before we can forward it to our handler.

Click the Add button under the Application Mappings grid, and you'll get to the dialog box shown in Figure 5-3.

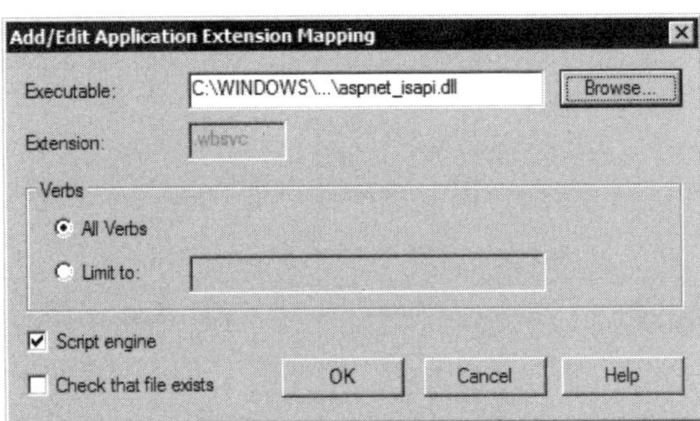

Figure 5-3 The Add/Edit Application Extension Mapping dialog box

The dialog box lets you specify two options:

- The Executable option points to the DLL that hosts the processing pipeline for the request. In our case, it's ASP.NET. Click Browse and navigate to *WindowsDirectory*\Microsoft.NET\Framework*Version*\aspnet_isapi.dll, where *Version* is the build of .NET you're using.

- The Extension option contains the file extension you want to use. In our case, it's .wbsvc (including the period).

  Finally, deselect the Check That File Exists check box and click OK.

> **Tip** Because of a bug in the IIS Administration tool, you sometimes can't click OK after you specify the Executable or Extension option. The cure is to click the text box containing the location of your pipeline DLL. The OK button will become enabled again, and you can proceed.

The second process to configure is the ASP.NET pipeline itself. You do this by creating a web.config file in the root directory of your virtual application (if there isn't one already) and adding a *<httpHandlers>* section to it:

```
<?xml version="1.0" encoding="UTF-8" ?>
<configuration>
    <system.web>
        <httpHandlers>
            <add verb="*" path="*.wbsvc"
                 type="wbsvcHandler, notashop.wscr.c5.wbsvc" />
        </httpHandlers>
    </system.web>
</configuration>
```

The *<add />* element maps all requests for files with the extension .wbsvc to the *wbsvcHandler* class in the assembly *notashop.wscr.c5.wbsvc*. Once you save the new web.config, copy *notashop.wscr.c5.wbsvc.dll* into the virtual application's bin directory. (If there isn't a bin directory, create it.) Try browsing to, for example, test.wbsvc in your Web application. Even though the file doesn't exist, our handler is passed the request for a .wbsvc page and returns the simple message we gave it.

Constraining the Mapping

The previous example is the most lenient mapping you can make to a handler. However, you can constrain it against a couple of criteria on the request. You can return a standard 404 File Not Found error if the .wbsvc file does not exist in the virtual application. To do this, you reselect the Check That File Exists check box in the Edit Application Extension Mapping dialog box for .wbsvc (as shown previously in Figure 5-3).

You can also limit the type of HTTP requests that make it through to the handler. Both IIS and the pipeline .config file allow you to specify the HTTP verbs—generally GET and POST—that you want to handle and those you don't.

In IIS, select the Limit To option in the Edit Application Extension Mapping dialog box and type **GET**, **POST** (as shown in Figure 5-4).

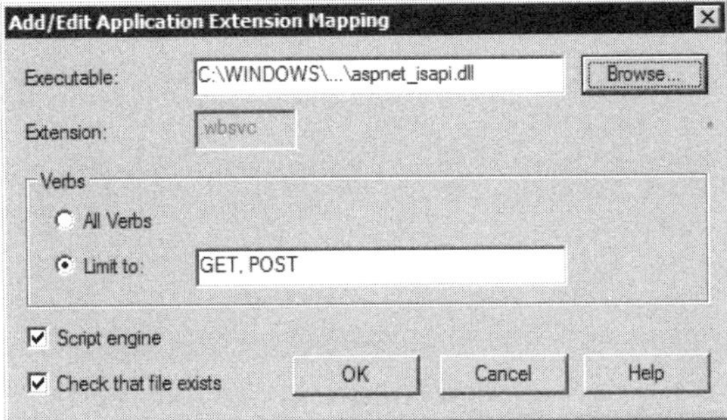

Figure 5-4 Restricting the HTTP request types allowed for a file extension.

In web.config, we can mirror this restriction by changing the verb attribute of our *<add />* elements from * (representing all verbs) to, for example, *"GET, POST"*.

```
<add verb="GET, POST" path="*.wbsvc"
     type="wbsvcHandler, notashop.wscr.c5.wbsvc" />
```

Note that IIS and web.config must agree that the request type should be forwarded to the handler before it actually is. If IIS forbids it, the client is returned a 403.1 Forbidden error. If web.config forbids it, you get a 404 Resource Not Found error.

The HTTP Pipeline

At this point, we need to step back a little and look at the bigger picture. We know our handler has access to the *HttpContext* object for the request, but how? Why does web.config work as it does? Why did we map .wbsvc to aspnet_isapi.dll in IIS? Can we extend the mapping to apply to every Web application that IIS is hosting? The answers to these questions and many others surrounding extending the .NET Web Services framework lie in understanding how a HTTP request is processed by IIS and then ASP.NET.

From IIS to ASP.NET

Once an ASP.NET request has been allowed through your server's firewall, typically via port 80 for HTTP or port 443 for HTTPS, your Web server picks it up and routes the request to the appropriate server-side pipeline for processing. In the case of IIS, it consults the Application Mappings list for the Web application the request is targeting and passes it to whichever version of aspnet_isapi.dll you're using.

This DLL then forwards the request through a named pipe to the ASP.NET worker process, aspnet_wp.exe, which hosts a common language runtime (CLR) instance. It provides an application domain for each virtual application that IIS maintains. In this way, each application is isolated from the rest. The request is passed into the pipeline in the appropriate application domain and processed (as shown in Figure 5-5). Finally, IIS retrieves the response generated from the pipeline and sends it back as appropriate.

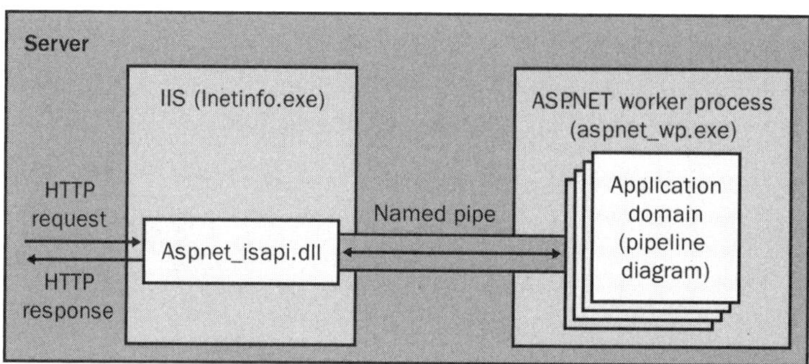

Figure 5-5 How an ASP.NET request is passed to ASP.NET by IIS

You can configure as much of the operation of the worker process as needed. Every new application domain is created and operates under the settings laid out in the global machine.config file (and your application-specific web.config), which initializes the ASP.NET worker process. For example, each process is designed to handle requests indefinitely, but you can change the *<processModel />* element in machine.config to specify a finite lifetime after which a process will be transparently replaced with a new instance of itself.

> **Important** IIS 6.0, which ships with Microsoft Windows Server 2003, brings some fairly large changes to this arrangement. Most notably, you can isolate separate applications in separate processes rather than having them grouped in a single process (as is the case in IIS 5.*x*). It also contains a kernel-mode HTTP listener, which can bypass aspnet_isapi.dll and send ASP.NET requests straight to the worker process.

You'll find machine.config in *WindowsDirectory*\Microsoft.NET\Framework*Version*\CONFIG. We'll look more at .config files and the Web service–related entries within them shortly.

Inside the ASP.NET HTTP Pipeline

If we look more closely at the HTTP pipeline that the ASP.NET worker process maintains for every application domain, you can find our handlers and more. Programmatically, the pipeline is implemented by classes in the *System.Web* namespace (as shown in Figure 5-6) and configured using machine.config with any application-specific settings given in web.config.

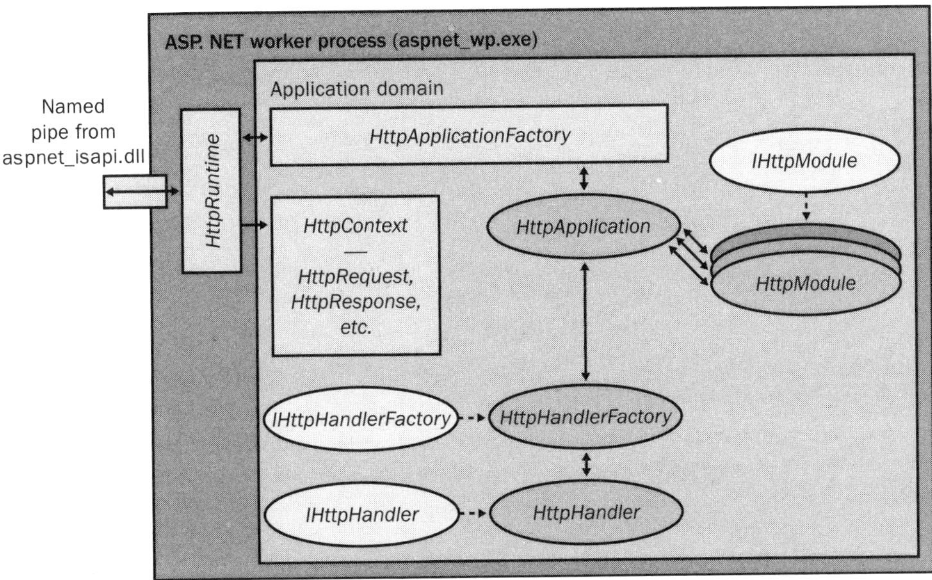

Figure 5-6 The ASP.NET HTTP pipeline. Read-only classes are drawn as rectangles.

A new request is marshaled from IIS to the beginning of the appropriate pipeline by an instance of *HttpWorkerRequest*.

At the top of the pipeline is *HttpRuntime*. It does two things:

- It sends a request to the *HttpApplicationFactory* object to generate an *HttpApplication* object representing the Web application containing the requested file or Web service. The *HttpApplicationFactory* object generates the *HttpApplication* object by retrieving it from a pool that the *HttpApplicationFactory* object controls or by instantiating a new object if the pool is not yet full.

- It creates an *HttpContext* object associated with the request. This wraps all the information pertinent to it (*Response*, *Request*, *Server*, and so forth) into a simple object model that is then available to the rest of the pipeline for state maintenance, reference, and reaction. The *HttpContext* object is passed automatically into the *ProcessRequest* method in your handler and can be retrieved by any other method using the static *HttpContext.Current* property.

The *HttpRuntime*, *HttpApplicationFactory*, and *HttpContext* classes implement the top half of the processing pipeline, which can't be altered. While you're writing handlers, the only evidence of the existence of these classes will be the *HttpContext* object passed into the *ProcessRequest* method. In contrast, the four objects in the bottom half of the pipeline provide you with hooks into the pipeline, giving you a good deal of control over the request and how it is processed:

- *HttpApplication* provides application- and session-level state information to the modules and handlers that process the request. It also keeps track via machine.config and web.config of exactly which modules and which handler will do that processing, by looking in the *<httpModules />* and *<httpHandlers />* elements of those files, respectively. Finally, it exposes several events within the pipeline that can be hooked into by adding code to the global.asax file for the Web application.
- Modules, which must implement *IHttpModule*, can view and alter the content of request and response messages as they flow through the pipeline. Indeed, any number of modules can work over a request before it reaches its intended handler. For example, two of the predefined modules in machine.config take care of the authentication and authorization of requests, respectively.

> **Note** Modules are the .NET equivalent of ISAPI filters. We'll revisit them in Chapter 10. They are the key to extending the Web method programming layer of .NET's Web service programming framework.

- Handlers receive the request after it has been appropriately processed by any modules. The handler that receives a request is implemented by the class given in web.config (or machine.config, if it's not application-specific).
- A handler factory instantiates a handler if the handler doesn't yet exist or is marked as not reusable. Alternatively, a handler can be instantiated directly. If it's marked as reusable and an instance already exists, the handler will be reused. We'll look at handler factories in more detail shortly.

Once a response to the request has been generated by the handler, it can be processed again by a module or two before it passes back up the pipeline, into IIS, and out to whatever client made the initial request.

Configuring the Pipeline for Your Application

Customizing the pipeline for your application boils down to working with the various .config files on your system. The machine.config file defines the default settings for the pipeline, and anything you override or add in the web.config file for your Web application must be based on the defaults. Be especially careful if you're working with nested Web applications. Each application should have its own web.config file, and the overall settings for a child application will be the "sum total" of machine.config, all of its parents' web.config files, and its own web.config file, as shown in Figure 5-7.

Actual pipeline settings for WebApp2 =
machine.config + web.config(WebApp1) + web.config(WebApp2)

Figure 5-7 A child application's pipeline settings are the sum of the root's settings, its parent's settings, and its own.

If you open machine.config, you can find the settings for ASP.NET under *<configuration>/<system.web>*. The file contains brief documentation next to each setting to identify possible settings and what they do, but you can find clearer, more detailed explanations in the .NET SDK documentation at *ms-help://MS.NETFrameworkSDK/cpgenref/html/gngrfaspnetconfigurationsectionschema.htm*.

The three sections we're particularly interested in as Web service developers are *<httpHandlers/>*, *<httpModules/>*, and *<webServices/>*. The last of these presents the settings for ASP.NET Web service pages built using Web methods. They don't help us at this lower level, but it's worth noting that *<webServices>/<protocols>* lets you specify what types of requests these Web services will accept, and *<webServices>/<WsdlHelpGenerator>* lets you specify a new documentation page for them. You can find the default documentation page at *WindowsDirectory*\Microsoft.NET\Framework\ *Version*\CONFIG\ DefaultWsdlHelpGenerator.aspx.

<httpHandlers/> and *<httpModules/>* can contain the following three subelements:

- *<add/>*, which adds a module or a handler to the application, as in *<add verb="*" path="*.ashx" type="System.Web.UI.SimpleHandlerFactory"/>*
- *<remove />*, which removes a module or a handler from the application that has already been defined globally or in a parent application, as in *<remove verb="*" path="*.ashx" />*
- *<clear />*, which removes every handler or module from the application

Using the Predefined HTTP Handlers

Make sure you know exactly what *<remove />* and *<clear />* do. For instance, *<remove verb="*" path="*.ashx" />* does not disallow requests to handler files—it removes any knowledge ASP.NET has of how to process them. Adding the above line to an application's web.config and browsing to an .ashx file returns the entire source code in that particular file rather than a 404 File Not Found error or 403.1 Forbidden error, as was probably intended.

If you're looking to return a standard error for a certain file or file extension, use the handlers that .NET has already defined. These aren't particularly well documented, but Table 5-1 shows you which handler produces which error if you add the following line to your web.config and use the handler name in place of *PredefinedHandlerName*.

```
<add verb="*" path="your.path" type="System.Web.PredefinedHandlerName" />
```

Table 5-1 Errors Returned by Predefined .NET Handlers

Handler	Resulting Error Code and Message	Notes
HttpForbiddenHandler	HTTP 403: This type of page has been expressly forbidden.	N/A
HttpMethodNotAllowedHandler	HTTP 405: 'GET' is forbidden.	Change the verb in *<add/>* to restrict specific HTTP request methods.
HttpNotFoundHandler	HTTP 404: This resource cannot be found.	N/A
HttpNotImplementedHandler	HTTP 501: 'GET' *.extension is not implemented.	Change the verb in *<add/>* to restrict specific HTTP request methods.

At this point, we need to cut and run from everything but HTTP-SOAP requests. We might want to include online documentation for our service handlers, but the implementation of such pages is pretty trivial and, as you've seen, trivial to associate with a simple HTTP-GET request. However, with respect to actually conversing with the handler, HTTP-POST and HTTP-GET both have drawbacks:

- Neither binding provides for the sending of header information specific to the conversation between client and service.
- HTTP-GET doesn't support the sending of complex types as name-value pairs in the query string.
- You cannot ensure that the data contained in a message is correctly typed with either HTTP-GET or HTTP-POST.
- Only the return parameter of the Web method can be returned using HTTP-GET or HTTP-POST. ASP.NET doesn't support encoding in/out or out parameters within the message returned to the client as a result of an HTTP-GET or HTTP-POST request.

For debugging purposes, both bindings can be useful, but on a full, live server, you should lock down access to your services as much as possible. Prohibiting all except HTTP-SOAP requests is recommended for both Web method and handler-based services.

Working with XML Directly

You've learned how to build a basic handler, how it works, and how requests come to it through the ASP.NET pipeline. Now we need to deal with SOAP requests and building SOAP responses in kind, and that means incorporating some XML handling into our service handlers.

If you'll recall, one of the first reasons you saw for working with the handler API rather than a serializer was so you could work in XML directly. There are several other good reasons:

- If you're working only with text, there's no point in using the serializer.
- You might want to work with a new standard (for example, XML 1.1 or SOAP 1.2) that the serializer doesn't support yet.
- You might want to append some processing to your SOAP message that's specific to your service and that the generic serializer can't handle. For example, you can make sure the message was validated against the message schema before you touch it, or you can handle encoded images inside or attached to your message.

We'll look specifically at how to use the two main .NET XML APIs to process incoming SOAP messages and generate SOAP responses—that is, how to approximate what the serializer does in the default Web service handler. Each of these XML APIs—the XML streaming API (not to be confused with the Simple API for XML) and the XML Document Object Model (DOM) API—has its pros and cons, which we'll discuss as we go along.

Using the XML Streaming API

Let's take an example called XmlHandler1, which you'll find included with this book's sample code. The client sends our handler the name of an album and the artist who recorded it for storage in a public database. Rather than deserializing the two strings into, for example, a *RecordDetails* object containing two string fields, we'll use our own handler (XmlHandler1) to pull the data straight out of the request message and add it to the database accordingly using .NET's XML streaming API.

Let's assume we've already published a schema (you'll find it in the sample code as AlbumEntry.xsd) for this service that specifies the following format for SOAP request messages:

```
<?xml version="1.0" encoding="utf-8"?>
<soap:Envelope xmlns:soap="http://schemas.xmlsoap.org/soap/envelope/"
```

```
    xmlns:xsi="http://www.w3.org/2001/XMLSchema-instance"
    xmlns:xsd="http://www.w3.org/2001/XMLSchema">
<soap:Body>
    <AddRecord xmlns="http://www.notashop.com/wscr">
        <album>Name_of_album_here</album>
        <artist>Name_of_artist_here</artist>
    </AddRecord>
</soap:Body>
</soap:Envelope>
```

And this format for response messages:

```
<?xml version="1.0" encoding="utf-8"?>
<soap:Envelope xmlns:soap="http://schemas.xmlsoap.org/soap/envelope/"
               xmlns:xsi="http://www.w3.org/2001/XMLSchema-instance"
               xmlns:xsd="http://www.w3.org/2001/XMLSchema">
<soap:Body>
    <AddRecordResponse xmlns="http://www.notashop.com/wscr">
        <AddRecordResult>Response_message</AddRecordResult>
    </AddRecordResponse>
</soap:Body>
</soap:Envelope>
```

The code for *ProcessRequest* in XmlHandler1.ashx has exactly the same shape as in SimpleHandler2.ashx (listed earlier, in the section "Accounting for Request Types"), with the execution of the *AddRecord* SOAP action reflecting the two steps the server needs to take to process the request and send a response. (Remember, there's no serialization.)

```
if (context.Request.Headers["SOAPAction"] == "AddRecord")
{
    string ResponseMessage = "";
    ResponseMessage = AddRecord(context.Request.InputStream);
    SendAddRecordResponse(context.Response.OutputStream,
        ResponseMessage);
}
```

The SOAP request message can always be found in the *InputStream* property of the current *HttpRequest* object, and it's this stream we send to our method to retrieve and process the message. The *AddRecord* method returns a string as an acknowledgement message, which *SendAddRecordResponse* places inside a SOAP response message, pushing it down the stream to the server's response back to the client:

```
private string AddRecord(Stream SOAPRequest)
{
    XmlTextReader RequestReader;
    string Response = "";
    string album = "";
```

```
    string artist = "";
    //Create new XmlTextReader object from InputStream of HTTP Request
    RequestReader = new XmlTextReader(SOAPRequest);
```

Inside *AddRecord*, we use the XML streaming API to pull out the album and artist. Specifically, we use an *XmlTextReader* object to work through the SOAP request sent by the client:

```
    try
    {
        //Iterate through document nodes
        while(RequestReader.Read())
        {
            // Filter out nodetypes and concatenate text types accordingly.
            if (RequestReader.LocalName == "album")
            {
                album = RequestReader.ReadString();
            }
            if (RequestReader.LocalName == "artist")
            {
                artist = RequestReader.ReadString();
            }
        }
        Response = album + " by " + artist +
                   " has been added to the record database.";
    }
    catch(Exception err)
    {
        Response = "Error occurred while reading request message: "
            + err.ToString();
    }
    return Response;
}
```

The actual work we do here is simple—iterating through the elements in the SOAP request until we find those we want and saving their text content into the appropriate variable. We don't need to worry about character encoding either because the reader discovers and deals with it automatically.

We could create the response by writing XML tags directly into a string. In this case, checking well-formedness and escaping reserved characters would be our responsibility. We'll use an *XmlTextWriter* object instead. Note that in the constructor of the *XmlTextWriter* object we must specify an encoding if we need something other than the default of UTF-8.

```
private void SendAddRecordResponse
    (Stream responseStream, string message)
{
    //Create XmlTextWriter to build SOAP request
    XmlTextWriter soapWriter =
        new XmlTextWriter(responseStream, Encoding.ASCII);
```

The rest of this method writes out the SOAP response almost verbatim, using the *XmlTextWriter* object's write methods to create the elements and set up their namespaces:

```
    //Write Xml Declaration
 soapWriter.WriteStartDocument();

    //Write Envelope Element
    soapWriter.WriteStartElement("env", "Envelope",
                "http://schemas.xmlsoap.org/soap/envelope/");
    soapWriter.WriteAttributeString("xmlns","xsi",null,
                "http://www.w3.org/2001/XMLSchema-instance");
    soapWriter.WriteAttributeString("xmlns","xsd",null,
                "http://www.w3.org/2001/XmlSchema");

    //Write Body Element
    soapWriter.WriteStartElement("Body",
                "http://schemas.xmlsoap.org/soap/envelope/");

    //Write AddRecordResponse Element
    soapWriter.WriteStartElement(null, "AddRecordResponse",
                "http://www.notashop.com/wscr");

    //Write AddRecordResult elements
    soapWriter.WriteElementString("AddRecordResult",
                "http://www.notashop.com/wscr", message);

    //Close All Elements
    soapWriter.WriteEndElement();
    soapWriter.WriteEndElement();
    soapWriter.WriteEndElement();
    soapWriter.WriteEndDocument();
```

Finally, we close the *Response* stream so the response is sent:

```
    //Write to file and close
    soapWriter.Close();
}
```

Which XML API?

In more complex situations, you need to address the question of which .NET XML API to use in your handler services. Even in our trivial example, you could argue that it would be better to use the XML DOM API rather than the XML streaming API. In *AddRecord*, for example, we could use the DOM API to move directly to the elements we need rather than iterate through the entire SOAP request. As ever, it's a case of weighing the pros and cons and using the solution that seems best. With that in mind, here are some of the arguments for either API.

The advantages of the DOM API are as follows:

- It's a random access API rather than forward-only, which means you can access particular document fragments—such as Web method parameters—in any order.
- It's a better choice for complex queries. The DOM API uses XPath statements to identify a group of XML nodes for assessment. You can be very specific if you use XPath correctly.
- It's easier to create a SOAP response that's based on the contents of the SOAP request.
- You can use the *XmlNodeChangedEventArgs* class to enforce business rules while the request is being processed by the server.

And, on the flip side, the advantages of the streaming API are

- It can start processing the SOAP request immediately. The DOM API must first parse the request into memory as a tree before you can start to use it.
- The larger the SOAP request, the more resources the DOM API uses to deal with it compared to the streaming API—for the reason noted above.
- It's better suited to reading through data that has been serialized from a data source (that is, a table or set of tables converted into XML).
- It's better suited to working with XML asynchronously than the DOM API. That is, it can start reading through a SOAP request before it has all been retrieved and write a response in which the data to be included is also retrieved asynchronously.

One "feature" the APIs share, however, is the inability to interpret default namespaces correctly. Take, for example, our sample SOAP request:

```
<soap:Body>
    <AddRecord xmlns="http://www.notashop.com/wscr">
        <album>Accelerated Evolution</album>
        <artist>Devin Townsend</artist>
    </AddRecord>
</soap:Body>
```

Both APIs correctly identify that the *<Body>* element belongs to the namespace identified by the prefix *soap*. Unfortunately, both return the information that *<AddRecord>*, *<album>*, and *<artist>* have no namespace at all, not even the default one, as is actually the case. The solution is to qualify every element in your request with a prefix rather than use a default namespace.

Using the XML DOM API

In this next example—called SchemaHandler1.ashx in the sample code—we'll combine the strengths of both APIs and rewrite our previous example so it does the following:

- Processes and returns messages that do not use a default namespace. Instead, the (previously default) namespace is associated with the prefix *a*.

  ```
  <soap:Body>
      <a:AddRecord xmlns:a="http://www.notashop.com/wscr">
          <a:album>Accelerated Evolution</a:album>
          <a:artist>Devin Townsend</a:artist>
      </a:AddRecord>
  </soap:Body>
  ```

- Validates the request message against our schema, AlbumEntry.xsd, and the SOAP 1.1 schema using an *XmlValidatingReader* object.
- Uses the XML DOM API to handle the processing of the request and the construction of a response.
- Sends a correctly formatted SOAP fault message back to the client if something goes wrong.

With a validation process in our handler against a schema we've created, the handler is now stricter than the default ASP.NET Web service handler. However, if you're validating incoming requests, they should be doc/literal requests rather than RPC/encoded requests. Doc/literal requests are literally schema-defined and therefore leave no ambiguities in their contents. In contrast, RPC/encoded requests include machine-generated information from client to server that must be accommodated in your schema using wildcards, thus weakening the validation process (the more wildcards your schema contains, the less effective it is) and hindering your ability to control what's actually sent to your Web service.

Adding Error Handling

Although the general structure of the handler hasn't actually changed, we've added a new *try/catch* statement to keep track of whether an error occurs while the request is being processed:

```
case "text/xml":
    if (context.Request.Headers["SOAPAction"] == "AddRecord")
    {
        string ResponseMessage = "";
        try
        {
            ResponseMessage = AddRecord(context.Request.InputStream);
            SendAddRecordResponse(ResponseMessage,
                context.Response.OutputStream);
        }
        catch(Exception e)
        {
            ResponseMessage = "Error occurred in AddRecord: "
                + e.Message;
            GenerateSoapError(ResponseMessage,
                context.Response.OutputStream);
        }
    }
    else
    {
        GenerateSoapError("You made a HTTP-SOAP request "
            + "for a method that doesn't exist",
            context.Response.OutputStream);
    }
    break;
```

The *GenerateSoapError* method uses the DOM API to create a new SOAP message containing details of the problem we've encountered and then an *XmlTextWriter* object to channel it back into the appropriate *Response* stream:

```
private void GenerateSoapError(string message, Stream responseStream)
{
    XmlDocument doc = new XmlDocument();
```

Taking our own advice, neither success nor failure responses use a default namespace, making sure that every element has a valid prefix:

```
    //Write Envelope Element
    XmlElement envelope = doc.CreateElement("env", "Envelope",
```

```
        "http://schemas.xmlsoap.org/soap/envelope/");
    doc.AppendChild(envelope);

    //Write Body Element
    XmlElement soapBody = doc.CreateElement("env:Body",
        "http://schemas.xmlsoap.org/soap/envelope/");
    envelope.AppendChild(soapBody);

    //Write Fault Element
    XmlElement soapFault = doc.CreateElement("env:Fault",
        "http://schemas.xmlsoap.org/soap/envelope/");
    soapBody.AppendChild(soapFault);
```

For brevity's sake, this example includes only the *<faultString>* element in the SOAP fault message. We encourage you to extend it to include the remaining *<faultcode>*, *<faultactor>*, and *<detail>* elements.

```
    //Write FaultString Element
    XmlElement faultString = doc.CreateElement("env:FaultString",
        "http://schemas.xmlsoap.org/soap/envelope/");
    faultString.InnerText = message;
    soapFault.AppendChild(faultString);
```

The cooperation between the streaming API and the DOM API here is in the *WriteTo* method. Once the fault message has been constructed as an *XmlDocument* object (a tree structure), the *WriteTo* method serializes this into the literal text that the writer can deal with:

```
    XmlTextWriter soapWriter =
        new XmlTextWriter(responseStream, Encoding.ASCII);
    soapWriter.Formatting = Formatting.Indented;
    doc.WriteTo(soapWriter);
    soapWriter.Close();
}
```

The same strategy is used to create a successful SOAP response and send it on its way in *SendAddRecordResponse*, so we'll move on and cover the processing of the request message in *AddRecord*.

Adding Validation

The actual code to check that a SOAP request message (or indeed any XML document) is valid against a schema is straightforward. Here are the steps:

1. Create a new *XmlValidatingReader* object against the message.
2. Set its *ValidationType* property to *Schema* and tell it where to find the appropriate schema.

3. Provide some mechanism to catch any validation errors that might occur as the message is read by the reader.

And that's it. An *XmlValidatingReader* object includes a hook to a single event handler that's called if a validation error occurs. If it isn't implemented and a validation error occurs, a simple *Exception* occurs instead. We use this latter approach to catch any errors:

```
private string AddRecord(Stream SOAPRequest){
    string album, artist, Response = "";

    XmlTextReader tr = new XmlTextReader(SOAPRequest);
    XmlValidatingReader vr = new XmlValidatingReader(tr);
    vr.ValidationType = ValidationType.Schema;
```

Don't worry about your SOAP message containing elements across several namespaces. The *XmlValidatingReader* class allows you to declare as many schema documents as are required using its *Schemas* property. The *XmlValidatingReader* class also validates (fragments of) XML documents against document type definitions (DTDs) and XML-Data Reduced (XDR) schemas if required, but not all at once; you can specify only one *ValidationType* at a time. The only tricky part might be actually locating the schema in the first place. Chapter 6 gives more information on locating schemas that are not your own, but for quick reference, the SOAP 1.1 schema is one of the few that can be found at the address given as its namespace URI: *http://schemas.xmlsoap.org/soap/envelope*. We retrieved a local copy and saved it in the application directory as SoapSchema.xsd.

```
    vr.Schemas.Add("http://www.notashop.com/wscr",
            "http://localhost/wscr/05/schemahandler/AlbumEntry.xsd");
    vr.Schemas.Add("http://schemas.xmlsoap.org/soap/envelope/",
            "http://localhost/wscr/05/schemahandler/SOAPSchema.xsd");
```

To use the DOM API, we need to link the *Reader* object we've set up with a new *XmlDocument* object. Fortunately, one of the overloaded versions of the *XmlDocument.Load* method does just that:

```
    XmlDocument doc = new XmlDocument();
    doc.Load(vr);
```

The DOM API provides several document context objects that make life easier when you're working with an *XmlDocument* object. One such context object is *XmlNamespaceManager*, which eliminates the need to specify the namespace URI associated with every element in our document. Instead, we can associate the URI with a prefix and then use that prefix rather than the URI in the XPath expressions we use to extract the artist and album name to be stored in our database:

```
    XmlNamespaceManager ns = new XmlNamespaceManager(doc.NameTable);
    ns.AddNamespace("a", "http://www.notashop.com/wscr");
    ns.AddNamespace("env","http://schemas.xmlsoap.org/soap/envelope/");

    album = doc.SelectSingleNode
      ("/env:Envelope/env:Body/a:AddRecord/a:album/text()", ns).Value;
    artist = doc.SelectSingleNode
     ("/env:Envelope/env:Body/a:AddRecord/a:artist/text()", ns).Value;
    Response = album + " by " + artist +
        " has been added to the record database.";
    return Response;
}
```

Two More Handler Classes

At the beginning of this chapter, we noted that not all our handlers need to inherit and implement the *IHttpHandler* interface. We have two other options:

- Inheriting from *IHttpAsyncHandler*, which lets you create an asynchronous service
- Inheriting from *IHttpHandlerFactory*, which lets you create a factory class that decides, given various pieces of information, what type of handler will deal with a particular request and instantiates one accordingly

We'll briefly look at these next.

IHttpAsyncHandler

HTTP is a synchronous protocol, so you might not associate it with asynchronous behavior in the same way you would, say, Simple Mail Transfer Protocol (SMTP). Nevertheless, the handler API provides for handlers with asynchronous responses to their requests. If you've included asynchronous calls in your programs before, you'll be happy to know that you use the same programming model to implement those calls against the handler.

In our case, that means a call to the handler is made and the request is processed asynchronously, waiting for a callback to be made signaling that the process is at an end and the response can be written back to the client. For example, a handler service adjudicating a game of battleships would respond asynchronously to each client in turn, waiting for one to make a move before it responded to the previous move from the other.

Your asynchronous handler class will inherit four methods from *IHttpAsyncHandler*:

- ***BeginProcessRequest(HttpContext context, AsyncCallback cb, Object extraData)*** This method starts the processing of the request. It takes as arguments the *HttpContext* object for the request, the method to be called back when the processing is complete, and any extra data needed to complete the processing. It returns an *IAsyncResult* object containing the current status of the process.
- ***EndProcessRequest(IAsyncResult result)*** This method performs any cleanup required after the request has been processed. It takes as an argument the current status of the processing.
- ***IsReusable* and *ProcessRequest(HttpContext context)*** These methods are inherited from *IHttpHandler* and work in the same way. Note that *ProcessRequest* must be present but doesn't need to be called.

We'll cover asynchronous Web service programming at the Web method level in Chapter 7. You'll find a simple example of an asynchronous handler in the .NET Framework documentation at *ms-help://MS.NETFrameworkSDK/cpguidenf/html/cpconhttphandlerregistration.htm*. You'll also find a full introduction to asynchronous programming in the SDK at *ms-help://MS.NETFrameworkSDK/cpguidenf/html/cpovrasynchronousprogrammingoverview.htm*.

IHttpHandlerFactory

As the name *IHttpHandlerFactory* suggests, a class that implements this interface is not a handler in itself but offers an alternative (and arguably more elegant) way to deal with requests into a Web service. Thus far, we've developed a handler that discerns how the service is being requested and calls a method to give an appropriate response. A handler factory class discerns how the service is being requested and creates a handler to give the appropriate response—a similar tactic but with different implications. In the former situation, we're reusing large handler objects designed to deal with all eventualities. In the latter, we're reusing much smaller handlers built for a specific request—HTTP-GET, HTTP-POST, synchronous, asynchronous, and so on. When you scale up the number of requests and performance becomes an issue, the *HandlerFactory* might be the way to go.

IHttpHandlerFactory contains two methods:

- *GetHandler(HttpContext context, string requestType, string url, string pathTranslated)*, which returns a handler object to the pipeline that will process the given request. It takes as parameters the *HttpContext* object for the current request, the HTTP request type (GET, POST, and so on), and the location of the requested file given as a URL and local file path.
- *ReleaseHandler(IHttpHandler handler)*, which releases a handler no longer being used back to the factory class so it can be reused when required.

Like *ProcessRequest* in our handler classes thus far, *GetHandler* might well need only a couple of *if* statements to figure out what it needs to do, as in this example:

```
class HandlerFactory : IHttpHandlerFactory
{
    ⋮
    public IHttpHandler GetHandler(HttpContext context,
        string requestType, String url, String pathTranslated)
    {
        IHttpHandler handlerToReturn;
        switch (requestType.ToLower())
        {
            case "get":
                handlerToReturn = new HttpGetHandler();
                break;
            case "post":
                switch (context.Request.ContentType)
                {
                    case "text/plain":
                    case "application/x-www-form-urlencoded":
                        handlerToReturn = new HttpPostHandler();
                        break;
                    case "text/xml":
                        handlerToReturn = new HttpSoapHandler();
                        break;
                    default:
                        throw new Exception
                            ("Plain text, form or SOAP POST requests "
                                + "only please.");
                }
                break;
```

```
                default:
                    throw new Exception("GET or POST requests "
                        + "only please");
            }
            return handlerToReturn;
        }
        :
}
```

The logic here works in exactly the same way as in previous examples; it's left to you to implement each of the handler classes (which inherit from *IHttpHandler* or *IHttpAsyncHandler*, of course). Likewise, you can register an association between the factory class and a file extension in your web.config in the same way you did with "single" handler classes.

Coding Differences Between the Handler API and the Web Method API

Using variations on the code shown thus far, your handler-cum-service should now be parsing requests and generating responses without a problem. The question is what to do with the message after it has been parsed. Any further code you write inside your handler should be identical to the code written at the Web method level because you're past the serialization stage that the built-in handler takes cares of for you in normal use, shouldn't it?

Yes and no. The Web method API still has a few "weaknesses" that you can fix by using the handler API instead. Two of the weaknesses are in the interchange between client proxy class and service:

- As Scott Short demonstrates in his book *Building XML Web Services for the .NET Platform* (Microsoft Press, 2002), ASP.NET is "somewhat inconsistent when handling parameters passed by reference to a Web method through a proxy class. Web methods can lose both the identities and the values of parameters passed by reference before they are passed back to the client."
- Only the return parameter can be passed back to the client. ASP.NET doesn't support encoding in/out or out parameters within the message returned to the client as a result of an HTTP GET or POST request.

You should also be aware of some differences when you work with the *HttpContext* object for the current request. When you work with the Web method API, having your class inherit from *System.Web.WebServices.WebService* usually gives you access to the standard ASP.NET objects that you already have access to in the handler API via the context object passed through to the *ProcessRequest* method. Likewise, you can usually access the context object using the static *HttpContext.Current* property as well. However, any methods marked as *OneWay* by the *[SoapRpcMethod]* or *[SoapDocumentMethod]* attributes do not get access to the *HttpContext* object at all. Furthermore, the Web method API never gains access to the *Request* or *Response* property of the *HttpContext* object, as the handler API does.

There's also the small issue of creating the WSDL file and some documentation for your service. At 62 KB, the Web method API's defaultwsdlgenerator.aspx is one of the most involved pages you'll come across—imitating it probably isn't worth it. Instead, roll your own WSDL and documentation for each service or group of methods.

Taking Care with Session State

Last but not least are a couple of provisos when you want to make use of session state variables within your services or handlers. A page request from a browser to a server includes the Session ID in either the URI if it's a GET request or in an HTTP header if it's a POST request. Logically, it follows that you should be able to parallel this and keep the Session ID either in the URI or in the SOAP header to keep track of the session associated with the request, but neither method is supported by the Web method API.

Of course, if you use a custom client and handler, you can roll our own state management solution, using whichever implementation suits the situation best. On the server side, session and application-level variables are accessed just as they are on a standard ASP.NET page. The only trick to be aware of is to mark your class as needing access to those variables. This you can do by implementing one of two interfaces:

- *IReadOnlySessionState*, which denotes that your class doesn't need to alter session state variables but does need to read them
- *IRequiresSessionState*, which denotes that your class requires both read and write access to the Web application's session state variables

Neither interface contains any methods.

Custom Clients

Back in Figure 5-1, you saw that the proxy class you can generate from a Web service's WSDL file also abstracts over a pair of message processing and serialization routines. Like those on the server side, they might become undesirable, too, so you need to know how to write our own proxy classes for the client.

The process is a great deal like working on the server side except you're working with the *System.Net* namespace rather than *System.Web*. As Figure 5-8 shows, it's just a case of knowing which objects to work with.

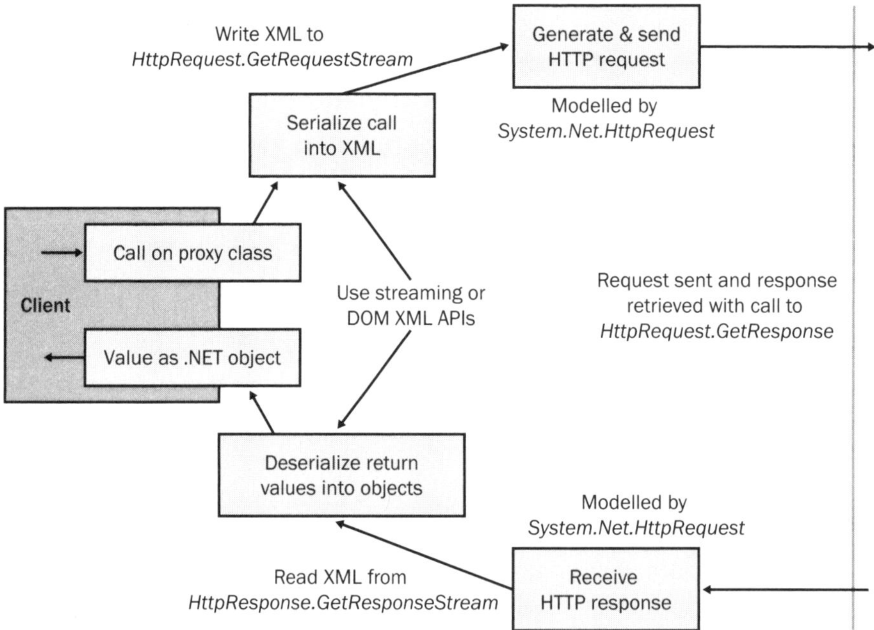

Figure 5-8 You can implement the client-side interaction with Web services using *System.Net.*

- You read and write the SOAP requests and responses by using the streaming and DOM APIs in the same way you do on the server. Of course, we're now writing the request and reading the response.
- An HTTP request is modeled by *System.Net.HttpWebRequest*. The standard HTTP headers are given as class properties, and any non-standard ones, such as SOAPAction, can be appended to its *Headers* collection. You can retrieve the stream that will contain the HTTP request body by using the *HttpWebRequest* object's *GetRequest-Stream* method.

- Once the request has been prepared, you send it using the *HttpWebRequest.GetResponse* method. This returns a *HttpWebResponse* object that represents the corresponding response from the server.
- You can retrieve the stream containing the SOAP response in the body of the HTTP message by using the *HttpWebResponse.GetResponseStream* method.

Let's take an example and see this in action. We'll build a client for *SchemaHandler1.ashx*, which we built earlier. If you'll recall, the handler expects a SOAP request containing the name of an album and the artist that recorded it and returns a message string saying whether the operation was successful on the server. From a user-interface point of view, the client is very simple (as shown in Figure 5-9). We need a couple of text boxes where the user can enter the album (*txtAlbum*) and artist (*txtArtist*) details, a submit button (*btnGo*) to send the SOAP request, and some means of displaying the results. In this case, we've chosen a simple label control (*lblResponse*) to display them verbatim.

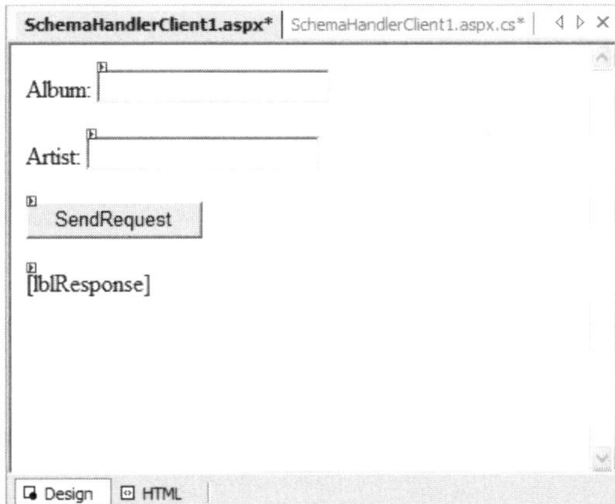

Figure 5-9 The user-interface elements of the client don't need to be very complex.

The submit button's *Click* event handler sets everything in motion and neatly abstracts the steps needed on the client into three simple operations:

```
private void btnGo_Click(object sender, System.EventArgs e)
{
```

First we create an *HttpWebRequest* object for our message with the static method *Create* inherited from its parent class. *WebRequest* is an abstract class built without any specific transport protocol in mind, so we need to cast it to an instance of its subclass:

```
    //Create web request object
    HttpWebRequest soapRequest = (HttpWebRequest)WebRequest.Create(
        "http://localhost/wscr/"
        + "05/schemahandler/SchemaHandler1.ashx");
```

Then it's a case of building the request and retrieving the response for display:

```
    HttpWebResponse soapResponse = BuildAndSendSOAPRequest(soapRequest);
    lblResponse.Text = ReadDocument(soapResponse.GetResponseStream());
}
```

Building an HTTP request containing a SOAP message requires the same actions as building a SOAP message but with the addition of setting the HTTP headers as required. The *BuildAndSendSOAPRequest* method in our example client demonstrates this well:

```
private HttpWebResponse BuildAndSendSOAPRequest(HttpWebRequest webreq)
{
```

As mentioned earlier, the standard headers are exposed as read-write properties of the *HttpWebRequest* object and any custom headers must be added to the *Headers* collection. Here, of course, we need to add a SOAPAction header. It's worth noting that the *HttpWebRequest* object supports the use of cookies for a state management system via its *CookieContainer* property.

```
    //Add HTTP headers to request
    webreq.Method = "POST";
    webreq.ContentType = "text/xml";
    webreq.Headers.Add("SOAPAction", "AddRecord");
```

With the headers set as required, it's just a matter of flowing the contents of the HTTP message body into the stream exposed by *GetRequestStream*. In this case, that's the SOAP request we want to send, and we'll do that with an *XmlTextWriter* object:

```
    //Create XmlTextWriter to build SOAP request
    XmlTextWriter soapWriter =
        new XmlTextWriter(webreq.GetRequestStream(), Encoding.ASCII);

    //Write Xml Declaration
    soapWriter.WriteStartDocument();

    //Write SOAP Envelope and Body Elements
    soapWriter.WriteStartElement("env", "Envelope",
        "http://schemas.xmlsoap.org/soap/envelope/");
```

```
    soapWriter.WriteStartElement("Body",
        "http://schemas.xmlsoap.org/soap/envelope/");

    //Write AddRecord Element
    soapWriter.WriteStartElement("a", "AddRecord",
        "http://www.notashop.com/wscr");

    //Write Album and artist elements
    soapWriter.WriteElementString("album",
        "http://www.notashop.com/wscr", txtAlbum.Text);
    soapWriter.WriteElementString("artist",
        "http://www.notashop.com/wscr", txtArtist.Text);

    //End Element
    soapWriter.WriteEndElement();
    soapWriter.WriteEndElement();
    soapWriter.WriteEndElement();

       //End XML Document
    soapWriter.WriteEndDocument();
```

Once your message is complete, you post it to the target URI with a call to *GetResponse*. This returns a *WebResponse* object, which, as before, you can cast into an *HttpWebResponse* object to gain a little more control. Note that you must *Close* the *Writer* object before you call *GetResponse* or it will return an exception.

```
    //Write to file and close
    soapWriter.Close();

    return (HttpWebResponse)webreq.GetResponse();
}
```

If the server fails to respond or returns a status code other than 200 OK, *GetResponse* throws a *WebException*, which you can handle in a *try/catch* block. *WebException* objects have two properties beyond those of a generic *Exception* object that are useful to us:

- *Response*, which contains the actual error message from the server
- *Status*, which contains the HTTP response code that the server sent back

Assuming that all has gone well, our client now has a reply from the server encapsulated in an *HttpWebRequest* object, the body of which is available as a *Stream* from its *GetResponseStream* method. In our simple client, we call a method that pulls out the entire SOAP message from the stream and sends it to the waiting label control:

```
lblResponse.Text = ReadDocument(soapResponse.GetResponseStream());
⋮
private string ReadDocument(Stream ResponseStream)
{
    XmlTextReader responseReader = new XmlTextReader(ResponseStream);
    responseReader.MoveToContent();
    string XmlString = responseReader.ReadOuterXml();
    responseReader.Close();
    return XmlString;
}
```

The SOAP tags are ignored by the browser, but the text message—whether success or error—is not, so we have our feedback from the service. It's a quick hack but demonstrates the idea nicely. In real-world situations, you can parse the results of the response back out into your application using either of the XML APIs we've discussed, or you might use XSL to transform it into something more pleasing to the eye.

Summary

In this chapter, you learned that the .NET Framework contains a second, lower-level handler API with which you can create Web services. Because it works at a lower level, it offers more control over how the service works with requests and responses, but you are not given any help behind the scenes as you are with the higher-level Web method API. On the other hand, the Web method API has several weaknesses that can be remedied if you use handlers instead.

You also learned how ASP.NET models its request pipeline, the endpoint of which is the handler. In Chapter 10, you'll see how you can use HTTP modules to extend the Web method API, and in Chapter 13 you'll learn how the Web Services Enhancements 1.0 kit sits over the pipeline to implement new features for Web services developers—such as routing and better security.

6

Writing Schemas for Your Services

Have you ever talked to people with really thick regional accents? They might be offering you a drink, but by the time you realize that, they'll already have bought themselves a round, missed you out, and it'll be your turn next.

"England and America are two countries separated by the same language."

—George Bernard Shaw

As Shaw suggests, there are even larger problems than accent. The word *pants*, for example, means different things in the United States than in the U.K.; unless you get the context right, your words might be misconstrued.

The same problem happens with Web services. Both client and server speak in SOAP, but they might disagree on the XML grammar used in the message payload—the context, if you will. Fortunately for Web service developers, there's a way to specify the message's context as it is sent to and from the client—by writing a schema for the message and obeying the rules that schema lays out.

In this chapter, then, we'll look at the following topics:

- The importance of schemas to Web service developers and to communication between client and server
- The components of a schema and how to write a schema for your messages

- Incorporating a schema into a Web service
- Implementing the .NET Framework equivalent of writing a Web service schema explicitly: annotating your classes

Alas for tourists, there's no real equivalent to a schema for dealing with regional accents or local idioms. Polite laughter and respect for your host are the best you can do to get "back in context."

The Role of Schemas in Web Services

Exactly what role do schemas play in Web services? Well, a client already knows the basic structure of a SOAP message because it's the same (*<envelope>*, *<header>*, *<body>*) whatever Web service it's calling. What it doesn't know is how the message payload should be structured or typed or how a response will be phrased in return. Schemas allow you to specify that structure, and by including the schemas for both request and response messages in the service's WSDL document, you give the client easy access to this information. On the server side, using schemas to define your message payload means you can validate your messages and use reflection to generate documentation and class definitions for your service.

Schemas also let you strongly type each element of the request and response. This is important for two reasons:

- You can ensure that the right kind of information is stored in each element. For example, if an element is set to an integer, you can check that its text content can be cast to an integer rather than a double and has no alphabetical characters. You can't calculate the area of a square if its height has been sent to you as "52 rabbits"—that would make no sense.
- You can arbitrate between platforms how the value should be stored. Consider the situation in which a .NET server sends a value of type *Integer* back to a Visual Basic 6.0 client. In Visual Basic 6.0, an *Integer* is a 16-bit number, but in Visual Basic .NET, it's 32-bit. If 32 bits are sent when 16 bits are expected, you'll get overflow errors unless the service can state categorically that it will be sending a 32-bit number to the client, which can adjust accordingly.

You can arbitrate between platforms because the XML Schema specification includes its own platform-neutral type system—the XML Schema Definition (XSD) type system. Defined as part of the XML Schema 1.0 standard that was released in May 2001 (*http://www.w3.org/TR/xmlschema-2/*), the XSD type system includes a set of 47 predefined types (described in full in Appendix A) and a language for defining new types, which we'll look at shortly.

You can create a schema for your Web service in two ways:

- Write one explicitly in your text editor or IDE
- Write one implicitly by tagging your service class with the special attributes that the .NET Framework makes available

If you choose the first approach, you can use a nice little .NET tool called xsd.exe that takes your schema and generates bare server and client classes for a Web service whose messages obey that schema. However, the second option requires less work to incorporate the schema into the service (it's just an extension of using the Web method API introduced in Chapter 2), but it doesn't give you as much control as writing your own schema.

> **Note** As noted in Chapter 2, if you're writing a service that uses Section 5 encoding, the message structure will be influenced by SOAP's own encoding rules. More on this later.

Writing a Schema Explicitly

A schema is just like any other XML document—it has a root element, it should be well formed and valid, and so on—but a schema's purpose is unique. You are rigidly defining the contents of a namespace in XML—that is, the valid elements in the namespace and the types of those elements. You can define elements that contain text or have attributes and are considered to be of a simple type. You can define elements that contain other elements and are considered to be of a complex type. Either way, you have to define the elements and their types.

A single schema typically defines all the contents of a namespace, but several schemas can work together for the same purpose, much as multiple cascading style sheets can define the style of an HTML page.

XML documents written to obey schemas are called *schema instance documents*. SOAP messages are fine examples of schema instance documents—they need the SOAP schema to validate the SOAP message framework, and they need your schema to validate the message payload. As the name suggests, the relationship between schema and instance document is comparable to that of class and object. One is an instance of the other.

The Root *<schema>* Element

At the root of all schemas is the *<schema>* element. It has several attributes that you can use to "reference" other schemas and define the shape of the instance documents that will follow the schema. Every type and element definition you write for the schema will be a descendent of this element. The following code illustrates the use of the *<schema>* element:

```
<xs:schema targetNamespace="http://www.notashop.com/wscr"
  elementFormDefault="qualified"
  attributeFormDefault="qualified"
  xmlns:tns="http://www.notashop.com/wscr"
  xmlns:xs="http://www.w3.org/2001/XMLSchema"
>
  <!-- all type and element definitions go here -->
</xs:schema>
```

The key tasks in this code are to identify the namespace whose contents the schema is defining—by using the *targetNamespace* attribute—and to reference your new types and elements within the schema—by using the *xmlns* attribute to set a prefix for the namespace. By convention, this prefix is usually *tns*—short for target namespace. You can also add references to any other schemas that yours will use, by using *xmlns* as you would in any other XML document. For example, to use the built-in *xsd* types, you include the line *xmlns:xs="http://www.w3.org/2001/ XMLSchema"*. Note that *xs* and *xsd* are the usual prefixes for the XSD schema. Table 6-1 describes the two namespaces most commonly used with schemas.

Table 6-1 Schema and Schema Instance Namespace URLs

Namespace URL	Description
http://www.w3.org/2001/XMLSchema	References all the possible constructs in a schema document
http://www.w3.org/2001/XMLSchema-instance	References all the schema constructs allowed in a schema instance document

With our namespaces defined in the schema, we can also specify whether the elements and attributes in our schema's instance documents should be qualified with a prefix, by using the *elementFormDefault* and *attributeFormDefault* attributes of the *<schema>* element—that is, we specify whether the elements and attributes will be part of a namespace other than the default one. By default, *elementFormDefault* and *attributeFormDefault* are both set to *unqualified*, which means they will not. Setting them to *qualified*, as in our example, means they will. Note that you can override this default setting on a per-element or per-attribute basis by using their *form* attribute. (More on this later.)

> **Tip** .NET strays from the schema standard in the default setting for the *elementFormDefault* attribute. The schema generator used by the .NET Web services framework sets *elementFormDefault* to *qualified* by default.

Chapter 5 noted that qualifying every element and doing away with the default namespace in an XML document is a good thing. This is doubly true when you work with schemas, for two reasons:

- Everything declared in a schema is either part of the given *targetNamespace* or is not part of any namespace. Qualifying your declarations should remind you of this.
- You risk some troublesome scoping issues when you define elements that contain other elements. We'll discuss them later when we come to complex types, but these risks are removed if you do not rely on a default namespace.

Associating Schemas with Instance Documents

Before we start defining types and elements, let's consider a couple of other questions posed in Chapter 5: How do we associate an instance document with its schema? And how do we find the actual schema for a given namespace?

Annoyingly, there is no standard way of doing either, but typically the first problem is tackled programmatically at run time. For example, you've seen that we add schemas to an *XmlValidatingReader* object's *Schemas* property for the instance document to be validated against. The only trick is to find the actual schema document. A few schemas can be found at the location given by the namespace URL they represent—the SOAP schema is a good example. Others can be found by checking the instance document for an *xsi:schemaLocation* attribute, as in this example:

```
<a:AddRecord xmlns:a="http://www.notashop.com/wscr"
  xmlns:xsi="http://www.w3.org/2001/XMLSchema-instance"
```

```
  xsi:schemaLocation="http://www.notashop.com/wscr/AlbumEntry.xsd">
  <a:album>Devin Townsend</a:album>
  <a:artist>Accelerated Evolution</a:artist>
</a:AddRecord>
```

The *schemaLocation* attribute is a whitespace-delimited list of namespaces in the instance document and the locations of the schemas that govern them. Again, your schema validator might not know what to do with the hints you provide, but as Chapter 5 showed, you have some space in the handler API to remedy this. You can also use an *xsi:noNamespaceSchemaLocation* attribute to reference schemas with no namespaces, but again you should avoid defining elements without namespaces for reasons we've already given.

Declaring Elements

You define new elements in your namespace by using the *<element>* element in a schema. At a minimum, you supply a *name* for the element and the *type* of information it contains. Your new name must follow XML naming conventions, and its type should be one of the 47 XSD types documented in Appendix A or a custom type defined in this schema or another schema. For example

```
<xs:element type="xs:string" name="album" />
<xs:element type="xs:gYear" name="yearOfRelease" />
```

Elements declared as children of the *<schema>* element are considered *global declarations* and can be used in other schemas and anywhere else in the same schema. If an element is declared as a child of some other part of the schema (usually a type definition), it is considered *local* to that part and cannot be referenced outside of it. With respect to SOAP messages, your schema should contain definitions for the root elements of both the request messages and the response messages your Web service will use. For instance, have another look at the WSDL file for the first Web service we created in this book, *http://localhost/wscr/01/simple1.asmx?wsdl*. You'll find the following:

```
<s:schema elementFormDefault="qualified"
  targetNamespace="http://www.notashop.com/wscr">
  <s:element name="WakeUp">
    ⋮
  </s:element>
  <s:element name="WakeUpResponse">
    ⋮
  </s:element>
</s:schema>
```

Don't forget that you're writing a schema to reflect the messages you want sent between client and server. Stay true to that.

Adding Restrictions

Once you declare the basic element, you can add the following basic attributes to it, which qualify how it will appear in instance documents that follow your schema:

- ***maxOccurs* and *minOccurs*** Govern how many times the element can appear in an instance document. By default, both are set to *1*, so the element can appear only once.
- ***default*** Specifies a default value for an element, where it is possible to give one.
- ***fixed*** Specifies a fixed value for an element, where it is possible to give one. Note that *default* and *fixed* cannot be used together for the same element.
- ***form*** Specifies whether this element must be fully qualified by a namespace URL in an instance document. This is the per-element override for the schema's *elementFormDefault* attribute you saw earlier. You can set the *form* attribute to *qualified* or *unqualified*.

Note that *maxOccurs* and *minOccurs* can be applied only to local element declarations. Likewise, there's no need to set *form* to *qualified* for the root elements of your instance documents because this is assumed to be the case. Let's expand on the ideas in Chapter 2 for adding band and album details to a music database:

```
<xs:element type="xs:gYear" name="yearOfRelease" default="2003" />
<xs:element type="xs:string" name="formerBandName"
            minOccurs="0" maxOccurs="2"/>
```

In this example, *<yearOfRelease>* defaults to 2003 if it isn't specified in our album submission. Meanwhile, *<formerBandName>* is optional, but it can occur up to twice in one instance document to cover any names the band formerly used.

Empty and Nillable Elements

Just as you can define a variable to be empty or null, you can do the same with elements in your schema. An empty element in this case is one that has no text content or child elements, although it can have attributes—for example, *
*. This translates into *<xs:element>* either not having a *type* or having a *type* that has no local elements or text nodes. For example

```
<xs:element name="ThisIsEmpty" />
```

If you or your client need to convey the concept of a null value in your SOAP messages, you can identify in your schema which elements might need to be null by setting the *nillable* attribute of their *<element>* declaration to *true*. By default, this attribute is set to *false*. Therefore, if we want to make it possible but not mandatory to submit an album cover to our database, we can declare the element in this way in the schema:

```
<xs:element name="albumCover" nillable="true" type="xs:base64binary"/>
```

If a client doesn't have a scan of the cover to submit, it can translate the null value for the image into the following:

```
<a:albumCover xmlns:xsi="http://www.w3.org/2001/XMLSchema-instance"
              xmlns:a="http://www.notashop.com/wscr"
              xsi:nil="true" />
```

The *<albumCover>* element remains valid even though it doesn't contain a base64-encoded binary string because *xsi:nil* is set to *true*.

Declaring Attributes

You define attributes in much the same way as you do elements, except you use the *<attribute>* element in your schema. For example

```
<xs:attribute name="noOfPlayers" type="xs:byte" use="optional" />
<xs:attribute name="nationality" type="xs:string" default="British" />
```

Like *<element>*, *<attribute>* also has *name*, *type*, *form*, *default*, and *final* attributes, each with the purpose discussed earlier. *maxOccurs* and *minOccurs* are not used, however, because it can be assumed that you'll be using that attribute either once or not at all. In their place is the *use* attribute, which can be set to *optional*, *required*, or *prohibited*.

We can also make the same distinction between global and local attribute definitions. Attributes defined as children of the root *<schema>* element are global and can be referenced by other schemas and any type in the schemas that contains it. You should use the *ref* attribute rather than *name* if you want to reference a global attribute from another schema. For example

```
<xs:schema targetNamespace="http://www.notashop.com/wscr"
  xmlns:tns="http://www.notashop.com/wscr"
  xmlns:xs="http://www.w3.org/2001/XMLSchema"
  xmlns:soap="http://schemas.xmlsoap.org/soap/envelope/">
  <xs:attribute ref="soap:mustUnderstand" default="1" />
</xs:schema>
```

An instance document based against your schema can then validly use the *<soap:mustUnderstand>* attribute as your schema wants.

A local attribute definition is one given as a child of some element other than the root *<schema>* element, most likely a type definition. Like local element definitions, they are specific to that type and cannot be referenced elsewhere.

Declaring Custom Types

So far, we've assumed that the types of the elements and attributes in our SOAP messages all correspond to one of the built-in XSD types, but that won't always be the case. One of the most powerful aspects of the XSD type system is that it lets you derive custom types from those already defined and reuse those types, much as you do in .NET. Custom types are neatly divided into two categories:

- **Simple types** These describe textual data. That is, they can be applied only to text-only elements or attributes. They are derivations of other simple types by restriction, by list, or by union.
- **Complex types** These describe structured data. That is, they contain attributes and other elements to create a nested structure in an instance document.

As shown in Appendix A, the built-in XSD types are all simple types derived from one root type called *anyType*. Each derived type is a restriction of its parent. For example, the definition of the *byte* type shows that it is just a subset of the values allowed in the *short* type.

Custom Simple Types

You can create your own simple types as restrictions, lists, and unions of existing simple types. In our music database scenario, this is useful in several cases. For example, we can assume that we won't be including records issued during or before World War II, so we can create a new type to reflect this:

```
<xs:schema targetNamespace="http://www.notashop.com/wscr"
    xmlns:tns="http://www.notashop.com/wscr"
    xmlns:xs="http://www.w3.org/2001/XMLSchema">

  <xs:element name="yearOfRelease" type="tns:postWar" />
  <xs:simpleType name="postWar">
    <xs:restriction base="xs:gYear">
        <xs:minExclusive value="1945" />
    </xs:restriction>
  </xs:simpleType>
</xs:schema>
```

In this case, we've defined a type called *postwar*, which is a restricted version of the *gYear* data type, denoted by the *<restriction>* element's *base* attribute. Values of this type can only be years from 1946 onward. Note that when we create an element of that type, we reference it as *tns:postWar*. Don't forget that we are defining types within a target namespace and that they must be fully qualified in a schema so they aren't treated as part of another namespace or as having no namespace at all.

In our example, we've used the *minExclusive* constraint to define how the original type will be restricted to create ours. There are actually 12 of these constraints, or *facets*, as they are properly known, as listed in Table 6-2.

Table 6-2 Schema Simple Type Constraints

Facet	Description
enumeration	Allows you to create a set of literal values that elements of that type might be given. This mirrors the .NET *enum* construct.
fractionDigits	Sets the maximum number of digits a number can have to the right of the decimal point. Must be equal to or less than the value for *totalDigits* if both are used in the same restriction.
length	Specifies the number of characters in a string, number of items in a list, or number of octets in a binary type. This facet cannot be used with *minLength* or *maxLength*.
maxExclusive	Sets a boundary that values of the new type cannot equal or exceed. *maxExclusive* must be less than the maximum value of the original type.
maxInclusive	Sets a boundary that values of the new type cannot exceed but can equal. *maxInclusive* must be less than the maximum value of the original type.
maxLength	Sets an upper limit on the length of a value in the new type. Applies to strings, lists, and binary types.
minExclusive	Sets a boundary that values of the new type cannot equal or be less than. *minExclusive* must be greater than the minimum value of the original type.
minInclusive	Sets a boundary that values of the new type cannot be less than but can equal. *minInclusive* must be greater than the minimum value of the original type.
minLength	Sets the lower limit for the length of a value in the new type. Applies to strings, lists, and binary types.
pattern	Introduces a regular expression pattern that values of the new type must match.

Table 6-2 Schema Simple Type Constraints

Facet	Description
totalDigits	Sets the maximum total number of digits a number can have. Must be greater than or equal to the value of *fractionDigits* if both are used in the same restriction.
whiteSpace	Defines how whitespace characters are treated inside string-based types. This attribute has three possible values: ***preserve*** Whitespace characters remain as written. ***replace*** All carriage return, line feed, and tab characters are turned into space characters. ***collapse*** Same as *replace*, but with all leading and trailing spaces removed and any sequence of two or more spaces reduced to one.

If you take a look at Appendix A, you'll see that each XSD type entry includes a list of the facets that are applicable to it. You can derive your own simple type by using those facets to restrict the XSD type. As long as the facets are valid for your base type, you can use a combination of them to create your custom type.

> **Tip** You can specify patterns on types, but you cannot specify a restriction on an element based on the value of another element. This is beyond the capabilities of schemas. Extension projects such as Schematron.NET (*http://sourceforge.net/projects/dotnetopensrc*), however, allow these additional checks to be made.

From a Web service point of view, it's easier to serialize custom simple types, which are restrictions of their base types, than types that are unions or lists. Take, for example, an enumerated type:

```
<xs:element name="albumFormat" type="tns:formatTypes" />
<xs:simpleType name="formatTypes">
  <xs:restriction base="xs:string">
    <xs:enumeration value="CD" />
    <xs:enumeration value="Tape" />
    <xs:enumeration value="Vinyl" />
    <xs:enumeration value="Minidisc" />
  </xs:restriction>
</xs:simpleType>
```

As noted before, this new type would map very well to a .NET *enum* construct. The *<albumFormat>* element defined here can take one of the four given values as its text value. However, if the element contains a list of enumerated values, as shown here, we're a little stuck:

```
<xs:element name="albumFormats" type="tns:formatList" />
<xs:simpleType name="formatList">
  <xs:list itemType="tns:format" />
</xs:simpleType>
```

Deriving by list means that elements of this new type might contain several values in the base type, separated by some whitespace character. In our example, then, valid values for the element *<albumFormats>* include:

```
<x:albumFormats>CD Vinyl</x:albumFormats>
<x:albumFormats>Tape Minidisc CD</x:albumFormats>
```

There is no .NET type that translates directly to or from a list such as this, other than a string. We have the same translation problems if we create a new simple type by *union*:

```
<xs:simpleType name="dayAndDate">
  <xs:union memberTypes="xs:string xs:date" />
</xs:simpleType>
```

An element of type *tns:dayAndDate* is hard to translate into a single .NET variable that can store the same data with the same meaning.

Complex Types

You've seen how to define elements, attributes, and simple types. By creating new complex types, you can combine all three and start to build a rich and meaningful set of messages for your Web services. For example, the SOAP schema defines a SOAP *<envelope>* element to contain a header, a body, and a section following the body that can contain anything at all. It can also contain any attribute defined in a different schema. Here's a portion of the SOAP Envelope schema:

```
<xs:element name="Envelope" type="tns:Envelope" />
<xs:complexType name="Envelope" >
  <xs:sequence>
    <xs:element ref="tns:Header" minOccurs="0" />
    <xs:element ref="tns:Body" minOccurs="1" />
    <xs:any namespace="##other" minOccurs="0"
      maxOccurs="unbounded" processContents="lax" />
  </xs:sequence>
  <xs:anyAttribute namespace="##other" processContents="lax" />
</xs:complexType>
```

We'll come to the wildcard elements, *<any>* and *<anyAttribute>*, in a moment, but let's first turn to the *<complexType>* element. Every complex type definition in a schema starts with a *<complexType>* element, which can be given a *name* if it is a global type declaration to be used elsewhere. Under this element, we can specify one of three ways to construct our complex type:

- ***<sequence>*** Defines the order in which the child elements must appear, if they appear at all
- ***<choice>*** Defines a group of elements from which exactly one might appear in the instance document
- ***<all>*** Denotes that all of the elements defined will appear, but that they might appear in any order as subelements of the complex typed element

Your chosen construction method should be written in as the child element of *<complexType>* and contain the group of elements that the complex type encompasses. For example, we could define the request message payload element for our album submission Web service as follows:

```
<xs:element name="albumSubmission" type="tns:albumEntryType" />
<xs:complexType name="albumEntryType">
  <xs:sequence>
    <xs:element ref="tns:artist" minOccurs="1" />
    <xs:element ref="tns:album" minOccurs="1" />
    <xs:element name="releaseDate" type="tns:dayAndDate" />
  </xs:sequence>
</xs:complexType>
```

Our incoming messages would then all have to look something like this:

```
<a:albumSubmission xmlns:a="http://www.notashop.com/wscr">
  <a:artist>Helmet</a:artist>
  <a:album>Meantime</a:album>
  <a:releaseDate>June 1991</a:releaseDate>
</a:albumSubmission>
```

Note that we have quite a few options when defining the group of elements within the sequence. We can

- Reuse a global element by using *ref*
- Define a new local element by using *name*
- Nest another *sequence* or *choice* (but not *all*) group within the current one
- Include wildcards in place of elements

As you saw in the definition of the SOAP *<envelope>* element, you can use *<any>* as a wildcard to indicate that any element can appear in its place given certain constraints that are expressed as the attributes of *<any>*, as shown in Table 6-3.

Table 6-3 Wildcard Constraints

Attribute	Default Value	Description
maxOccurs	*1*	Specifies the maximum number of times elements satisfying the wildcard can appear in an instance of this type in this context. *maxOccurs* can be set to *unbounded* or any number greater than or equal to 0.
minOccurs	*1*	Specifies the minimum number of times elements satisfying the wildcard can appear in an instance of this type in this context. The value for *minOccurs* must be equal to or less than that of *maxOccurs*.
namespace	*##any*	Specifies which namespace the element(s) taking the place of the wildcard must belong to. This attribute has five possible values: ***##target-Namespace*** Elements from the target namespace given in the schema can be used. ***##local*** Only elements with no namespace can be used. ***URI*** Only elements from the given namespace URI can be used. ***##other*** Any elements defined in a namespace other than the schema's target namespace can be used. ***##any*** Any element, with or without a namespace, can be used.
processContents	*strict*	Specifies whether the validator should locate the appropriate schema to validate elements replacing the wildcard. There are three possible values. ***lax*** Validate the elements if the appropriate schema is available; otherwise, don't worry about them. ***skip*** Don't try to validate the elements. ***strict*** The validator must locate the schema for the element and validate it.

If you'll recall the definition of a SOAP envelope that you saw earlier, we can decode the first wildcard stuck after the SOAP *<body>* element:

```
<xs:any namespace="##other" minOccurs="0"
        maxOccurs="unbounded" processContents="lax" />
```

This code states that a SOAP envelope can contain any number of elements after the *<body>* element as long as they are not elements from the SOAP namespace. If any elements are present in a SOAP message that is to be validated, they will be validated if a schema is at hand; with no schema present, the validator will just carry on as if the message is valid.

In addition to subelements, we can also use our *<complexType>* definition to attach attributes to an element. If we need to do this, our attribute declarations must follow the *<sequence>*, *<choice>*, or *<all>* construction defined in the complex type. For example, we can add a *sender* attribute to our album submission to identify who sent us the information:

```
<xs:complexType name="albumEntryType">
  <xs:sequence>
    ⋮
  </xs:sequence>
  <xs:attribute name="sender" type="tns:emailAddress" use="required" />
</xs:complexType>
```

There is also a wildcard for attributes that we can add to a complex type called *<anyAttribute>*. You saw this in action in the SOAP schema. We can control how wild *<anyAttribute>* is with the *namespace* and *processContents* attributes as defined in Table 6-3. *minOccurs* and *maxOccurs* do not exist for *<anyAttribute>*.

Simple, Mixed, and Complex Content in Complex Types

Thus far, we've looked solely at complex types that contain only child elements and possibly attributes. However, complex types can also contain a text value. A type's content can be categorized based on the different combinations of child elements, attributes, and text values that it can have, as follows:

- ***Complex content*** Child elements and possible attributes
- ***Simple content*** Attributes and optionally a text element
- ***Mixed content*** Child elements, a text element, and optionally some attributes

Unless told otherwise, a schema validator assumes that a complex type definition contains complex content. This is not difficult to remember, but if need be, we can make this statement explicit by adding a *<complexContent>* element around our group of child elements:

```
<xs:element name="albumSubmission" type="tns:albumEntryType" />
<xs:complexType name="albumEntryType">
  <xs:complexContent>
    <xs:extension>
```

```
        <xs:sequence>
          <xs:element ref="tns:artist" minOccurs="1" />
          <xs:element ref="tns:album" minOccurs="1" />
          <xs:element name="releaseDate" type="tns:dayAndDate" />
        </xs:sequence>
        <xs:attribute name="sender"
          type="tns:emailAddress" use="required" />
      </xs:extension>
    </xs:complexContent>
</xs:complexType>
```

Immediately inside *<complexContent>*, we must state whether the type is an extension or a restriction of its base type by using *<restriction>* or *<extension>* elements—for example, *<xs:restriction base="xs:albumInfo" />*. By default, the type is assumed to be an extension of its base type; if *base* is not specified, the base type is assumed to be *anyType*. All element groups and attribute definitions must be set inside the *<restriction>* or *<extension>* elements.

> **Important** Whether your new *complexType* is an extension or a restriction of its base type, the new type must be substitutable for its base type without any problems.

For complex types with simple content, we just replace *<complexContent>* with *<simpleContent>*:

```
<xs:element name="bandMember" type="tns:bandMemberType" />
<xs:complexType name="bandMemberType">
  <xs:simpleContent>
    <xs:extension base="xs:string">
      <xs:attribute name="plays" type="tns:instrument" />
    </xs:extension>
  </xs:simpleContent>
</xs:complexType>
```

This declaration states that the element *<bandMember>* will contain a string as text content and have an attribute called *plays* of type *tns:instrument*, as in this example:

```
<x:bandMember plays="guitar voice">Devin Townsend</x:bandMember>
```

A complex type with mixed content contains both subelements and text; you indicate this type by setting the *<complexType>* element's *mixed* attribute to *true*, as in this example:

```
<xs:complexType name="amixedType" mixed="true">
  <xs:sequence>
    <xs:element name="highlight" type="xs:string" />
  </xs:sequence>
</xs:complexType>
```

Complex types are serialized to classes and structures in .NET, so each subelement is translated into a data field or class member. Types containing mixed content are therefore seldom used, if at all, to define messages between services and their clients.

Anonymous Types

The simple and complex types we've defined to this point have all been global type declarations to be placed under the root *<schema>* element and referenced elsewhere by the names we've given them. However, it's entirely feasible to create local types without a name that are specific to a particular element. These types are anonymous and cannot be referenced elsewhere. For example, we can use two anonymous types to define the response from our album entry service:

```
<xs:element name="submissionReceipt">
```

The first defines the two elements that a response must contain:

```
  <xs:complexType>
    <xs:sequence>
      <xs:element name="message" type="xs:string" />
      <xs:element name="albumID">
```

The second defines a pattern for the value of *albumID*. In this case, *albumID* must contain a GUID:

```
        <xs:simpleType>
          <xs:restriction base="xs:string">
            <xs:pattern
              value="[0-9A-F]{8}-[0-9A-F]{4}-[0-9A-F]{4}-[0-9A-F]{4}-→
  [0-9A-F]{12}"
          </xs:restriction>
        </xs:simpleType>
      </xs:element>
    </xs:sequence>
  </xs:complexType>
</xs:element>
```

Element and Attribute Groups

You can use one other shortcut when writing your schema. If you're using the same set of elements or attributes in your complex types, you can define an element group by using *<group>* or define an attribute group by using an *<attributeGroup>* containing those items, and then you just reference the group. For example

```
<xs:element type="tns:albumType" name="album" />

<xs:complexType name="albumType">
  <xs:simpleContent>
    <xs:extension base="xs:string">
      <xs:attributeGroup ref="tns:albumProperties" />
    </xs:extension>
  </xs:simpleContent>
</xs:complexType>

<xs:attributeGroup name="albumProperties">
  <xs:attribute name="noOfTracks" type="xs:byte" />
  <xs:attribute name="runningTime" type="xs:duration" />
</xs:attributeGroup>
```

As with elements, attributes, and types, you can define groups with global scope so they can be reused elsewhere by referencing them with a *ref* instead of a *name*. Local group definitions remain specific to the definition in which they are created.

Namespace Scoping Issues

Earlier in this chapter, we mentioned a couple of potential namespace scoping issues that you might encounter if you rely on using default namespaces. Here's an example:

```
<xs:schema targetNamespace="http://www.notashop.com/wscr"
  xmlns:tns="http://www.notashop.com/wscr"
  xmlns:xs="http://www.w3.org/2001/XMLSchema">

  <xs:element type="xs:string" name="artist" />

  <xs:element name="albumSubmission">
    <xs:complexType>
      <xs:sequence>
        <xs:element ref="tns:artist" />
        <xs:element name="album" type="xs:string"/>
      </xs:sequence>
    </xs:complexType>
  </xs:element>
</xs:schema>
```

As you'll recall, everything declared in a schema is either part of the given *targetNamespace* or part of no namespace at all. All local declarations, such as that of *album*, fall into the latter category unless you set their *form* attribute to *qualified* or set the appropriate global *xxxFormDefault* attribute. If you do neither of these, creating instance documents becomes a little tricky.

The following code establishes nicely that the *<album>* element does not belong to the namespace *http://www.notashop.com/wscr*:

```
<x:albumSubmission xmlns:x="http://www.notashop.com/wscr">
  <x:artist>Tool</x:artist>
  <album>Lateralus</album>
</x:albumSubmission>
```

The distinction is lost if we use a default namespace:

```
<albumSubmission xmlns="http://www.notashop.com/wscr">
    <artist>Tool</artist>
    <album>Lateralus</album>
</albumSubmission>
```

This instance document is actually invalid because *<album>* is not associated with the default namespace—it is has no namespace at all. You can acknowledge this by changing the *<album>* element to read as follows:

```
<album xmlns="">Lateralus</album>
```

However, the neatest solution is to ensure that instances of local declarations are associated with the target namespace for the schema. That is, we set their *form* attribute or the appropriate global *xxxFormDefault* attribute to *qualified*. With this done in the schema, both examples become valid.

Advanced Schema Features

You've seen that defining new types means that the new type inherits the characteristics of the base type and either extends or restricts its definition. The XML Schema allows you to create an even richer inheritance model for instance documents in one of two ways:

- You can declare an element to be of an abstract base type and thus declare the instance of the element to be of one of the types that derives from the base type.
- You can specify a substitution group for an abstract type. An element of the base type will then take the form of one of the types in the substitution group.

To complement these polymorphic features, you can restrict which derived types an element can be assigned. You do this by specifying how the base type can be derived, if at all, and by blocking certain types of derivation on a per-element basis.

Unfortunately, because of a bug, the XML serializer library doesn't correctly form instance documents against schemas that use these features. Therefore, we'll skip the actual details for now. If you'd like to learn more about these schema features, check out Aaron Skonnard's article "Understanding XML Schema" at *http://msdn.microsoft.com/webservices.*

Incorporating a Schema into Your Web Service

Now that we've got our pristine schema that details request and response messages for our Web service, what do we do with it? How do we turn schemas into Web methods? Three approaches are available:

- Use the .NET Framework's XML Schema Definition tool, xsd.exe, to generate classes that mirror the schema. We can then create a Web service project as usual and add the classes to the project.
- Write a WSDL file around the schema and use .NET's wsdl.exe tool to generate the entire Web service code and a client proxy class as well, if required.
- Use xsd.exe to generate classes as described in the first suggestion, but continue to work in the handler API and create our own serialization solution. We can then continue to validate the messages against our schema as we receive them.

As you'll soon learn, the serializer's inability to capture all the subtleties of a schema that we've handwritten means that the most accurate way of incorporating our own schema as a blueprint for messages is the third suggestion in the list. However, if a schema is basic enough, the other two methods will be fine.

Using the XML Schema Definition Tool

The XML Schema Definition tool, or xsd.exe, generates .NET classes from schema files and generates schema files from .NET class libraries. To do this, it uses the same serializer as .NET's Web service framework.

To demonstrate how it works, we've prepared a pretty straightforward schema for our album submission service called AlbumService.xsd. You can find it in the code samples for this book. It looks like this:

```
<?xml version="1.0" encoding="utf-8" ?>
<xs:schema targetNamespace="http://www.notashop.com/wscr"
```

```
  elementFormDefault="qualified"
  xmlns:tns="http://www.notashop.com/wscr"
  xmlns:xs="http://www.w3.org/2001/XMLSchema">

  <!-- Root element and type for request messages -->
  <xs:element name="albumSubmission" type="tns:albumSubmission" />
  <xs:complexType name="albumSubmission">
    <xs:sequence minOccurs="1" maxOccurs="5">
      <xs:element name="artist" type="xs:string" />
      <xs:element name="album" type="tns:album" />
    </xs:sequence>
    <xs:attribute name="sender" type="xs:string" use="required" />
  </xs:complexType>

  <!-- Root element and type for response messages -->
  <xs:element name="submissionReceipt" type="tns:submissionReceipt" />
  <xs:complexType name="submissionReceipt">
    <xs:sequence minOccurs="1" maxOccurs="5">
      <xs:element name="message" type="xs:string" />
      <xs:element name="albumID">
        <xs:simpleType>
          <xs:restriction base="xs:string">
            <xs:pattern
              value="[0-9A-F]{8}(-[0-9A-F]{4}){3}-[0-9A-F]{12}" />
          </xs:restriction>
        </xs:simpleType>
      </xs:element>
    </xs:sequence>
  </xs:complexType>

  <!-- Other Global declarations -->
  <xs:attributeGroup name="albumProperties">
    <xs:attribute name="noOfTracks"
                  type="xs:unsignedByte" use="required" />
    <xs:attribute name="runningTime"
                  type="xs:duration" use="optional" />
  </xs:attributeGroup>

  <xs:complexType name="album">
    <xs:simpleContent>
      <xs:extension base="xs:string">
        <xs:attributeGroup ref="tns:albumProperties" />
      </xs:extension>
    </xs:simpleContent>
  </xs:complexType>
</xs:schema>
```

Our goal here is to generate .NET classes that reflect each complex type for inclusion in our Web service. Xsd.exe is command-line only, so open up the Visual Studio .NET command prompt from the Start menu and navigate to where you've stored the schema. Now type enter the following command and press Enter:

```
xsd.exe /classes AlbumService.xsd
```

If all goes well, you'll be presented with a new file, AlbumService.cs, containing our new classes. For example, the complex type for our *<albumSubmission>* element has been translated into the following tagged class:

```
[System.Xml.Serialization.XmlTypeAttribute(
    Namespace="http://www.notashop.com/wscr")]
[System.Xml.Serialization.XmlRootAttribute(
    Namespace="http://www.notashop.com/wscr", IsNullable=false)]
public class albumSubmission {

    [System.Xml.Serialization.XmlElementAttribute("artist")]
    public string[] artist;

    [System.Xml.Serialization.XmlElementAttribute("album")]
    public album[] album;

    [System.Xml.Serialization.XmlAttributeAttribute()]
    public string sender;
}
```

You saw the serialization tags for Web service classes in Chapter 2, and we'll look at them again in the next section, but for now note how the multiple occurrences of artist and album are accommodated as arrays. This is the standard way of translating elements that can appear more than once in an instance document into a .NET type.

Create a new C# Web service project in Visual Studio .NET called xsdToService at *http://localhost/wscr/06*. All you need to do is copy the classes in AlbumService.cs over to xsdToService.asmx.cs and write a Web method that makes use of them. For clarity's sake, we've written one here that returns a simple message and GUID to the client for each album and artist submitted:

```
[WebMethod]
public submissionReceipt SubmitAlbum(albumSubmission aSub)
{
    submissionReceipt sRec = new submissionReceipt();
    sRec.albumID=new string[aSub.album.Length];
    sRec.message=new string[aSub.album.Length];
    for (int i=0; i< aSub.album.Length; i++)
    {
```

```
        sRec.message[i]= aSub.album[i].Value.ToString() + " by " +
            aSub.artist[i].ToString() + " received";
        sRec.albumID[i]= System.Guid.NewGuid().ToString();
    }
    return sRec;
}
```

Lo and behold, we have a working Web service. You can test it against the simple client page called xsdToServiceClient.asmx, which is among the sample files.

What the Serializer Doesn't Do

The real test is whether the schema in the WSDL file for our new service is at least similar to the one we started out with. Granted, if we use the Web method API, we'll never see the actual format of the SOAP messages because .NET handles them for us, but we designed the schema as the basis for the service. It would be nice to know that it's preserved to at least some degree. Open a browser window and look at the schema at *http://localhost/wscr/06/xsdToService/xsdToService.asmx?wsdl*. It's the same as what you'd get if you were to compile AlbumService.cs and then generate a schema from the resulting DLL file using xsd.exe.

It appears that some detail has been lost, and in an inconsistent fashion. Of the two attributes we defined as "required," only one—*noOfTracks*—is still required. The other, *sender*, no longer has a *use* attribute, so it reverts to the default of *optional*. Our attribute group has gone, written out in full where appropriate by .NET, and the GUID pattern we gave to *AlbumID* has disappeared, leaving that particular element as just a string.

Most noticeably, the sequence of elements in our request type has been changed from

```
<xs:sequence minOccurs="1" maxOccurs="5">
  <xs:element name="artist" type="xs:string" />
  <xs:element name="album" type="tns:album" />
</xs:sequence>
```

to

```
<s:sequence>
  <s:element minOccurs="0" maxOccurs="unbounded" name="artist"
    type="s:string" />
  <s:element minOccurs="0" maxOccurs="unbounded" name="album"
    type="s1:album" />
</s:sequence>
```

Our instance document now looks like

```
<aSub sender="string" xmlns="http://www.notashop.com/wscr">
  <artist>string</artist>
  <artist>string</artist>
  <album noOfTracks="unsignedByte" runningTime="duration" />
  <album noOfTracks="unsignedByte" runningTime="duration" />
</aSub>
```

rather than the following, as was the original intention:

```
<aSub sender="string" xmlns="http://www.notashop.com/wscr">
  <artist>string</artist>
  <album noOfTracks="unsignedByte" runningTime="duration" />
  <artist>string</artist>
  <album noOfTracks="unsignedByte" runningTime="duration" />
</aSub>
```

Programmatically, it's just as easy to create messages in one style as the other, but it's easier to understand our original format. Note that the serializer is not perfect from schema to class or vice-versa. Just check that the key parts of the schema are still there. If they aren't, adjust the tags and types for the classes, as demonstrated in the next section.

Xsd.exe has a small set of options (listed in Table 6-4) that you can use to get more specific results than we did in our demonstration.

Table 6-4 Xsd.exe Options

Options	Description
/l or */language*	Specifies which .NET language the classes will be written in. The choices are *CS* (the default), *VB*, or *JS*.
/o or */outputdir*	Specifies which directory your class file will appear in.
/c or */classes*	Indicates that you want .NET classes reflecting the schema to be generated. Cannot be used at the same time as */d*.
/d or */dataset*	Indicates that you want to generate .NET classes derived from *System.Data.Dataset* that reflect the schema.
/e or */element*	Specifies which elements in the schema you want to generate classes for. You can use this flag more than once if required.
/n or */namespace*	Generates the classes for the schema within the given .NET namespace.
/u or */uri*	Indicates that you want to generate classes only against the elements defined within the given namespace URI.

Each option has a short and a long version. Options that have arguments must be separated from their argument by a colon, as shown here:

```
xsd.exe /l:VB /o:.\vbclasses /classes AlbumSchema.xsd
xsd.exe /u:http://www.notashop.com/wscr /e:album AlbumSchema.xsd
```

If you're generating a schema from a DLL or EXE file, you can use only */o* and a new flag, */t* (or */type*), which corresponds to */e* for schemas. You can use */t* to specify which classes you want to generate a schema for. For example:

```
xsd.exe /t:album AlbumService.dll
```

Using Wsdl.exe

The results you get using wsdl.exe to generate a Web service from your schema turn out to be truer to the schema than what you achieve using xsd.exe. However, the downside is that you first have to write the rest of your service's wsdl document before you can use it. Of course, having read Chapter 3, you're already an expert, so there's no problem. Don't forget that if you're basing a service on a schema, its binding should be doc/literal.

To save you time, we've written a WSDL document for the album entry service and saved it as AlbumService.wsdl in the wscr\06 folder of the book's sample code. You've encountered wsdl.exe before, so we won't waste time looking at the various switches we can use and we'll go straight to generating a service from our file:

1. Open a Visual Studio .NET command prompt and navigate to the folder on your machine containing AlbumService.wsdl.
2. Generate the service classes for the service by calling *wsdl.exe /server AlbumService.wsdl* at the prompt. Wsdl.exe produces a file called Albumdatabasesubmissionservice.cs to reflect the service's name in the .wsdl file.
3. Open Visual Studio .NET and create a new Web service project called wsdlToService at *http://localhost/wscr/06/wsdlToService*.
4. Delete all the code from the service's code view and paste in everything from Albumdatabasesubmissionservice.cs.

When asked to generate server classes based on a service's WSDL document, wsdl.exe generates an abstract class for the service and an abstract method for each Web method defined within it. Rather than inheriting this abstract base class, you can use a quick hack: delete the keyword *abstract* wherever it appears and implement each of the Web methods in the class. In our example, we have only one method—*SubmitAlbum*. It might not surprise you to learn that its implementation is similar to its counterpart that we built using xsd.exe.

```
[System.Web.Services.WebMethodAttribute()]
⋮
[return: System.Xml.Serialization.XmlElementAttribute("message")]
public string[] submitAlbum (
    [System.Xml.Serialization.XmlElementAttribute("artist")]
    string[] artist,
    [System.Xml.Serialization.XmlElementAttribute("album")]
    album[] album,
    [System.Xml.Serialization.XmlAttributeAttribute()]
    string sender,
    [System.Xml.Serialization.XmlElementAttribute("albumID")]
    out string[] albumID)
{
    albumID=new string[artist.Length];
    string[] message=new string[artist.Length];
    for (int i=0; i< artist.Length; i++)
    {
        message[i]= album[i].Value.ToString() + " by " +
            artist[i].ToString() + " received";
        albumID[i]= System.Guid.NewGuid().ToString();
    }
    return message;
}
```

Most obvious here is that wsdl.exe didn't generate classes for the response. Instead of sending back the convenient *submissionReceipt* object to the client, as in our previous example, we have to use *out* parameters to return any piece of information beyond the first. The actual implementation is easier to write because we don't need to encapsulate it inside a *submissionReceipt* object, but it's harder to read—the many tags that qualify this method are spelled out in full, making it somewhat unwieldy.

After you make those changes to the service's code, you build the service and browse over to *http://localhost/wscr/06/wsdlToService/wsdlToService.asmx?wsdl*. The schema has no extra elements defined in it, as was the case with xsd.exe, although the same changes do occur in our complex type definitions. For the most part, the WSDL remains unchanged except to reflect the name of the class we generated from the original file and the location of the Web service.

It looks like wsdl.exe is the best choice for incorporating a schema written from scratch into a Web service project. It remains truer to the original schema even if it does suffer from the serializer's inability to mirror class with schema.

> **Tip** The serializer doesn't mirror class with schema for quite a few schema constructs, as you've seen. We already mentioned that substitution groups cause problems, but so do complex types defined by choice. From class to schema and back, object graphs cause the most problems, but even something as simple as a public property isn't transitive through the serializer. It becomes a public field on the return trip from XML. Check to see how the Web method layer works with (or against) your code and take appropriate steps.

SOAP, WSDL, Encoding, and Styles

Back when SOAP 1.1 was introduced, the W3C hadn't finished working on the XML Schema standard. However, the creators of SOAP knew that schema should be used to describe the body of a SOAP message. Not wanting to wait around for the release of XML Schema, they created a schema-like type system and allowed a distinction to be made between messages templated by schemas (literal messages) and those using their stopgap type system (encoded messages). Section 5 encoding, as the stopgap is known, is part of the SOAP 1.1 spec and lays out its own wrapper types in an attempt to mirror the XSD type system. It was used heavily for a while but is now being dropped in favor of using schemas.

WSDL also makes a distinction between document-style messages, which adhere to a schema, and RPC-style messages, which take the form of a remote procedure call (RPC) and include operating system and runtime-specific information for use by the recipient. When SOAP was first designed, it was with RPC messages in mind, but over time document-style messages have been acknowledged as the way forward.

The *System.Xml.Serialization* namespace contains a number of attributes we can use to tag our Web service class and members to identify the type of service and what type of encoding the serializer should use. Based on that information, the serializer generates the service's WSDL document, which includes the service's schema. In the next section, we'll look at the serialization attributes you can use with .NET classes to generate schemas for document/literal messages (the default style in .NET)—this is the scenario we've already explored in this chapter by writing our own schema. Then we'll look at attributes you can use to influence the layout of services that use Section 5 encoding. In the final section of the chapter, we'll look at the *System.Runtime* serializer as an alternative to the System.Xml serializer when you work with a Web service in a .NET-only environment.

Writing Schemas Implicitly

You now know that the System.Xml serializer you use to serialize and deserialize messages can only do so much—it can translate (sometimes erroneously) the intention of your schema into an equivalent it can handle.

Back in Chapter 2, and again in this chapter, you've seen that we can tag members of our Web service class to influence how the class is serialized and the shape of the schema generated for the service. In this section, we'll look at exactly what these tags do. They work in the same way regardless of whether you are working with an existing class and writing a schema implicitly through tagging or have started with a schema and are trying to get the .NET serializer to be a little truer to your vision.

To demonstrate what each tag does, we'll start by building a Web service with a deliberately obfuscated set of classes and methods that mirror the AlbumSubmission service you've already seen, and we'll use our tags to give them meaning. In the sample code, you'll find the classes we'll use in the file BareServiceClass.cs. For example, the *albumSubmission* class now looks like this:

```
public class requestClass
{
    public string[] ReqElement1;
    public subclass[] ReqElement2;
    public string ReqAttribute1;
}
```

If you copy the classes and method into a new Web service project in Visual Studio .NET (you'll find such a project called TagService in the sample code) and open the WSDL file in your browser, you'll see that the service works fine, albeit unintelligibly. Actually, at this stage the serializer is more clever than you might imagine. Earlier you saw how xsd.exe turned our *AlbumID* GUID element into a plain string. By writing the class first, we can state that we want to use a *System.Guid* in our response class. The serializer notes this in the service's schema not as a plain string but as a string with a pattern matching a GUID!

```
<s:simpleType name="guid">
  <s:restriction base="s:string">
    <s:pattern value="[0-9a-fA-F]{8}-[0-9a-fA-F]{4}-[0-9a-fA-F]{4}-➥
      [0-9a-fA-F]{4}-[0-9a-fA-F]{12}" />
  </s:restriction>
</s:simpleType>
```

If a class involved in your Web service contains something that the serializer can't handle, this will be obvious the first time you try to browse to it. An ASP.NET error page will appear, telling you what class caused the problem. In general, numerical and string-based classes are fine, as are those that inherit from *ICollection* and *IEnumerable*. For those that don't, you can experiment with the *IXmlSerializable* interface, which we'll cover later.

Working with Document/Literal Services

Unless told otherwise, .NET assumes that every Web service and method is of the document/literal variety. However, if you want to make this explicit, you have two options:

- Add a *[SoapDocumentService]* attribute to your Web service class. Any Web method in the class will be serialized as document/literal by default.
- Add a *[SoapDocumentMethod]* attribute to your class method in addition to the *[WebMethod]* attribute.

Both attributes can be found in the *System.Web.Services.Protocols* namespace, so don't forget to reference it if you use them. We'll look at *[SoapDocumentMethod]* and *[WebMethod]* in more detail when we cover tagging methods, but first let's look at the other defaults that *[SoapDocumentService]* affords us.

Setting Service Defaults with *[SoapDocumentService]*

The *[SoapDocumentService]* attribute has three parameters that set defaults across all the Web methods defined in the class it has tagged. These are listed in Table 6-5.

Table 6-5 Properties of the *[SoapDocumentService]* Attribute

Property	Description
ParameterStyle	Sets whether the parameters and return values for the methods in the service will be contained within a single element (which is itself a child of the SOAP *<body>* element, the default) when serialized or whether they will each be written separately as children of *<body>*.
RoutingStyle	Sets whether the method called should be specified in the *SOAPAction* header (the default) or by the first element in the request message.
Use	Sets whether the serializer encodes the messages using XSD types (the default) or Section 5 types.

RoutingStyle and *Use* are self-explanatory, but *ParameterStyle* could do with a bit more explanation. We'll take our *SubmitAlbum* method as an example. By default, the *System.Xml* serializer creates a schema that specifies a request message with this structure:

```
<soap:body>
  <SubmitAlbum>
    <albumSubmission>
      <artist>Tool</artist>
      <album>Lateralus</album>
    </albumSubmission>
  </SubmitAlbum>
</soap:body>
```

As you can see, the serializer creates a wrapper element identified by the method's name unless we tell it otherwise. This setting can be written explicitly as follows:

```
[SoapDocumentService(ParameterStyle=SoapParameterStyle.Wrapped)]
```

The alternative is to set *ParameterStyle* to *SoapParameterStyle.Bare*, which removes the *<SubmitAlbum>* wrapper element:

```
<soap:body>
  <albumSubmission>
    <artist>Tool</artist>
    <album>Lateralus</album>
  </albumSubmission>
</soap:body>
```

ParameterStyle is also a property of the *[SoapDocumentMethod]* attribute; it allows you to override the service default on a per-method basis.

One other default to mention here is that .NET sets the *elementFormDefault* attribute for all its autogenerated service schemas to *qualified*. You cannot change this—which is good—but you can override it per element or attribute, as you'll soon see.

Identifying the Service with *[WebService]*

We used the *[WebService]* attribute as far back as Chapter 1, but what does it actually do behind the scenes? Recall that it has three attributes:

- ***Namespace*** Sets the *targetNamespace* for our service's schema to something other than *http://tempuri.org*. It is important to set this to our own namespace.
- ***Name*** Sets the *<service>* name attribute in your service's WSDL document.

- ***Description*** Sets the *<service>/<description>* element in your service's WSDL document.

Name and *Description* are less important to the serialization of messages than *Namespace*. Remember, however, that the *Namespace* attribute is important to the outward appearance of your service's documentation page.

Taking what we've learned, let's return to our TagService project and add the following to our service class declaration:

```
[WebService(Name="Album Submission Service",
    Namespace="http://www.notashop.com/wscr",
    Description="Submit an album to the database")]
[SoapDocumentService(ParameterStyle=SoapParameterStyle.Wrapped)]
public class Service1 : System.Web.Services.WebService
{
    ⋮
}
```

With respect to the schema and serialization, we've set the namespace for the service and decided on the outer element for request and response messages.

> **Important** From here on, we'll look only at attributes that work with document/literal services. If you tag a service with *[SoapRpcService]* or *[SoapDocumentService use="encoded"]* or tag a method with *[SoapRpcMethod]* or *[SoapDocumentMethod use="encoded"]*, none of the subsequent *[Xml...]* attributes will be taken into consideration by the serializer.

Setting XML Elements with *[XmlElement]*

The *System.Xml* serializer treats all public fields and properties of classes involved in Web methods in exactly the same way: it turns them into elements in your request and response messages and gives each element the same name as the field or property. In our TagService project, the serializer takes our request class

```
public class requestClass
{
    public string[] ReqElement1;
    public subclass[] ReqElement2;
    public string ReqAttribute1;
}
```

and presents us with the following schema:

```
<s:complexType name="requestClass">
  <s:sequence>
    <s:element minOccurs="0" maxOccurs="1"
               name="ReqElement1" type="s0:ArrayOfString" />
    <s:element minOccurs="0" maxOccurs="1"
               name="ReqElement2" type="s0:ArrayOfSubclass" />
    <s:element minOccurs="0" maxOccurs="1"
               name="ReqAttribute1" type="s:string" />
  </s:sequence>
</s:complexType>
```

We'll soon look at how to alter this so the serializer can recognize fields and properties as element attributes and text fields. In the meantime, we can tag those fields and properties that are meant to be elements with the *[XmlElement]* attribute to alter how they are represented in the service's schema:

```
[XmlElement(ElementName="Artist")]
public string[] ReqElement1;

[XmlElement(ElementName="Album")]
public subclass[] ReqElement2;
```

We can also use *[XmlElement]* to set how the parameters of a Web method are represented in the schema:

```
[ return: XmlElement("SubmissionReceipt")]
public responseClass RunThisMethod(
    [XmlElement("AlbumSubmission")] requestClass rC)
```

This approach is especially useful if the method takes parameters of a primitive type because it gives us a way to control their representation. Note, however, that *[XmlRoot]* and *[SoapDocumentMethod]* also give you the same control here, as you'll see later. If for no other reason than clarity, it's easier to use these other attributes than a gaggle of *[XmlElement]* tags around the method signature.

The *XmlElement* has six properties, as shown in Table 6-6.

Table 6-6 Properties of the *[XmlElement]* Attribute

Property	**Description**
DataType	Sets the XSD *type* for the element
ElementName	Sets the element's *name*
Form	Sets the element's *form* attribute in the schema to *qualified* (the default) or *unqualified*

Table 6-6 Properties of the *[XmlElement]* Attribute

Property	Description
IsNullable	Sets the element's *nillable* attribute in the schema to *true* or *false* (the default) and thus sets whether the tagged item can be set to null
Namespace	Sets the namespace for the element
Type	Identifies the .NET type for a specific element

The first five of these attributes are easy to understand. If we tag one of the *requestClass* fields as shown here

```
[XmlElement(ElementName="Artist", DataType="normalizedString",
    Form=XmlSchemaForm.Unqualified, IsNullable=true,
    Namespace="http://www.notashop.com/wscr")]
public string[] ReqElement1;
```

the serializer produces the following entry for it in the service's schema, pretty much as we'd expect:

```
<s:schema elementFormDefault="qualified"
          targetNamespace="http://www.notashop.com/wscr">
  ⋮
  <s:element minOccurs="0" maxOccurs="unbounded" form="unqualified"
             name="Artist" nillable="true" type="s:normalizedString" />
  ⋮
</s:schema>
```

If the namespace given in the *namespace* attribute differs from the *targetNamespace* of the schema, the serializer will create a second schema in the service's WSDL file for that namespace. This second schema will contain the definition for the element and will be imported into the original schema for the service.

The *Type* attribute needs explanation but is easier to demonstrate. Suppose you have a field of type *System.Object*, which you expect will store a value of some derived type, let's say a string. You can use the *Type* attribute to indicate the type that the service will expect or deliver in this field. So the following

```
[XmlElement(Type=typeof(string))]
public System.Object obj;
```

will appear in the corresponding schema as you see here:

```
<s:element minOccurs="0" maxOccurs="1" name="obj" type="s:string" />
```

Note that you can't use *Type* against a field or property that is itself a primitive type. Also, *Type* must specify a *derivation* of the class member's original type.

Setting XML Attributes with *[XmlAttribute]*

If you'd prefer that a class member (a field or a property) be represented as an attribute of the element representing the class, you can inform the serializer by tagging the member with an *[XmlAttribute]* attribute. For example, in our TagService example the *requestClass* class has a field named *reqAttribute1* that is being turned into an element by the serializer and that we'd prefer to be an attribute. If we tag the class like so

```
public class requestClass
{
    [XmlElement(ElementName="Artist")]
    public string[] ReqElement1;

    [XmlElement(ElementName="Album")]
    public subclass[] ReqElement2;

    [XmlAttribute(AttributeName="Sender")]
    public string ReqAttribute1;
}
```

the serializer reshapes the service's schema to accommodate our wishes:

```
<s:complexType name="requestClass">
  <s:sequence>
    <s:element minOccurs="0" maxOccurs="unbounded"
               name="Artist" type="s:string" />
    <s:element minOccurs="0" maxOccurs="unbounded"
               name="Album" type="s0:subclass" />
  </s:sequence>
  <s:attribute name="Sender" type="s:string" />
</s:complexType>
```

The *[XmlAttribute]* attribute has four properties, as shown in Table 6-7.

Table 6-7 Properties of the *[XmlAttribute]* Attribute

Property	Description
AttributeName	Sets the attribute's *name*
DataType	Sets the XSD *type* of the attribute's value

Table 6-7 Properties of the *[XmlAttribute]* Attribute

Property	Description
Form	Sets the element's *form* attribute in the schema to *qualified* (the default) or *unqualified*
Namespace	Sets the attribute's namespace

Each property works the same as the corresponding properties for the *[XmlElement]* attribute. Tagging *reqAttribute1* like so

```
[XmlAttribute(AttributeName="Sender", DataType="token",
    Form=XmlSchemaForm.Unqualified,
    Namespace="http://www.notashop.com/wscr")]
public string ReqAttribute1;
```

produces the following entry in the service schema:

```
<s:attribute form="unqualified" name="Sender" type="s:token" />
```

Note that an error will occur if you use *[XmlAttribute]* to set an attribute's *form* to *unqualified* and its namespace to a URI other than the value of *target-Namespace*.

> **Caution** Because of a bug in the documentation page, setting an attribute's form to *qualified* and its namespace to a URI that isn't the *targetNamespace* causes the attribute to disappear from the sample request or response message that it appears in.

Last but not least, there's no reliable way to use these serialization attributes to indicate that an attribute is required in a message (that is, to set an *<attribute>* element's *use* attribute to *required* in the service schema). It appears, however, that the serializer adds *use=required* to attribute declarations at random, so be careful.

Setting Text Nodes with *[XmlText]*

You saw earlier that schemas can define complex types containing elements, attributes, and text values. You know how to identify which class members should be serialized as elements and which should be serialized as attributes, so we're left with how to identify which class member represents the type's text node. We do this by tagging it with the *[XmlText]* attribute.

In our TagService example, the *subclass* class has a field member named *subTextValue1* that we'd like to associate with the text value of the type that will represent it. If we tag the class like so

```
public class subclass
{
    [XmlAttribute(AttributeName="noOfTracks", DataType="unsignedByte")]
    public System.Byte subAttribute1;

    [XmlAttribute(AttributeName="RunningTime")]
    public string subAttribute2;

    [XmlText(DataType="normalizedString")]
    public string subTextValue1;
}
```

the definition of the subclass complex type will change from a sequence of three elements to the following:

```
<s:complexType name="subclass">
  <s:simpleContent>
    <s:extension base="s:normalizedString">
      <s:attribute name="noOfTracks"
                   type="s:unsignedByte" use="required" />
      <s:attribute name="RunningTime" type="s:string" />
    </s:extension>
  </s:simpleContent>
</s:complexType>
```

Curiously, the documentation page's sample request message does not show that elements of this type can contain text, but the schema does, and that's what matters. Table 6-8 shows the properties you can set in the *[XmlText]* attribute. You've seen how they both work before.

Table 6-8 Properties of the *[XmlText]* Attribute

Property	Description
DataType	Sets the XSD type of the text or the base type being extended by the new *<complexType>* definition
Type	Identifies the .NET type for a specific element

Don't forget that a type can have only one text node, so you can tag only one class member with *[XmlText]*; otherwise, you get an error.

Setting WildCards with *[XmlAnyElement]* and *[XmlAnyAttribute]*

The *<any>* and *<anyAttribute>* wildcards in XML Schema offer a fair amount of control over what XML can replace them inside a complex type, but their equivalent .NET attributes, *[XmlAnyElement]* and *[XmlAnyAttribute]*, are somewhat less flexible. Adding the following to our service classes

```
[XmlAnyAttribute]
public XmlAttribute[] WildcardAttributes;

[XmlAnyElement]
public XmlElement[] WildcardElements;
```

produces the corresponding wildcards in the service schema:

```
<s:any minOccurs="0" maxOccurs="unbounded" />
<s:anyAttribute />
```

There is no way to influence the *namespace* or *process-Contents* attributes of either element. Each of the elements and attributes sent in messages in place of the wildcards is stored in the arrays of *XmlAttribute* and *XmlElement* objects declared in the class. This is the only way to set up a wildcard. How you process the contents of those arrays is up to you. *[XmlAnyAttribute]* has no additional properties, but *[XmlAnyElement]* has two, as detailed in Table 6-9.

Table 6-9 Properties of the *[XmlAnyElement]* Attribute

Property	Description
Name	Sets the name of a wrapper element for the elements templated by the wildcard. If the property is not specified, the array captures any elements not covered by the schema.
Namespace	Sets the namespace for the wildcard wrapper element. The *Name* property for *[XmlAnyElement]* must be also be set if this property is used; otherwise, an error will occur.

Applying a name to a wildcard element has a notable effect on the service schema. Let's say we add *(Name="IceCream")* to the *[XmlAnyElement]* attribute. The wildcard entry changes from *<s:any minOccurs="0" maxOccurs="unbounded" />* to this:

```
<s:element minOccurs="0" maxOccurs="unbounded" name="IceCream">
  <s:complexType mixed="true">
    <s:sequence>
      <s:any maxOccurs="unbounded" />
    </s:sequence>
```

```
    <s:anyAttribute />
  </s:complexType>
</s:element>
```

Because of a bug in .NET, *[XmlAnyAttribute]* clashes with the *[XmlText]* attribute. If a class contains two members, each tagged with one of these attributes, the resulting mixed-content complex type definition in the service schema will not contain an *<anyAttribute />* wildcard element.

Bypassing Class Members with *[XmlIgnore]*

We've looked at tagging class members that will be elements, attributes, and text, but what if we don't want a class member to be part of the message at all? We use the *[XmlIgnore]* attribute. Tagging a class member with *[XmlIgnore]* tells the serializer not to include it in the service schema, as in this example:

```
[XmlIgnore]
public string thisWontBeSerialized;
```

[XmlIgnore] has no properties.

Finalizing Message Class Definitions with *[XmlRoot]* and *[XmlType]*

When the serializer creates the schema for a method's request and response messages, the root element for each is defined by the method declaration in the service class. For example, in our TagService project, we have one method, which is declared as follows:

```
[WebMethod]
public responseClass RunThisMethod(requestClass rC)
{
    ⋮
}
```

In the service schema, the request class parameter becomes the root of the request message and the response class becomes the root of the response:

```
<s:element name="rC" type="s0:requestClass" />
<s:element name="RunThisMethodResult" nillable="true"
  type="s0:responseClass" />
```

Note that if the method were to have more than one parameter, each parameter would become a "root" element and you might want to use the wrapper element you can elicit from the *[SoapDocumentMethod]* or *[SoapDocumentService]* attributes as the root of your message. To do so, you set the *ParameterStyle* attribute of either attribute to *SoapParameterStyle.Wrapped*. This also applies to the situation in which the method has a return class and out parameters.

You can modify the schema definition for each root type by attaching the *[XmlRoot]* attribute to its class definition. For example:

```
[XmlRoot(ElementName="AlbumSubmission")]
public class requestClass
{
    ⋮
}

[XmlRoot(ElementName="SubmissionReceipt")]
public class responseClass
{
    ⋮
}
```

Adding these tags changes the schema definitions for the message roots to the following:

```
<s:element name="AlbumSubmission"
           nillable="true" type="s0:requestClass" />
<s:element name="SubmissionReceipt"
           nillable="true" type="s0:responseClass" />
```

Table 6-10 lists the properties you can set with the *[XmlRoot]* attribute.

Table 6-10 Properties of the *[XmlRoot]* Attribute

Property	Description
DataType	Sets the XSD *type* of the root element
ElementName	Sets the *name* of the root element
IsNullable	Set's the root element's *nillable* attribute in the schema to *true* (the default) or *false* and thus whether the tagged item can be set to null.
Namespace	Sets the namespace of the root element.

Tagging a subclass with the *[XmlRoot]* attribute has no effect on the service schema. Instead of *[XmlRoot]*, you must use *[XmlType]* attribute. It has three properties, which are detailed in Table 6-11.

Table 6-11 Properties of the *[XmlType]* Attribute

Property	Description
IncludeInSchema	Indicates whether the type definition should be included in the schema for the service
Namespace	Sets the namespace for the type definition
TypeName	Sets the name for the type definition

Customizing Enumerations with *[XmlEnum]*

We noted earlier that the serializer can generate schema types for numerical .NET classes, string-based classes, and classes that inherit from *ICollection* and *IEnumerable*. Let's consider basic enumerations first. In our TagService example, we declare a field in the subclass class to take values from an enumeration we've defined called *enumTypes*:

```
[XmlElement(ElementName="AlbumFormat")]
public enumTypes subEnum1;
⋮
public enum enumTypes
{
    CD, Vinyl, MD
}
```

By default, the enumeration and the field are translated into the following schema definitions:

```
<s:element minOccurs="1" maxOccurs="1"
           name="AlbumFormat" type="s0:enumTypes" />
⋮
<s:simpleType name="enumTypes">
<s:restriction base="s:string">
  <s:enumeration value="CD" />
  <s:enumeration value="Vinyl" />
  <s:enumeration value="MD" />
</s:restriction>
</s:simpleType>
```

As noted earlier, the schema *<enumeration>* element does indeed translate well to enumerations in .NET. The *[XmlElement]* works as usual except that you can't specify a *DataType* for it because the class member you're tagging isn't of a primitive type.

The *[XmlEnum]* attribute tags a value of the enumeration type. It has one property, *Name*, which you use to give the enumeration value a different name in the schema. For example

```
public enum enumTypes
{
    [XmlEnum(Name="Compact Disc")] CD,
    [XmlEnum(Name="Vinyl LP Record")] Vinyl,
    [XmlEnum(Name="Minidisc")] MD
}
```

With this attribute included, the enumeration's simple type in the schema changes to the following:

```
<s:simpleType name="enumTypes">
  <s:restriction base="s:string">
    <s:enumeration value="Compact Disc" />
    <s:enumeration value="Vinyl LP Record" />
    <s:enumeration value="Minidisc" />
  </s:restriction>
</s:simpleType>
```

The serializer ensures that one value is serialized or deserialized into its corresponding value as needed.

Customizing Arrays with *[XmlArray]* and *[XmlArrayItem]*

The array is the last .NET type we'll look at. It corresponds to a unique entry in a schema. By default, a class member that is an array is represented in a service schema by an element that can occur any number of times. In our TagService example, our *responseClass* class has the string array member, *respElement1*:

```
public string[] respElement1;
```

The corresponding schema entry looks like this:

```
<s:element minOccurs="0" maxOccurs="unbounded"
         name="respElement1" type="s:string" />
```

Arrays are the only .NET constructs for which the serializer generates *minOccurs* and *maxOccurs* attributes in a schema. You cannot change them, but you can alter the structure of the schema element that corresponds to the array by using the *[XmlArray]* and *[XmlArrayItem]* attributes.

The *[XmlArray]* attribute creates a wrapper around the elements representing the items in the array. If we tag *respElement1* with *[XmlArray]*, its schema entry changes from the single element declaration you saw earlier to the following:

```
<s:element minOccurs="0" maxOccurs="1" name="respElement1"
  type="s0:ArrayOfString" />
⋮
<s:complexType name="ArrayOfString">
  <s:sequence>
    <s:element minOccurs="0" maxOccurs="unbounded" name="string"
               nillable="true" type="s:string" />
  </s:sequence>
</s:complexType>
```

The *[XmlArray]* attribute has four properties that affect the *respElement1* wrapper element, as shown in Table 6-12.

Table 6-12 Properties of the *[XmlArray]* Attribute

Property	Description
ElementName	Sets the *name* of the wrapper element
Form	Sets the wrapper element's *form* attribute in the schema to *qualified* (the default) or *unqualified*
IsNullable	Sets the wrapper element's *nillable* attribute in the schema to *true* (the default) or *false*, and thus whether the array as a whole can be set to null
Namespace	Sets the *namespace* attribute for the wrapper element

If we tag *respElement1* with an *[XmlArrayItem]* attribute in addition to *[XmlArray]*, we also get control over the elements representing the items in our array:

```
[XmlArray]
[XmlArrayItem(ElementName="Message")]
public string[] respElement1;
```

The inclusion of the second attribute changes the complex type definition representing the array to the following:

```
<s:complexType name="ArrayOfString">
  <s:sequence>
    <s:element minOccurs="0" maxOccurs="unbounded"
               name="Message" nillable="true" type="s:string" />
  </s:sequence>
</s:complexType>
```

The *[XmlArrayItem]* attribute has seven properties, as detailed in Table 6-13.

Table 6-13 Properties of the *[XmlArrayItem]* Attribute

Property	Description
DataType	Sets the XSD *type* of the element representing an array item
ElementName	Sets the *name* of the element representing an array item
Form	Sets the *form* attribute for the element representing an array item to *qualified* (the default) or *unqualified*
IsNullable	Sets the *nillable* attribute for the wrapper element to *true* (the default) or *false*, and thus whether the array as a whole can be set to null

Table 6-13 Properties of the *[XmlArrayItem]* Attribute

Property	Description
Namespace	Sets the *namespace* for the element representing an array item
NestingLevel	For multidimensional arrays, indicates the nesting level for each dimension
Type	Identifies the .NET type of the item in the array

The *NestingLevel* attribute indicates to the serializer which dimensions of a multidimensional array should be nested in which. For example:

```
[XmlArray]
[XmlArrayItem(ElementName = "breadth", NestingLevel = 0)]
[XmlArrayItem(ElementName = "width", NestingLevel = 1)]
[XmlArrayItem(ElementName = "height", NestingLevel = 2)]
public int[][][] BoxDimensions;
```

In this case, the *BoxDimensions* field is serialized into the following format:

```
<BoxDimensions>
  <breadth>
    <width>
      <height>int</height>
      <height>int</height>
    </width>
    <width>
      <height>int</height>
      <height>int</height>
    </width>
  </breadth>
  <breadth>
    ⋮
  </breadth>
</BoxDimensions>
```

The default value for *NestingLevel* is *0*, so there is no need to apply this attribute to single dimensional arrays.

Marker Interfaces for *[XmlArray]* and *[XmlArrayItem]*

Although their names suggest that they are only for tagging arrays, the *[XmlArray]* and *[XmlArrayItem]* attributes can be used to tag most classes that implement the *IEnumerable* interface. By default, then, this statement can be stretched to include most classes that implement *ICollection* because the former must be implemented for the latter to work. You'll find a bare-bones example that shows this called ISerializeService in the chapter's sample code.

Note, however, that this statement cannot be stretched to include all classes that implement *ICollection*. The attributes and, indeed, the serializer will produce errors if the class implements certain other interfaces. For example, tagging a hash table will produce an error because it implements *IDictionary* in addition to *ICollection* and *IEnumerable*.

Creating Choices with *[XmlElement]* and *[XmlChoiceIdentifier]*

As you saw when we discussed writing schemas explicitly, complex types with complex content can be derived by using *<sequence>*, *<choice>*, or *<all>* elements. Thus far, you've seen the serializer produce only sequences of elements. It is possible to create a *<choice>*, which we'll see now, but there is no way to imply *<all>*.

In our TagService example, suppose we want to distinguish between soloists and bands. Rather than create an extra service for each scenario, we can just change the name of the element in the request message from *<Artist>* to *<SoloSinger>* or to *<Band>*, with the contents remaining the same. In an XML schema, this is represented by a *<choice>*; we can write this implicitly in our class by tagging multiple *[XmlElement]* attributes to the same class member. For example:

```
[XmlElement(ElementName="SoloSinger")]
[XmlElement(ElementName="Band")]
public string ReqElement1;
```

The serializer now creates a *<choice>*-based complex type definition but has no way to maintain a record of what choice has been made. Thus it produces an error unless the class member is also tagged with an *[XmlChoiceIdentifier]* attribute that identifies a helper variable to maintain that record:

```
[XmlElement(ElementName="SoloSinger")]
[XmlElement(ElementName="Band")]
[XmlChoiceIdentifier("performerType")]
public string ReqElement1;
```

That helper variable must represent an enumeration containing one value for each choice of element:

```
[XmlIgnore]
public PerformerTypes performerType;

[XmlType(IncludeInSchema=false)]
public enum PerformerTypes
{
    SoloSinger, Band
}
```

With this helper variable added to our service but not included in the service schema itself, the serializer indeed creates a *<choice>* of our two elements in the service schema:

```
<s:complexType name="requestClass">
  <s:sequence>
     <s:choice minOccurs="1" maxOccurs="1">
        <s:element minOccurs="0" maxOccurs="1"
                   name="SoloSinger" type="s:string" />
        <s:element minOccurs="0" maxOccurs="1"
                   name="Band" type="s:string" />
     </s:choice>
     <s:element minOccurs="0" maxOccurs="unbounded"
                name="Album" type="s0:subclass" />
  </s:sequence>
  <s:attribute name="Sender" type="s:string" />
</s:complexType>
```

If a request containing a choice is deserialized into classes, the serializer sets the value of the helper variable. If you want to serialize a class containing a choice into XML, you must set the helper variable yourself before starting the serialization.

Wrapping It All Up with *[SoapDocumentMethod]*

Last but not least, we come to the Web methods themselves and how they influence the service schema. As you'll recall from our look at *[XmlRoot]*, the serializer uses a class method's signature to derive a "wrapper element" for request and response messages that encapsulates elements representing the method's parameters and return values, respectively. So, by default, the request message takes this shape:

```
<soap:envelope>
  <soap:body>
    <methodname> ... </methodname>
  </soap:body>
</soap:envelope>
```

and the response to that has this shape by default:

```
<soap:envelope>
  <soap:body>
    <methodnameResponse> ... </methodnameResponse>
  </soap:body>
</soap:envelope>
```

Tagging a class method with *[SoapDocumentMethod]* affects only these wrapper elements. However, it first specifies that the request and response messages for this element be defined by a schema in the service's WSDL file. The

[SoapDocumentMethod] attribute has nine attributes, as listed in Table 6-14. Of those, *Action*, *Binding*, and *OneWay* affect only the method's representation in the service's WSDL document, but we've included them for completeness.

Table 6-14 Properties of the *[SoapDocMethod]* Attribute

Property	Description
Action	Sets the SOAPAction value required in the request message to access this method.
Binding	Sets the binding to be used for the method. The binding is identified elsewhere in the class by a *WebServiceBinding* attribute.
OneWay	Sets whether the server must produce a response to the method request.
ParameterStyle	Sets whether the *<methodname>* and *<methodnameResponse>* wrapper elements should exist in messages to and from the service. Possible values are *SoapParameterStyle.Wrapped* (the default) for yes and *SoapParameterStyle.Bare* for no. This value overrides any default set with the *[SoapDocumentService]* attribute.
RequestElementName	If wrapper elements are to be used, this sets the *name* of the wrapper element for the request message.
RequestNamespace	If wrapper elements are to be used, this sets the *namespace* of the wrapper element for the request message.
ResponseElementName	If wrapper elements are to be used, this sets the *name* of the wrapper element for the response message.
ResponseNamespace	If wrapper elements are to be used, this sets the *namespace* of the wrapper element for the response message.
Use	Sets whether the message parts are encoded against a schema (literal) or SOAP Section 5 encoding (encoded). This overrides any default set by using the *[SoapDocumentService]* attribute.

Serialization Attributes for Encoded Services

If you need to create a service whose methods use Section 5 encoding rather than XSD types, tag the service class with *[SoapDocumentService (Use=SoapBindingUse.Encoded)]* or *[SoapRpcService]*. The serializer doesn't support RPC/literal methods, so it's assumed that you'll use Section 5 encoding with RPC-style messages. If you need to set up encoding on individual methods in your service, you can tag them with *[SoapDocumentMethod (Use=SoapBindingUse.Encoded)]* or *[SoapRpcMethod]*.

By default, the structure of an encoded method is quite a bit larger than that of the equivalent document/literal method. It's also more difficult to establish what you need to include in the message if you're writing a custom client. However, like the *[Xml...]* attributes, a handful of *[Soap...]* attributes let us alter the template for an encoded method's request and response messages to at least give us a fighting chance.

In fact, they all do the same job as their *[Xml...]* counterparts and affect the same part of the schema for our methods. We won't go through them all individually, but Table 6-15 shows the *[Soap...]* attributes, the *[Xml...]* attributes they correspond to, and a list of the properties you can include in the *[Soap...]* attributes. These have the equivalent effect as the properties of the same name for the *[Xml...]* attributes.

Table 6-15 XML Serialization Attributes

Section 5 Encoding Attribute	Literal Message Attribute	Properties	Description
SoapAttribute	*XmlAttribute*	*AttributeName, DataType, Namespace*	Specifies that the tagged item should be serialized as an attribute and how
SoapElement	*XmlElement*	*DataType, ElementName, IsNullable*	Specifies that the tagged item should be serialized as an element and how
SoapEnum	*XmlEnum*	*Name*	Sets how the tagged value in an enumeration will be serialized
SoapIgnore	*XmlIgnore*	*SoapIgnore* has no properties	Specifies that the tagged item should not be serialized
SoapInclude	*XmlInclude*	*Type*	Specifies that elements of the tagged class can be substituted by elements of the named subclasses
SoapType	*XmlType*	*IncludeInSchema, Namespace, TypeName*	Specifies that the tagged item should be serialized as an XML type and how

There are no equivalents to *[XmlAnyAttribute]*, *[XmlAnyElement]*, *[XmlArray]*, *[XmlArrayItem]*, *[XmlChoiceIdentifier]*, *[XmlRoot]*, or *[XmlText]*.

If you take our obfuscated set of classes and method (in BareServiceClass.cs) and add them to an encoded service, you can experiment to confirm what they each do. You'll see this in the example service called TagEncService in the sample code.

Serializer-Unfriendly Classes

You saw in the section on marker interfaces for *[XmlArray]* how the serializer used by the Web method API chokes on classes that inherit certain interfaces. If you're happy to use the Handler API to create a custom serialization solution for the class, you can get around the issue that way. If not, your class should inherit from the *IXmlSerializable* interface in the .NET Framework; this interface will provide hints to the serializer on how to work with it. Its signature is as follows:

```
public interface IXmlSerializable
{
    System.Xml.Schema.XmlSchema GetSchema();
    void ReadXml(System.Xml.XmlReader reader);
    void WriteXml(System.Xml.XmlWriter writer);
}
```

Unfortunately, *IXmlSerializable* is listed for internal use within .NET only. We can surmise, however, that *GetSchema* will be called when the WSDL and schema is generated for the service, that *ReadXml* will be called when you receive an XML message, and that *WriteXml* will be called when the class needs to be serialized into a message.

> **Tip** Only one class inherits from the *IXmlSerializable* interface in the .NET framework—*System.Data.DataSet*. You might want to disassemble that class and study how it implements the three *IXmlSerializable* methods.

The Other .NET Serializer

A final note on schemas and serialization: The .NET Framework has two serializers, not one. Only one—that found in *System.Xml.Serialization*—is built into the Web method API and is used by xsd.exe to generate schemas for services and XML messages on demand. The other—the one found in *System.Runtime.Serialization*—is more generic. It allows you to define exactly how classes are serialized by using the *IFormatter* interface. The two built-in implementations of this interface specify a binary-based and a SOAP-based result, respectively.

If this second serializer can generate SOAP, why not use it instead of the default? Because for our purposes, the *System.Xml* serializer prioritizes the use of XSD types and schemas over what .NET types a class can use. If, for example, the request class contains a .NET type that cannot be translated into a *<complexType>* in the service schema, it will be disallowed. This requirement means the service has a platform-independent interface and clients can hold conversations with it regardless of the platform they are based on. On the other hand, the *System.Runtime* serializer gives preference to .NET types over XSD and handles classes that cannot be translated into schemas, which means it can handle and distinguish the likes of public and private data, pointers, object graphs, and polymorphism, but services that use it can be used only where both server and client are running .NET.

If you are working in a .NET-only environment (which belies one of the aims of Web services), you might want to consider throwing away the Web method API and using the Handler API with *System.Runtime.Serialization*. However, you're heading into the realm of Remoting, which is out of the scope of this book. Look for a copy of the *Visual Basic. NET Serialization Handbook* by Andy Olson, Matjaz Juric, Adil Rehan, and Eric Lippert (Wrox Press, 2002). It covers everything you could possibly want to know about using serializers, and then some.

Summary

In this chapter, you learned that Web services use an XML schema in their WSDL documents to dictate the shape and content of the request and response messages to the methods they expose. This schema document is written to a W3C standard and allows you to strongly type each element in the message in a platform-independent way. This means you can avoid type clashes when Web services and their clients are on different platforms.

You also learned that you can incorporate schemas into your .NET XML Web Services in two ways:

- You can design your messages, write the schemas for them, and then use xsd.exe or wsdl.exe to generate classes that you can incorporate into your code.
- You can start with code and use .NET's serialization attributes to adjust the schema that is autogenerated for you into something closer to what you want.

You also learned that the serializer built into the Web method API—found in the *System.Xml.Serialization* namespace—doesn't always maintain the schema you intended and that it sometimes trips up on .NET classes you want to use.

If you use the Handler API, you can implement your own serialization routines and use your own specific schemas. If you use the serializer found in the *System.Runtime.Serialization* namespace, you can use any .NET class you want in your messages, but you should restrict yourself to a .NET-only environment.

Part II

Building on the Core

7 Creating Web Methods

In Microsoft .NET, the heart of a Web service is its Web methods. Within a Web method, everything that a Web service does is defined. Web methods are the .NET way of specifying which parts of a class are to be exposed as a Web service. In the first four chapters, we looked at the technologies and standards that apply to any Web service, not just those that use .NET as a framework. In Chapter 5, we looked at how some of these standards are implemented in .NET, how to build custom handlers, and which .NET classes are of particular use to the Web services developer. In Chapter 6, we looked at how objects and data are serialized for transmission via a Web service.

With the preliminary work done, it's time for a detailed look at building Web methods and at what the Microsoft Visual Studio .NET abstraction boils down to underneath. We'll look at how much control you have over the serializer and how you can customize Web methods using the built-in attributes. (Usually the attributes change some aspect of the service's .wsdl file.) We'll also discuss several of these attributes again in later chapters. Last, but not least, we'll look at how you can debug and deploy your Web service and make it available for discovery.

Building a Web Method

By adding a public *WebMethod* attribute to your code, you indicate that the code should be exposed as part of your Web service. Six attributes, along with the *WebMethod* directive, let you modify aspects of your code by allowing you to enable sessions or allowing you to specify how long information is held in the cache. Before we delve into the Web method itself, let's look at the overall Web services model (which we looked at briefly in Chapter 1 when we built our first example Web service).

The XML Web Service Code Model

Web services have two logical parts: the entry point (normally the .asmx file) and the code that supplies the Web service functionality (which is located in the .asmx file, in a separate code-behind file, or in separate assemblies). Building an XML Web service in ASP.NET requires either two or three basic steps:

- Creating an .asmx file
- Adding a *@WebService* directive to the file (if you're not using Visual Studio .NET)
- Creating the methods within the Web service

If you've created a new .asmx file using Visual Studio .NET, the *@WebService* directive is created automatically. It tells the compiler the name of the class file to use as an entry point for the Web service. The *@WebService* directive (not to be confused with the *WebService* attribute) is placed at the head of the file. Together with the .asmx file, the *@WebService* directive provides a URL for access to the Web service.

The *@WebService* Processing Directive

We mentioned in Chapter 1 that the *@WebService* processing directive has four attributes: *language*, *code behind*, *class*, and *debug*. This directive defines the values of the attributes within a particular .asmx file. An example directive is as follows:

```
<%@ WebService class="RecordStore.Service1" language="C#"
    codebehind="RecordStore.Service1.cs" debug="true" %>
```

We'll now examine each of the attributes in turn.

class Attribute

The *class* attribute specifies which class should be exposed directly as an XML Web service. This class is automatically compiled the first time the Web service is accessed. A Web service can be made up of many classes, not all of them necessarily exposed as Web services. The *class* attribute is required when you use the *WebService* directive.

The class can also be contained within an assembly. If it is, the assembly file must be located in the bin directory, which itself must be in the Web application's root folder. The *class* attribute can be any valid, fully qualified class name.

codeBehind Attribute

The *codeBehind* attribute specifies that a separate file should be used for the source code for compiling the Web service, when the class specified in the class attribute does not contain it. This is the same principle of code-behind as that commonly seen in Web forms, where presentational HTML is separated out from the actual ASP.NET code behind it.

language Attribute

The *language* attribute specifies the programming language the class was written in. You must specify this attribute if the Web service code is contained in an .asmx file. This attribute tells the compiler which language compiler should be used to compile the class. Any .NET language can be specified for this attribute, and a shortened version is often supplied. The most common abbreviations are JS for JScript .NET, VB for Visual Basic .NET, and C# for C# .NET. You can add extra languages on top of those by adding them to the machine.config file as a *<compiler>* element in the *<compilation>* section. At typical entry for the C# compiler looks like this:

```
<compilation debug="false" explicit="true" defaultLanguage="vb">
  <compiler language="c#;cs;csharp" extension=".cs"
    type="Microsoft.CSharp.CSharpCodeProvider, System, ¬
      Version=1.0.3300.0, Culture=neutral, PublicKeyToken=b77a5c561934e089"
    warningLevel="1" />
  ⋮
```

The *compilation* element sets the default language to Visual Basic .NET, so if you want to use C#, you must set the language attribute in the *@WebService* directive. The *<compiler>* element specifies the acceptable abbreviations for the language, the extension that classes written in this language should contain, and information about the assembly itself.

You can also add a list of assemblies in the *<compilation>* section. You specify these assemblies using an *<add>* element, which requires *assembly*, *version*, *culture*, and *PublicKeyToken* attributes. A typical entry for the *System* namespace in machine.config looks like this:

```
<add assembly="System, Version=1.0.3300.0, Culture=neutral,
  PublicKeyToken=b77a5c561934e089"/>
```

The last assembly defined by an *add* element is as follows:

```
<add assembly="*"/>
```

This *<add>* element specifies any assembly name not listed, so missing assemblies can be searched for at run time.

debug Attribute

The *debug* attribute is by default set to *false*; set it to *true* if the code is to be compiled with debugging symbols. If it is set to *false*, the debugging symbols will be omitted.

Web Service Classes and Namespaces

Once you add a directive, you must expose your class to the Web by using the attributes provided in the *System.Web.Services.WebService* class. This class defines an optional base class for the Web service. It also allows access to common ASP.NET objects such as *Application* and *State*.

The *WebService* class is part of the *System.Web.Services* namespace. This namespace consists of classes used to transmit data from the client to the Web services. The types contained are used to map SOAP messages to method invocations. This namespace also contains the *WebServiceAttribute* and *WebMethodAttribute* classes, which we will use to expose our Web service's functionality. These two attributes will also feature somewhere within your code when you create Web services. The *WebService* attribute provides a mechanism for documenting your Web service, and the *WebMethod* attribute exposes to the Web the particular method to be called.

The *WebService* Attribute

The *WebService* attribute is used less often than the *WebMethod* attribute. It is placed before the class declaration and is used primarily to set the namespace of the Web service. It takes three properties: *Name*, *Namespace*, and *Description*. Here is a *WebService* attribute that defines a namespace for the class *Service1*:

```
[WebService (Name="Record Store Web Service",
    Namespace="http://www.notashop.com/wscr",
    Description="A web service which exposes the "
    + "stock of the record store to the web")]
public class Service1 : System.Web.Services.WebService
{
   ⋮
}
```

By default, ASP.NET templates don't include a *WebService* attribute.

Next we'll look at the three public properties of the *WebService* attribute: *Name*, *Namespace*, and *Description*.

Name Property

The *Name* property defines the name of the XML Web service. It is also reflected in the WSDL description of the service. When you use this attribute, avoid including spaces because the white space is reflected as *_x0020_* in any schema names. For example, the name *Record Store* (instead of *RecordStore*) would turn up as *Record_x0020_Store* in your WSDL and other related XML documents.

Namespace Property

The *Namespace* property defines the namespace for the server; if it is not set, the namespace defaults to *http://tempuri.org*. This property is also reflected in the WSDL description of the service. The default namespace used in this chapter (and in the rest of this book) is *http://www.notashop.com/wscr*.

Description Property

The *Description* property provides the text to describe the XML Web service. It is also reflected in the WSDL description of the service.

The *WebService* attribute has no other unique public properties and methods; all other methods are inherited from the attribute or object classes.

The *WebMethod* Attribute

The *WebMethod* attribute is the attribute you use to create your Web services. By attaching a *[WebMethod]* header in C# to a public method or by using *<WebMethod>* in Visual Basic .NET, you indicate that you want to expose the functionality of that method as a Web service. In fact, methods are the only functionality you can expose using a Web service; if you try to expose gettable or settable properties, .NET will assume that they are methods and will rename them accordingly.

Once created and compiled, a Web method can be invoked by a client using the very names set up in the classes and methods on the server side. The simplest approach is to simply add a *WebMethod* attribute in front of your method call. You saw this in Chapter 2, with a call that takes a number and a percentage and returns the percentage:

```
namespace PercentService
public class Service1:
{
    [WebMethod]
    public double CalcPercent(int Percent, double Number)
    {
        double Value = (Number / 100) * Percent;
        return Value;
    }
}
```

The Web method is then exposed and can be called from within a Windows Forms or ASP.NET Web Forms client application via the proxy class. (We'll look at these topics in the next chapter.)

```
PercentService.Service1 WebProxy= new PercentService.Service1();
double Total = WebProxy.CalcPercent(25, 5);
```

A new instance of the Web service called *WebProxy* is created from the proxy class, and then the Web method is called from the proxy class, just like a normal method, along with the arguments to be passed to it.

Although we didn't specify any properties for the *WebMethod* attribute in this short example, certain values are passed to the Web method by default, as you'll soon see.

Configuring Web Methods Using Attributes

You can alter or tweak the behavior of your Web method by using the properties of the *WebMethod* attribute. Two of the six properties simply document the Web method; the other four change aspects of your Web service's functionality.

The properties of attributes are specified within parentheses, as in this C# example:

```
[WebMethod(Description="Calculates the percentage value "
    + "given a percentage and a number")]
```

In Visual Basic .NET, attribute properties need an extra colon before the equals operator:

```
<WebMethod(Description:="Calculates the percentage value " _
    & "given a percentage and a number")>
```

Let's take a closer look at each of these properties.

Description Property

The *Description* property contains a plain-text description of your Web method. This information is then reflected in the WSDL description of the service.

MessageName Property

Use the *MessageName* property to add the name of your Web method. This information is also reflected in the WSDL description of the service.

EnableSession Property

The *EnableSession* property enables the state management mechanism, allowing Web services to make use of the ASP.NET application and session objects. In ASP.NET (as in classic ASP), the server creates a single application object for each application and a number of session objects, one for each unique session opened by the client.

If this property is set to *true*, session state can be accessed via *HTTPContext.Current.Session*. It can also be accessed via a *WebService.Session* property if the *WebService* base class has been inherited. When you use sessions, the Web service sends a unique Session ID (stored in a cookie), which must be returned by the client with the next request. The session can then be identified, and the data associated with that session can be accessed on the server. (This can be done in a number of ways, which we will look at later.)

The downside of the *EnableSession* property is that it can decrease performance considerably. By default, it is set to *false*. We'll study this property and the whole concept of session management and Web services in greater detail later in this chapter.

CacheDuration Property

The *CacheDuration* property sets the number of seconds that the output from a Web method will be stored in memory. The output is stored as a request/response pair, which is held in the cache. During this period of time, any further requests to the same Web method, with the same parameter values, will result in the output being sent from the cache without the Web method being invoked. Setting this property to 0, the default, disables caching of the results.

The cache stores each request and response within a hash table in memory, to reduce the amount of server resources required. Caching can be useful if you are returning data from a data source that doesn't actually affect the contents of the data store—such as when you are requesting a stock price or when you are asking frequently for data that doesn't change much (such as articles in an online magazine).

However, in most situations that involve a large range of possible requests, caching doesn't improve performance greatly because the cache isn't actually used, and a new journey is required to invoke the Web method and get back a new response. The more often the Web method is called, the larger and less efficient the hash table becomes. At other times, such as when you write to an event log, it is not possible to use the cache. The best kind of data to cache is read-only data.

TransactionOption Property

You use the *TransactionOption* property to set the level of support for .NET distributed transactions. Distributed transactions are a series of actions grouped into a logical whole. In .NET, transactions are supported via the *Systems.EnterpriseServices* namespace. As transactions take place over HTTP, a Web service can take part only as the root object of the transaction—in other words, all the components participating in the transaction must be called from one Web method.

The five possible settings for enabling the level of transaction support through *TransactionOption* basically boil down to two groups. The first group specifies that the Web method should not be run within the scope of the transaction and should be disabled, and the second group specifies that a new transaction is required. In each group, the individual settings don't provide any unique functionality despite the five different names.

- ***Disabled*** Disables transactions for the Web method.
- ***NotSupported*** Disables transactions for the Web method.
- ***Supported*** Disables transactions for the Web method.
- ***Required*** Requires a new transaction to be created. The new transaction is created for the Web method.
- ***RequiresNew*** Requires a new transaction to be created. The Web service is created within a new transaction.

The transaction releases its resources on successful completion. It can be aborted only by the throwing of an exception or the calling of the *SetAbort* method of the *System.EnterpriseServices.ContextUtil* class.

BufferResponse Property

The *BufferResponse* property allows the response to be kept in a memory buffer until the buffer is full or the response has been completed. If this property is set to *true*, the default, the entire response is buffered before it is sent to the client. This behavior helps minimize the amount of communication needed between the client and the Web server, Microsoft Internet Information Services (IIS).

A *BufferResponse* setting of *true* might not be desirable when large amounts of data are sent back by the Web method. In Chapter 2, you saw how a dataset can be sent back by a Web method; the dataset involved was relatively small, but you could see that if it had returned more than a couple of columns and rows, together with the SOAP needed to wrap it, a large amount of data would have been involved.

If you set the *BufferResponse* property to *false*, the response is sent back to the client as it is serialized, in chunks of 16 KB. You'll generally want this property set to the default, except for users who are browsing the service via an ASP.NET client; instead of making them wait for all the data to be sent, you can show them some of the data while the page is loading.

An Example Application

Having considered the basic makeup of a Web service, let's look at how to fill in the functionality by adding Web service logic to a Web method. We'll build a couple of Web methods that will crop up throughout this and the next chapter.

We'll use the record store database example from Chapter 2, but this time we'll provide more functionality than the ability to browse the database. In fact, we'll ape the abilities of Microsoft's Window Media Player to demonstrate how Web services are used in Windows Media Player to provide vital aspects of the functionality, such as the ability to provide details about a CD (artist, artist biography, discography, cover information, and so on).

Windows Media Player isn't the only software that provides this functionality; plenty of other software, such as MusicMatch Jukebox, also provides it. All of these players use Web services to leverage existing repositories of CD information, such as track listings and album covers, and they match this information to what is being played on the application, whether it be an MP3 file, a CD, or a DVD. The response is typically timely enough and invisible enough to give novices the impression that no external call to the Web has been made. This is a particularly common and suitable application of Web services—and for the Web methods on which .NET Web services depend.

In the next chapter, we'll create our own media player application by embedding Windows Media Player into a client application. Our small application will be able to identify and return information about CDs.

In this chapter, we'll create a Web service that the client application will use. We'll select two categories of information that Windows Media Player typically accesses on the Web and build two Web methods. The first Web method will expose an artist biography for each record, and the second will display a stored image of a CD cover when a user places a CD in the CD player and starts the application. You'll see how the Web methods both return straightforward text from a database in the form of a string and also something more complex in the form of an image returned as a byte array.

Our application will first check to see whether it can identify the record; if it can, it will check to see if there is an entry for it in our database, using the identifier and using our own Web services for details. If the application can't identify the artist or record, we will just return the information we can find. This might be a tracklisting and album title, or it might be nothing at all.

The first problem we face is how to uniquely identify CDs when they are placed in the CD tray. This issue has been a source of controversy among companies that initially provided tools to solve the issue as freeware and then added copyright handles at a later point. We'll use an .ocx file from freedb.org and embed this into a Windows Forms client; the tool from freedb.org will provide a useful wrapper to keep hidden the low-level basics of reading from the CD and identifying the CD.

The Example Web Service

We start by creating our .asmx file. First we need to add the classes that we will reference in the Web method. These are

```
using System.Web.Services.Protocols;
using System.Data.OleDb;
```

Then we place our Web service definition just before the *Service1* class definition:

```
[WebService (Name="RecordStoreWebService",
    Namespace="http://www.notashop.com/wscr",
    Description="A Web service which exposes the details "
        + "about an LP and its cover")]
public class Service1 : System.Web.Services.WebService
{
    ⋮
```

We place our Web methods in the *Service1* class definition.

The Example Web Methods

The first Web method, *GetBio*, takes a string containing the unique identifier of the CD and returns a string containing biographical information from our SQL database. The Web method returns the corresponding Biography field from the Biography table:

```
[WebMethod(Description="Gets the Artist's associated Biography")]
public string GetBio(string Id)
{
    OleDbConnection objConnection;
    OleDbCommand objCommand;
    string [] ArtistBio;
    string ArtistB;
    ArtistBio = new String[10];
    string strConnect;
    string strCommand;
    OleDbDataReader DataReader1;
    int i=1;
    strConnect = "Provider=SQLOLEDB.1;Password='';"
        + "Persist Security Info=True;User ID=sa;"
        + "Initial Catalog=dansrecordsSQL;Data Source=CHRISUHOME";
    strCommand = "SELECT Biography From Biography WHERE "
        + "Id='" + Id + "'";
    // Provide your own server's connection information here
 objConnection = new OleDbConnection(strConnect);
    objConnection.Open();
```

```
    objCommand = new OleDbCommand(strCommand, objConnection);
    DataReader1 = objCommand.ExecuteReader();
    while (DataReader1.Read())
    {
        ArtistBio[i] = DataReader1.GetString(0).ToString();
        i++;
    }
    DataReader1.Close();
    objConnection.Close();
    ArtistB = ArtistBio[1];
    return ArtistB;
}
```

Our Web method accepts a string—the identifier of the CD—and returns a string after querying the database by using the *OleDbConnection* and *OleDbCommand* objects and by using an *OleDbDataReader* object to return the information from the query. The query is then read into an array from which the returned string is taken. We've chosen a string within this Web method for reasons of interoperability.

Our Web method uses a data reader. In Chapter 9, you'll see that returning a data set causes problems for all client applications that are not .NET applications. To circumvent this limitation, we'll briefly use the data reader to read the biographical information into an array, and then we'll store the contents of the array in a string.

The second Web method is more complex. The Web service is provided with the identifier of the CD and must supply an image. Images are stored in BLOB format within a database, but that immediately poses the problem of how to retrieve information from the database and supply it to the Web method. We have to translate the image into a byte array and return this to the client. The client must translate the byte array back into image, which can be displayed on the form. (We won't worry about how the client deals with this information until the next chapter; we simply want the Web method to return a byte array.) Here's the code that achieves this:

```
[WebMethod(Description="Gets the Artist's or CD's Associated Picture")]
public byte[] GetPic(string Id)
{
    OleDbConnection objConnection;
    OleDbCommand objCommand;
    string strConnect;
    string strCommand;
    strConnect = "Provider=SQLOLEDB.1;Password='';"
        + "Persist Security Info=True;User ID=sa;"
        + "Initial Catalog=dansrecordsSQL;Data Source=CHRISUHOME";
```

```
    // Provide your own server's connection information here
  strCommand = "SELECT CoverPic From AlbumDetails "
        + "WHERE Id = '" + Id + "'";
    objConnection = new OleDbConnection(strConnect);
    objConnection.Open();
    objCommand = new OleDbCommand(strCommand, objConnection);
    // Convert stream to byte array
    OleDbDataAdapter da = new OleDbDataAdapter(objCommand);
    DataSet ds = new DataSet();
    da.Fill(ds, "AlbumDetails");
    int count = ds.Tables["AlbumDetails"].Rows.Count;

    if(count>0)
    {
        Byte[] BLOBPicByteArray =  new Byte[0];
        BLOBPicByteArray=(Byte[])
            (ds.Tables["AlbumDetails"].Rows[count - 1]["CoverPic"]);
        objConnection.Close();
        return BLOBPicByteArray;
    }
    else
    {
        Byte[] BLOBPicByteArray =  new Byte[0];
        objConnection.Close();
        return BLOBPicByteArray;
    }
}
```

> **Caution** How the image is placed in the AlbumDetails table affects the functionality of the Web method. If you use a Microsoft Access front end at any point to insert the images into the database, by default an OLE container will be inserted around the image, and this will cause the Web method to return an error because it expects an image rather than an OLE container. To work around this, you can insert the image using pure SQL statements or create a small procedure that inserts the image as BLOB data via the form. We supply a small method for doing this together with the code you can download for the book.

This method is more complex than the first one; the code required to extract the image from the database is similar, but once the image has been identified, it has to be read as a stream of bytes into a byte array. The mechanics by which the requisite piece of data is identified is pretty much the same as with the first method—the connection and command objects are used to execute a SQL query against the database—but we'll use the more flexible *DataAdapter* object to return the result of our data query before reading the stream of bytes into the byte array.

You can now browse the .asmx file, and you should get details on the two Web methods that have just been created, as Figure 7-1 shows.

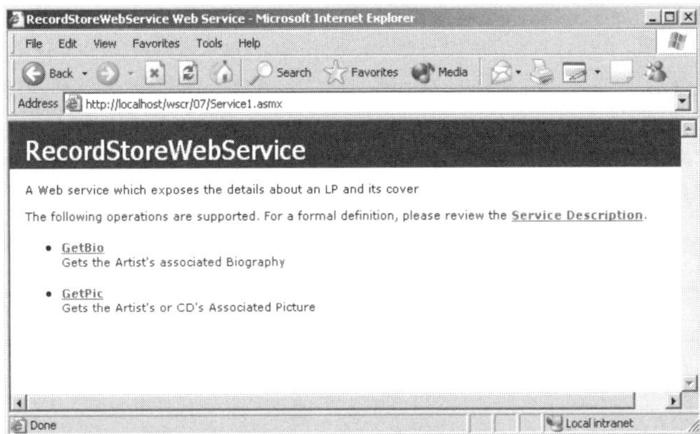

Figure 7-1 Browsing the Service1.asmx file of RecordStoreWebService

If you set up the example MSDE/SQL database, you should also be able to send a test request and get a response back. We now have two Web methods that provide the required functionality. We haven't supplied the Web methods with any extra attribute settings because we know that the Web methods will not need to use session handling, caching, or transactions in any form. However, creating a class and exposing it as a Web method isn't the end of the story. We have to consider how this information will be encoded, how to keep track of state, how the functionality of the Web service will be affected by configuration files, and how to deploy and debug the Web service.

Tweaking Your Web Methods

You can tweak your Web methods by directly altering them using properties of the *WebMethod* attribute or of related attributes or by altering the WSDL document produced by the Web service. By altering the WSDL document, you alter the definition of the service and therefore the service itself.

WSDL and Web Methods

We'll start by reexamining the relationship between the WSDL document and our Web methods and then move on to how we can alter the WSDL document to interact with and use the Web service meaningfully. We discussed the workings of WSDL in detail in Chapter 3, but we need to revisit some details and investigate them in greater depth.

When you assign something in a *WebService* or *WebMethod* attribute, a corresponding entry is created in the WSDL document. If we look at the lengthy WSDL document created for our *GetBio* Web method, we can isolate some specific points. We'll go through the WSDL document that is automatically created when you browse the Web service and add a *?wsdl* query string to the end of it.

The document begins with the initial namespace definitions:

```
<?xml version="1.0" encoding="utf-8" ?>
<definitions xmlns:http="http://schemas.xmlsoap.org/wsdl/http/"
  xmlns:soap="http://schemas.xmlsoap.org/wsdl/soap/"
  xmlns:s="http://www.w3.org/2001/XMLSchema"
  xmlns:s0="http://www.notashop.com/wscr"
  xmlns:soapenc="http://schemas.xmlsoap.org/soap/encoding/"
  xmlns:tm="http://microsoft.com/wsdl/mime/textMatching/"
  xmlns:mime="http://schemas.xmlsoap.org/wsdl/mime/"
  targetNamespace="http://www.notashop.com/wscr"
  xmlns="http://schemas.xmlsoap.org/wsdl/">
```

The *targetNamespace* attribute is set to the namespace that was defined in the *WebService* attribute in the class. Under the namespace definitions is the *<types>* element. As you saw in Chapter 3, the *<types>* element contains the schema. By default, this is an XML schema, but you can use other type systems. Here is the schema that contains the rules for serializing the data contained in our two Web methods:

```
<types>
  <s:schema elementFormDefault="qualified"
    targetNamespace="http://www.notashop.com/wscr">
    <s:element name="GetBio">
      <s:complexType>
        <s:sequence>
          <s:element minOccurs="0" maxOccurs="1" name="Id"
            type="s:string" />
        </s:sequence>
      </s:complexType>
    </s:element>
    <s:element name="GetBioResponse">
      <s:complexType>
        <s:sequence>
```

```
          <s:element minOccurs="0" maxOccurs="1" name="GetBioResult"
            type="s:string" />
        </s:sequence>
      </s:complexType>
    </s:element>
    <s:element name="GetPic">
      <s:complexType>
        <s:sequence>
          <s:element minOccurs="0" maxOccurs="1" name="Id"
              type="s:string" />
        </s:sequence>
      </s:complexType>
    </s:element>
    <s:element name="GetPicResponse">
      <s:complexType>
        <s:sequence>
          <s:element minOccurs="0" maxOccurs="1" name="GetPicResult"
            type="s:base64Binary" />
        </s:sequence>
      </s:complexType>
    </s:element>
    <s:element name="string" nillable="true" type="s:string" />
    <s:element name="base64Binary" nillable="true" type="s:base64Binary" />
  </s:schema>
</types>
```

The *GetBio* Web method takes a string and returns a string. The string is named *Id* in the Web method, and you can see quite clearly that this is reflected in the *<s:element>* element. It returns the result via a *<s:element>* named *GetBioResult*. Both of these elements are strings, which again reflects the makeup of our Web method.

The second of our two Web methods, *GetPic*, takes a string and returns a byte array. *GetPic* has the same RPC-style structure as *GetBio* and does little different other than return its data, a byte array, in a different format.

Next in the WSDL document is the *<message>* element. This element contains a definition of all the types that the Web service is capable of receiving. We haven't amended the defaults in any way (this is done via the .NET .config files, which we will look at shortly). In .NET version 1.1, our Web service can receive only SOAP responses because only the SOAP protocol is enabled in machine.config—in .NET 1.0, you might well see extra code with sections for HTTP-POST and HTTP-GET as well:

```
<message name="GetBioSoapIn">
  <part name="parameters" element="s0:GetBio" />
</message>
```

```
<message name="GetBioSoapOut">
  <part name="parameters" element="s0:GetBioResponse" />
</message>
<message name="GetPicSoapIn">
  <part name="parameters" element="s0:GetPic" />
</message>
<message name="GetPicSoapOut">
  <part name="parameters" element="s0:GetPicResponse" />
</message>
```

For each format the Web service can receive and send information in, there is a *<message>* element that contains a part *<element>* that contains the type of data and the corresponding schema element that is being returned.

Next up is the *<portType>* element, which groups the different operations. It creates an abstract definition that combines each of our Web method names (*GetBio* and *GetPic*) with each type of operation:

```
<portType name="RecordStoreWebServiceSoap">
  <operation name="GetBio">
    <documentation>Gets the Artist's associated Biography</documentation>
    <input message="s0:GetBioSoapIn" />
    <output message="s0:GetBioSoapOut" />
  </operation>
  <operation name="GetPic">
    <documentation>
      Gets the Artist's or CD's Associated Picture
    </documentation>
    <input message="s0:GetPicSoapIn" />
    <output message="s0:GetPicSoapOut" />
  </operation>
</portType>
```

Notice that a documentation element is created for each *<operation>* element, and that this documentation element contains whatever we put in the *Description* attribute of our Web method.

The *<binding>* element describes information about the transport protocols and message formatting. The definitions also contain the number of communications across the network needed to make a correspondence. Each operation makes only one request and requires one response. If you are using another protocol, such as SMTP, more than one operation is required. The *<binding>* element contains extension elements that define the method of transport and supply the namespace defined within the Web method as part of the SOAP transfer:

```
<binding name="RecordStoreWebServiceSoap"
  type="s0:RecordStoreWebServiceSoap">
  <soap:binding transport="http://schemas.xmlsoap.org/soap/http"
    style="document" />
  <operation name="GetBio">
    <soap:operation soapAction="http://www.notashop.com/wscr/GetBio"
      style="document" />
    <input>
      <soap:body use="literal" />
    </input>
    <output>
      <soap:body use="literal" />
    </output>
  </operation>
  <operation name="GetPic">
    <soap:operation soapAction="http://www.notashop.com/wscr/GetPic"
      style="document" />
    <input>
      <soap:body use="literal" />
    </input>
    <output>
      <soap:body use="literal" />
    </output>
  </operation>
</binding>
```

The final part of the WSDL document is the *<service>* element. This element contains a *<port>* element that defines the address via which the Web service can be invoked. Details are given for invocation via the SOAP method only in .NET 1.1:

```
  <service name="RecordStoreWebService">
    <documentation>A Web service which exposes the details about an LP
      and its cover
    </documentation>
    <port name="RecordStoreWebServiceSoap"
      binding="s0:RecordStoreWebServiceSoap">
      <soap:address location="http://localhost/StoreService/Service1.asmx" />
    </port>
  </service>

</definitions>
```

So we've got our Web methods, and you've seen how what we put in them is reflected in the WSDL document. However, plenty of other attributes are available for altering the content of our WSDL document.

Doc-Lit vs. RPC Encoding

In Chapter 2, we looked at the two styles of formatting SOAP messages. You can set the style of the formatting using the *[SoapDocumentService]* or the *[SoapRpcService]* attribute. We also looked at the difference between straight document-literal-style messages, in which the aim is to exchange document-oriented messages between client and server, and RPC encoding, which enables a procedure/method call type of functionality. Many Web services (including our example in this chapter) rely on a request/response scenario, but the document-literal style is fast becoming commonplace because it is more straightforward to use and can do everything that the RPC encoding style can do.

You can supply *[SoapDocumentService]* and *[SoapRpcService]* attributes after the *[WebService]* attribute. These attributes alter the information supplied in the WSDL information under the *<binding>* element. By default, the *[SoapDocumentService]* attribute is used, but we can add a *[SoapRpcService]* attribute to our example code to alter the WSDL in the following way:

```
<binding name="RecordStoreWebServiceSoap"
  type="tns:RecordStoreWebServiceSoap">
  <soap:binding transport="http://schemas.xmlsoap.org/soap/http"
    style="rpc" />
  <operation name="GetBio">
    <soap:operation soapAction="http://www.notashop.com/wscr/GetBio"
      style="rpc" />
    <input>
      <soap:body use="encoded" namespace="http://www.notashop.com/wscr"
        encodingStyle="http://schemas.xmlsoap.org/soap/encoding/" />
    </input>
    <output>
      <soap:body use="encoded" namespace="http://www.notashop.com/wscr"
        encodingStyle="http://schemas.xmlsoap.org/soap/encoding/" />
    </output>
  </operation>
  <operation name="GetPic">
    <soap:operation soapAction="http://www.notashop.com/wscr/GetPic"
      style="rpc" />
    <input>
      <soap:body use="encoded" namespace="http://www.notashop.com/wscr"
        encodingStyle="http://schemas.xmlsoap.org/soap/encoding/" />
    </input>
    <output>
      <soap:body use="encoded" namespace="http://www.notashop.com/wscr"
        encodingStyle="http://schemas.xmlsoap.org/soap/encoding/" />
    </output>
  </operation>
</binding>
```

Little changes in the WSDL for our example application if we do this and the number of operations remains the same. However, extra information about using the RPC-encoded style is added into the *<soap:body>* statement.

If you don't want these styles to apply to the whole Web service, you can use the *[SoapDocumentMethod]* and *[SoapRpcMethod]* attributes instead; for a method, these are specified after the *[WebMethod]* attribute. They can be used to override the values set up with the *[WebService]* attribute.

We won't dig too much farther into the WSDL here—we've covered it previously, and we simply want to demonstrate how our Web methods affect and alter the contents of the WSDL document.

Configuring Web Methods

A quick recap, then: We've built our Web service and given it two Web methods. We've looked at the WSDL document created automatically as part of the Web service. The content of the WSDL document depends partly on what happens within the Web method itself. However, the Web method isn't the only object that can affect the contents of the WSDL document. It's also possible to alter how the Web service and Web method work via the configuration files.

One major new feature in the .NET Framework was the XML configuration files, which store configuration information pertinent to both the .NET Framework and ASP.NET. You can use these configuration files to manage certain aspects of Web methods. Two main configuration files are used in .NET:

- Machine.config, which is used to configure information for the server and is used throughout all of your applications. It is the file from which all other configuration files can inherit their settings. It can be found at \Windows\Microsoft.Net\Framework*version*\Config.
- Web.config, which is used to control application-specific information and should be found in the virtual root directory of the Web application. There might be more than one web.config file per application, with one file overriding another web.config file's settings, along with any conflicting settings within the machine.config file. Web.config files apply configuration settings to all child directories unless other web.config files are beneath them.

The configuration files are simple XML files that allow alteration of the IIS metabase via various tags.

The Machine.config File

Machine.config is where a lot of the ASP.NET service's functionality is enabled or disabled. This file allows you to take care of a number of tasks, from the setting of permissions in IIS to the enabling of protocols for use by Web services. There is a single version of machine.config for each version of ASP.NET that has been installed, to ensure some backward compatibility with future versions. All ASP.NET applications use this file for default properties and behaviors.

We're interested in the behaviors of this file that affect Web services, so it makes sense to focus on the *<webServices>* element and the sections it supports.

Protocols

If you look under the *<webServices>* element in your machine.config file, you'll see a list of the protocols that .asmx files support:

```
<webServices>
  <protocols>
    <add name="HttpSoap1.2"/>
    <add name="HttpSoap"/>
    <!-- <add name="HttpPost"/> -->
    <!-- <add name="HttpGet"/> -->
    <add name="Documentation"/>
  </protocols>
  ⋮
</webServices>
```

In .NET 1.1, only one protocol is supported by default. You can add others by changing the add element as follows:

```
<webServices>
  <protocols>
    <remove name="HttpSoap1.2"/>
    <add name="HttpSoap"/>
    <add name="HttpPost"/>
    <add name="HttpGet"/>
    <add name="Documentation"/>
  </protocols>
  ⋮
</webServices>
```

This action adds support for the HTTP-POST and HTTP-GET protocols for the whole server. You can remove support for any protocol by using the *<remove>* element and using the *name* attribute to specify the name of the protocol you want to remove.

Documentation

In addition to the three protocols, there is also a documentation protocol. It allows you to customize the documentation page that appears when you navigate to an .asmx endpoint. You can change it by means of the *<wsdlHelpGenerator>* element under the *<webServices>* element:

```
<webServices>
  ⋮
  <wsdlHelpGenerator href="defaultWsdlHelpGenerator.aspx" />
```

This element displays the HTML documentation. When you run a Web service, you see the test page by default, and the *href* attribute will default to indicate a local file called defaultWsdlHelpGenerator.aspx. If we run this page without altering it for our RecordStore test service, we'll see the page shown earlier, in Figure 7-1, in the section "The Example Web Methods."

By changing the setting in machine.config, you can substitute this page for your own page or an upgraded version of the defaultWsdlHelpGenerator.aspx page.

In addition to the *protocols* element, in the machine.config file you will also find the *soapExtensionTypes*, *soapExtensionReflectorTypes*, *soapExtensionImporterTypes*, and *serviceDescriptionFormatExtensionTypes* elements. These elements are used to register SOAP extensions, reflectors, and importers for use in the WSDL generation and proxy-client generation processes. These elements are poorly documented, but you can use them to add custom attributes to Web methods and provide access to these custom attributes on the client. For example, you can use them to add security attributes to import other XML schemas, such as the XML-Encryption and XML-Signature documents to help with proper authentication. The MSDN documentation specifies that these properties are not to be used by developers directly from code and should be left empty, but this isn't entirely accurate because they do provide useful functionality.

The Web.config File

You can use the web.config file to modify settings from machine.config or to extend and define its own settings. The web.config file is commonly used to override settings from machine.config or other web.config files; it has an element you can use within the *<protocols>* element to wipe the protocol information specified in parent configuration files.

The *<clear />* tag clears all settings inherited from a machine.config or web.config file. You can place this element at the head of the file and then add any protocol definitions after it, as in this example:

```
<webServices>
  <protocols>
    <clear />
    <add name="SOAP"/>
```

It is a good idea to use the *<clear />* element because by default your Web service might be using the HTTP-POST and HTTP-GET protocols to transmit your Web service as well as SOAP, and this might not only affect the performance of your Web service but also make it more insecure. Also, for reasons of interoperability, it might be preferable to just use SOAP because SOAP is the standard protocol for Web service transfer and HTTP-POST and HTTP-GET are not.

You can also use the web.config file to enable debugging, by setting the compilation tag's *debug* attribute to *true*. You do this within the *<system.web>* tag as follows:

```
<configuration>
  <system.web>
    <compilation debug="true"/>
  </system.web>
</configuration>
```

Another setting of interest in the web.config file is the *appSettings* tag. This tag allows the addition of custom application data, such as DSN details or information to enable Active Directory settings. You can add custom application data by using an *add* tag within the *AppSettings* tag, which takes *key* and *value* attributes:

```
<configuration>
  <appSettings>
    <add key="key" value="value" />
  </appSettings>
</configuration>
```

You can use the *appSettings* tag to dynamically specify the URL of a Web service at run time. This might be useful if you've tested a Web service on your own machine and need to change the name to deploy it on a client's server or if you have several versions of a Web service and you want the user to be able to choose among them.

> **Important** You can also access the files you add to the *appSettings* element programmatically via a shortcut, by including the *System.Configuration* namespace and then specifying the following:
>
> ```
> string example;
> example = ConfigurationSettings.AppSettings["URL"];
> ```

To dynamically specify the URL of a Web service, you have to jump through a few hoops. First you have to change the URL Behavior setting for the

Web service from Static to Dynamic. To do so, you select the Web reference in Solution Explorer and then change the setting for URL Behavior in the Properties pane. This adds an *appSetting* entry to the app.config file in this fashion:

```
<appSettings>
  <add key="WebApp.localhost.Service1"
    value="http://localhost/wscr/07/RecordStore/Service1.asmx/">
</appSettings>
```

Next you must create an installer class that will override the *install* method of the class and modify the web.config file itself. This installer class must log the installation and locate the correct web.config file, which will then be added to the project as a custom action. (Custom actions are the actions requested by code that couldn't be performed during installation.) You must create a project that includes the installer class and a dialog box that allows users to dynamically select the location of the Web service they want to run.

Generally, altering the .config files that affect Web methods isn't a big issue, but it does alter the contents of the WSDL document, too.

Now let's look at the other way to alter Web services—via attributes.

Managing State

We mentioned the *EnableSession* attribute, which can be applied to the *WebMethod* attribute to enable session handling, and we showed how it allows access to the *Application* and *Session* objects via the *System.Web.Services* namespace. However, session handling with Web services is not nearly as straightforward as just using the *Session* and *Application* objects and hoping for the best. It merits a larger discussion in its own right.

One potential conundrum when you create a Web application is how to maintain state while using the inherently stateless protocol HTTP. Of course, with Web services this generally shouldn't be a concern because normally you won't need to keep track of state, but sometimes even Web services require a method for remembering state. For example, your Web service might need to make multiple connections to a client. Or, when you're using transactions, your Web service might need to remember, for a transaction, the state of each process that involves the service.

Throughout the brief history of Web applications, the Web developer has had three choices in this matter: maintaining state on the server, maintaining state on the client, or abandoning the information completely when a connection is closed or cut off. The tradeoff is between making the code simpler (by maintaining state on the server or client) and making the code perform optimally (not keeping track of state at all).

You keep track of state in a Web service by exposing the ASP.NET *Application* and *Session* objects. In fact, the methods for accessing these objects are very straightforward.

You can expose the *Session* and *Application* objects in two ways:

- By inheriting from the *WebService* class contained in the *System.Web.Services* namespace.
- By accessing the *HttpContext* object via the *HttpContext* class's *Current* property. The *HttpContext* object allows you to access all "classic" ASP objects.

Before we rush into looking at how to do this, let's consider the circumstances under which you should keep track of state.

When Should You Maintain State?

Maintaining state isn't always necessary when you use Web services, and indeed the additional overhead needed to maintain state can often greatly delay and damage a service, so think carefully before you implement state management. If at all possible, your Web service should be stateless.

If you consider the following example, you'll see why it is often preferable to forget about state. To keep track of state, you could update the property of a particular object and access it whenever you need to, but this isn't at all straightforward. For starters, Web methods support only methods, not property procedures, so the following code would be illegal:

```
public class Artist: System.Web.Services.WebService
{
    [WebMethod]
    public string Biography
    {
        get
        {
            return Biography;
        }
        set
        {
            Biography = "A short history";
        }
    }
}
```

Any proxy class generated would not contain the necessary properties. Instead, you must enable the *Session* property of each property accessor individually, setting the *EnableSession* property to *true* as follows. (Again, this code is illegal; we're using it just for theoretical purposes.)

```
public class Artist:System.Web.Services.WebService
{
    public string Biography;
    {
        [WebMethod(EnableSession = true)]
        get
        {
            return (string) Session["Biography"];
        }
        [WebMethod(EnableSession = true)]
        set
        {
            Session["Biography"] = "A short history";
        }
    }
}
```

We created a *Session* variable, *Biography*, in which we stored our value. To return a value from it, we explicitly cast the *Session* variable as a string. However, even if this solution were to work, it would undermine the advantages provided by Web services. If you want to get or set the property value, you must make a separate method call over the Internet for each call, and this will affect your Web service's performance. Also, using *Session* information like this is artificial. *Artist.get_Biography* isn't tied to *Session["Biography"]* by any other way than the Web method, so when the Web method is finished, the *Session* variable persists until it times out or the session is concluded. Also, because session variables are related to separate cookies with their own session IDs, in some situations you might need to use two separate Session IDs, such as for banking transactions, and this can cause further performance problems.

Rather than list the situations in which you shouldn't keep track of state, it's probably easier to list the times when you might use session management within a Web service:

- When your Web service requires information from a data source (as in our example application)
- When your Web service goes through a series of steps in a transaction that might have to be rolled back, depending on whether a step fails or succeeds

Even in these situations, good alternatives are available to using state management, as we will briefly touch on.

Maintaining State on the Server

You can store state on the server in three ways: by tracking state on a single server, by using an ASP.NET state service, or by using a SQL Server database.

In-Memory State

Classic ASP maintains state on a single server by using cookies on the client, which can then be referenced via the *Session* object. This practice is the fastest way of maintaining state but also the most liable to breakage. If the ASP/ASP.NET process gets stopped, all associated information is lost. The information can also be lost if a request to one server is sent to a different one instead.

Out-of-Process State

You can use two out-of-process state services with ASP.NET to keep track of state. The advantage of this approach is that it can be used over several servers, and state isn't as vulnerable to being lost if the ASP/ASP.NET process is killed. The main problem with keeping track of out-of-state session processes is that using either service is much slower than maintaining in-memory state. The two types of out-of-process state are

- **StateServer** An ASP.NET state service can be tracked via the Microsoft Management Console (MMC).
- **SQLServer** SQLServer uses stored procedures, which must first be installed via the SQL Server Manager.

You typically use these forms of state management only when you're using a Web farm configuration together with several servers. In fact, in-process session state is the only form of state management currently available in the .NET Framework. So we'll concentrate on using state in Web services via ASP.NET.

Integrating ASP.NET's Built-in State Facility into Web Services

One great downside of using sessions with classic ASP was that underneath all the wrapping it still relied on cookies to do its work. A user who turned off cookies would lose any benefit of sessions—and likely the entire functionality of the Web application as well. ASP.NET allows you to send cookieless information by munging the session state information to a URL that allows the user to reconnect to the session information.

For you to use session state, a *SessionStateModule* object must be present in the application. (It is by default.) You can then alter information about the session using the *sessionState* element in the machine.config file on the server.

The *sessionState* element has six attributes:

- ***mode*** You can set this attribute to *Off*, *InProc*, *StateServer*, or *SQLServer*. It specifies where the session state information is to be held. These are basically the scenarios we have discussed; either session state handling is turned off or the information can be stored in process via the StateServer service or in a SQL database.
- ***cookieless*** This attribute specifies whether to use "classic ASP" session cookies (*false* is the default setting) or whether to use the new ASP.NET cookieless munging procedure.
- ***timeout*** Indicates how long, in minutes, the session can be idle before it is terminated.
- ***stateConnectionString*** Specifies the location and port of the session state server.
- ***sqlConnectionString*** Specifies the location of the SQL Server.
- ***stateNetworkTimeout*** Specifies the number of seconds the TCP/IP network connection between the Web server and the state server can be idle before the session is abandoned.

You alter these settings for the whole application via the configuration file and then you can enable a session for each Web method by using the *EnableSession* attribute and setting it to *true*.

Two types of state can be enabled for a session. We'll look at them next.

Application State

The *Application* object allows you to maintain *application state* by letting you store session information for the whole application. The *Application* object doesn't have to be explicitly enabled; it is already available via the *Context* object, so any class deriving from the *WebService* class will automatically have access to the *Application* object.

The best way to demonstrate this is to build a simple example Web method. This Web method contains two pieces of information: an artist and a specific title the artist has performed. The Web service will store the name of the artist and then add the title to that artist information.

The code that does this task is broken down into two classes. The first class has two Web methods. The first Web method that is exposed stores the Artist's Name in the *Application* object, under the variable "*Artist*". The second method allows the user to retrieve the artist's name.

```
public class SetArtist:System.Web.Services.WebService
{
    [WebMethod]
    public string SetArtistName(string Artist)
    {
        Application.Add("Artist", ArtistName);
        return ((string) Application["Artist"]);
    }
    [WebMethod]
    public string GetArtistName()
    {
        return((string) Application["Artist"]);
    }
}
```

This Web service uses the inherited Web service class to provide access to the *Application* object. You can just as easily use the second method of accessing the *Application* object's state via the *HttpContext* object. We can write a second class, *SetArtist* class, that concatenates the title to the artist's name in the *Application* object, by using the *HttpContext* object as follows:

```
public class SetTitle:System.Web.Services.WebService
{
    [WebMethod]
    public string AddTitle(string Title)
    {
        HttpContext ConObj = HttpContext.Current;
        ConObj.Application["Artist"] =
            (string) ConObj.Application["Artist"] + Title;
        return ((string) ConObj.Application["Artist"]);
    }
}
```

We use the *Current* property of the *HttpContext* object to return a reference to the *Application* object.

Session State

The main difference between using session state instead of application state is that we have to explicitly enable the *Session* object by setting the *EnableSession* property of the Web method to *True*. Then all we need to do is substitute the occurrence of the *Application* object for the *Session* object in our first class:

```
public class SetArtist:System.Web.Services.WebService
{
    [WebMethod(EnableSession = True)]
    public string SetArtistName(string Artist)
```

```
    {
        Session.Add("Artist", ArtistName);
        return ((string) Session["Artist"]);
    }
    [WebMethod(EnableSession = True)]
    public string GetArtistName()
    {
        return((string) Session["Artist"]);
    }
}
```

and in our second class:

```
public class SetTitle:System.Web.Services.WebService
{
    [WebMethod(EnableSession = True)]
    public string AddTitle(string Title)
    {
        HttpContext ConObj = HttpContext.Current;
        ConObj.Session["Artist"] =
            (string) ConObj.Session["Artist"] + Title;
        return ((string) ConObj.Session["Artist"]);
    }
}
```

As mentioned earlier, the *Session* object doesn't offer an ideal solution because each time the Web service is called, a new session is invoked.

Custom Cookies

The final way you can use ASP.NET to monitor state information on the client is to store it in a cookie and submit it along with each request. If you are certain that your clients will have cookies enabled, you can use this method.

You can create a cookie and insert the relevant information into it and send it to the client, by using the *Response* object. Then, in a future Web method call, you can use the *Request* object to retrieve it. Both the *Request* and *Response* objects can be accessed via the *Context* object.

The code to store this session information is as follows:

```
public class SetArtist:System.Web.Services.WebService
{
    [WebMethod]
    public string SetArtistName(string Artist)
    {
        HttpCookie CustomCookie = new HttpCookie("artist");
        CustomCookie.Values.Add("Artist", "The Monkees");
        Context.Response.AppendCookie(CustomCookie)
    }
```

The code to retrieve it looks like this:

```
[WebMethod]
public string GetArtistName()
{
    HttpCookie CustomCookie = Context.Response.Cookies("artist");
    if(cookie.Values["artist"] == "The Monkees")
    {
        string message = "I'm a believer";
    }
    return message;
}
```

In this way, you can handle session state transparently and easily on the client. This can be a good solution if the information being stored doesn't have to be secure, is only textual information, and is restricted to using HTTP.

Asynchronous Web Services

Web services also provide an ideal model for the remote calling of methods just as if they were present on the client's machine. By default, calls to a Web service made from ASP.NET clients or from Windows Forms applications are synchronous and rely on immediate responses. However, even over the shortest distances some lag is likely, so in some situations it's far better to get your client to poll the Web service and then come back later to pick up the response. The .NET Framework provides good support for this kind of asynchronous operation.

Some situations are much better suited to asynchronous operations than others. Any kind of operation in which the Web service might be blocked by a thread that must wait on specific information before continuing is not suited to asynchronous services. However, when you call a Web service that might take a long time to return a result, but the information isn't critical to the continuation of the thread—as is likely in most situations in which a Web service is called over the Internet—asynchronous calls are the preferable solution. With an asynchronous call, your application can continue executing a thread after having issued a call for the Web service and won't be held up by the lack of response. Situations in which this is useful are those involving a transaction or those that require the use of a user interface, where the lack of response might freeze the interface.

This model of asynchronous consumption might seem to have no bearing on the Web method itself. Whether a service is called asynchronously doesn't directly affect the Web method because the call happens via the client and proxy class (as you shall see in the next chapter). However, there are some concerns relating to asynchronous behavior when you need your Web service to return information about work in progress, such as the status of a download or installation. In theory, your method will run from start to finish and not return any information until it has finished the job at hand.

The *OneWay* Property

The simplest trick for writing an asynchronous Web method is to use the *OneWay* property, which is part of the *SoapRpcMethod* attribute. Setting this property to *true* enables the client to return immediately because it won't be waiting for a response value. In other words, the client doesn't have to wait for the Web service to finish processing.

The Web service does this by returning a 202 HTTP status code, which indicates to the client that the service has started and that the client doesn't need to come back and check that the service has finished. Instead, the Web service usually writes a value to a database, which can be picked up at a later time. *OneWay* methods aren't allowed to have a return value for this obvious reason.

One possible application of the *OneWay* method is on a random-number generator. A Web service that has to generate thousands of sequences of unique random numbers (for lotto cards, for example) might take hours to complete, so you wouldn't want the Web service's client hanging around this long for an answer.

To set up this attribute, you can do the following:

```
public class GenerateRandomNumber: WebService
{
    [SoapRpcMethod(OneWay=true)]
    [WebMethod]
    public void Generate()
    {
        //Logic for generating random number sequences
    }
    ⋮
```

As with most simple solutions, this has flaws. For example, you cannot uniquely identify which service kick-started the process. You might be able to identify a particular user, but what happens if that user makes several calls to the Web service? There is no way around this, so a better solution is needed.

Dividing the Labor

Another way to implement asynchronous services is to write several Web methods and get each Web method to perform a different action within the Web service. The task has to be started by one Web method and finished by another, but then you can get around the problem of not being able to return a value because one Web method can call another, and then a second can return a value.

Threading

The big issue when you use multiple Web methods is guaranteeing a secure and safe way of accessing the information. If you consider that several Web methods will be running every time the service is called and that the service can be called many times, you need some sort of locking procedure to guarantee a particular Web method's exclusive access to a resource.

WS-Routing

WS-Routing is a SOAP-based protocol that allows the asynchronous routing of SOAP messages. It adds information to the SOAP header that describes the path from initial sender to ultimate receiver via intermediaries.

The proposal for WS-Routing was launched in late 2001 and hasn't been updated since. It provides a framework for one-way and two-way messaging and allows for the continuation of long-running dialogs. We look at WS-Routing in some more detail in Chapter 14.

Versioning with XSLT

When providing versioning for classes and assemblies, most programmers typically rely on Windows and Visual Studio .NET to do the dirty work. However, when it comes to the task of keeping your other bits and pieces, such as schemas, associated with the Web service so that you can easily tell which is the most up-to-date version, a little more effort is required. Extensible Stylesheet Language Transformations (XSLT) is an ideal tool for versioning because it allows you to write style sheets in XSLT to transform one XML document into another. It is a programming language in its own right; an XSLT processor can take an XML document and an XML source file containing the XSLT document and perform a transformation that renders a new version of the XML document.

The advantage of this approach is that if a request is made to a new version of a Web service and the request is formatted for an old version of the service, instead of throwing out the request you can upgrade it to keep the original request unchanged. Before we do this, we need to look at how XML documents are versioned and then at how to use XSLT transformations to upgrade them.

Versioning XML Documents

XML documents are generally versioned in one of two ways: by adding a version attribute to the XML document or by placing the versioning information within a namespace. You can use XSLT with either approach, or indeed with both approaches at the same time, but the namespace approach is preferable. An example XML fragment shows the difference. The first fragment uses a version attribute:

```
<?xml version="1.0"?>
<album version="1.1">
  <title>
    <titlename>Rated R</titlename>
  </title>
</album>
```

Conceptually, this is the less "pure" method because the version attribute is in essence just tagged onto unrelated code.

The version information is more typically included at the end of a namespace declaration:

```
<?xml version="1.0"?>
<album xmlns="http://www.notashop.com/wscr/albums/1.1">
  <title>
    <titlename>Rated R</titlename>
  </title>
</album>
```

An alternative version using namespaces is also commonly used—instead of using a version number, you include a datestamp as part of the namespace:

```
<?xml version="1.0"?>
<album xmlns="http://www.notashop.com/wscr/albums/2003/03/07">
  <title>
    <titlename>Rated R</titlename>
  </title>
</album>
```

The namespace definition is not without its own drawbacks, though. Any time a namespace is changed, each user of the namespaces is forced to support each slight change in the namespace along with the original namespace. One solution is to not change the namespace URI when only small changes are made to the XML document.

If we have a versioning procedure for our XML documents, then, how do we go about upgrading from one document to another?

Upgrading an XML Document with XSLT

When an upgraded document is released, you will have the old version and an up-to-date version. Accompanying the new version should be an XSLT document that performs the upgrade. First you check the new XML document and version against the old one. You run the XSLT transformation on the original XML document to the next one. Typically, one XSLT transformation handles each incremental upgrade. So one transformation is required to get from version 1.0. to version 1.1. Also, when the transformation is performed, it must change the corresponding version attribute or namespace in the document to reflect this.

An Example Transformation

Let's say our new version of the service requires a *recordLabel* element to be supplied as part of a request. This would clearly alter the XML schema and would be an ideal application of an XSLT transformation. This example adds a *recordLabel* element to the album element:

```
<xsl:stylesheet version="1.0"
  xmlns:xsl="http://www.w3.org/1999/XSL/Transform">

  <xsl:output method="xml" version="1.0"
    doctype-system="RecordStore.xsd" indent="yes" encoding="utf-8"/>

  <xsl:template match="RecordStore">
    <RecordStore version="1.1">
      <xsl:apply-templates/>
    </RecordStore>
  </xsl:template>

  <xsl:template match="album">
    <album>
      <recordLabel>false</recordLabel>
      <xsl:apply-templates/>
    </album>
  </xsl:template>

  <xsl:template match="*">
    <xsl:copy-of select="."/>
  </xsl:template>

</xsl:stylesheet>
```

This XSLT program/transformation contains a number of instructions known as *templates*. The main step of any transformation is to find a rule in the template that matches the root node of the source document. When the template is instantiated, instructions in the template are executed and a results document is created.

Writing XSLT Programs

We can write the XSLT program in two ways: in an ASP style or by using multi-template transformations.

ASP

XSLT can function much like classic ASP does. ASP dynamically generates new content based on a mixture of HTML and ASP code each time the ASP page is called. XSLT works in a similar way. You can put the XSLT calls between the HTML elements, and XSLT can dynamically generate data by leaving placeholders in the code in the form of curly braces: {}. Dynamic text is generated from the XSLT instructions. XSLT instructions accommodate common programming constructs such as loops and conditional branches. We won't get into the XSLT syntax here because XSLT is a pretty complex language in its own right.

Unfortunately, this method really only looks after simple transformations, which might be adequate for basic transformations against a known document structure but is not adequate for more complex transformations.

Multitemplate Transformations

Using multitemplate transformations is more complex but provides superior functionality. As you saw earlier in the section titled "An Example Transformation," you can separate transformations into separate pieces of logic known as templates. You can then apply templates in a procedural programming type of format or even in a declarative style.

You can name and call templates just as you would functions, or you can associate them with a pattern. These patterns are called by the XSLT processor and contain a mixture of static content and XSLT instructions. The syntax for patterns is based on a subset of XPath. The template is placed in the root transformation element.

Again, we won't go into specific XPath and XSLT syntax—this is just a brief overview of how you might go about upgrading your Web services.

Getting Your Web Method to Work

We've looked at the attributes involved in creating a Web method, and, broadly speaking, our Web service is now complete. But although the code is finished, that's not all we need to do by a long shot.

Debugging

After you create the Web method, you have no guarantee that it will work immediately, and even if it does run correctly, you have no guarantee that it will necessarily work in the future. There are no golden rules for how to proceed if things go belly-up with your Web server, but you can follow a common set of guidelines to minimize the effects of any errors that creep in. We'll look at those as well as some situations that most developers will encounter at some point.

Exceptions

Intelligently handling exceptions is probably the best way to ensure that your Web services work as intended. When an error occurs in a Web service, the following protocol is observed:

- .NET catches the error.
- The error information is serialized within a SOAP message.
- When the client receives the SOAP response, it throws the exception.

The type of exception raised is *SoapException* because the error message information is supplied in the body of the SOAP message. Quite often you will be invited to inspect the *StackTrace* object for further information relating to your error. The *StackTrace* object is accessible via the *Exception* object.

To exert greater control, you can get the Web method to raise an error itself, by explicitly throwing an exception. You are often better off throwing your own exceptions, because then you can get the Web service to behave in a predictable way when faced with a certain situation.

You saw in Chapter 2 that faults can be serialized in a SOAP fault message and that this message is displayed on the client. When designing Web methods, you should always account for every situation or every possible user entry. If an unexpected value is encountered, you can follow a particular course of action rather than letting the Web service encounter an error itself (such as a divide-by-zero error). For example, if you're running a piece of code that relies on one of a particular range of inputs from a user, all possible values should be anticipated:

```
[WebMethod]
public string Input(string userInput)
{
    int amount;
    switch(userInput)
    {
        case 1:
            amount=1;
            break;
        case 2:
            amount=20;
            break;
        case 3:
            amount=30;
            break;
```

```
        default:
            throw new SoapException("Invalid Amount supplied",
                SoapException.ClientFaultCode);
    }
    :
```

As you also saw in Chapter 2, you can add extra information about the exception being thrown via the *Message*, *Code*, *Actor*, *Detail*, and *OtherElements* properties of the *SoapException* object to let the user know exactly why the exception was thrown.

Error Logging

Debugging relies on the tracing of errors. When you write a Web service, you should be sure that any errors encountered are written to a log so they can be checked later.

.NET allows you to write and retrieve log entry information via the *EventLog* class. This class allows access to security, system, and application logs. If you are logging events from your Web service, the application log is the correct place to record them. The *EventLog* class is accessed via the *System.Diagnostics* namespace. You can log errors by placing them in a *try/catch* construct. For example, here's a piece of code that tries to write more numbers into an array than the number of elements that the array can hold:

```
[WebMethod]
public void ErrorLogging()
{
    try
    {
        int[] testarray = new int[5];
        for(int i=0; i++; i<=10)
        {
            testarray[i] = i+1;
        }
    }
    catch (Exception err)
    {
        EventLog Applog = new EventLog();
        Applog.Source = "ErrorGenerator";
        Applog.WriteEntry(err.Message, EventLogEntryType.Error);
    }
}
```

This code writes the contents of the exception from the application to the *EventLog* object. The event is logged as type *EventLogEntryType.Error*. The *Source* property of the *EventLog* object allows you to specify the name of the application that threw the error.

The *EventLog* class has the following properties (not including inherited ones):

- ***EnableRaisingEvents*** Specifies whether the *EventLog* instance will receive *EntryWritten* event notifications (which are generated whenever an event is written to the log)
- ***Entries*** Gets the contents of the event log in the form of a collection
- ***Log*** Specifies the name of the log to be written to or read from
- ***LogDisplayName*** Gets the event log's "friendly" name
- ***MachineName*** Specifies the names of the machine on which the event log is located
- ***Source*** Specifies the name of the application to be used when writing events to the log
- ***SynchronizingObject*** Gets or sets the object used to marshal the event handler calls that are issued when an event is generated by an *EventLog* entry being written

The *EventLog* class has the following methods (not including inherited ones):

- ***BeginInit*** Begins the initialization of an event log at run time
- ***Clear*** Clears all entries from the specified event log
- ***Close*** Closes the event log
- ***CreateEventSource*** Gives permission to a particular application to be able to write to an event log
- ***Delete*** Deletes the event log
- ***DeleteEventSource*** Removes permission to a particular application to be able to write to an event log
- ***EndInit*** Ends the initialization of an event log at run time
- ***Exists*** Returns a value depending on whether a specified log exists
- ***GetEventLogs*** Creates an array of event logs
- ***LogNameFromSourceName*** Retrieves the name of the EventLog given an application/source name

- ***SourceExists*** Checks the registry to see if the application that claims to have generated the event actually exists
- ***WriteEntry*** Writes an entry to the event log

Anyone can write to error logs, so they are prone to deletion, amendments, or overwriting by other applications and are not good permanent stores for such information.

To retrieve information from the error log, you can create another Web method that returns the appropriate information from the *EventLog* object. You can return the information in whatever format you want, ranging from a *DataSet* object to a more straightforward array. This example populates an array with the retrieved event log information:

```
[WebMethod]
public void RetrieveLog()
{
    EventLog log = new EventLog("Application1");
    string[][] ErrorLogArray = new string[10][2];
    int i=0;
    foreach (EventLogEntry entry in log.Entries)
    {
        if (entry.Source == "ErrorGenerator")
        {
            ErrorLogArray[i][0] = entry.Message;
            ErrorLogArray[i++][1] = entry.TimeGenerated;
        }
    }
    ⋮
```

Deployment

Deploying a Web service might feel like the final stretch of a project, but if you don't get it right, it won't work correctly on the machine it's intended to run on. When I was deploying my first-ever project for my first client after becoming self-employed, I deployed a random batch generator that worked perfectly but used the Common Dialog OCX, which of course isn't available on machines that don't have Visual Basic installed. It took a good half-hour of discussions with the client to ascertain that the code wasn't broken and that the problem was easily fixable. Motto: do it right the first time!

Visual Studio .NET offers facilities for creating a deployment project that builds an .msi file containing all the necessary dependencies and Web server configurations. The .msi file also registers the assemblies, making certain not to overwrite newer copies of them. The .msi file should be copied to the Web server and run. Once run, the application should be correctly set up to work and broadcast the Web service.

Deployment Using Visual Studio .NET

To add a deployment project to a solution, you choose Add Project from the File menu, and then choose New Project. In the Add New Project dialog box, select the Setup And Deployment Projects folder, then select the Web Setup Project template, and supply an appropriate name and location, as shown in Figure 7-2.

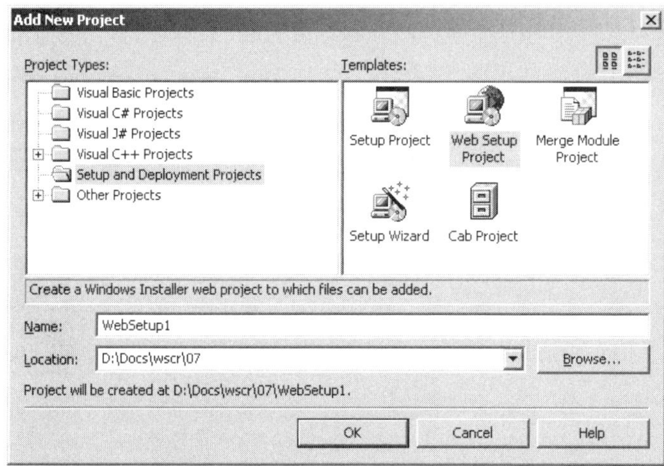

Figure 7-2 Visual Studio .NET's Add New Project dialog box with the Web Setup Project template selected

The tree view that appears on the right lists two nodes: File System On Target Machine and Web Application Folder. Right-click Web Application Folder and choose Add from the shortcut menu. Then select Project Output to configure various options, such as which assemblies to include (as shown in Figure 7-3).

If you select the primary output for each file and select the appropriate configuration setup, you can select from among the configurations you set up and examine any detected dependencies.

When you deploy an XML Web service, you must be sure that the .asmx file and any associated assemblies not included as part of the .NET Framework are included as a part of the deployment. They must be placed in the virtual directory of the application and the bin folder of the virtual directory, respectively.

For example, for the Recordstore example, the .asmx file could be located at \Inetpub\wwwroot\Recordstore\service1.asmx. Assemblies would be found at \Inetpub\wwwroot\Recordstore\bin\RecordStoreProxy.dll.

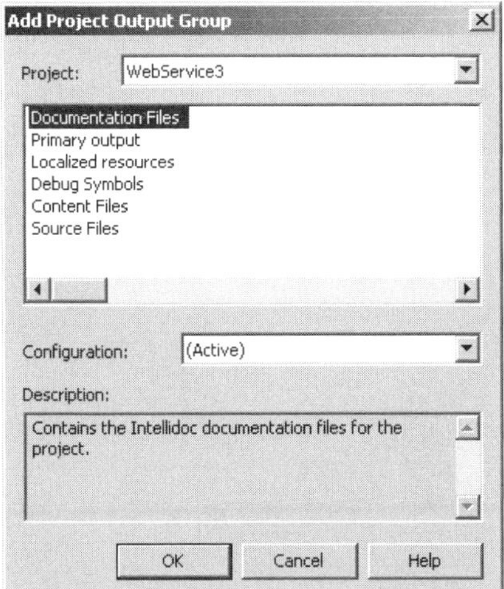

Figure 7-3 The Visual Studio .NET Add Project Output Group dialog box

If all of the target machines that the Web service is to be deployed on use the .NET Framework, it is possible to identify some deployment files that are included by default in the .msi installation file and exclude them in Solution Explorer so they are not included. When you run the .msi file, it will automatically update the setting for the Web server and the web.config file if you changed it in any way.

Deployment Using Code-Behind

Deployment might seem straightforward with Visual Studio .NET—in fact, just by building a solution, you can deploy a project, but what if you deploy using code-behind files? In this case, you need to take care of certain tasks when you configure how Visual Studio .NET will interact with IIS. Or, if you don't use Visual Studio .NET at all and deploy the Web service directly to the Web server, you must deal with some issues.

FrontPage Server Extensions

Microsoft FrontPage Server Extensions are a notoriously unreliable piece of technology that allows the transfer of code directly from Visual Studio .NET to the Web server using the HTTP protocol. Previous versions could be broken if an FTP tool was used to conduct the transfer of files, and they posed security risks and often require a server to be restarted to make them work. You can install them as part of IIS or download them from Microsoft's own site. You can manage them from the IIS Management Console, by right-clicking the Default Web Site icon, selecting All Tasks, and then selecting Configure Server Extensions.

UNC

Using the Universal Naming Convention (UNC), you can share files across the network. Using UNC is much faster than using FrontPage extensions. UNC involves a network resource being identified by a three-part name consisting of the server name, the share name, and the file path, as in *\\contoso\wwwroot$\RecordStore*. You can choose UNC access for access to your Web server in place of Front Page Extensions, and, in fact, by default Visual Studio .NET will attempt to access your Web server via UNC.

Deployment via IIS

Of course, just by creating a virtual application on an IIS server that is available to an intranet or extranet, you can deploy a Web service as well. When you set up a new virtual application on IIS, you can manually add a bin folder and place any assemblies that the Web service needs in this folder. .NET will automatically look first in this folder for assemblies.

Discovery of the Web Service

Once the service has been deployed, it's still not fully functioning. It's like creating a Web site and then hoping people will happen to visit. Unless you've got paranormal powers of persuasion, you could wait a long time. We've already talked about the UDDI repository in Chapter 4 and how Web services can be registered there, and then how they can be searched for via a directory of different companies and organizations. We also looked at the other alternative in Microsoft's DISCO protocol, which allows you to discover the different Web services running on a single machine. The times that you'd use these methods varies depending on what you intend to do with the Web service and who you're intending to reach. We'll start with a quick look at how DISCO might be used for our Web service.

DISCO

If your Web methods are intended to be consumed by people other than the ones who regularly browse your machine, registering the service on the UDDI registry instead of using DISCO would be a more appropriate solution for discovery of the service. However before you open the service to the general public, it's a good idea to check that you can find it first on our own server and that it is exposed in the correct fashion—and for this purpose, DISCO is better suited.

In Chapter 4, we mentioned that there are three types of documents: the .disco file, in which the endpoint of the service is known and which contains details about a single web service; the .disco file that is generated when you append the *?disco* query string to a .asmx Web service file, allowing you to treat the Web service itself as a discovery document; and the .vsdisco file, in which the endpoint of the Web service isn't known and which is helpful when you need to discover different Web services on your server. By default, the dynamic discovery capability that enables .vsdisco files to work is turned off for security reasons. To use .vsdisco files, you need to enable dynamic discovery in the machine.config file by uncommenting the line in .NET 1.0:

```
<!--
  <add verb="*" path="*.vsdisco"
    type="System.Web.Services.Discovery.DiscoveryRequestHandler, ↵
      System.Web.Services, Version=1.0.3300.0, Culture=neutral, ↵
      PublicKeyToken=b03f5f7f11d50a3a" validate="false"/>
-->
```

Then you can let Visual Studio .NET create the file that will iterate through all the paths for you.

You can create your own static discovery document (.disco file) as follows. Add a new item within Visual Studio .NET to your Web service project, and select Static Discovery File. The document for static discovery of the example Web service would look like this:

```
<?xml version="1.0"?>
<discovery xmlns="http://schemas.xmlsoap.org/disco/">
  <contractRef
   ref=" http://www.notashop.com/wscr/07/disco/service1.asmx?wsdl"
   docRef=" http://www.notashop.com/wscr/07/disco/service1.asmx"
   xmlns="http://schemas.xmlsoap.org/disco/scl/" />
  <discoveryRef
   ref="http://www.notashop.com/wscr/07/disco/simple/default.disco" />
  <discoveryRef
   ref="http://www.notashop.com/wscr/07/disco/soap/default.vsdisco" />
  <schemaRef
   ref="http://www.notashop.com/wscr/07/disco/soap/schema.xsd" />
</discovery>
```

A static discovery document for our example Web service requires just three elements: *<contractRef>*, which specifies the service we wish to make available; *<discoveryRef>*, which references other discovery documents; and the *<schemaRef>* element, which is used to connect to the Web service's schema.

DISCO works much better on a small, local scale, allowing you to discover services running on a local computer and to browse them. Another advantage is that UDDI requires registration with the Microsoft server, whereas DISCO doesn't. However, for any large-scale Web service, you'll probably want to use a registry of some sort; the UDDI is the probable discovery mode of choice.

UDDI

You can think of UDDI as a giant telephone directory of Web services. If you want to reach a particular person using a telephone directory, you might struggle if you had only her address. UDDI, however, addresses the problem of locating services when you don't know the provider.

If you go to the UDDI site at *http://uddi.microsoft.com* and choose Register from the left-hand menu, you can register the service. You must register your company first and supply a verifiable e-mail address. Then you can go to the Publish section of the site and, under the Providers tab, you can add a service and details about your service. Chapter 4 explains the process in more detail.

WS-Inspection

WS-Inspection, a part of the Global XML Web Services Architecture (GXA), offers another alternative for Web service discovery. It is a set of rules governing how Web service–related information should be made available for consumption. The proposed recommendation is currently in working-draft status on W3C's site, but it will move away from UDDI's business-centric approach and offer the discovery and description of services at a more functional level to the customer. That is, it is intended to allow users to scour Web sites for their Web service offerings, via descriptions of Web services. It aims to allow referencing of Web service descriptions in a more organized fashion. In theory, a customer will be able to interrogate a company's Web server for a list of available Web services. WS-Inspection also aims to provide a method whereby search engines can tag and reference the services offered.

The WS-Inspection specification hasn't been changed since November 2001; the current version of the specification can be found at *http://msdn.microsoft.com/library/default.asp?url=/library/en-us/dnglobspec/html/ws-inspection.asp*.

Summary

In this chapter, we briefly looked at all aspects of creating Web methods, steering clear of any discussion of how the service will be consumed (except in our practical example). We started with an overall view of the XML Web service model, and we looked at creating an .asmx file, adding an *@WebService* directive, and then adding the functionality for the Web methods. We looked at attributes that affect the WSDL that is produced, and you saw how changes in the configuration files can be used to affect the WSDL.

Next we considered how state can be managed within a Web method and what to consider when you write asynchronous services. We discussed how to look after the upgrading of your Web service, and we discussed methods for debugging and deploying your Web service and putting it up for discovery. This chapter reiterated some material from previous chapters as part of the overview of how to create a Web method. In the next chapter, we'll look at the other end of the process: how the service will be consumed.

8

Consuming Web Services

It seems almost perverse that we've spent the last seven chapters talking about how to create Web services but we've virtually ignored the subject of most interest to end users—how to consume and make use of Web services. We've analyzed each section of the pipeline, from the creation of the class to the method and format of the transmission of the Web service—but without the ability to harvest information at the other end, all these elements are as good as useless. In places, we've been so wrapped up with the method of delivering information fromjmnh the Web service that we've sometimes either provided client code without any guidance for what it does or omitted client code altogether from our sample Web methods. It's time to remedy the situation and talk about Web services from the point of view of consumption.

Types of Clients

To consume a Web service, you need a client. The client provides the interface through which a user can connect to a Web service. The client can take a variety of forms. With a small, dedicated Web client, a user might run an application (such as a stock ticker or an Amazon sales position ticker) and specify that the client application connect once every 15 minutes for an update. Or the client might be something less obtrusive, such as an antivirus program that automatically runs on your taskbar, periodically checking its parent site for the latest updates. Or the client might even be the Windows update mechanism itself.

Of course, not all clients have to be executable applications—they can just as easily be Web Forms, such as those that return maps when supplied with a ZIP or postal code, or a set of news channels downloaded onto a browser on a personal digital assistant (PDA) with the most relevant headlines. Clients don't even have to be restricted to using Web Forms or to being Web browser–based applications. Applications such as multimedia or MP3 players might use Web services as a sideline to the main functionality—say, to download extra information about the media being played. Another example might be a flight simulator application that connects to the Internet to download the latest weather conditions so users can experience within the simulation the actual weather patterns outside.

Any application capable of receiving XML across HTTP can consume a Web service. That means the role of Web services can be much broader than you might initially assume. Beyond applications that connect to the Web, download information, and then close down, Web services can improve the usefulness of any client and the overall richness of the user experience. In fact, many clients exist just to provide an interface with already existing Web services; users might never have to build a Web service for themselves.

We'll start by looking at the existing model that .NET uses for Web service consumption. Then we'll examine how a client can discover a Web service and look at how to build different types of clients.

The .NET Model of Web Service Consumption

In .NET, the process of consuming a Web service is deliberately made very simple. To consume a Web service, you must accomplish the following tasks:

1. Discover the Web service.
2. Create a proxy class for the Web service.
3. Include a namespace in the client's code so the proxy class can be referenced by the client.
4. Create an instance of the proxy class in the client.
5. Access the Web methods via the proxy class in the client so that the client can use the Web service.

We'll reference this model as we build our clients. Despite the varying types of clients, they all use this basic model.

Finding and Consuming a Web Service

If you can't find a Web service, you cannot consume it, so this first step is fundamental. The process that the service provider and the consumer must go through to consume a Web service can be summed up in three words—*publish*, *find*, and *bind*. The service provider publishes details about the service in the service registry and provides information to the consumer about how to bind to the service after finding it.

> **Tip** IBM has proposed adding a repository of Web service ratings and recommendations to this process. There are currently no facilities for choosing between Web services that appear to offer the same function. The idea is to add some sort of "review" process whereby Web services can be compared and consumers can make more informed choices. This repository would be freely browsable by consumers and would be linked back to the service registry. IBM's proposal can be found in a document on the company's Web site:
>
> *http://www-106.ibm.com/developerworks/webservices/library/ws-qual/?dwzone=webservices.*

This model isn't the only way to consume Web services, but it is the most common. However, it is also common for the consumer to know exactly where the Web service is and bypass the service registry entirely. Next we'll discuss the most popular ways to discover services.

Discovering a Web Service

If a consumer already has the URL of a service, all he has to do is supply it. In Microsoft Visual Studio .NET, if you add a Web reference to your project and then supply the URL, this is enough for consumers to "discover" your service. For example, in the previous chapter we used *http://localhost/wscr/07/RecordStore/Service1.asmx*. We can simply add a reference to it, as shown in Figure 8-1.

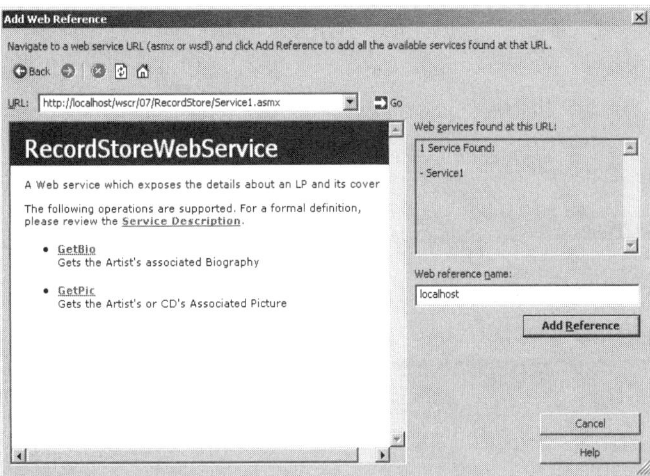

Figure 8-1 Visual Studio .NET's Add Web Reference dialog box

This rather haphazard method certainly works, but if your company is looking to expose Web services and charge for their use, you won't want to rely on this fairly arbitrary method of discovery. Given that the WS-Inspection standard is some ways away from being fully implemented, you will probably use one of the two most popular methods, UDDI and Microsoft Discovery (DISCO).

UDDI

An implementation of Universal Description, Discovery, and Integration (UDDI) is held on a Microsoft server at *http://uddi.microsoft.com*. It is by no means the only registry, but it is perhaps the most visible portal for searching for Web services. It was started by Microsoft and IBM and is supported by Visual Studio .NET, Microsoft Office XP and later, and Microsoft Windows Server 2003 Enterprise Edition (in which UDDI services have become an integral part of the operating system). The UDDI registry provides a directory of business services and also a set of test Web services that developers can use as they develop their applications.

UDDI has two aims—to provide a method of describing a Web service, making the description meaningful enough to be useful during searches, and to provide a facility to make the descriptions useful enough that you can interact with a service while not knowing much about it.

Microsoft anticipates that most developers will use UDDI in two ways:

- **Developer reuse** The UDDI services provide all the necessary information when a developer wants to repeatedly use some programmatic resources within an application.
- **Dynamic configuration** Applications can connect to a UDDI service at run time for various configuration information about the services they use.

When you go to add a Web reference to your projects in Visual Studio .NET, you can follow one of two links straight to the UDDI registry. From the registry you can search by service name, by provider name, or by one of the following categorization schemes:

- **ntis-gov:sic:1987** Standard Industrial Classification
- **unspsc-org:unspsc:3-1** United Nations Standard Products and Services Code System
- **unspsc-org:unspsc** Universal Standard Products and Services Classification
- **uddi-org:iso-ch:3166:1999** Geographic Taxonomy

- **microsoft-com:geoweb:2000** Geographic Taxonomy
- **ntis-gov:naics:1997** North American Industry Classification System
- **VS Web Service Search Categorization** Visual Studio .NET's own categorization scheme

Once you locate a Web service URL from a scheme, you just add the Web reference to include it. Not a lot of services are in the registry yet, so don't be surprised if your search for a particular type of service doesn't turn up anything or if the WSDL interface hasn't been made available.

You can also search for services directly from one of four tabs on the Microsoft UDDI site. Once you obtain the service you're looking for, you can go back to Visual Studio .NET and add the URL as a Web reference to the project. We looked at UDDI in detail in Chapter 4, so we won't examine it further here.

DISCO

The other option is to use DISCO. DISCO is a Microsoft protocol for enabling a client to discover all Web services available on a particular machine and obtain information about a particular Web service. When you create a Web service in Visual Studio .NET, the IDE and the .NET Framework can create a set of XML files that hold information about the Web service. Those files have the following filename extensions:

- **.disco** Contains information such as the link to the actual Web service, the location of the Web service's WSDL document, a link to the Web service's documentation, and a link to an XSD file that describes the Web service (not used in version 1.1 of the .NET Framework). An .asmx Web service creates this file automatically when you browse the URL of the Web service with the *?disco* query string. The *?disco* query string is used in static discovery when you know the location of the Web service but want to know more details about the service.
- **.vsdisco** Contains information for dynamic discovery when you don't know the URL of a particular Web service but you do know the endpoint of the Web service provider. Dynamic discovery must be specifically enabled; you can instruct ASP.NET to navigate through particular folders looking for Web services. When you create a new project, a .vsdisco file is automatically created for you.
- **.map** Created by the client when you add a Web reference to a project. The .map file contains links to Web service resources such as the WSDL and DISCO files. It is regenerated every time you update the Web reference. It is mainly used to help you find copies of original files.

From the client's point of view, the .vsdisco file is the one that has real bearing on the discovery of a service. If you want to consume a Web service, you need to know the location of it.

If you supply a .vsdisco filename when you add a Web reference, you'll get a list of available Web services. By default, dynamic discovery is disabled in Visual Studio .NET and the .NET Framework 1.1, so if you want to use dynamic discovery, you must enable it by making a change in the machine.config file. To enable dynamic discovery, uncomment the applicable line under *<httphandlers>*. Another factor that prevents clients from finding Web services is that, in the .NET Framework 1.1, the HTTP-GET protocol is also no longer enabled by default.

For a client to discover a Web service, then, you must provide the URL of the .vsdisco file, dynamic discovery must be specifically enabled on that machine, and the HTTP-GET protocol must be enabled as well.

Finding the Schema and WSDL for the Service

It isn't enough to have the URL of the Web service—you also need the location of the schema and the WSDL of the service. Whenever a Web service is exposed for consumption, a WSDL document is generated. This document is either pregenerated or generated on demand if you add the suffix *?wsdl* to the URL for the .asmx file. The WSDL document acts as a contract between a provider and a consumer for how a Web service is exposed and how it is to be consumed.

We covered WSDL in detail in Chapter 3. The WSDL file is simply an XML file that indicates the schema, the method(s) to call, and the data type(s) returned. However, you must supply the WSDL file to be able to generate a proxy client class.

The Proxy Client

We mentioned proxy classes in earlier chapters, but now we need to look more closely at them because they form the critical bridge between the Web service and Web client. The proxy classes abstract the dirty work of making a SOAP call (and the like) via various .NET types. Proxy classes allow developers to integrate the Web service logic into different applications without having to build the code from the ground up.

When a client application calls a method in a Web service, the proxy is involved as follows:

1. The application calls a function in the proxy class, passing any relevant parameters.
2. The proxy class creates the request that will be sent to the Web service using the parameters supplied.

3. The proxy sends the function call to the Web service whether the service is on a local machine, an intranet, or the Web.
4. The Web service executes the function and returns a result in XML.
5. The proxy class receives the results and parses the XML returned by the Web service retrieving the data.
6. The proxy passes the data to your application.

The role of the proxy class is really to imitate the interface of the Web service. All of the methods that a Web service exposes must be exposed by the proxy class. The proxy class takes care of all the data marshaling, so the developer has to worry only about how to use the data received from the Web service.

You can build a proxy client class three ways. The first two approaches generate it for you automatically (as you saw in Chapter 1).

- Use the wsdl.exe tool to build it.
- Use Visual Studio .NET's Add Web Reference dialog box to point to the WSDL document generated from the .asmx file.
- Build it manually.

Most people opt to generate the proxy because it is easier and commonly offers all of the functionality you need anyway. The proxy client basically sits beside the client and handles any interaction with the properties and methods of the Web service. The Web service client has no concept of dealing with a remote service because the client's method calls are really calls to the local proxy that are relayed by the proxy to the Web service. For each Web method, three methods are generated in the corresponding proxy class.

If you used wsdl.exe to generate the proxy client for the RecordStore Web service created in Chapter 7, you'll find that the portion of the proxy file that relates to the *GetBio* Web method looks like this:

```
public RecordStoreWebService() {
    this.Url = "http://localhost/wscr/07/RecordStore/Service1.asmx";
}

/// <remarks/>
[System.Web.Services.Protocols.SoapRpcMethodAttribute(
    "http://www.notashop.com/wscr/GetBio",
    RequestNamespace="http://www.notashop.com/wscr",
    ResponseNamespace="http://www.notashop.com/wscr")]
public string GetBio(string Id) {
    object[] results = this.Invoke("GetBio", new object[] {
                Id});
    return ((string)(results[0]));
}
```

```
/// <remarks/>
public System.IAsyncResult BeginGetBio(string Id,
    System.AsyncCallback callback, object asyncState) {
    return this.BeginInvoke("GetBio", new object[] {
                Id}, callback, asyncState);
}

/// <remarks/>
public string EndGetBio(System.IAsyncResult asyncResult) {
    object[] results = this.EndInvoke(asyncResult);
    return ((string)(results[0]));
}
```

This code contains a definition that holds the URL of the service, followed by three method definitions. These method definitions all contain calls to the same *GetBio* Web method. One is the *GetBio* method, which can be used to synchronously call our Web service, and the other two are *BeginGetBio* and *EndGetBio*, which you won't use unless you asynchronously call the Web service. We'll deal with asynchronous calls later in the chapter. This proxy client just takes the calls from the clients, relays them to the service, and returns any data to the client from the service.

Now let's shift our focus to how to build a client to consume the Web service.

Building a Client

We mentioned earlier that just about any type of client can consume a Web service. The first question you might ask is, "When do I use a particular type of client?" The answer depends partly on the application that's using the Web service and partly on the way the Web service is made available. For example, our Media Player application (discussed in Chapter 7) would be an unsuitable Web Forms client because you wouldn't want a Web page to have access to your CD drive. On the other hand, if you were developing a Web Forms application that required users to enter their address, you wouldn't want to have them download a separate .exe file to find the postal code—you would expect the postal code logic to dovetail seamlessly within your Web Forms.

We'll look at a variety of scenarios that require different kinds of clients. We'll start with a basic Web Forms application.

A Basic Web Forms Client

For this example, we'll use an existing Web service from the UDDI registry. The Web service we'll use is a weather forecasting Web service from *WebserviceX.NET* (*http://www.webservicex.net*), which returns the current weather for a locality when supplied with a ZIP Code. Our example application will simply ask the user to supply a ZIP Code, submit it to the Web service, and then process the XML response that the Web service returns and display it in a readable format.

In Visual Studio .NET, we start by creating a new solution and building an ASP.NET Web application. We add the following URL as a Web reference: *http://www.webservicex.net/usweather.asmx*. We then rename this reference *WeatherFetcher* in Visual Studio .NET, as shown in Figure 8-2, for easier reference in our code.

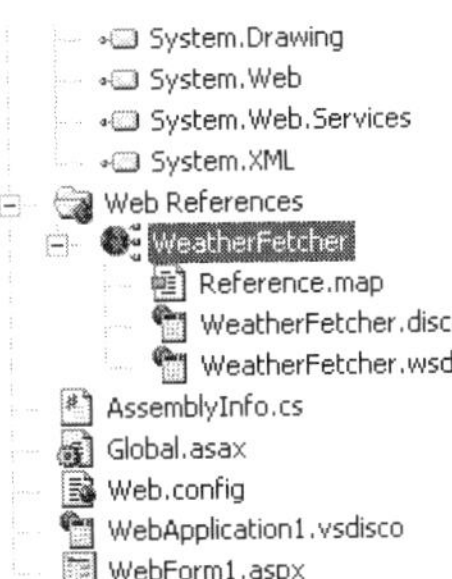

Figure 8-2 Newly added WeatherFetcher Web reference

Next we create a Web Form in Visual Studio .NET that takes one text box for the weather, one button to submit the details, and two labels—one to describe the contents of the text box and one for the output from the service (as shown in Figure 8-3).

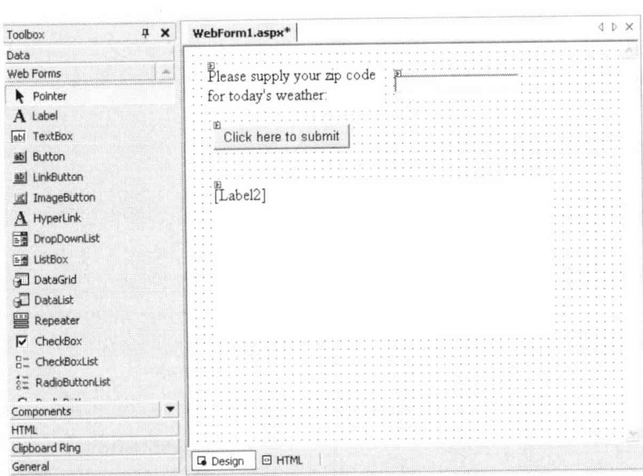

Figure 8-3 Building a form for the USWeather Web service client in Visual Studio .NET

This ASP.NET form produces something roughly resembling the following ASP.NET code:

```
<%@ Page language="c#" Codebehind="WebForm1.aspx.cs" AutoEventWireup="false" In
herits="WebApplication1.WebForm1" %>
<!DOCTYPE HTML PUBLIC "-//W3C//DTD HTML 4.0 Transitional//EN" >
<HTML>
    <HEAD>
    <title>WebForm1</title>
        <meta name="GENERATOR" Content="Microsoft Visual Studio 7.0">
        <meta name="CODE_LANGUAGE" Content="C#">
        <meta name="vs_defaultClientScript" content="JavaScript">
        <meta name="vs_targetSchema"
         content="http://schemas.microsoft.com/intellisense/ie5">
    </HEAD>
    <body MS_POSITIONING="GridLayout">
        <form id="Form1" method="post" runat="server">
            <asp:TextBox id="TextBox1"
             style="Z-INDEX: 101; LEFT: 209px; POSITION: absolute; TOP: 29px"
             runat="server" Width="125px"
             Height="18px">
            </asp:TextBox>
            <asp:Label id="Label1"
             style="Z-INDEX: 102; LEFT: 23px; POSITION: absolute; TOP: 19px"
             runat="server" Width="170px"
             Height="39px">
                Please supply your zip code for today's weather:
            </asp:Label>
            <asp:Button id="Button1"
             style="Z-INDEX: 103; LEFT: 28px; POSITION: absolute; TOP: 77px"
             runat="server" Width="136px"
             Text="Click here to submit">
            </asp:Button>
            <asp:Label id="Label2"
             style="Z-INDEX: 104;LEFT: 28px; POSITION: absolute; TOP: 135px"
             runat="server" Width="333px" Height="147px">
            </asp:Label>
        </form>
    </body>
</HTML>
```

When you use third-party Web services, everything is done for you when you add the Web reference to the machine. It's like having the object on your machine, with the proxy class already generated for you. So, the first three requirements of our .NET Web services consumption model have been satisfied. All we need to do is add the code that takes the content of the text box and supplies it to the Web service, and then returns the result from the service to the Web form.

If you supply the following code to the Web form button's event handler and then compile and run it, the client will provide the weather conditions in detail for any ZIP Code in the United States that the user submits:

```
⋮
using System.Xml;
⋮
private void Button1_Click(object sender, System.EventArgs e)
{
    WeatherFetcher.USWeather USW = new WeatherFetcher.USWeather();
    XmlDocument doc = new XmlDocument();
    doc.LoadXml(USW.GetWeatherReport(TextBox1.Text));
    foreach (XmlNode node in doc)
    {
        XmlNodeReader noderead = new XmlNodeReader(node);
        while(noderead.Read())
        {
            if(noderead.NodeType == XmlNodeType.Element)
            {
                string elementnode, nodecontents;
                nodecontents = noderead.ReadString();

                if (nodecontents == "")
                {
                    nodecontents = noderead.Value.ToString();
                    noderead.ReadOuterXml();
                }
                elementnode = noderead.Name;
                Label2.Text += elementnode + " - "
                        + nodecontents + "<br>";
            }
        }
    }
}
```

Only three lines of code are required to do the work:

```
FetchWeather.USWeather USW = new FetchWeather.USWeather();
    XmlDocument doc = new XmlDocument();
    doc.LoadXml(USW.GetWeatherReport(TextBox1.Text));
```

The first line generates an instance of the object, the second line creates an instance of an *XmlDocument* class, and the third line reads the result of the Web service request into the *XmlDocument* object. The rest of the code formats the answer the Web service returns—the Web service returns the answer as a single string, but this string is an XML document with the following format:

```
<Weather>
  <City></City>
  <State></State>
```

```
    <County></County>
    <Fahrenheit></Fahrenheit>
    <Celsius></Celsius>
    <Condition></Condition>
    <Humidity></Humidity>
    <Wind></Wind>
    <Sunrise></Sunrise>
    <Sunset></Sunset>
    <DailyReport>
      <Day></Day>
      <HighFahrenheit></HighFahrenheit>
      <HighCelsius></HighCelsius>
      <LowFahrenheit></LowFahrenheit>
      <LowCelsius></LowCelsius>
    </DailyReport>
  </Weather>
```

We have to process this XML document to display formatted output to the user, as shown in Figure 8-4—otherwise the information will appear all jumbled in one large string.

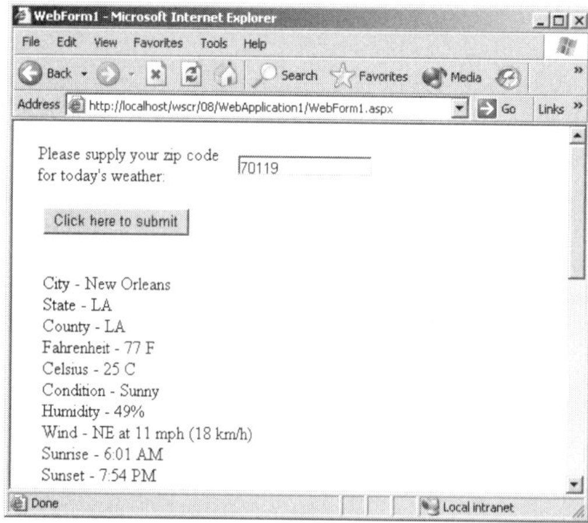

Figure 8-4 USWeather Web service client displaying formatted results

We use the XML Document Object Model (DOM) to iterate through each element, displaying the element name followed by the contents of that element. We do this by examining each node in the XML document and seeing if it is an element:

```
foreach (XmlNode node in doc)
{
    XmlNodeReader noderead = new XmlNodeReader(node);
    while(noderead.Read())
    {
        if(noderead.NodeType == XmlNodeType.Element)
```

If it is an element, we read its name and contents into the corresponding string variables *elementnode* and *nodecontents* and display them in *Label2*.

You don't have to take any special considerations into account with Web Form clients because the HTTP request and responses are handled in the normal way by .NET. Exceptions are also handled by the client.

A Basic Windows Forms Client

For our Windows Forms client, we'll create a client to consume the two example Web methods that we created in the previous chapter. This is the final extension of our media player example. Our completed media player won't actually play any CDs (although it wouldn't be difficult to add a control enabling our application to play a CD). Instead, it will simply identify the CD placed in the drive and return information about the CD and the artist involved back to the user, from both the freedb.org database (which contains only album titles and track listings) and from our own database.

In the previous chapter, we discussed how to identify the CD. We used an .ocx file provided on the freedb.org site (*http://www.freedb.org*), which returns a unique identifier from the CD. This file also returns simple information, such as the artist's name and the CD title, as properties. We extended the functionality of the .ocx file by creating two Web methods. The first allowed us to extract the extra biographical details about the artist, and the second allowed us to download a .jpg file from our own database via our Web methods.

> **Important** We're using a freeware .ocx file supplied by Jon F. Zahornacky and Peter Schmiedseder to access the freedb.org database; the file is located at *http://www.freedb.org*, in the Downloads section under Miscellaneous. The freedb.org site houses a database that contains the unique identifiers for millions of CDs, plus track listings for each CD. The .ocx component can generate the unique identifier for a CD when supplied with that CD and can match it to the details stored in the database. You must register the uFREEDB.ocx file on your machine before Visual Studio .NET can use it.

The client code is quite lengthy in this case, but the basic five steps we outlined for the consumption of Web services at the start of the chapter still hold true. The rest of the code simply manipulates the data made available from the Web service and presents it in an easily digestible format for the user. To sum up how the application works: The user inserts a CD and starts the application. She clicks Search and the client retrieves the artist name, track list, and title information from the freedb.org database. The client then uses the unique identifier, employed as a primary key in our local database, to retrieve the biographical details for the artist. Also, the client uses the unique identifier to retrieve a picture from our local database.

For all of this to work, the client must be set up correctly. You must also have created the two Web methods in Chapter 7 and be running Microsoft SQL Server 7.0/2000 or Microsoft SQL Server Desktop Engine (MSDE) and have downloaded a copy of the RecordStore database from the Microsoft Press site.

To create the client, we create a new Windows Forms application and add four labels, one button, and one picture box to *Form1*. Add the picture box on the left side, between labels 1 and 2. You'll need to add the Windows Media Player component to the project. To do this, right-click on the toolbox in the Forms Designer and select Add/Remove Items from the shortcut menu. In the Customize Toolbox dialog box, click on the COM Components tab and select the Windows Media Player component, as shown in Figure 8-5.

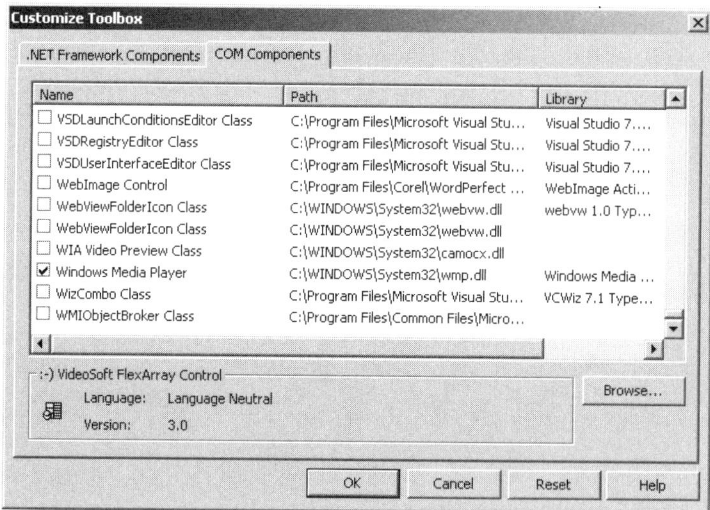

Figure 8-5 Using Visual Studio .NET's Customize Toolbox dialog box to add the Windows Media Player component to a project

Now you can drag the Windows Media Player control from the Forms Designer toolbox into the form. Set the control's *Visible* property to *False* because you don't want it to appear on the box. Next, download uFREEDB 1.6.2 from the Downloads area of *http://www.freedb.org*, extract the file uFREEDB.ocx, add it to the toolbox (in the same way you added the Windows Media Player control), and drag the uFREEDB control onto the form. Finally, clear the label controls of any text and change the button's label so the button text is *Search*. Before the label controls are cleared, the form will look something like that shown in Figure 8-6.

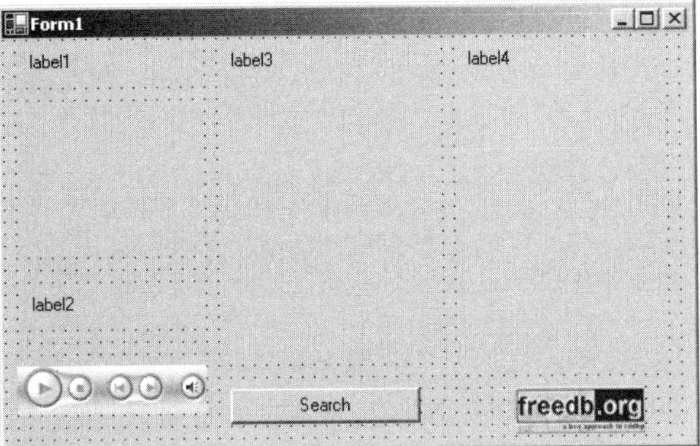

Figure 8-6 Forms Designer view of the main form of the Windows Forms Web service client

We then add references to the following namespaces at the beginning of the forms code:

```
using System.IO;
using System.Drawing.Imaging;
using FREEDBControl;
```

Next we add a Web reference to the form pointing to our Web services and rename this *Bio*. We then click on the button handler and add the following code to connect with our Web service:

```
public void button1_Click(object sender, System.EventArgs e)
{
    // Code required to make FreeDB Control work
    uCDDBMatchCode sts = new uCDDBMatchCode();
    bool notallow = false;
    axuFREEDB1.set_AllowSubmission(ref notallow);
    string em = "your.email@goes.here.com";
    axuFREEDB1.set_EmailAddress(ref em);

    // Code initializing values for control
    string artist;
    string title;
    string Id;
    sts = axuFREEDB1.LookupMediaByToc(axuFREEDB1.GetMediaTOC("D"));
    // Change above letter to whatever your CD drive is.
    artist = axuFREEDB1.GetArtistName;
    title = axuFREEDB1.GetAlbumName;
  Id = axuFREEDB1.GetMediaID;
    // Check to see what the artist name is
    if(axWindowsMediaPlayer1.cdromCollection.Item(0)
        .Playlist.getItemInfo(axWindowsMediaPlayer1
        .cdromCollection.Item(0).Playlist.get_attributeName(1))
```

```
            == "Unknown Artist")
        {
            //Unknown Artist
            MessageBox.Show("Item not in Windows Media Player db.");
        }
        else if (axWindowsMediaPlayer1.cdromCollection.Item(0)
            .Playlist.getItemInfo(axWindowsMediaPlayer1
                .cdromCollection.Item(0).Playlist.get_attributeName(1))
            == "No Disc in Drive")
        {
            MessageBox.Show("No CD in drive");
        }
        else
        {
            // Known artist
            Bio.Service1 ws = new Bio.Service1();
            label4.Text = ws.GetBio(Id);
            try
            {
                MemoryStream BLOBDataStream = new
                    MemoryStream(ws.GetPic(Id));
                pictureBox1.Image=Image.FromStream(BLOBDataStream);
            }
            catch(Exception ex)
            {
                MessageBox.Show(ex.Message);
            }
            label1.Text = artist;
            label2.Text = title;
            label3.Text = "";
    int counter = axWindowsMediaPlayer1.cdromCollection
                .Item(0).Playlist.attributeCount;

            for(int i = 1;
                i <= axWindowsMediaPlayer1
                    .cdromCollection.Item(0).Playlist.count-1;
                i++)
            {
                label3.Text += axWindowsMediaPlayer1.cdromCollection.Item(0)
                    .Playlist.get_Item(i).name + "\n";
            }
        }
    }
```

The code for the client is relatively straightforward, but we need to examine two aspects of the uFREEDB control because without them our code cannot work properly. First, you need to submit a functioning e-mail address before you can query the database. Without this code, you won't get a response. The second issue is that the artist name and the title name are returned by the *GetArtistName* and *GetTitleName* properties, and these are supplied as parameters to our local Web methods.

We also use the Windows Media Player control and query the *Playlist* object of this control to determine whether a CD is in the drive. As mentioned in Chapter 7, Windows Media Player already provides the ability to extract biographical details and pictures from a Web service at a lower level, but the point of this example is to demonstrate how you can do this yourself and how you can use your own Web services to provide this information.

When you look at our client code, it should be evident that only after we have identified the CD and have determined that the artist is contained within the Freedb.org do we get a chance to query our Web method. The code underneath the *// Known artist* comment is where the Web service functionality begins. Going back to our five-step model for building a client, the form already inherits from the application namespace, so we don't need to add anything extra. By adding a Web reference, we have "discovered" the Web methods and have also created a proxy client.

We can then query our Web service by querying the proxy client as follows:

```
Bio.Service1 ws = new Bio.Service1();
```

Then we can access the Web methods as "normal" methods:

```
label2.Text = ws.GetBio(Id);
```

The code calls our *GetBio* Web method and displays the results as text in the label control. The second Web method retrieves an image from the database. This is slightly more complex because it requires us to use a binary large object (BLOB) and read the image in from a data stream:

```
try
{
    MemoryStream BLOBDataStream = new
        MemoryStream(ws.GetPic(Id));
    pictureBox1.Image = Image.FromStream(BLOBDataStream);
}
catch(Exception ex)
{
    MessageBox.Show(ex.Message);
}
```

We enclose the code to do this within a *try/catch* block because reading from a data stream can lead to unexpected exceptions (exceptions not caused by errors in our code). The client application reads the data that our Web service returns, which the Web service fetches from a database, into a *MemoryStream* object. The *MemoryStream* object is then used to create an *Image* object that is assigned to the *Image* property of the picture box on our client. The rest of the code following this simply uses the existing uFREEDB and Windows Media Player controls on the form to supply extra information about the CD.

For the example to fully work, the CD must be located in both the freedb.org database and our own database. If it isn't in the latter, the biographical details and picture won't be displayed.

To run the example and see it in action, you don't have to find a CD contained in our CD database—you can use a "dummy entry" by changing the following lines in the client and putting any audio CD you have in the CD drive:

```
artist = axuFREEDB1.GetArtistName;
title = axuFREEDB1.GetAlbumName;
id = axuFREEDB1.GetMediaID;
```

to

```
artist = "Shane DeSeranno";
title = "Vacant and Happy";
Id = "r23q3t4h";
```

Figure 8-7 shows what the code displays:

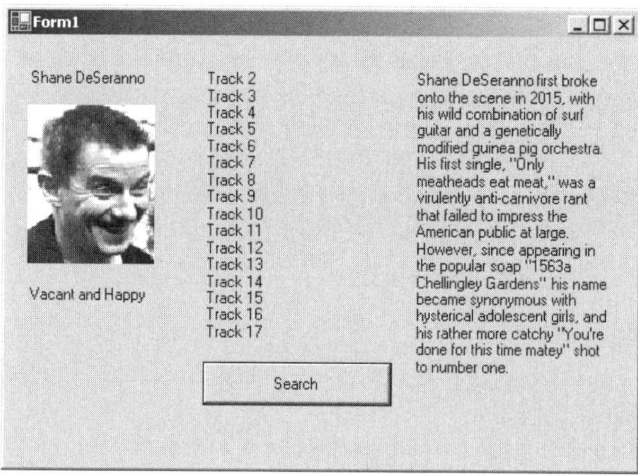

Figure 8-7 The famous Shane DeSeranno—vacant and happy

The picture from our *GetPic* Web method is inserted on the left and the biographical details from our *GetBio* Web method are displayed on the right. Despite the extra window-dressing to make our client richer, the actual communication with the Web service itself remains very straightforward. The client deals with the request/response nature of the service, just as it did within the Web Forms application, and it also allows the user to accommodate any exceptions that arise via normal structures such as a *try/catch* block.

Other Scenarios

Windows Forms clients and Web Forms clients will account for the majority of consumers of Web services, but plenty of other scenarios are possible. We'll provide a brief overview of some of them.

A Basic Interfaceless Client

We've assumed so far that our client has a user interface, but in fact it doesn't have to. In other words, your Web client might be an automated service or a background process. The interfaceless client is an attractive option if the results of the Web service do not need to be displayed on screen. For instance, a Really Simple Syndication (RSS) aggregator (RSS being the XML format used to share news headlines and stories among sites) stores its subscribed feeds until the user actually needs them. In this case, the Web service's client ultimately has a user interface, but you can imagine a client that runs unattended at given times, downloading the details to the aggregator.

Once again, this kind of service doesn't need anything special on top—it deals with the service in the normal request/response way and can also handle any exceptions thrown.

Dealing with Multipart Messages

Another scenario is one in which the WSDL specifies how a message must be constructed if it has more than one element. For example, the message might involve a SOAP message and binary object. How can clients deal with this and the attachments?

Here you can use the new Web Services Enhancements (WSE) extensions. The WS-Attachments specification and the Direct Internet Message Encapsulation (DIME) format enable you to attach documents outside of the SOAP envelope instead of having to serialize them and transfer them as part of the SOAP body, as we did in our Windows Forms client example. DIME lets you encapsulate items such as .zip files, images, documents, or XML files as a series of records. You can send a series of records and then use your Web client at the other end to retrieve and manipulate them. This is a significant subject area—you'll find more details about DIME in Chapter 12.

Solicit/Response Conversations

Request/response isn't the only kind of two-way conversation. If the server initiates the conversation, it is known as solicit/response, in which case your client is acting as a listener. In a one-way case, the client is almost an event handler.

An example of this is a one-way alert. Microsoft recently introduced a facility for .NET alerts at *http://alerts.microsoft.com/Alerts/Default.aspx* whereby users can sign up to receive messages, such as reminders on a calendar or special offers from approved companies. These alerts are forwarded on to an instant messenger client, an e-mail client, or a mobile device, at times that are convenient for the user and via a method chosen by the user.

A Web service client in this case reacts to an event when one is generated by the server, downloads the appropriate information from the Web service, and displays it.

Non-Client/Server Setups

We've talked about fairly simple client/server setups over HTTP, but there are also situations in which the connection isn't a simple server-to-client setup over a synchronous protocol (in other words, that doesn't use HTTP). For example, consider the following two scenarios:

- **Scenario 1** The client is an intermediary point that forwards the message, possibly over another protocol. You deal with this scenario by using the HTTP SOAPAction and SOAP envelope headers. We covered this topic in Chapter 2.
- **Scenario 2** The client communicates asynchronously with the server using the asynchronous methods generated in the proxy class by wsdl.exe. These asynchronous calls can occur over Simple Mail Transfer Protocol (SMTP) or Microsoft Message Queue (MSMQ). The binding is specified in the WSDL.

In all of these situations, our five-point model for consuming a Web service applies. We haven't yet considered asynchronous consumption in our clients—we'll discuss that next.

One-Way Requests and Asynchronous Consumption

It is perfectly valid for a Web services client to make a request of a service without expecting a response. For instance, the client might want to make a request to a Web service and come back later to get a response, getting on with other work in the meantime. (You might find your application performing inefficiently if it waits for a response the whole time.)

Of course, not all Web services are suitable for asynchronous calls. For instance, any situation in which the client is likely to be waiting on a response from the Web service before it can continue is not a good candidate for asynchronous invocation. However, with long-running tasks you might consider calling the Web service asynchronously; the decision is made in the client, not in the Web service. To be able to call a Web service asynchronously, you must use a couple of methods exposed by the proxy class, which we'll introduce next.

BeginInvoke and *EndInvoke* Methods

Within every automatically generated Web service proxy class are the *BeginInvoke* and *EndInvoke* methods, which enable asynchronous access. The *BeginInvoke* method is there to call a Web service, but it doesn't wait for a response. The *EndInvoke* method allows you to return the response to get the results. These two methods are used in combination to provide asynchronous services, but in reality they are just separate asynchronous calls to your Web service.

The *BeginInvoke* method returns an object of type *System.Web.Services.Protocols.WebClientAsyncResult*. This object allows you to check the status of your Web service request and to handle multiple calls to the same Web service.

If we dig into the proxy class of our example, the *GetBio* Web method, we can see that the *BeginInvoke* method is sandwiched in a *BeginGetBio* method:

```
public System.IAsyncResult BeginGetBio(string Id,
    System.AsyncCallback callback, object asyncState)
{
    return this.BeginInvoke("GetBio", new object[] {Id},
           callback, asyncState);
}
```

Just as there are *BeginGetBio* and *EndGetBio* methods for the *GetBio* Web method in the proxy class, each Web method has a *BeginWebMethod* call and an *EndWebMethod* call within the proxy class. These can be called directly from within the client. In fact, any method can be called asynchronously when you use these methods.

You can actually use two approaches to call Web services asynchronously:

- Call a Web method that initiates requests and returns a status based on whether the Web service has completed.
- Call a Web method that initiates requests and uses callbacks to send results.

We'll examine these approaches next.

Polling

The first way of calling a Web method asynchronously, by calling a corresponding *Begin* method in the proxy class and then checking occasionally to see if the service has completed, is known as *polling*. The *BeginWebMethod* and *EndWebMethod* classes provide the polling interface. Here's how it all works: When called, the *BeginWebMethod* class returns an *IAsyncState* object. This object is used to decide when the method has completed. In the *GetBio* proxy class, the return type of the function is *System.IAsyncResult*. You can check the *IAsyncState.IsComplete* property to see whether it is *true* or *false*. If it is true, you can call the *EndWebMethod* class, supplying the *IAsyncState* object as a parameter.

> **More Info** You can specify two extra parameters of the *BeginWebMethod* to provide a callback (described shortly). When using polling, however, you can leave these blank.

One advantage of making asynchronous Web service calls is that you can call several methods at the same time. We mentioned earlier that the *IAsyncResult* object provides this functionality. This is because for each *BeginWebMethod* call, a different *IAsyncResult* object is generated, and to be able to invoke the *EndWebMethod* call, you have to provide the correct *IAsyncResult* object to the Web service.

WaitHandle Objects

You can use *WaitHandle* objects in conjunction with polling. *WaitHandle* objects wait for the response from the service to complete before allowing processing to continue. You can submit several requests and then decide to wait for one or more of them to return before you carry on processing. To implement the requests, you use the *System.Threading.WaitHandle* object to block one of the executing threads, by calling a delay. *WaitHandle* objects are useful when you want to make asynchronous calls and you want to do processing after the call but do not want the client to return before it has received all of the data from Web service.

An Example of an Asynchronous Web Service Call

Although there is no need to call our weather Web service asynchronously, to keep the code simple and to the point, we will do just that. We will call the service asynchronously by clicking one button and then get the client to pick up the result by clicking another. We can then go back and modify the code so we can call several methods simultaneously.

First we create a Web form with one text box and two buttons in Visual Studio .NET, as shown in Figure 8-8.

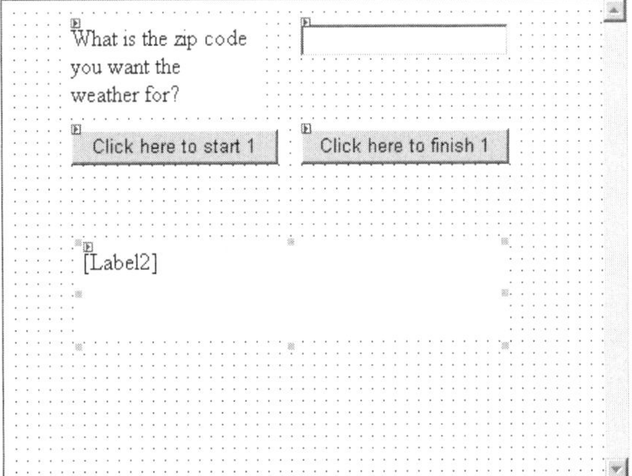

Figure 8-8 Designing a Web Forms application that calls a Web service asynchronously

We create a static variable to hold the *IAsyncResult* object and also add event handler code for the two buttons we've created:

```
static IAsyncResult tempHolder1;
WeatherFetcher.USWeather USW = new WeatherFetcher.USWeather();
:
private void Button1_Click(object sender, System.EventArgs e)
{
    Button1.Enabled = false;
    tempHolder1 = USW.BeginGetWeatherReport(TextBox1.Text, null, null);
}
private void Button2_Click(object sender, System.EventArgs e)
{
    if (tempHolder1.IsCompleted)
    {
        Label2.Text += USW.EndGetWeatherReport(tempHolder1) +"<br>";
        Button1.Enabled=true;
        tempHolder1 = null;
    }
    else
    {
        Label2.Text += "1 is Still completing...";
    }
}
```

Button 1's event handler disables the button when it is clicked and then calls *GetWeatherReport* asynchronously and stores the *IAsyncResult* object in *tempHolder1*. Button 2's event handler checks to see whether the *tempHolder1* object's *IsCompleted* property is *true*. If it is, the event handler displays the raw

XML result in the *Label2* control, enables the *Button1* control, and sets *tempHolder1* to *null* because further calls can cause exceptions.

If you run the program and type a ZIP Code and submit it, the answer isn't returned, as shown in Figure 8-9. To get the answer, you must first click the Click Here To Finish button.

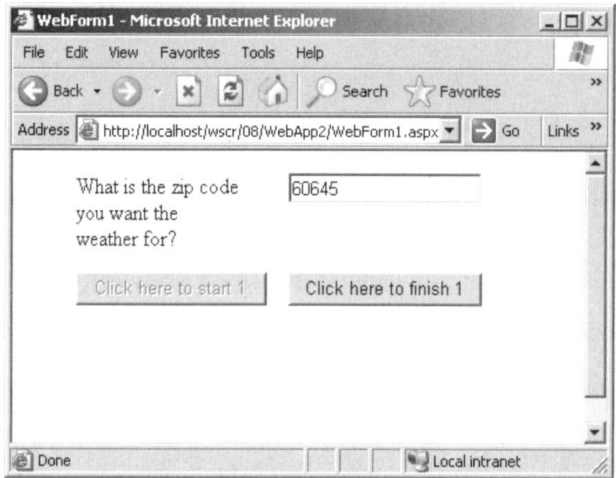

Figure 8-9 Asynchronous USWeather Web service client in action

Let's ramp up the example a little and see how we can call the Web service asynchronously and return the results in a different order. We add another four buttons to the form so it looks like Figure 8-10.

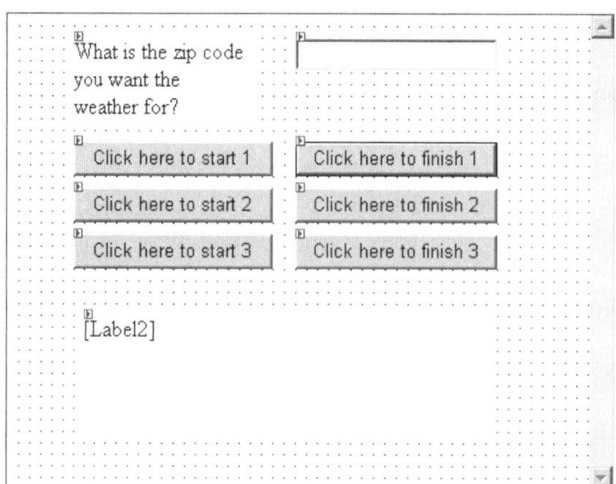

Figure 8-10 Designing a Web Forms application that calls a Web service asynchronously and that allows the calls to complete out of order

We add a couple more *IAsyncResult* definitions to our existing one:

```
static IAsyncResult tempHolder1;
static IAsyncResult tempHolder2;
static IAsyncResult tempHolder3;
```

Then we add the following code to these new button event handlers:

```
private void Button3_Click(object sender, System.EventArgs e)
{
    Button3.Enabled = false;
    tempHolder2 = USW.BeginGetWeatherReport(TextBox1.Text, null, null);
}
private void Button5_Click(object sender, System.EventArgs e)
{
    Button5.Enabled = false;
    tempHolder3 = USW.BeginGetWeatherReport(TextBox1.Text, null, null);
}
private void Button4_Click(object sender, System.EventArgs e)
{
    if (tempHolder2.IsCompleted)
    {
        Label2.Text += USW.EndGetWeatherReport(tempHolder2) +"<br>";
        Button3.Enabled=true;
        tempHolder2 = null;
    }
    else
    {
        Label2.Text += "2 is still completing...";
    }
}
private void Button6_Click(object sender, System.EventArgs e)
{
    if (tempHolder3.IsCompleted)
    {
        Label2.Text += USW.EndGetWeatherReport(tempHolder3) +"<br>";
        Button5.Enabled=true;
        tempHolder3 = null;
    }
    else
    {
        Label2.Text += " 3 is still completing...";
    }
}
```

We can now submit a different ZIP Code to the Web service with each of the buttons and then return the results in a different order by clicking the corresponding finish button. Figure 8-11 shows that we've submitted 60645 first, then

95472, and finally 98052 (the Redmond ZIP Code). We've received the return data in the opposite order, starting with the weather information for Redmond.

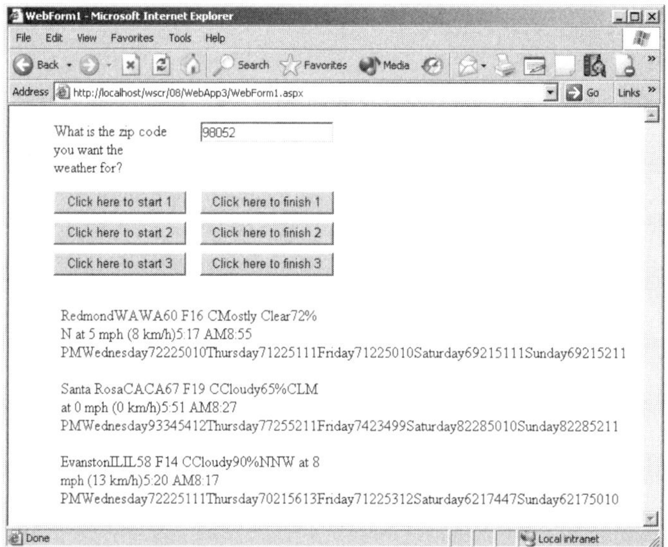

Figure 8-11 Calling a Web method several times with different data and then receiving the results out of order

This is still a rather primitive way of invoking asynchronous calls, however; instead of polling the service to see if it has completed, you might prefer to use the method described next.

Callbacks

An alternative to polling is callbacks. Callbacks wait for a response from the service and then process the response along with the Web service. Callbacks are used to notify your client that some event has occurred. The Web service has to respond to the client when a particular event has taken place. .NET uses delegates to handle communication between the Web service and client when you use callbacks. The callback holds information about a single method. The *BeginInvoke* and *EndInvoke* methods are used with callbacks. The *BeginInvoke* method commences the asynchronous call, using a different thread from the calling method. On top of the parameters for the Web method, the *BeginInvoke* method takes another two parameters:

- An *IAsyncState* object that contains context information for the callback
- An *AsyncCallback* delegate that enables the callback method to be invoked on completion of the Web method

The *BeginInvoke* method returns an *IAsyncResult* object. This object has an *IAsyncDelegate* property. The property contains the delegate object that was invoked by the original Web service call. When *EndInvoke* is used, the *AsyncResult* object is passed as a parameter to it, and *EndInvoke* returns the expected values from the Web service.

You can create a callback by attaching an *AsyncCallback* delegate to your method. This variable is then passed to the *BeginWebMethod* method as an extra parameter.

Amending Our Example to Use Callbacks

We can change our example so it uses callbacks. First we delete all but the first button on the form and the corresponding event handlers that we added to the end of the previous example.

Next we amend the code for the first button's event handler as follows:

```
private void Button1_Click(object sender, System.EventArgs e)
{
    Button1.Enabled = false;
    AsyncCallback callBack = new AsyncCallback(MyCallBack);
    USW.BeginGetWeatherReport(TextBox1.Text, callBack, USW);
    Label2.Text = "Web Service called...";
}
```

We also add the following method to the code for the callback:

```
public void MyCallBack(IAsyncResult AsyncResult)
{
    string ReturnValue;
    ReturnValue = USW.EndGetWeatherReport(AsyncResult);
    Label2.Text += "<br>" + "Weather Report = " + ReturnValue;
        Button1.Enabled = true;
}
```

For all intents and purposes, our client works in the same way as it did when we used polling. The difference is that the *MyCallBack* method now retrieves the result instead of the second button's event handler retrieving it.

The drawback is that unlike with the multiple methods example, if several calls are made, the method has no way of knowing which method made the request. We've avoided this by passing the proxy class instance as the third parameter to the service.

Other issues crop up with callbacks that relate to threading (mainly that callbacks can end up executing different threads that then run concurrently with other parts of your application, which might not be desirable). However, we won't delve into these issues because we simply want to show a simple example that uses callbacks.

When the Client Doesn't Use .NET

All of the types of clients we've looked at in this chapter assume that you have the .NET Framework installed, but not all people will have it. Interoperability is the key to Web services, so you need to know how to build clients around a .NET Web service when .NET is not available on the client. We'll focus on two common scenarios, one in which the developer is using a legacy Visual Studio language such as Visual Basic 6.0 or Visual C++ 6.0, and one in which the developer is using ASP.

Consuming a Web Service from Old COM Applications

There are two common ways of enabling your COM applications to consume a Web service. You can use the SOAP Toolkit to build in the functionality, or you can get Microsoft XML Core Services (MSXML) to do it for you. We'll look briefly at both. Once again, we'll use our weather report example, but this time we'll call it using a Visual Basic 6.0 application to show how you can use either approach.

Using the SOAP Toolkit

The SOAP Toolkit is a handy add-on that allows you to add Web services to your COM applications and components. It provides a COM-based API that can be used with languages such as Visual Basic 6.0 and Visual C++ 6.0. The SOAP Toolkit is currently in its third revision, and the latest version (3.0 as of this writing) is available for free from Microsoft at *http://msdn.microsoft.com/library/default.asp?URL=/downloads/list/websrv.asp*.

You can use the SOAP Toolkit 3.0 to both create clients capable of connecting to Web services and to expose methods from existing COM applications as Web services. The Toolkit consists of two main components—a client-side component called SOAPClient, which can invoke operations described in the WSDL document, and a server-side component that maps the Web service methods to COM object method calls. This second component allows you to expose your Web services. In this chapter, we'll focus only on the SOAPClient component.

For our example, we just need to create a standard .exe file. As we did with the Web Forms application, we simply add a text box, a button, and two labels. Before we can add any code, we must supply a reference to the SOAP Type Library 3.0 using the References dialog box, as shown in Figure 8-12. This will ensure that the SOAPClient component is available for use in Visual Basic 6.0.

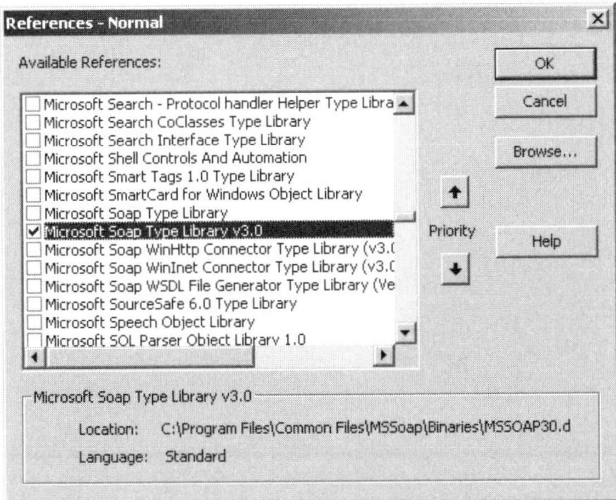

Figure 8-12 Supplying a reference

For the sorting of the XML code that is returned by the Web service, we should also add the MSXML 3.0 or 4.0 library (depending on which is available). We then add the following code to the button's click event handler:

```
Private Sub Command1_Click()


    Dim SOAP As MSSOAPLib30.SoapClient30
    Set SOAP = New MSSOAPLib30.SoapClient30
    SOAP.MSSoapInit "http://www.webservicex.net/usweather.asmx?WSDL"
    Dim weather As String
    weather = SOAP.GetWeatherReport(Text1.Text)
    Dim strDoc As String
    strDoc = ""
    Dim XMLDocument As MSXML2.DOMDocument
    Set XMLDocument = New MSXML2.DOMDocument

    XMLDocument.LoadXml (weather)
    Set XMLRoot = XMLDocument.documentElement

    For loop1 = 0 To XMLRoot.childNodes.length - 1
        Set XMLParentNode = XMLRoot.childNodes(loop1)

        For loop2 = 0 To XMLParentNode.childNodes.length - 1
            Set XMLNode = XMLParentNode.childNodes(loop2)
            If XMLNode.nodeName = "#text" Then


                strDoc = strDoc + XMLNode.parentNode.nodeName + " - " _
                    + XMLNode.Text + vbCrLf
```

```
                Else
                    strDoc = strDoc + XMLNode.nodeName + " - " _
                        + XMLNode.Text + vbCrLf
                End If
            Next
        Next
Label2.Caption = strDoc
End Sub
```

The code is simple enough: after the error handler, the first two lines just create an instance of the *SoapClient30* object called *SOAP*. We load the WSDL of the service into the object, and then we can call the methods of the Web service, just as we would in .NET.

In fact, the *SoapClient30* object takes three parameters, all as strings. The first is the WSDL reference to the Web service, the second is the port name, and the third is the WSML file. The second and third parameters are optional if you specify only a WSDL document containing one service with one SOAP port. For this example, we supplied only the first parameter. The second part of the code just iterates through the elements in the XML that is returned, displaying the element followed by the text.

When you run the code, it returns the information to your application as shown in Figure 8-13.

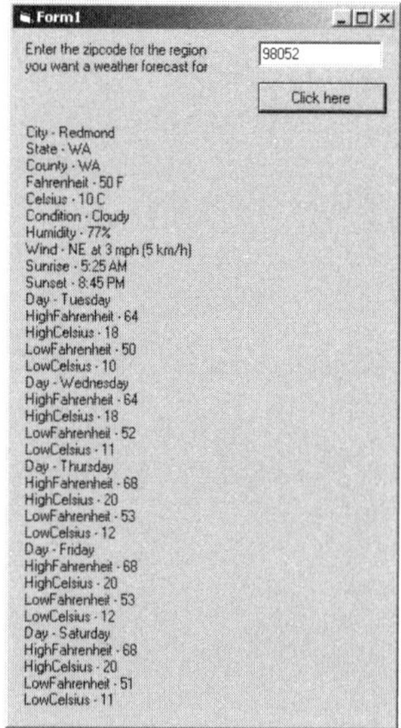

Figure 8-13 Legacy Visual Basic 6.0 application accessing a .NET Web service

Error handling is also done slightly differently in a COM client because you must rely on the SOAP *Client* object to get information from the SOAP *Fault* element for you. You can add an *On Error Go To* section to the code to return this information, followed by an error handler section:

```
On Error Goto Err
⋮
Err:
    Dim errMsg As String
    Msg = Err.Description + vbcrlf _
        + "Fault Code -" + soap.FaultCode + vbcrlf
    Msg = Msg + "Fault String -" + soap.FaultString
    MsgBox msg, vbCritical
```

This code should enable you to more elegantly handle any problems with the Web service that might arise.

Using MSXML

Using MSXML to consume the Web service is just as easy. You don't need a reference to the SOAP Type Library—you just need the reference to the MSXML library. The code varies only slightly:

```
Private Sub Command1_Click()
    Dim XMLDocument As MSXML2.DOMDocument
    Set XMLDocument = New DOMDocument
    XMLDocument.async = False
    Dim wsURL As String
    wsURL = "http://www.webservicex.net/usweather.asmx" _
        + "/GetWeatherReport?zipcode=" + Text1.Text
    Label2.Caption = wsURL
    XMLDocument.Load (wsURL)
    Dim strDoc As String
    strDoc = ""
    Dim strDoc2 As String
    strDoc2 = ""
    strDoc2 = XMLDocument.lastChild.Text
    Dim XMLDocument2 As MSXML2.DOMDocument
    Set XMLDocument2 = New MSXML2.DOMDocument
    XMLDocument2.LoadXml (strDoc2)
    Set XMLRoot = XMLDocument2.documentElement

    For loop1 = 0 To XMLRoot.childNodes.length - 1
        Set XMLParentNode = XMLRoot.childNodes(loop1)

        For loop2 = 0 To XMLParentNode.childNodes.length - 1
            Set XMLNode = XMLParentNode.childNodes(loop2)
            If XMLNode.nodeName = "#text" Then
```

```
                strDoc = strDoc + XMLNode.parentNode.nodeName + " - " _
                    + XMLNode.Text + vbCrLf
            Else
                strDoc = strDoc + XMLNode.nodeName + " - " _
                    + XMLNode.Text +  vbCrLf
            End If
    Next
Next

Label2.Caption = strDoc

End Sub
```

We created an instance of the *MSXML2.DOMDocument* object, set its *async* property to *false* to enable the document to finish loading before processing continues, and then we supplied the whole URL of the particular Web method along with the query information and used the *load* method to load the resulting text. However, as you can see if you query the method directly by browsing the URL *http://www.webservicex.net/usweather.asmx/GetWeatherReport?zipcode=98052*, the XML is in fact wrapped in a <*string*> element (as shown in Figure 8-14).

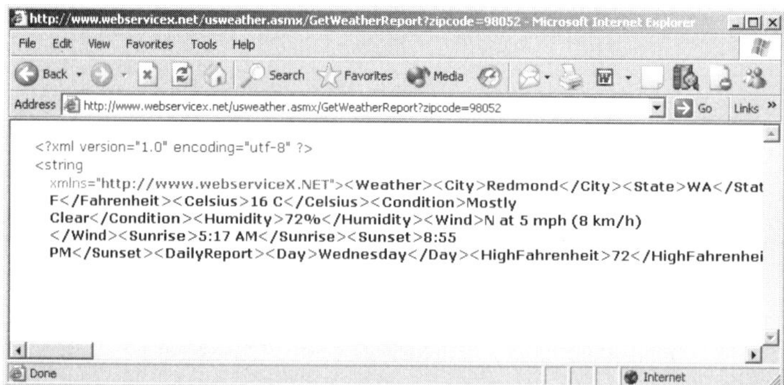

Figure 8-14 Viewing the XML returned by the USWeather Web service in Internet Explorer

The XML elements returned from the Web service have to be extricated from the <*string*> element (something .NET can be made to do automatically with its extended XML classes) before they can be separated out. To do this, we create a second *DOMDocument* object and read the last child from the first *DOMDocument* object into it before we can iterate through each element, separating out the element names and matching them with the data they contain.

Despite the extra layer of work required with this particular Web service (not all Web services would return their information in this way), it is still straightforward to return the data from the Web service to our Visual Basic 6.0 client.

Using ASP 2.0 and 3.0

Since Microsoft Internet Information Services (IIS) 3.0, classic ASP has been standard on most Windows platforms. (Windows ME and Windows XP Home Edition are the notable exceptions, but it is possible to install Personal Web Server, which comes with ASP, on Windows ME.) It's also a given that most Windows Internet service providers (ISPs) will use IIS. Unfortunately, not all ISPs will have upgraded to .NET, and among those that have upgraded, plenty will charge more for the use of .NET-based facilities. Therefore, many small businesses and home consumers will still be using ASP instead of ASP.NET. Fortunately, it's possible—and easy—to add Web services to classic ASP pages.

If we go back to our Web Form weather forecast example from earlier in this chapter, it's a simple task to change the ASP.NET client to ASP. Of course, we have to move back to ASP's classic request/response two-page structure, something that's been done away with in ASP.NET, but otherwise there isn't much difference.

The first page is an HTML form that takes the ZIP Code and submits it to our ASP page:

```
<html>
  <head>
  </head>
  <body>
    Enter the zip code of the region you want a weather forecast for:
    <form method="get" action="aspwebservice.asp">
      <input type="text" name="zipcode">
      <input type="submit" value="Click here">
    </form>
  </body>
</html>
```

There's nothing special in this page—just a simple text box control called zipcode and a button for submitting the HTML form. The HTML form is submitted using the HTTP-GET method, and the page that is called up is aspwebservice.asp. It's the ASP code in this page that's of most interest to us:

```
<%@language = JScript%>
<html>
<head>
<%
```

```
    var userRequest = Server.CreateObject("MSXML2.XMLHTTP")
    var XMLDocument = Server.CreateObject("MSXML2.DOMDocument")
    var XMLDocument2 = Server.CreateObject("MSXML2.DOMDocument")
    XMLDocument.async = false
    var webservURL = "http://www.webservicex.net/usweather.asmx/"
        + "GetWeatherReport?ZipCode=" + Request.QueryString("Zipcode")
    userRequest.Open ("GET", webservURL, false)
    userRequest.Send()

    var strDoc = ""
XMLDocument.load(userRequest.responseXML)
    var strDocument = XMLDocument.lastChild.text
    XMLDocument2.loadXML(strDocument)
    XMLRoot = XMLDocument2.documentElement

    for (loop1=0; loop1 <= XMLRoot.childNodes.length-1; loop1++)
    {
        XMLParentNode = XMLRoot.childNodes(loop1);
        for (loop2=0; loop2<=XMLParentNode.childNodes.length-1; loop2++)
        {
            XMLNode = XMLParentNode.childNodes(loop2);
            if (XMLNode.nodeName == "#text")
            {
                strDoc += "<b>" + XMLNode.parentNode.nodeName +
                    "</b> - " + XMLNode.text + "<br>"
            }
            else
            {
                strDoc += "<b>" + XMLNode.nodeName + "</b> - " +
                    XMLNode.text + "<br>"
            }
        }
    }

    userRequest = null
    XMLDocument = null
%>
</head>
<body>
The weather forecast is:
<br>
<br>
<%
    Response.Write(strDoc)
%>
</body>
</html>
```

As you can see, we're using JScript—it's closer to the C# we've been using in the Web Forms example. The first seven lines do all the work. The first three lines create instances of three new objects:

```
var userRequest = Server.CreateObject("MSXML2.XMLHTTP")
var XMLDocument = Server.CreateObject("MSXML.DOMDocument")
var XMLDocument2 = Server.CreateObject("MSXML2.DOMDocument")
```

The first object, *XMLHTTP*, allows a client to make a request, receive a response, and parse that response using the XML document model. This is really the only significant difference from our Web Forms example, in which you could query an instantiation of the proxy class directly. Here we just send a request to our Web service and get the response back as an XML document.

The second object is an instance of *XMLDocument*. This second object is used to store the XML that is returned by the response of the Web service. The third object is a second instance of *XMLDocument*. When the response is sent back by the Web service, it wraps the XML tags in a *<string>* element, and it's impossible to navigate this structure because it uses XMLDOM; with the more complex XML processing facilities of .NET, this wasn't an issue. We now have to split out this XML as text and load it into a second XML document, minus the *<string>* tag, before we can navigate it.

Next we have to configure the objects correctly so we can send a request to the Web service:

```
XMLDocument.async = false;
var webservURL = "http://www.webservicex.net/usweather.asmx/"
    + "GetWeatherReport?ZipCode=" + Request.QueryString("Zipcode")
```

XMLDocument has an *async* property that must be set to *false* so the code will wait for the *XMLDocument* object to be loaded in its entirety before processing it. We create a URL to query the service with. This URL is made up of the service name followed by the name of the method, *GetWeatherReport*, followed by the request we want to submit to the Web service. The query string has the name *ZipCode* and takes its value from the reply the user posted in the HTML form. In the next two lines, we submit the request using the URL and *false* property, via the HTTP-GET protocol:

```
userRequest.Open("GET", webservURL, false);
    userRequest.Send();
```

The response is then loaded into the *XMLDocument* object, and a text version of that response is displayed on the page. In Figure 8-15, we supply the ZIP Code 60645 for the Evanston district of Illinois.

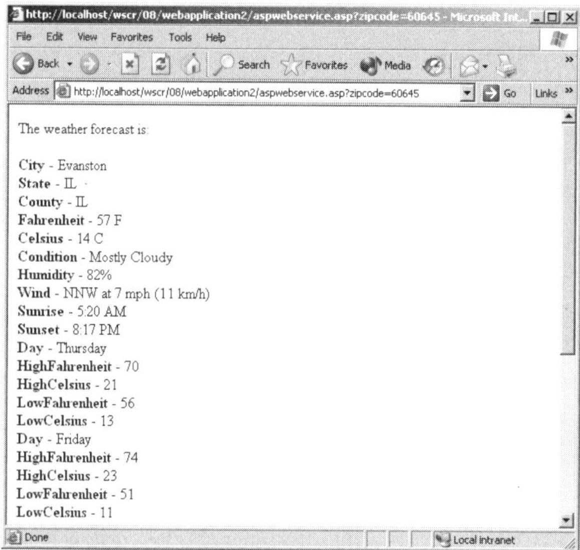

Figure 8-15 ASP Web service client

Once again, we've also used the DOM to separate out each element so we can view them all on the screen in a readable format. You can choose to process the XML that is returned in any way you like—we've chosen to make the element names bold.

As you can see, it's relatively easy to query a Web service using ASP and then parse the XML response and display it in an ASP page.

Working with XML in the Client

Last but not least, the information that your client is returning might be only part of the story. In Chapter 6, you saw examples in which we needed the XML itself from the client, not the actual objects. We covered the XML APIs in earlier chapters, so here we'll focus instead on manipulating the XML we receive using XSLT transformations to help create our interface.

With our weather reporting Web service, you've seen how we can return the XML and mold it into a roughly presentable format. However, we can use XSLT to improve the interface even more.

Using XSLT for User Interface Purposes

To use XSLT in the client, you send a source XML document and an XSLT style sheet to the browser and get the browser to apply the XSLT transformation for you. One problem is that only the most recent browsers (such as Internet Explorer 6.0 and later, Netscape 6.0 and later, and Mozilla) support the XSLT 1.0 standard. We'll assume that you're using one of these browsers.

In the Web Forms example, we supply the following code for button 1's event handler:

```
⋮
using System.Xml.Xsl;
using System.Xml;
using System.Xml.XPath;
⋮
private void Button1_Click(object sender, System.EventArgs e)
{
    XmlDocument doc = new XmlDocument();
    doc.LoadXml(USW.GetWeatherReport(TextBox1.Text));
    doc.Save("C:\\test.xml");
    XPathDocument doct = new XPathDocument("C:\\test.xml");
    XslTransform xslt = new XslTransform();
    xslt.Load("C:\\xsltfile.xslt");
    XmlReader xmlReader = xslt.Transform(doct,null);
    xmlReader.MoveToContent();
    this.Label2.Text = xmlReader.ReadOuterXml();
    xmlReader.Close();
}
```

Next we create a new XSLT file with the following code, which should be saved as xsltfile.xslt to an appropriate location. (We've used the root C:\ folder for simplicity.)

```
<xsl:stylesheet xmlns:xsl="http://www.w3.org/1999/XSL/Transform" version="1.0">
    <xsl:output method="html" indent="no"/>

    <xsl:template match="/">
        <html>
            <body>
                <xsl:apply-templates />
            </body>
        </html>
    </xsl:template>
```

```
        <xsl:template match="Weather">
            <table bgcolor="efefef" cellpadding="5" width="640">
                <tr>
                    <td>
                        City:
                            <b>
                                <xsl:value-of select="City" />
                            </b>

                    </td>
                    <td>
                        State:
                        <xsl:value-of select="State" />
                    </td>
                    <td>
                        County:
                        <xsl:value-of select="County" />
                    </td>
                </tr>
                <tr>
                    <td>Fahrenheit:
                        <xsl:value-of select="Fahrenheit" />
                    </td>
                    <td>Celsius:
                        <xsl:value-of select="Celsius" />
                    </td>
                    <td>Condition:
                        <xsl:value-of select="Condition" />
                    </td>
                </tr>
                <tr>
                    <td>Humidity:
                        <xsl:value-of select="Humidity" />
                    </td>
                    <td>Wind:
                        <xsl:value-of select="Wind" />
                    </td>
                    <td>Sunrise/Sunset:
                         <xsl:value-of select="Sunrise" />/
                        <xsl:value-of select="Sunset" />
                    </td>
                </tr>
            </table>
        </xsl:template>
    </xsl:stylesheet>
```

When you run the application now, you get the result shown in Figure 8-16.

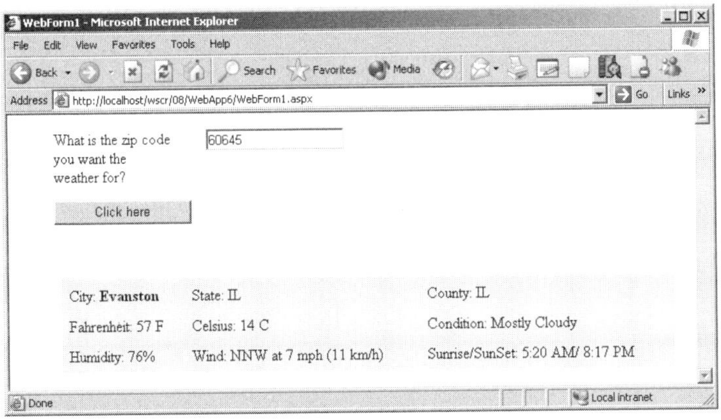

Figure 8-16 Web service client application using XSLT

We get this result because our transformation has been applied to the XML returned by the Web service. In our code, we started by loading the response from our *XMLDocument* object. From there we saved it into an actual file:

```
XmlDocument doc = new XmlDocument();
doc.LoadXml(USW.GetWeatherReport(TextBox1.Text));
doc.Save("C:\\test.xml");
```

This is a fairly crude way to get an *XPathDocument* object to accept the XML format returned by the Web service. As noted earlier, the document is returned within a string element, but loading it into an *XMLDocument* object and saving it breaks it out of this element. Next we load the document into the *XPathDocument* object, which is passed as a parameter to the *Transform* method, which performs the simple transformation on the XML file.

```
XPathDocument doct = new XPathDocument("C:\\test.xml");
```

We then create an *XslTransform* object and load our XSLT style sheet into it:

```
XslTransform xslt = new XslTransform();
xslt.Load("C:\\xsltfile.xslt");
```

Next we create an *XmlReader* object and read results of our transformation into it. Finally, we display contents of the *XmlReader* object in our label control:

```
XmlReader xmlReader = xslt.Transform(doct,null);
xmlReader.MoveToContent();
this.Label2.Text = xmlReader.ReadOuterXml();
xmlReader.Close();
```

This code returns the results to the user.

Using XSLT for Noninterface Purposes

You can also use XSLT to alter parts of the client other than the interface. For instance, you can use XSLT for versioning, such as when a new version of a Web service produces a response format that is different from the old version of the Web service. We looked at this subject in the previous chapter.

Summary

In this chapter, we investigated ways to consume Web services. We started with an overview of the five-step model that .NET uses for consuming Web services: discover the Web service, create a proxy class for the Web service, include a namespace in the client code, create an instance of the proxy class in the client, and access the Web methods via the proxy. We examined all five steps in the course of the chapter. We started with a brief reminder of how to discover Web services before moving on to the building of the client itself.

We considered a variety of possible clients, from the standard, straightforward Web Forms and Windows Forms applications to more esoteric ones that use the SOAP Toolkit, classic ASP, and JScript. We also considered some nonstandard situations, such as using the client to call the service asynchronously or where no user interface existed.

We examined the creation of Web methods in Chapter 7 and looked at clients in this chapter, so it's at last time to focus on the third part of the equation: the data stores between which the Web method and the client must interact. In the next chapter, we will look at how to use ADO.NET to provide the necessary wrapper for such communications.

9

ADO.NET and Web Services

As you saw in earlier chapters, Web services can be extremely useful for accessing data stored in databases. In Chapter 2, for example, we used a Web service to access a music database, retrieving the albums released by a specified artist. To do this, we sent a *DataSet* object via a Web method.

Of course, you can do an awful lot more with the combination of data access and Web services. For starters, you'll probably want to update data as well as extract it. You might also want to access other data sources, such as XML files, data stored in Active Directory, or even files stored on servers. Web services allow you to expose data from a plethora of sources, both current and legacy, via a single, standard interface.

In this chapter, we'll take a closer look at where Microsoft ADO.NET fits in with Web services. We'll start with a look at basic techniques and ways of streamlining performance and dealing with disparate clients. This involves repackaging data and even avoiding *DataSet* objects altogether in some cases to make the XML that the client receives as simple as possible. You'll also see how to use XML for SQL Server (SQLXML) to obtain XML straight out of a Microsoft SQL Server database, without having to go through an intermediate *DataSet* object representation.

We'll then look at how to use ADO.NET in combination with other, more advanced, techniques, including accessing data stored in locations other than a database. This will involve looking at the XPath and XQuery specifications, which enable you to locate information within the body of an XML file.

Data Access Using ADO.NET

ADO.NET is the standard way to access data in databases in Microsoft .NET. However, the framework is extensible, and, as you'll see later in this chapter, ADO.NET can actually do a whole lot more if you're willing to put in the effort.

Whichever data provider you use, whether it's one of the four supplied in the framework (SQL Server, OLE DB, Oracle, and ODBC) or another, you're likely to get at your data using a *DataReader* or *DataSet* object. Both have advantages and disadvantages. We'll look at using both of these technologies in conjunction with Web services.

DataReader Objects

DataReader objects are the simplest and quickest way to get at your data. You typically use a *DataReader* object in the following way:

1. Open a connection to a database.
2. Execute a command to obtain a reader.
3. Use the reader to extract the results of the command, one row at a time.
4. Close the connection.

In code it looks like this:

```
SqlConnection conn = new SqlConnection(ConnectionString);
SqlCommand cmd = new SqlCommand(CommandText, conn);
conn.Open();
SqlDataReader reader = cmd.ExecuteReader(CommandBehavior.Default);
while (reader.Read())
{
    // extract data from reader.
}
conn.Close();
```

Here we use the SQL Server provider for illustrative purposes, but the principles are the same for the OLE DB provider and other .NET data providers. The command you execute (*CommandText*, in the previous code) might be a SQL *SELECT* statement, a stored procedure, or something provider-specific. Obviously, if you're executing a command that doesn't return data (perhaps a simple *DELETE* statement), you don't need to use a *DataReader*, but when you're reading data from a database, you do.

When you're exposing data for read-only access, *DataReader* objects are extremely powerful. For one thing, they enable you to access data up to four times faster than when you use a *DataSet* object. They are also great at repackaging data into whatever form you want. For example, let's say you have a Web method that obtains title and price data about a list of books. Rather than returning a *DataSet* object, which (as you've seen in previous chapters) can result in a lot of superfluous information, you can return an array of classes (or structures). A suitable *Book* class is shown here:

```
public class Book
{
    private string title;
    private float price;

    public Book()
    {
    }

    public string Title
    {
        get
        {
            return title;
        }
        set
        {
            title = value;
        }
    }

    public float Price
    {
        get
        {
            return price;
        }
        set
        {
            price = value;
        }
    }
}
```

Packaging data into an array of this type (*Book*) is simple. The following Web method takes data from the SQL Server sample database called pubs. The actual data isn't that important because we're primarily concerned with the code here. The only point worth noting is that the *NULL* values in the Price column necessitate a check for *DBNull* values—hence the additional code in the *while* loop.

```
[WebMethod]
public Book[] GetBooks()
{
    SqlConnection conn =
        new SqlConnection("Server=SQL Server Name;User=sa;DataBase=pubs");
    SqlCommand cmd = new SqlCommand("SELECT Title, Price FROM Titles",
        conn);
    conn.Open();
    SqlDataReader reader = cmd.ExecuteReader(CommandBehavior.Default);
    ArrayList booksToReturn = new ArrayList();
        int index = 0;
    while (reader.Read())
    {
        Book newBook = new Book();
        newBook.Title = reader["Title"] as string;
        if (reader["Price"].GetType() != typeof(DBNull))
        {
            newBook.Price = Convert.ToSingle(reader["Price"]);
        }
        else
        {
            newBook.Price = -1;
        }
        booksToReturn.Add(newBook);
        index++;
    }
    conn.Close();
    return booksToReturn.ToArray(typeof(Book)) as Book[];
}
```

Note Using an *ArrayList* object in this way isn't always the most efficient approach because this class resizes itself as necessary, copying objects to a larger array when it needs to. It might be more efficient to first find out how many records will be returned by the query, perhaps via the SQL *Count* function. You can then initialize an array of the right size before reading data. However, this work should really be done as part of a transaction because the data might change between the request to find out how many records there are and the request to read them. For our purposes here, we'll ignore the performance hit of the *ArrayList* object, which will be far less than the performance hit of passing data over the Internet via a Web service anyway.

The SOAP returned by this Web method contains XML like this:

```
<ArrayOfBook ...>
  <Book>
    <Title>The Busy Executive's Database Guide</Title>
    <Price>19.99</Price>
  </Book>
  <Book>
    <Title>Cooking with Computers: Surreptitious Balance Sheets</Title>
    <Price>11.95</Price>
  </Book>
  ⋮
</ArrayOfBook>
```

This XML can be interpreted easily by any client, regardless of what language is used. .NET makes it easy to read the data straight into a *Book* array form, but this isn't a necessity.

Another advantage of using an array of objects like this is that you can easily modify the XML that's generated—using XML serialization attributes, for example:

```
public class Book
{
    ⋮
    [XmlAttribute]
    public string Title
    {
        ⋮
    }

    [XmlAttribute]
    public float Price
    {
        ⋮
    }
}
```

This simple modification has an immediate and dramatic effect on the XML generated:

```
<ArrayOfBook ...>
  <Book Title="The Busy Executive's Database Guide"
        Price="19.99" />
  <Book Title="Cooking with Computers: Surreptitious Balance Sheets"
        Price="11.95" />
  ⋮
</ArrayOfBook>
```

Applying XML serialization attributes in this way can make it even easier for disparate clients to consume data.

So, to summarize, *DataReader* objects are great for speedy read-only access of data, and they make it easy to obtain data in a variety of formats for use by clients. However, in some situations, particularly when you're dealing with "fat" .NET clients, *DataSet* objects are the way to go, as you'll see in the next section.

DataSet Objects

The other way to extract data from a database via ADO.NET is to use a *DataSet* object. (Admittedly, you can get scalar results using a *Command* object, and *DataSet* objects use *DataReader* objects internally, but in essence that statement is true.) *DataSet* objects are fairly heavyweight beasts, exposing far more functionality than you might need, but they certainly have their uses. In particular, when you're dealing with .NET clients of Web services, the concept of a "disconnected data set" can be extremely useful. Clients can obtain a data set, bind it to a DataGrid or other bindable control, edit data quickly and easily, and inform a Web service of the changes—all with relatively simple code. *DataSet* objects include members that deal with concurrency, too, so often you can make changes to the data source intelligently. Of course, having disconnected *DataSet* objects taken from a database that changes rapidly has its own problems—the client-side copy of the data might go out of date quickly—but these problems are surmountable.

The decision to use a *DataSet* object, though, should never be taken lightly, particularly when Web services are involved. Often a combination of *DataReader* objects and *Command* objects that access stored procedures is preferable (in particular, as noted above, when you can't rely on clients being .NET clients).

The basic code for using a *DataSet* object is as follows:

```
SqlConnection conn = new SqlConnection(ConnectionString);
SqlDataAdapter adapter = new SqlDataAdapter(SelectCommand, conn);
DataSet ds = new DataSet();
conn.Open();
adapter.Fill(ds, TableToFill);
conn.Close();
```

Here *TableToFill* is the name of the table in *ds* that will contain the result of the query. By default, the name will be something like *Table1*, so it's usually worth being explicit here, to make it easier to reference our data.

Subsequent code can examine and modify data, although you can't transmit changes back to the database without supplying insert, update, and delete commands to the *DataAdapter* object. One way of doing this is to use the *SqlCommandBuilder* class as follows:

```
SqlConnection conn = new SqlConnection(ConnectionString);
SqlDataAdapter adapter = new SqlDataAdapter(SelectCommand, conn);
SqlCommandBuilder builder = new SqlCommandBuilder(adapter);
DataSet ds = new DataSet();
conn.Open();
adapter.Fill(ds, TableToFill);
conn.Close();
```

This procedure works fine and allows you to use code as follows:

```
conn.Open();
adapter.Update(ds, TableToUpdateFrom);
conn.Close();
```

However, the *SqlCommandBuilder* class is far from perfect. For starters, it works only if the string for the *SelectCommand* property of the data adapter returns primary key data. This isn't such a problem—the *SelectCommand* string usually does this. What's worse is the format of the commands generated. For example, our command builder generates the following *DeleteCommand* string:

```
DELETE FROM Titles WHERE
( (title_id = @p1)
AND ((@p2 = 1 AND Title IS NULL) OR (Title = @p3))
AND ((@p4 = 1 AND Price IS NULL) OR (Price = @p5)) )
```

Although this command works fine, the following would suffice:

```
DELETE FROM Titles WHERE title_id = @p1
```

The *UpdateCommand* string that the command builder generates is of a similar form, including plenty of redundant information, although the *InsertCommand* string is more like what we'd expect to see.

So, you can get better performance by adding *Insert*, *Update*, and *Delete* commands manually, but even with their problems the command builders can be a useful shortcut in basic situations.

Briefly, then, let's look at what happens when we return the same data as in the previous section, but using a *DataSet* object instead. This time, the Web method code is as follows:

```
[WebMethod]
public DataSet GetBooks()
{
    SqlConnection conn =
        new SqlConnection("Server=SQL Server Name;User=sa;DataBase=pubs");
    SqlDataAdapter adapter =
        new SqlDataAdapter("SELECT Title, Price FROM Titles", conn);
```

```
        DataSet ds = new DataSet();
        conn.Open();
        adapter.Fill(ds, "Books");
        conn.Close();
        return ds;
    }
```

And here is the XML result:

```
<DataSet xmlns="...">
  <xs:schema id="NewDataSet" xmlns=""
             xmlns:xs="http://www.w3.org/2001/XMLSchema"
             xmlns:msdata="urn:schemas-microsoft-com:xml-msdata">
    <xs:element name="NewDataSet" msdata:IsDataSet="true"
                msdata:Locale="en-GB">
      <xs:complexType>
        <xs:choice maxOccurs="unbounded">
          <xs:element name="Books">
            <xs:complexType>
              <xs:sequence>
                <xs:element name="Title" type="xs:string" minOccurs="0" />
                <xs:element name="Price" type="xs:decimal" minOccurs="0" />
              </xs:sequence>
            </xs:complexType>
          </xs:element>
        </xs:choice>
      </xs:complexType>
    </xs:element>
  </xs:schema>
  <diffgr:diffgram xmlns:msdata="urn:schemas-microsoft-com:xml-msdata"
                   xmlns:diffgr="urn:schemas-microsoft-com:xml-diffgram-v1">
    <NewDataSet xmlns="">
      <Books diffgr:id="Books1" msdata:rowOrder="0">
        <Title>The Busy Executive's Database Guide</Title>
        <Price>19.9900</Price>
      </Books>
      <Books diffgr:id="Books2" msdata:rowOrder="1">
        <Title>Cooking with Computers: Surreptitious Balance Sheets</Title>
        <Price>11.9500</Price>
      </Books>
      ⋮
    </NewDataSet>
  </diffgr:diffgram>
</DataSet>
```

There's nothing wrong with this XML, but it does seem awfully lengthy, especially compared to the XML in the previous section. This data includes schema information for the *DataSet* object and full contents with DiffGram information (as described in the next section), which is fine if we want to reconstitute a *DataSet* object on the client side, but it's overkill if all we want is the data!

The way *DataSet* objects (and other behavioral types) are serialized is impossible to describe using WSDL. This has implications when you're using non-.NET clients, which might rely completely on WSDL to generate types to hold returned data. In such cases, it might be necessary to create your own type based on the .NET *DataSet* class, which can be counterproductive.

Finally, before we look at DiffGrams in more detail, it's worth pointing out that you do have some control over the XML generated when a *DataSet* object is serialized via the *ColumnMapping* property of each column. As you can see in the following example, you can set this property to a value from the *MappingType* enumeration, effectively customizing the XML as we did in the last section with XML serialization attributes:

```
[WebMethod]
public DataSet GetBooks()
{
    SqlConnection conn =
        new SqlConnection("Server=SQL Server Name;User=sa;DataBase=pubs");
    SqlDataAdapter adapter =
        new SqlDataAdapter("SELECT Title, Price FROM Titles", conn);
    DataSet ds = new DataSet();
    conn.Open();
    adapter.Fill(ds, "Books");
    conn.Close();
    ds.Tables[0].Columns[0].ColumnMapping = MappingType.Attribute;
    ds.Tables[0].Columns[1].ColumnMapping = MappingType.Attribute;
    return ds;
}
```

This code changes the XML as follows:

```
:
<NewDataSet xmlns="">
  <Books diffgr:id="Books1" msdata:rowOrder="0"
         Title="The Busy Executive's Database Guide"
         Price="19.9900" />
  <Books diffgr:id="Books2" msdata:rowOrder="1"
         Title="Cooking with Computers: Surreptitious Balance Sheets"
         Price="11.9500" />
  :
</NewDataSet>
:
```

We don't have as much control here—we can't make as many kinds of modifications as we can with XML serialization attributes. Also, when we send *DataSet* objects via a Web service, we typically expect the client to understand what a *DataSet* object is and be able to use it, so one could argue that modifying the intermediate exchange XML isn't that useful. This functionality of *DataSet* classes is more useful for reading and writing data from XML files, where specific schema information must be adhered to.

DiffGrams

The .NET Framework uses DiffGrams to communicate modifications made to *DataSet* objects so that you can update data sources without having to send all the data in a *DataSet* object back to the server. Instead, you just need information concerning which data has changed, which decreases the volume of information transmitted.

DataSet objects maintain DiffGram information without any intervention on your part. However, to use them effectively with Web services, you must use them explicitly because, by default, sending a modified *DataSet* object to a Web service not only includes DiffGram information, but it also includes all the information in the *DataSet* object. To send just the DiffGram information, you must use the *GetChanges* method of the *DataSet* object. Consider the following simple console code:

```
SqlConnection conn =
    new SqlConnection("Server=SQL Server Name;User=sa;DataBase=pubs");
SqlDataAdapter adapter =
    new SqlDataAdapter("SELECT title_id, Title, Price FROM Titles",conn);
SqlCommandBuilder builder = new SqlCommandBuilder(adapter);
DataSet ds = new DataSet();
conn.Open();
adapter.Fill(ds, "Books");
conn.Close();

DataRow dr = ds.Tables[0].NewRow();
dr["title_id"] = 99;
dr["Title"] = "A new book about fishing.";
dr["Price"] = 33.33;
ds.Tables[0].Rows.Add(dr);

ds.WriteXml(Console.Out, XmlWriteMode.DiffGram);
```

This code takes a *DataSet* object, adds data to it, and then writes out the XML representation of the object using the *XmlWriteMode.DiffGram* mode, which is exactly what happens if you pass a *DataSet* to or from a Web method (but without being wrapped in other XML, including the *DataSet* schema). We could of course do this via a Web service, but this code is simpler and does what we want.

The XML displayed by this code is as follows:

```
<diffgr:diffgram xmlns:msdata="urn:schemas-microsoft-com:xml-msdata"
                 xmlns:diffgr="urn:schemas-microsoft-com:xml-diffgram-v1">
  <NewDataSet>
    <Books diffgr:id="Books1" msdata:rowOrder="0">
      <title_id>BU1032</title_id>
      <Title>The Busy Executive's Database Guide</Title>
      <Price>19.9900</Price>
    </Books>
    ⋮
    <Books diffgr:id="Books19" msdata:rowOrder="18"
           diffgr:hasChanges="inserted">
      <title_id>99</title_id>
      <Title>A new book about fishing.</Title>
      <Price>33.33</Price>
    </Books>
  </NewDataSet>
</diffgr:diffgram>
```

Here we see every record in the *DataSet* object displayed, including the new one. However, you can see that this is a modified *DataSet* object—the last record, which we just added, has the *diffgr:hasChanges="inserted"* attribute.

Alternatively, if we use the *GetChanges* method, as follows, we get just the XML for the new row in the *<diffgr:diffgram>* element. We also get any other changes, such as updated or deleted rows.

```
ds.GetChanges().WriteXml(Console.Out, XmlWriteMode.DiffGram);
```

What this means is that our client-side code shouldn't use code such as this:

```
myWebService.UpdateData(myUpdatedDataSet);
```

Instead, we should use code like this:

```
myWebService.UpdateData(myUpdatedDataSet.GetChanges());
```

This won't affect the processing required by the Web service because only the changes are required to update data, but it sends a lot less XML down the wire. However, making this change can speed things up a great deal if you're dealing with large amounts of data—this is especially important in asymmetric bandwidth situations, where minimizing data sent to a Web service is crucial.

Typed *DataSet* Objects

You can use typed *DataSet* objects to create strongly typed classes, which make data access easier. An XSD schema is examined and used to create the code for a class that inherits from the *DataSet* class, and that includes various properties and methods that simplify the code dealing with data. For example, rather than having a plain old *DataRow* object and having to use code such as this:

```
string myName = myDataRow["Name"] as string;
```

we can use this code instead:

```
string myName = myTypedDataRow.Name;
```

This approach makes the code much easier to work with and is surprisingly easy to set up. If you haven't used typed *DataSet* objects before, now is the time to try them out—you won't be disappointed. To get you up and running, here's a quick example, called TypedDataSetExample, which you can find in the chapter's sample files.

To add a typed *DataSet* to a project, you simply select the *DataSet* type when you add a new item. This adds an .xsd schema file that appears in Solution Explorer, plus a couple of files that don't appear there unless you have the Show All Files option selected. The reason these files don't normally appear is that the files (a class file and a resource file) are generated automatically based on the contents of the schema.

Microsoft Visual Studio .NET includes a graphical editor for typed *DataSet* schema files, which includes—and this is the bit I really like—the ability to drag and drop tables (and even views) from Server Explorer to create the required schema information for your data source.

This approach is used in the TypedDataSetExample, which has a typed *DataSet* named *CDDBDataSet* generated from the Records table in DansRecords.mdb. The schema is shown graphically, as shown in Figure 9-1.

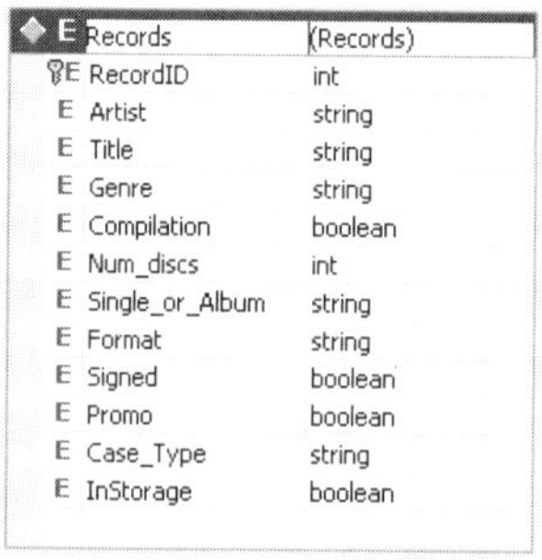

E Records	(Records)
E RecordID	int
E Artist	string
E Title	string
E Genre	string
E Compilation	boolean
E Num_discs	int
E Single_or_Album	string
E Format	string
E Signed	boolean
E Promo	boolean
E Case_Type	string
E InStorage	boolean

Figure 9-1 Schema created from the Records table in DansRecords.mdb

This typed *DataSet* is used in code as follows:

```
OleDbConnection conn =
    new OleDbConnection(@"Provider=Microsoft.Jet.OLEDB.4.0;"
        + "User ID=Admin;"
        + @"Data Source=C:\WSCR\dansrecords.mdb;");
OleDbDataAdapter adapter =
    new OleDbDataAdapter("SELECT RecordID, Artist, Title, Genre, "
        + "Compilation, Num_discs, Single_or_Album, Format, Signed, "
        + "Promo, Case_Type, InStorage "
        + "FROM Records WHERE Artist = 'Ezio'", conn);
CDDBDataSet ds = new CDDBDataSet();
conn.Open();
adapter.Fill(ds, "Records");
conn.Close();

foreach (CDDBDataSet.RecordsRow dataRow in ds.Records)
{
    Console.WriteLine("Artist: '{0}' Title: '{1}'", dataRow.Artist,
        dataRow.Title);
}
Console.WriteLine();

ds.WriteXml(Console.Out);

Console.ReadLine();
```

The first section of output code shows how easy it is to use the typed *DataSet* object, including a very readable *foreach* format. The code simply outputs the Artist and Title fields for the two records found. Next we output the XML, which looks pretty much like the XML we'd get from the other kind of *DataSet* object.

In fact, the advantages of using typed *DataSet* objects are purely cosmetic. They're great when you're writing code, but when you use them with Web services the pros and cons are pretty much the same as when you use standard *DataSet* objects. The only real difference is that the client also has access to the new class—assuming we're talking about a .NET client. And let's face it, there's not much point in using *DataSet* objects, standard or typed, for non-.NET clients.

ADO.NET Data Access Recommendations

In the past few sections, we've looked at when to use *DataReader* objects and when to use *DataSet* objects for Web service data access. However, we also have to consider what exactly we expose to clients, keeping in mind that we might not have so much control over who has access to our Web services—at least not until we cover security in later chapters. It is quite possible to give people too much control over your data, and unless you're careful, you could lose control of the data.

One common problem, which you really should try to avoid, is exposing a Web method as shown here:

```
[WebMethod]
public DataSet GetRecordById(string idString)
{
    SqlConnection conn = new SqlConnection(ConnectionString);
    SqlDataAdapter adapter = new SqlDataAdapter(
        "SELECT * FROM MyTable WHERE Id = " + idString, conn);
    DataSet ds = new DataSet();
    conn.Open();
    adapter.Fill(ds, "Records");
    conn.Close();
    return ds;
}
```

This syntax leaves you wide open to what is known as a SQL Insertion (or SQL Injection) attack. Even though you expect clients to supply just an ID value here, nothing can stop them from doing something like this:

```
MyService.GetRecordById("REC001; DROP TABLE MyTable;");
```

This approach can lead to disastrous results! Now, it's worth pointing out that this sort of thing is database management system (DBMS)–specific. Microsoft Access, for example, doesn't allow you to execute batches of SQL statements, so it isn't so vulnerable to this problem. SQL Server, though, does allow you to execute batches of SQL statements. So take precautions!

There are two ways around this vulnerability. First, you can parse the string, checking for dangerous SQL. However, this can be tricky (even with regular expressions) and is not recommended. The other, far easier, way is to use parameterized commands. The previous code can be rewritten as follows:

```
[WebMethod]
public DataSet GetRecordById(string idString)
{
    SqlConnection conn = new SqlConnection(ConnectionString);
    SqlDataAdapter adapter =
        new SqlDataAdapter("SELECT * FROM MyTable WHERE Id = @id", conn);
    adapter.SelectCommand.Parameters.Add("@id", SqlDbType.VarChar);
    adapter.SelectCommand.Parameters["@id"].Value = idString;
    DataSet ds = new DataSet();
    conn.Open();
    adapter.Fill(ds, "Records");
    conn.Close();
    return ds;
}
```

This means the parameter will be automatically parsed, and you are shielded from extra SQL.

Because it's best to use commands, I also recommend that you use stored procedures (if available) as well. In fact, I advocate stored procedures for *every* action taken on a database—and I'm not alone in making this recommendation. Apart from not being vulnerable to SQL Insertion attacks, stored procedures have other advantages. DBMSs tend to be optimized for stored procedures, which are compiled inside the DBMS and will run faster. They also make your code easier to understand—less SQL text is distributed among your code—and provide a centralized location for SQL statement modification. Rather than having to change multiple SQL statements every time you modify a commonly used select command, all you do is change it in one place.

To round off this section, then, here's a summary of recommendations for using ADO.NET in Web services:

- Where possible, use *DataReader* objects for better performance.
- Repackage data into arrays of simple types to cut down on the volume of XML transmitted and make it easier for non-.NET clients to use your Web methods.
- When you use *DataSet* objects, use the *GetChanges* method on the client to avoid sending data that isn't required to the Web service.
- In situations where you might use *DataSet* objects, use typed *DataSet* objects. The extra work you put in to create them will pay you back a hundredfold when you come to use them.
- Be sure that your data access code is SQL Insertion–proof.
- Always use stored procedures if you can.

If you follow all this advice, your data access Web service will be a much happier data access Web service, and your data will thank you for it.

Using ADO.NET to Access Custom Data Sources

Out-of-the-box ADO.NET is great, and when used properly it is easy to use and powerful. However, you can get even more out of this technology if you're prepared to put in some work. One possibility is to expose all sorts of data, not just data stored in databases, via ADO.NET. You can do this by creating your own data provider and exposing whatever data you want in a standardized ADO.NET way.

Custom Providers

We'll look at an example of a custom ADO.NET data provider that exposes files and directory information on your local network (in the FileSystemDataProvider project in the chapter's sample code) and allows files to be downloaded as *byte* arrays. To keep things simple, we'll implement only read functionality and look only at the names of files and directories, but the principles you'll learn along the way will also apply when you have bigger needs. More important, you'll see how to create a custom data provider for any data source.

FileSystemDataProvider

To create an assembly that can be called a basic data provider, you must implement certain interfaces, all found in the *System.Data* namespace. Table 9-1 shows these interfaces, along with the classes that implement them in the FileSystemDataProvider library.

Table 9-1 FileSystemDataProvider Implementation of Data-Provider Interfaces

Interface	Description	Implementing Class in FileSystemDataProvider
IDbConnection	Data source connection	*FSConnection*
IDbCommand	Command or query for manipulating your data source	*FSCommand*
IDataReader	Forward-only, read access to data	*FSDataReader*
IDataAdapter	The link between data and a *DataSet* object	*FSDataAdapter*

In addition, if you want to use parameterized commands, you must implement the interfaces listed in Table 9-2.

Table 9-2 Data-Provider Interfaces for Parameterized-Command Support

Interface	Description	Implementing Class in FileSystemDataProvider
IDataParameter	Single parameter	N/A
IDataParameterCollection	Collection of parameters	N/A

The two interfaces listed in Table 9-2 aren't implemented in FileSystemDataProvider, although it wouldn't be much of a chore to add them. We've omitted them in the sample code purely for space considerations.

In addition to the four classes listed in Table 9-1, FileSystemDataProvider also includes the types listed in Table 9-3.

Table 9-3 FileSystemDataProvider Types

Type	Description
FSException	Provider-specific exception class that inherits from *DataException*. Functions as a standard exception class, with no custom properties.
FSInfo	Intermediate class for storing file or directory information. Has *Name* and *Type* properties. *Name* is a string property, and *Type* is a *FSInfoType* property. (See below.)
FSInfoType	Enumeration of possible *FSInfo* types: *FSInfoType.File* and *FSInfoType.Directory*.

We won't look at the code for these types in this chapter because they're so simple.

You can write data providers in a way that allows data sources to be queried using standard SQL syntax, although that might mean writing an awful lot of code. To keep things simple, FileSystemDataProvider understands the commands listed in Table 9-4.

Table 9-4 FileSystemDataProvider Commands

Command	Description
GetDirectory [path]	Obtains the contents (files and directories) of the connection-configured root directory or a subdirectory indicated by the optional *path* parameter. To restrict the portion of the directory that can be examined, this command doesn't recognize .. in *path*.
GetFile path	Obtains information about one or more files matching *path*; wildcards are permitted.

In addition, the *FSDataReader* class allows the current file to be obtained in byte form.

FSConnection

The *FSConnection* class, as noted earlier, is responsible for maintaining a connection to a data source, in this case the file system. This is achieved via an instance of the *System.IO.DirectoryInfo* class.

In ADO.NET, connections are usually initialized with a connection string; we'll keep this concept. The connection string in this case is a path to a directory, which is what the *DirectoryInfo* instance will point to. Also, connections can be either open or closed; data access is permitted only when the connection is open. Although the *DirectoryInfo* class has no analogue to the "open" and "closed" states, we'll implement our own open/closed states for the purposes of consistency.

We'll need to implement plenty of members of the *IDbConnection* interface, but several of them relate to functionality we don't need, including transactional support (two versions of *BeginTransaction*), changing databases and getting database names (*ChangeDatabase* and the *Database* property), and using a timeout period (*ConnectionTimeout*). We'll set these members to do nothing or raise a *NotSupportedException*, since they don't really apply in the context of this example or the technology we are using to achieve our results.

We'll walk through the rest of the code, starting with the private members for holding state information, and two constructors:

```
public class FSConnection : IDbConnection
{
    private ConnectionState connectionState;
    private String connectionString;
    private DirectoryInfo dirInfo;

    public FSConnection() : this("")
    {
    }

    public FSConnection(string newConnectionString)
    {
        connectionState = ConnectionState.Closed;
        connectionString = newConnectionString;
    }
```

The *connectionState* and *connectionString* members are accessible via public properties; the *ConnectionState* property is read only, and the *ConnectionString* property can be modified only if the connection is closed:

```
public System.Data.ConnectionState State
{
    get
    {
        return connectionState;
    }
}
```

```
public string ConnectionString
{
    get
    {
        return connectionString;
    }
    set
    {
        if (connectionState == ConnectionState.Closed)
        {
            connectionString = value;
        }
        else
        {
            throw new FSException("Cannot set the connection string unless"
                + " the connection is closed.");
        }
    }
}
```

The private member, *dirInfo*, isn't publicly accessible, but it must be available to other classes in the assembly, so we'll make it internal:

```
internal DirectoryInfo DirInfo
{
    get
    {
        return dirInfo;
    }
}
```

Next we have *Open* and *Close* methods for controlling the connection; *Open* instantiates the *dirInfo* member, and *Close* clears it:

```
public void Open()
{
    try
    {
        dirInfo = new DirectoryInfo(connectionString);
        connectionState = ConnectionState.Open;
    }
    catch
    {
        throw new FSException("Cannot open connection.");
    }
}
```

```
    public void Close()
    {
        dirInfo = null;
        connectionState = ConnectionState.Closed;
    }
```

Once a connection is "open," other classes in the assembly can use the *DirInfo* property to access files and use *ChangeDirectory* to change the private *dirInfo* member:

```
    internal void ChangeDirectory(string newDir)
    {
        if (newDir.IndexOf("..") != -1)
        {
            throw new FSException("Cannot use '..'.");
        }
        if (connectionState == ConnectionState.Closed)
        {
            throw new FSException("Connection is closed.");
        }
        dirInfo = new DirectoryInfo(newDir);
    }
```

Finally, we have two methods for creating commands, both of which return *FSCommand* instances:

```
    public IDbCommand CreateCommand()
    {
        FSCommand newCommand = new FSCommand();
        newCommand.Connection = this;
        return newCommand;
    }

    public FSCommand CreateCommand(String commandText)
    {
        FSCommand newCommand = new FSCommand(commandText);
        newCommand.Connection = this;
        return newCommand;
    }

    ...other members omitted...
}
```

FSCommand

Next we come to the class responsible for executing commands against the connection, *FSCommand*.

Once again, there are several *IDbCommand* members that we won't implement. They include the *Transaction* property, the *Cancel* method, and the

Prepare method (for transactional support); the *ExecuteScalar* and *ExecuteNonQuery* methods and the *CommandTimeout* property; and the *CreateParameter* method (for parameter support). There are also two members that return fixed values and don't allow other values to be set: *CommandType*, which is always *CommandType.Text*, and *UpdateRowSource*, which determines mapping between returned parameters and the *DataSet* object and is always *UpdateRowSource.None*.

The code for this class starts with the private state members we require and two simple constructors:

```
public class FSCommand : IDbCommand
{
    private FSConnection connection;
    private String commandText;

    public FSCommand(): this("GetDirectory")
    {
    }

    public FSCommand(String newCommandText)
    {
        commandText = newCommandText;
    }
```

We also have two simple property accessors, *Connection* and *CommandText*, to access the private members, although there is no real need to show these here.

The real work of this class is done in the *ExecuteReader* method. The code for this method starts by ensuring that the command is in a position to execute by checking for an open connection:

```
public IDataReader ExecuteReader(System.Data.CommandBehavior behavior)
{
    if (connection == null)
    {
        throw new FSException ("No connection associated with this command.");
    }
    if (connection.State != ConnectionState.Open)
    {
        throw new FSException("Connection not open.");
    }
```

Next we analyze the command string by using a regular expression to split the command (*GetDirectory* or *GetFile*) from the parameter used (if any). We throw an exception if no command exists, and we get the command and parameter if it does. We also declare an *FSDataReader* variable for returning the reader result of the command:

```
Regex pattern =
    .new Regex("\\s*(?<Command>\\S*)\\s*(?<Parameter>\\S*)\\s*",
        RegexOptions.IgnoreCase);
Match splitString = pattern.Match(commandText);
if (!splitString.Success)
{
    throw new FSException("Must supply a command.");
}
string cmdCommand = splitString.Groups["Command"].Value;
string cmdParameter = splitString.Groups["Parameter"].Value;
FSDataReader reader = null;
```

Next we check the command type and take action accordingly. If the command is *GetDirectory*, we change the directory using *FSConnection.ChangeDirectory* if necessary, and then we get the directory information using *DirectoryInfo.GetFileSystemInfos*, passing the result to the *Data* property of *FSDataReader*. (See the next section.)

```
switch (cmdCommand.ToLower())
{
    case "getdirectory" :
        try
        {
            if (cmdParameter != "")
            {
                connection.ChangeDirectory(
                    connection.DirInfo.FullName + cmdParameter);
            }
            reader = new FSDataReader(connection);
            reader.Data = connection.DirInfo.GetFileSystemInfos();
        }
        catch (System.IO.IOException)
        {
            throw new FSException("No such directory.");
        }
        catch (System.ArgumentException)
        {
            throw new FSException("Bad directory name.");
        }
        break;
```

The *GetFile* command requires a parameter (filename), so we throw an exception if nothing is supplied. If we do have a parameter, we split the path info from the filename, change the directory to the correct location, and execute the command, getting a reader in the same way as for *GetDirectory*:

```
        case "getfile" :
            try
            {
                if (cmdParameter == "")
                {
                    throw new FSException("Must specify a filename.");
                }
                if (cmdParameter.IndexOf('\\') != -1)
                {
                    connection.ChangeDirectory(
                        connection.DirInfo.FullName
                            + cmdParameter.Substring(0,
                                cmdParameter.LastIndexOf('\\') + 1));
                }
                reader = new FSDataReader(connection);
                reader.Data = connection.DirInfo.GetFiles(
                    cmdParameter.Substring(
                        cmdParameter.LastIndexOf('\\') + 1));
                if (reader.RecordsAffected == 0)
                {
                    throw new FSException("No files found.");
                }
            }
            catch (System.IO.IOException)
            {
                throw new FSException("No such directory.");
            }
            catch (System.ArgumentException)
            {
                throw new FSException("Bad directory name.");
            }
            break;
        default:
            throw new FSException("Unknown command.");
    }
    return reader;
}
```

There is also another version of *ExecuteReader* that works without needing a value for the *CommandBehavior* parameter (which we don't use anyway, so we just pass a *CommandBehavior.Default* value to the version of this method shown above), and that completes the code for this class:

```
IDataReader System.Data.IDbCommand.ExecuteReader()
{
    return ExecuteReader(CommandBehavior.Default);
}
```

```
    ...other members omitted...
}
```

FSDataReader

Now we come to the class that allows us read access to the data returned by *FSCommand* execution, *FSDataReader*. As usual, the code starts with private state-holding members and two constructors (both internal because this class cannot be created independently):

```
public class FSDataReader : IDataReader
{
    private FileSystemInfo[] data;
    private FileSystemInfo currentData;
    private FSInfo currentDataInfo;
    private int index;
    private FSConnection connection;
    private bool isClosed;
    private bool readMethodCalled;

    internal FSDataReader()
    {
        isClosed = true;
        readMethodCalled = false;
        index = 0;
    }

    internal FSDataReader(FSConnection connectionRef)
    {
        connection = connectionRef;
        isClosed = false;
        readMethodCalled = false;
        index = 0;
    }
```

The state members are

- ***data*** A *FileSystemInfo* array containing directory members, initialized by *FSCommand* via the internal property *Data*
- ***currentData*** The *FileSystemInfo* object representing the current file or directory
- ***currentDataInfo*** An *FSInfo* representation of *currentData*
- ***index*** The index of the current record within the data
- ***connection*** A reference to the associated connection

- ***isClosed*** A Boolean value indicating whether the reader is closed
- ***readMethodCalled*** A Boolean value indicating whether *Read* has been called, which is necessary to initialize data

The most important method in this class is *Read* (from *IDataReader*), which advances the current data through the *FileSystemInfo* array containing all the file and directory objects returned by *FSCommand*. First we check whether the reader is open, which it will be if it was initialized with a connection; if there is any data to examine, we read the data. We assign the current *FileSystemInfo* object to *currentData*. Then we check to see whether the record being examined is a directory by checking the type of the *FileSystemInfo* object to see if it is actually a *DirectoryInfo* instance. We then initialize the *currentDataInfo* member accordingly. (*FSInfo* requires this information.)

```
public bool Read()
{
    if (!isClosed)
    {
        if (data != null)
        {
            if (index < data.Length)
            {
                currentData = data[index];
                if (currentData.GetType() == typeof(DirectoryInfo))
                {
                    currentDataInfo = new FSInfo(currentData.Name,
                                                 FSInfoType.Directory);
                }
                else
                {
                    currentDataInfo = new FSInfo(currentData.Name,
                                                 FSInfoType.File);
                }
```

Next we advance the index so it's ready for the next time *Read* is called, set *readMethodCalled* to *true*, and return a *true* result. Alternatively, if no data is found, a *false* value is returned so the client knows to stop reading data.

```
                index++;
                readMethodCalled = true;
                return true;
            }
            else
            {
                return false;
            }
        }
```

Finally, we have exception-throwing code in case the reader isn't properly initialized:

```
            else
            {
                throw new FSException("No data loaded.");
            }
        }
        else
        {
            throw new FSException("Reader is closed.");
        }
    }
```

The rest of the *IDataReader* members (and the *IDataRecord* members, which must be implemented if we implement *IDataReader*) are concerned with getting information about the current record or are concerned with the data in general, and none of them concern us that much. Some have been implemented, and others haven't, based on whether they are applicable to *FSInfo* data. (Most of them aren't, such as *GetGuid*.)

The data can be examined using members of these interfaces that are implemented, but we would expect clients of this class to use the custom methods *GetFSInfo* (to access the current file info) and *GetFile* (which returns a *byte* of the current file). *GetFSInfo* simply returns *currentDataInfo* as appropriate (that is, if the reader is properly initialized):

```
    public FSInfo GetFSInfo()
    {
        if (!isClosed)
        {
            if (readMethodCalled)
            {
                return currentDataInfo;
            }
            else
            {
                throw new FSException("Must call Read() to initialize data.");
            }
        }
        else
        {
            throw new FSException("Reader is closed.");
        }
    }
```

GetFile loads the current file into a byte array using file stream classes and returns it as follows:

```
    public byte[] GetFile()
    {
        if (!isClosed)
        {
            if (readMethodCalled && currentDataInfo.Type == FSInfoType.File)
            {
                FileInfo currentFile = currentData as FileInfo;
                FileStream stream = currentFile.OpenRead();
                BinaryReader reader = new BinaryReader(stream);
                byte[] fileData = new byte[stream.Length];
                for (long currentByte = 0; currentByte < stream.Length;
                    currentByte++)
                {
                    fileData[currentByte] = reader.ReadByte();
                }
                reader.Close();
                stream.Close();
                return fileData;
            }
            else
            {
                throw new FSException("Must call Read() to initialize data.");
            }
        }
        else
        {
            throw new FSException("Reader is closed.");
        }
    }

    ...other members omitted...
}
```

The code so far is all we need to access our data source. However, to make it a proper data provider, we must provide a way to obtain data in *DataSet* form, which requires *FSDataAdapter*.

FSDataAdapter

FSDataAdapter has only one private state member (and an associated public property accessor, which we won't look at here):

```
public class FSDataAdapter : IDataAdapter
{
    private FSCommand fillCommand;
```

This member holds the command used to fill a *DataSet* with results. Typically, *DataAdapter* classes also have commands for data modification, but we're creating a read-only provider here, so we don't need to worry about them.

Next we have some constructors, which require varying numbers of parameters and supply the usual .NET data-provider versatility in how classes are used:

```
public FSDataAdapter() : this(new FSCommand())
{
}

public FSDataAdapter(FSCommand newFillCommand)
{
    fillCommand = newFillCommand;
}

public FSDataAdapter(FSCommand newFillCommand,
    FSConnection newConnection)
{
    fillCommand = newFillCommand;
    fillCommand.Connection = newConnection;
}
```

Next we come to the *IDataAdapter* members. Most of these aren't required for this data provider. *TableMappings*, which determines what happens if unmapped data raises errors, simply returns *null*. *MissingSchemaAction*, which determines whether schema information is added to the *DataSet* even if no data is present, is always *MissingSchemaAction.Add* (which means that schema information is added). *MissingMapping* action is always *MissingMappingAction.Passthrough*, which means that unmapped data (if any) is added to the *DataSet* without complaint. *Update*, which is used by the adapter to make changes to a data source based on DiffGram information, isn't required, and it throws a *NotSupportedException*.

None of this, though, affects the real meat of this class, which is the *FillSchema* and *Fill* methods. They are responsible for setting the *DataSet* object's schema information and filling the *DataSet* object with data, respectively.

FillSchema sets the schema information by creating a new table, setting column information (the filename is used as a primary key—filenames are unique within a directory by definition, after all), and adding the table to the *DataSet* object as a new table named FSInfo. Note that we always use this table name for adding to the *DataSet*, so clients never have to supply one when *Fill* is called.

```
public DataTable[] FillSchema(DataSet dataSet,
                              System.Data.SchemaType schemaType)
{
    DataTable[] tables = new DataTable[1];
```

```
        tables[0] = new DataTable("FSInfo");
        tables[0].Columns.Add("Name", typeof(String));
        tables[0].Columns.Add("Type", typeof(String));
        DataColumn[] primaryKeys = new DataColumn[1];
        primaryKeys[0] = tables[0].Columns["Name"];
        tables[0].PrimaryKey = primaryKeys;

        if (dataSet.Tables.Contains("FSInfo"))
        {
            dataSet.Tables.Remove("FSInfo");
        }
        dataSet.Tables.Add(tables[0]);
        return tables;
    }
```

Fill simply uses the stored *fillCommand* command to read data and stores it into the FSInfo table initialized in *FillSchema*:

```
    public int Fill(DataSet dataSet)
    {
        FillSchema(dataSet, SchemaType.Mapped);
        DataTable FSInfoTable = dataSet.Tables["FSInfo"];
        FSDataReader reader = fillCommand.ExecuteReader(
            CommandBehavior.Default) as FSDataReader;
        FSInfo inf = null;
        while (reader.Read())
        {
            inf = reader.GetFSInfo();
            DataRow newRow = FSInfoTable.NewRow();
            newRow["Name"] = inf.Name;
            newRow["Type"] = inf.Type.ToString();
            FSInfoTable.Rows.Add(newRow);
        }
        dataSet.AcceptChanges();
        return 0;
    }

    ...other members omitted...
}
```

And that completes our data provider.

A Windows Client for FileSystemDataProvider

Before exposing file system data via a Web service, we should check that everything is working by using a simple Windows application. This is good practice and makes the code easier to debug—plus, we can make the application use a Web service rather than using the provider directly with relatively few modifications.

We won't look at how to create this application because it uses standard Windows Forms techniques; you can view the code at your leisure in the files that come with this book. We will, however, examine the data access–specific parts and discuss the basic concepts behind the application. Figure 9-2 shows the application in action.

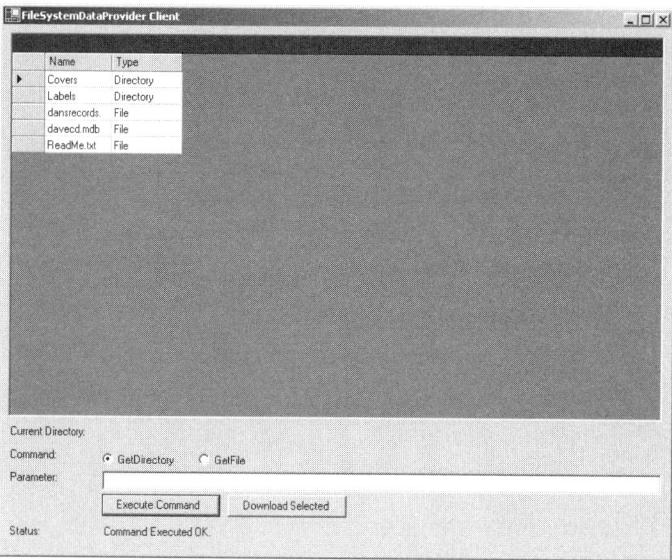

Figure 9-2 A Windows Forms client application for FileSystemDataProvider

The user can choose to execute a *GetDirectory* or a *GetFile* command and optionally supply a parameter. The DataGrid display will show the files using a *DataSet* object obtained using an *FSDataAdapter* object configured with the command entered.

In addition to allowing you to enter commands manually, the application allows you to select and download files by using the Download Selected button. This button uses a *GetFile* command and then calls the *GetFile* method of the *FSDataReader* class to get the file data, and the data can then be saved by using a *SaveFileDialog* object.

> **Note** Because this is a local windows application, you aren't really downloading files at all, you're just copying them from one place to another. However, we'll be modifying this application to use a Web service shortly, where the Download File button makes more sense.

Feedback is also supplied in the Current Directory and Status labels, which show which directory is being examined (information that is also used when files are downloaded) and what operations the application carries out, respectively.

Note that the root directory of the data is hardcoded into the application, in the constructor. Although this isn't strictly necessary, it fits in with the design methodology for the data provider. The idea is to expose a selection of files and directories below a common root and not allow .. to be used, to avoid exposing other data. When we tie the provider into a Web service shortly, we will hardcode this root directory into the Web service, but for now (because this information isn't appropriate inside the provider itself) we'll set it in the client application.

In addition to the *rootPath* private state member, the application has a private state variable called *results*, which stores the *DataSet* filled by *FSDataAdapter*. The rest of the code in the application is contained in the event handlers for the two buttons.

Let's first look at *executeButton_click*, which is executed when the user clicks Execute Command. We start by initializing the connection:

```
private void executeButton_Click(object sender, System.EventArgs e)
{
    try
    {
        FSConnection conn = new FSConnection(rootPath);
        FSCommand cmd = null;
```

We then check for the command type selected and use this to construct a *FSCommand* instance:

```
        if (getDirectoryButton.Checked)
        {
            cmd = conn.CreateCommand("GetDirectory "
                      + parameterTextBox.Text);
        }
        else
        {
            cmd = conn.CreateCommand("GetFile "
                      + parameterTextBox.Text);
        }
```

Next we use the command to create an *FSDataAdapter*, use this adapter to fill results, bind the data to the DataGrid, and set the status labels:

```
        FSDataAdapter da = new FSDataAdapter(cmd, conn);
        results = new DataSet();
        conn.Open();
        da.Fill(results);
```

```
            conn.Close();
            resultGrid.DataSource = results;
            resultGrid.DataMember = "FSInfo";
            statusLabel.Text = "Command Executed OK.";
            if (getDirectoryButton.Checked)
            {
                directoryLabel.Text = parameterTextBox.Text;
            }
            else
            {
                directoryLabel.Text = parameterTextBox.Text.Substring(0,
                    parameterTextBox.Text.LastIndexOf('\\') + 1);
            }
        }
```

If anything goes wrong in the code, we'll receive an *FSException* (never a *NotSupportedException* because we aren't using the unimplemented members). If this occurs, we can use the text to set the status and abort:

```
        catch (FSException ex)
        {
            results = null;
            resultGrid.DataSource = null;
            statusLabel.Text = ex.Message;
        }
    }
```

Next we have *downloadButton_Click*, which is called when the user clicks the Download File button. This code checks for results and for a selected file (not directory) before creating and executing a command to initialize an *FSDataReader*. Note also that the current directory information is taken from the *directoryLabel* label, which is written to when *GetDirectory* is executed:

```
private void downloadButton_Click(object sender, System.EventArgs e)
{
    try
    {
        if (results != null && resultGrid.CurrentRowIndex != -1)
        {
            DataRow selectedRow =
            results.Tables["FSInfo"].Rows[resultGrid.CurrentRowIndex];
            String rowName = selectedRow.ItemArray[0] as String;
            String rowType = selectedRow.ItemArray[1] as String;
            if (rowType == "Directory")
            {
                statusLabel.Text = "Cannot download whole directories.";
                return;
            }
```

```
            FSConnection conn = new FSConnection(rootPath);
            FSCommand cmd = conn.CreateCommand("GetFile "
                + directoryLabel.Text
                + "\\" + rowName);
            conn.Open();
            FSDataReader reader = cmd.ExecuteReader(
                CommandBehavior.Default) as FSDataReader;
```

Downloading the file involves checking for the presence of the file using *FSDataReader.Read* (in case the directory listing has changed for some reason), prompting the user for a file path to save to, and then saving the file using standard streaming code:

```
            if (reader.Read())
            {
                byte[] fileData = reader.GetFile();
                saveFileDialog1.FileName = rowName;
                if (saveFileDialog1.ShowDialog() == DialogResult.OK)
                {
                    FileInfo newFile = new FileInfo(
                        saveFileDialog1.FileName);
                    FileStream fs = newFile.Create();
                    BinaryWriter writer = new BinaryWriter(fs);
                    writer.Write(fileData);
                    writer.Flush();
                    writer.Close();
                    statusLabel.Text = "File downloaded successfully.";
                }
            }
            else
            {
                statusLabel.Text = "File not available.";
            }
```

Finally, we have code to close the connection and we have exception-handling code—which is very much like the exception-handling code in *executeButton_click*:

```
            conn.Close();
        }
    }
    catch (FSException ex)
    {
        statusLabel.Text = ex.Message;
    }
}
```

To use the application, you simply set the directory in the constructor to a directory on your computer (or on another computer with a drive letter configured) and play away. Some sample data is included in the code for this chapter. Figure 9-3 shows a download in action.

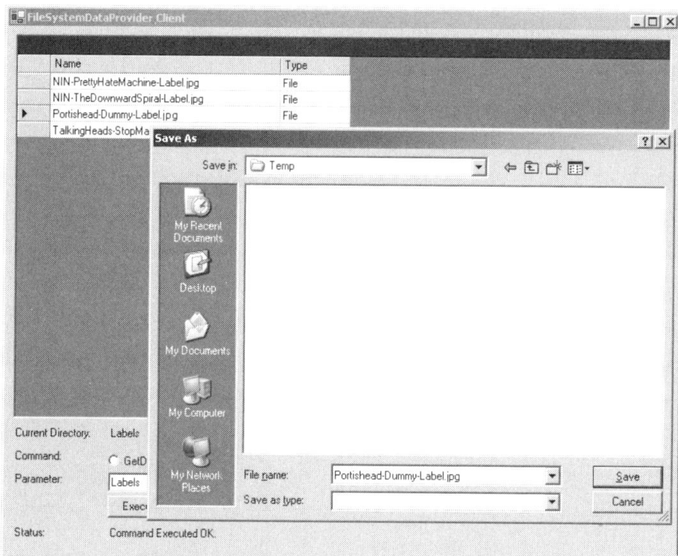

Figure 9-3 The FileSystemDataProvider client application downloading a file

Using FileSystemDataProvider via a Web Service

Now that we've done most of the legwork, it's time to put some of the concepts we've covered into practice and look at a Web service for accessing FileSystemDataProvider. We'll do this by modifying the Windows client from the previous section to use a Web service called FSDPWebService.asmx.

We're using a "fat" client, which understands *DataSet* objects, so we'll pass the data as a *DataSet* object. Furthermore, because we can and because it illustrates an earlier point, we'll pass the data as a typed *DataSet* object. Now, you might wonder why we didn't use a typed *DataSet* object directly in FileSystemDataProvider. There are three reasons for this. First, we had to conform to the interface signature for *IDataAdapter.Fill*, which uses a regular *DataSet* object. (We could have added a custom method for this, however, so it doesn't really matter.) Second, *DataAdapter* objects are supposed to work with any *DataSet* object. We can include *FSInfo* data in any *DataSet* object, even one that stores other types of data at the same time. Again, though, we could have provided an alternative. Third, and perhaps most important, we wanted our typed *DataSet* object to be used with user interface components, and the data provider sits firmly in the business layer. Making the typed *DataSet* type visible to a business layer isn't a problem, but making it visible through the business layer to user interface components can lead into tricky waters.

Instead, we introduced the typed *DataSet* object in the business layer, making it visible to the user interface layer. This doesn't cause a problem when it comes to accessing the data layer because, as noted earlier, *DataReader* objects work with any *DataSet* objects—including, of course, objects that inherit from *DataSet*, which is exactly what a typed *DataSet* object is.

Let's start, then, by looking at this typed *DataSet* class, called *FSDataSet*, which is in the FSDPWebServices project in the sample code for this book. Unfortunately, because this isn't a standard data connection, we can't drag and drop a table as we did before. Instead, we have to build the schema manually. The result is shown in Figure 9-4.

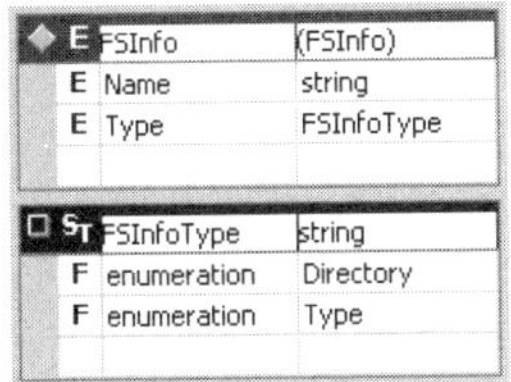

Figure 9-4 The schema for *FSDataSet* shown in the Visual Studio .NET Schema view

This schema consists of one element, *<FSInfo>*, which contains *<Name>* and *<Type>* elements, where *<Name>* is a string and *<Type>* is the *SimpleType FSInfoType*. *FSInfoType* has two constraints set, which restrict the possible string values to *Directory* and *Type*. In XML, this schema is as follows:

```
<?xml version="1.0" encoding="utf-8" ?>
<xs:schema id="FSDataSet"
  targetNamespace="http://www.notashop.com/wscr/FSDataSet.xsd"
  elementFormDefault="qualified" attributeFormDefault="qualified"
  xmlns="http://www.notashop.com/wscr/FSDataSet.xsd"
  xmlns:mstnshttp://www.notashop.com/wscr/FSDataSet.xsd"
  xmlns:xs="http://www.w3.org/2001/XMLSchema"
  xmlns:msdata="urn:schemas-microsoft-com:xml-msdata">
  <xs:element name="FSDataSet" msdata:IsDataSet="true">
    <xs:complexType>
      <xs:choice maxOccurs="unbounded">
        <xs:element name="FSInfo">
          <xs:complexType>
            <xs:sequence>
```

```
              <xs:element name="Name" type="xs:string" minOccurs="0" />
              <xs:element name="Type" type="FSInfoType" minOccurs="0" />
            </xs:sequence>
          </xs:complexType>
        </xs:element>
      </xs:choice>
    </xs:complexType>
  </xs:element>
  <xs:simpleType name="FSInfoType">
    <xs:restriction base="xs:string">
      <xs:enumeration value="Directory" />
      <xs:enumeration value="Type" />
    </xs:restriction>
  </xs:simpleType>
</xs:schema>
```

This code defines the type *FSDataSet*, which we will use in the code for both the Web service and the new Windows client.

Now let's look at the Web service code, FSDPWebService.asmx.cs. We start by putting the service in our standard namespace:

```
[WebService(Namespace="http://www.notashop.cm/wscr")]
public class FSDPWebService : System.Web.Services.WebService
{
```

As mentioned earlier, we hardcode the root directory for file transfer in the Web service, initialized in the constructor:

```
    private string rootDirectory;

    public FSDPWebService()
    {
        //CODEGEN: This call is required by
        //the ASP.NET Web Services Designer
        InitializeComponent();

        rootDirectory = "C:\\WSCR\\CDDBInfo\\";
    }
```

Next we have some more standard Web service code, then our three Web methods: *GetDirectory* for using the *GetDirectory* command, *GetFile* for using the *GetFile* command, and *DownloadFile* for getting files in *byte* form. Here's the *GetDirectory* Web method:

```
    [WebMethod]
    public FSDataSet GetDirectory(string directory)
    {
        FSConnection conn = new FSConnection(rootDirectory);
        FSCommand cmd = conn.CreateCommand("GetDirectory " + directory);
```

```
        FSDataAdapter adapter = new FSDataAdapter(cmd, conn);
        FSDataSet results = new FSDataSet();
        conn.Open();
        adapter.Fill(results);
        conn.Close();
        return results;
    }
```

This follows the standard code we used earlier to use our custom data provider. The only new thing here is that we use an *FSDataSet* object rather than a plain *DataSet* object. Note that once we've defined this type we can use an object of the type as if it were a plain *DataSet* object. We don't have to add any extra code.

Then we have *GetFile*:

```
    [WebMethod]
    public FSDataSet GetFile(string searchString)
    {
        FSConnection conn = new FSConnection(rootDirectory);
        FSCommand cmd = conn.CreateCommand("GetFile " + searchString);
        FSDataAdapter adapter = new FSDataAdapter(cmd, conn);
        FSDataSet results = new FSDataSet();
        conn.Open();
        adapter.Fill(results);
        conn.Close();
        return results;
    }
```

Again, this is standard code that now uses an *FSDataSet*.

Finally, here's the *DownloadFile* method:

```
    [WebMethod]
    public byte[] DownloadFile(string filename)
    {
        FSConnection conn = new FSConnection(rootDirectory);
        FSCommand cmd = conn.CreateCommand("GetFile " + filename);
        conn.Open();
        FSDataReader reader = cmd.ExecuteReader(CommandBehavior.Default)
          as FSDataReader;
        if (!reader.Read())
        {
            return null;
        }
        byte[] returnVal = reader.GetFile();
        conn.Close();
        return returnVal;
    }
}
```

Once more, we see code that's almost identical to that in our earlier Windows client. We get the file into a *byte* array and return it. Simple.

Next we turn to the client for this Web service. As mentioned earlier, we're basing the client on FSDPWinFormClient but hooking up a Web reference to the new Web service and using that rather than referencing FileSystemDataProvider.

The first code change, other than the namespace referenced in the *using* statement that gives the client access to our file system data, is simply to remove the root directory configured in the client because this is now handled by the Web service. Next we have changes to our two handlers. First, the *executeButton_Click* handler:

```
private void executeButton_Click(object sender, System.EventArgs e)
{
    try
    {
        FSDPWebService service = new FSDPWebService();
        if (getDirectoryButton.Checked)
        {
            results = service.GetDirectory(parameterTextBox.Text);
        }
        else
        {
            results = service.GetFile(parameterTextBox.Text);
        }
        resultGrid.DataSource = results;
        resultGrid.DataMember = "FSInfo";
        statusLabel.Text = "Command Executed OK.";
        if (getDirectoryButton.Checked)
        {
            directoryLabel.Text = parameterTextBox.Text;
        }
        else
        {
            directoryLabel.Text = parameterTextBox.Text.Substring(0,
              parameterTextBox.Text.LastIndexOf('\\') + 1);
        }
    }
    catch (SoapException ex)
    {
        results = null;
        resultGrid.DataSource = null;
        Regex pattern =
            new Regex("\\S*FSException: (?<Message>[a-zA-Z0-9 ]*)",
            RegexOptions.Multiline);
        Match splitString = pattern.Match(ex.Message);
        if (!splitString.Success)
```

```
            {
                statusLabel.Text = ex.Message;
            }
            else
            {
                statusLabel.Text =  splitString.Groups["Message"].Value;
            }
        }
    }
```

Here we change the data access classes used to use the Web service, and the exception-handling code to catch exceptions of type *SoapException*. To extract just the message from the *FSException* that is the precursor to the *SoapException* message, we use another simple *RegEx* expression. To see why this is required, try setting *statusLabel.Text* to *ex.Message* for all exceptions. You'll see a lot of text that isn't very useful!

Next, we have the *downloadButton_Click* button handler:

```
private void downloadButton_Click(object sender, System.EventArgs e)
{
    try
    {
        if (results != null && resultGrid.CurrentRowIndex != -1)
        {
            DataRow selectedRow = results.Tables["FSInfo"]
                .Rows[resultGrid.CurrentRowIndex];
            String rowName = selectedRow.ItemArray[0] as String;
            String rowType = selectedRow.ItemArray[1] as String;
            if (rowType == "Directory")
            {
                statusLabel.Text = "Cannot download whole directories.";
                return;
            }
            FSDPWebService service = new FSDPWebService();
            byte[] fileData = service.DownloadFile(directoryLabel.Text
                + "\\" + rowName);
            saveFileDialog1.FileName = rowName;
            if (saveFileDialog1.ShowDialog() == DialogResult.OK)
            {
                FileInfo newFile = new FileInfo(
                    saveFileDialog1.FileName);
                FileStream fs = newFile.Create();
                BinaryWriter writer = new BinaryWriter(fs);
                writer.Write(fileData);
                writer.Flush();
                writer.Close();
                statusLabel.Text = "File downloaded successfully.";
```

```
                }
            }
        }
        catch (SoapException ex)
        {
            Regex pattern =
                new Regex(@"\S*FSException: (?<Message>[a-zA-Z0-9 ]*)",
                    RegexOptions.Multiline);
            Match splitString = pattern.Match(ex.Message);
            if (!splitString.Success)
            {
                statusLabel.Text = ex.Message;
            }
            else
            {
                statusLabel.Text =  splitString.Groups["Message"].Value;
            }
        }
    }
```

Much more was removed from this method than put in. We now have much simpler syntax because the *byte* array from the source file is obtained by the Web service. We just have to save it to disk, using the same code as before. The only other change to the code is to modify the exception handling as before.

And there we have it. A fully functional custom ADO.NET provider accessed via a Web service, using typed *DataSet* objects suitable for a .NET Windows client. This enables the client to make use of the full *DataSet* functionality to manipulate file system data, which is great in situations like this, where we can use a DataGrid control with ease.

A Final Note

Before moving on, it's worth noting one important thing, which we'll examine in more depth in Chapter 11. The Web service is responsible for accessing the directory containing the downloadable files. This means that security plays a part—the Web service itself must have access to these files. Now, you might have noticed that in our example we used the directory C:\WSCR\CDDBInfo\—that is, not a directory below wwwroot, but one elsewhere on the file system. And we didn't receive a security error. In fact—and this is the key thing we'll be looking at later—ASP.NET (including ASP.NET Web services) is given a high degree of security privilege by default. But this can be a dangerous thing. Admittedly, the data provider used here is read only, but people can still get access to private data if you aren't careful. What we really need to do is to impose a greater level of control over what ASP.NET can and can't do, and you'll see how to do that in Chapter 11.

XML Data

So far we've looked at how ADO.NET can be used to access data and how XML plays a big part. Whenever you serialize a *DataSet* object, you get XML, which the client uses to rebuild the *DataSet* object. If we repackage data or pass simple types, we still get XML.

Of course, sometimes the source data itself is XML. You might be storing data in an XML document rather than a database, or you might access a data source that is exposed as XML. In addition, you might want to expose legacy data as XML yourself rather than use a custom ADO.NET provider. Fortunately, the .NET Framework provides powerful tools for manipulating XML because XML is crucial to the functioning of .NET as a whole.

We'll look at four topics related to XML data in relation to Web services:

- Querying XML data sources (getting data out of XML documents)
- Addressing a *DataSet* object as XML (using XML techniques to access data in an ADO.NET *DataSet* object)
- SQLXML (getting data out of a database in XML form)
- Exposing other data as XML (using an XML representation of legacy/custom data as a data source)

Querying XML Data Sources

XML has been with us for a few years now, and in that time a wealth of new standards and technologies have emerged. Every time someone thinks of a question like "How can we individually address elements in an XML document?" or "How can we link XML documents together?," someone comes up with an answer. The only problem is that the goalposts keep moving as standards evolve. The World Wide Web Consortium (*http://www.w3.org/*) maintains most XML standards, which go through a process of evaluation to move from draft form to recommendation form. As I write this sentence, in fact, I've learned that the XPointer framework (an extension of XPath that allows a finer-grained level of text selection) has become a recommendation. Not many implementations of XPointer are available right now—but by the time you read this, they're sure to be more widespread.

For the moment, though, the main XML access technology that you can use in .NET is XPath. We won't go into the details here because this isn't the place for such a discussion, but we'll give a quick example. The following code is taken from the XMLQuerying project in the code for this book, and it starts by loading an XML document that contains the same data as DansRecords.mdb: DansRecords.xml.

```
XmlDocument doc = new XmlDocument();
doc.Load(@"c:\WSCR\DansRecords.xml");
```

To access this data via XPath, we can create an *XPathNavigator* object from the document root:

```
XmlNode root = doc.DocumentElement;
XPathNavigator navigator = root.CreateNavigator();
```

To get the results of an XPath expression, we create an *XPathExpression*. (We could just use a string, but this class gives us additional options, such as the alphabetic sorting used here.)

```
XPathExpression expression = navigator.Compile(@"//Artist");
expression.AddSort(".", XmlSortOrder.Ascending, XmlCaseOrder.None, "",
                   XmlDataType.Text);
```

We get results back in the form of an *XPathNodeIterator*:

```
XPathNodeIterator iterator = navigator.Select(expression);
```

Next we use the *XPathNodeIterator.MoveNext* method to work our way through the data (in this case, all the *<Artist>* elements), and we process it at our leisure:

```
string artist = "";
string lastArtist = "";
int multiple = 1;
while (iterator.MoveNext())
{
    artist = iterator.Current.Value;
    if (artist == lastArtist)
    {
        multiple++;
    }
    else
    {
        if (multiple > 1)
        {
            Console.WriteLine(" (x{0})", multiple);
            multiple = 1;
        }
        else
        {
            Console.WriteLine();
        }
        Console.Write(iterator.Current.Value);
```

```
    }
    lastArtist = artist;
}
```

The result of this code lists all the artists in the database, counting how many entries they have. (The code relies on the fact that the data is sorted.)

Obviously, we can do a whole lot with XPath, and we strongly advise you to read up on its powerful syntax.

The other current possibility in .NET XML processing is XQuery, which is for executing queries against XML documents, but this technology is still in the early stages of development. You'll find the W3C working draft for XQuery at *http://www.w3.org/TR/xquery/*.

Addressing a *DataSet* as XML

.NET was created with XML data in mind, and that thinking is apparent throughout ADO.NET. As you've seen, serializing a *DataSet* object as XML happens automatically (although you can, of course, control this or even do it all yourself if you prefer). Not only that, but you can easily get an XML representation of a *DataSet* object in code (including schema information and so forth), using an *XmlDataDocument* class.

The following code, from the XMLDataSetQuerying project available with this chapter's sample code, shows just how easy this is:

```
OleDbConnection conn = new OleDbConnection(
    @"Provider=Microsoft.Jet.OLEDB.4.0;"
    + @"User ID=Admin;Data Source=C:\WSCR\dansrecords.mdb;");
OleDbDataAdapter adapter = new OleDbDataAdapter("SELECT RecordID, Artist, "
    + "Title, Genre, Compilation, Num_discs, Single_or_Album, Format, "
    + "Signed, Promo, Case_Type, InStorage FROM Records", conn);
DataSet ds = new DataSet();
conn.Open();
adapter.Fill(ds, "Records");
conn.Close();
XmlDataDocument doc = new XmlDataDocument(ds);
```

After we have our data, we just pass the *DataSet* object to the *XmlDataDocument* constructor. Then we can do whatever we like with this XML, treating it much like any other XML document: navigate it, add, remove, or update nodes, transform it using XSLT, or serialize it to XML. Any change applied to the XML document is reflected live in the data set, and vice versa. The example code simply executes the same XPath expression as in the *XMLQuerying* example, so we won't repeat it here.

SQLXML

If you are using a SQL Server 2000 data source, you have another option at your disposal. By installing SQLXML, you can extend the XML capabilities of the DBMS in several ways, including adding *FOR XML* to the SQL *SELECT* statement syntax. This enables you to run queries and get data back directly as XML.

Let's look at a quick example of this, from the SQLXMLExample project. We start by initializing a new *XmlDocument* object for storing our results, and then we set up our connection and *FOR XML* query:

```
XmlDocument doc = new XmlDocument();

SqlConnection conn = new SqlConnection(
    "Server=ALTAR1;User=sa;DataBase=pubs");
SqlCommand cmd = conn.CreateCommand();
cmd.CommandText = "SELECT * FROM Titles FOR XML AUTO";
```

The *AUTO* keyword lets SQL Server decide how to format the results. Next we use the *SqlCommand.ExecuteXmlReader* method to obtain an *XmlReader* object on our results (*not* a *SqlDataReader* object):

```
conn.Open();
XmlReader reader = cmd.ExecuteXmlReader();
```

Then we access the results and close the connection. Bear in mind that we can't just load XML straight into an *XmlDocument* object using this *XmlReader* object because the results of this query don't constitute well-formed XML—there is no single document root element. Instead, we have a collection of results in individual elements. One way of dealing with this, which is used in the example, is to construct our own XML using a *StringBuilder*, wrapping the results in a *<QueryResult>* element:

```
StringBuilder sb = new StringBuilder();
sb.Append("<QueryResult>");
if (reader.Read())
{
    while (!reader.EOF)
    {
        sb.Append(reader.ReadOuterXml());
        reader.Skip();
    }
}
conn.Close();
sb.Append("</QueryResult>");
```

The XML that this generates can be loaded into an *XmlDocument* object, and in our example we simply write the document to the screen:

```
doc.LoadXml(sb.ToString());
doc.Save(Console.Out);
```

As with the other technologies we've looked at, a whole lot more is possible by using *FOR XML* queries and SQLXML as a whole. If this solution fits your needs, it is well worth a look. You can even configure Microsoft Internet Information Services (IIS) to execute commands using URL format, effectively accessing SQL Server over the Web as a Web service, but without using .NET Web services. However, this veers away from the topic of this book somewhat, so we won't cover it here.

Exposing Other Data as XML

As mentioned throughout this chapter, you need not limit yourself to databases and XML documents when it comes to data access. As we did earlier with a custom provider, you can expose sources such as file system data, and you can make full use of XML querying capabilities as well as ADO.NET. In fact, it can often be worthwhile to skip ADO.NET and take a pure XML route, although this comes with its own challenges.

One approach is to derive a class from *XPathNavigator*, implementing the various members as appropriate to your data source. An excellent example of this can be found on Aaron Skonnard's Web site, at *http://staff.develop.com/aarons/xmllinks.htm*. He provides a library of customized *XPathNavigator* classes that are suitable for using XPath to query file system, registry, assembly, and other data sources.

Summary

In this chapter, we looked primarily at ADO.NET data access as applied to .NET Web services. You saw how the various ADO.NET techniques fit in with Web services, and you saw tips on how to use them to expose data via Web methods.

You learned how to use *DataReader* objects for fast, read-only access, and how to use them to shape data into simpler forms, which can be advantageous for both .NET and non-.NET clients. Next we turned to *DataSet* objects, discussing where to use them or avoid them, as well as looking in a little more depth at how DiffGrams work and why you should use typed *DataSet* objects wherever possible.

In addition, you saw how ADO.NET can be extended such that legacy or custom data can be exposed via a Web service in a standardized way. This was illustrated with a custom ADO.NET provider that can be used to query file system data. This was a read-only implementation, but the basic principles behind custom data providers are clear.

We also had a brief tour through the topic of XML data. You saw how XML data sources can be queried directly and how ADO.NET *DataSet* objects can be treated (and queried) as XML. For SQL Server users, we also looked at a shortcut—SQLXML. And for hardcore programmers, we briefly discussed customized ways to treat other data sources as XML.

10

Extending the Web Services Framework

The key to software design is to take a problem or a task and divide it into the actions that must be taken to solve the problem or complete the task. Sometimes those component actions must be further divided until each action is a simple unit that can be implemented as a class method or a single line of code.

The problem that this book addresses can be summed up as "how to deliver a Microsoft .NET solution that exposes operations as methods that are available publicly as a Web service." If we apply the simple tenet of division to this problem, we can see that in the ASP.NET infrastructure Web methods should do only what they were intended to do. On a live production server, security, logging facilities, quality-of-service regulation, and other features must be implemented as part of the infrastructure and not as part of the service.

In this chapter, we'll look at two kinds of components you can attach to a Web application: HTTP modules and SOAP extensions. Each type of component influences a different period in a SOAP request's life cycle. We will discuss how they differ, how to build them, and when to use them. Like the HTTP handlers you saw in Chapter 5, both allow you to get closer to the actual processing logic that the Web method API deals with and "protects" you from. Using one or even both in tandem, you can intercept requests before they are processed by the handler *and* intercept the responses before they make their way back to the client.

Just because you have access to the message doesn't mean your components will necessarily alter that message. They might carry out administrative tasks such as logging, tracing, and validating.

HTTP Modules vs. SOAP Extensions

Before we start coding, it's worth understanding the differences between the two types of components. Both allow you to process a request message before the Web method is actually called and to process the response before it leaves the Web server and is returned to the client—but at different points in the message's life cycle.

A Message's Life Cycle

As you'll recall from Chapter 5, SOAP messages use the same pipeline as requests for ASP.NET pages to get to the service they are destined for.

A request is guided by Microsoft Internet Information Services (IIS) into the application domain of the Web application the target service is a part of. The *HttpRuntime* object generates an *HttpApplication* object to maintain the state of the application, if one doesn't already exist, and it generates an *HttpContext* object that maintains information specific to the request in the application. When the *HttpApplication* object receives the request, it checks machine.config to see whether any *HttpModule* objects should be created to perform preprocessing and to see which *HttpHandler* object will actually handle the request. When the *HttpHandler* object has prepared a response to the request, those *HttpModule* objects might also postprocess the response message, if needed, before the *HttpApplication* object sends it back to the client. This cycle is depicted in Figure 10-1.

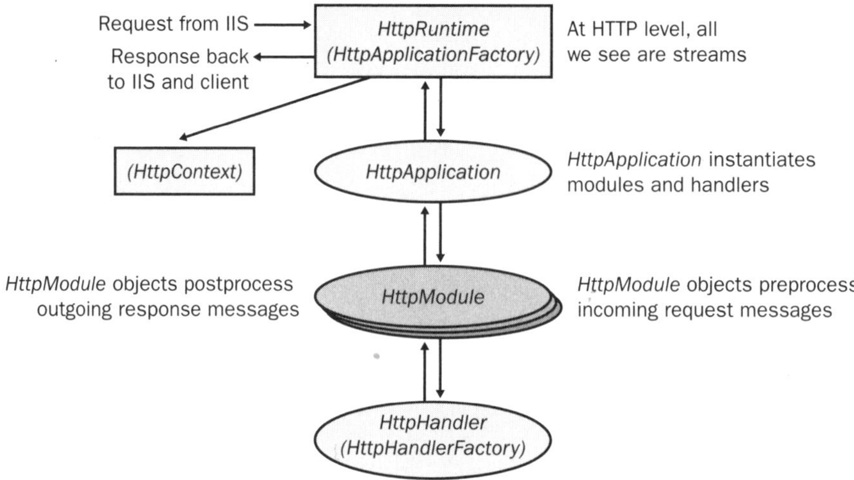

Figure 10-1 A closer look at HTTP modules in the grand scheme of the ASP.NET pipeline

It's easy to see from this description where HTTP modules fit into the scheme of things. They work at the HTTP level and are implemented as autonomous parts of the ASP.NET pipeline. That is, if the .config file for a Web application includes an HTTP module in the pipeline, the HTTP module gets a crack at every message going in or out of the application's pipeline, irrespective of the handler that will deal with the request or the target of the message.

SOAP extensions work at a different level. In fact, they bolt onto the default ASMX handler provided by ASP.NET and are therefore not easy to use in conjunction with your own handlers. Once the *HttpApplication* object has requested an instance of the ASMX handler from the ASP.NET *WebServiceHandlerFactory* class, that handler checks to see whether any extensions have been defined within the application. Each extension that is present and that is applicable to the request gets access to objects representing the request and response messages themselves rather than the streams carrying them. Figure 10-2 shows how extensions fit into the message life cycle.

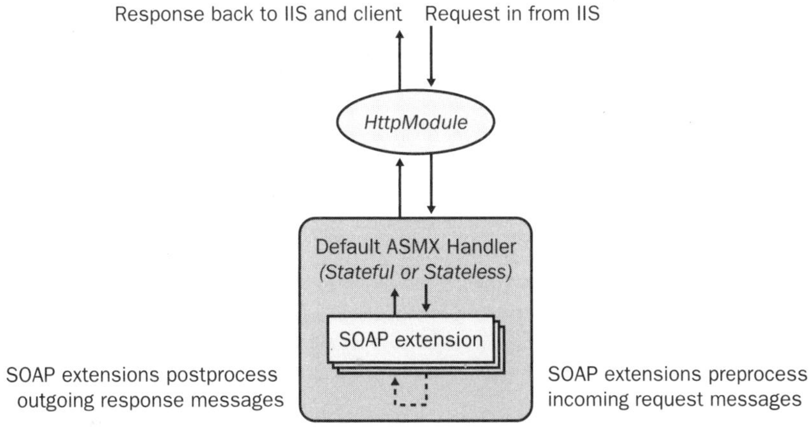

Figure 10-2 SOAP extensions work within the default ASMX handlers.

SOAP extensions are more adaptable than HTTP modules. You can set them up to work autonomously with every response and request, just like HTTP modules, or you can apply them declaratively to individual methods exposed by a Web service. The second option offers flexibility that HTTP modules can't provide. You can also use SOAP extensions on the client side when required. For instance, there would be little point in decompressing a SOAP request on the server side if it were not compressed by the client first. You can write a single extension and apply it on both the client side and the server side.

Practical Applications

Modules and extensions are suited to different tasks because they have different levels of access, autonomy, and applicability. Modules, for instance, give you access to the HTTP request and response messages in their entirety—not just the SOAP message in their body (if a SOAP message is to be found). Also, modules are specific not to Web services but to the Web applications that contain them. They react to a request for any item in a Web application, not just items with an .asmx file extension.

Uses for modules include the following:

- Implementing security (authentication, authorization, or encryption of HTTP messages)
- Caching responses
- Acting as an intermediary and routing requests to a different server
- Making the handling of the request a transaction
- Parsing HTTP headers for some reason other than those listed here
- Logging and tracing requests
- Logging server response times to requests
- Incorporating performance counters in the Web application

In contrast, an extension is the last code to see the request before the method is called and the first to see the method's response. It has access only to the SOAP message (that is, no access to HTTP information), but it can access it as the XML contents of a stream (like a module does) and as the message is deserialized into .NET classes and objects. Extensions should thus implement small tasks, specific to a Web service or perhaps to just a Web method. They can do more than encapsulate a business rule, but a business rule is a good indication of the complexity of the tasks you should take on with extensions.

Uses for SOAP extensions include the following:

- Implementing security (encrypting and decrypting the SOAP message payload)
- Compressing and decompressing the SOAP message
- Converting messages intended for old versions of the method to the current version
- Parsing SOAP headers for some reason other than those already listed here

- Validating SOAP messages against their schemas
- Applying business rules to request parameters and return values

These lists of uses are not exhaustive, but they should get you thinking about which components might best serve your application. The remainder of this chapter will look at how each is implemented.

Building HTTP Modules

In this section, we'll create a very simple example, deploy it, and then go back and look more closely at the process, filling in the gaps we left along the way.

A Simple Example

Our straightforward HTTP module example will show how an HTTP module can send a request back to a client before processing has even begun. Open Visual Studio .NET, create a new class library project called SimpleModule, add a reference to the System.Web.dll assembly, and add the following code:

```
using System;
using System.Web;

public class SimpleModule : IHttpModule
{
    public void Init(HttpApplication webApp)
    {
        webApp.BeginRequest += new EventHandler(webApp_BeginRequest);
    }

    public void Dispose()
    {
    }

    private void webApp_BeginRequest(object sender, EventArgs e)
    {
        HttpApplication webApp = (HttpApplication)sender;
        HttpContext context = webApp.Context;
        webApp.CompleteRequest();
        context.Response.StatusCode = 403;
        context.Response.StatusDescription =
                "Requests to this application are forbidden";
    }
}
```

Save the code as SimpleModule.cs and compile it into an assembly called Notashop.Wscr.C10.SimpleModule.dll. You can do this by setting the assembly name to Notashop.Wscr.C10.SimpleModule on the project's property pages before building the class. The module is now ready to be deployed. Remember that a module reacts to any request within its Web application, so we'll create a simple ASP.NET page rather than a Web service, which will more clearly show the module in action.

Create a new Web application project in Visual Studio .NET at *http://localhost/wscr/10/testwebapp*. Rename webform1.aspx to TestWebPage.aspx and add the following HTML:

```
<body>
    <form id="Form1" method="post" runat="server">
        <p style="color:red">
            This is a test page. The handler produced a response here.
        </p>
    </form>
</body>
```

It doesn't matter what the page actually does for this example, but it will be handy to have a marker here for two reasons:

- To prove that this SimpleModule doesn't allow the test page to execute and print the text.
- To mark when the ASP.NET handler actually processes the code in the page. HTTP modules let you handle events before and after processing, so a marker is useful for identifying which event occurs when.

Like any other library file, the one containing our module will be accessible to us only if we place it in the Web application's bin directory or in the global assembly cache (GAC). Copy Notashop.Wscr.C10.SimpleModule.dll into the TestWebApp\bin directory. All that's left to do is tell the application of our module's existence. We do this in a .config file.

Open the web.config file for the TestWebApp application, add the following code, and then save it:

```
<?xml version="1.0" encoding="utf-8" ?>
<configuration>
  <system.web>
    <httpModules>
      <add name="SimpleModule"
           type="SimpleModule, Notashop.Wscr.c10.SimpleModule" />
    </httpModules>
  </system.web>
</configuration>
```

Our module—which should respond to all client requests to the Web application with a 403 Forbidden message—is now in place and is tied into the ASP.NET pipeline. We have only to test it by opening up a browser and trying to access *http://localhost/wscr/10/testwebapp/TestWebPage.aspx*. Sure enough, the module kicks in and we get a familiar page, as shown in Figure 10-3.

Figure 10-3 Our SimpleModule successfully blocks requests with a 403 Forbidden response.

Our first module is written, deployed, and working in less than five pages. Now let's go back and figure out how it all works.

The *IHttpModule* Interface

Building a module involves writing a class that inherits and implements the *System.Web.IHttpModule* interface, plus a number of event handlers:

```
using System;
using System.Web;

public class SimpleModule : IHttpModule
{
    ⋮
}
```

The class inherits two methods from *IHttpModule* that we must implement:

- ***Init*** This method is called when the module is first initialized in the pipeline. It connects the module to events exposed by the *HttpApplication* object that represents the Web application the request has targeted. The handlers for these events are where the actual work is done by the module. In our SimpleModule example, we use *Init* to create a handler for the *BeginRequest* event. In the next section, we'll look at all the events that can be handled. *Init* has one parameter—the *HttpApplication* object—and returns nothing:

```
public void Init(HttpApplication webApp)
{
    webApp.BeginRequest += new EventHandler(webApp_BeginRequest);
}
```

- ***Dispose*** This method is called when the module is removed from the pipeline. It frees any resources, apart from memory, that the module might have been using. It takes no parameters:

```
public void Dispose()
{
}
```

Finally, we need to implement each event handler we set up in *Init*. Remember that we're working at the HTTP level, so access to and information about the request and its response must be through the *HttpApplication* object or the *HttpContext* object for the request. The first of these is passed as the first parameter in our event handlers, and the second is made available via the *HttpApplication.Context* property or the *HttpContext* object's own static property, *Current*.

In our example, we use the *HttpApplication* object's *CompleteRequest* method to abort the processing of the request before it has even begun, and we use the *HttpContext* object to qualify the response to the client with a status code and description, as shown in the following code. One downside of using HTTP modules rather than SOAP extensions is that you must handle errors explicitly. In extensions, an exception generates a SOAP fault automatically.

```
private void webApp_BeginRequest(object sender, EventArgs e)
{
    HttpApplication webApp = (HttpApplication)sender;
    HttpContext context = webApp.Context;
    webApp.CompleteRequest();
    context.Response.StatusCode = 403;
    context.Response.StatusDescription =
        "Requests to this application are forbidden";
}
```

At the moment, we're accepting on blind faith that the *BeginRequest* event will be triggered before processing begins. Next we'll take a closer look at the events we can hook into and when they occur.

Events Exposed by Modules

The *HttpApplication* object for your Web application exposes 14 events, each occurring at a significant point in the journey of a request or response message through the ASP.NET pipeline. Six occur before the request is passed to the handler. In chronological order, the 14 events are

- ***BeginRequest*** Indicates that a new request has arrived.
- ***AuthenticateRequest*** Indicates that the request is ready to be authenticated by the Windows authentication module.
- ***AuthorizeRequest*** Indicates that the request is ready to be authorized by the Windows authorization module.
- ***ResolveRequestCache*** Indicates the point at which a module should check whether the response to this request is in the cache. If it is, the response can be drawn from there and sent back to the client, bypassing the need to send the request to the handler.
- ***AcquireRequestState*** Indicates that the handler for the request has been instantiated and has loaded the current state of the application and session before processing the request.
- ***PreRequestHandlerExecute*** Indicates that the handler is about to be passed the request and executed to produce a response.

Each event, with the exception of the security-related events *AuthenticateRequest* and *AuthorizeRequest*, has a counterpart that occurs as the request is sent back to the client. In order of occurrence, they are

- ***PostRequestHandlerExecute*** Indicates that the handler has finished processing the request and has produced a response to be sent back to the client.
- ***ReleaseRequestState*** Indicates that the session and application state, as revised by the processing of the request, is ready to be saved.
- ***UpdateRequestCache*** Indicates that the response is ready to be added to the output cache for later use.
- ***EndRequest*** Indicates that the request is ready to be sent to the client. Note that *EndRequest* is raised as soon as a module calls *HttpApplication.CompleteRequest*.
- ***Disposed*** Indicates that the response message has left the ASP.NET pipeline and is on its way back to the client.

Last but not least, *HttpApplication* defines three events that can occur at any time, depending on what the module is doing:

- ***PreSendRequestHeaders*** Indicates that the HTTP headers for the response are about to be sent to the client. It can be triggered by a call to *Response.Flush* or *HttpApplication.CompleteRequest*, for example.
- ***PreSendRequestContent*** Indicates that the content of the response is about to be sent to the client. It usually follows *PreSend-RequestHeaders*.
- ***Error*** Indicates that an error has occurred in the module.

Figure 10-4 shows the path that a request and its response take through these events in a module.

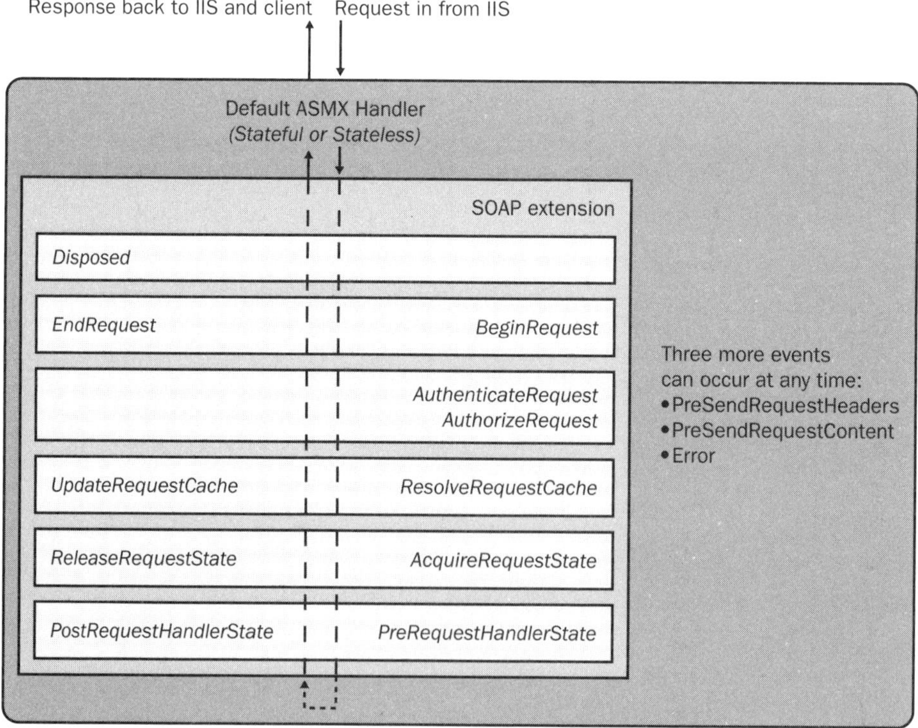

Figure 10-4 The events exposed by the *HttpApplication* object, in chronological order

For a demonstration, you can look at a module called EventListModule, which is in the TestWebApp sample application. The code is in EventList-

Module.cs. The module hooks into every event we named and simply writes to the test page that the event has occurred. For example, here's the code for the *UpdateRequestCache* event:

```
private void webApp_UpdateRequestCache(object sender, EventArgs e)
{
    HttpContext context = HttpContext.Current;
    context.Response.Write("<p>EventListModule: "
        + "UpdateRequestCache fired</p>");
}
```

We simply add the following entry for EventListModule to the web.config file for TestWebApp and comment out the entry we made earlier for Simple-Module:

```
<add name="EventListModule"
     type="EventListModule, Notashop.Wscr.c10.EventListModule" />
```

If we browse to TestWebPage.aspx, we should see a complete list of events that have occurred during the request for the page, as shown in Figure 10-5.

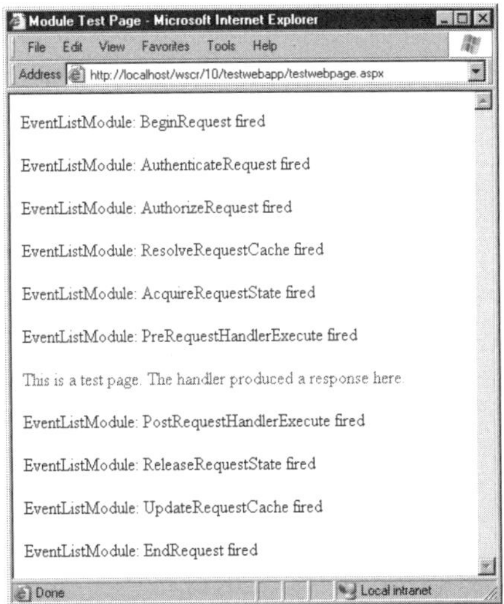

Figure 10-5 EventListModule in action

Adding Asynchronous Events

Thus far, we have considered only the events that occur in synchronous Web applications, but what if the application is asynchronous? The *HttpApplication* object exposes 10 events that mark the progress of an asynchronous request and its response through the application. They are the equivalent to the 10 synchronous events that are not *Disposed*, *Error*, *PreSendRequestHeaders*, or *Pre-*

SendRequestContent. As before, we set up our handlers for any asynchronous events we want to trap in *Init*, but in a slightly different fashion. So far we've used the following shortcut notation:

```
webApp.BeginRequest += new EventHandler(webApp_BeginRequest);
```

To set up an asynchronous event in a module, we must call the appropriate method exposed by the *HttpApplication* object. For example, if we want to handle the *BeginRequest* event asynchronously, we must create a handler for the beginning of the event and a second handler for the end of the event, and we must make the following call in *Init*:

```
webApp.AddOnBeginRequestAsync(beginHandler, endHandler);
```

The method names all take the form *AddOn*EventName*Async(beginhandler, endhandler)*.

Deploying a Module to a Web Application

After you write a module and compile it into a DLL file, deploying it into a Web application is straightforward, as you've seen. You follow three simple steps:

1. Copy the DLL to the Web application's bin directory or add it to the GAC.
2. Add an entry for the module to the application's web.config file.
3. Restart or rebuild the application.

You don't need any help for steps 1 and 3, but you might for adding the web.config entry. As you'll recall from Chapter 5, web.config is where you can add new components to the ASP.NET pipeline for an application and remove any that are present by default because they are set in the global machine.config file. For HTTP modules, we need to add an entry under *<configuration>/<system.web>/<httpModules>*; as with handlers, we have three subelements we can use:

- ***<add />*** This subelement adds a module into the pipeline. It has two attributes. You can use *name* to provide a friendly name for the module, which you can then use to reference the module in global.asax; you can use *type* to specify the module's class name and the assembly that contains it, as in *<add name="MyModule" type="ModuleClass, ModuleAssembly" />*.
- ***<remove />*** This subelement removes a module from the application that has been defined globally or in a parent application. For

example, machine.config defines seven modules to be included in every application. To remove, say, the UrlAuthorization module, we can add *<remove name="UrlAuthorization"/>* to our web.config file. The *name* attribute in this case is the friendly name given to the module when it was added originally.

- ***<clear />*** This subelement removes every module from the application.

When ASP.NET reads web.config, it performs the instructions it finds there in order, from top to bottom. If we set web.config to read as follows, ASP.NET will remove the seven modules added to our application's pipeline by default in machine.config. We can then add our own modules.

```
<?xml version="1.0" encoding="utf-8" ?>
<configuration>
    <system.web>
        <httpModules>
            <clear />
            <add name="SimpleModule"
                 type="SimpleModule, Notashop.Wscr.c10.SimpleModule" />
        </httpModules>
    </system.web>
</configuration>
```

If the *<clear/>* and *<add/>* elements were switched in this code, ASP.NET would add our module into the pipeline and then remove both it and the seven default modules.

Multiple Modules in One Application

Knowing that an ASP.NET application has by default a number of modules attached to it brings up some interesting questions: How do modules coexist in a pipeline? What happens if two or more handle the same event? Does one have precedence over another? The answers depend on the order in which you add modules to the pipeline. If two modules contain handlers for the same event, the module added first to the pipeline will have its handler called first.

Note that you can also handle all 14 events that are accessible to the module in the global.asax file for your application. Visual Studio .NET autogenerates empty handlers for some of them, but you can access all of them by creating a method with the following signature:

```
protected void Application_EventName(Object sender, EventArgs e)
{
    ⋮
}
```

In fact, we can go a step further and access any event exposed by a module in global.asax by creating a method with the following signature:

```
protected void FriendlyModuleName_OnEventName(Object sender, EventArgs e)
{
    ⋮
}
```

Any event handlers defined in global.asax are triggered last, after every corresponding handler defined in an application's modules. To demonstrate this, the sample code includes a copy of EventListModule called SecondListModule that we can add to our TestWebApp application. Also, a couple of event handlers are defined in the application's global.asax.cs file that we can uncomment for this demonstration. With EventListModule added before SecondListModule in web.config, EventListModule will always send its event message before SecondListModule, which in turn will always precede messages from handlers in global.asax (as shown in Figure 10-6).

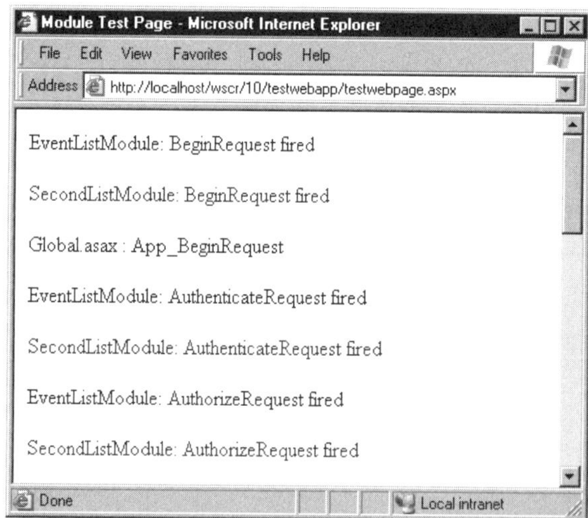

Figure 10-6 Events are always handled in order by multiple modules and global.asax.

A Final Module Example

Our final example before we turn our attention to SOAP extensions measures the response time for a request between the point at which ASP.NET receives the request and the point at which it sends the response back to the client. It's a nice little demonstration of using the *Items* property of *HttpContext* to maintain pipeline state information. *Items* stores information about a specific request as a key/value pair. This information persists for the lifetime of the request, and the response can be accessed by any module or handler that knows to look for it.

You'll find the code for this module saved as ResponseTimeModule.cs in the sample code. The strategy is simple. We create two event handlers for our module. The first handles the *BeginRequest* event, saving the current time in the *Items* request state:

```
private void webApp_BeginRequest(object sender, EventArgs e)
{
    HttpApplication webApp = (HttpApplication)sender;
    HttpContext context = webApp.Context;
    context.Items.Add("Start", System.DateTime.Now);
}
```

The second event handler triggers at the *EndRequest* event, gets the current time, and finds the difference between it and the time stored previously. The result is the response time of the server, which is added to the page before it is sent back to the client:

```
private void webApp_EndRequest(object sender, EventArgs e)
{
    HttpApplication webApp = (HttpApplication)sender;
    HttpContext context = webApp.Context;
    System.DateTime then = (System.DateTime)context.Items["Start"];
    string responseTime = (System.DateTime.Now - then).ToString();
    context.Response.Write("<p>It took " + responseTime +
                           " to send the request back to you.</p>");
}
```

Note that we didn't calculate the response time in the *Disposed* event. At that point, the response would already be on its way to the client, so we wouldn't be able to add the time to the page for the client to see. We could use *Disposed* if we were logging response times on the server.

Building SOAP Extensions

Like HTTP modules, SOAP extensions have access to the SOAP request message and its corresponding SOAP response message for processing before they move on to the handler and the client, respectively. However, unlike HTTP modules, which are always constructed in the same way, the strategy for coding a SOAP extension can vary based on two factors:

- Whether the extension will work autonomously for every request to a Web service or will work only against certain methods

- Whether the extension will alter or add to the contents of the message it intercepts

Next we'll look at extensions for three scenarios, each of which adds new code to old code and which together demonstrate everything you need to write SOAP extensions successfully. The code needed for a fourth scenario, an autonomous extension that alters a message, can be extrapolated from the other three.

An Autonomous SOAP Extension

As we did with modules, our first example is the simplest scenario for a SOAP extension—one that works autonomously and does not alter the contents of the request or response. We'll build it, deploy it, and then go back over it to fill in the gaps we left along the way. As with modules, this means building an extension that blocks all requests for Web services in a Web application. Unlike with modules, this means raising a SOAP fault to be sent back to the client rather than stopping processing altogether. Don't forget that we're working with SOAP rather than HTTP. To emphasize the similarity in construction and deployment between the two, we'll even use the same instructions as last time. You'll see that the only real difference at this level is the test setup.

Open Visual Studio .NET and create a class library project called SimpleExtension. Add references to *System.Web* and *System.Web.Services* to the project, and then add the following code:

```
using System;
using System.IO;
using System.Web;
using System.Web.Services.Protocols;

public class SimpleExtension : SoapExtension
{
    public override object GetInitializer(Type serviceType)
    {
        return null;
    }

    public override object GetInitializer(LogicalMethodInfo methodInfo,
        SoapExtensionAttribute attribute)
    {
        return null;
    }

    public override void Initialize(object initializer)
    {
```

```
            return;
        }

        public override void ProcessMessage(SoapMessage message)
        {
            switch(message.Stage)
            {
                case SoapMessageStage.BeforeDeserialize:
                    throw new SoapException("This service is not available",
                        SoapException.ClientFaultCode);
                    break;

                case SoapMessageStage.AfterDeserialize:
                    break;

                case SoapMessageStage.BeforeSerialize:
                    break;

                case SoapMessageStage.AfterSerialize:
                    break;

                default:
                    break;
            }
        }
    }
```

Save the code as SimpleExtension.cs and compile it into an assembly called Notashop.Wscr.C10.SimpleExtension.dll. You can do this by setting the assembly name on the project's property pages before building the class.

Add a new Web service called TestWebSvc.asmx to our TestWebApp project in Visual Studio .NET and uncomment the *HelloWorld* Web method. It doesn't matter what the service actually does for this example, but it does matter how we access it. An extension bolts onto the default ASMX handler and comes into play only when we deal with SOAP messages to and from the server. Just using the default test page won't trigger an extension because the test page uses only HTTP-POST requests to access the service, so we have to generate a proxy class for the service and build a client page around it. You'll find TestClient.aspx all ready for you among the code samples, but if you prefer to do the work yourself, here are the steps:

1. Add a Web reference to TestWebSvc.asmx to the TestWebApp project.
2. Add an ASP.NET page called TestClient.aspx to the TestWebApp project.

3. Add a button called *btnGoProxy* and a label called *lblResponse* to TestClient.aspx.

4. Create an event handler for clicking the button, and then add the following code:

```
private void btnGoProxy_Click(object sender, System.EventArgs e)
{
    TestWebApp.localhost.TestWebSvc proxy =
        new TestWebApp.localhost.TestWebSvc();
    lblResponse.Text = proxy.HelloWorld();
}
```

We can now test our SOAP extension and deploy it. We deploy by following the same steps as for deploying a module:

1. Copy the SOAP extension DLL file into the TestWebApp\bin directory or the GAC.
2. Tell the Web application that the SOAP extension exists by adding an entry for it in the application's web.config file.
3. Restart or rebuild the application.

Steps 1 and 3 are straightforward enough. Step 2 requires opening up web.config and adding the following:

```
<?xml version="1.0" encoding="utf-8" ?>
<configuration>
  <system.web>
    ⋮
    <webServices>
      <soapExtensionTypes>
        <add type="SimpleExtension, Notashop.Wscr.C10.SimpleExtension"
             priority = "1" group ="0" />
      </soapExtensionTypes>
    </webServices>
  </system.web>
</configuration>
```

If you're still using the web.config file from the previous section, just add the *<webServices>* element and its contents after the *<httpModules>* element, which you should comment out. The extension should now be deployed and working. To test it, open testclient.aspx in a browser and click the button. The client will call the service, SimpleExtension, which will run and produce an error as expected (as shown in Figure 10-7).

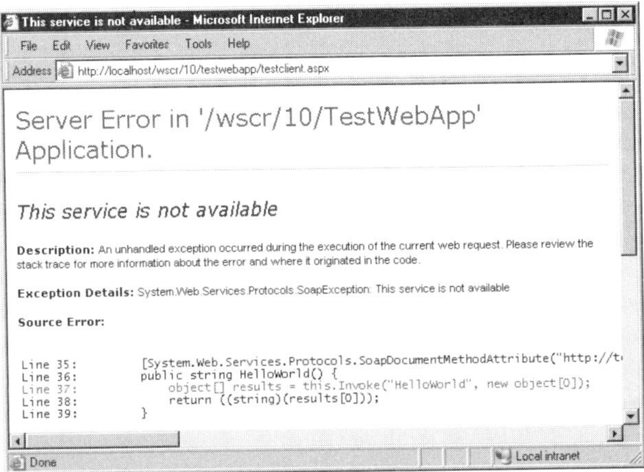

Figure 10-7 SimpleExtension blocks SOAP requests with a SOAP fault.

This error is not a particularly elegant response, but the proxy and Microsoft Internet Explorer know how to display it to give you the clearest information. Our TestClient page has a second button, which sends a custom-built request to TestWebSvc. The extension creates the same SOAP fault, but the results are much less clear in the browser; it looks like an Internal Server Error (code 500) has occurred.

Let's go back and look at the key pieces of our extension.

The *SoapExtension* Class

Creating a SOAP extension means writing a class that inherits from the *System.Web.Services.Protocols.SoapExtension* class and overriding the methods it contains:

```
using System;
using System.IO;
using System.Web;
using System.Web.Services.Protocols;

public class SimpleExtension : SoapExtension
{
```

Two methods, *GetInitializer* and *Initialize*, work together to make available any information the extension needs while a message is being processed. In this simple example, we don't need any preset data to raise an error, so we've left the methods empty. But note that *GetInitializer* (both overloads) and *Initialize*, shown here, must be overridden before the extension will compile.

```
public override object GetInitializer(Type serviceType)
{
    return null;
}

public override object GetInitializer(LogicalMethodInfo methodInfo,
                                      SoapExtensionAttribute attribute)
{
    return null;
}

public override void Initialize(object initializer)
{
    return;
}
```

We'll return to these two methods and their unique symbiotic relationship a little later on.

The *SoapExtension* class has a third method called *ChainStream*, which you don't need to override unless you're planning to alter the contents of the SOAP messages. For now, this isn't the case, so *ChainStream* isn't implemented. However, it's useful to know that it exists.

Overriding *ProcessMessage*

The *ProcessMessage* method is where the extension does all its work; it is called four times by ASP.NET during a message's lifetime. Its parameter is a *SoapMessage* object that represents the contents of and metadata for the request and the corresponding response the extension is processing. The two key properties of the *SoapMessage* object are *SoapMessage.Stream* and *SoapMessage.Stage*. The *Stream* property provides direct access to the stream containing the message (much like *HttpContext.Response.GetOutputStream* and *HttpContext.Request.GetInputStream*), and the *Stage* property defines the four stages during the processing of the request when we can do something. That is, it defines the equivalent of four events that we can hook into. The only difference is that we hook into them using a *case* statement rather than event handlers. Whenever ASP.NET calls *ProcessMessage*, it has already updated the *Stage* property to reflect the current state of processing and so the extension acts accordingly, as the following code illustrates.

```
public override void ProcessMessage(SoapMessage message)
{
    switch(message.Stage)
    {
```

```
            case SoapMessageStage.BeforeDeserialize:
                throw new SoapException("This service is not available",
                    SoapException.ClientFaultCode);
                break;

            case SoapMessageStage.AfterDeserialize:
                break;

            case SoapMessageStage.BeforeSerialize:
                break;

            case SoapMessageStage.AfterSerialize:
                break;

            default:
                break;
        }
    }
}
```

Here are the four stages represented by the *SoapMessage.Stage* property:

- ***BeforeDeserialize*** Indicates that the SOAP request message is about to be deserialized into a *SoapMessage* object. You can still access it as XML here.
- ***AfterDeserialize*** Indicates that the request has been deserialized into objects. Information contained in the XML message can now be accessed through the *SoapMessage* object that was passed to *ProcessMessage* as a parameter.
- ***BeforeSerialize*** Indicates that the *SoapMessage* object is about to be serialized into a SOAP response message.
- ***AfterSerialize*** Indicates that the SOAP response message has been created and is ready to be sent back through the pipeline and out to the client.

Our simple example merely throws an exception of type *SoapException* the first chance it gets, but nontrivial extensions will use the *SoapMessage* object parameter to pull data pertaining to the request and response and react to it. The only caveat is that some of its properties and methods are valid only some of the time. Table 10-1 describes the properties and methods of the *SoapMessage* object.

Table 10-1 Useful Properties and Methods of the *SoapMessage* Object

Property or Method	What It Returns	When It's Available
Action property	The HTTP *SOAPAction* header for the request.	All stages
ContentType property	The HTTP *Content-Type* of the request (read-only) or response (read/write). The default is *text\xml*.	*AfterDeserialize* *BeforeSerialize*
Exception property	The exception of type *SoapException* that was raised during the request. It is *null* if no exception has occurred.	All stages
Headers property	A *SoapHeaderCollection* list containing the headers in the request or response message.	All stages, but it contains content only at *AfterDeserialize* and *BeforeSerialize*
MethodInfo property	A *LogicalMethodInfo* object containing information about the Web service class method being called by the SOAP request.	All stages, but it contains content only at *AfterDeserialize* and *BeforeSerialize*
OneWay property	Boolean value indicating whether the request is one way (*true*) or expects a response (*false*).	All stages
Stage property	The current stage of message processing.	N/A
Stream property	The stream containing the SOAP request or SOAP response message. Note that this is read-only.	All stages
Url property	The URL of the Web service.	All stages
GetInParameterValue(int i) method	The *i*th parameter of the call to the Web method.	*AfterDeserialize*
GetOutParameterValue(int i) method	The *i*th out parameter of the call to the Web method.	*BeforeSerialize*
GetReturnValue method	The return value of the call to the Web method.	*BeforeSerialize*

As noted back in our first module example, you must produce a SOAP fault in an HTTP module by hand, but a SOAP extension produces it automatically when we throw a *SoapException*.

Deploying Autonomous SOAP Extensions

You can deploy a SOAP extension in your Web application in two ways. If the SOAP extension should process every request made to every Web service method in your application, you add an entry to the application's web.config file. If the SOAP extension should process only requests to specified methods, you associate the extension with a custom attribute and tag the specified methods with the attribute.

Our example is of the former type. Here's how we add an entry to the web.config file:

```
<configuration>
    <system.web>
        <webServices>
            <soapExtensionTypes>
              <add type="SimpleExtension, Notashop.Wscr.C10.SimpleExtension"
                   priority = "1" group ="0" />
            </soapExtensionTypes>
        </webServices>
    </system.web>
</configuration>
```

The ASP.NET configuration schema allows only an *<add />* element under *<soapExtensionTypes>* and no *<remove />* or *<clear />* elements, as it does for HTTP modules. (This might be because ASP.NET doesn't come with any SOAP extensions straight out of the box; it comes with only HTTP modules.) *<add />* has three attributes: *type* lets you specify the extension's class name and the assembly it is in, and *priority* and *group* pertain to the situation in which more than one extension is deployed in the same Web application.

Multiple Extensions in One Application

Although .NET doesn't define any SOAP extensions, it doesn't preclude the deployment of multiple extensions in a single Web application. But how will they coexist? The answer lies with their *priority* and *group* values.

All extensions, regardless of how they work, have a priority value. For applications that use multiple SOAP extensions, the order in which their methods run is determined by their priority. The methods are grouped together (all the *GetInitializer* methods first, then all the *Initialize* methods, and so on), but in order of priority (low to high). The only exception is when you call *ProcessMessage* for the *BeforeSerialize* and *AfterSerialize* stages, in which case the extension calls are prioritized from high to low. An extension's group is related to its priority and can be 0 or 1; extensions in group 0 run before extensions in group 1, regardless of their priority level. In the case of a tie (same priority, same group), ASP.NET goes by the order in which the extensions were declared.

Figure 10-8 shows the order in which a SOAP extension calls its methods and the priority level an extension must have for its methods to be called first.

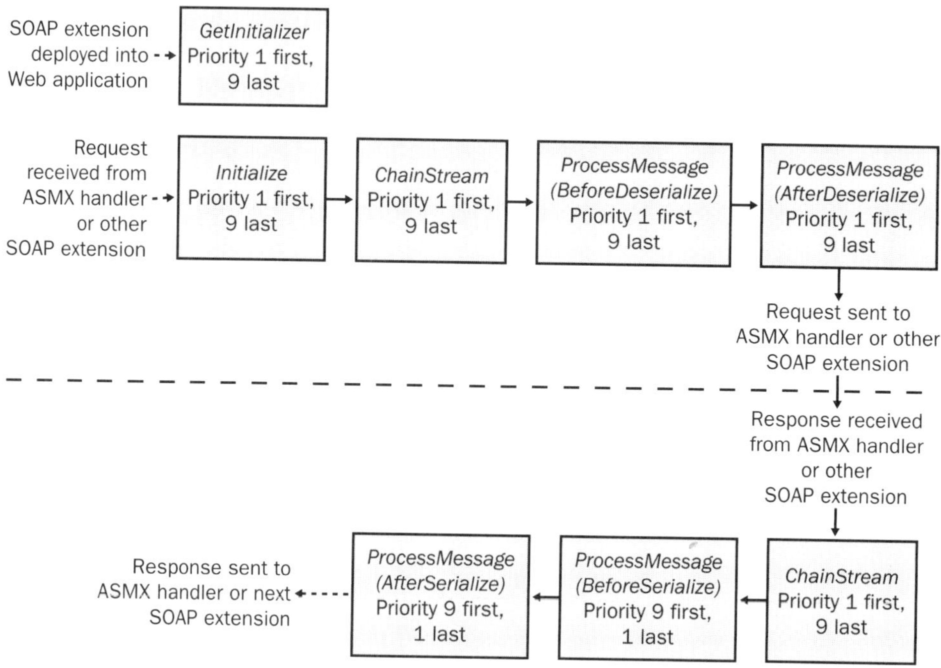

Figure 10-8 The order of method calls during the life of a SOAP extension

A Targetable SOAP Extension

As mentioned earlier, you should use the second type of SOAP extension deployment into a Web application if the extension should process only requests to methods that you identify. You associate the methods with a custom attribute that you create, and you tag the methods with the attribute. For example, we'll create an extension that checks whether one integer parameter is less than another when a method is called. It's a simple example of an extension implementing checks on the request in addition to validating it with the schema, a concept we introduced in Chapter 6.

In our sample Web service, we'll add a new Web method that simply returns the sum of two integers, as follows. The *[LessThan]* attribute requires the names of two parameters in the method call on which to perform the check. The first parameter should be less than the second, or an error will occur.

```
[WebMethod]
[LessThan("a", "b")]
public int add(int a, int b)
{
    return a + b;
}
```

The code that implements the attribute and extension can be found in LessThanExtension.cs in the sample code for this chapter.

Creating a SOAP Extension Attribute

To create a new attribute to trigger your extension, you create a class that inherits from *System.Web.Services.Protocols.SoapExtensionAttribute* and override its two properties: *ExtensionType* and *Priority*. The *ExtensionType* property returns the .NET class of the extension that the attribute is attached to, and *Priority* gets or sets the priority of the extension:

```
[AttributeUsage(AttributeTargets.Method)]
public class LessThanAttribute : SoapExtensionAttribute
{
    private int priority = 9;

    public override Type ExtensionType
    {
        get { return typeof(LessThanExtension); }
    }

    public override int Priority
    {
        get { return priority; }
        set { priority = value; }
    }
```

An attribute need not have parameters, but if it does, their values will be passed into the attribute's constructor. You must supply a different constructor for each combination of properties the attribute can have. Our example has just the one variation, in which the attribute is initialized with the names of two parameters that we'll store in two class properties. When a *SoapExtension* is initialized, it is passed the *SoapExtensionAttribute* class attached to it and can pull those names out for comparison:

```
    public string ParamName1;
    public string ParamName2;

    public LessThanAttribute(string param1, string param2)
    {
        this.ParamName1 = param1;
```

```
        this.ParamName2 = param2;
    }
}
```

That's it for the *SoapExtensionAttribute* class. Next we'll look at how to tie the attributes to their associated extensions.

Creating the SOAP Extension

Our *LessThanExtension* class has the same structure as *SimpleExtension* but needs to get the names of the parameters to compare them to the attribute that tagged the method. To do this, we must implement one of the *GetInitializer* overrides that gives us that access. It takes two arguments: a *LogicalMethodInfo* object, which represents the attributes and metadata of the method the attribute has tagged, and the custom attribute class we created in the last section. Note that the custom attribute class is passed to *GetInitializer* as a generic *SoapExtensionAttribute* object, so we must cast it to a *LessThanAttribute* object before we can access it.

```
public override object GetInitializer(
    LogicalMethodInfo methodInfo, SoapExtensionAttribute attribute)
{
    LessThanAttribute lta = (LessThanAttribute)attribute;
    // Error traps removed for clarity
    return new string[]{lta.ParamName1, lta.ParamName2};
}
```

GetInitializer runs only at one point in the lifetime of a Web application—the first time the extension is deployed (compiled) into the Web application. It executes and returns to ASP.NET an object known as an *initializer*, which is cached and passed to *Initialize* every time a Web method to be parsed by the SOAP extension is invoked. It is *Initialize* that creates an instance of the *SoapExtension* class and calls *ProcessMessage* to check or alter the SOAP messages. In our case, *Initialize* populates the extension's member fields with the name of the parameters to check:

```
public override void Initialize(object initializer)
{
    ParameterName1 = ((string[])initializer)[0];
    ParameterName2 = ((string[])initializer)[1];
}
```

Understanding *GetInitializer* and *Initialize*

Why the elaborate two-step initialization? Why not just have *Initialize* set everything up when a *SoapExtension* object is initialized? The answer is to improve performance. A *SoapExtension* object is created every time a Web service method is invoked, but if its constructor has a lot to do, a performance hit might result if the method is invoked frequently. Our example extension needs only two string properties to be populated, but what if it were to require a set of namespaces and their schemas to be downloaded from the Web each time? Even the fastest connections would see the extension start to jam up if it had to download six different schemas every time a method was called.

To improve performance, we run the generic initialization code in *GetInitializer* only once for the lifetime of the application. The *initializer* object it returns to ASP.NET for caching contains the information (such as schemas, connection strings, and datasets) that *Initialize* needs to initialize a new instance of the extension object. Figure 10-9 shows this relationship.

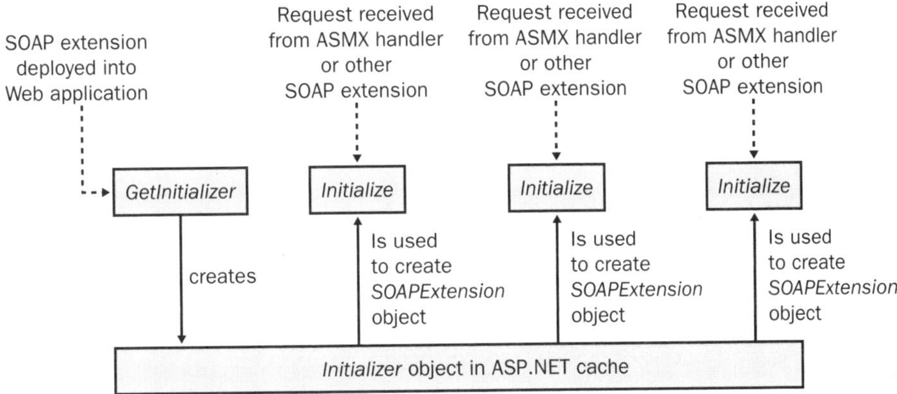

Figure 10-9 *GetInitializer* is called only once, but *Initialize* is called frequently. The *initializer* object remains in the ASP.NET cache throughout.

Two questions remain about *GetInitializer*:

- **Why are there two versions of *GetInitializer*?** The two versions of *GetInitializer* correspond to the two scenarios we've discussed. Regardless of whether the extension alters the SOAP messages, if it is attached to methods with a custom attribute, *GetInitializer(methodInfo, attribute)* will be called to create the *initializer* object. If the extension works autonomously over all Web service methods in the application, it will call *GetInitializer(serviceType)*. Of course, you can implement both versions in your extension, but only one will be called, depending on how the extension was deployed.

- **What happens to the *initializer* object if an extension attribute contains different parameter values for different methods? Do the contents of the object change according to which method is called?** The contents of an *initializer* object do not change over time. Instead of having one *initializer* per extension class, *GetInitializer* is called and an *initializer* is created and cached for each method tagged by the extension's attribute. When a method is invoked, ASP.NET passes *Initialize* the appropriate *initializer* object for the method.

Completing the Extension

Now that we're clear on how our *LessThanExtension* object will be initialized, we just need to implement the *ProcessMessage* method, shown in the following code, before we can deploy the extension.

```
public override void ProcessMessage(SoapMessage message)
{
    switch (message.Stage)
    {
        case SoapMessageStage.BeforeDeserialize:
            break;
```

Our task is to check whether one of the integer parameters in the call to a Web method is less than another. *GetInitializer* has already checked that the named parameters are integers, so all we need to do is retrieve their values and compare them. Details of all a method's parameters can be found in the *SoapMessage* object, but only after the SOAP request to the method has been deserialized. Here's the *ProcessMessage* code for the *AfterDeserialize* stage:

```
        case SoapMessageStage.AfterDeserialize:
            int pvalue1 = 0; bool foundval1 = false;
            int pvalue2 = 0; bool foundval2 = false;
            ParameterInfo[] inParams = message.MethodInfo.InParameters;
            for (int i=0; i<inParams.Length ; i++)
            {
                if (inParams[i].Name == ParameterName1)
                {
                    pvalue1 = (int)message.GetInParameterValue(i);
                    foundval1 = true;
                }
                if (inParams[i].Name == ParameterName2)
                {
                    pvalue2 = (int)message.GetInParameterValue(i);
                    foundval2 = true;
                }
            }
```

The *SoapMessage.MethodInfo.InParameters* property returns an array of *ParameterInfo* objects. Each of these contains the name, value, and type of a parameter, among other properties. However, there's no way to retrieve a parameter's value given just its name. We have to iterate through the array until we find the parameters we need.

Upon retrieving the value of the parameter, we test the two flags we set to make sure we have values to compare. If one or both haven't been set, we raise an error:

```
            if (!foundval1)
            {
                string errormsg = "Couldn't find a value for "
                    + ParameterName1 + ". Does it exist?";
                throw new SoapException(errormsg,
                    SoapException.ServerFaultCode);
            }
            if (!foundval2)
            {
                string errormsg = "Couldn't find a value for "
                    + ParameterName2 + ". Does it exist?";
                throw new SoapException(errormsg,
                    SoapException.ServerFaultCode);
            }
```

Last but not least, we make the comparison and raise an error if parameter 1 is greater than or equal to parameter 2:

```
            if (pvalue1>=pvalue2)
            {
                string errormsg = ParameterName1 + " must be less than "
                    + ParameterName2 + " for this Web method to run";
                throw new SoapException(errormsg,
                    SoapException.ClientFaultCode);
            }
            break;

        case SoapMessageStage.BeforeSerialize:
            break;

        case SoapMessageStage.AfterSerialize:
            break;

        default:
            break;

    }
}
```

To deploy our targetable SOAP extension, all we need to do is add its class file (and the attribute's class file, too, if it is separate) to the Web application project and rebuild it. To test it, we need to regenerate the proxy class for TestWebSvc.asmx and add an extra button and some text boxes to Test-Client.aspx. The text boxes will take hold of the parameters for the *add* method, and the button will send a message to the method with the following code in its *onClick* event handler:

```
private void btnAdd_Click(object sender, System.EventArgs e)
{
    TestWebApp.localhost.TestWebSvc addproxy =
        new TestWebApp.localhost.TestWebSvc();
    int a = int.Parse(txtA.Text);
    int b = int.Parse(txtB.Text);
    lblResponse.Text = (addproxy.add(a, b)).ToString();
}
```

Our new SOAP extension will return an error from *add* if parameter *a* is not less than parameter *b*. Try sending equal values to *add*. The extension will kick in and return a SOAP fault message, as expected (as shown in Figure 10-10).

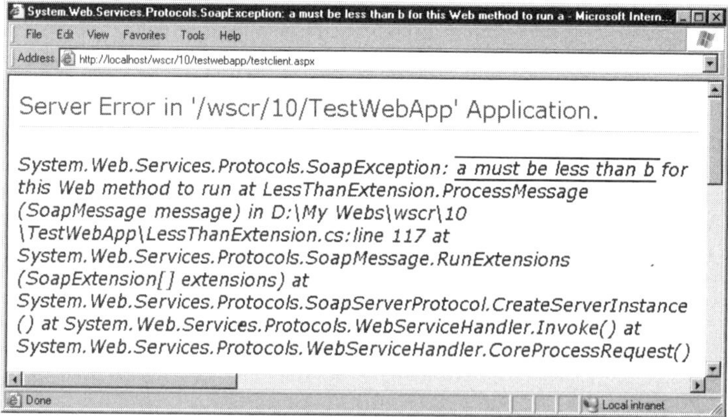

Figure 10-10 The LessThanExtension SOAP extension in action

Changing the SOAP Message Using Your Extension

Thus far, we've covered only extensions that inspect the contents of a SOAP message and then do something else. Now we'll look at how to add to or change the message itself. You might want to do this, for example, if you want to compress and decompress or encrypt and decrypt the SOAP message for transmission across the wire or if you want to change the shape of the message to conform to a new version of the Web service.

> **More Info** The next chapter includes a great example of an encryption extension that alters the SOAP message. We'll cover the theory here, and you can see the full implementation in Chapter 11.

The key to using an extension in this way is working with the stream containing the raw requests and responses. When we're working in *ProcessMessage*, we can access the stream in the *SoapMessage.Stream* property. The only problem is that the stream is read-only, so if we want to alter its contents, we have to pull them out and copy them into another stream. This presents another problem. How do we tell the handler to use the stream with the new contents for any future processing? The answer is simple: we use the *ChainStream* method.

Implementing *ChainStream*

The method signature for *ChainStream* looks like this:

```
public override Stream ChainStream(Stream stream)
{
}
```

The read-only stream it presents as the parameter contains the content you want to alter. The stream it expects as a return value is a new read-write stream that it will hook up to the message's destination in place of the old one. Thus a simple implementation of *ChainStream* in an extension class looks like this:

```
public class AnExtension : SoapExtension
{
    public Stream currentStream;
    public Stream newStream;
    public override Stream ChainStream(Stream stream)
    {
        currentStream = stream;
        newStream = new MemoryStream();
        return newStream;
    }
    ⋮
}
```

Remember that all *ChainStream* does is present the SOAP extension with a new stream that points at the message's recipient. The actual processing of the current stream's contents and the subsequent writing to the new stream must be done during one of the four calls to *ProcessMessage*. For this task, *Process-*

Message needs access to both streams, and the simplest way to give it that access is to store the streams in member variables, as we did earlier.

With *ChainStream* set up, all that's left to do is to implement *ProcessMessage* itself. If you're developing an extension for encrypting or compressing a SOAP message, you should access *currentStream*, process it, and copy the results into *newStream* at the *BeforeDeserialize* and *AfterSerialize* stages. In outline form, this looks something like the following:

```
public override void ProcessMessage(SoapMessage message)
{
    switch(message.Stage)
    {
        case SoapMessageStage.BeforeDeserialize:
            DecodeAndCopyRequestStream(currentStream, newStream);
            break;
        case SoapMessageStage.AfterDeserialize:
            break;
        case SoapMessageStage.BeforeSerialize:
            break;
        case SoapMessageStage.AfterSerialize:
            EncodeAndCopyResponseStream(currentStream, newStream);
            break;
        default:
            throw new Exception("Invalid stage");
    }
}
```

Extensions that alter the content of the request or its response can be deployed as either autonomous or targetable SOAP extensions.

SOAP Extensions on the Client

A dog is not just for Christmas, and a SOAP extension isn't just for the server. If you consider an extension that decrypts a request and encrypts a response, you'll realize that there's not much point in it existing on the server if it doesn't also exist on the client where it will encrypt requests and decrypt responses. Fortunately, you can incorporate a targetable SOAP extension into your client by using Visual Studio .NET, in just five easy steps:

1. Generate a proxy class (Web reference) to the Web service for your client project.
2. Add the class files for your extension and its attribute to your client project.

3. Open the class file for your proxy class—usually called reference.cs—and tag the methods that need processing by your extension with its attribute.
4. Save reference.cs and build your client as you normally would.
5. Compile and run the extension.

> **Important** If you regenerate the proxy class for a Web service, you lose any changes made to incorporate the extension into the client and you'll have to add the attributes again.

By and large, an extension written for the server will work as expected on the client without any code modifications. This is because the four message stages in *ProcessMessage* are in a different order on the client. *ProcessMessage* generates a request and receives a response in this order: *BeforeSerialize*, *AfterSerialize*, *BeforeDeserialize*, *AfterDeserialize*. However, if the extension really needs to know whether it's working on the client or the server, you can find out in *ProcessMessage* by calling *typeof* on its *SoapMessage* parameter. The *typeof* operator will return *SoapServerMessage* if the extension is on the server, and it will return *SoapClientMessage* if the extension is on the client. Both these classes inherit from *SoapMessage*.

Again, you'll find a full example of adding a SOAP extension to the client in the next chapter.

Summary

As you've seen in this chapter, HTTP modules and SOAP extensions have a fair amount in common. For example, they are both relatively simple to implement and can be reused in any number of Web applications. You can even use them together in the same application. However, they both come with a tradeoff between power and flexibility, which will affect your choice of which one to use in your projects.

HTTP modules have full access to the processing of any HTTP request or response related to an application, but they can't be deployed on a client. They are "all or nothing" in two ways: they process either every request and response or none at all, and the onus is on you to code every aspect of the module's workings.

SOAP extensions, on the other hand, use ASP.NET's WebMethod API. This means you get help with certain aspects of your coding (such as error handling) and can develop your applications faster. SOAP extensions give you a choice of deployment options—autonomous or targetable—on the server, and they can be included on the client as well. Their flexibility comes with some disadvantages, however. They work only with SOAP requests to Web services, and only requests that are handled by the default ASMX handler. That means you can't even test them with the service's default documentation page.

We looked at the differences between HTTP modules and SOAP extensions and discussed the tasks best suited to each. Both give you access to a set of events that you can hook into and perform a task. You also learned how to set a pecking order among multiple modules in the same application by using the *priority* attribute, and how to use the same approach when you use multiple extensions in one place.

Finally, we looked at the key properties and methods you must implement for your modules and extensions to work. You learned what they do, when to use them, and how they tie into the lifetime of the SOAP message they are processing.

In later chapters, you'll see that quite a few of the higher-level tasks for the Web services framework are implemented using one or both of these add-on components. You'll also find some components of both types scattered about on the Web. Check out *http://www.newtelligence.com/* for a good start, and go to *http://www.newtelligence.com/downloads/SoapExtensionWizard-0-1.zip* for a handy SOAP extension wizard for Visual Studio .NET.

11

General Security

Security is, has always been, and always will be a huge and often nebulous topic. Whatever we do on our computers, whether it be writing documents, developing code, or just daily calendar-keeping, security is an issue. And when we throw the Internet into the mix, security becomes even more crucial.

As a Web service developer, you have a lot to keep in mind. In this chapter, we'll consider how to make Web services as secure as possible and examine the two aspects of security that apply to Web services:

- **Authentication** Determining who a user is, usually via a username/password combination
- **Authorization** Determining whether a user has permission to perform a task

We'll start with a brief overview of Microsoft Windows security because Windows is the operating system that our .NET Web services will interact with. Then we'll look at how users can be authenticated by Web services—by using Windows security or by using a custom method. This will involve an examination of Microsoft Internet Information Services (IIS) authentication methods.

Next we'll look at how authorization fits in and how to determine whether users (Windows users or otherwise) are allowed to do certain things. We'll also look at what ASP.NET Web services are allowed to do by default and how to grant them greater privileges by running them in alternative accounts or by using account impersonation.

Whenever you pass user credentials and other sensitive information around the Web, you must consider ways to secure those communications. We'll look at two ways: using SSL connections and using our own cryptography techniques.

Windows Security

We could devote hundreds of pages to Windows security, but this isn't the place for such a treatise. Instead, we'll skim through the important features, most of which you're probably familiar with already.

All versions of Windows manage security in terms of users and groups. The exact mechanism varies because Active Directory might play a part, users might be local or maintained by a server, and users might have varying amounts of information attached. However, every user must have a username and a password.

You control access to various resources via access control lists (ACLs) and grant it on a per-user or per-group basis (where all users belonging to a group get the security privileges of that group). For example, files have ACLs that match up users and groups with the ability to read from the file, write to the file, and so on. File ACLs are usually hierarchical—permissions applied to one directory propagate down to subdirectories. However, propagated privileges can be overridden by file-specific ones.

Windows also maintains some special user accounts that are used internally. The System account, for example, is used to run processes that the user isn't involved with. Most often this account applies to Windows services and the inner workings of the operating system. Without such accounts, not much would be possible without a user logging in. It would be a bit of a pain, for example, if you had to log in to make Microsoft SQL Server work. This would also mean that such services would get only the same privileges as you do, which might not be enough to function.

By default, ASP.NET Web services run in one of these special accounts, with the username ASPNET. We'll look at the implications later in the chapter.

Authentication in ASP.NET

The default behavior of an ASP.NET Web application or Web service is to ignore user identity and simply operate under the ASPNET account. For many purposes this is fine, particularly when the Web service is intended for public consumption. However, sometimes you need to know who people are before you perform certain tasks. It is even possible to force ASP.NET to impersonate a user—any tasks performed are performed under the account of that user, with that user's privileges.

The easiest way to get access to authentication features via ASP.NET is to use those already built in to IIS. You can let IIS authenticate users, and then you can pass this information to your Web application.

The other alternatives in ASP.NET are to use Forms, Microsoft Passport, or custom authentication. Of these, only custom authentication really applies to Web services because Forms and Passport both rely on more of a Web Forms front end. Forms authentication requires you to provide a login form and a list of accounts to authenticate against as part of the web.config file for the application. Passport is currently in a state of flux, but possibilities are emerging. Currently, the signup process for a passport authenticated Web application involves information such as Web pages to redirect to once authenticated, where to find corporate files such as licensing agreements, and so on, none of which are applicable to Web services. It is, however, possible to implement a system whereby a passport authenticated Web site is used to obtain a Kerberos ticket to be passed with a Web service request, but we won't cover this here because of possible imminent changes in Passport functionality. Also, if you do use such an approach, you won't actually be using Passport to authenticate Web service users—you will be implementing custom authentication.

To control the authentication method used by an ASP.NET application, including Web service applications, you can modify the *<authentication>* element in web.config:

```
<authentication mode="authenticationMode" />
```

The value of *authenticationMode* can be

- ***None*** No authentication will be performed by ASP.NET. Choose this option when you implement your own custom authentication method.
- ***Windows*** IIS authentication will be used. To configure this further, you must configure the application through IIS management, as discussed in the next section.
- ***Forms*** ASP.NET Forms-based authentication will be used. As discussed above, this isn't appropriate for Web services.
- ***Passport*** Passport authentication will be used. Again, as things stand, this isn't applicable to Web services.

IIS Authentication

IIS can authenticate users in a number of ways:

- **Anonymous access** No authentication is performed.
- **Basic authentication** Authentication is in the form of a plain text username and password combination sent by the client.

- **Digest authentication** A challenge/response mechanism whereby a hash of the user's password rather than plain text is transmitted.
- **Integrated** A Windows-specific challenge/response mechanism that uses hashes. Similar to digest authentication.
- **Client certificates** Users are identified by a digitally signed key.

We'll look at each of these authentication methods in the sections that follow, with the exception of client certificates, which we'll look at in Chapter 15. First, though, some general information. When a user is authenticated by IIS, a *System.Security.Principal.WindowsPrincipal* object is created that represents the user. This object supports the *IPrincipal* interface, which is made accessible to the Web service through the request context information, via *Context.User*. Basic information concerning the user is available via the *IPrincipal.Identity* property, which is an *IIdentity* interface. For users authenticated via IIS, it is possible to cast the *Context.User* and *Context.User.Identity* references into *WindowsPrincipal* and *WindowsIdentity* objects, respectively, where Windows-specific implementations can be manipulated.

In the following sections, we'll use some example code to illustrate how these authentication methods work and show basic use of the user information via the classes outlined above. This code is contained in the Authentication-Methods solution in the sample code. This solution contains a client Windows Forms application called AuthenticationClient, which passes authentication details to one of two Web services, also included in the solution. The Web services are contained in the projects IISAuthenticationWebServices and Custom-AuthenticationWebServices, and are both called AuthenticatedService. We'll examine these services and the client that calls them as necessary.

Anonymous Access

The simplest authentication instruction to pass to IIS is "don't bother authenticating users." This is useful when we don't need authentication, and it is the behavior you've seen up to this point in the book. To enable anonymous access (or reenable it, since it is enabled by default) we must modify the properties for the Web service application in IIS Manager. To do this, open the IIS application's Properties dialog box, click on the Directory Security tab, and click the Edit button in the Anonymous Access And Authentication Control group. Clicking the Edit button will bring up the Authentication Methods dialog box shown in Figure 11-1.

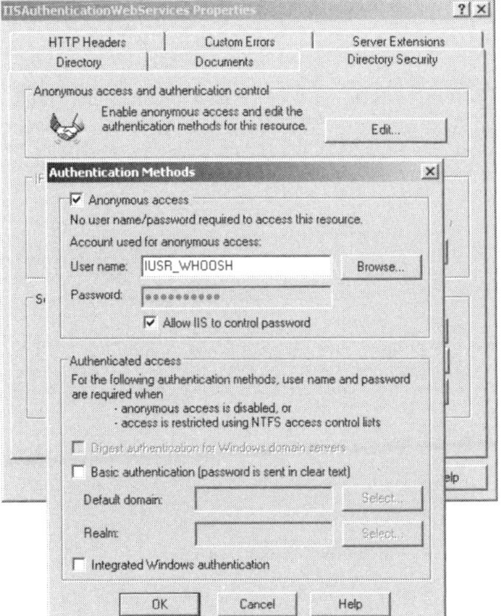

Figure 11-1 Configuring authentication methods in IIS Manager

The AuthenticatedService service in IISAuthenticationWebServices attempts to obtain information about the authenticated user, which the service returns in an array of five strings. The first three of these strings are extracted from the *WindowsIdentity* object for the user as follows:

```
[WebMethod]
public string[] GetAuthenticationDetails()
{
    string[] returnValues = new string[5];
    returnValues[0] = Context.User.Identity.AuthenticationType;
    returnValues[1] = Context.User.Identity.Name;
    returnValues[2] = Context.User.Identity.IsAuthenticated.ToString();
```

Even though we are using anonymous access, this object still exists—it just won't be associated with a user (as you'll see shortly).

Next the service attempts to read from and write to a file using the user account for the logged in user. Unless we modify the access permissions for the files and directories concerned, this file access will fail for anonymous authentication, causing the Authentication Client application to display the screen shown in Figure 11-2.

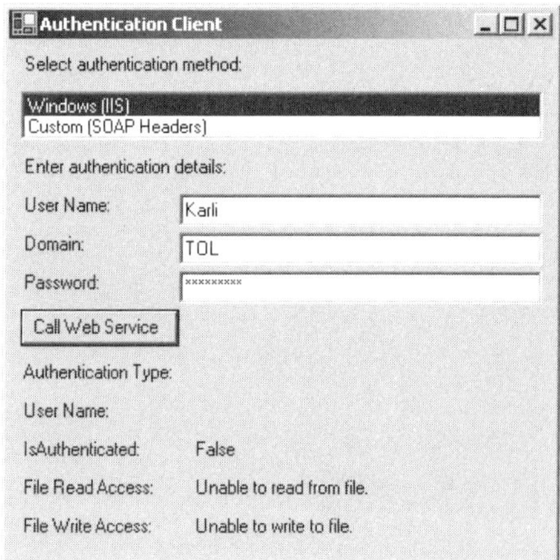

Figure 11-2 The Authentication Client application accessing a Web service using anonymous authentication

Note that the Authentication Type and User Name fields are empty strings, whereas the IsAuthenticated field is False, denoting that the user hasn't been authenticated.

Basic Authentication

You can select Basic authentication from the same properties window in IIS Manager where you select anonymous access. When you do this, a warning appears, pointing out that Basic authentication can be a security risk in unsecured communications. Later in the chapter, we'll look at secure communications in more detail, but for now we're just looking at how authentication works, so we can ignore this warning.

Once the IISAuthenticationWebServices application is configured for Basic authentication, we can try the Web service again, via the Windows client. This time the results will depend on what permissions the selected user has. For a local user or administrator, file access will probably be permitted. For a domain user with no local rights, file access will be restricted. Of course, you can change this by assigning different ACL permissions to your C:\Temp directory. For the user selected in Figure 11-3, TOL\Karli, we've assigned both read and write permissions to the directory.

The main bonus of Basic authentication is that it is a feature of the HTTP 1.0 specification, which means it is available to the widest variety of client operating systems. However, the security risk is that it involves plain text, as mentioned above, and without some form of encryption this information might be vulnerable to Internet spying.

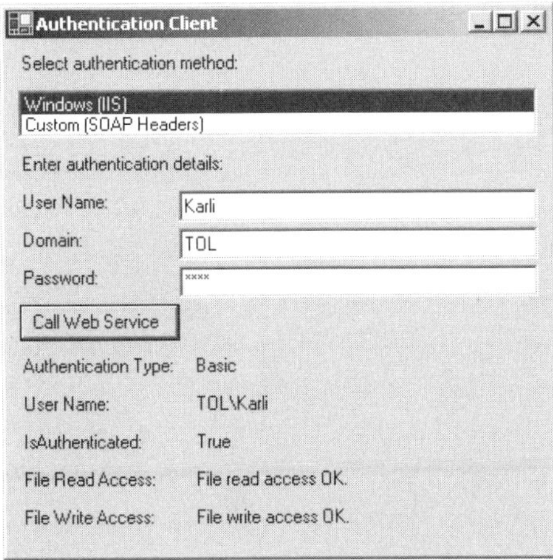

Figure 11-3 The Authentication Client application accessing a Web service using Basic authentication

Before moving on, it's worth looking at how the client application sends the authentication information to the service. The code for this is as follows:

```
private void CallIISAuthenticatedWebService()
{
    try
    {
        IISAuthenticationWebServices.AuthenticatedService service =
            new IISAuthenticationWebServices.AuthenticatedService();

        NetworkCredential credential =
            new NetworkCredential(userNameBox.Text, passwordBox.Text,
                                  domainBox.Text);
        service.Credentials = credential;

        fillResults(service.GetAuthenticationDetails());
    }
    catch (Exception ex)
    {
        MessageBox.Show("Access denied! Exception details: "
                        + ex.Message, "Access Denied",
                        MessageBoxButtons.OK, MessageBoxIcon.Error);
    }
}
```

We use a *System.Net.NetworkCredential* object, which we assign to the *Credentials* property of the instance of the AuthenticatedService Web service.

The proxy class uses this information to populate the required HTTP headers for Basic authentication.

This same code can be used for Digest and Integrated authentication.

Digest Authentication

Digest authentication is similar to Basic authentication but doesn't directly expose password information. However, even though snoopers cannot discover the information, it is still vulnerable to attack if the communications channel isn't secured—the hashed information sent to IIS can be obtained and copied in such a way that other people can impersonate an authorized user. Nevertheless, Digest authentication provides better security than Basic authentication.

To use Digest authentication, you must be using an Active Directory–administered domain because it works only with Active Directory user accounts. User accounts must also be Digest enabled. This involves selecting the Store Password Using Reversible Encryption option, which you can do through the Active Directory Users and Computers MMC snap-in, and resetting the passwords.

Once configured, though, Digest authentication operates in much the same way as Basic authentication. Figure 11-4 shows the result using Digest authentication.

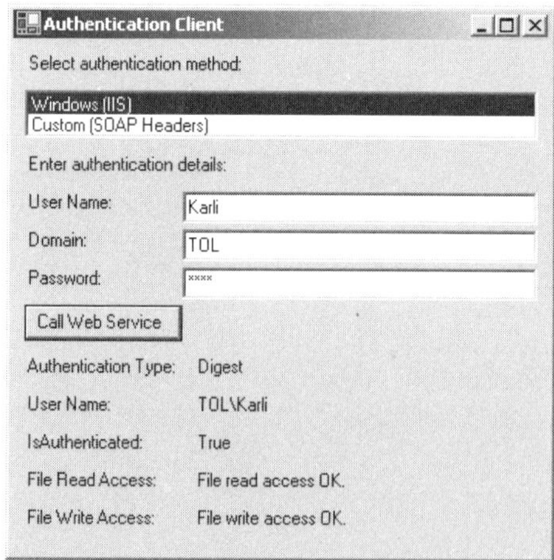

Figure 11-4 The Authentication Client application accessing a Web service using Digest authentication

The only difference here as far as we're concerned is that the Authentication Type shows Digest. However, this makes little difference to the code we write to deal with user accounts in the rest of our Web service.

Functionally, the problem with this authentication method is that it is supported only by Microsoft Internet Explorer 5.0 and later, and it doesn't tie into the Kerberos security system. Of course, we aren't using a Web browser front end, so this isn't a problem for Web services.

Integrated Authentication

Integrated authentication is a great choice for intranet environments and can be very secure. It does have its problems, though. For a start, this type of authentication is difficult to use through a firewall or proxy. (It is possible, but it might involve an additional security risk.) It is usable with Internet Explorer 2.0 and later via a Web site or a Web service interface, and it works with Kerberos for Internet Explorer 5.0 and later.

The results using this type of authentication are shown in Figure 11-5.

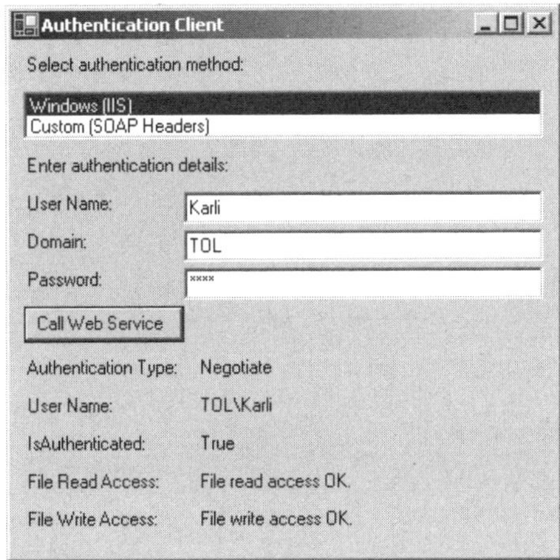

Figure 11-5 The Authentication Client application accessing a Web service using Integrated authentication

Again, the results are similar, apart from the change of Authentication Type to Negotiate. Using the Negotiate HTTP header to let the client know what to do is one of two modes that Integrated authentication can use. The other, for less sophisticated clients, is NTLM challenge/response mode. The results are the same, but Kerberos isn't used.

Custom Authentication

Custom authentication can mean many things because you can implement it in innumerable ways. The main reason for using this type of authentication is that you don't have to rely on Windows user accounts; this can be advantageous when you don't want to assign every user of your Web service such an account. Instead, you can use a table of users stored in a database somewhere, perhaps specific to an application that the Web service is a part of. For example, let's say you have an e-commerce application, and users place orders using a Windows application front end. You might make use of user information stored in a customer database to obtain information when users browse catalog listings or place orders with a credit card.

We'll look at one scheme that has become quite popular and would be appropriate to the scenario just outlined—exchanging authentication information via SOAP headers.

The situation is as follows:

1. The user obtains a security token via an authorizing Web service.
2. The user uses this token in a custom SOAP header in requests to a separate Web service.
3. The token either expires after a set period, or it can be forced to expire when the user logs out.

The advantage to this approach is that only the authorizing Web service needs to be accessed securely if we are careful. One way to be careful, which is used in the next example, is to assemble the token using the IP address used by the user, so that even if the token is stolen it cannot easily be used to spoof the user account.

The code in the CustomAuthenticationWebServices project has a single Web method in Logon.asmx called *GetToken* to illustrate step 1:

```
[WebMethod]
public string GetToken(string userName, string password)
{
    // validate username / password combination.

    string userIP = Context.Request.UserHostAddress;
    Guid newToken = Guid.NewGuid();
    OleDbConnection conn =
        new OleDbConnection(@"Provider=Microsoft.Jet.OLEDB.4.0;" +
        @"User ID=Admin;Data Source=C:\Inetpub\wwwroot\wscr\11\" +
        @"CustomAuthenticationWebServices\bin\WSCRLogons.mdb;");
    OleDbCommand cmd = conn.CreateCommand();
    cmd.CommandText = "INSERT INTO Logons (Token, IP, Created, UserName)" +
        " VALUES ('" + newToken.ToString() + "', '" + userIP + "', '" +
        DateTime.Now.ToUniversalTime() + "', '" + userName + "')";
    conn.Open();
    cmd.ExecuteNonQuery();
    conn.Close();
    return newToken.ToString();
}
```

This method doesn't actually validate the username/password combination, although this would be simple to add, but it does generate and store a token. It does this in a simple database table called Logons in the file WSCR-Logons.mdb, which is structured as follows:

Column	Type
Token	Text (primary key)
IP	Text
Created	Date/Time
UserName	Text

The token obtained is a *Guid* value and is passed back to the client. This token can then be used in a custom SOAP header called *TokenHeader*:

```
public class TokenHeader : SoapHeader
{
    public string Token;

    public TokenHeader()
    {
    }
}
```

As you saw in Chapter 2, we associate this header with our Web method by adding a public field of the header type (type *TokenHeader* in this case) to the other Web service, AuthenticatedService.asmx, and using the *SoapHeader* attribute on the Web method that uses the header:

```
public TokenHeader tokenHeader;

[WebMethod]
[SoapHeader("tokenHeader", Direction=SoapHeaderDirection.In)]
public string[] GetAuthenticationDetails()
{
    string userName = CheckLogin();
    string[] returnValues = new string[5];
    returnValues[0] = "Custom";
    returnValues[1] = userName;
    returnValues[2] = "True";
    returnValues[3] = "N/A";
    returnValues[4] = "N/A";
    return returnValues;
}
```

Note that we don't bother with the file access checking that we mentioned (but didn't look at in detail) earlier. This is because we are not attempting to match up the custom user information with a Windows account, so it makes no sense to worry about it.

The important functionality here is in *CheckLogin*:

```
private string CheckLogin()
{
    if (tokenHeader == null)
    {
        throw new Exception("SOAP header tokenHeader not supplied.");
    }

    string userIP = Context.Request.UserHostAddress;

    OleDbConnection conn = new OleDbConnection(
        "Provider=Microsoft.Jet.OLEDB.4.0;User ID=Admin;" +
        @"Data Source=C:\Inetpub\wwwroot\wscr\11\" +
        @"CustomAuthenticationWebServices\bin\WSCRLogons.mdb;");
    OleDbCommand cmd = conn.CreateCommand();
    cmd.CommandText = "SELECT Token, IP, Created, UserName " +
        "FROM Logons WHERE Token = '" + tokenHeader.Token + "'";
    conn.Open();
    OleDbDataReader reader = cmd.ExecuteReader(
        CommandBehavior.CloseConnection);
    if (!reader.Read())
    {
        reader.Close();
        throw new Exception("Not logged in.");
    }
    if ((string)reader["IP"] != userIP)
    {
        reader.Close();
        throw new Exception("Not logged in.");
    }
    if ((DateTime)reader["Created"] > DateTime.Now.AddHours(1))
    {
        reader.Close();
        throw new Exception("Login expired.");
    }
    return (string)reader["UserName"];
}
```

This method attempts to get data from the database entry with the specified GUID. If no such entry exists, an exception is thrown. If the data does exist but the IP used is different for this request, an exception is thrown. If the token is valid but a set amount of time has elapsed since its creation (one hour in this code), an exception is thrown. Otherwise, the method returns the username of the user.

Note that a number of things are not implemented in this example. First, no provision is made for validating the username and password, as noted earlier. Also, no tokens are ever removed from the database if they are invalid, although this isn't necessarily a problem. Finally, it might be nice to use a SOAP extension class to do the job of *CheckLogin*, thus avoiding having to call the method from every Web method that requires a token. You can even implement this in such a way that you create a custom user information object that supports the *IIdentity* interface, which would be available to code in the Web service.

Anyway, back to our client. The code that uses this custom authenticated Web service follows. First we use Logon.asmx to obtain a token:

```
private void CallCustomAuthenticatedWebService()
{
    try
    {
        CustomAuthenticationLogon.Logon logonService =
            new CustomAuthenticationLogon.Logon();
        string token = logonService.GetToken(userNameBox.Text,
            passwordBox.Text);
```

Next we use this token to create a *TokenHeader* object for passing to the Web service via a SOAP header:

```
        CustomAuthenticationWebServices.AuthenticatedService mainService =
            new CustomAuthenticationWebServices.AuthenticatedService();
        CustomAuthenticationWebServices.TokenHeader header =
            new CustomAuthenticationWebServices.TokenHeader();
        header.Token = token;
        mainService.TokenHeaderValue = header;
```

Then we call the Web method we're interested in:

```
        fillResults(mainService.GetAuthenticationDetails());
    }
    catch (System.Net.WebException ex)
    {
        MessageBox.Show("Access denied! Exception details: " +
            ex.Message, "Access Denied", MessageBoxButtons.OK,
            MessageBoxIcon.Error);
    }
}
```

Typically, we need to call the *GetToken* Web method of Logon.asmx only once. When we have a token, we don't need to get another one, at least until we log out or the token expires. Also, it's probably a good idea to store the proxy object for AuthenticatedService.asmx somewhere because once we set the TokenHeader header, there is no need to do it again—it will be passed in all subsequent Web method calls.

Before moving on, it's worth pointing out the criticisms that some people have with this type of authentication. Perhaps the main problem is that it doesn't follow the "self-describing" guidelines for Web services. Without knowing how the scheme works, it would be impossible to use. Still, this hardly seems that important because you'd need to be an authorized user in the first place, in which case you'd probably be using a client application that was aware of this functionality. The other concern is that this involves more than one roundtrip to access a Web method, and method calls involve sending a token with each request. Still, it is only one extra call, and not a whole lot of extra data is sent in each request. With the performance we are accustomed to on the Internet, this isn't that much of a problem.

Now for security concerns. Obviously, the first logon request must be secure, to avoid letting slip any private details. However, there is no need to pass subsequent requests over a secure channel, so only Logon.asmx needs to be secured. Of course, as we will discuss later in this chapter, this scheme doesn't prevent data returned by AuthenticatedService.asmx from being exposed, but there are ways around this.

Manually Logging On to a Windows Account

Unfortunately, there is no simple way to take a username and a password and use them to log on to a Windows account. To log on to a Windows account, we are forced to use the Win32 API via Interop. However, this will mean that we can hook up the custom authentication sample from the last section to Windows user accounts. The following code, from Win32LogonUserWrapper.cs, exposes the Win32 API method we need (*LogonUser*) via a static method:

```
using System;
using System.Runtime.InteropServices;
using System.Security.Principal;

namespace NotAShop.WSCR.Chapter11.CustomAuthenticationWebServices
{
    public enum LogonType
    {
        Interactive = 2,
        Network = 3,
        Batch = 4,
        Service = 5,
        Unlock = 7,
        NetworkCleartext = 8,
```

```
        NewCredentials = 9
    }

    public enum LogonProvider
    {
        Default = 0,
        WindowsNT35 = 1,
        WindowsNT4 = 2,
        WindowsNT5 = 3
    }

    public class Win32LogonUserWrapper
    {
        [DllImport("advapi32.dll")]
        private static extern bool LogonUser(String lpszUsername, String
            lpszDomain, String lpszPassword, LogonType dwLogonType,
            LogonProvider dwLogonProvider, out IntPtr phToken);

        private Win32LogonUserWrapper()
        {
        }

        public static WindowsPrincipal GetPrincipal(string userName,
            string password)
        {
            IntPtr token;
            if (!LogonUser(userName, "TOL", password, LogonType.Network,
                LogonProvider.Default, out token))
            {
                return null;
            }
            WindowsIdentity identity = new WindowsIdentity(token);
            return new WindowsPrincipal(identity);
        }
    }
}
```

Here the domain name is hardcoded, but we could just as easily take it from a Web method parameter. The key thing is that the code returns either a *WindowsPrincipal* object for the user or *null*. We can integrate this into the Logon.asmx Web service with little difficulty:

```
[WebMethod]
public string GetToken(string userName, string password)
{
    if (Win32LogonUserWrapper.GetPrincipal(userName, password) == null)
        throw new System.Net.WebException("Invalid credentials.");
```

```
string userIP = Context.Request.UserHostAddress;
:
```

We can also store the token retrieved by the *LogonUser* function so that we can re-create the *WindowsPrincipal* object in calls to AuthenticatedService.asmx and have access to the user account there.

Authorization in ASP.NET

Let's look at how authorization fits in with ASP.NET. First we'll look at the permissions that .NET Web services themselves have and how to customize this behavior. Then we'll look at how to use user account information to control which tasks Web services can perform. This discussion will cover the concept of user account impersonation, whereby Web services carry out tasks using the logged in account. Finally, we'll discuss how to restrict access to Web services based on user information.

ASP.NET Process Identity

As mentioned earlier, the default behavior for ASP.NET Web services is to execute under the ASPNET account. This means that any actions you take, such as database access, file manipulation, registry modifications, and so on, are carried out under this account. This can be good or bad, depending on the way your service works. The ASPNET account has restricted access, which means you can be fairly certain that the Web service can't do anything dangerous, but at the same time it might be tricky to get at the information you want using this account.

This isn't necessarily a problem because, as you'll see in a later section, you can often avoid the ASP.NET process identity account entirely. However, this can sometimes be an important problem, especially in simple services that don't perform authentication, so we should look at how to change this process.

ASP.NET Process Identity Configuration

The machine.config file on your .NET Web server (found in \Windows\Microsoft.NET\Framework\<Version>\CONFIG\ in default installations) contains the following element:

```
<processModel enable="true" timeout="Infinite" idleTimeout="Infinite"
  shutdownTimeout="0:00:05" requestLimit="Infinite"
  requestQueueLimit="5000" restartQueueLimit="10" memoryLimit="60"
  webGarden="false" cpuMask="0xffffffff" userName="machine"
  password="AutoGenerate" logLevel="Errors" clientConnectedCheck="0:00:05"
  comAuthenticationLevel="Connect" comImpersonationLevel="Impersonate"
  responseDeadlockInterval="00:03:00" maxWorkerThreads="20"
  maxIoThreads="20"/>
```

The two emphasized attributes, *userName* and *password*, are responsible for setting the ASP.NET process identity account. The *userName* attribute can be set to *machine* to use the ASPNET account, *SYSTEM* to use the System account, or any other username you like. If a value other than *machine* or *SYSTEM* is specified, the account password must be entered in *password* rather than the special value *AutoGenerate*.

Any account specified must have the following minimum security settings:

- Read access to the Windows\Microsoft.NET\Framework\<Version> directory as well as read/write access to the Temporary ASP.NET Files directory contained there
- Read/write access to the Windows\Temp directory and read access to the Windows\Assembly directory (the global assembly cache)
- Read access to the Web site root directory, typically inetpub\wwwroot for the default Web site
- Read access to a Web application directory that will run under this account

Bear in mind, though, that modifying these *userName* and *password* settings can be dangerous. If you set the ASP.NET process identity to use the System account or a system administrator account, Web services will have permission to do pretty much anything. Even a slight misstep in your Web service code then can open the door to malicious attacks. In general, the ASPNET account is fine because when we want additional permissions it isn't too tricky to obtain them by other means. Rather than changing this setting to a user with a slightly higher level of permissions than ASPNET, it is usually easier to simply add permissions to the ASPNET account—as long as we're not talking about potentially lethal permissions. Giving the ASPNET account rights to write to a specific temporary directory or to an access database so data can be updated is generally fine.

To avoid exposing the username and password for a specified account in plain text, you can store these details in the registry in an encrypted format, by using the Windows API *CryptProtectData* function. You can then set the *userName* and *password* attributes as follows:

```
<processModel ...
  userName="registry:HKLM\<SubKey>\,userName"
  password="registry:HKLM\<SubKey>\,password"
  ... />
```

<SubKey> refers to the key containing the two binary values *userName* and *password*, which hold the encrypted information.

> **Tip** If you want to store these details in the registry in an encrypted format, the aspnet_setreg.exe utility can be useful because it can encrypt the required data and add it to the registry automatically. You can download this utility from *http://support.microsoft.com/default.aspx?scid=kb%3ben-us%3b329290*.

Authorizing Users

Authorization typically consists of checking whether a user is a member of a certain group (such as Administrators, Group Managers, and so on) and then carrying out an action using the ASP.NET process identity or the identity of the logged-in user (if the user is mapped to a Windows user account).

Role Membership

Users who have Windows accounts can be members of Windows groups such as Administrators or Users. Other types of users can also be divided into roles or groups, either by virtue of what they are or by some custom scheme that you have devised. Either way, you can use the *IPrincipal.IsInRole* method to check membership.

You simply pass a string to the method and get a Boolean result, as in this code:

```
if (Context.User.IsInRole("Customers"))
{
    // do something that requires Customers permissions
}
```

Alternatively, if you are using a *WindowsPrincipal*, you can use overloaded versions of this method to check for such roles, including a version that uses values from the *WindowsBuiltInRole* enumeration. These values include *WindowsBuiltInRole.User* and *WindowsBuiltInRole.Administrator*.

Note that checking for roles doesn't necessarily mean that you can then carry out tasks on behalf of these roles. You are still tied to the security privileges of the ASP.NET process identity account (or lack thereof). However, one way around this restriction is to use impersonation.

Impersonation

Impersonation means running code as if it were under the account of a user other than the ASP.NET process identity. You can use impersonation to expose files and other resources that aren't generally accessible by Web services, for example. We know that we are doing this for authenticated users only, so we can be reasonably sure that nothing bad will happen. (Of course, some resources should never be exposed except to highly trusted individuals!)

You can implement impersonation in two ways. One way is to configure it in the web.config file of a Web application or a Web service, and the other is to use code inside a Web method. The advantage of the former approach is that you don't have to do much work at all—you just say "go ahead and use the such-and-such account to execute this service." The latter approach is more versatile and fits in better with non-IIS authenticated services.

Let's start by looking at the first configuration approach, which involves the use of the *<identity>* element. By default this element has an *impersonate* attribute of *false*:

```
<identity impersonate="false" />
```

When you set this attribute to *true*, you can use impersonation with whatever account has been authenticated using IIS. This can be very useful in combination with the IIS authentication methods we examined earlier.

> **Important** If you use anonymous access, the Web service will run under the anonymous account configured by IIS, which is IUSR_*MachineName* by default, *not* ASPNET.

Alternatively, you can use the *<identity>* element to specify that a specific account should be used to run the application, by using the *userName* and *password* attributes:

```
<identity impersonate="true" userName="Keith Chegwin"
  password="PlaysPop"/>
```

> **Tip** The aspnet_setreg.exe utility we referred to earlier can also be used to encrypt username and password data for use in impersonation.

From code, we can impersonate a Windows user using the *WindowsIdentity.Impersonate* method, which returns a *WindowsImpersonationContext* object. Between the *Impersonate* call and a call to *WindowsImpersonationContext.Undo*, code will run under the impersonated account.

This is the method used in the IISAuthenticatedServices Authenticated-Service.asmx Web service we examined earlier. We call the *Impersonate* method for authenticated users as follows:

```
WindowsIdentity identity = null;
WindowsImpersonationContext context = null;
if (Context.User.Identity.IsAuthenticated)
{
    identity = Context.User.Identity as WindowsIdentity;
    context = identity.Impersonate();
}
```

The next section of code attempts to read from and write to a file, all of which will take place under the account being impersonated:

```
try
{
    FileStream fs = new FileStream("C:\\Temp\\Test.txt", FileMode.Open,
        FileAccess.Read);
    StreamReader reader = new StreamReader(fs);
    returnValues[3] = reader.ReadToEnd();
    reader.Close();
}
catch
{
    returnValues[3] = "Unable to read from file.";
}
try
{
    FileStream fs = new FileStream("C:\\Temp\\Test2.txt", FileMode.Create,
        FileAccess.Write);
    StreamWriter writer = new StreamWriter(fs);
    writer.WriteLine("File write access OK.");
    writer.Close();
    returnValues[4] = "File write access OK.";
}
catch
{
    returnValues[4] = "Unable to write to file.";
}
```

Finally, the code stops impersonating the account by using the *Undo* method:

```
if (Context.User.Identity.IsAuthenticated)
{
    context.Undo();
}
```

Note that this code will use the ASPNET account if no user is authenticated.

Controlling Access to Services

One quick and easy method of authorization is to configure Web services to permit only certain users or groups. You can set up this type of authorization by using the *<authorization>* element in web.config. This element can contain *<allow>* and *<deny>* elements, each of which can specify comma-separated lists of users, roles, and HTTP verbs that can have access to the Web application (using the *users*, *roles*, and *verbs* attributes). For example, the following grants access to the Web application only to users in the Managers role:

```
<authorization>
  <allow roles = "Managers"/>
  <deny roles = "*"/>
</authorization>
```

> **Tip** Users are matched against *<allow>* and *<deny>* elements in the order they are listed.

The *** wildcard refers to all users, and the *?* wildcard can be used to refer to users that haven't been authenticated.

Secure Communication

Many of the examples in this chapter have involved passing sensitive information over the Internet, such as unencrypted usernames and passwords. Although some of the authentication methods, such as Digest authentication, attempt to accommodate this, there is no substitute for encryption. By ensuring that nobody can listen in on the exchange of information you make with a Web service, you can ensure security. This applies not only to the passwords you send to a Web service but also to the information you receive in return, which might be just as sensitive.

The simplest means of achieving security is to use Secure Sockets Layer (SSL) encryption, which means using the HTTPS protocol. Alternatively, you can implement your own encryption scheme. We'll look at both of these approaches.

SSL

To use SSL encryption, your Web server must be configured with a server certificate. A certificate is essentially a combination of a public key that clients can use to encrypt information and a private key for the Web server to decrypt information. (The public key *cannot* be used to decrypt data.) Server certificates are also digitally signed by a certification authority that identifies where they come from. It is possible to generate your own certificates, but for customer confidence it is usually better to obtain one from a third party such as *VeriSign*. Users won't receive a warning message if they use a certificate from a known authority because the digital signatures are (for all practical purposes) universally recognized.

We won't go through the details of obtaining and installing a server certificate—instructions are widely available. Instead, we'll assume that you have installed a server certificate, and we'll look at setting up secure communication with a Web service.

With a server certificate in place, we can access any of our Web services over SSL simply by replacing the *http:* part of the URL used to reference them with *https:*. However, in some cases (such as the Logon.asmx Web service we used earlier in our custom authentication example) we need to restrict access to *only* SSL. To do this, we just check a box in IIS Manager for the file or directory we want to restrict access to, as shown in Figure 11-6.

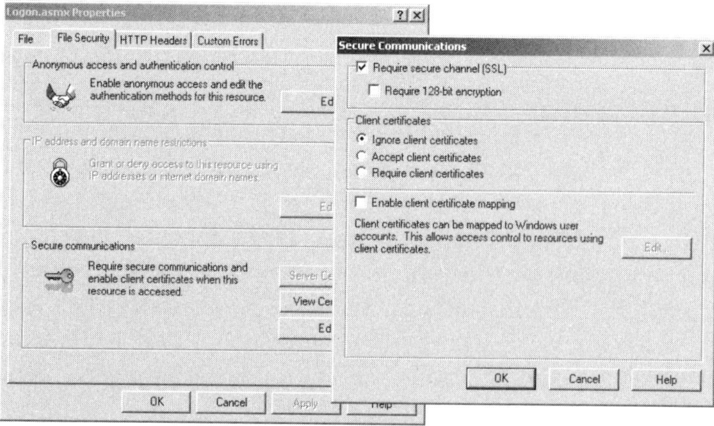

Figure 11-6 Configuring a Web service to require SSL access

> **Note** If you have a server certificate installed, the Secure Communications dialog box allows you to configure client certificate mapping and to specify whether client certificates will be used. We'll look at this type of authentication in more depth in Chapter 15.

Using SSL is an effective way to achieve secure communication, but this approach isn't perfect. Perhaps the biggest problem is with performance—especially when you're dealing with large amounts of data. Asymmetric encryption, although extremely secure, isn't the speediest thing in the world. If performance isn't an issue, go ahead and use SSL for all your Web service communications; otherwise, think carefully before you do.

One final point: Web service code is capable of determining whether HTTPS is being used, by examining the *Context.Request.IsSecureConnection* property. This is a Boolean value that is *true* if an SSL connection has been made to the Web service, and *false* otherwise. Typically, we use this property as follows:

```
[WebMethod]
public string GetToken(string userName, string password)
{
    if (!this.Context.Request.IsSecureConnection)
        throw new System.Net.WebException("Secure connection required.");
    ⋮
```

Of course, by this point the client will already have exposed its security details, but at least it will go no further!

Custom Cryptography

There are many ways around the performance problems of SSL. One solution is to use SSL to exchange a shared symmetric key and use plain HTTP to exchange messages encrypted using that key. Another solution is to encrypt only the sensitive parts of the SOAP messages that are sent back and forth.

Next we'll look at one way of doing this—by creating a SOAP extension that allows the encryption and decryption of portions of the SOAP message by way of XPath selection of sensitive elements.

Encrypting Portions of a SOAP Message

The code for this SOAP extension is in the WebServiceEncryptionExtension project in the sample code. As with all SOAP extensions, this one defines an attribute for applying to Web methods and defines the *SoapExtension*-derived class for carrying out the extension's actions.

The code for the attribute, *EncryptMessageAttribute*, is as follows:

```
[AttributeUsage(AttributeTargets.Method)]
public class EncryptMessageAttribute : SoapExtensionAttribute
{
    private string[] xPathExpressionArray = new string[] {
        "/soap:Envelope"};

    public override Type ExtensionType
    {
        get
        {
            return typeof(EncryptMessage);
        }
    }

    public override int Priority
    {
        get
        {
            return 0;
        }
        set
        {
        }
    }

    public string XPathEncryption
    {
        get
        {
            StringBuilder sb = new StringBuilder();
            foreach (string query in xPathExpressionArray)
            {
                sb.Append(query);
                sb.Append(',');
            }
            return sb.ToString(0, sb.Length - 1);
        }
        set
        {
```

```
            xPathExpressionArray = value.Split(',');
        }
    }

    internal string[] XPathExpressionArray
    {
        get
        {
            return xPathExpressionArray;
        }
    }
}
```

The only nonstandard code here is for the public *XPathEncryption* property, which you can use to control the behavior of the encryption extension. This is set via a comma-separated list of values but is stored as an array of strings, and it is made available internally (that is, to the SOAP extension class) in this format. By default, the extension encrypts everything contained in *<soap:Envelope>*, although this is more than you'll need in most cases.

Next we have the extension class itself, *EncryptMessage*; its private members are as follows:

```
public class EncryptMessage : SoapExtension
{
    private Stream oldStream;
    private MemoryStream newStream;
    private byte[] key = {1, 2, 3, 4, 5, 6, 7, 8};
    private byte[] iv = {1, 2, 3, 4, 5, 6, 7, 8};
    private string[] xPathExpressionArray;
```

The *oldStream* and *newStream* objects are used in the *ChainStream* method, which follows the standard syntax for stream manipulation in SOAP extensions:

```
    public override Stream ChainStream(Stream stream)
    {
        oldStream = stream;
        newStream = new MemoryStream();
        return newStream;
    }
```

The *key* and *iv* members are used as a key for encryption purposes. (This class obviously doesn't implement a particularly strong encryption method—only an easily-guessed 64-bit key is used—but you can easily modify that sort of thing in production code.) *xPathExpressionArray* is extracted from the attribute we examined previously in the initialization code for the class.

```
public override object GetInitializer(Type serviceType)
{
    return typeof(EncryptMessage);
}

public override object GetInitializer(LogicalMethodInfo methodInfo,
    SoapExtensionAttribute attribute)
{
    return attribute;
}

public override void Initialize(object initializer)
{
    EncryptMessageAttribute attribute =
      initializer as EncryptMessageAttribute;

    xPathExpressionArray = attribute.XPathExpressionArray;
}
```

Next we have *ProcessMessage*, which calls either *Encrypt* or *Decrypt*, depending on the message stage:

```
public override void ProcessMessage(SoapMessage message)
{
    switch (message.Stage)
    {
        case SoapMessageStage.BeforeSerialize:
            break;

        case SoapMessageStage.AfterSerialize:
            Encrypt();
            break;

        case SoapMessageStage.BeforeDeserialize:
            Decrypt();
            break;

        case SoapMessageStage.AfterDeserialize:
            break;

        default:
            throw new ArgumentException("Invalid SOAP Message Stage.");
    }
}
```

Encrypt starts by loading the formatted SOAP document from the stream *newStream* into an XML document:

```
public void Encrypt()
{
    // get newStream into XML document
    newStream.Position = 0;
    XmlTextReader reader = new XmlTextReader(newStream);
    XmlDocument doc = new XmlDocument();
    doc.Load(reader);
```

> **Note** The code for this chapter includes a simple logging facility in *Encrypt* and *Decrypt*, which you can uncomment if you want to see the results of this encryption in action.

Next we iterate through each of the nodes selected by each of the XPath expressions in *xPathExpressionArray*, encrypting the data using *EncryptString*, which we'll look at shortly:

```
    // manipulate XML
    XmlNamespaceManager nsMan = new XmlNamespaceManager(doc.NameTable);
    nsMan.AddNamespace("soap",
        "http://schemas.xmlsoap.org/soap/envelope/");
    foreach (string xPathQuery in xPathExpressionArray)
    {
        XmlNodeList nodesToEncrypt =
            doc.SelectNodes(xPathQuery, nsMan);
        foreach (XmlNode nodeToEncrypt in nodesToEncrypt)
        {
            nodeToEncrypt.InnerXml =
                EncryptString(nodeToEncrypt.InnerXml);
        }
    }
```

When the XML is encrypted, we copy the XML data back into *newStream* and then copy *newStream* to *oldStream* to send the encrypted data:

```
    // put manipulated XML into newStream
    newStream.Position = 0;
    XmlTextWriter writer = new XmlTextWriter(newStream, Encoding.UTF8);
    doc.Save(writer);

    newStream.Position = 0;
    Copy(newStream, oldStream);
}
```

The *Copy* method called here simply copies data from one stream to another as follows:

```
private void Copy(Stream from, Stream to)
{
    TextReader reader = new StreamReader(from);
    TextWriter writer = new StreamWriter(to);
    writer.Write(reader.ReadToEnd());
    writer.Flush();
}
```

Decrypt contains similar code to *Encrypt*. We start by loading the encrypted data into a new *MemoryStream* called *tempStream* and converting this data into XML:

```
public void Decrypt()
{
    // copy original stream into tempStream
    MemoryStream tempStream = new MemoryStream();
    Copy(oldStream, tempStream);
    // get tempStream into XML document
    tempStream.Position = 0;
    XmlTextReader reader = new XmlTextReader(tempStream);
    XmlDocument doc = new XmlDocument();
    doc.Load(reader);
```

Next we use *DecryptString* to get back the original XML data:

```
    // manipulate XML
    XmlNamespaceManager nsMan = new XmlNamespaceManager(doc.NameTable);
    nsMan.AddNamespace("soap",
        "http://schemas.xmlsoap.org/soap/envelope/");
    foreach (string xPathQuery in xPathExpressionArray)
    {
        XmlNodeList nodesToEncrypt =
            doc.SelectNodes(xPathQuery, nsMan);
        foreach (XmlNode nodeToEncrypt in nodesToEncrypt)
        {
            nodeToEncrypt.InnerXml =
                DecryptString(nodeToEncrypt.InnerXml);
        }
    }
```

Finally we fill *tempStream* with the unencrypted XML data and then copy the data into *newStream* so it is ready for processing by the Web service:

```
    // put manipulated XML into tempStream
    tempStream = new MemoryStream();
    XmlTextWriter writer =
        new XmlTextWriter(tempStream, Encoding.UTF8);
```

```
        doc.Save(writer);

        // copy manipulated stream to newStream
        tempStream.Position = 0;
        Copy(tempStream, newStream);

        newStream.Position = 0;
    }
```

The next two methods, *EncryptString* and *DecryptString*, can be replaced to use any type of encryption you like. In this example, we encrypt and decrypt using a 64-bit DES scheme (hence the *key* and *iv* members we examined earlier). The original string is encrypted into a byte array, the byte array is serialized into an XML document, and the encoded string is extracted from this XML document:

```
    private string EncryptString(string sourceString)
    {
        // get memory stream for encrypted data
        MemoryStream encryptedStream = new MemoryStream();

        // get encryptor and encryption stream
        DESCryptoServiceProvider encryptor =
            new DESCryptoServiceProvider();
        CryptoStream encryptionStream =
            new CryptoStream(encryptedStream,
                encryptor.CreateEncryptor(key, iv),
                CryptoStreamMode.Write);

        // encrypt bytes from newStream
        byte[] sourceBytes = Encoding.UTF8.GetBytes(sourceString);
        encryptionStream.Write(sourceBytes, 0, sourceBytes.Length);
        encryptionStream.FlushFinalBlock();

        // Serialize
        XmlSerializer serializer = new XmlSerializer(typeof(byte[]));
        StringBuilder sb = new StringBuilder();
        TextWriter writer = new StringWriter(sb);
        serializer.Serialize(writer, encryptedStream.ToArray());
        writer.Flush();

        // Extract relevant XML
        XmlDocument doc = new XmlDocument();
        doc.LoadXml(sb.ToString());

        return doc.DocumentElement.InnerXml;
    }
```

DecryptString reverses this process. It starts by wrapping the encoded string in the XML required for it to be deserialized, the data is then deserialized into a *byte* array, and finally this *byte* array is interpreted using UTF-8 encoding to obtain the decrypted data:

```
    private string DecryptString(string sourceString)
    {
        // Deserialize
        sourceString =
            "<?xml version=\"1.0\" encoding=\"utf-16\"?><base64Binary>" +
            sourceString + "</base64Binary>";
        XmlSerializer deSerializer = new XmlSerializer(typeof(byte[]));
        TextReader reader = new StringReader(sourceString);
        byte[] sourceBytes = deSerializer.Deserialize(reader) as byte[];

        // get new memory stream for decrypted data
        MemoryStream tempStream = new MemoryStream();

        // get  decryptor and decryption stream
        DESCryptoServiceProvider decryptor = new DESCryptoServiceProvider();
        CryptoStream decryptionStream =
            new CryptoStream(tempStream,
                decryptor.CreateDecryptor(key, iv),
                CryptoStreamMode.Write);

        // decrypt data
        decryptionStream.Write(sourceBytes, 0, sourceBytes.Length);
        decryptionStream.FlushFinalBlock();

        return Encoding.UTF8.GetString(tempStream.ToArray());
    }
}
```

Now all we need to do is to test this code. The code samples include a Web service called EncryptedService.asmx, which uses the following Web method:

```
[WebMethod]
[EncryptMessage(XPathEncryption="//soap:Body/*/*")]
public string GetBankAccountPassword()
{
    return "Cerberus";
}
```

This simple Web method is marked with the *EncryptMessage* attribute, which uses the XPath expression *"//soap:Body/*/*"* to specify that children of children of the *<soap:Body>* element should be encrypted, which in effect means that the *<GetBankAccountPasswordResult>* element of the response SOAP message will be encrypted.

> **Tip** Try replacing the XPath expression "*//soap:Body/*/**" with other search strings or even omitting the parameter entirely to encrypt the entire contents of *<soap:Envelope>*.

Next comes the only really tricky part of this example—this SOAP extension must be applied to both the Web service *and* the client (specifically, to the proxy class that the client uses to call the Web method). This is tricky because we are likely to be dealing with autogenerated code for this proxy, which is re-created every time we use the Add Web Reference or wsdl.exe tools.

We need to modify the proxy code in the hidden file Reference.cs as follows:

```
using System.Diagnostics;
using System.Xml.Serialization;
using System;
using System.Web.Services.Protocols;
using System.ComponentModel;
using System.Web.Services;
using NotAShop.WSCR.Chapter11.WebServiceEncryptionExtension;

[...]
public class EncryptedService :
    System.Web.Services.Protocols.SoapHttpClientProtocol
{
    ⋮
    [...]
    [EncryptMessage(XPathEncryption="//soap:Body/*/*")]
    public string GetBankAccountPassword()
    {
        object[] results = this.Invoke("GetBankAccountPassword",
            new object[0]);
        return ((string)(results[0]));
    }
```

Now the client code to call the Web method is simply this:

```
EncryptedService service = new EncryptedService();
Console.WriteLine(service.GetBankAccountPassword());
```

> **Tip** Stepping through the SOAP extension code on the server side can be a little tricky. Try putting a breakpoint in the second line of the client code shown above, and before resuming execution attach to the aspnet_wp.exe process. That way, you should be able to step through into the more interesting code.

Concerns with Custom Cryptography

The biggest problem with custom cryptography is accommodating non-.NET clients. We wrapped our cryptographic code inside a SOAP extension that is really only usable by .NET code. The key required for decryption isn't available externally, so clients might have a problem. One way around this is to exchange keys using a different secure method, such as SSL, and to write custom client-side code to consume the Web service.

However, we still have a problem: the XML passed between server and client might not be a valid SOAP message, and even if it is, it might not match up with the WSDL description for the Web service. This might confuse clients who expect such a message or confuse intermediate nodes that are responsible for processing SOAP headers.

Despite these problems, though, custom cryptography can be useful in corporate systems—especially when you need to pass large amounts of data—because not everything needs to be encrypted. It can also be a great help when you pass security details in a SOAP header because we can use the attribute with an XPath expression that encodes just that portion of the SOAP message.

Summary

In this chapter, we looked at general security concerns with .NET Web services. We started with a general discussion of Windows security and how to use IIS to authenticate users prior to Web service execution. We also discussed how to use each of the IIS authentication methods and examined the differences between them.

We also looked at other types of authentication that don't involve IIS, including a wrapper class for a Win32 function to log on Windows users.

Next we turned our attention to authentication, looking at the permissions that users can possess to access resources. You can test this by looking at role membership, or you can simply impersonate the user to gain access to whatever resources the associated Windows account has access to. Alternatively, you can use the account that ASP.NET runs under to access resources; you can configure this for a higher level of access to ASP.NET applications.

The last part of the chapter was concerned with secure communication. First we looked at SSL and how to use the HTTPS protocol to set up secure communication between Web services and clients. We also considered that SSL isn't always the best option, and to address these concerns we put together a custom cryptography extension for Web services using the SOAP protocol.

You might be pleased to know that the latest SOAP and Web service developments have made many of the challenges discussed in this chapter a little easier. In the next few chapters, we'll look at these additions, most importantly the Global XML Web Services Architecture (GXA). It is worth noting, though, that the principles we covered in this chapter apply to all the techniques you will see in those later chapters.

Part III

Enhancing the Web Services Framework

12

The Global XML Web Services Architecture

In the previous 11 chapters, we looked at Web services from the perspective of what is available in version 1.1 of the .NET runtime. You learned that we can use SOAP, WSDL, and UDDI to implement Web services and use them in the real world, but we're still limited in what we can do with the basic facilities provided by the .NET runtime. We don't have a standardized security model, we have no concept of timely delivery of requests, and using attachments is fraught with difficulties—among other problems.

We could produce our own solutions to such problems, but this would tie us to those solutions—if we wanted any of our customers to use our Web services, they would be forced to implement solutions that follow the arbitrary design decisions we've made. In most cases, our solutions would be proprietary and would provide no interoperability with solutions to the same problems written by other developers.

What we need is a series of specifications that build on SOAP, WSDL, and UDDI and provide standardized solutions to all of the problems we're likely to encounter.

To this end, Microsoft and IBM introduced a plan, available at *http://www.w3.org/2001/03/WSWS-popa/paper51*, for the evolution of Web services at the W3C Workshop on Web Services in April 2001. After this workshop, the work was formalized and expanded into the Global XML Web Services Architecture (GXA).

The Microsoft site devoted to GXA, at *http://msdn.microsoft.com/webservices/understanding/gxa/default.aspx*, is quite comprehensive. It not only provides details of all of the specifications released so far, but it also provides links to articles that expand on the specifications. The complete list of specifications and their revisions is shown in Table 12-1.

Table 12-1 The GXA Specifications

Release Date	Specification	Namespace
October 2001	WS-Referral	*/2001/10/referral*
October 2001	WS-Routing	*/rp*
November 2001	WS-Inspection	*/2001/10/inspection*
April 2002	WS-Security	*/2002/04/secext*
June 2002	WS-Attachments	
August 2002	WS-Security (with Addendum)	*/2002/07/secext*
August 2002	WS-Timestamp	*/2002/07/utility*
August 2002	WS-Coordination	*/2002/08/wscoor*
August 2002	WS-Transaction	*/2002/08/wsba*
		/2002/08/wstx
December 2002	WS-Policy	*/2002/12/policy*
December 2002	WS-Security (with Addendum and WS-SecurityPolicy Addendum)	*/2002/12/secext*
March 2003	WS-Addressing	*/2003/03/addressing*
March 2003	WS-ReliableMessaging	*/2002/03/rm*

WS-Timestamp, defined as part of the April 2002 release of the WS-Security specification, isn't strictly a specification in its own right. It is however used in most of the subsequent specifications and is referred to as WS-Timestamp so it makes more sense to use its common name.

You can see from the table that there have been two revisions of the WS-Security specification. The Addendum clarifies some of the ambiguous parts of the original WS-Security specification; the WS-SecurityPolicy Addendum adds various policies (using the WS-Policy specification) that apply to Web services.

GXA Specifications in WSE

As you saw in Table 12-1, 11 specifications currently fall under the GXA banner. We'll first look at the five that are implemented in the Web Service Enhancements (WSE) package and in the next three chapters we'll go into these in a lot more detail.

We'll provide enough detail that when we look at the WSE implementation of these specifications, you can appreciate what is going on and will have a basic understanding of the various XML constructs that are passed to and from Web services.

We'll look at the remaining six specifications later in the chapter.

WS-Attachments

The WS-Attachments specification is different from the other specifications in that there is no WS-Attachments specification document as such. Instead, the WS-Attachments specification is a GXA name for the IETF-defined Direct Internet Message Encapsulation (DIME) specification.

> **Note** The DIME specification was an IETF Internet draft that never made it to RFC status. WS-Attachments is based on the last released version of the DIME specification and can be found at *http://msdn.microsoft.com/library/en-us/dnglobspec/html/draft-nielsen-dime-soap-01.txt*. When you use DIME for the WS-Attachments specification, no changes are made to the way DIME messages are constructed and transmitted. The only stipulation for WS-Attachments is that the SOAP envelope of the message be encapsulated in the first DIME record in the DIME message, with any attachments added as subsequent DIME records.

The DIME specification is a method of encapsulating data (a payload, in DIME parlance) in any format in a binary message that follows a specified structure.

A DIME message basically consists of a series of DIME records or DIME record chunks. A DIME record has a maximum size of 2^32-1 bytes and if the payload is bigger than what can be accommodated in a single DIME record, it will be split across several DIME record chunks.

All of the work to construct and deconstruct DIME messages is handled by the framework you use, but it is worthwhile to understand how a DIME message and the DIME records and DIME record chunks that it contains are constructed.

DIME Messages

As we said earlier, the DIME message consists of a series of DIME records or DIME record chunks, which we'll look at shortly. What we're interested in here is the organization of these records and record chunks into the overall message.

A DIME message is, fundamentally, a single binary stream with the details of what is encoded being left to the record and record chunk constructs. When you transmit a DIME message, you set the media type of the message to *application/dime* and hope that the receiver understands this media type and knows how to decode the DIME message you've sent.

Within the message, you simply place the records and record chunks in the order you want them to be received, and you specify the first object and the final object in the message—you don't use object numbering because the order of the objects in the message is determined by their position. A schematic look at a DIME message is shown in Figure 12-1.

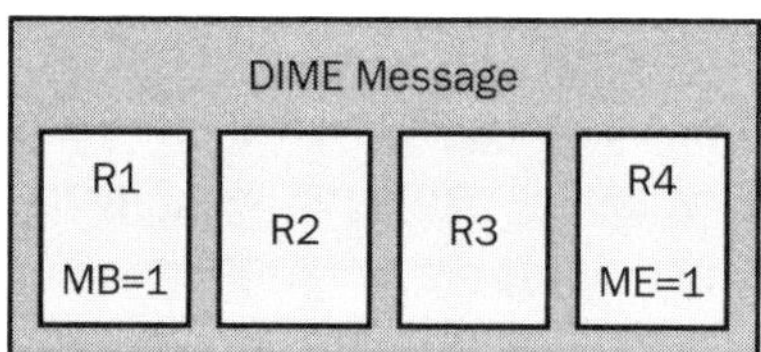

Figure 12-1 A simple DIME message

As you can see, the message has four DIME records (R1 to R4). We also set two of the DIME record flags to indicate the start and end of the message, respectively. We use the *MB* flag to specify the first record in the message, and we use the *ME* flag to specify the final record in the message.

DIME Records

The overall structure of a DIME record is shown in Figure 12-2.

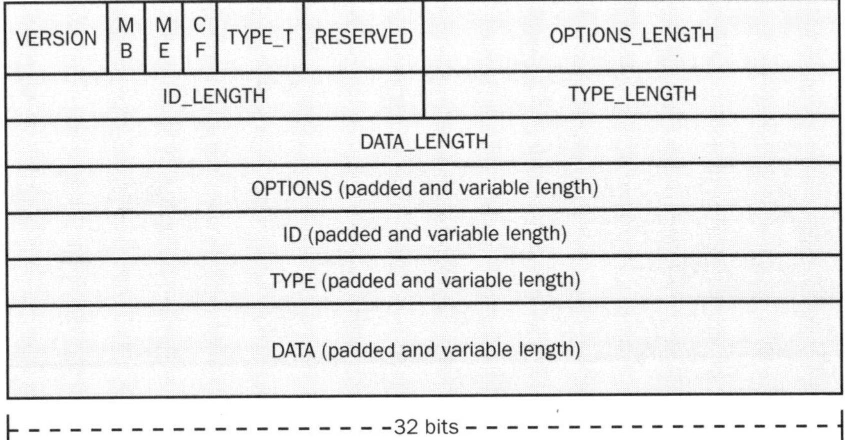

Figure 12-2 The DIME record structure

RESERVED
function:

- ***VERSION*** Specifies the version of the DIME record format you're using. This is an unsigned 5-bit integer; at present, only the value *1* is defined.
- ***MB*** If set, this single bit specifies that this DIME record is the first record in the message.
- ***ME*** If set, this single bit specifies that this DIME record is the final record in the message.
- ***CF*** A single bit that is set when a payload is split across several DIME record chunks.
- ***TYPE_T*** A 4-bit integer that is used to specify what the TYPE field will contain. The two values you'll use most often are *media-type* (1) and *absoluteURI* (2). You use *media-type* when the record contains a payload that has a MIME type, and you use the *absoluteURI* value when you're dealing with a type that is specified by a URI (such as a SOAP envelope).
- ***RESERVED*** A 4-bit field that is reserved for future use and must be set to 0.

- ***OPTIONS_LENGTH*, *ID_LENGTH* and *TYPE_LENGTH*** Unsigned 16-bit integers that specify the length of the *OPTIONS*, *ID*, and *TYPE* fields, respectively (minus any padding that is required). If any of these values are set to 0, the field whose length they specify will not be present in the record.
- ***DATA_LENGTH*** A 32-bit unsigned field that specifies the length of the DATA field.
- ***OPTIONS*** A variable-length field, padded to the next 16 bits, that contains various optional properties for the DIME record. In the current release of the DIME specification, this field doesn't contain any meaningful information.
- ***ID*** A variable-length field, padded to the next 16 bits, that contains a unique ID for the record. In most cases, this will not actually be present in the record and the *ID_LENGTH* field will be set to 0.
- ***TYPE*** A variable-length field, padded to the next 16 bits, that contains the type of the record. This flag must be valid for the type system specified by the *TYPE_T* flag.
- ***DATA*** A variable-length field, padded to the next 16 bits, that contains the actual data for the record.

DIME Record Chunks

As we implied earlier, a DIME record chunk is simply a DIME record with several of the flags that specify the DIME record set slightly differently. For a DIME record chunk, the following fields are set:

- ***CF*** You set this flag to 1 to indicate that the record is actually a record chunk.
- ***TYPE_T*, *TYPE_LENGTH*, and *TYPE*** For the first record chunk, you set these values as you do for a normal DIME record, but for all following chunks the *TYPE_T* value must be set to *unchanged* (0) and the *TYPE_LENGTH* flag must be set to 0. We have a zero-length type field, so we can't specify the *TYPE* field.

You place the data in the DATA field as you do for normal DIME records, and the data can be split arbitrarily by the sender. The recipient is responsible for interpreting the flags set for the record and combining all of the record chunks, in the correct order, to retrieve the original data.

WS-Security

The WS-Security specification was one of the first specifications released under the GXA banner and is the one that has been most emphasized since it was released.

> **Note** The first draft of the WS-Security specification was released on April 5, 2002, and was amended by the WS-Security Addendum on August 18, 2002. This addendum tidied up a few inconsistencies in the original specification and can be considered the base implementation of WS-Security. The specification is in the *http://schemas.xmlsoap.org/2002/07/secext* namespace and is usually given the *wsse* prefix.

You can achieve a measure of security by using a transport protocol that has built-in security (such as HTTPS, which uses SSL to provide an encrypted channel between the client and the server), but the WS-Security specification provides security across any transport protocol you want to use.

The WS-Security specification provides security to the messages transmitted between clients and Web services by using message authentication, integrity, and confidentiality.

Although WS-Security provides a framework for adding security details to messages and for securing those messages, the actual details of how to ensure the integrity and confidentiality of messages is contained in two W3C recommendations that we'll look at shortly. The basic WS-Security specification is also the basis for a whole raft of additional specifications that we'll look at when we discuss the specifications released after the WS-Security specification.

Security Tokens

The entire WS-Security implementation is based on the use of security tokens. A *security token* is a structure that encapsulates the security credentials of a message transmitter.

The WS-Security specification defines two types of security token—a signed security token that has been endorsed by a specific authority (such as X509 certificates and Kerberos tickets) and an unsigned security token that has not been endorsed by a third party.

The unsigned security token defined in the WS-Security specification is *<wsse:UsernameToken>*; you can use this token to pass username and password details for authentication.

The signed security token, *<wsse:BinarySecurityToken>*, is used to encapsulate any binary security tokens (such as X509 certificates and Kerberos tickets) or any security token that is in a non-XML format.

<wsse:UsernameToken> element The *<wsse:UsernameToken>* element is unsigned and allows you to pass a username and password combination with the message, which can then be read by the recipient of the message and used to authenticate the sender. The structure of *<wsse:UsernameToken>* is as follows:

```
<wsse:UsernameToken
 xmlns:wsu="http://schemas.xmlsoap.org/ws/2002/07/utility"
 wsu:Id="...">
  <wsse:Username>...</wsse:Username>
  <wsse:Password Type="...">...</wsse:Password>
  <wsse:Nonce EncodingType="...">...</wsse:Nonce>
  <wsu:Created>...</wsu:Created>
</wsse:UsernameToken>
```

The *<wsse:Username>* and *<wsse:Password>* elements allow you to specify the username and password. Sending a plaintext password is not particularly secure, but using the *Type* attribute of the *<wsse:Password>* element, you can specify that the password is actually a digest value encoded using the SHA1 hash algorithm.

Using a digest value for the password is still not secure because the relationship between the password and the digest value of the password is well known. For this reason, the *<wsse:Nonce>* and *<wsu:Created>* elements were added in the WS-Security Addendum. You can use these elements to provide additional security to the password by providing a digest password that is a combination of the real password as well as the values of the *<wsse:Nonce>* and *<wsu:Created>* elements.

The extra features defined in the WS-Security Addendum do solve several security problems, but the relationship between the password digest and the real password is still well known. We can calculate the real password relatively easily knowing the different elements in the *<wsse:UsernameToken>* element.

If you're using a secure channel, however, and the security used by the channel meets your requirements, you can use *<wsse:UsernameToken>* security to authenticate the user. But if you need to send messages across a nonsecure channel, you have to use a more secure mechanism such as X509 certificates or Kerberos tickets.

<wsse:BinarySecurityToken> element The *<wsse:BinarySecurityToken>* element is used to pass security tokens that are binary in nature or are non-XML. The current release of the specification defines three types of binary security token—X509 certificates and two types of Kerberos ticket—but the current implementation of WSE allows you to use only X509 certificates. We'll therefore concentrate our discussion on X509 certificates.

A typical *<wsse:BinarySecurityToken>* is defined as follows:

```
<wsse:BinarySecurityToken ValueType="..." EncodingType="..."
 xmlns:wsu="http://schemas.xmlsoap.org/ws/2002/07/utility"
 wsu:Id="...">
  ...
</wsse:BinarySecurityToken>
```

As you can see, the *<wsse:BinarySecurityToken>* has three attributes and these allow us to specify what the security token is. We define the type of the security token in the *ValueType* attribute and specify how it is encoded in the *EncodingType* attribute. Then *wsu:Id* attribute is used to provide a unique identifier that is used when we sign and encrypt the messages we're sending.

The content of the *<wsse:BinarySecurityToken>* element is the textual representation of the security token. Using the type and encoding specified by the *ValueType* and *EncodingType* attributes, the recipient of the message can reconstruct the security token.

Authentication

As you've seen, the WS-Security specification allows you to authenticate the message that is received. Unfortunately, this process is susceptible to all of the security problems that are prevalent on the Internet. Without proper security provided by the transport protocol, the information you enter is easy to steal. If you're not using a secure transport protocol, message authentication on its own will not provide any security and you'll need to look at the sections titled "Integrity Through Signing" and "Confidentiality Through Encryption."

When you authenticate a message, you simply add the security token to the message in the *<wsse:Security>* SOAP header, as follows:

```
<soap:Header>
  <wsse:Security soap:mustUnderstand="1"
   xmlns:wsse="http://schemas.xmlsoap.org/ws/2002/07/secext">
    <wsse:UsernameToken
     xmlns:wsu="http://schemas.xmlsoap.org/ws/2002/07/utility"
     wsu:Id="SecurityToken-99b9ace3-426d-412b-bcb2-f12f29362474">
      <wsse:Username>test1</wsse:Username>
      <wsse:Password Type="wsse:PasswordText">pass1</wsse:Password>
      <wsse:Nonce>EgWWZYqwaf5Dr5+5ZkZp9A==</wsse:Nonce>
      <wsu:Created>2003-04-14T19:32:32Z</wsu:Created>
    </wsse:UsernameToken>
  </wsse:Security>
</soap:Header>
```

Although we added a username and password combination using the *<wsse:UsernameToken>* element, you can also use *<wsse:BinarySecurityToken>* for authentication. However, if you're using X509 certificates, there isn't much point because you have to pass the public part of the certificate, and this is freely available.

If you're using a secure transport protocol, using a username and password combination to authenticate the sender of the message can still be perfectly viable, depending on the level of security provided by the transport protocol.

Integrity Through Signing

As we've said, the WS-Security specification provides a framework for security. The details about how to ensure the integrity of the messages that are sent are contained in the W3C XML Signature Syntax and Processing recommendation (at *http://www.w3.org/TR/xmldsig-core/*). This is quite a weighty document, at over 60 pages, and trying to distill the entire recommendation into a couple of paragraphs (or even a couple of pages) would be nearly impossible. Therefore, we'll just look at how the recommendation applies to X509 certificates.

> **Note** When you sign a message using X509 certificates, a hash is generated of the content of the message. This hash value is then encrypted using the private key of the X509 certificate and attached to the message. Because of the way X509 certificates work, only the public key of the X509 certificate can verify that the private key was used for encryption. If you can verify that the private key was used for encryption, you can be sure of the integrity of the message. The recipient of the message also generates the hash value for the content of the message and compares this to the hash value that was received and then decrypted. If the two hash values don't match, message integrity has been lost—the message might have been intentionally altered by a hacker, it might have been corrupted, or something else might have occurred to modify the message. Whatever has happened to the message, it isn't the same as when it was sent and should be rejected.

When you sign a message using WSE and X509 certificates, it is advisable to add the public part of the X509 certificate to the message. This allows the recipient of the message to immediately verify the signature of the message without having to retrieve the public key of the X509 certificate from a public key server. When we add the public part of the X509 certificate, we add a *<wsse:BinarySecurityToken>* element to the *<wsse:Security>* SOAP header.

```
<wsse:BinarySecurityToken ValueType="wsse:X509v3"
 EncodingType="wsse:Base64Binary"
 xmlns:wsu="http://schemas.xmlsoap.org/ws/2002/07/utility"
 wsu:Id="SecurityToken-8a104aa6-b736-44ab-a768-5b0a5a6c018f">
  MIIBuj...N5jy8=
</wsse:BinarySecurityToken>
```

A <*Signature*> element is also added as defined in the XML Signature Syntax and Processing recommendation. This element contains the details of the signature and points to the key needed to verify the signature.

```
<Signature xmlns="http://www.w3.org/2000/09/xmldsig#">
  <SignedInfo>
    <CanonicalizationMethod
     Algorithm="http://www.w3.org/2001/10/xml-exc-c14n#" />
    <SignatureMethod
     Algorithm="http://www.w3.org/2000/09/xmldsig#rsa-sha1" />
    <Reference URI="#Id-64ebe2b9-c5a6-4730-afcb-407e3da6c1fc">
      <Transforms>
        <Transform Algorithm="http://www.w3.org/2001/10/xml-exc-c14n#" />
      </Transforms>
      <DigestMethod Algorithm="http://www.w3.org/2000/09/xmldsig#sha1" />
      <DigestValue>PTo973... LIxYCg=</DigestValue>
    </Reference>
  </SignedInfo>
  <SignatureValue>c4ux/X.../xHwA=</SignatureValue>
  <KeyInfo>
    <wsse:SecurityTokenReference>
      <wsse:Reference
       URI="#SecurityToken-8a104aa6-b736-44ab-a768-5b0a5a6c018f" />
    </wsse:SecurityTokenReference>
  </KeyInfo>
</Signature>
```

A discussion of all of the elements specified here is beyond the scope of this chapter. Full details of these elements, as well as the elements not used here, can be found in the W3C recommendation. We'll only briefly look at the elements used here:

- ***<SignedInfo>*** Contains the details of how the signature is generated in the <*CanonicalizationMethod*> and <*SignatureMethod*> elements.
- ***<Reference>*** This element within <*SignedInfo*> details the element that is signed, and the *URI* attribute contains the unique identifier that identifies the signed element.
- ***<SignatureValue>*** Contains the actual signature for the message.

- ***<KeyInfo>*** Allows details specifying the location of the key that is needed to verify the signature. If you added the public key of the X509 certificate to the message, this element will contain a *<wsse:SecurityTokenReference>* element that points at the correct *<wsse:BinarySecurityToken>* element.

When you sign the message, the body of the message changes very little; all that is added is a *wsu:Id* attribute that allows the link between the signature and the signed element to be established:

```
<soap:Body wsu:Id="Id-64ebe2b9-c5a6-4730-afcb-407e3da6c1fc"
 xmlns:wsu="http://schemas.xmlsoap.org/ws/2002/07/utility">
  <Echo xmlns="http://www.notashop.com/wscr">
    <strMessage>THIS IS A TEST MESSAGE</strMessage>
  </Echo>
</soap:Body>
```

Confidentiality Through Encryption

In addition to ensuring that a message hasn't been changed, you might also want to ensure that only the recipient of the message can see what the message contains. You can accomplish this by encrypting the contents of the message. As with signing a message, the actual details of how to encrypt a message are contained in a W3C recommendation—in this case the XML Encryption Syntax and Processing recommendation (at *http://www.w3.org/TR/xmlenc-core/*). Although not as large as the signature recommendation, this document still comes in at nearly 50 pages. We'll look only at the basics of how to encrypt messages using X509 certificates.

> **Note** When you encrypt a message using X509 certificates, the body of the message is encrypted using the public key of the message recipient. Due to the way X509 certificates work, only the private key of the X509 certificate can decrypt a message that was encrypted using the public key.

To encrypt a message, you add an *<xenc:EncryptedKey>* element to the message. This element contains all of the details needed to decrypt the message, except for the encryption algorithm used:

```
<xenc:EncryptedKey Type="http://www.w3.org/2001/04/xmlenc#EncryptedKey"
 xmlns:xenc="http://www.w3.org/2001/04/xmlenc#">
  <xenc:EncryptionMethod
```

```
  Algorithm="http://www.w3.org/2001/04/xmlenc#rsa-1_5" />
  <KeyInfo xmlns="http://www.w3.org/2000/09/xmldsig#">
    <wsse:SecurityTokenReference>
      <wsse:KeyIdentifier ValueType="wsse:X509v3">
        kMhUMx...AoBTw=
      </wsse:KeyIdentifier>
    </wsse:SecurityTokenReference>
  </KeyInfo>
  <xenc:CipherData>
    <xenc:CipherValue>JeTKQL...=</xenc:CipherValue>
  </xenc:CipherData>
  <xenc:ReferenceList>
    <xenc:DataReference
     URI="#EncryptedContent-8e7ec57a-5911-4f42-8a96-317eac913ad5" />
  </xenc:ReferenceList>
</xenc:EncryptedKey>
```

As with signing, a discussion of all of the elements specified here is beyond the scope of this chapter. Full details of these elements, as well as the elements not used here, can be found in the W3C recommendation. We'll look only briefly at the elements used here:

- ***<KeyInfo>*** Contains the details of the public key that was used to encrypt the message. Rather than point at a *<wsse:BinarySecurity-Token>* element, you actually store the identifier of the public key in a *<wsse:KeyIdentifier>* element. This is not the complete public key; it is a pointer that the recipient can use to determine which key was used to encrypt the message.
- ***<xenc:ReferenceList>*** Used in the same way as the *<Reference>* element when you sign the message and the *URI* attribute of the *<xenc:DataReference>* element points at the encrypted part of the message.

When you encrypt a message (as opposed to when you simply sign a message), the entire contents of the message are modified. Or, more precisely, the content of the *<soap:Body>* element is replaced by a *<xenc:EncryptedData>* element:

```
<soap:Body xmlns:wsu="http://schemas.xmlsoap.org/ws/2002/07/utility"
 wsu:Id="Id-0ae9b58f-2cc6-478a-9b7a-f1d840e794cd">
  <xenc:EncryptedData Type="http://www.w3.org/2001/04/xmlenc#Content"
   Id="EncryptedContent-8e7ec57a-5911-4f42-8a96-317eac913ad5"
   xmlns:xenc="http://www.w3.org/2001/04/xmlenc#">
    <xenc:EncryptionMethod
```

```
      Algorithm="http://www.w3.org/2001/04/xmlenc#tripledes-cbc" />
    <xenc:CipherData>
      <xenc:CipherValue>IiyPs7...oZmA==</xenc:CipherValue>
    </xenc:CipherData>
  </xenc:EncryptedData>
</soap:Body>
```

The *<xenc:EncryptedData>* element contains an encrypted version of the body of the message. The *<xenc:EncryptionMethod>* element contains details about the encryption algorithm used, and the *<xenc:CipherData>* element contains the actual encrypted version of the body within the *<xenc:CipherValue>* element.

Signing and Encrypting Messages

Although we've looked separately at signing messages and encrypting messages, it is possible to both sign and encrypt the same message.

When you send a message, it is signed before it is encrypted; when the message is received, it must be decrypted before the signature is verified. If you attempt to do these in the wrong order, the signature check will fail because the encrypted version of the message body will have a different signature than the unencrypted version.

WS-Timestamp

As we mentioned earlier, WS-Timestamp is not a specification document in its own right but is still important in the grand scheme of things. It is often called a specification in various documents, so we'll treat it as such.

The WS-Timestamp specification defines a new element, *<wsu:Timestamp>*, that allows timing information to be added to messages.

> **Note** The WS-Timestamp specification was first released in the Security Addendum published by IBM, Microsoft, and VeriSign on August 20, 2002. This version of the specification is in the *http://schemas.xmlsoap.org/ws/2002/07/utility* namespace and usually takes the *wsu* prefix.

The *<wsu:Timestamp>* Element

The structure of the *<wsu:Timestamp>* header is as follows:

```
<wsu:Timestamp>
  <wsu:Created ValueType="...">...</wsu:Created>
```

```
  <wsu:Expires ValueType="...">...</wsu:Expires>
  <wsu:Received Actor="..." Delay="..." ValueType="...">...</wsu:Received>
  ⋮
  <wsu:Received Actor="..." Delay="..." ValueType="...">...</wsu:Received>
</wsu:Timestamp>
```

The *<wsu:Created>* and *<wsu:Expires>* elements can be added by the sender of the message. They indicate the time that the message was created and the time that it should be considered expired. You can also specify the *ValueType* attribute, which indicates the type of time data; if you don't specify it, it will default to *xsd:dateTime*, which is suitable for most purposes.

The *<wsu:Timestamp>* header can also contain multiple *<wsu:Received>* elements, which contain details of any intermediaries that the message passed through on the way to the ultimate recipient. You can have one *<wsu:Received>* element for each intermediary that the message passed through. In addition to the *ValueType* attribute, this element can also have the *Actor* and *Delay* attributes. *Actor* is a required attribute and matches the details in the *<wsrp:via>* element as specified in the WS-Routing specification (described shortly). The *Delay* attribute is used to express, in milliseconds, the delay incurred by the message because of this intermediary.

For all three elements, you specify the time as the content of the element, in UTC format.

WS-Routing and WS-Referral

We've covered three of the specifications implemented by WSE, and now it's time to look at the other two. We'll talk about both in this section. They rely so much on each other that it is next to impossible to talk about one without talking about the other.

Having said that, you can use one specification without the other. In fact, you can use WS-Routing with a different configuration mechanism, and you can use WS-Referral with another path control model. Granted, no specifications are available that you can use instead of WS-Routing and WS-Referral, but the opportunity is there for someone to write them.

WS-Routing

The WS-Routing specification defines a mechanism for exchanging messages between a sender and a recipient via a set of intermediaries. In addition to defining the forward path for these messages, the specification also defines an optional reverse path that you can use to enable two-way messaging that can be used when the underlying transport protocol does not have an intrinsic return path.

> **Note** The WS-Routing specification is a Microsoft-only specification. It was released as a replacement for the SOAP-RP specification on October 23, 2001. This specification is in the *http://schemas.xmlsoap.org/rp/* namespace and usually takes the *wsrp* prefix.

WS-Routing defines a platform-neutral mechanism for routing messages from an initial sender to an ultimate recipient via any number of intermediaries. You define a SOAP header, *<wsrp:path>*, that specifies the complete routing details for the message, and you define a set of rules that must be followed to route the message along the specified path.

Although we have three different definitions for the points that a message will take from the sender to the receiver (sender, recipient, and intermediary), all of them can be considered endpoints, and they all follow the same rules for routing the message. Only when the endpoint processes the *<wsrp:path>* element and applies the routing rules does it know what it should do with the message and which of the three types of endpoint it ultimately belongs to.

The WS-Routing specification is transport neutral and can be bound to any transport protocol. Unlike with the other specifications, the transport protocols you can use are lower-level than SOAP—SOAP is not strictly a transport protocol because it sits on an underlying transport (such as HTTP, TCP, FTP, or SMTP). At the moment, you can build only Web services that operate across the HTTP protocol, although the WS-Routing specification defines bindings for the TCP and UDP protocols as well.

***<wsrp:path>* element** The *<wsrp:path>* element is at the heart of what you can do with the WS-Routing specification. It is added to the SOAP header of the message to be routed. This element allows you to specify where a message is from, where it is going, and the route it should take from the initial sender to the ultimate recipient.

The complete structure of the *<wsrp:path>* element is as follows:

```
<wsrp:path>
  <wsrp:action>...</wsrp:action>
  <wsrp:from>...</wsrp:from>
  <wsrp:to>...</wsrp:to>
  <wsrp:fwd>
    <wsrp:via>...</wsrp:via>
    ⋮
    <wsrp:via>...</wsrp:via>
  </wsrp:fwd>
```

```
  <wsrp:rev>
    <wsrp:via>...</wsrp:via>
    ⋮
    <wsrp:via>...</wsrp:via>
  </wsrp:rev>
  <wsrp:id>...</wsrp:id>
  <wsrp:relatesTo>...</wsrp:relatesTo>
</wsrp:path>
```

It's not hard to tell what a lot of the elements do, but for others the meaning is not so clear. We'll look briefly at each element.

The *<wsrp:action>* element indicates the intent of the message, much like the SOAPAction HTTP header does. It must be added by the initial sender of the message and shouldn't be modified on its path to the ultimate recipient.

As their names suggest, the *<wsrp:from>* and *<wsrp:to>* elements specify the initial sender and the ultimate recipient of the message, respectively, and both are optional. If you don't specify them, the details in the *<wsrp:fwd>* and *<wsrp:rev>* elements will be used to route the message, as you'll see when we look at the routing rules.

The *<wsrp:fwd>* and *<wsrp:rev>* elements specify the forward and reverse paths for the message, respectively—with the caveat that if the transport protocol has an intrinsic reverse path, as is the case with HTTP, you don't need to specify the reverse path. Both of these elements contain child *<wsrp:via>* elements that contain an ordered list of intermediaries between the initial sender and the ultimate recipient of the message.

The final two elements are *<wsrp:id>* and *<wsrp:relatesTo>*. The *<wsrp:id>* element is required; it specifies a unique ID for the message. The *<wsrp:relatesTo>* element specifies that a message has some relationship with another message—for example, that it is the response to a request.

The routing rules Now that we've looked at the *<wsrp:path>* element, it's time to look at the rules that determine how the message is actually routed. Only two sets of rules are actually used for routing—the sending rules that are followed when a message is sent and the receiving rules that are followed when a message is received. The initial sender of the message will folllow only the sending rules and the ultimate recipient will follow only the receiving rules. However, as we'll shortly see, an intermediary will follow the receiving rules first, then the sending rules.

When creating a message for routing, the sender must ensure that a route is specified in the message—either in the *<wsrp:to>* element, the *<wsrp:fwd>* element, or a combination of the two. The message must be sent first to the *<wsrp:via>* element in the *<wsrp:fwd>* element, and if there is no *<wsrp:fwd>* element, the message must be sent to the *<wsrp:to>* element.

When a message is received that has a *<wsrp:path>* header in the SOAP header, it has either reached its ultimate destination or it needs to be routed to the next endpoint. The process depends on whether there is a *<wsrp:fwd>* element in the *<wsrp:path>* header.

- If no *<wsrp:fwd>* element is present or the element contains no *<wsrp:via>* elements, the message has probably reached its ultimate destination and you must look at the *<wsrp:to>* element. If the *<wsrp:to>* element matches the current endpoint, the message has reached its ultimate destination. If the *<wsrp:to>* element does not exist or does not match the current endpoint, an error has occurred and a fault must be sent back to the initial sender.
- If a *<wsrp:fwd>* element is present and contains one or more *<wsrp:via>* elements, the message must be routed. If the first *<wsrp:via>* element does not indicate the current endpoint, an error has occurred and a fault must be returned to the original sender. If the first *<wsrp:via>* element does match the current endpoint, you might have to route the message to another endpoint. If any other *<wsrp:via>* elements are present or if the message contains a *<wsrp:to>* element, this endpoint is an intermediary and the rules described in the next list must be followed. If neither of these elements can provide details of an endpoint, the current endpoint is the ultimate destination.

When the two previous rules are followed, an endpoint can determine whether it is an intermediary. It is an intermediary if it has to send the message on to another endpoint. In this case, it must also follow these additional rules:

- The intermediary must remove the *<wsrp:via>* element referring to itself from the *<wsrp:fwd>* element.
- The intermediary can add extra endpoints to the forward path. You can use custom logic to determine the extra endpoints, or you can use details provided by the WS-Referral specification to determine those extra endpoints.
- If a *<wsrp:rev>* element is present, the *<wsrp:via>* element that was removed from the *<wsrp:fwd>* element should be placed first in the *<wsrp:rev>* element, before any existing *<wsrp:via>* elements.
- If one or more *<wsrp:via>* elements are in the *<wsrp:fwd>* path, you must send the message to the address specified in the first *<wsrp:via>* element.

- If no *<wsrp:via>* elements are in the *<wsrp:fwd>* path, you must send the message to the address specified in the *<wsrp:to>* element.

These rules might seem complex, but as you'll see when we look at routing in Chapter 14, they provide a lot of scope for routing messages and performing various processing tasks at the intermediaries along the way.

WS-Referral

You know from our discussion of WS-Routing how messages are routed and how the routing information is added to the message in the *<wsrp:path>* element. WS-Referral is a complementary specification that allows you to amend routing details for an endpoint.

> **Note** The WS-Referral specification is a Microsoft-only specification and was released on October 23, 2001. This specification is in the *http://schemas.xmlsoap.org/2001/10/referral/* namespace and usually takes the *r* prefix.

With WS-Referral, you can modify the routing details for an endpoint and delegate a given URL or part of a URL to a different endpoint than that originally specified. What WS-Referral does not do is guarantee the trustworthiness of the information specified—you have to implement a separate trust mechanism to verify that the WS-Referral details can be trusted.

The WS-Referral specification defines the *<r:ref>* element, which you can use to specify the configuration details for a router. We'll briefly discuss the structure of this element in a moment, and you'll see it in action in Chapter 14 when we look at server-controlled routing.

The WS-Referral specification also defines mechanisms for endpoints to query other endpoints for their routing information and for endpoints to request that the routing information for an endpoint be modified. These are quite advanced topics. The current release of WSE doesn't support that functionality, so you can refer to the specification for a description of these mechanisms.

***<r:ref>* element** The *<r:ref>* element appears complex at first but is really very simple. Its structure is as follows:

```
<r:ref>
  <r:for>
    <r:exact>...</r:exact>
    <r:prefix>...</r:prefix>
```

```
  </r:for>
  <r:if>
    <r:ttl>...</r:ttl>
  </r:if>
  <r:go>
    <r:via>...</r:via>
  </r:go>
  <r:refId>...</r:refId>
  <r:desc>
    <r:refAddr>...</r:refAddr>
  </r:desc>
</r:ref>
```

This might look complex, but it can be summarized as "if the conditions in the *<r:for>* element are met, send the message to one of the *<r:via>* child elements of the *<r:go>* element." You can easily tell what many of the child elements of *<r:ref>* actually do, but for completeness we'll briefly describe each of them.

The *<r:for>* element contains the details of the addresses this referral instruction applies to. The *<r:exact>* element specifies an exact URL, and the *<r:prefix>* element specifies the start of a URL to which you want all matching requests to be routed.

The *<r:if>* element specifies the conditions under which you want the referral instruction to be valid. The *<r:ttl>* element specifies the time, in milliseconds, that the referral instruction is valid—after the specified time, the referral instruction is discarded.

The *<r:via>* child elements of *<r:go>* specify the routes that a message can take from this endpoint. If multiple *<r:via>* elements are present, the endpoint can choose which *<r:via>* element to route the message to—the order of the *<r:via>* elements is irrelevant.

The *<r:refId>* element supplies a unique identity for this referral instruction. It is required.

The final element in the referral instruction, *<r:desc>*, can contain useful additional information about the WS-Referral statement.

There is another element that we haven't shown. The *<r:if>* element has another possible child element, *<r:invalidates>*, as shown here:

```
<r:if>
  <r:invalidates>
    <r:rid>...</r:rid>
  </r:invalidates>
</r:if>
```

You can use the *<r:invalidates>* element to change the existing routing details by either removing the details altogether or specifying a replacement for an existing route. By specifying the ID that was used in the *<r:refId>* element for the *<r:rid>* element, you can replace the route that was previously defined. If you have a *<r:via>* element in the *<r:go>* element, the existing route is replaced and if you have an empty *<r:go>* element, the route will be removed.

Other GXA Specifications

We've looked at the five GXA specifications that are implemented in WSE and are currently most relevant to us. As you'll recall from Table 12-1, the GXA portfolio has six other specifications, as well as a second addendum to the WS-Security specification.

It doesn't make sense to spend a great deal of time looking at these specifications because they have no implementation yet. (Some people would argue that even with an implementation, we still wouldn't really need to understand them.) We'll look at them briefly, and you can go to *http://msdn.microsoft.com/webservices/understanding/gxa/default.aspx* to see the complete specifications.

WS-Addressing

All of the Web services we've built so far have an address that belongs to the HTTP transport protocol (as in *http://host:port/file*). As the use of Web services becomes more prevalent, you're likely to want to use protocols that don't fit into the *protocol://host:port/file* paradigm. For example, what if you want to send a request to a Web service to a message queue?

The WS-Addressing specification solves this problem by defining two constructs that take the messaging information from the underlying transport protocol and represent it in a transport-neutral way.

The first construct we'll look at is the endpoint reference. An endpoint is any object that you can target with a request for a Web service, and the endpoint reference conveys all of the information required to access that endpoint.

The second construct that the WS-Addressing specification defines, the message information header, is used in messages to and from Web services. It allows the addressing of the message using an endpoint reference construct and also provide details of the message characteristics for the source and destination. It can also be used to provide a unique identity for a message.

WS-Addressing was in the most recent batch of specifications along with WS-ReliableMessaging and WS-ReliableMessaging is the only specification that makes use of it. As the other specifications are updated, they will likely use the WS-Addressing specification to provide standardized addressing across all the available transport protocols.

> **Note** The WS-Addressing specification was released as a public specification by BEA Systems, IBM, and Microsoft on March 13, 2003. This version of the specification is in the *http://schemas.xmlsoap.org/ws/2003/03/addressing* namespace and usually takes the *wsa* prefix.

WS-Coordination

The WS-Coordination specification provides a framework for distributed applications to coordinate their efforts. What it doesn't do is specify the coordination between the distributed applications—that is left to other specifications, such as WS-Transaction.

WS-Coordination defines a context for all of the details required to specify the coordination. You specify how long the coordination request will be valid, the coordination type, and the address details for the registration service that the remote applications will connect to in order to receive the details of the coordination.

The coordination type is a reference to the specifics of the coordination effort, which are defined in other specifications. The WS-Transaction specification, which we'll look at shortly, defines two coordination types; other specifications are free to define their own coordination types as required.

When the registration service receives a request, it returns the address details of the Web service to connect to as well as the specifics of the coordination effort. The WS-Coordination specification defines only the process of setting up the coordination—other specifications control what the coordination effort actually does.

> **Note** WS-Coordination is still a draft specification; the latest version was released by BEA Systems, IBM, and Microsoft on August 9, 2002. This version of the specification is in the *http://schemas.xmlsoap.org/ws/2002/08/wscoor* namespace and usually takes the *wscoor* prefix.

WS-Inspection

The WS-Inspection specification is a replacement for the Microsoft Discovery (DISCO) specification, which we looked at in Chapter 4.

You can think of the WS-Inspection specification as DISCO on steroids. Like DISCO, WS-Inspection lets you create documents that detail the Web services available at a particular location—although it does not specify the method used to describe the Web services. And as with DISCO, if you don't know the address of the Web service you're requesting, you still need to look at using some other mechanism, such as UDDI, to discover the Web service.

The WS-Inspection specification defines an inspection document that contains the details of the Web services that are available.

You saw in Chapter 4 why DISCO has fallen by the wayside and why we've moved to the use of UDDI to discover Web services. With WS-Inspection being almost a direct replacement for DISCO, it is hard to see where WS-Inspection really fits into the overall scheme of things. We still need UDDI to discover Web services when we know nothing about the Web service. A WS-Inspection document will probably end up as the document that is referenced from UDDI—you'll interrogate the WS-Inspection document to retrieve the WSDL definition of the Web service. This offers the best of both worlds—you'll have a reference to your Web service within the UDDI Directory, and you'll also have a local document that you can reference directly that contains the details of your Web service.

> **Note** The WS-Inspection specification was released as a public specification by IBM and Microsoft on November 1, 2001. This version of the specification is in the *http://schemas.xmlsoap.org/ws/2001/10/inspection* namespace and usually takes the *wsil* prefix.

WS-Policy

Although the GXA specifications we've discussed so far will allow you to develop complex Web services once they have a concrete implementation, they don't give you a way to inform users of your Web services that you are using the GXA specifications or to tell them your requirements. For example, a Web service might require all messages to be signed with an X509 certificate, but you need a way to communicate this requirement to users. This is where WS-Policy comes in.

WS-Policy allows you to define policy statements for Web services. A policy statement contains a series of policy assertions that detail what the Web service expects. The specification is open enough that you can define any assertions you want—from assertions that define what the Web service requires of the messages it receives all the way to assertions that deal with privacy policy and quality-of-service guarantees.

Although WS-Policy defines the framework for adding policy assertions to Web services, it does not define any assertions—that's up to the individual specifications. You'll see this when we look at WS-ReliableMessaging and the new version of WS-Security, which were released after the WS-Policy specification and define policy assertions that can be applied to Web services that implement those specifications.

> **Note** The WS-Policy framework was released as a public specification by BEA Systems, IBM, Microsoft, and SAP AG on December 18, 2002. This version of the specification is in the *http://schemas.xmlsoap.org/ws/2002/12/policy* namespace and usually takes the *wsp* prefix. In addition to the base WS-Policy specification, the complementary specifications WS-PolicyAssertions and WS-PolicyAttachment also use this namespace.

WS-PolicyAssertions

As we mentioned, the WS-Policy specification doesn't specify any assertions, but the complementary WS-PolicyAssertions specification defines four common assertions that you can use:

- **Language assertion** Lets you specify that the messages you receive must be in a given language (such as English or French) and specify whether you'll accept requests in a variety of languages.
- **MessagePredicate assertion** Lets you specify that all messages you receive must match some precondition that the sender should check before sending the message.
- **SpecVersion assertion** Lets you specify which version of a particular specification you're using. Different versions of a specification might handle certain elements differently, and this assertion lets you specify which version messages must be using.

- **TextEncoding assertion** Lets you specify that any messages sent must be encoded using a specific text format (such as ISO-8859-1 or UTF8).

WS-PolicyAttachment

Released at the same time as WS-Policy and WS-PolicyAssertions, the WS-PolicyAttachment specification defines a way to add assertions to WSDL and UDDI descriptions. It allows you to add your policy assertions at a higher level than the Web service so users can determine whether your Web service is suitable without having to interrogate the Web service directly to retrieve the policy assertions.

WS-ReliableMessaging

One problem with Web services is that they offer no reliable means of message delivery—if the delivery of a message fails, no mechanism is in place to automatically retry delivery. The WS-ReliableMessaging specification fills that gap.

WS-ReliableMessaging defines a mechanism for transferring messages reliably between a source and a destination and for an acknowledgement to be returned indicating that the message was delivered successfully.

A message transmitted from a source to a destination has an embedded sequence number (an incrementing integer). The sequence numbers control the overall process—the last message in the exchange is flagged as the last message, and the destination informs the source if any of the messages in the sequence were missed. The sender then retransmits any missed messages, and the destination acknowledges that the messages were received.

This specification was released after the WS-Policy specification and uses that framework to define its own policy assertions. The assertions defined by WS-Reliable detail your requirements—how many times a message send can be retried, how long a sequence is valid, the maximum gap between messages, and so on.

> **Note** The WS-ReliableMessaging specification was released by BEA Systems, IBM, Microsoft, and TIBCO Software on March 13, 2003. This version of the specification is in the *http://schemas.xmlsoap.org/ws/2003/03/rm* namespace and usually takes the *wsrm* prefix.

WS-Security

Two days after the release of the WS-Security specification, the "Security in a Web Services World" roadmap (available at *http://msdn.microsoft.com/library/en-us/dnwssecur/html/securitywhitepaper.asp*) was published. It details the way forward for security and provides an overview of six additional specifications built on top of the WS-Security specification that provide a more secure and flexible security framework.

Those six specifications include the WS-Policy specification, which we just looked at, and which the roadmap describes as a fundamental requirement for the future of security. Since the roadmap was released, the status of WS-Policy has been upgraded beyond being just a child of the WS-Security specification. The other five specifications still belong to the WS-Security fold.

In December 2002, simultaneous with the release of WS-Policy, a new version of the WS-Security specification was released. It consists of WS-SecurityPolicy, an addendum to WS-Security that defines various policy assertions, and WS-SecureConversation and WS-Trust, two of the five specifications in the roadmap released eight months earlier.

> **Note** WS-SecurityPolicy was released as a public specification by IBM, Microsoft, RSA Security, and VeriSign on December 18, 2002. This is an addendum to WS-Security and has the same prefix, *wsse*, as previous versions, but has a new namespace, *http://schemas.xmlsoap.org/ws/2002/12/secext*. WS-SecureConversation and WS-Trust also share this namespace and prefix.

In the next sections, we'll look at the released specifications in some detail. First, however, let's look at a brief description of the three as-yet unreleased specifications.

- **WS-Authorization** Describes how authorization policies for a Web service are specified and managed.
- **WS-Federation** Builds on the facilities provided by WS-Security, WS-Policy, WS-Trust, and WS-SecureConversation to provide federation between different security token issuers.
- **WS-Privacy** Uses a combination of WS-Security, WS-Policy, and WS-Trust to allow you to define privacy policies for Web services and use the WS-Trust specification to validate the privacy claims made by Web services and users.

WS-SecureConversation

Although the security mechanisms defined in the WS-Security specification (and its two addendums) allow you to provide authentication, signing, and encryption services, they are not ideal in terms of conducting conversations between two endpoints. WS-Security is susceptible to various security attacks—the longer the conversation between two endpoints, the greater the likelihood of the security of the conversation being compromised.

The WS-SecureConversation specification addresses several of these security issues by defining a mechanism for establishing and sharing security contexts and for deriving session keys from these contexts.

Before a conversation starts, a security context is created (by a security token service, by one of the endpoints, or by negotiation), and this context is used to generate session keys that are used to sign and encrypt the messages that form the conversation. These keys are created from details shared between the two endpoints and can be changed on an ad hoc basis; if the two endpoints use the same security context, the derived keys will be valid for both endpoints.

WS-SecurityPolicy

WS-SecurityPolicy is not really a specification; it is actually a second addendum to the WS-Security specification. WS-Security was released before WS-Policy, so this addendum details the policy assertions that apply to WS-Security.

Six policy assertions are defined in the addendum:

- **Confidentiality assertion** Specifies that certain parts of the message must be encrypted and specifies the required encryption method.
- **Integrity assertion** Specifies that certain parts of the message must be signed and specifies which type of signing is acceptable.
- **MessageAge assertion** Specifies the maximum elapsed time between a message being transmitted and being received.
- **SecurityHeader assertion** The *<wsse:Security>* SOAP header can contain a lot of different information, and this assertion allows you to specify the parts of the header that are required.
- **SecurityToken assertion** Specifies that the sender must attach a *SecurityToken* to the message. You can specify the type or types of *SecurityToken* that are acceptable.
- **Visibility assertion** Specifies that parts of the message must be unencrypted.

WS-Trust

We now have a fairly complete and usable security model for Web services, but we still have no means of requesting and issuing security tokens. So far we have had to acquire the security tokens by "offline" means—outside of the Web services processing model. WS-Trust addresses this by defining a mechanism for requesting and issuing security tokens.

WS-Transaction

When we looked at the WS-Coordination specification, we said that without other specifications you can't actually do an awful lot. The WS-Transaction specification is one of these other specifications.

WS-Transaction defines two new coordination types that allow you to perform transactions: the atomic transaction (AT) and business activity (BA) types.

Using the AT coordination type, you can specify that the coordination effort you're engaged in be a transaction and that all parts of the transaction must be successful before the results of the transaction are finalized. When you use atomic transactions, you're usually involved in a short interchange that requires little time and few resources.

In contrast, the BA coordination type allows you to define a far more complex transaction that involves multiple atomic transactions in what, for want of a better term, is a business process.

The distinction between an *atomic* transaction and a *business* process can be quite loose, but a business process, although atomic, doesn't really fit the abort-retry mechanism of atomic transactions. With a business process, you're more likely to want the overall process to continue even if one part of the process, an atomic transaction, fails.

> **Note** WS-Transaction is still a draft specification. The latest version was released by BEA Systems, IBM, and Microsoft on August 9, 2002. This version of the specification has two namespaces, *http://schemas.xmlsoap.org/ws/2002/08/wsba* and *http://schemas.xmlsoap.org/ws/2002/08/wstx*, and these take the *wsba* and *wstx* prefixes, respectively.

Summary

In this chapter, we took a quick look at the current specifications in the GXA portfolio. A lot of work is still going on in the Web services arena, so these specifications are not the end of the story.

In many cases, the GXA specifications provide only basic frameworks; other specifications must be defined to show the true worth of the GXA specifications. You saw this when we looked at the reliance of WS-Transaction on the WS-Coordination specification—WS-Coordination provides a framework, and WS-Transaction builds an implementation on top of it. In addition to Microsoft and IBM, a whole host of other companies and organizations are extending the specifications. For example, the OASIS WS-Security Technical Committee (*http://www.oasis-open.org/committees/tc_home.php?wg_abbrev=wss*) is working on the use of different security tokens in the WS-Security specification. The WS-Security specification currently defines the use of X509 certificates and Kerberos tickets; OASIS is working out the details of using Security Assertion Markup Language (SAML), XML Common Biometric Format (XCBF) and numerous other security tokens within the WS-Security framework.

In addition, it is all but guaranteed that the current specifications will be modified. Some of the earlier specifications have inconsistencies that need to be ironed out—we've already seen this with the first addendum to the WS-Security specification.

A lot of the specifications will also be reworked to remove inconsistencies caused by later specifications and to take advantage of the facilities available in the later specifications. For example, the WS-SecurityPolicy specification updated the WS-Security specification to be compatible with the WS-Policy specification. And with the release of WS-Addressing, we now have a common way to reference Web services; the earlier specifications can now abandon their own way of referring to Web services and use the common reference mechanism defined in WS-Addressing.

13

Web Service Enhancements

In the previous chapter, we looked at the specifications that make up the Global XML Architecture (GXA). Specifications without any implementation are pointless, so Microsoft has released the Web Service Enhancements (WSE) package, which implements five of the specifications.

In this chapter, we'll look at the underlying structure of WSE and how it integrates with the Microsoft .NET Web services infrastructure. As you'll soon see, WSE builds on what's already in place to provide an initial implementation of WS-Attachments, WS-Referral, WS-Routing, WS-Security, and WS-Timestamp.

We'll then take a look at WS-Attachments and the implementation of WS-Timestamp. In Chapter 14 we'll look at the possibilities for routing and referral, and in Chapter 15 we'll look at the security features that WS-Security offers.

Downloading and Installing WSE

WSE is not an integral part of the .NET runtime; you must download and install it separately. WSE 1.0 was released in January 2003, and Service Pack 1 was released in March 2003.

WSE 1.0 Service Pack 1 is more of a cumulative release than a service pack. Unlike Windows service packs, you don't have to install WSE 1.0 to install the service pack; WSE 1.0 Service Pack 1 is a complete package and includes WSE 1.0 with the updates from the service pack already applied. You can download it from *http://www.microsoft.com/downloads/details.aspx?FamilyID=06255a94-2635-4d29-a90c-28b282993a41*.

WSE 1.0 Service Pack 1 functions happily under both .NET 1.0 and .NET 1.1. The installation process is straightforward—you just click and go, except in one situation. If you installed the technology preview of WSE—the Web

Services Development Kit (WSDK), which is compatible only with .NET 1.0—and then installed .NET 1.1, you cannot immediately install WSE. The installation process for WSE will attempt to uninstall WSDK, but WSDK will install and uninstall only under .NET 1.0. If you have .NET 1.1 installed, the uninstall of WSDK will fail when it checks the version of the runtime and finds that .NET 1.1 is installed. The only solution is to uninstall .NET 1.1 and then uninstall WSDK. Once you're at a base .NET 1.0, you can install both WSE 1.0 SP1 and .NET 1.1 (in either order).

> **Note** The WSE classes are contained within the Microsoft.Web.Services.dll assembly that's added to the global assembly cache (GAC) and registered automatically with Microsoft Visual Studio .NET. You must add a reference to this assembly to all projects that use WSE and also add the correct namespace references to all source files that will use WSE. The root namespace for WSE is *Microsoft.Web.Services*; you might also have to add several child namespaces.

The Structure of WSE

Before we look at using WSE in code, you must have an understanding of how WSE integrates with the existing .NET Web service infrastructure. At its core, WSE is fundamentally a mechanism for applying advanced Web service protocols to a SOAP envelope. SOAP headers are written to an outgoing message or read from an incoming message, and the body of the message is modified as required.

WSE is implemented as a pipeline architecture that modifies the SOAP envelope of a message as it's sent or received, and the same architecture is used on both the client and the server. Although clients and servers use the same pipeline architecture, the point at which the message is passed through the pipeline is different. What the pipeline accomplishes is the same. We'll look at how WSE is integrated with the existing .NET implementation of Web services shortly.

The WSE Pipeline

As we've pointed out, WSE uses a pipeline to modify the SOAP envelopes that are transmitted between Web services. This pipeline is unique to WSE and is not to be confused with any of the other pipelines used by .NET.

In the pipeline is a series of filters that modify the SOAP envelopes—input filters for incoming messages and output filters for outgoing messages. All messages leaving a process are passed through the output filters, and all messages arriving at a process are passed through the input filters.

> **Note** The WSE documentation doesn't have a specific name for the collections of filters in the pipeline; it simply refers to them as *input filters* and *output filters*. We'll use *input pipeline* and *output pipeline* to refer to the groups of filters to avoid any confusion about whether we're talking about the groups or the individual filters in the groups.

As we mentioned, the current release of WSE implements five of the current GXA specifications. Four of them—WS-Referral, WS-Routing, WS-Security, and WS-Timestamp—are implemented as filters in the pipeline. The fifth, WS-Attachments, is implemented outside of the pipeline, as you'll soon see.

WSE also defines an additional filter that doesn't implement a GXA specification and that can be thought of as a "helper" filter. The Trace output filter allows you to easily capture the SOAP envelope that is being transmitted, and the Trace input filter allows the received SOAP envelope to be captured—a feature that's missing from the standard .NET Web services architecture.

The five sets of filters provided with WSE are listed in Table 13-1.

Table 13-1 Default Filters in WSE

Namespace	Input Filter	Output Filter
Diagnostics	*TraceInputFilter*	*TraceOutputFilter*
Referral	*ReferralInputFilter*	*ReferralOutputFilter*
Routing	*RoutingInputFilter*	*RoutingOutputFilter*
Security	*SecurityInputFilter*	*SecurityOutputFilter*
Timestamp	*TimestampInputFilter*	*TimestampOutputFilter*

By default, all of the filters in both the input and output WSE pipelines are enabled, although the Trace filters require some additional configuration before they will capture the SOAP envelopes.

The one specification that WSE supports that's not implemented as a filter is WS-Attachments. As you'll recall from Chapter 12, adding an attachment to a message requires the entire message to be constructed as a Direct Internet

Message Encapsulation (DIME) message with the SOAP envelope for the message being in the first DIME record. On sending a message, this can occur only after you've done all the processing on the message; on receiving a message, this must occur before you do any processing on the message. If the message to be sent doesn't have any attachments, you don't construct a DIME message; if the message you receive isn't a DIME message, you don't try to split it.

In Figure 13-1, you can see the filters that messages are passed through, as well as the point at which the DIME message, if required, is created or split.

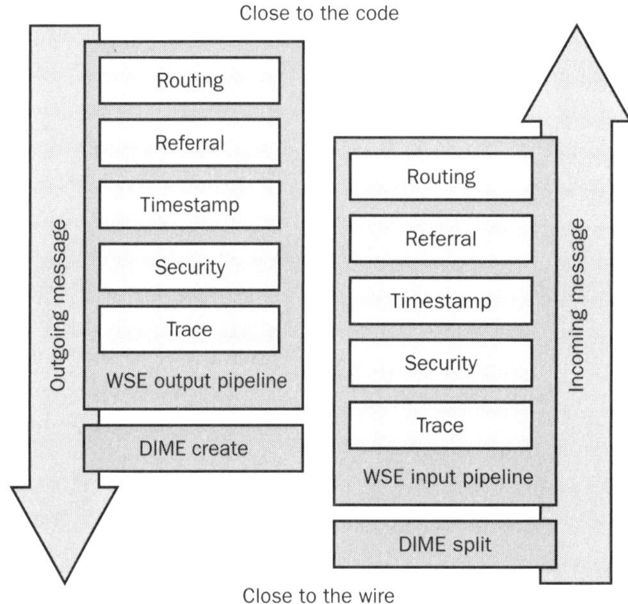

Figure 13-1 Message path through the WSE pipeline and the filters

As you can see in the figure, you process the filters in one direction for an outgoing message and in the other direction for an incoming message. You do this because you must remove details specific to a filter in the opposite order that they were applied to the message.

Consider the case in which you encrypt a message. When you send a message, you pass it through the output Security filter after it has already been through the Referral, Routing, and Timestamp output filters. As you'll see in Chapter 15, the Security filter encrypts everything that the message contains, including the details added by the other filters. (Well, this is not strictly true, as you'll see in Chapter 15, but for our purposes here it's close enough.) When you receive the message at the other end, you must remove the encryption before you can do anything with the message—the filters in the input pipeline can't process the message if all they have access to is the encrypted version of the message.

You can see that even though you have matching input and output filters, they perform significantly different tasks. Output filters take the settings you specify and use them to modify the message you're sending. Input filters extract the relevant information from the message, modify the message if required, and tell you their settings. If an input filter detects anything wrong with the format of the message (such as the Security input filter detecting an invalid security signature), it will raise an exception that's passed back to the client.

We mentioned that output filters allow "the settings" to control their operation and that input filters tell us "their settings," but we haven't explained the mechanism for doing this: the *SoapContext* object.

The *SoapContext* Object

WSE defines a new class, *SoapContext*, that allows you to interact with the filters in the pipeline. WSE uses a request *SoapContext* that is queried by output filters and a response *SoapContext* that is populated by input filters.

When you create a proxy for a Web service, the request *SoapContext* object is valid for the lifetime of the proxy—you can set values on the request *SoapContext* and use those settings for all calls to the Web service. Only one response *SoapContext* object is available, but this is overwritten with every call you make to the Web service.

> **Note** The request *SoapContext* object is valid for the lifetime of the proxy, but a problem occurs when you attempt to reuse attachments across multiple calls to the Web service. If you try to reuse an attachment, an *ObjectDisposedException* is thrown. You should avoid using the same proxy object to make multiple calls to a Web service that uses attachments because your code will generate an exception.

At the server, when a request is received, request and response *SoapContext* objects are created that exist only for the processing of that request. Each request to a Web service has its own *SoapContext* objects.

You'll see shortly when we look at the client and server specifics how you actually access the *SoapContext* objects. For now, the six most important properties of the *SoapContext* object are listed in Table 13-2.

Table 13-2 Important Properties of the *SoapContext* Object

Property	Description
Attachments	Lets you get or set the DIME attachments for the message.
Envelope	For incoming messages, retrieves the SOAP envelope, as a *SoapEnvelope* object, that the current *SoapContext* was populated from. For outgoing messages, this is undefined.
Path	Lets you get or set the routing information for the message.
Referrals	Lets you get or set the referral information for the message.
Security	Lets you get or set the security information for the message.
Timestamp	Lets you get or set the timestamp information for the message.

We'll look more closely at five of these properties later in this chapter and in the next two chapters. The sixth property, *Envelope*, returns the received SOAP envelope after it has been through the input pipeline. As we pointed out, input filters modify the message by removing the SOAP headers specific to WSE and change the body of the message according to the details contained in the relevant headers. The *SoapEnvelope* object that we retrieve contains the incoming message after it has been passed through the input pipeline and has been stripped of all the WSE-specific details.

WSE does a superb job of shielding you from having to interact with *SoapEnvelope* objects, and it populates the *SoapContext* object with the information that has been extracted. However, we'll have to deal with instances of *SoapEnvelope* when we create custom filters later in this chapter and when we create custom routers in Chapter 14.

The *SoapEnvelope* Object

The *SoapEnvelope* object is a representation of the message that is received. The SOAP envelope received is an XML document, so it makes sense that the *SoapEnvelope* object exposes the underlying envelope. It does this by inheriting from the *System.Xml.XmlDocument* class. You can interrogate this object using the standard methodology.

In addition to the properties and methods inherited from *System.Xml.XmlDocument*, the *SoapEnvelope* class exposes three properties that are shortcuts to the different parts of the XML document and make the task of using the *SoapEnvelope* class a little easier.

The *Body*, *Envelope*, and *Header* properties return *System.Xml.XmlElement* objects that contain the different parts of the SOAP envelope minus the element they're contained in. The *Body* property returns the SOAP body of the message without the *<soap:Body>* container element, *Envelope* returns the elements contained by *<soap:Envelope>*, and *Header* returns the elements contained by *<soap:Header>*.

WSE at the Client

When you're creating a proxy for a Web service, the tools provided by Visual Studio .NET and .NET generate a class that inherits from the *SoapHttpClientProtocol* base class. The proxy class exposes methods that represent the methods on the Web service, and these ultimately call the *Invoke* method on the *SoapHttpClientProtocol* base class.

WSE is integrated at the client side by a new class, *WebServicesClientProtocol*, that inherits from the *SoapHttpClientProtocol* class. If you use this as the base class for the Web service proxies, the messages you send and receive will automatically pass through the input and output pipelines. You'll see shortly how this actually happens; for now, just have faith that it does work.

The tools provided with Visual Studio .NET and the .NET Framework always build proxies that inherit from *SoapHttpClientProtocol*. You must manually change the autogenerated code to inherit from the *WebServicesClientProtocol* class instead.

> **Note** In addition to changing the class that the proxy inherits from when you first create the proxy, you must also change the class every time you update the reference to the Web service. This can quickly become very tedious—you'll soon see a tool that helps you overcome this problem.

Those are the only changes you must make to use WSE in a client application. You have access to the *SoapContext* objects by using two properties that the proxy inherits from *WebServicesClientProtocol*. The *RequestSoapContext* property of the proxy allows you to access the request *SoapContext*, and you have access to the response *SoapContext* by using the *ResponseSoapContext* property. You simply set the values on the *RequestSoapContext* and then call the method required on the proxy. When the method returns, you can check the *ResponseSoapContext* for the WSE details returned by the Web service.

To see how easy it is to use WSE on the client, have a look at the following code, taken from an upcoming example. The only change you need to make to the proxy code is shown in italic:

```
[System.Web.Services.WebServiceBindingAttribute(Name="DiagnosticsWSSoap",
 Namespace="http://www.notashop.com/wscr")]
public class DiagnosticsWSWse:
 Microsoft.Web.Services.WebServicesClientProtocol {
```

If you now look at the Object Browser in Visual Studio .NET, as shown in Figure 13-2, you can see that the proxy class does inherit from the correct class and that you have access to the request and response *SoapContext* objects via the *RequestSoapContext* and *ResponseSoapContext* properties.

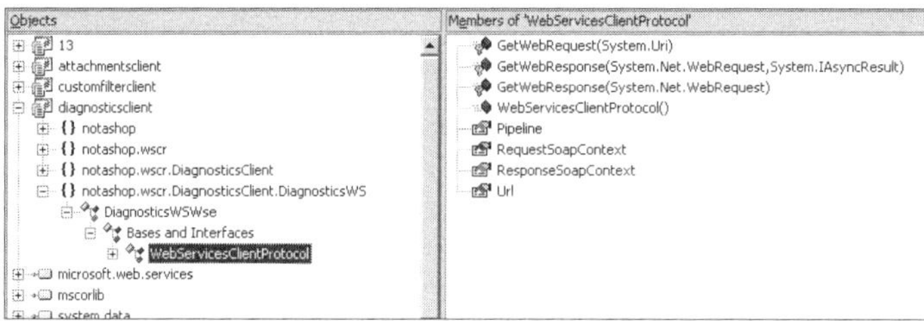

Figure 13-2 The proxy class after manual editing to support WSE

Under the Covers

When you use a proxy to access a Web service, you ultimately call the *Invoke* method of the proxy class. The proxy doesn't implement an *Invoke* method—what you actually call is the *Invoke* method of the base class. Before WSE this was the *Invoke* method of the *SoapHttpClientProtocol* class. With WSE, you use a different base class, *WebServicesClientProtocol*, for the proxies. As you can see in Figure 13-2, this class doesn't have an *Invoke* method. So how does this work? In the same way that a proxy calls the *Invoke* method on its base class—Inheritance!

WebServicesClientProtocol inherits from *SoapHttpClientProtocol*, and that class does have the *Invoke* method. When a call is made to *Invoke*, the call is handled by the first *Invoke* method that is found in the inheritance chain. In this case, it's the *Invoke* method of the *SoapHttpClientProtocol* class. However, to fully understand what's going on you need to look under the covers at what *Invoke* actually does.

Figure 13-3 shows a simplified view of the internal process of the *Invoke* method.

As you can see, the *Invoke* method calls the *GetWebRequest* method, which returns an *HttpWebRequest* object. You serialize the outgoing request into the *HttpWebRequest* object and then pass it into the *GetWebResponse* method, which uses the *HttpWebRequest* object to make the call to the Web service. On completion of the call to the Web service, *Invoke* is returned an *HttpWebResponse* object, from which we deserialized the returned message. There's nothing new here, and we already covered this in detail earlier in the book. What's important is how WSE builds on the existing structure and uses inheritance to facilitate the use of the input and output pipelines in the call to the Web service.

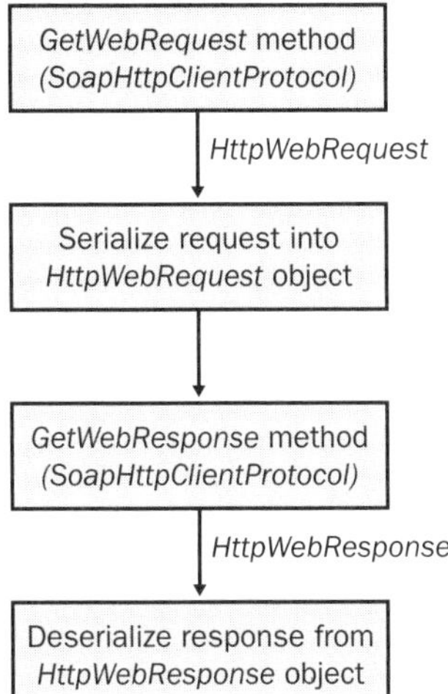

Figure 13-3 Internal architecture of *SoapHttpClientProtocol.Invoke*

Closer inspection of Figure 13-2 reveals that the *WebServicesClientProtocol* class implements its own *GetWebRequest* and *GetWebResponse* methods, and when *Invoke* makes a call to either of these methods, the versions implemented by *WebServicesClientProtocol* are called. This is the key to the integration of WSE with the existing Web service calling mechanism.

The *Invoke* method expects *GetWebRequest* and *GetWebResponse* to return *WebRequest* and *WebResponse* objects, respectively. You've seen that when you use the methods exposed by *SoapHttpClientProtocol*, it returns *HttpWebRequest* and *HttpWebResponse* objects instead, which are derived from the two classes that *Invoke* expects. Not surprisingly, WSE has its own derived classes that are used in place of *SoapWebRequest* and *SoapWebResponse*.

The *SoapWebRequest* and *SoapWebResponse* classes inherit from *WebRequest* and *WebResponse*, respectively, and implement the functionality required by WSE. The *GetWebRequest* method implemented by *WebServicesClientProtocol* returns a *SoapWebRequest* object, and *GetWebResponse* expects a *SoapWebRequest* object passed to it and returns a *SoapWebResponse* object. The *Invoke* method treats these in the same way that it does any other derived classes, and the call to the Web service is made and the WSE pipeline is used.

You also saw in Chapter 5 that it's possible to call Web services without creating a proxy class. We did this by creating an instance of the *HttpWebRequest* class and calling the *GetResponse* method. This made a call to the Web service and returned an *HttpWebResponse* object.

To manually call a Web service and still use WSE, you simply create a *SoapWebRequest* instead of an *HttpWebRequest*. When returning from the

GetResponse method, you're returned a *SoapWebResponse* object instead of an *HttpWebResponse* object.

And how do you access the *SoapContext* for the two new classes? Simple. The *SoapWebRequest* and *SoapWebResponse* classes each expose a *SoapContext* property that returns the *SoapContext* that's being used for the current operation.

WSE at the Server

Now that we've looked at how WSE is implemented on the client side, it's time to look at how it's implemented on the server. WSE on the server is implemented as a SOAP extension. We looked closely at SOAP extensions in Chapter 10.

You integrate the WSE Soap Extension into the .NET Web service infrastructure by simply adding the WSE Soap Extension class to the *<soapExtensionTypes>* element of the configuration file:

```
<configuration>
  <system.web>
    <webServices>
      <soapExtensionTypes>
        <!-- the TYPE attribute must be on one line  -->
        <add type="Microsoft.Web.Services.WebServicesExtension,→
          Microsoft.Web.Services,Version=1.0.0.0, Culture=neutral,→
          PublicKeyToken=31bf3856ad364e35" priority="1" group="0" />
      </soapExtensionTypes>
    </webServices>
  </system.web>
</configuration>
```

As with most configuration details in .NET, you can add the SOAP extension details to any of the configuration files you want, although the standard practice is to apply the configuration only at the level you need it. In most cases, this is the web.config file for the application that's hosting the Web services.

Note the use of the *priority* and *group* attributes in our SOAP extension addition to the configuration files. For WSE to function correctly, you must have it executed first (or last for outgoing messages) in the chain of SOAP extensions. Setting a priority of 1 and a group value of 0 indicates that you want to run the WSE SOAP extension with the highest possible priority. You can change these values and give the WSE SOAP extension any priority you want, but this can lead to unpredictable results.

That's it. You don't need to make any more changes to the server code, and the incoming and outgoing SOAP messages are passed through the input and output pipelines as part of the normal SOAP extensions process.

The one thing we're missing is access to the *SoapContext* objects used by the request and the response. Unlike on the client side, where you have direct access to them on the proxy class, you access them on the server by calling static methods of the *HttpSoapContext* class within the called method itself. We have static *RequestContext* and *ResponseContext* properties that return the *SoapContext* for the current call.

Under the Covers

When you use the WSE SOAP extension, *WebServicesExtension*, the process for calling the methods on the extension is the same as for all other SOAP extensions. The runtime makes repeated calls to the *ProcessMessage* method of the extension, passing in the *SoapMessage* object that's being handled; *WebServicesExtension* deals with two of these calls to pass the message through the pipeline.

ProcessMessage is first called with *SoapMessageStage* set to *BeforeDeserialize*. The *WebServicesExtension* instance takes the *SoapMessage* object and performs the necessary steps on it. If *SoapMessage* is a DIME message, it is split into its component parts and the SOAP envelope is passed through the input pipeline, populating the request *SoapContext* as it goes.

The handler continues with its normal processing cycle—it deserializes the message and calls the intended method—which has access to both the request *SoapContext* and the response *SoapContext*.

When the called method completes and control is passed back to the .NET runtime, *ProcessMessage* is called with *SoapMessageStage* set to *AfterSerialize* and performs the processing required for outgoing messages. The *SoapMessage* object is passed through the output pipeline using the details specified in the response *SoapContext* object and then converted to a DIME message if necessary.

The handler then does a little more processing, and the response is returned to the client.

The Web Settings Tool

Because manually changing proxy classes every time you add a new reference or update a reference can become very (very!) tedious, you can use an unsupported tool from Microsoft called the Web Settings Tool instead. (You can download it from *http://www.microsoft.com/downloads/details.aspx?FamilyID=e1924d29-e82d-4d9a-a945-3f074ce63c8b*.) This tool, an add-in to Visual Studio .NET, automates a lot of the mundane tasks that you need to perform when using WSE.

When generating proxies, the Web Settings Tool automatically creates a proxy that inherits from *WebServicesClientProtocol*—but only if the Microsoft.Web.Services DLL has been added as a reference to the project.

However, it doesn't do it in the same way as we did above when we changed the base class for the existing proxies.

Rather than modifying the proxy that's generated by Visual Studio .NET, the Web Settings Tool adds a second proxy to the same class file. This new proxy inherits from *WebServicesClientProtocol* and is distinguished from the standard proxy class by the appending of *Wse* to the name of the proxy. If you look at the Object Browser, as shown in Figure 13-4, you'll see that we now have two proxies—one for the normal Web service and one for the Web service that's using WSE.

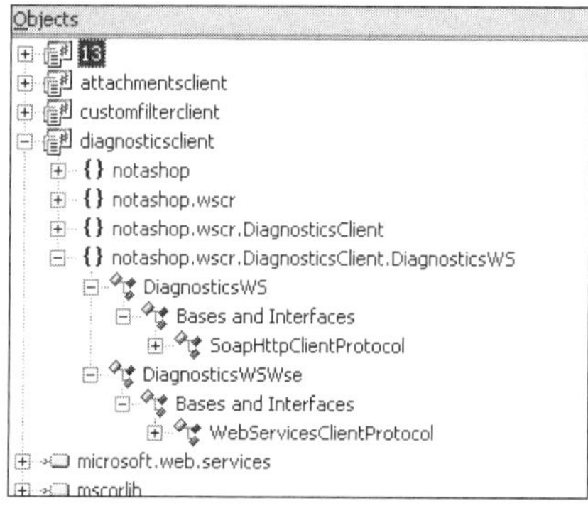

Figure 13-4 The Web Settings Tool generates the *DiagnosticsWSWse* class.

This method of creating the proxies might seem a little strange, but it actually makes more sense than simply changing every proxy you're using. By creating two proxies, you have the option of using the standard Web service infrastructure or the WSE-enabled infrastructure without any need to change configuration options. If you include references to standard Web services and WSE-enabled Web services in the same project, you can use whichever version of the proxy is correct. You don't have to worry about the tools creating the wrong type of proxy—both have been created, and you can simply use the one that's required.

The Web Settings Tool also allows you to graphically configure most of the configuration options for the filters and to automatically update the necessary configuration files. We could use the Web Settings Tool to manage the configuration of WSE, but we'll use it only to generate the correct proxies. To show you what's actually occurring with the configuration, we'll manually modify the configuration files as required.

Individual Configuration Options

Beyond configuring the client and server to actually use WSE, you might also need to configure some aspects of the behavior of the filters in the configuration files beyond what you can do with *SoapContext* objects.

All of the configuration details for the filters are required to be in a *<microsoft.web.services>* configuration element, and any configuration options you specify will apply equally to both input and output filters. This is not a standard section in the configuration files, so you must add details of the section to the configuration file (either web.config or an application configuration file) before you can use it:

```
<configuration>
  <configSections>
    <!-- the TYPE attribute must be on one line  -->
    <section name="microsoft.web.services"
     type="Microsoft.Web.Services.Configuration.WebServicesConfiguration,→
     Microsoft.Web.Services, Version=1.0.0.0, Culture=neutral,→
     PublicKeyToken=31bf3856ad364e35" />
  </configSections>
</configuration>
```

Now you can add the *<microsoft.web.services>* element to the configuration file and populate this with the details required by the individual filters. We'll cover these details shortly, when we look at the specifics of the filters.

Controlling the Filters in the Pipeline

As we pointed out earlier, all the filters are enabled by default, but in many cases this won't be what you need. Passing through unused filters adds overhead to the Web service call, and you might want to use different filters for incoming and outgoing messages. When we look at developing custom filters later in the chapter, you'll also see that you also need the ability to add and insert filters into the pipeline.

You gain access to the input and output pipelines by using the *InputFilters* and *OutputFilters* properties of the *FilterConfiguration* object exposed by the static *WebServicesConfiguration.FilterConfiguration* property. These properties return a *SoapInputFilterCollection* or a *SoapOutputFilterCollection* that derives from the *CollectionBase* class. The *CollectionBase* class provides methods to manipulate the collection; using these, you can add and remove filters from the pipeline.

> **Note** You also have access to a *SoapInputFilterCollection* and a *SoapOutputFilterCollection* object via the *Pipeline* property of the *WebServicesClientProtocol* class that's the base class of the proxies you use. It returns the filters that are in use for the current proxy and allows you to modify the filters that the current proxy is using without modifying the filters that the rest of the application is using. Only by changing the collections returned from the *WebServicesConfiguration.FilterConfiguration* property can you change the filters for the entire application.

You can easily view the filters that are present in the pipeline by iterating through the relevant collection. For example, if you want to view the input filters, you simply get the *SoapInputFilterCollection* object and iterate through its members:

```
// get the input filters
SoapInputFilterCollection inputFilters =
    WebServicesConfiguration.FilterConfiguration.InputFilters;

// loop through the filters
for (int x=0; x<inputFilters.Count; x++)
{
    Console.WriteLine(x + " - " + inputFilters[x].GetType());
}
```

To remove a filter, you simply call the *Remove* method of the filters collection and specify either the specific filter to remove or the type of filter to remove. Unless you're keeping references to the filters that you're creating, you should always use the *Remove* method that expects a filter type:

```
// get the input filters
SoapInputFilterCollection inputFilters =
    WebServicesConfiguration.FilterConfiguration.InputFilters;

// remove the Timestamp filter
inputFilters.Remove(typeof(TimestampInputFilter));
```

The *Remove* method iterates through the filters collection and removes the first instance of the type specified, shuffling the remaining filters up and filling the gap left by the removal. If there are multiple instances of a specific filter, you obviously need to call the *Remove* method multiple times.

If you now want to add a filter to the filters collection, you simply call the *Add* method of the filters collection and pass it a new instance of the filter you want to use. The use of the *Add* method will become clearer when we look at custom filters later in the chapter, but if you want to move the *Timestamp* filter to the end of the pipeline, you use the *Add* method in combination with the *Remove* method:

```
// get the input filters
SoapInputFilterCollection inputFilters =
    WebServicesConfiguration.FilterConfiguration.InputFilters;

// move the Timestamp filter to the end of the pipeline
inputFilters.Remove(typeof(TimestampInputFilter));
inputFilters.Add(new TimestampInputFilter());
```

The *Add* method always adds the filter to the end of the collection, but as you just saw, the pipelines are accessed in opposite directions depending on whether you're dealing with an outgoing request or an incoming request. For an outgoing request, the filter you've added is processed at the end of the pipeline; for an incoming request, the filter is processed at the start of the pipeline.

Simply adding the filter to the pipeline might not be what you want—you might want to place the filter at a specific location in the pipeline. You could remove all of the filters and then add them in the order you require, but it's much easier to use the *Insert* method of the filters collection to insert the filter at the given index:

```
// get the input filters
SoapInputFilterCollection inputFilters =
    WebServicesConfiguration.FilterConfiguration.InputFilters;

// move the Timestamp filter to the start of the pipeline
inputFilters.Remove(typeof(TimestampInputFilter));
inputFilters.Insert(0, new TimestampInputFilter());
```

This code moves the Timestamp filter to the first position in the pipeline (used first for outgoing messages, last for incoming messages), shuffling the remaining filters to accommodate the new filter.

Although we've looked exclusively at the input filters so far, the process for modifying (adding, removing, or inserting) output filters is exactly the same, except you start with a *SoapOutputFilterCollection* instead of a *SoapInputFilterCollection*.

> **Note** If you need to alter the filters collection, you must do so as soon as your application is initialized so all Web service calls will use the new pipeline. For clients, you do this in the initialization code; for server-based applications, you should do this in the *Application_Start* method in global.asax.

When you look at the upcoming Web services and client applications, you'll see that the filters that aren't being used have been removed—however, the Trace filters will always be running. For the Web services, this is done in the *Application_Start* method; for the clients, this is done in the constructor for the form after the call to *InitializeComponent*.

Adding Filters in the Configuration Files

You can also control the filters used by an application by specifying filters you want to add to the pipelines in the application configuration file. You can add filters to the pipeline, but you cannot remove filters from the pipeline, nor can you control the position at which new filters are added.

To add a filter to the pipelines, you simply add the details to the *<filters>* element of the configuration file. If you want to see the trace details for what went into the pipeline, as well as what comes out of the pipeline, you can add a second trace filter to both the input and the output pipelines. The default trace filters will catch one end of the pipeline, and the new trace filters you add will catch the other.

You add the new filters as follows:

```
<configuration>
  <microsoft.web.services>
    <filters>
      <input>
        <add type="Microsoft.Web.Services.Diagnostics.TraceInputFilter,¬
         Microsoft.Web.Services, Version=1.0.0.0, Culture=neutral,¬
         PublicKeyToken=31bf3856ad364e35" />
      </input>
      <output>
        <add type="Microsoft.Web.Services.Diagnostics.TraceOutputFilter,¬
         Microsoft.Web.Services, Version=1.0.0.0, Culture=neutral,¬
         PublicKeyToken=31bf3856ad364e35" />
      </output>
    </filters>
  </microsoft.web.services>
</configuration>
```

Now that you have filters at either end of the pipeline, whenever you have tracing turned on, you'll have two messages added to the trace file—one before the filters have processed the message and one after the filters have processed the message.

Recommended Filter Configuration

One problem with the ability to add filters in the configuration files is that third parties can add filters into the pipeline that you weren't expecting and that might cause problems. If you deliver a client application to a customer, for example, the customer can add its own filters to the pipeline.

We recommend that you remove all of the filters from the input and output pipelines by using the *Clear* method of the relevant filter collection. You can add back in the filters you require. We recommend adding the Trace filter back into the pipeline so you can turn on tracing for the application if needed—this provides a valuable diagnostic tool for the applications that don't perform as expected.

All of the filters in the pipeline have the ability to amend the SOAP envelope that you're passing, and as you'll see shortly, both the Timestamp and the Routing filter add details to the SOAP envelope if they're in the pipeline—even if you're not explicitly using the facilities they provide. If you're not using them, it's pointless to transmit the unnecessary data across the wire. Removing the unused filters from both the client and the server will minimize the overhead that WSE introduces.

The Trace Filters

We'll start our look at the filters that WSE gives us by looking at the Trace filters. These aren't part of the GXA architecture, but they fill a massive gap in the initial .NET Web services implementation.

> **Note** The Trace filters provide an ideal debugging tool even if you're not building a WSE-enabled application. Simply turn off all of the filters except the Trace filters, and you'll have instant debugging of the messages that are entering and leaving your client or service. In most cases this beats using the trace utility provided with the Microsoft SOAP Toolkit!

As we pointed out earlier, in the current release of WSE the Trace filters are enabled by default but need some additional configuration before they'll actually trace the input and output SOAP messages.

Within the *<microsoft.web.services>* configuration element, you simply add a *<diagnostics>* element that contains a *<trace>* element. Within the trace element, you specify whether the trace is enabled and the filenames of the input and output traces:

```
<diagnostics>
  <trace enabled="true" input="input.xml" output="output.xml" />
</diagnostics>
```

The application that's running, whether it's the ASP.NET process or a client application, must have permission to write to the location you've specified. Once you enable tracing, the input and output Trace filters are enabled, and they start writing what they're receiving and sending to the files you've specified. The only way you can trace one without the other is to physically remove the Trace filter from the pipeline. If you don't specify the input and output filenames, the defaults of *inputTrace.webinfo* and *outputTrace.webinfo* are used, respectively.

You can see the messages that are traced by launching and running the DiagnosticsClient application from the chapter's code samples. This simple example calls the *MakeMyDay* method of the Diagnostics Web service located at *http://localhost/wscr/13/diagnosticsws.asmx*. This method simply returns a string. There's nothing in this code you haven't already seen, but it's the action of the Trace filters we're interested in this time.

When the call is made to the Web service, the output.xml file is written to disk, as shown in Figure 13-5.

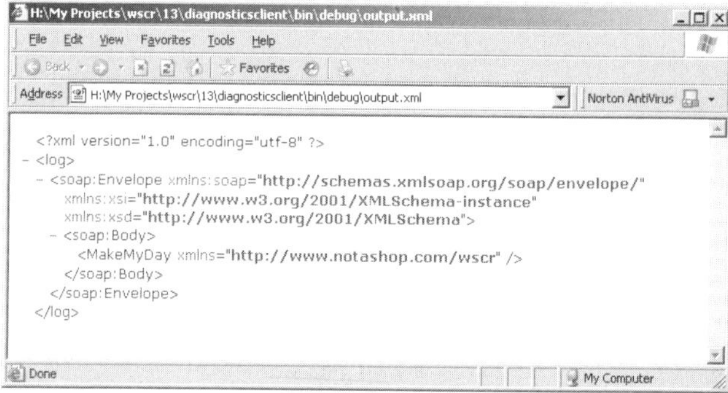

Figure 13-5 The SOAP envelope sent to the *MakeMyDay* method

The SOAP envelope that is output from the client is sent to the Web service. If you were to look at the input filter on the server, you'd see that exactly the same SOAP envelope arrives at the server.

The return from the call, the input to the client application, is shown in Figure 13-6. The *<MakeMyDayResult>* element in the SOAP body is returned, as expected, but a *<wsu:Timestamp>* element is also returned in the SOAP header. This is added by *TimestampOutputFilter*. (We'll look at this shortly.) If you were to look on the server, you'd see that the identical SOAP envelope was sent from the Web service.

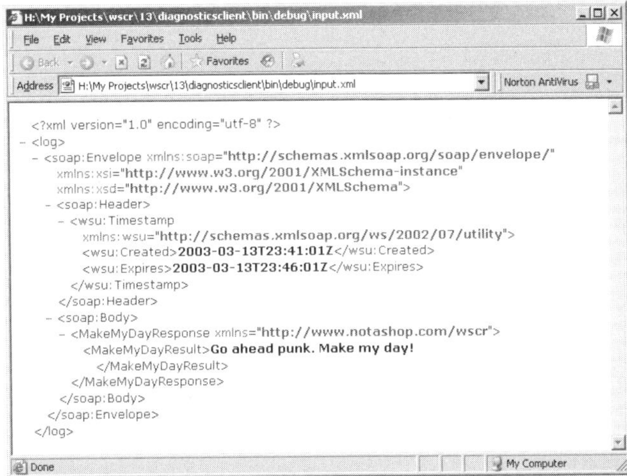

Figure 13-6 The SOAP envelope returned from the *MakeMyDay* method

There isn't a lot more to say about the Trace filters. You simply turn on the filters and specify the filenames of where you want the filters to go. When a call is made, the input and output filters are updated with a new *<soap:Envelope>* element that contains the relevant SOAP message.

As you'll soon see, however, there's one situation in which the Trace filters, which provide very good debugging facilities for the SOAP envelope, might not fulfil all your debugging requirements.

Working with Attachments

We've already talked about how attachments are added to a message and the resulting conversion to a DIME message. We'll consider how to add and process attachments by looking at a simple Web service that accepts an image attachment. The Attachments Web service, located at *http://localhost/wscr/13/attachmentsws.asmx*, has one method, *FlipMe*, that accepts the image and reverses the palette before returning the image to the client.

> **Note** The code here for modifying the image in the Web service method is far from ideal. It creates four versions of the same buffer, each in a slightly different format, which would play havoc with memory usage on the server if we were to attempt to scale up the application. We're using it here simply to show how attachments are passed between clients and servers.

This example removes all of the filters from the WSE pipeline except the Trace filters. We'll show that the Trace filters don't really help you when you're trying to debug an application that uses attachments.

If you open the AttachmentsClient application in sample code, you'll see a very simple form that allows the selection of an image by using the Browse button. The image is loaded and resized to fit the form. The important part occurs when you click the Flip Me button and a call to the Web service is made.

As with all Web service calls, the first thing you need to do is create an instance of the proxy class—in this case, the WSE-enabled version of the proxy. You then create a *MemoryStream* object that contains the image, retrieved as a JPEG, that you want to reverse:

```
// create the proxy
AttachmentsWSWse proxy = new AttachmentsWSWse();

// save the image as a stream
MemoryStream streamImage = new MemoryStream();
picMain.Image.Save(streamImage, ImageFormat.Jpeg);
```

Attachments in WSE are handled using streams, and everything you want to pass as a DIME attachment must be available as a stream. Because you can create streams from just about anything, this isn't a problem.

To add the image to our message, we can create a new *DimeAttachment* object. The constructor for *DimeAttachment* we're calling expects three parameters—the MIME type that we're creating, an enumeration value that specifies the type format of the attachment, and the stream that we want to create the attachment from. When creating a JPEG image attachment, we specify that the MIME type is *image/jpg* and that we're using a *MediaType*. As the final parameter, we pass the stream object we created earlier.

To add attachments to a request, you need to access the *Attachments* collection of the *RequestSoapContext* object of the proxy class. This returns a *DimeAttachmentCollection*—a class that's derived from the *CollectionBase* object. As with all classes that derive from *CollectionBase*, it offers access to an *Add* method. We can simply use this to add the attachment to the collection:

```
// add the stream to the response
DimeAttachment dimeAttach= new
    DimeAttachment("image/jpg", TypeFormatEnum.MediaType, streamImage);
proxy.RequestSoapContext.Attachments.Add(dimeAttach);
```

Once the attachment has been added to the message, we can make a call to the Web service by calling the *FlipMe* method of the proxy.

On the server, the *FlipMe* method first checks to see that only one attachment is attached to the message by accessing the *Count* property of the *DimeAttachmentCollection* exposed by *HttpSoapContext.RequestContext*:

```
if(HttpSoapContext.RequestContext.Attachments.Count == 1)
```

If we don't have one attachment, we don't do any more processing in the method. If we have exactly one attachment, we need to check that it is of the correct format.

You access individual members of the *Attachments* collection by using the *Item* property. This is also the indexer for the class, so we can use the shortened format for accessing the item we require:

```
DimeAttachment receivedItem=HttpSoapContext.RequestContext.Attachments[0];
```

Each item in the *Attachments* collection is a *DimeAttachment*, and this class exposes several properties that allow you to interrogate the attachment to determine what it actually is. This relies on the sender being truthful about what she's attached, however.

We'll use two of these properties, *Type* and *TypeFormat*. These expose the details that we passed to the constructor when we created the attachment at the client. We simply check that the *Type* and *TypeFormat* values of the *DimeAttachment* are what we expect:

```
if(receivedItem.TypeFormat == TypeFormatEnum.MediaType
    && receivedItem.Type == "image/jpg")
```

If the attachment is not of the correct format, we don't do any more processing. If it is the correct format, we process the received attachment.

The *DimeAttachment* class exposes a copy of the stream that we used at the server to create the attachment; this can be accessed by using the *Stream* property. It's a simple matter to use this property to extract the stream *receivedItem* and pass it to the constructor to create a new *Bitmap*:

```
// get the image
Bitmap imgReceived = new Bitmap(receivedItem.Stream);
```

Once we create the *Bitmap*, we can flip the palette by reversing the color of each pixel. This code isn't complex; it's not efficient, either, but it performs its intended task. You can see what it actually does in the sample code.

After we alter the image, we instantiate a new *DimeAttachment* and add it to the *ResponseContext*. This is exactly the same process we perform at the client.

```
// save the image as a stream
MemoryStream streamImage = new MemoryStream();
imgReceived.Save(streamImage, ImageFormat.Jpeg);

// add the stream to the response
DimeAttachment dimeAttach = new
    DimeAttachment("image/jpg", TypeFormatEnum.MediaType, streamImage);
HttpSoapContext.ResponseContext.Attachments.Add(dimeAttach);
```

On returning to the client, we now have the bitmap but with the palette reversed. We first check to see that there is only one attachment and that the attachment is of the correct type. We then retrieve the stream from the attachment and use this to create a new bitmap to replace the original image:

```
if(proxy.ResponseSoapContext.Attachments.Count == 1)
{
    DimeAttachment receivedItem = proxy.ResponseSoapContext.Attachments[0];

    if(receivedItem.TypeFormat == TypeFormatEnum.MediaType
        && receivedItem.Type == "image/jpg")
    {
        picMain.Image = new Bitmap(receivedItem.Stream);
    }
}
```

That's it. We've now sent an attachment to a Web service and received an attachment back from the Web service. All attachments follow the same process no matter what the type of the attachment.

When you send an attachment, you create a *DimeAttachment* object and add it to the *Attachments* collection of the request context. If you receive an attachment, you have to be a little more careful. You might not need to check for the correct number of attachments, but you usually need to check the type of the attachment. You can then extract the attachment as a stream and construct the original object as required.

Debugging Attachments

As you saw earlier, the process of converting an outgoing message into DIME format is handled outside of the filter pipeline. The Trace filters are in the pipeline and won't see that you have an attachment with your message.

If you open the output trace file for the previous application, as shown in Figure 13-7, you'll see that there is no reference to any DIME message. Nor can you see that we added a DIME attachment to the message.

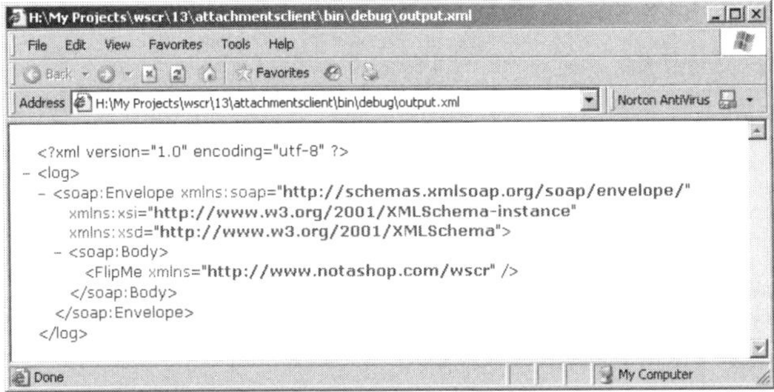

Figure 13-7 Trace filters don't show DIME messages.

If you think back to the point at which the DIME message is constructed, it's easy to see why you can't use the Trace filters. An outgoing message is converted to DIME after all the filters in the pipeline have been executed, and an incoming message is converted from DIME before any of the filters in the pipeline are executed. We need some other means to debug what is being sent across the wire.

The solution is a tool we dismissed earlier in the chapter—the trace utility from the SOAP Toolkit. You saw this tool in action in Chapter 2; we'll use it here to look at the structure of the DIME message that we're sending across the wire.

Figure 13-8 shows the trace utility view of the structure of the DIME message that's sent to the *FlipMe* method of the Attachments Web service.

By clicking on the Dime entry in the tree on the left, you can see the DIME structure of the message. At the top of the right pane, you can see that the DIME message actually contains two individual DIME records. If you look at the *<Type>* element for the two DIME records, you can see that the first record is a SOAP envelope and the second is an image.

We've seen the structure of the DIME message, but sometimes you want to see the actual contents of the message as well as the details of the SOAP envelope that makes up the first DIME record. You can do all of this using the trace utility.

Click on the Message # 1 entry in the tree on the left to show the SOAP envelope that was transmitted. It will be identical to the SOAP envelope seen by the output trace filter.

The HTTPHeaders entry lets you view the HTTP headers sent with the message, and you can see the actual binary message that was sent by clicking on the Binary entry.

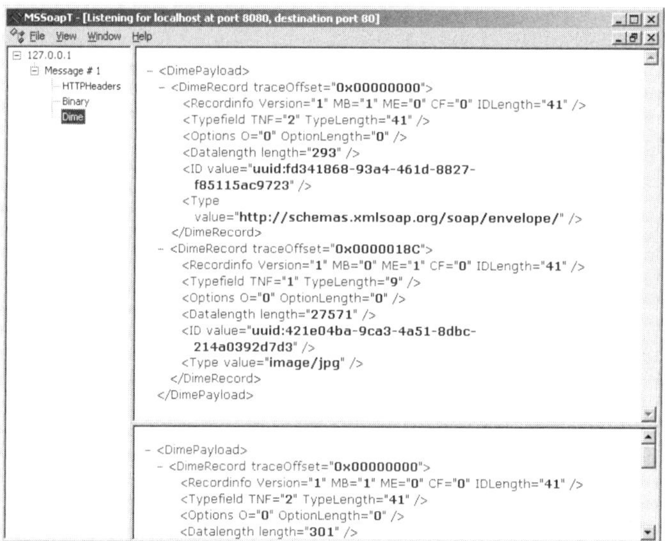

Figure 13-8 The trace utility allows you to debug DIME messages.

Using Timestamp Filters

The remaining filter we need to look at in this chapter is the Timestamp filter. Of the filters that are handled in WSE, it has the most basic task. The output filter adds the Timestamp SOAP header using the details in the request *SoapContext*, and the input filter checks that the Timestamp SOAP header is correctly formatted and raises an exception if the header is incorrect or if the message has expired.

Most of the work accomplished by the Timestamp filters is automatic, and the only thing you can really change is the time-to-live (TTL) setting for a message. The time the message is created and the time it expires are added to the SOAP message by the output filter, and the input filter checks that the expiry time is not before the current time.

We'll show the use of the Timestamp filters by building a simple application that allows the TTL for the message to be specified. This application uses the Timestamp Web service at *http://localhost/wscr/13/timestampws.asmx*. This Web service has one method, *Time*, that returns the Timestamp details from the received message as a string.

This Web service will automatically reject expired messages; by modifying the TTL of the message to a relatively small value, we can cause the message to be rejected by the Web service.

> **Note** Bear in mind two issues when you work with the Timestamp filters. First, all times are converted from local time to Coordinated Universal Time (UTC) format before they're used. For example, if the machine you're using is in Seattle (eight hours behind UTC), when you look at the time in the SOAP header it will appear eight hours ahead of local time.
>
> The second issue is that all times are based on the time of the machines involved and not on some magical Internet time—the filters always assume that the time on the local machine is correct. Problems can arise if the machines are set to the incorrect time or time zone. If, after conversion to UTC, the times on the two machines are more than five minutes apart, you'll have a problem—the default TTL for a message is five minutes, and all messages will appear to have expired.
>
> One solution is to ensure that the time zone on the machines is set correctly and then to synchronize the machine time with one of the Internet time servers. You can do this easily in Microsoft Windows XP and Windows 2003 Server.

If you open the TimestampClient application in the sample code, you'll see yet another simple form, as shown in Figure 13-9. This one allows the entry of the TTL value for the call and offers a Tell Me button that makes the call to the Web service.

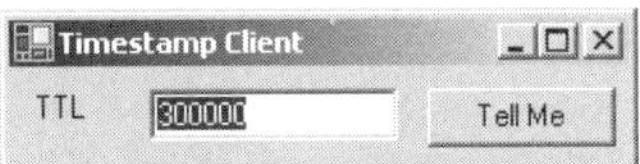

Figure 13-9 The TimestampClient application

The TTL value in the text box is set at 300000 milliseconds, or 5 minutes. This is the default value used by WSE; we've also used this as the default value on the form.

When the Tell Me button is clicked, the first thing we do is create an instance of the WSE-enabled version of the proxy:

```
TimestampWSWse proxy = new TimestampWSWse();
```

We then enclose the rest of the code for the method in a *try/catch* block so any exceptions that are raised are caught and displayed to the user. The TTL value for the request is set by parsing the value in the text box as an integer and setting the *Timestamp.Ttl* property of the request *SoapContext*. We then make the call to the *Time* method of the Web service as normal:

```
try
{
    // set the TTL of the request
    proxy.RequestSoapContext.Timestamp.Ttl = int.Parse(txtTTL.Text);

    // make the remote call
    MessageBox.Show(proxy.Time(), "Returned message");
}
catch(Exception error)
{
    MessageBox.Show(error.Message,"Error!!");
}
```

On the server, we first define the variables we need to use. We create a string, *strReturn*, to hold the message we're returning and a *SoapContext* object, *reqCon*, that is initialized to the current request *SoapContext*:

```
string strReturn;
SoapContext reqCon = HttpSoapContext.RequestContext;
```

We then use various properties of the *Timestamp* object returned from the *Timestamp* property of the *reqCon* object to extract the timestamp details from the incoming SOAP message. The *Timestamp* object has *Created* and *Expires* properties that return the relevant times. We use these to construct a "created at X, received at Y, would have expired at Z" message and return this to the caller:

```
// extract the details from the message
strReturn = "The message was created at " +
    reqCon.Timestamp.Created.ToString() + ", ";
strReturn = strReturn + "received at " + DateTime.Now.ToString() + " ";
strReturn = strReturn + "and would have expired at " +
    reqCon.Timestamp.Expires.ToString() + ".\n\n";
```

Two outcomes are possible from the Timestamp filters when we make a call to a Web service—the message passes through the filters without any problems or the message has expired and an exception is raised by the filter. We can simulate both of these scenarios using the *TimestampClient* application.

If we accept the default value of 300000 for the TTL value and click the Tell Me button, the Web service is called and a string is returned to the client, as shown in Figure 13-10.

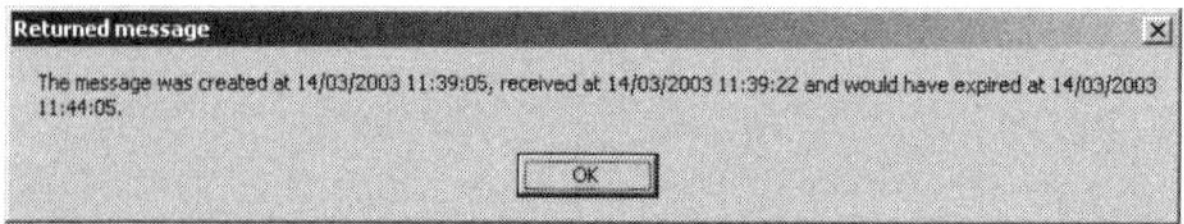

Figure 13-10 Message returned showing the Timestamp details

As you can see from Figure 13-10, the message was created at 11:39:05 on March 14, 2003. It would have expired five minutes later were it not for the fact that it was received at 11:39:22, 17 seconds after it was sent. You can see the created and expired details in this extract from the SOAP header:

```
<wsu:Timestamp xmlns:wsu="http://schemas.xmlsoap.org/ws/2002/07/utility">
  <wsu:Created>2003-03-14T11:39:05Z</wsu:Created>
  <wsu:Expires>2003-03-14T11:44:05Z</wsu:Expires>
</wsu:Timestamp>
```

The difference between the created and received times might seem long for such a simple request, but it was affected by two things. The server that the Web service is running on is about 10 seconds ahead of the machine on which the client was executed. It was also the first time the Web service was actually called, so extra overhead was incurred due to the compilation of the code on the server. A second click of the Tell Me button yielded a much more respectable 12-second difference (about 2 seconds if you ignore the 10-second difference in the clocks on the two machines).

You've seen what happens if the message is received within the specified TTL; now let's see what happens if the message has expired when it is received by the server. We can easily do this by specifying a very low value for the TTL. My personal favorite is 1—no request will ever take 1 millisecond to be transported and decoded.

Why not use 0 as the TTL? If you specify 0 as the TTL, you're not specifying a TTL of 0 milliseconds—you're actually specifying that you don't have a TTL. If you set a TTL of 0, you don't generate a *<wsu:Expires>* element—as you can see if you look at a fragment from the SOAP message that's generated:

```
<wsu:Timestamp xmlns:wsu="http://schemas.xmlsoap.org/ws/2002/07/utility">
  <wsu:Created>2003-03-14T11:42:38Z </wsu:Created>
</wsu:Timestamp>
```

And if you look at the message returned by the Web service, you can see that the expiration date has defaulted to an arbitrary value of December 31, 9999, at 23:59:59. You can see this in Figure 13-11.

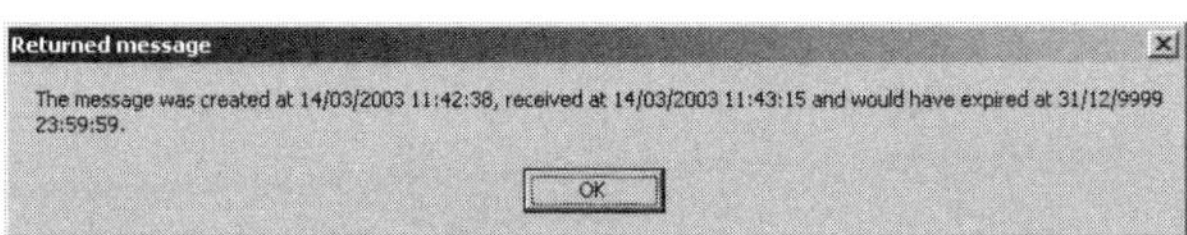

Figure 13-11 Timestamp details with no expiration date

After that digression, we still haven't seen an expired message being rejected. Set the TTL to 1 and click the Tell Me button. As you can see in Figure 13-12, the message has been rejected and a *TimestampFault* exception thrown.

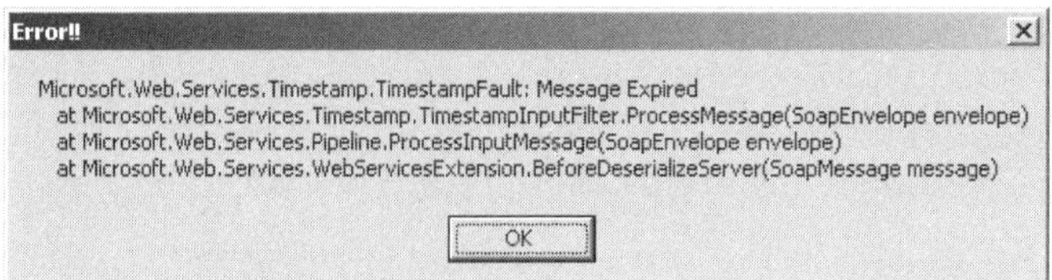

Figure 13-12 An expired message throws a *TimestampFault* exception.

We have one further thing to cover regarding Timestamps. When you route messages, the Timestamp filters add *<wsu:Received>* elements for each router that the message passes through. We'll cover routing in Chapter 14, and we'll also look at this aspect of the Timestamp filters there.

Creating Custom Filters

As you saw earlier in the chapter, it's possible to add and remove filters from the pipeline; we also briefly mentioned that it's possible to create your own filters. We'll now look at creating our own input and output filters that simply add a message to the event log; the message we'll log is simply the body of the message that we're sending and receiving.

Under the Covers

As we mentioned earlier, all filters used by WSE inherit from *SoapInputFilter* or *SoapOutputFilter*. We briefly explained how filters are actually called because you didn't need to understand the process by which the prewritten filters are called to use them. Now that we're developing our own filters, however, you do need to understand this in more detail.

If you look at the documentation for either of the filter base classes, you'll see that they have only one exposed method, *ProcessMessage*. This method has one parameter—an instance of the *SoapEnvelope* class—and we can use this to access the message we're working with. In this example, we're only reading from the *SoapEnvelope*, but nothing can stop a filter from modifying the *SoapEnvelope*. Any filters that are processed after this filter will receive the modified *SoapEnvelope*.

This is exactly what the existing filters do—they override the *ProcessMessage* method and perform their own logic. When an incoming filter processes a message, it interrogates the *SoapEnvelope* object and populates the correct *SoapContext* object. The input filter removes the details specific to it from the *SoapEnvelope* object—the *SecurityInputFilter* object unencrypts the message if necessary, the *TimestampInputFilter* object removes the timestamp details, and so forth. Output filters do the opposite and use the correct *SoapContext* object to modify the *SoapEnvelope* object, adding details specific to them—the *SecurityOutputFilter* object might encrypt the message, the *TimestampOutputFilter* object adds the timestamp details, and so on.

To write your own filter, you follow the same paradigm. You inherit from the correct base class and override the *ProcessMessage* method.

Building a Custom Filter

We first need to decide whether we're writing an input filter or an output filter. We can't write one filter and use this as both the input and the output filter; we must create a unique filter that derives from the correct base class.

We simply add a new class file to our project and create the two classes we require—one inheriting from *SoapInputFilter* and one from *SoapOutputFilter*. Within each derived class, we override the *ProcessMessage* method and call the *WriteToEventLog* static method on the *Logger* class (which you'll see shortly).

```
namespace CustomFilterClient
{
    public class EventLogInputFilter : SoapInputFilter
    {
        public override void ProcessMessage(SoapEnvelope envelope)
        {
            string strMessage = "INCOMING:\n\n " + envelope.InnerXml;
            Logger.WriteToEventLog(strMessage);
        }
    }

    public class EventLogOutputFilter : SoapOutputFilter
    {
        public override void ProcessMessage(SoapEnvelope envelope)
        {
            string strMessage = "OUTGOING:\n\n " + envelope.InnerXml;
            EventLogger.WriteToEventLog(strMessage);
        }
    }
}
```

Because we're performing the same function in both the input filter and the output filter, we've created another class, *Logger*, with one static method, *WriteToEventLog*, that writes a string we pass it into the event log. Having this in a separate method allows us to use the same logic in both the input and the output filters without repeating any code.

In the *WriteToEventLog* method, we simply take the string that has been passed as a parameter and write a new entry to the event log. We allow .NET to create the event source for us automatically when we create the *EventLog* instance, and we delete the event source after we've used it:

```
public class Logger
{
    public static void WriteToEventLog(string strMessage)
    {
        string strSource = "NotAShop.com";

        // create an event log object (auto creates event source)
        EventLog evLog = new EventLog("Application", ".", strSource);

        // write message to the event log
        evLog.WriteEntry(strMessage, EventLogEntryType.Information);

        // now delete the event source we created
        EventLog.DeleteEventSource(strSource);
    }
}
```

Adding a Custom Filter

As we stated briefly at the start of the chapter, you can add custom filters to the pipeline in two ways: you can add them to the end of the pipeline by using the configuration files, or you can add them programmatically at any point in the pipeline.

We'll add them programmatically because we want them to trap the actual SOAP message that's sent or received by the code—we're not interested in the changes that the other filters might have made to the SOAP envelope. We can do this easily by adding a new instance of the filter we require at position zero to the correct filter collection. We do this in the *Load* event of the client application's main form so it is set as soon as we start the application.

```
// add the custom input filter to the pipeline
SoapInputFilterCollection inputFilters =
    WebServicesConfiguration.FilterConfiguration.InputFilters;
inputFilters.Insert(0, new EventLogInputFilter());

// add the custom output filter to the pipeline
SoapOutputFilterCollection outputFilters =
    WebServicesConfiguration.FilterConfiguration.OutputFilters;
outputFilters.Insert(0, new EventLogOutputFilter());
```

> **Note** We're only showing the custom filter being added to the pipelines on the client, but the code to add the filters on the server is identical. Instead of adding it in the *Load* event of the form, you add it to the *Application_Start* event in the global.asax file for the service.

Custom Filters on the Client

We'll show the use of our custom filter by creating a new client application, CustomFilterClient, that calls the Timestamp and Diagnostics Web services that you saw earlier.

You've actually seen the four lines of client code to add the custom filters to the pipeline, but there's a little more to the client application than that. Figure 13-13 shows a drop-down list to select the service you want to call and an Execute button to call the service you've selected.

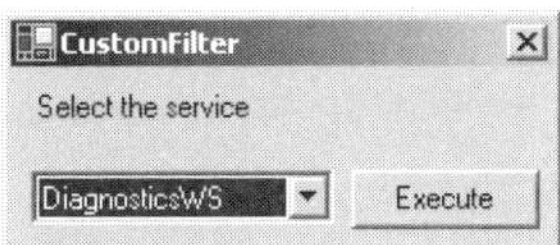

Figure 13-13 The CustomFilterClient application

Rather than write another Web service to show the custom filter in use, we'll use two of the services you've already seen in this chapter—the Diagnostics Web service, at *http://localhost/wscr/13/diagnosticsws.asmx*, and the Timestamp Web service, at *http://localhost/wscr/13/timestampws.asmx*.

The code to set up the five entries in the drop-down list is in the *Load* event for the form, after the code to add the custom filters to the pipeline. It's very simple and simply adds two entries and then sets the first entry as the selected entry:

```
// populate the drop down box
cboService.Items.Add("DiagnosticsWS");
cboService.Items.Add("TimestampWS");
cboService.SelectedIndex = 0;
```

The work done by the client is contained in the click event handler for the Execute button. We use exactly the same method for calling the remote services that we used previously. We determine which service has been selected and then create the correct proxy method. Once we create the proxy, we can call the correct method and return the results as a dialog box to the user:

```
switch (cboService.SelectedItem.ToString())
{
    case "DiagnosticsWS":
        DiagnosticsWSWse Dproxy = new DiagnosticsWSWse();
        MessageBox.Show(Dproxy.MakeMyDay(), "Returned message");
        break;
    case "TimestampWS":
        TimestampWSWse Tproxy = new TimestampWSWse();
        MessageBox.Show(Tproxy.Time(), "Returned message");
        break;
}
```

When you call any of the services, the call is made and you're not immediately aware that a custom filter has been used. If you look at the Event Viewer entries, as shown in Figure 13-14, you can see that the details have been written to the event log as we requested.

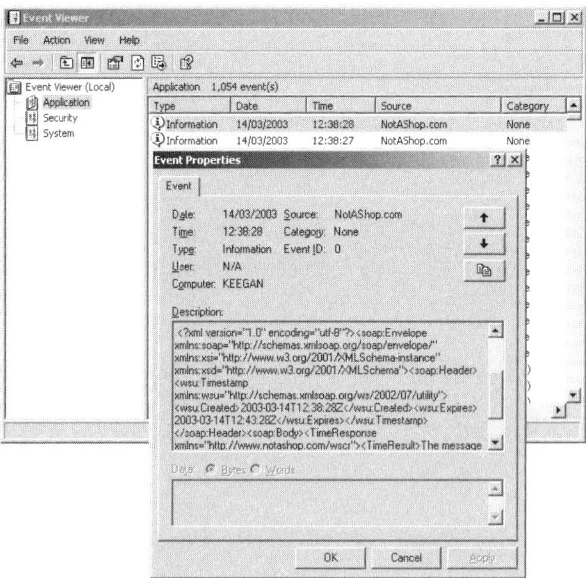

Figure 13-14 Entries written to event log by the custom filter

Summary

We've covered quite a lot of ground in this chapter, and we haven't even looked at the WS-Referral, WS-Routing, or WS-Security specifications yet. To recap, we looked at

- The specifications that the current release of WSE implements
- The structure of WSE—the pipeline and the filters—and its integration into the existing .NET Web service architecture, both at the client and the server
- The Trace filters and their value as a debugging tool, even if you're not using any of the other facilities provided by WSE
- How WSE handles attachments and the problems that DIME causes when you're debugging
- The Timestamp filters and how they allow you to track the timeliness of a message
- How to write your own custom filters

14

Routing and Referral

As you saw when we looked at the various specifications in Chapter 12, WS-Routing and WS-Referral allow you to control the path that your message takes to its ultimate destination.

You can route messages in three ways using the facilities provided by WS-Routing and WS-Referral. We'll look at each of these methods in turn.

We'll start by looking at server-controlled routing, in which the route the message takes is determined by the details specified in a referral cache at the server. The client that makes a request to a Web service is unaware that the request has been forwarded to another destination to be processed.

The second form of routing that we'll look at is a slight modification of server-controlled routing, in which the destination of the request is determined based on some other factor—the request might be forwarded to a different location depending on the time or day or the actual contents of the request. As with server-controlled routing, the client has no knowledge of the request being handled by a different destination than was requested.

The final form of routing we'll look at is client-controlled routing, in which the client specifies the route that it wants the message to take. Each step along the way gets a chance to interact with the message, and possibly alter the route of the message, before passing it on to the next step.

Before we look at any of these types of routing, however, you need to understand how Web Services Enhancements (WSE) deals with routing under the covers.

The *Path* Object

The cornerstone of your control over message routing is the *Path* object. This object contains the routing details for the current request, and WSE uses it to determine where the message is actually sent. Instances of the *Path* object are used in two places.

The first place that we see the *Path* object is within the *SoapContext* object that we looked at in Chapter 13. As you'll soon see when we look at the way that WSE implements routing, the usefulness of the *Path* object that is available within the *SoapContext* object is questionable. The *Path* object within the request's *SoapContext* object is populated by the Routing input filter from the routing details, but the *Path* object within the response's *SoapContext* object is undefined and cannot be altered. You can interrogate the *Path* object within the request's *SoapContext*, but unless you manually route the incoming message, all you have is a read-only copy of the routing information.

Not until you start using the routing facilities that WSE provides do you see a *Path* object that is useful. As you'll see in the next section, WSE provides a much more elegant way of implementing routers. Here's where the second instance of the *Path* object makes an appearance: when you're implementing a WSE router, you're passed an instance of the *Path* object that contains the outgoing path that messages leaving the router will take. We'll see this shortly.

The *Path* object effectively maps directly to the WS-Routing header that you saw in Chapter 12; properties are available that relate directly to the elements within the header. The three most commonly used properties are listed in Table 14-1.

Table 14-1 Properties of the *Path* Object (Partial List)

Property	Description
Fwd	Maps to the *<wsrp:fwd>* element and contains the forward path details of the message. This property returns a collection of *Via* elements that map to the contained *<wsrp:via>* elements.
Rev	Maps to the *<wsrp:rev>* element and contains the reverse path details of the message. This property returns a collection of *Via* elements that map to the contained *<wsrp:via>* elements.
To	Maps to the *<wsrp:to>* element and contains the ultimate destination of the message.

The *Path* object does contain a few other properties, as you'll see in the WSE documentation, but the three listed in the table are the ones we'll use when we use routers in this chapter.

How WSE Routing Works

Routing in WSE is implemented by using a custom HTTP handler for the requested URL that can route the incoming message to the next intermediary. In WSE, this custom handler is the *RoutingHandler* class.

When an incoming message is received, the Routing input filter parses the routing header and populates the *Path* object of the request's *SoapContext* object. Control is then passed to the *ProcessRequest* method of the *RoutingHandler* class; this is where all of the work to route the message occurs. The processes that occur in *ProcessRequest* are shown in Figure 14-1.

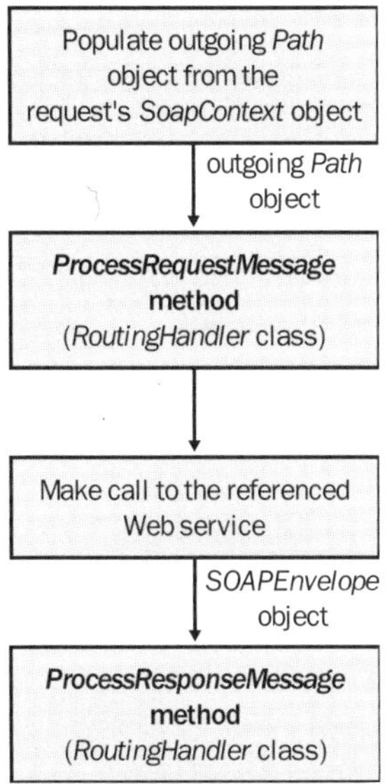

Figure 14-1 Internal architecture of the *RoutingHandler.ProcessRequest* method

Within *ProcessRequest*, we use the details in the *Path* object of the request's *SoapContext* object to create an outgoing *Path* object that contains the details about the route the message must take after it leaves this router. The outgoing *Path* object is basically a copy of the path specified by the request's *SoapContext* object, except that if the current router is the first *<wsrp:via>* element in the *<wsrp:fwd>* collection, it is moved from the *Fwd* collection to the *Rev* collection. (We want to keep details of the reverse path, and we don't want to reroute to the same router!)

The *ProcessRequestMessage* method is then called and is passed a copy of the outgoing *Path* object—if the outgoing *Path* object isn't populated, the

ProcessRequestMessage method checks the referral cache for any details for this router, and these are copied from the referral cache to the *Path* object.

When control is passed back to *ProcessMessage*, the returned *Path* object is interrogated to determine the next intermediary for the message. If there are any *Via* elements that can be routed, the first one in the collection is used; if there are no *Via* elements, a call is made to the router specified in the *To* element. If we can't determine a router that we can forward the message to, an exception of type *SoapHeaderException* is thrown.

Before making the call to the next router, the routing handler sets the *Path* object of the outgoing *SoapContext* object to the *Path* object returned from *ProcessRequestMessage*. The Routing output filter then uses the *Path* object to add the routing header to the request.

When control is returned from the next router, we call the *ProcessResponseMessage* method; the message returned from the remote call can then be modified if required.

All of this might seem a little complex for this early in the chapter, but you'll soon see that the way the different objects are integrated provides a vast range of options for controlling how you route messages.

Routing and HTTP

At the moment, the only transport protocols available for our Web services are HTTP and HTTPS. Due to the request/response nature of these protocols, we have a reverse path to the caller intrinsically defined, and we don't need to define the *<wsrp:rev>* elements in the routing header.

Although WS-Routing specifies the concept of a reverse path, when you use HTTP or HTTPS this path has no real meaning. It's only when we start looking at other protocols that don't have an intrinsic reverse path, such as Microsoft Message Queuing (MSMQ), that we need to concentrate on those details.

The current implementation of the routing input and output filters doesn't populate the reverse path details by default—if there is no *<wsrp:rev>* element in the incoming routing header, no *<wsrp:rev>* header will be added to the request to the next router. We can, however, force the filter to populate the *<wsrp:rev>* header, and when we look at client-controlled routing later in the chapter, you'll see that if we want to keep track of the route that our message has taken to reach its destination, we must force the use of the reverse path.

The Destination Web Services

For all of our routing scenarios, we'll use Web services that have exactly the same functionality. We're not concerned with what we can do at the destination Web service; we're concerned only with how the message arrives at that Web service.

Each Web service that we'll use exposes one method, *Echo*, which simply returns a string containing the URL of the executing Web service as well as the route that the message took to reach it.

The route is determined by looking at the *Path* object of the request's *SoapContext* object because this contains the route that the received message took.

We can interrogate the collections returned from the *Rev* and *Fwd* properties of the *Path* object and concatenate these to the return string, showing the route that the message took.

Server-Controlled Routing

Server-controlled routing is the easiest form of routing to implement. It simply allows you to forward a request to a different URL. This all happens without the knowledge of the client that is making the request to the Web service.

You can use this form of routing in several situations. You can use it to forward requests to a specific URL behind a firewall (although the wisdom of doing this would be questionable). Or you might use it if you know that the service you'll ultimately use is likely to move and you don't want to have to update all the clients when this occurs.

The Web Service

The Web service we'll use for this example can be found at *http://localhost/wscr/14/TellMe.asmx*. As we mentioned, this service exposes the *Echo* method that returns the URL of the executing Web service as well as the details of the route that the message took.

We could call this method directly, but we wouldn't see any routing details because our request obviously hasn't been routed to the ultimate destination. We must configure some routers first.

Server Configuration

As we discussed earlier, to use *RoutingHandler* we need to change the handler for the router we want to implement, and we add this handler in the same way that we would any other HTTP handler—in the *<httpHandlers>* section of the web.config file. We simply add an entry to *<httpHandlers>* for whatever filenames we want to handle. If we want to route all requests to Web services for a given application, we can use **.asmx* as the filename; if we want to route only a given request and allow all other requests to be handled by the default handler, we can specify a real filename for the handler, such as RouterA.asmx.

Also, nothing can stop us from specifying a completely new extension for the routers we want to use. We could allow all **.rp* requests, for instance, to be handled by *RouterHandler*. We covered HTTP handlers in more detail in Chapter 5, so if you want a lot more detail, have a look there.

For this first example, we have one router in place, at *http://localhost/wscr/14/RouterA.asmx*, that forwards any requests that it receives to the TellMe Web service, as shown in Figure 14-2.

Figure 14-2 Basic server-controlled routing scenario

If you look at the sample code for this chapter, you'll see that it does not include a RouterA.asmx file. (It does include a RouterA.wsdl file, but we'll come to that shortly.) All WSE routers are defined in web.config—they don't have a physical .asmx file. We configure the server to allow routing for the RouterA.asmx address by adding an HTTP handler for that address to web.config, as follows:

```
<!-- the TYPE attribute must be on one line  -->
<add verb="*" path="RouterA.asmx"
  type="Microsoft.Web.Services.Routing.RoutingHandler,→
  Microsoft.Web.Services, Version=1.0.0.0,→
  Culture=neutral, PublicKeyToken=31bf3856ad364e35" />
```

Once we add the router, we must also specify the details about where we want the request routed. We do this by creating a referral cache document that contains the details of where we want the message routed, specified as described in the WS-Referral specification. As you saw when we looked at WS-Referral in Chapter 12, to forward a request we simply use the *<r:exact>* element to specify what URL we're routing and a *<r:via>* element to specify where we want to route to:

```
<?xml version="1.0" ?>
<r:referrals xmlns:r="http://schemas.xmlsoap.org/ws/2001/10/referral">
  <r:ref>
    <r:for>
      <r:exact>
        http://localhost/wscr/14/RouterA.asmx
      </r:exact>
    </r:for>
    <r:if/>
    <r:go>
      <r:via>
```

```
        http://localhost/wscr/14/TellMe.asmx
      </r:via>
    </r:go>
    <r:refId>uuid:fa469956-0057-4e77-962a-81c5e292f2aa</r:refId>
  </r:ref>
</r:referrals>
```

We now need to tell the *RoutingHandler* that a referral cache is being used. As with all WSE configuration items, this is done in the *<microsoft.web.services>* element within web.config, as follows:

```
<referral>
  <cache name="referral.config" />
</referral>
```

The *name* attribute contains the filename of the file that contains the referral cache and is placed in the root of the application directory structure.

> **Note** When you use referral cache files, you must give the ASP.NET account write access to the file you're using—if you don't, the routing request to the server will return an *UnauthorizedAccessException*. Once the ASP.NET process opens this file, you cannot change its contents. If you're in a live environment, you obviously can't turn off the server to modify the file, and you need to change the file in place. To do this, you must create a new referral cache file on the server and then change the settings in web.config to point at this new file. Any new requests will immediately use the new referral cache file, and once all the existing requests have been processed, you can delete the old referral cache file.

We've now configured RouterA.asmx to forward all incoming requests to the real Web service at TellMe.asmx. However, one thing is still missing from a client perspective. We have no way of adding a reference to the Web service to our project because the router doesn't have an automatically generated WSDL document—the RouterA.wsdl file that we mentioned earlier now comes into play.

WSDL for the Router

As we mentioned earlier, a router doesn't have a real endpoint, so it is impossible to automatically generate a WSDL description of it. As we access the WSDL for the service across HTTP, we cannot automatically retrieve it because the router cannot route HTTP requests to retrieve the WSDL for the ultimate destination. If we try to retrieve the WSDL for the Web service in Microsoft Internet Explorer, we get an exception of type *NotSupportedException*, as shown in Figure 14-3.

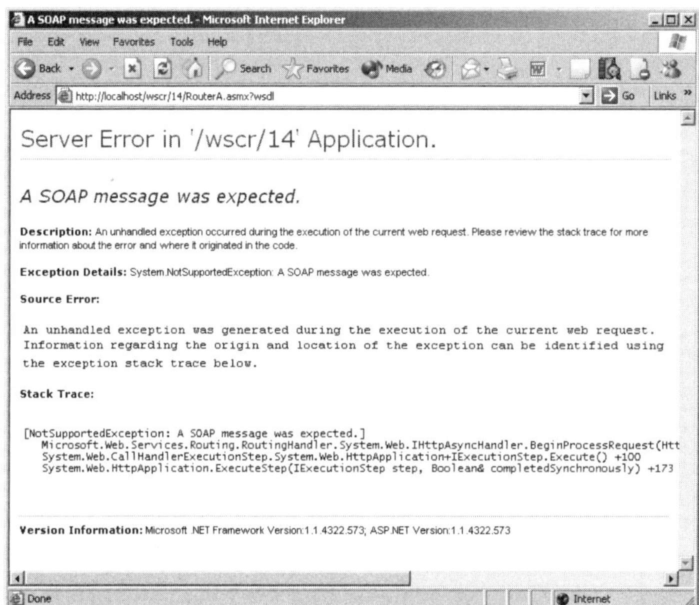

Figure 14-3 We can't view WSDL for a router.

We must therefore manually provide a WSDL document for the RouterA.asmx Web service that's based on TellMe.asmx, the real service we're routing to. We can do this quite easily by viewing the WSDL for TellMe.asmx, saving it, and changing the reference to TellMe to RouterA. This effort involves a simple Find and Replace within the WSDL document that we've saved. The Replace will change names and references in the *<portType>*, *<binding>*, *<service>*, and *<port>* elements in the WSDL as well as the *location* attribute of the *<soap:address>* element:

```
<soap:address
  location="http://localhost/wscr/14/RouterA.asmx" />
```

We could get away with changing only the *<soap:address>* element, but changing all references to the original Web service provides a further separation between the router and the service that will actually process the message.

We can use this modified WSDL file for the Web service instead of any automatically generated WSDL. For RouterA.asmx, this is the WSDL file that we mentioned earlier at *http://localhost/wscr/14/RouterA.wsdl*; we can use this to create the reference to the router.

> **Note** When you use static WSDL files, remember that the *<soap:address>* element must be manually changed to match the server that the Web service resides on. This is no longer changed automatically for you when you move between servers.

The Client

As far as the client is concerned, we're simply accessing a normal Web service. The whole point of routing in this manner is that the client is unaware that the request has been forwarded to another location for processing. We're not concerned with where the request is executed—only whether the request is executed correctly.

We can add a reference to *http://localhost/wscr/14/RouterA.wsdl* to the project, and the code that we use to access the Web service will be no different from any code we've already written.

You can see this in the RoutingClient application that is among the code samples for this chapter. This client application, which looks more complex than it actually is, demonstrates all the routing options we'll look at. Each of the three types of routing that we'll look at has its own tab—for now, we're interested only in the first tab, Server, as shown in Figure 14-4.

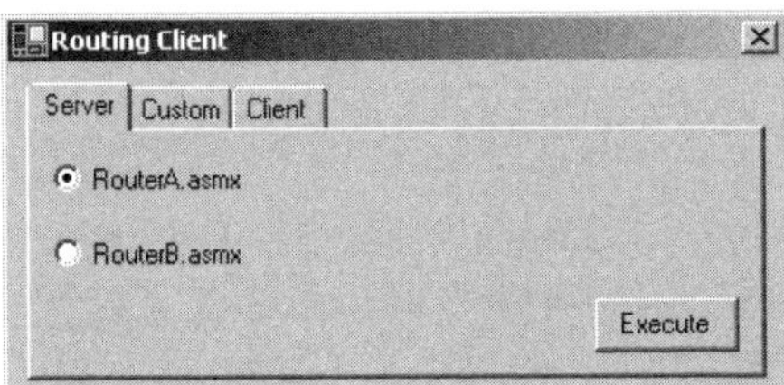

Figure 14-4 The RoutingClient application showing the server-controlled routing tab

As you can see, two option buttons allow you to specify which router you want to call. So far, we've looked at RouterA.asmx only, so for now you can ignore the RouterB.asmx option—we'll talk about it later. If we leave the RouterA.asmx option selected and click the Execute button, we'll call the RouterA.asmx service.

Within the event handler for the Execute button, we first check to see which option was selected and execute the correct block of code. As you can see in the following code, we then simply create an instance of the proxy class and call the *Echo* method. There is a little bit of error handling around the Web service call, but nothing that you haven't seen before.

```
if (radA.Checked == true)
{
    try
    {
        // create the proxy
        RouterAWse proxy = new RouterAWse();

        // call the proxy
        MessageBox.Show(proxy.Echo(), "Returned message");
    }
    catch (Exception error)
    {
        MessageBox.Show(error.Message, "Error!!");
    }
}
```

As you can see in Figure 14-5, if we run the above code we do indeed route to the location we specified in the referral cache.

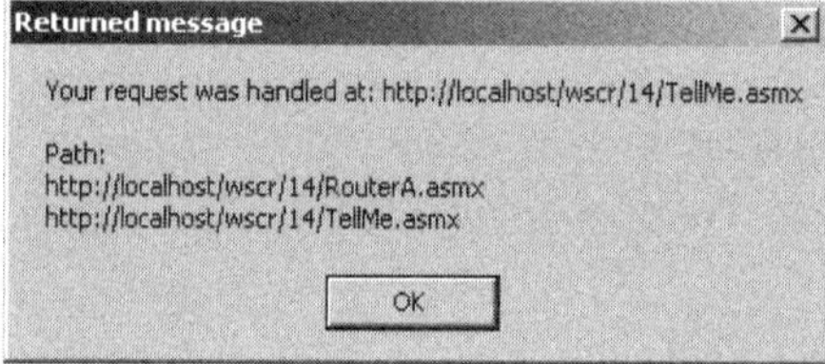

Figure 14-5 Return showing the path that was taken to TellMe.asmx

Although Figure 14-5 shows the client displaying routing details, it has a view of these only because we chose to return them to the client so we could show that the message was actually routed. In a real-life situation, we wouldn't pass these back to the client, and the message would appear to have been handled by the Web service that we called.

The SOAP Messages

The routing example we've been looking at so far takes the simplest possible form. However, changes are still made to the SOAP messages that are passed between the client and the Web service that ultimately handles the request.

When we send a message from the client, the Routing output filter adds a routing header that specifies the address we're actually sending the message to. As you'll recall from Chapter 12, these details are contained in the *<wsrp:to>* element of the *<wsrp:path>* element of the SOAP header:

```
<wsrp:to>http://localhost/wscr/14/routing/RouterA.asmx</wsrp:to>
```

After *RoutingHandler.ProcessRequest* calculates the correct outgoing path and the call is made to the next router, the Routing output filter populates the *<wsrp:path>* element with the correct details:

```
<wsrp:to>http://localhost/wscr/14/RouterA.asmx</wsrp:to>
<wsrp:fwd>
  <wsrp:via>
    http://localhost/wscr/14/TellMe.asmx
  </wsrp:via>
</wsrp:fwd>
```

Multiple Routers on the Same Server

Nothing prevents us from having several routers within the same application, all routing to different locations. However, if we have a chain of routers on the same machine, all controlled using the referral cache, the *RoutingHandler.ProcessRequestMessage* method will make some optimizations to the path that the message takes. Instead of travelling between the different routers, the message is simply passed directly to the final router in the chain.

This is not what we require, but it actually makes sense. Any routers referenced in the referral cache and handled by *RoutingHandler* have no other processing performed on them. Why would we pass a request through a series of routers that will do nothing but pass the message onto the next one in the chain?

You can see this in action if we use RouterB.asmx, which we sidestepped earlier. RouterB.asmx is configured in a chain with RouterC.asmx, which then calls TellMe.asmx, as shown in Figure 14-6.

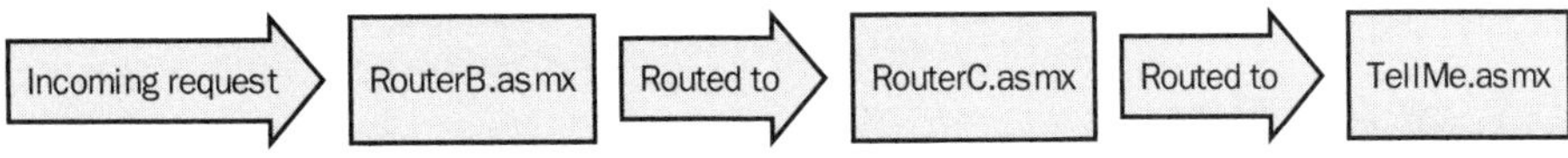

Figure 14-6 Server-controlled routing chain

On the server, we added handlers for the two routers to the web.config file, and we also added two new *<r:ref>* elements to the referral cache. If we hadn't, as soon as we tried to route through a router without an entry in the referral cache, we'd generate an exception of type *SoapHeaderException* because we'd have no routing details for the router we defined.

If we now run the *RoutingClient* application and select RouterB.asmx as the router, we can see that we don't actually go through RouterC.asmx—we go directly to BasicHandler.asmx. This is shown in Figure 14-7.

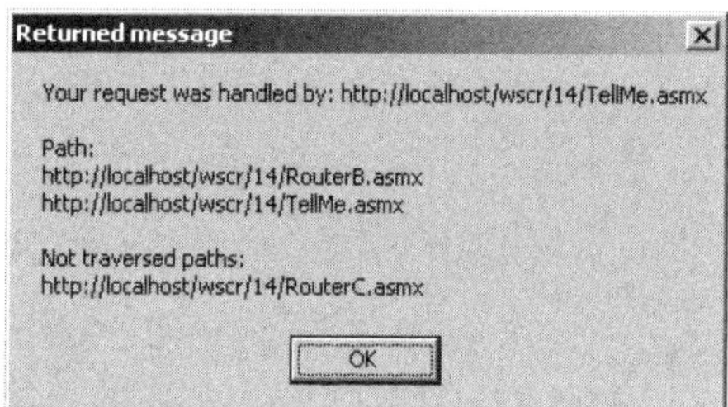

Figure 14-7 Routing chains on the same server are optimized.

Although *RoutingHandler* optimized the route we took, we haven't lost the actual route we should have taken from the *<wsrp:path>* header—if we were to lose it, we wouldn't be able to generate the list of paths that we missed in Figure 14-7. When the optimization takes place, the Routing input filter places the unused paths after the optimized path in the *<wsrp:fwd>* element, as you can see in this extract from the Trace filters on the server:

```
<wsrp:to>http://localhost/wscr/14/RouterB.asmx</wsrp:to>
<wsrp:fwd>
  <wsrp:via>
    http://localhost/wscr/14/TellMe.asmx
  </wsrp:via>
  <wsrp:via>
    http://localhost/wscr/14/RouterC.asmx
  </wsrp:via>
</wsrp:fwd>
```

We had only one missed path here—*RouterC.asmx*—but if we'd had more, they would also appear as elements in the *<wsrp:fwd>* element.

Custom Routing

In the previous section, we looked at server-controlled routing using the *RoutingHandler* HTTP handler. Another server-controlled routing option we can consider is routing the message based on the content of the message or some external factor.

We can easily accomplish this by deriving a new class from *RoutingHandler* and using this as the handler for the Web services we want to route.

By deriving from *RoutingHandler*, we gain the basic routing functionality that *RoutingHandler* provides. *ProcessRequestMessage* is called by *ProcessRequest* and we override the *ProcessRequestMessage* method to perform our custom routing; whatever *Path* details we specify will be used by the *ProcessRequest* method and the message will be routed to the correct destination.

For this example, we'll use a custom router that will route the incoming message to a different Web service, depending on the time of the day. We might use this sort of routing in a stock-trading scenario—depending on the time of day, we'd route to Tokyo, London, or New York.

Building the Custom Router

To build a custom router, we simply create a new class and set it to inherit from *RoutingHandler*—nothing more to it:

```
public class CustomRouter : Microsoft.Web.Services.Routing.RoutingHandler
{
    ⋮
}
```

We now have a custom router with all the functionality of *RoutingHandler*. We haven't overridden the *ProcessRequestMessage* and *ProcessResponseMessage* methods, so the custom router will have exactly the same functionality as the standard *RoutingHandler* class.

We'll look at what to do within our custom router in a moment. For now, we can leave it performing the same function as *RoutingHandler*. We'll first look at how to configure the server to use the custom router.

We inherited from a class that implements *IHttpHandler*, so we can simply use this derived class as the HTTP handler for whichever routers we require. In this case, we'll implement RouterD.asmx, which will use the code in our *CustomRouter* class:

```
<add path="RouterD.asmx" verb="*" type="_14.CustomRouter, 14" />
```

We've simply specified the type of the class in the normal manner; whenever a request is made to RouterD.asmx, an instance of our *CustomRouter* class is instantiated and the *ProcessRequest* method is called.

That's it! Our custom router is now configured to run on the server. If you try to connect to it, however, you'll get a *SoapHeaderException* message because the router doesn't have an entry in the referral cache—nor does it have routing details specified in the incoming message. We've built a custom router but we're still using the default routing provided by *RoutingHandler*.

As we pointed out earlier, we'll route the request from *http://localhost/wscr/14/RouterD.asmx* to a different Web service depending on the Coordinated Universal Time (UTC) time of day. Whichever Web service we route to will return its URL as well as the route that the request took to its destination. This is exactly the same as what we return from the TellMe.asmx service, which we looked at earlier.

Between midnight and 8 A.M. we'll route to Tokyo.asmx, between 8 A.M. and 4 P.M. we'll route to London.asmx, and between 4 P.M. and midnight we'll route to NewYork.asmx. This scenario is shown in Figure 14-8.

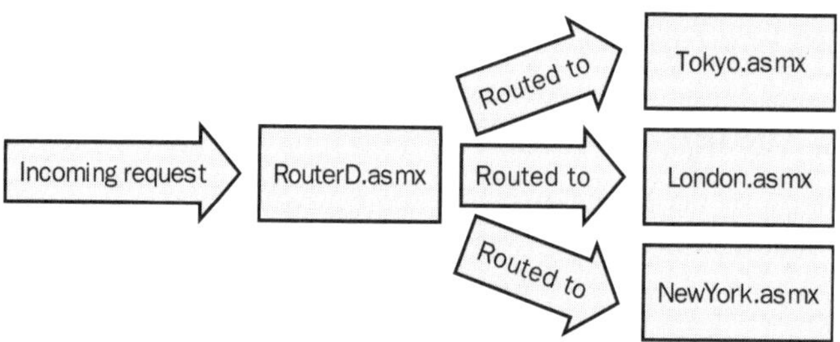

Figure 14-8 The custom routing scenario

The code to actually do the routing is really quite simple. In our example here, we're not actually using the content of the incoming request to determine the route—we're relying on the time of day to determine the route. We do, however, have access to the *SoapEnvelope* object for the incoming request, and we can interrogate this to determine the route, if required.

The code for the overridden *ProcessRequestMessage* is shown here:

```
protected override void ProcessRequestMessage(SoapEnvelope message,
    Path outgoingPath)
{
    Via destinationService;

    // get the time of day
    DateTime dateNow = DateTime.Now;

    // set the destination correctly
    if(dateNow.Hour >=0 && dateNow.Hour <8)
    {
        destinationService = new Via(TokyoUri);
    }
    else if(dateNow.Hour >=8 && dateNow.Hour <16)
    {
        destinationService = new Via(LondonUri);
    }
```

```
    else
    {
        destinationService = new Via(NewYorkUri);
    }

    // now go to the route we've specified
    outgoingPath.Fwd.Insert(0, destinationService);
}
```

This code is pretty standard. We have a series of conditions that check the time and set the *destinationService* object to the correct URL. To produce more maintainable code, we extract the URLs of the three Web services from web.config in the constructor for the class and store them as *TokyoUri*, *LondonUri*, and *NewYorkUri*.

Once we have a *Via* object that contains the details of the Web service that we're routing to, we can add this as the first element in the forward path.

That's how easy it is. After returning from *ProcessRequestMessage*, the first entry in the forward path is used and the message is routed to the correct destination.

Creating the Web Services

In our custom routing scenarios, we'll route to the Tokyo.asmx, London.asmx, and NewYork.asmx Web services. These must obviously share the same interface—otherwise, we couldn't route to them; they can have extra methods on them, but there wouldn't be much point to adding any because we can route only to methods that are common across all the Web services we're going to route to. In this case, they all have an *Echo* method that returns the URL of the executing Web service as well as the route that the message took to that service.

We could cut and paste the code for one Web service into another Web service relatively easily, but we could run into problems doing this. It's easy to mess up code when you cut and paste. As you saw in Chapter 4, .NET provides a solution to this problem—we can use the wsdl.exe command-line tool to generate a base class for all of the Web services we're using.

We can use the first Web service that's created as the basis for the abstract class. With a little name changing in the code, we have a base class, *BaseService*, that we can use as the basis for all three of the destination Web services—even the Web service that we used to generate the abstract base class. We simply use this class as the base class for our three Web services and override the *Echo* method with the correct version for the Web service.

WSDL for the Router

Generating the WSDL for a custom router is identical to creating the WSDL for a standard router. We save the WSDL for one of the destination Web services and modify it to match the details of the router we want to use.

The Client

The client that we're implementing is the second tab of the RoutingClient application, the Custom tab, as shown in Figure 14-9. We have only the Execute button on the tab because all the routing work occurs on the server.

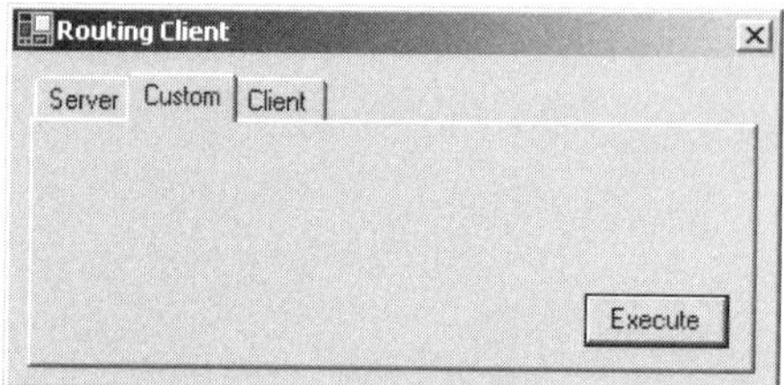

Figure 14-9 The RoutingClient application showing the Custom tab

The code for calling the Web service is no different from what you saw earlier in this chapter and in previous chapters. We simply create an instance of the proxy for the router and call the *Echo* method. The Web service we call tells us its URL as well as the route the message took to the server, as shown in Figure 14-10.

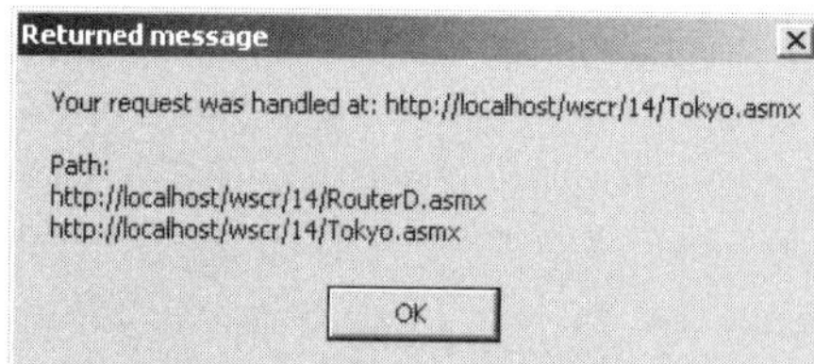

Figure 14-10 Returned message from Tokyo.asmx showing the path taken to the Web service

Nothing to it—all the work is done on the server!

The SOAP Messages

For custom routing, we follow the same paradigm we used for server-controlled routing in that the outgoing *Path* object is populated with the destination we want to route the message to.

When we make the call to the router, the SOAP message has only the *<wsrp:to>* element populated with the address of the Web service that we're calling:

```
<wsrp:to>http://localhost/wscr/14/RouterD.asmx</wsrp:to>
```

After we determine the correct outgoing path and the call has been made to the destination Web service, the Routing output filter populates the *<wsrp:path>* element. For the routing to Tokyo.asmx that we looked at earlier, the SOAP routing header would be populated as follows:

```
<wsrp:to>http://localhost/wscr/14/RouterD.asmx</wsrp:to>
<wsrp:fwd>
  <wsrp:via>
    http://localhost/wscr/14/Tokyo.asmx
  </wsrp:via>
</wsrp:fwd>
```

Client-Controlled Routing

In the two examples we've looked at so far, the server has controlled how the message is routed and the client is unaware that the message has been routed. There is also a third form of routing available: client-controlled routing. Client-controlled routing allows the client to specify the Web service it wants to call and to specify the route that the message takes to the destination Web service.

The Web Service

The Web service we'll use for this example is the same Web service we used for the server-controlled routing; it can be found at *http://localhost/wscr/14/TellMe.asmx*. It's the route to this Web service that we're interested in—not what the service does—so we can reuse the existing service without any problems.

Server Configuration

Configuration of a client-controlled router is similar to the configuration of a server-controlled router. We must add an HTTP handler to the web.config file for each router that we want to have available. In this example, we'll make three routers available—RouterE.asmx, RouterF.asmx, and RouterG.asmx—and we'll add three entries to the web.config file:

```
<!-- the TYPE attribute must be on one line  -->
<add verb="*" path="RouterE.asmx"
  type="Microsoft.Web.Services.Routing.RoutingHandler,→
  Microsoft.Web.Services, Version=1.0.0.0,→
  Culture=neutral, PublicKeyToken=31bf3856ad364e35" />
<add verb="*" path="RouterF.asmx"
  type="Microsoft.Web.Services.Routing.RoutingHandler,→
  Microsoft.Web.Services, Version=1.0.0.0,→
  Culture=neutral, PublicKeyToken=31bf3856ad364e35" />
<add verb="*" path="RouterG.asmx"
  type="Microsoft.Web.Services.Routing.RoutingHandler,→
  Microsoft.Web.Services, Version=1.0.0.0,→
  Culture=neutral, PublicKeyToken=31bf3856ad364e35" />
```

In a difference from server-controlled routing, however, we don't need to create entries in the referral cache. All of the routing details are contained in the incoming message, and the server has no knowledge of where an incoming message is to be routed next.

WSDL for the Routers

When we use client-controlled routing, we don't have to provide any WSDL for the routers we're using. The client application we're using creates a reference only to the Web service that is the final destination of the message and, as you'll see, it simply adds the routers that it wants to use to the forward path collection of the request's *SoapContext* object.

The Client

The client application is where all of the work to use the routers actually takes place, and it is here that the message's route to its final destination is configured. Within the RoutingClient application, we need to click on the Client tab, as shown in Figure 14-11.

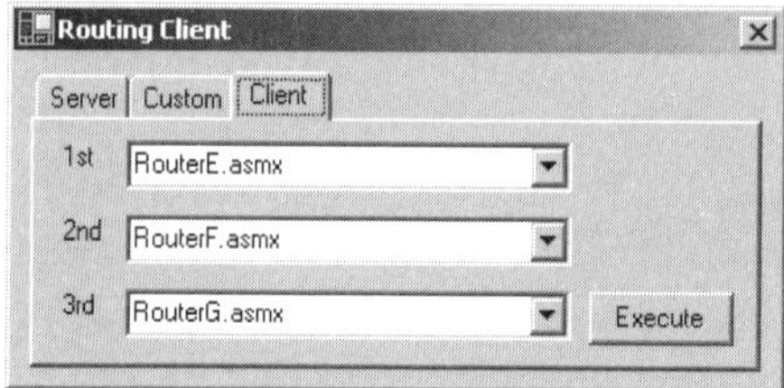

Figure 14-11 The RoutingClient application showing the client-controlled routing tab

As you can see in Figure 14-11, we can specify the three routes that we want the message to take to reach the destination Web service. In each of the combo boxes, we have the choice of RouterE.asmx, RouterF.asmx, or RouterG.asmx for that stage in the route. If we want, we can even send the message through the same router three times.

Clicking the Execute button runs the click event handler code for the button; it is here that we add the routing details.

We first create an instance of the proxy class for the Web service just as we would for any other proxy class. We then have to add the routing details to the message.

As you saw when we looked at the *Path* object, the forward path is contained in the *Fwd* property. This is a collection of *Via* objects, and we add a new *Via* object to the *Path* for each router that we want to add to the route. The *Via* object constructor requires a *Uri* object, so we create one of these inline, passing in the URL that we want to route the request through:

```
// add the route to the message
proxy.RequestSoapContext.Path.Fwd.Add(new Via(new
    Uri("http://localhost/wscr/14/" + cboFirst.Text)));
proxy.RequestSoapContext.Path.Fwd.Add(new Via(new
    Uri("http://localhost/wscr/14/" + cboSecond.Text)));
proxy.RequestSoapContext.Path.Fwd.Add(new Via(new
    Uri("http://localhost/wscr/14/" + cboThird.Text)));
```

To track the path that the message takes to its final destination, we must add a *<wsrp:rev>* element to the routing header. As we pointed out earlier, the HTTP protocol already has an intrinsic reverse path; a reverse path is not added to the routing header by default. We can override this by forcing a reverse path to be added to the routing header, and once the routers see this element in the header, they will populate it correctly.

We can't simply add an empty *Via* object to the *Rev* collection of the *Path* object because the *ViaCollection* that the *Rev* property exposes is not defined. We must create a new *ViaCollection* and set the *Rev* property.

```
// add a <wsrp:rev> element so that we can track the path
proxy.RequestSoapContext.Path.Rev = new ViaCollection();
```

We can then make the request to the proxy in the normal manner, by calling the *Echo* method.

If we leave the default routing options selected and call the destination Web service, the message will be routed to TellMe.asmx. If you look at Figure 14-12, you'll see that the message passes through RouterE.asmx, RouterF.asmx, and RouterG.asmx before it reaches its final destination.

Figure 14-12 Returned message showing the path that was taken to TellMe.asmx

The SOAP Messages

The routing header generated by the Routing output filter is similar to the routing headers we looked at when we discussed server-controlled and custom routing.

The client adds the route that the message takes to its final destination, so all of the details are present in the message that leaves the client. The *<wsrp:to>* element contains the final destination of the request, and the *<wsrp:fwd>* element contains a series of *<wsrp:via>* elements that contain the route that the message is to take. We also have an empty *<wsrp:rev>* element that will be populated as we pass through the routers. You can see this if you look at the message received by RouterE.asmx:

```
<wsrp:to>http://localhost/wscr/14/TellMe.asmx</wsrp:to>
<wsrp:fwd>
  <wsrp:via>http://localhost/wscr/14/RouterE.asmx</wsrp:via>
  <wsrp:via>http://localhost/wscr/14/RouterF.asmx</wsrp:via>
  <wsrp:via>http://localhost/wscr/14/RouterG.asmx</wsrp:via>
</wsrp:fwd>
<wsrp:rev />
```

RouterE.asmx forwards the message to RouterF.asmx and removes itself from the forward path. We have a *<wsrp:rev>* element, so it will add itself to the reverse path of the message. You can see this in the message received by RouterF.asmx:

```
<wsrp:to>http://localhost/wscr/14/TellMe.asmx</wsrp:to>
<wsrp:fwd>
  <wsrp:via>http://localhost/wscr/14/RouterF.asmx</wsrp:via>
  <wsrp:via>http://localhost/wscr/14/RouterG.asmx</wsrp:via>
</wsrp:fwd>
<wsrp:rev>
  <wsrp:via>http://localhost/wscr/14/RouterE.asmx</wsrp:via>
</wsrp:rev>
```

RouterF.asmx and RouterG.asmx perform the same task of moving themselves from the forward path to the reverse path and sending the message to the next router. RouterG.asmx forwards the message to the final destination service, which is contained in the *<wsrp:to>* element, because there are no more entries in the forward path, as you can see if you look at the routing header received by TellMe.asmx:

```
<wsrp:to>http://localhost/wscr/14/TellMe.asmx</wsrp:to>
<wsrp:rev>
  <wsrp:via>http://localhost/wscr/14/RouterG.asmx</wsrp:via>
  <wsrp:via>http://localhost/wscr/14/RouterF.asmx</wsrp:via>
  <wsrp:via>http://localhost/wscr/14/RouterE.asmx</wsrp:via>
</wsrp:rev>
```

Working Routers

The routers we've looked at so far have all met the standard definition of a router—receive a request and forward it on to a new destination. However, we introduced a little variety into this paradigm when we looked at custom routers—rather than simply routing the message to a predetermined location, we performed some processing to determine the route.

We still haven't covered every possible scenario. When we looked at client-controlled routing, you saw that this approach would be pointless unless the routers actually did some work. Otherwise, we could just jump directly to the ultimate destination.

What we need is a new type of router, a "working router," that performs a real processing task and uses routing information that is specified elsewhere—either in the referral cache or in the routing header in the incoming message.

To create a working router, we follow the same process as for a custom router—we derive a new router from *RoutingHandler* and override the *ProcessRequestMessage* method. The difference between a custom router and a working router is that in a working router we don't specify any routing details within the overridden *ProcessRequestMessage* method.

If we're using client-controlled routing and we want to have a working router, we can simply create a derived class that specifies no routing details because all of the information to route the message is already contained with the *Path* object that *ProcessRequestMessage* receives. The basic approach is as follows:

```
public class WorkingRouter : Microsoft.Web.Services.Routing.RoutingHandler
{
```

```
    protected override void ProcessRequestMessage(SoapEnvelope message,
        Path outgoingPath)
    {
        // do some work here
    }
}
```

For server-controlled routing, the process isn't as simple as with client-controlled routing because the referral details are manipulated by the *ProcessRequestMessage* method that we've overridden. Within our overridden class, we need to call the *ProcessRequestMessage* on the base class to determine the route from the referral cache:

```
public class WorkingRouter : Microsoft.Web.Services.Routing.RoutingHandler
{
    protected override void ProcessRequestMessage(SoapEnvelope message,
        Path outgoingPath)
    {
        // do some work here
        // get the routing information from the referral cache
        base.ProcessRequestMessage(message, outgoingPath);
    }
}
```

If we're not sure whether the router will exist in a server-controlled or a client-controlled situation, we must use the server-controlled version of the working router. As you'll recall, if we have routing details already specified, any details we specify in a referral cache are ignored.

Routing and Timestamps

When we looked at timestamps in the previous chapter, we mentioned that routing also affects the timestamps that are generated. When we route requests to Web services using any of the routing methods discussed in this chapter, we also record the timestamp details for the router in a *<wsu:received>* element in the timestamp header.

Thankfully, the Timestamp filters handle this automatically; whenever we pass through a router, a *Received* element is added to the timestamp header containing the time the message was received as well as how long the message was delayed by the router.

If we turn on the Timestamp filters for our Web services, every router that is passed through on the way to the final destination will have a *<wsu:Received>* element added to the timestamp header. As an example, the following is the timestamp header that is received at TellMe.asmx when we pass the message through RouterA.asmx:

```
<wsu:Timestamp xmlns:wsu="http://schemas.xmlsoap.org/ws/2002/07/utility">
  <wsu:Created>2003-02-26T22:01:58Z</wsu:Created>
  <wsu:Expires>2003-02-26T22:06:58Z</wsu:Expires>
  <wsu:Received
    Actor="http://localhost/wscr/14/RouterA.asmx"
    Delay="30234">
    2003-02-26T22:02:08Z
  </wsu:Received>
</wsu:Timestamp>
```

Summary

In this chapter, we looked at the facilities available in WSE from the WS-Routing and WS-Referral specifications. We looked at allowing the server or the client to determine the path that a message takes to its final destination by using the referral cache on the server or routing details specified in the incoming message.

We also briefly discussed how to create routers on the server that can determine the destination of a request based on either the content of the incoming message or some external factor. In our example, we routed the message based on the time of day, but you're not really limited in how you can route messages.

We also discussed creating routers that, in addition to using the details specified in the referral cache or in the incoming message, perform their own tasks before allowing the message to be routed to its final destination.

15

Web Service Security

In the last two chapters, we looked in depth at WSE but purposely left the coverage of WSE and security until this chapter. You learned the general principles of security for Web services in Chapter 11, and now we'll look at what WSE brings to the party.

At this point in the evolution of Web services, we are likely to use only one transport protocol—SOAP over HTTP. HTTP can also have a measure of security applied to it at the transport layer, HTTPS, and we can use this underneath SOAP to provide some level of protection for Web service calls.

However, as we've mentioned, the various Web service specifications are written from a protocol-agnostic point of view, and not all of these other protocols have "intrinsic security." If you were to use SMTP, FTP, or Microsoft Message Queuing (MSMQ) as the transport protocol for your messages, you would lose the SSL security that HTTPS provides. The WS-Security specification addresses this shortcoming by allowing you to apply security requirements to messages you're transmitting irrespective of the protocol used.

Before we look at any code, however, let's look at our security requirements.

Security Requirements

As mentioned in Chapter 12, you have basically three requirements for securing the messages that pass between Web services. We looked at the changes that the WS-Security specification makes to the SOAP messages to enforce these requirements. We'll quickly recap the requirements here before looking at the implementation of the WS-Security specification.

- **Authenticity** You must be able to authenticate the sender of the message to confirm that person's identity. You can do this by attaching your security credentials to the message you're sending. However, without an intrinsic security mechanism in the transport protocol, authentication by itself is not enough—a hacker can intercept the message, modify the content of that message, and send it on to the intended recipient. The recipient will be unaware that any changes have been made to the message, which will appear authentic. Without a security mechanism in the transport protocol, you have no message security.
- **Integrity** You must be able to ensure that a message has not been altered on its way to the recipient. You can do this by signing the message with the security credentials of the sender. Any changes to the message en route to the recipient will invalidate the signature of the message, and the message will be rejected. If a message is received with a signature intact, you can assume that message integrity has been maintained and that the signer of the message was the sender. As a consequence or proving that the integrity of the message hasn't been compromised, we've also authenticated the sender of the message.
- **Confidentiality** Beyond ensuring message integrity and confirming the identity of the sender, you can also encrypt a message to keep its contents confidential. You do this using the security credentials of the recipient. If you're using a transport protocol such as HTTPS, which is encrypted automatically, you don't have to worry about the confidentiality of the message because this is handled by the transport protocol.

We'll look at each of these requirements in turn, as they relate to the security credentials that WSE allows you to use.

Username and Password Security

If you've used the Internet at all, you've almost certainly registered with a Web site and entered a username and password to access various parts of that site. Such Web sites can range from e-commerce applications that require signing in before a purchase can be completed to Web sites that restrict access to certain areas of content. WSE allows you to use usernames and passwords as security credentials, but this approach is not very secure. To verify that the credentials are correct, you must pass both the username and the password with the message, but a hacker still has ample opportunity to intercept the message and modify it.

Granted, you can use password digests instead of a normal password, which improves security slightly, but the relationship between a password and its digest is relatively simple—especially compared to the relationship between the public and private parts of an X509 certificate, which we'll look at shortly.

Of course, it is completely insecure to use username and password security credentials across a transport protocol that isn't secure. If you must use username and password credentials, you must also use a secure transport protocol such as HTTPS—the messages between the client and the Web service will be encrypted automatically by the runtime, which means that a hacker cannot interpret the intercepted messages and the need for signing and manually encrypting messages is removed.

X509 Certificate Security

As we've pointed out, sending username and password security credentials across a nonsecure transport protocol is completely insecure. And as bindings for more transport protocols are released, the probability that you'll want to use a transport protocol without an intrinsic security mechanism will increase. Therefore, you're likely to want a more secure security-credential mechanism that will be consistent across a wide variety of transport protocols. WSE supports the use of X509 certificates for this purpose.

X509 certificates are managed by a third-party issuer, such as VeriSign, and are granted only to people and organizations that have passed strict security checks. In what is known as a *trust chain*, you can trust any X509 certificates that an issuer has granted if you trust that issuer.

> **Note** X509 certificates combine a public key and a private key that together allow you to sign and encrypt messages that you want to send. You make the public key available to anyone who wants it and keep the private key secret. The relationship between the public and private keys is such that you can use the public key to decrypt something encrypted with the private key, and you can use the private key to decrypt something encrypted with the public key. Although there is a relationship between the two keys, it is impossible to deduce the private key from the public key in a reasonable amount of time, so you can be assured of the security of the system.

In a difference from username and password credentials, you can use X509 certificates to fulfill all three of the security requirements we've discussed. However, due to the nature of X509 certificates, you cannot guarantee any level of security if you use the certificate for authentication. With X509 certificates, the only part of the certificate you can make available is the public key, and this is used as the security credential for authentication. However, the public key is, well, public—and anyone can use it and attempt to spoof your identity. Even when you use a secure transport protocol, this problem still exists. So if you want to use X509 certificates as the security credentials for your Web services, you must ensure that the messages are signed before they are transmitted to the Web service. You can then be sure that the message has not been altered and also confirm the authenticity of the message.

When a sender signs a message, the sender generates a hash of the message, uses his private key to encrypt the hash, and attaches the encrypted hash to the message. Upon receiving a signed message, the recipient generates the hash for the message, decrypts the sender's hash using the sender's public key, and compares the two hashes. If the two hash values are different, the message has been altered.

Using X509 certificates to encrypt a message also uses the relationship between the pubic and private keys to ensure the security of the message. The sender encrypts the message using the recipient's public key and sends the encrypted message. Only the recipient possesses the corresponding private key that can be used to decrypt the message.

Generating Test X509 Certificates

Before you can go live with a Web service that uses X509 certificates, you must obviously have a certificate from a trusted source. But for testing purposes, you can create test certificates that don't have a trust chain that is validated to a trusted source. In all other respects, the test certificates you generate are identical to real certificates.

To generate a test certificate, you can use the makecert tool provided in the current release of the Microsoft .NET SDK. Using this tool, you can create certificates and add them to the correct certificate store. Each user has a separate certificate store, referred to as the Current User store, that is available only to that user; there is also a certificate store, the Local Computer store, that is available to all users of the machine. When you use WSE, it is assumed that the certificates are in the Local Computer certificate store, but as you'll see shortly, it is possible for WSE to be configured to access the Current User certificate store instead.

> **Note** The makecert tool provided in the current release of the .NET SDK does not correctly create certificates that are added to the Local Computer certificate store. Although the certificate will appear in the Local Computer certificate store, the private key of the certificate will be added to the Current User certificate store for the user that ran the makecert tool. Therefore, the private key won't be available to anyone other than the user who created the certificate. To create valid test certificates, you must obtain the fully functional version of the tool from the Platform SDK. You can download this by navigating to *http://www.microsoft.com/msdownload/platformsdk/sdkupdate/update.htm* and downloading the Build Environment from the Core SDK.

Using the makecert tool is relatively easy, except for a couple of gotchas that you should be aware of. First, when you use test certificates, you must tell the security filters that you're allowing test certificates to be used. If you don't do this, the certificates will be invalid because they don't have a trust chain back to a trusted source. You inform the security filters by adding an entry to the configuration file for the application:

```
<microsoft.web.services>
  <security>
    <x509 allowTestRoot="true" />
  </security>
</microsoft.web.services>
```

Second, when you create a test certificate, you must specify the *-sky "exchange"* and *–sk "unique name"* parameters. The *–sk* parameter value must be unique for the machine on which the certificate is used. When you purchase a certificate this occurs automatically, but when you're testing it is easy to create a certificate that doesn't have a unique value.

To create a certificate, you simply specify which store you want the certificate to be created in, by using the *–sr* option, and what part of the store you want the certificate to be created in, by using the *–ss* option. You specify the name of the certificate, according to the X500 standard, by using the *–n* option.

Client Configuration

Let's create a certificate for the current user, Joe Bloggs:

```
makecert -sky "exchange" -sk "joebloggs" -sr CurrentUser -ss My→
    -n "CN=Joe Bloggs"
```

This creates the key in the Personal folder of the Current User certificate store. The name option simply specifies the common name of the user; this is extracted and used as the *Issued To* parameter when you look at the certificate.

Many more options are available in the makecert tool, but for our purposes we don't need to consider them. You can refer to the documentation for a full list.

You can view the certificates that the current user has installed in two ways: through Internet Explorer or through the Certificates snap-in to the Microsoft Management Console (MMC). In Internet Explorer, you view the certificates via the Content tab of the Internet Options dialog box. Clicking the Certificates button opens the Certificates dialog box, which lists the certificates installed, as shown in Figure 15-1.

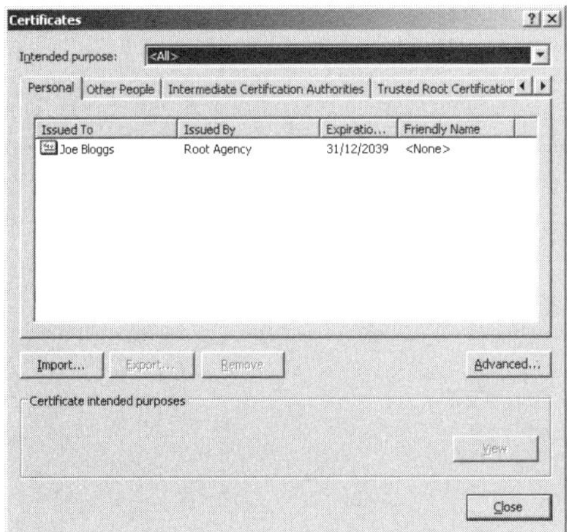

Figure 15-1 Viewing certificates for the current user

Although we've installed the certificate and can use it for signing, it still cannot be used to decrypt messages that we receive. WSE assumes that the X509 certificates it will use are in the Local Computer store, whereas a user's X509 certificate will be in the Current User certificate store. You must configure client applications to look in the Current User store and not the Local Computer store. We can do this in the configuration file for the client application by using the *storeLocation* attribute of the *<x509>* element within the *<security>* section:

```
<microsoft.web.services>
  <security>
    <x509 allowTestRoot="true" storeLocation="CurrentUser" />
  </security>
</microsoft.web.services>
```

This configuration forces WSE to look for certificates in the Current User store and also allows test certificates.

Server Configuration

Creating certificates for the server is no more difficult than creating a certificate for the client. We can use the same command that we used when we created a client certificate, but we'll specify the Local Computer store rather than the Current User store:

```
makecert -sky "exchange" -sk "notashop.com" -sr LocalMachine -ss My
    -n "CN=NotAShop.com"
```

Before we can use this certificate, we must also give the ASP.NET process permission to read the certificate from disk. But finding the certificate that we want to allow the ASP.NET process to use is not as easy as it could be.

All of the certificates for the Local Machine are stored in the C:\Documents and Settings\All Users\Application Data\Microsoft\Crypto\RSA\Machine Keys directory, and we must find the one that we've just created. However, the filenames in this directory are GUIDs and have no relationship to the real name of the certificate. We're left to determine which is the correct certificate by looking at the creation date for the files. We then have to give the ASP.NET account full control of the file in question.

You can view the certificates that are installed for the local machine by using the Certificates MMC snap-in. Add the snap-in, and select Computer Account when you're prompted for the account for which to manage certificates. Figure 15-2 shows the MMC displaying the NotAShop.com certificate in the Local Computer certificate store.

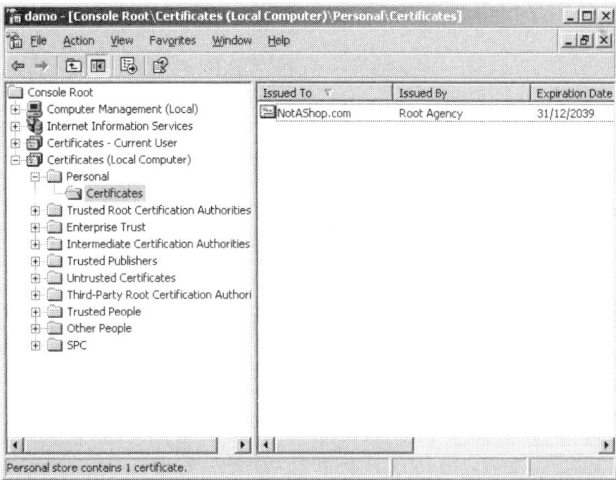

Figure 15-2 Viewing certificates in the Local Computer certificate store

We can now sign and decrypt using this certificate without any further configuration changes. However, we must make the public key of the certificate available to users so they can use it to encrypt messages to send to the server. You can do this from the Certificates MMC snap-in by choosing Export from the All Tasks shortcut menu for that certificate. This launches the Certificate Export Wizard, which allows you to export the certificate, and you can then make this available for users to download and install on their machines. But be careful: if you have the option to export the private key, select No!

Importing X509 Certificates

The easiest way to import a certificate is to right-click on the certificate file in Windows Explorer and choose Install Certificate from the shortcut menu. This starts the Certificate Import Wizard, which allows you to add the certificate to the Current User certificate store. You can allow the wizard to determine which folder to place the certificate in, or you can select the folder yourself.

You can also import certificates through the Certificates MMC snap-in; if we want to import certificates into the Local Computer certificate store, you have to take this route. If you right-click on a folder in the Current User certificate store or the Local Computer certificate store and then from the shortcut menu choose All Tasks and then Import, the Certificate Import Wizard will launch. You select the certificate you want to import, and then you can let the wizard determine the best folder for the certificate or you can select the folder yourself.

Getting Real X509 Certificates

So far, we've looked only at using test certificates at the client and the server. As a user of a site that requires messages to be signed with an X509 certificate, you must purchase a personal certificate before a site will trust you. If you're responsible for Web services that require the use of an X509 certificate, you must also purchase a certificate for the server. We'll look at both of these options.

Personal Certificates

Personal certificates, commonly referred to as *digital IDs*, are available from a number of sources, but the most widely used digital IDs are supplied by VeriSign. The VeriSign digital ID homepage is at *http://www.verisign.com/products/class1/index.html*.

The process of purchasing a VeriSign digital ID is largely automated and simply requires that you fill in payment details as well as the details about the user to whom the certificate is to be issued. Completing the purchasing process automatically installs the certificate in the Personal folder of the Current User certificate store.

Server Certificates

Although you can purchase a personal certificate and use it at the server, it makes more sense to use certificates that are designed expressly for the purposes of securing communication with a server—SSL certificates. Chances are that if you're building Web services that are secure, you'll also have a Web site that requires secure communication; you can use the existing SSL certificate to implement security for your Web services.

SSL certificates are provided by several companies, and the process of purchasing and installing real SSL certificates is relatively straightforward. Most SSL certificates in use today are provided by VeriSign; full details of the purchase and installation process are available at *http://www.verisign.com/products/site/index.html.*

When an SSL certificate is installed on a server, the certificate is added to the Personal folder of the Local Computer store and the public key can be exported and made available for users of your Web services. The only thing you have to remember is to update the available public key whenever the SSL certificate is renewed.

Using Other Security Credentials

The WS-Security specification is open enough to allow you to use any form of security for securing messages that you send. The specification categorizes the credentials you supply as username and password credentials or binary credentials. As you've seen, the current release of WSE supports the use of username and password credentials as well as X509 certificates but it also allows you to use any security credentials you want.

We won't look at custom security credentials in any detail in this chapter because this is a topic for only the most advanced users. We'll briefly discuss how to define your own custom security credentials when we look at using shared secrets for encrypting messages, but for most purposes X509 certificates will meet all of your security needs, so we'll mainly focus on them.

The *SecurityToken* Class

The heart of the WSE implementation of WS-Security is the *SecurityToken* class. This is an abstract class that is used as the base class for all the security credentials that can be used with WSE. As you can see in Table 15-1, this base class provides the necessary infrastructure for signing and encrypting messages.

Table 15-1 Properties of the *SecurityToken* Class

Property	Description
AuthenticationKey	Gets the key that can be used to verify the signature of a message
DecryptionKey	Gets the key that will be used to decrypt a message
EncryptionKey	Gets the key that will be used to encrypt a message
Id	Gets or sets a unique identifier for the *SecurityToken* object
SignatureKey	Gets the key that is used to sign a message
SupportsDataEncryption	Returns *true* if the *SecurityToken* can be used for encryption
SupportsDigitalSignature	Returns *true* if the security token can be used for signing messages

Unless you're creating your own custom security credentials, you'll rarely, if ever, need to use any of the properties shown in Table 15-1. As you'll soon see, WSE does a wonderful job of shielding you from having to interrogate the *SecurityToken* instances to retrieve the keys for a different task—you simply add the *SecurityToken* to the request *SoapContext*, and WSE takes care of retrieving the correct keys.

As you saw earlier, WSE supports two types of security credentials, which translate into two derived classes, *UsernameToken* and *X509SecurityToken*. However, as you'll recall from Chapter 12, we have a *<wsse:BinarySecurityToken>* defined that encapsulates any security credentials that are binary in nature, and this includes the X509 certificates. The class hierarchy in WSE also follows this pattern and defines another abstract class, *BinarySecurityToken*, that derives from *SecurityToken* and is used as the base class for the *X509SecurityToken* class.

The relationship between the classes is shown in Figure 15-3.

Figure 15-3 *SecurityToken* inheritance

The classes derived from *SecurityToken* become more specific as you move further down the inheritance hierarchy, and each derived class adds more specific properties to the properties provided by the *SecurityToken* class.

As you'd expect, the *UsernameToken* class has *Username* and *Password* properties that allow a username and a password to be specified as well as *PasswordOption* and *Nonce* properties that allow you to provide a very basic level of security to the password.

Although the *BinarySecurityToken* is abstract and you can never create an instance of the class, it does provide the basic framework for all binary tokens—it has properties for specifying the type of the token and how the token is encoded, as well as properties for setting the raw binary for the token.

On top of the methods provided by *BinarySecurityToken*, the *X509SecurityToken* class provides only one other property of its own—the *Certificate* property, which allows the certificate that the security token is based on to be retrieved or specified.

We briefly talked about the individual properties and derived classes of the *SecurityToken* class. You'll rarely need to deal with them directly. Both the *UsernameToken* and *X509SecurityToken* classes provide constructors that configure the required properties correctly; you can simply create the correct *SecurityToken* derived class and allow WSE to handle all the low-level details.

Message Authentication

The first of our three security requirements is message authenticity, and as you've seen, it is not wise to rely on authentication alone unless you use username and password credentials and a transport protocol with intrinsic security.

To show the problems that can occur if you use authentication as the sole means of security for a Web service, we'll build a client application, AuthenticationClient, that interacts with a simple Web service. The user interface of the application is shown in Figure 15-4.

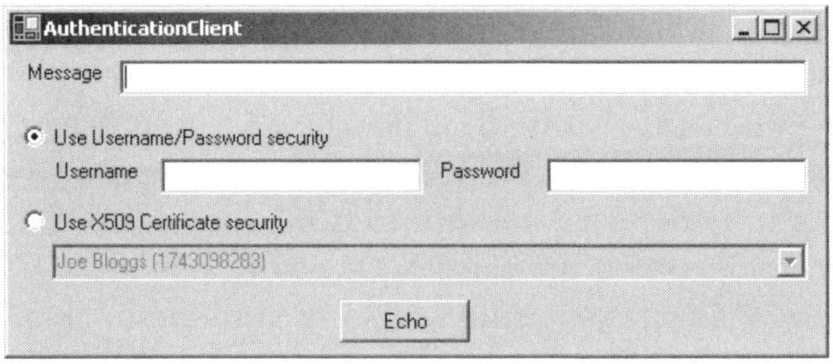

Figure 15-4 The AuthenticationClient application

The AuthenticationClient application allows you to send a message to a Web service and pass along the authentication details with the message. The Web service, at *http://localhost/wscr/15/authenticationws.asmx*, exposes one method, *Echo*, that accepts a message as a string and returns this message to the caller with details of the security information that it has been able to extract from the service.

The Client

It is relatively easy to add the authentication details to the message we're sending—it takes just two lines of code. We said earlier that it's easy to add security credentials to a message, and now you can see how easy it really is. However, we must take care of several housekeeping tasks before we add the credentials to the message.

First, as in all our WSE examples, we'll remove the filters that we won't use. In this case, we'll remove the Referral, Routing, and Timestamp filters from both the input and output pipelines. You saw this code several times in the last two chapters, so we won't repeat it here.

Although we can enter a username and password combination to use as the security credentials, we also have the option of using an X509 certificate. As you know, this provides no security whatsoever, but for completeness we'll allow the user to add the public part of the X509 certificate to the message in this example. This also gives you the chance to look at the code for retrieving X509 certificates from the certificate store.

Retrieving Certificates from the Certificate Store

As mentioned, you can specify which folder in the certificate store you want to store the certificates. WSE provides easy access to the certificate store using static methods of the *X509CertificateStore* class. You can use the *CurrentUserStore* and *LocalMachineStore* methods to return an instance of the *X509CertificateStore* class, which you can use to access the Current User certificate store and the Local Computer certificate store, respectively. You can then use the other methods of the *X509CertificateStore* class to interrogate the store to retrieve the certificates you need.

This isn't the end of the story, though. The X509 certificates are actually stored in a subfolder of the certificate store, so you must decide which part of the store you want to retrieve the certificates from. As you'll recall from Figure 15-2, there are 10 folders you can place X509 certificates into, 9 of which are common to the Local Computer certificate store and the Current User certificate store. WSE allows you to access the 5 most useful of these store folders programmatically, by using public fields of the *X509CertificateStore* class (as described in Table 15-2).

Table 15-2 Public Fields of *X509CertificateStore*

Field	Certificate Store Folder
CAStore	Intermediate Certification Authorities
MyStore	Personal
RootStore	Trusted Root Certification Authorities
TrustStore	Enterprise Trust
UnTrustedStore	Untrusted Certificates

You can place any X509 certificates you have into any of the available folders, although it makes sense to put personal certificates in the Personal folder. It also pays to have a place to put certificates you receive from other people. Ideally, they'd go in the Other People folder, but you can't access that programmatically. You have to use a different store. Out of the five that are available, the one that best suits our purpose in this example is the Enterprise Trust folder. As you'll see later in the chapter, this is where we'll put other people's certificates that we have received.

Now it's time to interrogate the store to retrieve the certificates that are available. The AuthenticationClient application, as you saw in Figure 15-4, allows you to select an X509 certificate from a drop-down list, which you populate by interrogating the certificate store. In the examples available in the sample code, this is done in the *Load* event for the main form of the application.

We first create an instance of the *X509CertificateStore* class and populate it with the certificates from the correct store. We do this by calling the *CurrentUserStore* static method on the *X509CertificateStore* class and specifying which part of the store we want. In this case, we want the Personal part of the store, so we specify a value of *X509CertificateStore.MyStore*. We then call the *OpenRead* method to open the store for read-only access:

```
// specify and open the correct certificate store
X509CertificateStore certStore = X509CertificateStore.CurrentUserStore
    (X509CertificateStore.MyStore);
certStore.OpenRead();
```

Now that we have an open reference to the correct certificate store folder, we can interrogate the store. The *X509CertificateStore* class has four methods you can use to search for a certificate, but in this case we want to retrieve all of the available certificates, so we'll use the *Certificates* property. This returns a collection of *X509Certificate* objects that correspond, not surprisingly, to the certificates that are available. We can iterate through the collection of certificates and add these to the list box on the form:

```
// loop through the collection and get the certificates
foreach(X509Certificate certCertificate in certStore.Certificates)
{
    // add the certificate to the combo box
    cboX509.Items.Add(X509.GetCommonName(certCertificate.GetName()));
}
```

As you'll see from the *Add* method of the *Items* collection of the *ComboBox* object, we first call a helper function to give us the common name of the certificate. The *GetName* method of the *X509* class returns the complete X500 string for the certificate; we're interested only in the Issued To part. The *GetCommonName* method of the helper class simply manipulates the string and retrieves the part we're interested in.

We then close the open connection to the certificate store and, if we've populated the list, automatically select the first entry:

```
// close the open store
certStore.Close();

// select the first entry
if(cboX509.Items.Count != 0) cboX509.SelectedIndex = 0;
```

Now that the *ComboBox* object is populated, we can get to the really important code—the code that adds the security credentials to the outgoing message.

Adding the *SecurityToken* to the Message

Once the application has launched, the user can enter the message that the server is to echo back. The security credentials must also be selected—either a username and password combination or an X509 certificate from the list box. Clicking the Echo button executes the click handler for the button.

Within the click handler is an enclosing *try/catch* loop that traps any exceptions raised by the code and displays the exception details to the user. In reality, we'd need more complex error handling to provide a better user experience, but for now we're only interested in the code that's directly related to security.

The first thing we do is create the two objects we'll need for the rest of the click handler. The first object is the Web service proxy object we've come to expect. We'll look at the Web service for this example shortly; here we're interested in the second object, *secClientToken*.

The *secClientToken* object is an instance of the *SecurityToken* class. As you saw earlier, this is a base class for several derived classes; we can use it to hold instances of any of the derived classes. This allows us to use the same code to add any type of security credential—WSE takes care of retrieving the correct parts of the credential for the action that it is currently performing:

```
// create the proxy class
AuthenticationWSWse proxy = new AuthenticationWSWse();

// declare the token that represents the client
SecurityToken secClientToken;
```

We then check to see which type of security credential we're providing, by using the status of the option buttons on the form.

If you're providing username and password credentials, you create a new instance of the *UsernameToken* class and specify the username and password to the constructor. You also tell the constructor what you want done with the password you're sending—you can pass no password, a plain-text password, or a hashed password (as shown here).

```
// create the username token
secClientToken = new UsernameToken(txtUsername.Text, txtPassword.Text,
    PasswordOption.SendHashed);
```

If you're using an X509 certificate, things are a little more complex because you must first retrieve the certificate you want to use from the Certificate Store. We added only the certificate name to the list box, not an instance of the certificate, so we need to retrieve the certificate from the store again.

To retrieve the correct certificate from the store, we use the *FindCertificateBySubjectString* method of the *X509CertificateStore* class. This method performs a search, using the text we specify, on all the certificates in the open certificate store folder. We pass to this method the text of the currently selected item in the list box and the method returns a collection of certificates that contain the text we're searching for. If several certificates have similar names, the collection might contain several different entities and more checking might be needed to ensure that we've retrieved the correct certificate. In this case, we'll assume that the first certificate in the collection is the one that we require:

```
// get the certificate we selected from the store
X509Certificate certCertificate = certStore.FindCertificateBySubjectString
    (cboX509.Text)[0];
```

Once the certificate has been retrieved, we can use it to construct a new *X509SecurityToken* by passing the *X509Certificate* to the *X509SecurityToken* constructor. After creating the security token, we close the connection to the certificate store:

```
// create the X509 token
secClientToken = new X509SecurityToken(certCertificate);

// close the certificate store
certStore.Close();
```

Whichever path the code took through the code, we now have a valid *SecurityToken* object that we add to the *Tokens* collection of the *Security* property of the request's *SoapContext* object. Then we make the call to the Web service, passing the message we want echoed:

```
// add the token to the message
proxy.RequestSoapContext.Security.Tokens.Add(secClientToken);

// make the call
MessageBox.Show(proxy.Echo(txtMessage.Text), "Returned message");
```

As the message is passed through the output pipeline, the Security output filter takes the contents of the *Security.Tokens* collection of the request's *SoapContext* object and adds them as *<wsse:UsernameToken>* or *<wsse:BinarySecurityToken>* elements to the *<wsse:Security>* security SOAP header (as you saw in Chapter 12).

The Web Service

On arriving at the Web service, the Security input filter extracts any *<wsse:UsernameToken>* and *<wsse:BinarySecurityToken>* elements from the *<wsse:Security>* header and reconstructs the *Security.Tokens* collection in the request's *SoapContext* object. We can then access this to retrieve the security credentials of the sender.

The first thing the Web service does is create a variable to hold the message that we'll return to the client and a variable to hold the request's *SoapContext*. We then check, as we do with all of our WSE-enabled code, that the request has a *SoapContext*:

```
string strResponse = "";

// get the request context
SoapContext reqContext = HttpSoapContext.RequestContext;

// must be a WSE message
if (reqContext == null)
    throw new ApplicationException("No WSE details discovered");
```

We then check that we've actually received authentication details in the message by checking that the *Security.Tokens* collection isn't empty. If it is, we don't have the details of any tokens to add to the message, and we return a message telling the user that we didn't receive any authentication details and echo the message back to the sender.

If we do have authentication information, we iterate through the collection of security tokens and extract the correct details. We cast the base *SecurityToken* to the correct type and extract the details we need from it.

For the *UsernameToken* object, we simply want to get the *Username* property, but for the *X509SecurityToken* object, we want the common name of the certificate, so we pass the results of the *GetName* method to the *X509.GetCommonName* helper method:

```
// we've got a message with authentication
strResponse = "The following message had authentication details from ";

// add the details to the message
foreach(SecurityToken secToken in reqContext.Security.Tokens)
{
    if (secToken is UsernameToken)
    {
        strResponse = strResponse + ((UsernameToken)secToken).Username;
    }

    if (secToken is X509SecurityToken)
    {
        strResponse = strResponse + X509.GetCommonName
            (((X509SecurityToken)secToken).Certificate.GetName());
    }
}
```

The received message is then added to the message we generated and is returned to the sender:

```
// now add the incoming message to the response
strResponse = strResponse + strMessage;

// now return the response to the caller
return (strResponse);
```

Verifying Username and Password Credentials

The one thing we haven't discussed is how the authentication details are validated by the Web service. If you're using X509 certificates as the credentials, no checking is done by the Security input filter to validate the certificate you passed—another nail in the coffin of using X509 certificates for authentication!

If you're using username and password security credentials, once you receive a *<wsse:UsernameToken>*, you must verify that the username and password are correct. If you don't pass a password, no authentication check is made and the user is assumed to be authentic.

To authenticate the username and password combinations received at the Web service, you must provide an implementation of the *IPasswordProvider* interface—if you don't, any requests that contain username and password credentials will be rejected and an exception of type *ConfigurationException* will be thrown. The *IPasswordProvider* interface has one method, *GetPassword*, that accepts the username that is being authenticated and requires the password to be returned. WSE then accepts or rejects the security credentials by comparing the password that was received in the message to the password returned from the *GetPassword* method.

The *GetPassword* method can be as complex or as simple as is required by the application. In our example Web service, we have only two valid user accounts and a simple *switch/case* statement that returns a hardcoded password:

```
public class authPassword : IPasswordProvider
{
    public string GetPassword(UsernameToken token)
    {
        switch (token.Username)
        {
            case "user1":
                return ("pass1");
            case "user2":
                return ("pass2");
            default:
                return (null);
        }
    }
}
```

We must inform the Security input filter of the details for our implementation of the *IPasswordProvider* interface. We do this in the configuration file:

```
<microsoft.web.services>
  <security>
    <passwordProvider type="_15.authPassword, 15" />
  </security>
</microsoft.web.services>
```

Once we configure WSE to use our implementation of *IPasswordProvider*, all requests to the Web service that have username and password credentials attached will cause the *authPassword* class to be instantiated and the *GetPassword* method to be called.

> **Note** As you've probably guessed, the *GetPassword* method presents us with a problem. We're most likely to store the passwords for a user in one-way encrypted form—be it in Active Directory, an SQL Server database, or any of a number of other locations. The *GetPassword* method must return the plain-text password so WSE can compare it to the password that is received. We have only one solution at present, and that is to store the passwords in plain text—this is possible in an SQL Server database but is generally not recommended.

Security Problems

As we pointed out earlier, you encounter several security problems when you use authentication as the sole means of security for your application. You've seen that using username and password credentials requires you to have a pretty insecure method of storing the passwords at the server, and unless you're using a secure transport protocol, the messages you send can be intercepted and modified relatively easily.

If you're using a secure transport protocol such as HTTPS, the message you send can use username and password security credentials, and you can be sure that your password will be kept secure—well, as secure as your credit card number was the last time you made an online purchase.

You already know that when you use X509 certificates for authentication they don't provide any security whatsoever because you're using the public part of the certificate, which is open to anyone who wants it.

The sample code for this chapter contains a public certificate for a fictitious user, Anne Bloggs, at *http://localhost/wscr/15/annebloggs.cer*. Anne has made her public certificate freely available so you can encrypt messages to her if you need to. If an unscrupulous person receives Anne's public certificate, he can quite easily spoof her identity if a Web service relies purely on authentication using X509 certificates. Go ahead and add the public certificate to the Personal folder of the Current User certificate store, and you'll see that you can use this as the security credentials of the Web service. Not very secure at all!

If you want to use X509 certificates, you must force the signing of the message and check for this when the message is received. As you'll see shortly, this approach doesn't involve much more work, but it is a lot more secure because it relies on the private part of the X509 certificate, which is hopefully still private.

Message Signing and Encrypting

As you know, using authentication really provides no security for the message transfer between the client and the server. You can move to a secure transport protocol (such as HTTPS) in many cases, but you might not want to go to the expense of purchasing an SSL certificate, or you might actually use a transport protocol that cannot be secured at the transport layer (such as SMTP). In these cases, you have to look at the two other options: message signing and encrypting.

You can sign a message using username and password credentials. However, as we pointed out earlier, the relationship between the username and the password is relatively trivial—it would be easy to intercept the message and retrieve the password used to sign the message, thereby destroying any security. Because you're unlikely to ever use username and password credentials to sign a message, we won't implement this approach in our example—the WSE documentation has full details of how to sign the message using these credentials. However, we will allow the signing of messages using X509 certificates.

If you're worried about the confidentiality of the message, you can also encrypt it so that only the intended recipient can see the contents. You cannot use username and password credentials to encrypt the message because these details are specific to the sender and, as you'll see, you need to rely on details specific to the recipient so you can encrypt the message to that person's requirements.

The Web service we'll use for this example can be found at *http://localhost/wscr/15/x509ws.asmx*. As in the previous Web service example, this one allows you to send a message that is echoed back, but in this case it also checks whether the message was signed and encrypted. In addition, if the message that is received is encrypted and signed, the returned message will be encrypted to the X509 certificate that signed the message—ensuring that only the person who sent the message can see what the returned message contains.

Required Certificates

To use this example, you must generate two certificates—one for the client and one for the server. The details of how to create both client and server certificates were covered earlier in the chapter.

Once the server certificate has been added to the Local Computer certificate store, the public key for the certificate must be exported and added to the Enterprise Trust folder of the Current User certificate store.

In the real world, the client and server would be on separate machines, but for our examples we're running both the client and the server on the same machine. Rather than having the client application access the Local Computer certificate store, we've chosen to place the public keys in the Enterprise Trust folder of the Current User certificate store. This is more likely to occur in the real world. Only administrators can add certificates to the Local Computer certificate store—others can't add to the Local Computer certificate store, but they can add to the Enterprise Trust folder of their own certificate store.

The Client

The client for this example is the X509Client application, which you'll find among the book's sample code. The user interface for the application is shown in Figure 15-5. As you can see, it allows you to enter a message you want echoed as well as specify whether you want the message signed or encrypted using X509 certificates that you specify.

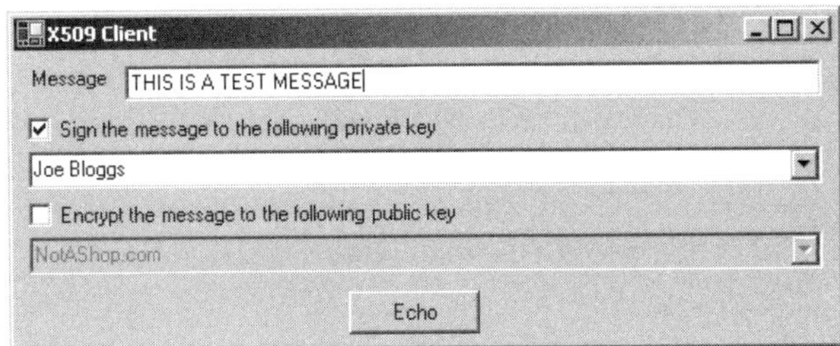

Figure 15-5 The X509Client application

The two list boxes are populated as the form is loaded, in the same way as in the AuthenticationClient application except that the encryption list box is populated from the Enterprise Trust folder of the Current User certificate store rather than from the Personal folder.

After you enter the message you want to echo and select the signing and encrypting options along with the X509 certificates you want to use, the click handler for the Echo button is called.

If you're signing the message, you open the Personal folder of the Current User certificate store and retrieve the selected certificate. We'll create an *X509SecurityToken* object from the certificate and add this to the message, as we did when we used X509 certificates for authentication:

```
// open the current user certificate store
X509CertificateStore certStore = X509CertificateStore.CurrentUserStore
    (X509CertificateStore.MyStore);
certStore.OpenRead();

// get the certificate and create the security token
X509Certificate certSignCertificate =
```

```
    certStore.FindCertificateBySubjectString(cboCertsSign.Text)[0];
X509SecurityToken secSignToken = new
    X509SecurityToken(certSignCertificate);

// add public key to message
proxy.RequestSoapContext.Security.Tokens.Add(secSignToken);
```

Although we said earlier that adding the public key of an X509 certificate to the message is pointless, we added it here to simplify the work that has to occur on the server. To check the message signature, the server needs to know the public key of the signer of the message. If the client adds the public key to the message, the Web service won't need to have every public key that is to be used stored on the server. The Security input filter automatically uses the public key in the message to verify the signature of that message, and the Security output filter can then use this public key to encrypt the message back to the caller, as you'll soon see.

To sign the message, we create a *Signature* object, passing in the *SecurityToken* object that we're using, and we add this to the *Security.Elements* collection of the request's *SoapContext* object. Finally, we close the certificate store.

```
// create the signing details and add to the message
Signature certSignature = new Signature(secSignToken);
proxy.RequestSoapContext.Security.Elements.Add(certSignature);

// close the certificate store
certStore.Close();
```

The code to encrypt the message is similar to the code that we use for signing, as you can see in the following listing:

```
// open the local machine certificate store
X509CertificateStore certStore = X509CertificateStore.CurrentUserStore
    (X509CertificateStore.TrustStore);
certStore.OpenRead();

// get the certificate and create the security token
X509Certificate certEncryptCertificate =
    certStore.FindCertificateBySubjectString(cboCertsEncrypt.Text)[0];
X509SecurityToken secEncryptToken = new
    X509SecurityToken(certEncryptCertificate);

//  create the encryption details and add to the message
EncryptedData encData = new EncryptedData(secEncryptToken);
proxy.RequestSoapContext.Security.Elements.Add(encData);

// close the certificate store
certStore.Close();
```

We open the Enterprise Trust folder rather than the Personal folder, retrieve the certificate we're after, and use this to create an *X509SecurityToken*. Whereas when we signed the message we created a *Signature* element, here we create an *EncryptedData* object and add this to the *Security.Elements* collection.

That's all there is to it—WSE hides from us all of the intricacies of requesting the keys to sign and encrypt the message from the *SecurityToken*. By simply adding *Signature* or *EncryptedData* objects to the *Security.Elements* collection of the request *SoapContext*, we've specified that we want the message signed and encrypted and provided the information required to do so.

If we add a *Signature* object to the *Security.Elements* collection, the Security output filter will sign the message using the private key of the X509 certificate we used to create the *Signature* object, by adding a *<wsse:Signature>* element to the Security SOAP header and modifying the SOAP body to reference the *<wsse:Signature>* that was added. If we add an *EncryptedData* object to *Security.Elements*, the Security output filter will encrypt the message using the public key of the X509 certificate that we used to create the *EncryptedData* object, by adding an *<wsse:EncryptedKey>* element to the SOAP header and replacing the plain-text SOAP body with the encrypted version. We looked at the changes that the Security output filter makes to the SOAP message in Chapter 12, so we won't go into any specific details here.

The Web Service

On arrival at the Web service, the Security input filter checks that all the security details for the message are correct before control is passed to the method that was called. During the checking process, the request's *SoapContext* object is populated with the details as they are extracted from the incoming message.

The Security input filter verifies the message signature using the public key that was attached to the message—or, if that public key is not available, the filter looks in the Personal folder of the Local Computer certificate store for a certificate that matches the required public key. If there are any problems with the signing, the filter raises an exception.

If necessary, the filter also decrypts the message, searching for the private key in the Personal folder of the Local Computer certificate store by default. As you saw earlier, you can configure WSE to look in the Personal folder of the Current User certificate store. If a private key cannot be found to decrypt the message, an exception is raised automatically.

Once the security details have been verified, control is passed to the called method, and it is up to the method to enforce the necessary security requirements (whether the message has to be signed, and so forth).

Our sample Web service won't enforce any security requirements; it will simply return to the caller an indication of whether the message the service received was signed or encrypted or both. If the message was both signed and encrypted, the Web service will also encrypt the return message using the X509 certificate that signed the message that was received.

Once control has been passed to the correct method, the first thing the method checks (as with all the other WSE-enabled Web services) is that a request *SoapContext* object is available. If the WSE message is properly formatted, the method will then check how many objects are in the *Security.Elements* collection of the request's *SoapContext* object. If there are zero elements, we know that the message was neither signed nor encrypted, and we can simply echo the received message back to the caller.

If we find objects in the *Security.Elements* collection, we know that the message has been signed or encrypted and we can then proceed to check what was done to the message.

We first create three local variables that are used to store the information that we retrieve from the incoming message. We have Boolean flags that are set to *true* if the incoming message is encrypted or signed and an *X509SecurityToken* that contains the token that signed the message. (We'll need this if we determine that the response message is to be encrypted.)

```
bool boolEncrypted = false;
bool boolSigned = false;
X509SecurityToken secSigningToken = null;
```

We then iterate through the *Security.Elements* collection and check to see what type of object that we're looking at.

If we have a *Signature* object, we know that the message has been signed. We used the default options for what part of the message we're signing, and you'll see later in the chapter how to sign the different parts of the message. For now, all you need to know is that the body of the message is signed by default, and that you check that this is the case. To perform this check, we perform a bitwise AND with the *SignatureOptions* property of the *Signature* object and the *IncludeSoapBody* value from the *SignatureOptions* enumeration. If we don't get a zero value, we know that the message body was signed. If the message was signed, we set the Boolean flag to *true* and store the *SecurityToken* corresponding to the *Signature* object:

```
// is this a signature element
if(secElement is Signature)
{
    // cast to a real signature object
    Signature secSignature = (Signature)secElement;
```

```
    // is the body signed
    if ((secSignature.SignatureOptions
         & SignatureOptions.IncludeSoapBody) != 0)
    {
        // set the flag that we need
        boolSigned = true;

        // get the encryption token that we need
        secSigningToken = (X509SecurityToken)secSignature.SecurityToken;
    }
}
```

The process for checking that the message was encrypted is similar to that for checking that it was signed. If the object we're looking at is an *EncryptedData* object, we know that the message has been encrypted and we can perform the necessary checks to see what was encrypted. As with signing the message, we use the default settings for what parts of the message are encrypted, and we check the *TargetElement.LocalName* of the *EncryptedData* object to determine whether the body element is encrypted. If it is, we set the Boolean flag to *true*.

```
// is this an encryption element
if(secElement is EncryptedData)
{
    EncryptedData secEncrypted = (EncryptedData)secElement;

    // is the body of the message encrypted
    if(secEncrypted.TargetElement.LocalName == "Body")
    {
        boolEncrypted = true;
    }
}
```

Once we step through the *Security.Elements* collection, we create the return message for the method using the two Boolean flags to modify the string—this is just some simple code that checks which Boolean flags are set and appends different parts to the output string.

After we create the message that we'll return to the caller, we decide whether to encrypt the message. If the request was encrypted and we have a public token for the caller (which will be the case if the message was signed), we encrypt the return message using the available public key:

```
// do we need to encrypt the return
if(boolEncrypted == true && boolSigned == true)
{
    EncryptedData encData = new EncryptedData(secSigningToken);
    respContext.Security.Elements.Add(encData);
}
```

Shared Key Encryption

The approach to encryption that we looked at in the previous section is *asymmetric encryption*—the keys to encrypt and decrypt the message are different. We used X509 certificates as the basis for the encryption and used the different parts of the certificate to encrypt and decrypt the message. It is also possible to encrypt and decrypt messages *symmetrically*—using the same key for decryption that you use for encryption. However, this relies on the transmission of the shared key having taken place between the client and the server. Whereas you can make the public key of the X509 certificate available for everyone to use and feel safe in the knowledge that only the holder of the private key can decrypt the messages sent, when you use shared key encryption you must ensure that the key is kept as secure as possible because all senders can decrypt data that is encrypted using the shared key. If you have a shared key that is known to everyone, you effectively have no encryption at all.

To use a shared key to encrypt the message, you create an *EncryptionKey* object and use it rather than an *X509SecurityToken* object to initialize the *EncryptedData* object. You can add this *EncryptedData* object to the *Security.Elements* collection, as we did earlier.

When you create the encryption key, you can use any of the algorithms that descend from the *SymmetricAlgorithm* class in the *System.Security.Cryptography* namespace. The current release of .NET includes implementations of the DES, RC2, Rijndael, and Triple-DES algorithms, but only two of these, Triple-DES and Rijndael, can be used as the basis for our shared encryption key.

> **Note** A full discussion of symmetric encryption and the algorithms provided by .NET in the *System.Security.Cryptography* namespace is beyond the scope of this book. A good reference tome for cryptography is *Applied Cryptography: Protocols, Algorithms, and Source Code in C, Second Edition* by Bruce Schneier (John Wiley & Sons, 1996). It's in C rather than C# and is slightly out-of-date, but it contains everything you need to know to get started with cryptography. Also, several articles on encryption and what is provided by .NET are available on the MSDN site—a good starting point is at *http://msdn.microsoft.com/library/en-us/cpguide/html/cpconcryptographyoverview.asp*.

For this example, we'll create a new client application, SharedKeyClient, and a new Web service at *http://localhost/wscr/15/sharedkeyws.asmx*. We'll encrypt only the message to the server and return the results as plain text, but as you'll see, the process by which we tell WSE that we want to encrypt the message is simple—and not a lot of code changes are required to encrypt the return.

The Shared Key

We'll use the Rijndael algorithm as our shared key; all of the code for generating the necessary encryption and decryption keys is in the *SharedKey* class in the helper DLL. To use a shared key, we need to create instances of the *SymmetricEncryptionKey* and *SymmetricDecryptionKey* classes that we can use to encrypt and decrypt the messages that we're sending. As with X509 certificates, most of the work to encrypt and decrypt the messages is handled automatically by WSE, and all we need to provide is the correct keys.

To create the keys, we simply pass the correct algorithm to the constructor of the *SymmetricEncryptionKey* or *SymmetricDecryptionKey* class. We're using a shared key, and we're using the same algorithm for both the encryption and decryption keys, so we place this code into its own method that can be called as required. Within this method we create the algorithm and set the key and initialization vector to whatever values we choose. (You should make a better choice than we have here!) The code for this method follows.

```
private static SymmetricAlgorithm getAlgorithm()
{
    // create instance of the correct algorithm
    SymmetricAlgorithm algo = new RijndaelManaged();

    // set the key and IV for the algorithm
    byte[] keyBytes = {1,2,4,8,16,32,64,128,128,64,32,16,8,4,2,1};
    byte[] ivBytes =  {2,4,6,8,10,12,14};
    algo.Key = keyBytes;
    algo.IV = ivBytes;

    // return the algorithm
    return (algo);
}
```

We can then use the algorithm that is returned to create the correct decryption and encryption keys that we need.

To create the encryption key, we create a new instance of the *SymmetricEncryptionKey* class and pass the algorithm that we're using to the constructor. We must also add a *KeyInfo* clause to the key so that when we come to decrypt the message we know which encryption algorithm we used. The *KeyInfoName* object that we add as the clause can be any arbitrary value, but we must ensure that both the client and the server are using the same name.

```
public static EncryptionKey GetEncryptionKey()
{
    // create new EncryptionKey
    SymmetricEncryptionKey keyEncrypt = new
        SymmetricEncryptionKey(getAlgorithm());

    // add the ID details to the key
    KeyInfoName keyName = new KeyInfoName();
    keyName.Value  = "www.notashop.com/wscr encrypted";
    keyEncrypt.KeyInfo.AddClause(keyName);

    // return the EncryptionKey in question
    return keyEncrypt;
}
```

Creating the decryption key is a lot simpler because the determination of which key we need to use has already been made before the call to create the key. We simply create a new instance of the *SymmetricDecryptionKey* class, passing the correct algorithm to the constructor:

```
public static DecryptionKey GetDecryptionKey()
{
    // create new DecryptionKey and return
    return (new SymmetricDecryptionKey(getAlgorithm()));
}
```

The Client

The client application we'll use for this example follows the same process as the clients we used for the earlier examples in this chapter. We simply enter the message we want the server to echo back and click the Echo button. Unlike in the other examples, however, we don't have to specify how we want the message encrypted—all the messages we send will be encrypted to the encryption key that is hardcoded at both the client and the server.

The code for encrypting the message is the same as the code you saw for encrypting the message using an X509 certificate, except instead of using the X509 certificate you use the key that you retrieve from the helper class to generate the *EncryptedData* object:

```
// create the proxy class
SharedKeysWSWse proxy = new SharedKeysWSWse();

// get the encryption key
EncryptionKey keyEncrypt = SharedKey.GetEncryptionKey();

//  create the encryption details and add to the message
```

```
EncryptedData encData = new EncryptedData(keyEncrypt);
proxy.RequestSoapContext.Security.Elements.Add(encData);

// make the call
MessageBox.Show(proxy.Echo(txtMessage.Text), "Returned message");
```

As we pointed out earlier, all of the work required to encrypt the message is handed internally by WSE.

The Web Service

When we looked at decrypting messages that were encrypted using X509 certificates, you saw that you don't have to write any code on the server for the decryption to take place. The decryption is performed automatically by the Security input filter, and control is passed to the calling method only if the decryption is successful.

When you use shared keys for encryption, the decryption also takes place automatically, but you have to let the Security input filter know what the encryption key is so it knows how to decrypt the message. You do this by creating a class that implements the *IDecryptionKeyProvider* interface.

This interface exposes one method, *GetDecryptionKey*, which returns the key that will decrypt the message that has been received. The key is determined from the *KeyInfo* element that is passed to the method.

Within the *KeyInfo* object is a series of *KeyInfoClause* elements that correspond to the details that have been added to the encryption key. We iterate through each of these to determine the key that we need to provide the key for:

```
public DecryptionKey GetDecryptionKey(string algorithmUri, KeyInfo keyInfo)
{
    foreach ( KeyInfoClause clause in keyInfo )
    {
```

In the earlier code we added a *KeyInfoName* element to the encryption key, and now we'll look for that key. If we find this key, we'll return the decryption key provided by the helper class; if we find a key that we can't decode, we'll throw an exception.

```
        // are we using a shared encryption key
        if ( clause is KeyInfoName )
        {
            switch (((KeyInfoName)clause).Value)
            {
                case "www.notashop.com/wscr encrypted":
                {
                    return(SharedKey.GetDecryptionKey());
                }
```

```
                default:
                {
                    throw new ApplicationException
                        ("Unsupported encryption key");
                }
            }
        }
```

If we're worried only about being able to decrypt messages that are encrypted using shared keys, simply adding new *case* statements to the above code will handle all possible situations. But if we need to be able to decrypt X509 certificates within the same application, as we have for the four Web services we've used in this chapter, we must add another piece of code to the loop through the *KeyInfo* collection.

Adding a handler for the *IDecryptionKeyProvider* interface to an application removes the application's ability to automatically decrypt messages. We need to be able to handle the situation in which we receive a message encrypted using an X509 certificate. We simply look for a *SecurityTokenReference* and determine whether it is an X509 certificate. If it is, we create an instance of the default implementation of the *IDecryptionKeyProvider* interface, the *DecryptionKeyProvider* class, and call the *GetDecryptionKey* method, passing in the parameters we received:

```
        // manually handle X509 Security as
        // we've broken the default handler
        if (clause is SecurityTokenReference)
        {
            switch(((SecurityTokenReference)clause)
                      .KeyIdentifier.ValueType.Name)
            {
                case "X509v3":
                {
                    DecryptionKeyProvider Decryptor =
                        new DecryptionKeyProvider();
                    return(Decryptor.GetDecryptionKey
                        (algorithmUri,keyInfo));
                }
                default:
                {
                    throw new ApplicationException
                        ("Unsupported encryption key");
                }
            }
        }
    }
```

If we go through the loop without finding any keys in the message, something has gone wrong and we won't be able to decrypt the message. We throw an exception that will be passed to the caller:

```
    // if we get here we can't decode the message
    throw new ApplicationException("Unknown encryption key");
}
```

Although we now have a method to provide the decryption key, we still haven't hooked it to the Security input filter. To do this, we must add an entry to the *<security>* element in the configuration file. We add a *<decryptionKeyProvider>* element that points at the correct type to instantiate:

```
<security>
  <decryptionKeyProvider type="notashop.wscr.Helper.DecryptKey, Helper" />
</security>
```

Signing and Encrypting Parts of the Message

So far when we've looked at signing and encrypting messages that we're sending, we've accepted the defaults for what part of each message is signed and encrypted. In most cases, this is fine because you won't need to specify other parts of the message for signing or encrypting.

However, in some cases you'll want to sign or encrypt other parts of the message. A prime example is when you use SOAP headers. The header might contain information that you need to secure, and the default options won't do this. You need to be able to modify the default signing and encrypting options for the message. Thankfully, WSE allows you to do just that.

We'll build an example, PartsClient, that sends a message containing a SOAP header to the Web service at *http://localhost/wscr/15/partsws.asmx*. The example allows you to specify the header you're sending and then choose to sign or encrypt the message. On receiving the message, the Web service displays the details of the header and then iterates through the signature and encryption details to tell you what was signed or encrypted.

Signing Parts of the Message

As you've seen, when you sign a SOAP message using the defaults, you sign the body of the message. The defaults for signing actually go further than this—you actually sign six other elements within the message.

If you've enabled the Routing and Timestamp output filters, you also sign the parts of the SOAP header that they add to the message. For the Routing filter, you sign the *action*, *from*, *id*, and *to* elements; for the Timestamp filter, you sign the *created* and *expires* elements. In most cases these will satisfy your requirements, but if you need to change what is signed by default, you can modify the *SignatureOptions* property of the *Signature* object that you're signing with.

The *SignatureOptions* property is a bit field that allows you to specify which parts of the message you want to sign. There is also a *SignatureOptions* enumeration that allows you to easily specify what you want to sign by combining the different values of the enumeration. These values are described in Table 15-3.

Table 15-3 The *SignatureOptions* Enumeration

Member	Description
IncludeNone	Do not sign anything in the message.
IncludePath	Sign the entire WS-Routing header.
IncludePathAction	Sign the *action* element of the WS-Routing header.
IncludePathFrom	Sign the *from* element of the WS-Routing header.
IncludePathId	Sign the *id* element of the WS-Routing header.
IncludePathTo	Sign the *to* element of the WS-Routing header.
IncludeSoapBody	Sign the body of the message.
IncludeTimestamp	Sign the entire WS-Timestamp header.
IncludeTimestampCreated	Sign the *created* element of the WS-Timestamp header.
IncludeTimestampExpires	Sign the *expires* element of the WS-Timestamp header.

If you choose not to sign the entire body of the message or you need to sign any SOAP headers that you add to the message, you must specify individually what parts of the message you want to sign. You'll see in the next example how to do this.

Encrypting Parts of the Message

When you encrypt a message, the only part of the message that is encrypted by default is the message body. Unlike signing parts of the message, when you encrypt a message you make the encrypted part unreadable. Encrypting certain parts of the message, such as the WS-Routing headers, would generate a message that might be incorrect. For example, only the ultimate recipient of the message can decrypt the message, so any routers that the message had to pass through would not be able to read the necessary SOAP header.

You might, however, need to encrypt SOAP headers that you add to the message to ensure that the contents of that header cannot be read. As you'll soon see, WSE allows you to specify what you want to encrypt.

The Client

PartsClient, the client we'll use for this example, is similar to X509Client, which we looked at earlier. It allows you to specify the message you want the Web service to echo and to specify whether to sign or encrypt the message using X509 certificates. As you can see in Figure 15-6, you can also specify a Number header.

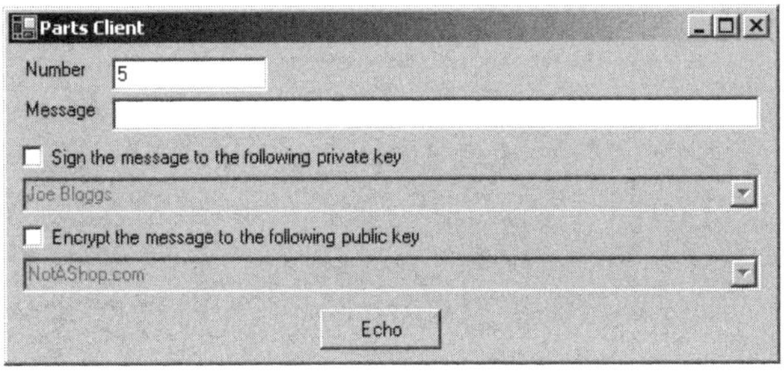

Figure 15-6 The PartsClient application

Most of the code for encrypting and signing the message is the same as what you saw for the X509Client. We just need to add code to tell WSE that we want to sign and encrypt the new header that we've added.

As you'll see when we look at the code for the Web service, we have a header with two exposed properties—*Id* and *Number*. The *Number* property is the value that we want to pass as the header, and the *Id* property is a value that we use to tell WSE which element we want to sign or encrypt. Without the *Id* property, we'd have no way of telling WSE which element we're referring to. As in the WS-Security specification, the ID of an element must be a unique valid GUID prefixed with *Id:*, and we can use *Guid.NewGuid* to retrieve one. We populate the header with the correct details and store the GUID we just created so we can use it to tell WSE that we want to sign and encrypt the header:

```
// create the GUID that we need for the header
string headerId = "Id:" + Guid.NewGuid().ToString();

// create the header and add it to the call to the proxy
NumberHeader numHeader = new NumberHeader();
numHeader.Id = headerId;
numHeader.Number = txtNumber.Text;
proxy.NumberHeaderValue = numHeader;
```

To sign this header, we create a reference to the ID of the element we want to sign and add it to the signature we're using to sign the message. The reference to the element that we want to sign is an instance of the *Reference* class, and we use the GUID that we defined earlier and prefix it with the # symbol:

```
// create the signing details
certSignature = new Signature(secSignToken);

// we want to sign the header
Reference refHeader = new Reference("#" + headerId);
certSignature.AddReference(refHeader);

// now add the signature to the message
proxy.RequestSoapContext.Security.Elements.Add(certSignature);
```

Unlike signing, where we can use the existing signature and simply use this to sign an additional part of the message when we are encrypting, we have to create a completely new instance of the *EncryptedData* class, specifying which element we want to encrypt. To do this, we call a different version of the *EncryptedData* constructor, passing in the ID of the element we want to encrypt as well as the *SecurityToken* we want to use:

```
// encrypt the default message elements
encData = new EncryptedData(secEncryptToken);
proxy.RequestSoapContext.Security.Elements.Add(encData);

// we also want to encrypt the header
encData = new EncryptedData(secEncryptToken, "#" + headerId);
proxy.RequestSoapContext.Security.Elements.Add(encData);
```

We've told WSE to sign and encrypt the body of the message and the header that we added to the message, and we can call the proxy in the same way we always have.

The Web Service

When the message gets to the server, the Security input filter goes through its normal process and checks the signature of the message and decrypts the parts of the message that need decrypting, populating the request's *SoapContext* as it goes.

As with the X509Client application, we can loop through the *Security.Elements* collection of the request *SoapContext* to extract the security information that was added to the message.

If the item in the *Security.Elements* collection is a *Signature* object, we know that at least part of the message was signed. We loop through the *Signed-*

Info.References collection of the signature to determine what parts of the message were signed, and we use the *TargetElement.Name* to return the namespace prefixed element that was signed. We simply concatenate the element name to a string that contains all of the elements in the message that are signed:

```
if(secElement is Signature)
{
    // cast to a real Signature object
    Signature secSignature = (Signature)secElement;

    // loop through each element in the message
    foreach (Reference refElement in secSignature.SignedInfo.References)
    {
        // add the prefixed name to the output string
        strSigned = strSigned + refElement.TargetElement.Name + ", ";
    }

    // at least some of the message was signed
    boolSigned= true;
}
```

When we check the encrypted details, we use roughly the same process. Each element that is encrypted has its own entry in the *Security.Elements* collection. We cast the element to an *EncryptedData* object and retrieve the data from the *TargetElement.Name* property of the *EncryptedData* object:

```
if(secElement is EncryptedData)
{
    // cast to a real EncryptedData object
    EncryptedData secEncrypted = (EncryptedData)secElement;

    // add the prefixed name to the output string
    strEncrypted = strEncrypted + secEncrypted.TargetElement.Name + ", ";

    // at least some of the message was encrypted
    boolEncrypted = true;
}
```

We then use the Boolean flags that were set to create the message that is returned to the caller.

Summary

WS-Security is open enough to let you use a wide variety of security credentials for securing your Web services. You learned in this chapter that you can use username and password credentials across a secure transport protocol—without that secure transport protocol, this form of security is useless.

We also looked at using X509 certificates for signing and encrypting messages. We discussed how to ensure the integrity and confidentiality of messages across unsecured transport protocols without requiring any major work by the developer.

We briefly looked at using shared encryption keys to encrypt messages, and we used a simple algorithm to illustrate the process.

We closed the chapter by looking at signing and encrypting parts of the message other than those that are signed and encrypted by default.

Much work is being done on security in the Web services world. Microsoft has provided a good first step along the path and has provided tools to secure messages to and from Web services using X509 and SSL certificates. However, as you saw in Chapter 12, the WS-Security specification allows any type of binary security credential to be used, and other vendors and standards bodies are starting to provide alternatives to X509 certificates. For example, the OASIS WS-Security Technical Committee (at *http://www.oasis-open.org/committees/tc_home.php?wg_abbrev=wss*) is working on the use of different security tokens in the WS-Security specification. The WS-Security specification explicitly defines the use of X509 certificates and Kerberos security tokens, and OASIS is working out the details of using Security Assertion Markup Language (SAML), XML Common Biometric Format (XCBF), and a whole host of other security tokens within the WS-Security framework.

16

Looking to the Future

In this final chapter of the book, we'll look beyond what exists now to what will or might exist in the future. What is being developed that could inspire the world to use Web services on a wider scale? Will a standard practice emerge for implementing the Web service layer of an enterprise application, and if so, what might it be? Specifically, we'll cover these topics:

- The tasks that standards bodies and developers have ahead of them before Web services can become a truly viable and rich framework for distributed applications
- The problems that currently hamper cross-platform interoperability and their remedies

As with any kind of forecasting, what we say here might well be out of date by the time you read it. The contents of beta products continue to change until the products are released, standards face ongoing problems with intellectual property rights and patents, and release dates are ever slipping. Who's to say that someone won't discover or develop something tomorrow that makes Web services obsolete?

That said, let's get on with it.

The Standards

Work continues apace on the core Web standards we've covered in this book (and plenty more) in an effort to give the Web services platform a richer function set to work with. Appropriately enough, the best overview of the standards work going on is in one of the standards being written at the moment: the working draft for a reference Web Services Architecture (WSA), which can be found at *http://www.w3.org/TR/ws-arch/*. The goal of the WSA is to describe a standard generic model for a Web services framework and the functionality it should provide. Like the Open Systems Interconnection (OSI) 802.1 network layer model, it's being written to show how the pieces of the framework should work and be linked together but doesn't prescribe any particular standard technology to implement them. (It does use SOAP, XML, and WSDL as examples, however.)

If you're wondering why the WSA is only in working draft form, consider that there isn't yet a unified view of what Web services should do or how they should work. That understanding is slowly coming together, however, and the World Wide Web Consortium (W3C) now feels confident that it can write a reference specification that won't need tearing up and rewriting six months down the line. Now that the plumbing is quite stable, it might not change shape again for quite a while.

The draft document describes the WSA in terms of a basic architecture—the plumbing that we know and love—and an extended architecture, which Microsoft, IBM, and several other companies are starting to work on. We'll look at the work being done on each of them in turn.

The Basic Architecture

The core part of the WSA (often referred to as "the plumbing" in this book) is currently implemented by the standards we investigated in Chapters 2, 3, 4, and 6. That is, the basic architecture includes the following technologies:

- The wire stack, where client and server can exchange messages
- The description stack, where a Web service can be described to the client
- The discovery agencies stack, where servers can publish Web services and clients can discover them

If you believe the word on the street, the plumbing has pretty much come together and is quite mature. However, of the six technologies shown in Figure 16-1 that make up the plumbing, only SOAP is not still being directly altered.

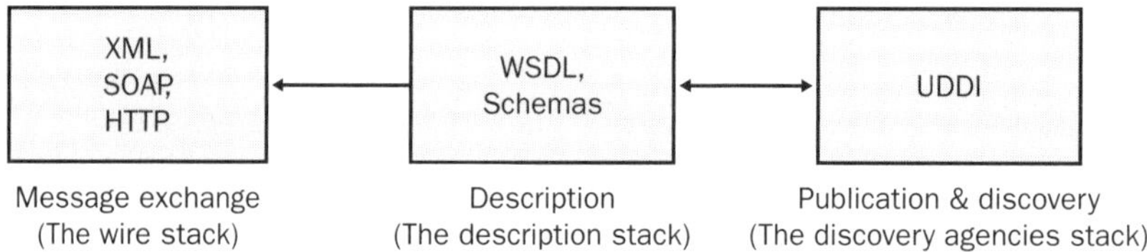

Figure 16-1 The basic plumbing of the WSA and the standards that currently implement it

The other technologies are being worked on either directly or by extension to increase their usefulness. Even the W3C states that it will continue to work on this basic architecture until the end of 2004. By then, either all the issues raised by the six technologies will have been addressed or something else will have taken their place. It's valid to argue that standards should be "frozen" before they become obsolete, but that's an argument for a different time. We need to stay in the present and consider the three tasks that the basic architecture defines: message exchange, service description, and publishing and discovery.

Message Exchange

Of the three tasks, message exchange, as executed in the wire stack, is in the best shape. XML has always been the choice for carrying messages, and with SOAP we have a simple yet flexible and extensible format for phrasing those messages. HTTP 1.1 will remain the transport protocol that SOAP binds to as a template in its specification, but work continues apace to produce standard bindings to other protocols as well, as you can see in Figure 16-2.

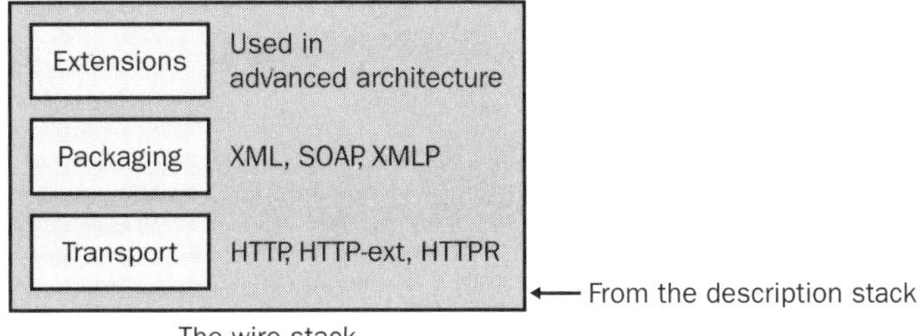

Figure 16-2 The wire stack and the technologies involved in each layer

XML and Unicode The W3C will release version 1.1 of the XML and Namespaces in XML specifications in 2003 to make use of Unicode 3.0. XML 1.0 disagrees with Unicode 2.0 slightly and the new version corrects that problem, but it is backward incompatible as a result.

From a Web services point of view, the inclusion of Unicode 3.0 in the XML space is welcome, but some issues (especially internationalization issues) still haven't been resolved. For example, a URI in an XML document can be written in any character set as long as that character set is identified in the processing instruction at the top of the document, but by specification (in RFC 2396 to be exact), URIs must be written in 7-bit ASCII. This is fine if you generally use the ASCII set of characters in daily life, but what if, for example, a Vietnamese developer wants to use a Namespace URI (corresponding to his schema) in his own character set? Converting his UTF 16–encoded URI for display in a browser down to ASCII would probably involve the browser changing at least every other character in the URI into an escape sequence that the browser could display. The readability and ease of use of a URI depends on the character set it originated in. When asked to write the URL for his services' schema on the back of his business card, should the Vietnamese developer write it in his native language or the escaped URL that the browser will understand?

You can find the XML 1.1 specification at *http://www.w3.org/TR/xml11/* and Namespaces in XML 1.1 at *http://www.w3.org/TR/xml-names11/*. A complete list of issues identified so far between Unicode and XML can be found at *http://www.w3.org/TR/unicode-xml*.

HTTP HTTP 1.1 has been the de facto standard for transferring messages and data across networks for six years. However, groups are working to add extensions to (or even replace) HTTP to help those who are trying to implement the extended architecture (which we'll look at shortly). The following projects aim to improve on or replace HTTP:

- The HTTP Extension Framework (*http://www.w3.org/Protocols/HTTP/ietf-http-ext/*)
- A purely XML-based protocol called XMLP (*http://www.w3.org/2000/xp/Group/*)
- A robust version of HTTP called Reliable HTTP (*http://www-106.ibm.com/ developerworks/library/ws-phtt*)

IBM is working on Reliable HTTP, which provides the reliability of robust messaging systems such as its own MQSeries. Developers whose Web services run over Reliable HTTP will be able to determine the quality of their service—an issue that is preeminent in the Extended WSA, as you'll see shortly.

Interestingly enough, these projects intersect neatly with others that affect or will affect the SOAP envelope. For example, if you send SOAP messages over Reliable HTTP to monitor the quality of Web service response, that functionality will be restricted to servers that can work with Reliable HTTP. If we can incorporate what Reliable HTTP does into a SOAP header with a little programming, we can have that quality of service across every protocol. Indeed, work on the HTTP Extension Framework at the W3C has been suspended, and using SOAP headers is one of the suggested alternatives.

SOAP The W3C's involvement in the creation of SOAP 1.2 is the first time the organization has had access to this standard, and it has tried to remove as much of the ambiguity from the specification as possible. For example, SOAP 1.2 uses the XML Infoset (*http://www.w3.org/TR/xml-infoset/*) to describe the contents of a SOAP message rather than the XML specification itself, in accordance with the WSA draft.

This effort has the desired effect of making it a lot harder for Web service toolkit developers to misinterpret what each piece of SOAP 1.2 should do—but at the cost of readability and, some would say, uniformity. (See *http://www.xml.com/pub/a/2002/11/20/ends.html* for the full argument.) SOAP 1.1 is simple to understand, while SOAP 1.2 has twice as many specification documents, which are themselves twice as long and twice as dense as those in SOAP 1.1. *S* now stands for "strict but still extensible" rather than "simple," it would seem.

You can find a full list of differences between SOAP 1.1 and 1.2 in the SOAP 1.2 Primer document (*http://www.w3.org/TR/2002/CR-soap12-part0-20021219/#L4697*). In brief, SOAP 1.2 does the following:

- Changes the SOAP media type to application/soap+xml, in line with RFC 3023, and it removes the SOAPAction HTTP header
- More strictly defines the use of the SOAP *<fault>* element and its child elements and clarifies which HTTP status code to use when
- Defines new syntax for use when sending SOAP messages via one or several intermediaries
- Includes the W3C Schema 1.0 Recommendation
- Tries to make the serialization of messages using SOAP encoding less complex
- Doesn't currently comply with the WSA draft because QNames might be used to identify certain items in a SOAP envelope rather than URIs

This last point isn't a specific feature of SOAP 1.2, but rather of the WSA draft. Indeed, the W3C XML Protocol Working Group, which looks after the SOAP standard, is working closely with the Web Services Architecture Working Group to marry the two. As you'll see in a minute, the latter group has also been quite busy trying to extend the reach of SOAP, with several adjoining specs for SOAP 1.2 addressing issues such as attaching items to SOAP messages and using SOAP headers to enable various security efforts.

Service Description

Compared to the wire stack, the description stack (shown in Figure 16-3) is almost in disarray. Developers are still learning what it should do. In the meantime, a lot of work remains to be done by the W3C before this part of the WSA is comprehensive. The XML Schema specification is very stable, but WSDL still needs some fairly major work. The top layer of the stack, collaboration description, will deal with describing how one Web service should interact with another, but little has been done about this yet. (More on this later.)

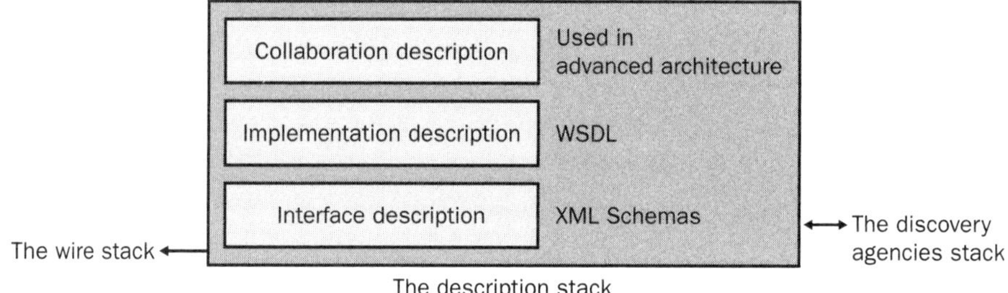

Figure 16-3 The WSA description stack

WSDL Like SOAP 1.2, WSDL 1.2 will be the first version of the standard written by the W3C. Unlike SOAP 1.1, however, WSDL 1.1 isn't almost complete. Indeed, it could be described as the spaghetti stuck to the wall after the contents of the brainstorm bowl have been thrown at it. No one knew exactly what WSDL should do when it was designed, so it was built to cover everything it should do and some things it shouldn't. Only since it has been tried out has it become clear what exactly it should do. One could argue, for instance, that WSDL's *<service>* and *<binding>* elements would be more at home in UDDI. The Web Services Description Working Group, which looks after the development of WSDL, therefore has four tasks ahead of it:

- Streamlining WSDL to do only what it must
- Making WSDL less ambiguous by describing the contents of a WSDL document in terms of the XML Infoset
- Adding binding support for SOAP 1.2 to WSDL
- Collaborating with the W3C Semantic Web Activity to develop a more meaningful description of a Web service (*http://www.w3.org/TR/2002/WD-owl-guide-20021104/*)

The last point is particularly interesting not only because it marks the first good, solid application of the semantic Web activity onto another area of the W3C but because it also represents cooperation rather than a clash between WSDL and UDDI. The taxonomy (classification) of the Web service described in UDDI will form part of the service's ontology (semantics) in WSDL. Exactly how this will be achieved is best left to the experts, but a WSDL document will eventually describe the context in which a Web service should be used as well as the interface it exposes—and that's a powerful thing.

Schemas As the W3C's only XML-based interface definition language, Schemas appear to have a secure role in the WSA that will remain so for quite a while. The first working draft of WSDL 1.2 provides for the use of RELAX NG documents and document type definitions (DTDs) in addition to Schemas, but more for convenience than anything else.

More interesting perhaps are the extensions to the Schema specification beyond the updates to match the latest version of XML. Schematron (*http://xml.ascc.net/xml/resource/schematron/schematron.html*), for example, allows you to put comparison constraints on the elements of a SOAP message in addition to the structure and strong typing that Schemas allow. You saw in Chapter 10 that you can accommodate that kind of constraint as a SOAP extension, but it would be far more powerful as a mandatory part of the WSA. An adjunct standard, perhaps?

Publishing and Discovery

The discovery agencies stack (shown in Figure 16-4) is in a completely different situation from the wire and discovery stacks in that no single component of the stack is yet accommodated by an actual standard.

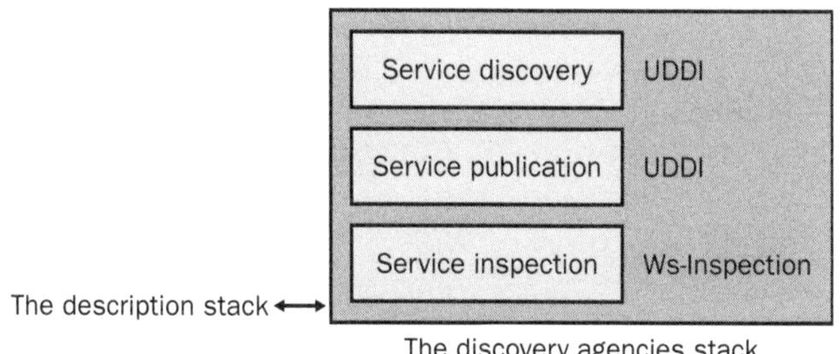

Figure 16-4 The current implementation of the discovery agencies stack is almost completely dependent on UDDI.

UDDI UDDI 3.0 was released in July 2002 by the UDDI Project (*http://www.uddi.org*) and subsequently handed over to OASIS (*http://www.oasis-open.org*) for standardization. Its adoption has been a little slow, even though compared to earlier versions UDDI 3.0 offers better integration with other standards and provides for private UDDI registries. Version 3.0 has grown a great deal compared with version 2.0 (11 APIs instead of 3), but most of the growth is related to interdirectory communication and handling the distribution of the registry between the three root directories. Version 3.0 does provide explicitly for private UDDI servers, but small local servers such as the new UDDI Server in Windows 2003 Server don't need the complexity of UDDI 3.0, which is why Windows 2003 Server supports only versions 1.0 and 2.0 of the UDDI API. You might not be surprised to learn that OASIS is working to make version 2.0 a standard first rather than version 3.0.

Discovery technologies can only ever be reactive to technologies in the description stack because their main purpose is to direct a user to the location of a service's description. A lot can be done to improve the publishing mechanism, security, and directory services of UDDI registries, but the standard itself will always need to be in line with the latest version of WSDL, WS-Data, or whatever the description is at the time. The W3C itself might be finished by 2004, but OASIS will probably work with UDDI for quite some time after. Just as the W3C is starting to look at the addition of semantic syntax to WSDL, so too will OASIS need to acknowledge that sooner or later users will want to scope out the intention of a service from a UDDI registry as well as its concrete details.

WS-Inspection WS-Inspection has been around since November 2001, but even though Microsoft created it with IBM, it hasn't paid much attention to WS-Inspection until recently, preferring to stick with the DISCO mechanism to browse for service descriptions on a network. IBM, meanwhile, handed over its Java implementation of WS-Inspection, WSIL4J, to the Apache group; it is now part of Apache Axis.

Essentially the next generation of DISCO, WS-Inspection sits on top of a network and draws into one predetermined place entries for the various services and their descriptions resident on a server or network. Microsoft will include WS-Inspection as part of its Web Services Enhancements (WSE) for Microsoft .NET download at some point to mirror its inclusion in the WS-* Interop group of specifications.

You can find out more about WS-Inspection at *http://msdn.microsoft.com/library/en-us/dnglobspec/html/wsinspecspecindex.asp*.

Users on the discovery stack It seems a bit inconsistent that the technology in the discovery stack is more advanced than that in the description stack if one relies on the other. How can the developers of WSDL just be figuring out what WSDL should do exactly while the UDDI Project already has a clear idea? If the aim of UDDI is to present a way to publicize and locate services' WSDL documents, why isn't it doing so? Ignoring the many hundred entries for "Hello World" services, the four root UDDI servers contain many times more entries for services than they do the WSDL documents for those services. Why? Because although the UDDI Project might know where it's going, service developers are more at ease with WSDL than they are with publishing information on a UDDI server. It would seem that the developers of UDDI need to talk more with the WSDL team, figure out which technology needs to do what, and then figure out how to get the service developers to do what they should—publish their WSDL documents on the UDDI server as part of the service's entry in the UDDI directory.

The Extended Architecture

As its name would suggest, the Extended Web Services Architecture strives to provide the functionality that developers expect from a mature distributed architecture framework. Implementing the basic architecture just gets the system up and running across the wire, but it's the pieces that bolt on top of it that make for a great system that people want to use. (See Figure 16-5.)

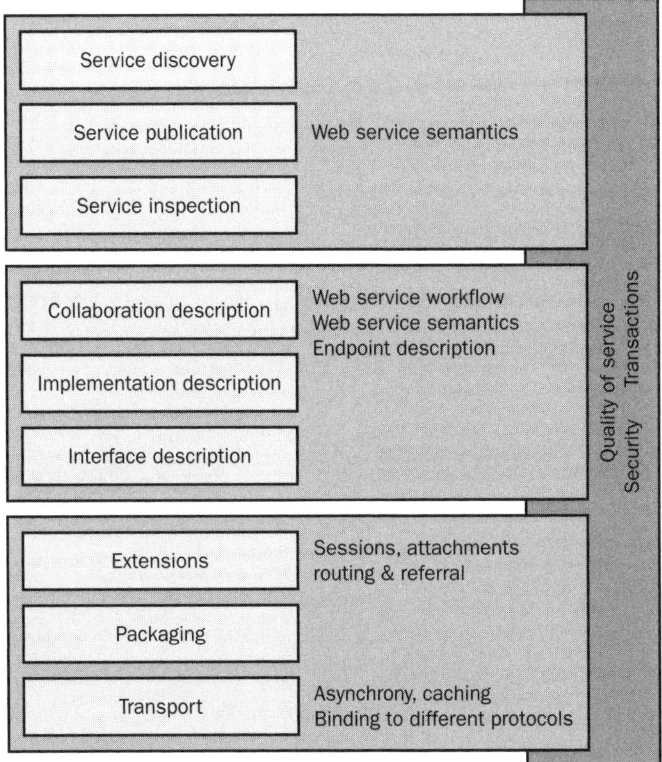

Figure 16-5 The Extended Web Services Architecture

The present WSA draft gives a partial list of the features that should be incorporated into Web services operations. These and several other features can be divided into two groups. The first group includes features that can be implemented within the operation stacks of the basic architecture:

- Asynchronous messaging
- Adding attachments to your messages
- Caching

- Binding to different protocols
- Sending messages via intermediaries
- Making Web services stateful within their parent application
- Cooperation between (the orchestration of) Web services

The second group consists of features that apply to every layer of the WSA:

- Security
- Transactions
- Quality of service

Web service developers with access to the .NET Framework and the Web Service Enhancements add-on pack for .NET already have access to some of these features, to one degree or another (as covered in Chapters 12 and 13).

Of course, Microsoft isn't the only one looking at the concepts and tasks to implement in the extended architecture. IBM/OASIS, Sun, and Hewlett-Packard have their own equivalents of the WS-* Interop initiative, but to keep confusion to a minimum, we'll concentrate solely on the W3C and Microsoft. If you're curious what the others are doing, check out *http://www.zapthink.com/reports/poster.html* or *http://webservices.xml.com/pub/a/ws/2002/01/09/soap.html* for a round-up and *http://www.xml.com/2003/02/12/deviant.html* for an overall view.

Wire Stack Extensions

SOAP was designed to be simple and extensible, and almost all the stack-specific extensions to the WSA shown earlier in Figure 16-5 are based on either the bindings of SOAP to protocols other than HTTP or the definitions of new features to be added in the SOAP *<header>* element.

HTTP remains the protocol of choice for communication over the Web, but in version 1.2 the SOAP standard for the first time explicitly states that it is independent of any transport mechanism. Systems have of course already used SOAP messages across other protocols, but there's now an opportunity to lay out standards for binding SOAP across a variety of transports. The W3C is already working on a standard binding for SOAP over e-mail (*http://www.w3.org/TR/soap12-email*), giving us true asynchronous messaging in addition to the ability to use HTTP messaging asynchronously. It wouldn't be a surprise to see it bound formally to a P2P protocol, such as Jabber or Groove; several proprietary messaging systems such as Microsoft Message Queuing (MSMQ) or the MQSeries; or even multicast protocols such as User Datagram Protocol (UDP) in the future (especially if you could present some use cases for the existence of those bindings).

On the SOAP *<header>* front, meanwhile, the WS-* Interop initiative is already looking to accommodate the rest of the wire stack extensions (attachments, routing, referral, and sessions). Indeed, in Chapter 13, you saw how the WSE pack implements these extensions using SOAP header elements to store the necessary information to carry out the relevant tasks. The W3C is also developing a standard for adding attachments to messages (*http://www.w3.org/TR/SOAP-attachments*) that complements Direct Internet Message Encapsulation (DIME).

Combining Web Services

As we noted earlier, the basic WSA defines a third row of the discovery stack that covers the collaboration, or *orchestration*, of Web services—that is, the combination of two or more Web services at run time in a business process that's invisible to the user. Because the implementation of a Web service is regarded as a software module or component, it would seem natural to create more complex services by adding together simple ones.

A combination of Web services could play one of several roles. Intraenterprise Web services might collaborate to present a single Web service interface to the public. Optionally, Web services from different enterprises might collaborate to perform machine-to-machine or business-to-business transactions. Alternatively, a workflow manager might call each Web service in turn to participate in a business process.

Microsoft's Biztalk Server takes this latter approach using the XLang (*http://www.gotdotnet.com/team/xml_wsspecs/xlang-c/default.htm*) language to orchestrate interchanges between services. On the broader front, the W3C has begun to tackle this issue quite late in the day. With several orchestration languages in the works—Web Services Flow Language, Business Process Modeling Language, and XLang—the standards body's new Web Services Choreography Group will have a tough time reconciling the ideas of each effort into a cohesive standard to sit next to WSDL. Indeed, it might have a worse time trying to resolve the many intellectual property issues that it is sure to face for having appeared so late at the party. You can read more on the problems facing Web services orchestration at *http://www.infoworld.com/article/02/07/05/020708plweborch_1.html.*

Universal Issues

On all three stacks the WSA must address three important concerns at all levels—security, transactions, and quality of service. To be sure, these will not be the only overarching concerns, but they are currently the most evident. The key will be to make sure that each stack addresses these issues and that they can be integrated quickly and safely with any new concern or technology that is introduced to the WSA as a whole.

Security

As with any other interchange that occurs across a wire, one of the primary concerns with using Web services is how secure you can make them. Can a SOAP message be kept confidential, its sender be authenticated, its security level be expressed, and its integrity be checked at the end of its journey? We've already spent a chapter looking at the various APIs and specs in the WS-* Interop group that deal with security, so here we'll just note two more points:

- No single security solution currently covers every aspect of the basic Web Services Architecture. For example, WS-Security covers how to send keys and encrypt with them but doesn't cover key exchange or maintenance. It is possible to implement the W3C's own XML Key Management System in ASP.NET, however (*http://msdn.microsoft.com/library/en-us/dnaspp/html/implementingxkms.asp*).
- Every new feature introduced in the extended architecture will likely require new security measures. For example, if you get two Web services to collaborate, how do you ensure that the request message and the response message remain secure as they're passed between the two? You would have to either make sure the collaboration language agrees with the security language or rewrite the security mechanism to account for the collaboration.

Transactions

You've learned in the course of this book that in .NET, Web services can take part in a transaction only as the root of a new transaction. If one transactional Web method calls another, each takes part in its own transaction. That's the current situation. The feature set for the extended WSA includes both session support and Web service collaboration, so transactions can potentially extend across Web services and perhaps even across applications. How to accommodate such long-running transactions—in particular, how to store the extended and distributed rollback information—is yet to be established. WS-* Interop includes WS-Transaction (which sits in the WS-Coordination framework), which starts to address this, but WS-Transaction and WS-Coordination haven't been implemented as part of WSE. Both are still in early development.

Quality of Service

Quality of service at a messaging level refers to the ability to send a message exactly as given and to send it only once to the given recipient and send an error back if this is not possible. Current efforts in this field include:

- Using Reliable HTTP as the underlying transport protocol (as discussed earlier) to provide for some measurement of the message's arrival and the communication of that measurement in the request/response headers
- IBM's Web Service Endpoint Language, which aims to provide an XML format for handling endpoint management, including quality of service, usage, and security characteristics to include in SOAP headers

Quality of service also implies that a server and its services guarantee a certain level of service. Web services must be able to specify dispute resolution authorities, provide references, perhaps even employ distributed reputation systems, and specify legally binding guarantees of service. The OASIS Web Services Reliable Messaging technical committee will be working on this (*http://www.oasis-open.org/committees/wsrm/*).

The March Toward Interoperability

As you can see, the house that SOAP built isn't quite the penthouse overlooking Central Park West just yet, but enough thought and effort is going into it that it should be quite something when it's finished. That is, if something else doesn't supercede it first.

In the meantime, a lot of developers and a lot of toolkits are trying to live under the one roof. True interoperability is (or at least should be) the focus of all Web service toolkits today, but most of them just don't work well together yet. A great deal of tweaking is inevitably required to get a service working against them all. Having standards helps a lot, but toolkit developers continue to find different ways to interpret them and, of course, they're always trying to include unique selling points in their kits that don't actually make the services created with those toolkits any more compatible with other kits or with services created elsewhere. .NET uniquely defines a documentation request type—for example, a GET request with no query string. Will Web service toolkits ever implement a single set of common functionality?

The efforts to improve Web service interoperability across the board include

- The SOAPBuilders community (*http://www.soapbuilders.org*), a project to get every platform and toolkit working with the others while adhering to ratified standards. It's worth noting that after three years, they're still trying to get SOAP encoding to reconcile across the board. More on this later.

- The Web Services Interoperability Organization (WS-I), an independent body that judges and guides toolkit vendors in their implementations of the standards. It has issued a document that outlines criteria for toolkits, along the lines of the WSA draft from the W3C. This Basic Profile document was released as a working draft in October 2002. You can find it at *http://www.ws-i.org/Profiles/Basic/2002-10/BasicProfile-1.0-WGD.htm.*

We're making an issue of this lack of compatibility between platforms because it is truly widespread—across every layer of the wire and description stacks. Here are some of the affected areas:

- **Transport layer** The SOAPAction HTTP header is mandatory, and its value must be surrounded by quotes, according to SOAP 1.1. However, some toolkits can't actually create the header or leave off the quotes.
- **Packaging layer** Some toolkits don't check for or even register the SOAP mustUnderstand header.
- **Interface definition layer** Different toolkits support different versions and different pieces of the Schema spec. The .NET serializer, for example, has a few problems with substitution groups.
- **Implementation description** Only a few toolkits support both doc/literal and RPC/encoded-style messages, and those do not all do it in the same way. Also, different toolkits generate different WSDL documents given the same service, and these documents must be altered before they are usable by a different toolkit. For example, wsdl.exe includes entries for HTTP-GET requests in .NET WSDL documents, which mean nothing to other toolkits.
- **Extended WSA** Each vendor's toolkit supports only its own solutions to its own problems.

Solutions

Some of these problems can be fixed by adhering to new standards as they come in, but a lot more might be solved by developers coming to the same conclusions about Web service development and changing their practices accordingly. Paying more attention to groups such as the WS-I and SOAPBuilders will definitely help.

A Freezing of Standards?

If organizations such as the WS-I are to succeed, they'll need a stable base from which to work, so why not freeze the standards that represent the basic architecture once they come in line with SOAP 1.2? That gives the ones lagging behind (WSDL 1.2, UDDI) time to catch up and the toolkit developers time to liaise with each other and with interoperability groups to sort out issues. A time to stand back and collaborate is overdue; the various standards groups need this, and the WS-I needs it to produce a standard worth more than the paper it's written on. Front-line developers could also focus on interoperation rather than stack alignment and marshaling details.

An interesting parallel exists here between WS-I and the Linux Standard Base (LSB) project (*http://www.linuxbase.org/*). The headache that LSB set out to alleviate was the increasing divergence in the content of the various Linux distributions that users can download (Red Hat, SuSe, Debian, and so on). A lot of extra effort was needed to accommodate new libraries and applications into the various distributions because they did not all contain the same compilers, graphics libraries, and so on. The LSB provided a reference set of packages for distributions to include. What's interesting is that the various distributors saw the wisdom of adhering to the base and adopted it accordingly. Who's to say that when the WSA or the WS-I's base profile becomes a standard that vendors will adhere to them? If real collaboration is involved, there's no reason why they wouldn't. The effort required to talk it out would be outweighed by the value produced.

Coding Practices

Meanwhile, we developers still have to produce the cross-platform applications we've told the managers we can build, and that won't get any easier unless we start following standard practices. DeveloperWorks has a nice set of articles identifying scenarios that best fit Web services (*http://www-106.ibm.com/developerworks/webservices/library/ws-bestcol.html*), but once you've realized that Web services are the way forward, where do you begin?

The .NET developer who just wants to create some private Web services for use internally can start off by adding the *[WebMethod]* attribute to a class method. A conscientious developer who doesn't know what type of clients his Web service will attract has to start off with designing request and response messages, and that means writing a schema. Using an operating system–independent type system means that you can at least start off without any type clashes in your messages even if the data types contained within them are deserialized in slightly different ways. In .NET, that means using single-dimension arrays and avoiding datasets, using complex types defined by *sequence* or *all* and avoiding those defined by *choice*, and definitely avoiding substitution groups and object graphs. Have a look again at Chapter 6 to see what the Schema type system and .NET agree on. You've already seen how to implement a schema validator as a handler or SOAPExtension, so we have the added bonus of being able to validate messages as they come in and discard those that aren't correct before they even finish their journey.

Once you design your schema, you need a WSDL document to wrap it in. All the toolkits can help you build a WSDL document around your service, but don't be afraid to look at the results. Working with a toolkit is great, but unless you know what it's doing (or not doing) for you, you'll come to a screeching halt when you let it do too much. It's like just working in design mode in Microsoft FrontPage and never looking at the HTML behind it. Don't forget that you're designing with commonality in mind, and your toolkit is writing your WSDL with just itself in mind. You might need to edit its efforts for the best results across the board. If you've had a good look at Chapter 3, you might even want to consider writing your own WSDL document from scratch.

One big difference among the WSDL produced by the various toolkits is the level of support the toolkits give to doc/literal and RPC/encoded-style messages. While it remains the default for some kits, RPC/encoded is quickly being recognized as a legacy style, supported for those who use Section 5 SOAP encoding. When SOAP 1.1 came out, most people saw SOAP as a simple RPC protocol that could easily work over the Internet with its firewalls and proxies. As a result, a rash of SOAP implementations mostly focused on RPC and on using Section 5 encoded messages. However, it's become apparent that doc/literal is a better fit for SOAP messaging because you have full control over the format of the message payload through the use of schemas. You can even use schema validation as a security feature of sorts: the SOAP schema does allow anything to be placed in its *<body>* element, after all, even a virus or a Trojan horse.

There's also the argument that it seems almost impossible to get RPC/encoded services working across every toolkit; the SOAPBuilders community has been trying for three years without much success. General thinking has it that RPC/encoded messages will slowly disappear in favor of doc/literal.

The key to making your services interoperable is to adhere to the standards as much as possible. Pay attention to details in the plumbing specs, and know what your toolkit does and doesn't do.

Data-Oriented Design Practices

Beyond the quest for interoperability, you might want to match the way you design your Web service–powered applications with the way they will work, and not try to align the way they work with how you're used to building applications. Normal class design goes out the window because the only exposed methods in your Web service API will be the Web methods.

The whole Web service architecture revolves around messages, or, if you want to view those messages as XML, data. You might serialize that data into and from objects, but Web services are not about objects. We continue to ignore the fact. .NET is object-oriented while Web services are message- or data-oriented.

The theory goes that if we start to design and build in the correct fashion, the need to comply with and eradicate ambiguities in standards and implementations will grow. The WS-I can help a lot in providing some simple tips to start you down the right road:

- Design messages, not methods. Start with the schema for your message and work outward, but don't forget to keep things simple.
- Don't try to reinvent the wheel. SOAP messages are XML, so make use of the XML vocabularies and standards that already exist. For example, why bother writing your own schema for a SQL query when you can place an XQuery in the body of the message and use the .NET extension classes for XQuery to execute them? Similarly, over 500 XML vocabularies are available for the various vertical markets out there. Why make your own if one already exists and is used by others? (Check out *http://www.zapthink.com* for a list.) Finally, don't forget to look at what XHTML has to offer—it's one of the most flexible XML vocabularies out there.

XML remains the key to working in this new fashion. It's the basis for every piece of the W3C's reference architecture and is data-oriented. Of course .NET, C++, and Java are still object-oriented, so will we ever be able to distance ourselves from the object-oriented paradigm? A company called Clear Methods saw this particular problem and siphoned (pun intended) a new, data-oriented language called Water that was designed specifically for Web service-based application development (*http://www.waterlang.org*). True to the nature of the problem, it's even written in XML and can be validated with a schema. Water has been available since the beginning of 2002 and been well received by those up to the challenge. Given that it's backed by Java, there's still that question of translation between object-oriented and data-oriented code under the covers, but Microsoft will have to face this problem as well as it develops X# (*http://www.microsoft-watch.com/article2/1,4248,766199,00.asp*)—a .NET-based competitor for Water.

Summary

Web services are not a panacea for all the programming woes of the world, but they offer a basis for a new kind of software and a new way to design software. The fun part, which we're only starting to scratch at, is exactly how that software will work and be designed. Currently, the possibilities for Web services are understood only within the context of existing solutions. Enterprise Application Integration continues to be the main motivational force behind Web services, but it won't remain that way. It won't be allowed to be.

The question remains—what does the future hold? Microsoft is incorporating Web services into practically all its software, and IBM and Sun aren't too far behind. But where will the truly new leaps in software come from? Web services over P2P? Will XML become omnipresent and require its own coprocessor? Will SOAP (or XMLP) make HTTP obsolete and become a transport in its own right? We're looking forward to finding out.

Part IV

Appendixes

The XSD Simple Types

The XML Schema Definition (XSD) language allows you to assign a type to any element in a schema instance document. This type can be one of the 47 built-in types (conceptual, primitive, and derived) covered here or a custom type. Custom types are derived from one of the built-in types or another custom type.

This appendix defines the value spaces for all 47 built-in types in the XML Schema specification (*http://www.w3.org/TR/xmlschema-2/*) and explains how they are related to each other and how new types can be derived from them.

Conceptual Types

At the top of the XSD type hierarchy is the type *anyType*. Every type, simple or complex, derives from *anyType*. The simple type *anySimpleType*, which derives directly from *anyType*, is the base from which the remaining 45 simple types derive. Types that derive directly from *anySimpleType* are known as *primitive types*. All other types, simple and complex, are known as *derived types*. Figure A-1 shows the relationship among the XSD conceptual types.

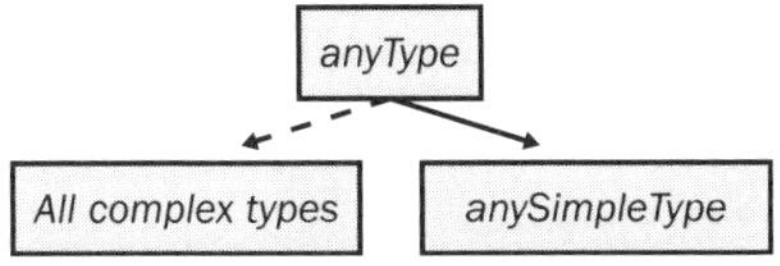

Figure A-1 The conceptual type hierarchy

Numeric Types

Numeric XSD types can be divided into primitive numeric types and derived numeric types. Figure A-2 shows the relationship among numeric types in the XSD type hierarchy, with the primitive numeric types appearing in ovals.

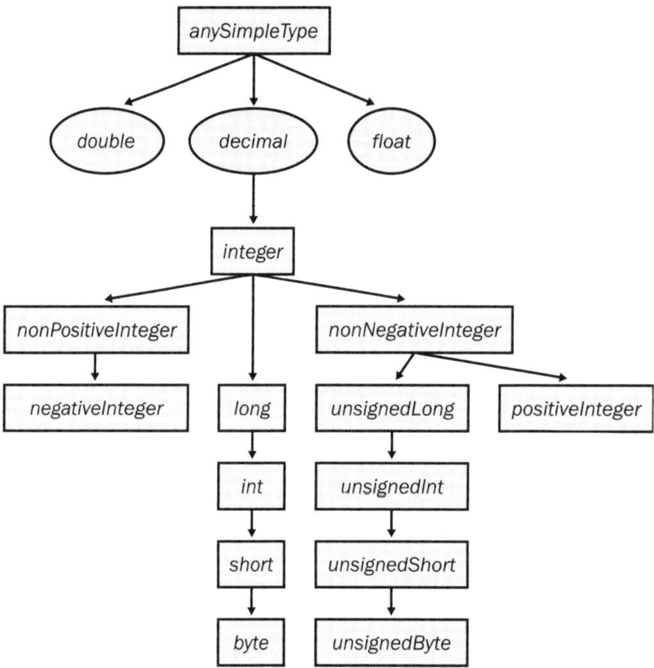

Figure A-2 The numeric type group; primitive types are in ovals.

Primitive Numeric Types

As you saw in Figure A-2, the primitive numeric types are *double*, *decimal*, and *float*. We'll look at each of these in some detail.

decimal

The *decimal* type represents the infinite set of all decimal numbers. It lexically covers all decimal numbers of finite length, optionally preceded by or trailed by any number of zeros. You can use + or – to indicate whether the number is positive or negative.

Base Type	Derived Type	SQL Server Type	.NET Type
anySimpleType	*integer*	*DECIMAL*	*System.Decimal*
Applicable Facets	*enumeration, fractionDigits, maxExclusive, minExclusive, maxInclusive, minInclusive, pattern, totalDigits, whiteSpace*		

Examples	`<dec>42</dec>`
	`<dec>+4567.8723</dec>`
	`<dec>-000023.2</dec>`		

double

The *double* type represents the set of Institute of Electrical and Electronics Engineers (IEEE) double-precision 64-bit floating-point numbers—the values from $+2^{53}\times2^{970}$ to 1×2^{-1075} and from -1×2^{-1075} to $-2^{53}\times2^{970}$. The *double* type also contains the values NaN, INF, 0, –0, –INF. The exponent section of the number should be represented with an uppercase E.

Base Type	Derived Type	SQL Server Type	.NET Type
anySimpleType	*None*	*FLOAT*	*System.Double*
Applicable Facets	*enumeration, maxExclusive, minExclusive, maxInclusive, minInclusive, pattern, whiteSpace*		

Examples	`<double>42</double>`
	`<double>4.5678723E3</double>`
	`<double>-000034.431000E-10</double>`		

float

The *float* type represents the set of IEEE single-precision 32-bit floating-point numbers—the values from $+2^{24}\times2^{104}$ to 1×2^{-149} and from -1×2^{-149} to $-2^{24}\times2^{104}$. Float also contains the values NaN, INF, 0, –0, –INF. The exponent section of the number should be represented with an uppercase E.

Base Type	Derived Type	SQL Server Type	.NET Type
anySimpleType	*None*	*REAL*	*System.Single*
Applicable Facets	*enumeration, maxExclusive, minExclusive, maxInclusive, minInclusive, pattern, whiteSpace*		

Examples	`<float>42</float>`
	`<float>4.5678723E3</float>`
	`<float>-000034.431000E-10</float>`		

Derived Numeric Types

Following are the rest of the numeric types.

integer

The *integer* type represents the infinite set of all decimal numbers that contain no digits after the decimal point. It lexically covers all integers of finite length, optionally preceded by any number of zeros. You can use + or – to indicate whether the number is positive or negative.

Base Type	Derived Type	SQL Server Type	.NET Type
decimal	*long, nonPositiveInteger, nonNegativeInteger*	*BIGINT*	*System.Decimal*
Applicable Facets	*enumeration, fractionDigits, maxExclusive, minExclusive, maxInclusive, minInclusive, pattern, totalDigits, whiteSpace*		

Examples	`<integer>42</integer>`
	`<integer>+4567</integer>`
	`<integer>-000023</integer>`		

long

The *long* type represents the set of all integers that can be stored as a signed integer in a 64-bit field—all integers between –9223372036854775808 and 9223372036854775807. You can use + or – to indicate whether the number is positive or negative.

Base Type	Derived Type	SQL Server Type	.NET Type
integer	*int*	*BIGINT*	*System.Int64*
Applicable Facets	*enumeration, fractionDigits, maxExclusive, minExclusive, maxInclusive, minInclusive, pattern, totalDigits, whiteSpace*		

Examples	`<long>0</long>`
	`<long>+123456789000</long>`
	`<long>-000023</long>`		

int

The *int* type represents the set of all integers that can be stored as a signed integer in a 32-bit field—all integers between 2147483647 and –2147483648. You can use + or – to indicate whether the number is positive or negative.

Base Type	Derived Type	SQL Server Type	.NET Type
long	*short*	*INT*	*System.Int32*
Applicable Facets	*enumeration, fractionDigits, maxExclusive, minExclusive, maxInclusive, minInclusive, pattern, totalDigits, whiteSpace*		

Examples	`<int>0</int>`
	`<int>+123456789</int>`
	`<int>-54</int>`		

short

The *short* type represents the set of all integers that can be stored as a signed integer in a 16-bit field—all integers between 32767 and –32768. You can use + or – to indicate whether the number is positive or negative.

Base Type	Derived Type	SQL Server Type	.NET Type
int	*byte*	*SMALLINT*	*System.Int16*
Applicable Facets	*enumeration, fractionDigits, maxExclusive, minExclusive, maxInclusive, minInclusive, pattern, totalDigits, whiteSpace*		

Examples	`<short>0</short>`
	`<short>+12345</short>`
	`<short>-54</short>`		

byte

The *byte* type represents the set of all integers that can be stored as a signed integer in a 8-bit field—all integers between 127 and –128. You can use + or – to indicate whether the number is positive or negative.

Base Type	Derived Type	SQL Server Type	.NET Type
short	*N/A*	*SMALLINT*	*System.SByte*
Applicable Facets	*enumeration, fractionDigits, maxExclusive, minExclusive, maxInclusive, minInclusive, pattern, totalDigits, whiteSpace*		

Examples	`<byte>0</byte>`
	`<byte>+123</byte>`
	`<byte>-54</byte>`		

nonPositiveInteger

The *nonPositiveInteger* type represents the infinite set of all integers between zero and negative infinity inclusive. It lexically covers all negative integers of finite length and zero, optionally preceded by any number of zeros.

Base Type	Derived Type	SQL Server Type	.NET Type
integer	*negativeInteger*	*BIGINT*	*System.Decimal*
Applicable Facets	*enumeration, fractionDigits, maxExclusive, minExclusive, maxInclusive, minInclusive, pattern, totalDigits, whiteSpace*		

Examples	`<npint>0</npint>`
	`<npint>-4567</npint>`
	`<npint>-000023</npint>`		

negativeInteger

The *negativeInteger* type represents the infinite set of all integers between -1 and negative infinity inclusive. It lexically covers all negative integers of finite length, optionally preceded by any number of zeros.

Base Type	Derived Type	SQL Server Type	.NET Type
nonPositiveInteger	N/A	*BIGINT*	*System.Decimal*
Applicable Facets	*enumeration, fractionDigits, maxExclusive, minExclusive, maxInclusive, minInclusive, pattern, totalDigits, whiteSpace*		
Examples	`<nint>-4567</nint>` `<nint>-000023</nint>`		

nonNegativeInteger

The *nonNegativeInteger* type represents the infinite set of all integers between zero and positive infinity inclusive. It lexically covers all positive integers of finite length and zero, optionally preceded by any number of zeros.

Base Type	Derived Type	SQL Server Type	.NET Type
integer	*positiveInteger, unsignedLong*	*BIGINT*	*System.Decimal*
Applicable Facets	*enumeration, fractionDigits, maxExclusive, minExclusive, maxInclusive, minInclusive, pattern, totalDigits, whiteSpace*		

Examples	`<nnint>0</nnint>`
	`<nnint>+4567</nnint>`
	`<nnint>000023</nnint>`		

positiveInteger

The *positiveInteger* type represents the infinite set of all integers between 1 and positive infinity inclusive. It lexically covers all positive integers of finite length, optionally preceded by any number of zeros. You can include a + sign.

Base Type	Derived Type	SQL Server Type	.NET Type
nonNegativeInteger	N/A	*BIGINT*	*System.Decimal*
Applicable Facets	*enumeration, fractionDigits, maxExclusive, minExclusive, maxInclusive, minInclusive, pattern, totalDigits, whiteSpace*		
Examples	`<pint>+4567</pint>` `<pint>000023</pint>`		

unsignedLong

The *unsignedLong* type represents the set of all nonnegative integers that can be stored in a 64-bit field—all integers between 0 and +18446744073709551615.

Base Type	Derived Type	SQL Server Type	.NET Type
nonNegativeInteger	*unsignedInt*	N/A	*System.UInt64*
Applicable Facets	*enumeration, fractionDigits, maxExclusive, minExclusive, maxInclusive, minInclusive, pattern, totalDigits, whiteSpace*		

Examples	`<ulong>0</ulong>`
	`<ulong>+09876554321000</ulong>`
	`<ulong>000023</ulong>`		

unsignedInt

The *unsignedInt* type represents the set of all nonnegative integers that can be stored in a 32-bit field—all integers between 0 and +4294967295.

Base Type	Derived Type	SQL Server Type	.NET Type
unsignedLong	*unsignedShort*	*BIGINT*	*System.UInt32*
Applicable Facets	*enumeration, fractionDigits, maxExclusive, minExclusive, maxInclusive, minInclusive, pattern, totalDigits, whiteSpace*		

Examples	`<uint>0</uint>`
	`<uint>+098765543</uint>`
	`<uint>000023</uint>`		

unsignedShort

The *unsignedShort* type represents the set of all nonnegative integers that can be stored in a 16-bit field—all integers between 0 and +65535.

Base Type	Derived Type	SQL Server Type	.NET Type
unsignedInt	*unsignedByte*	*INT*	*System.UInt16*
Applicable Facets	*enumeration, fractionDigits, maxExclusive, minExclusive, maxInclusive, minInclusive, pattern, totalDigits, whiteSpace*		

Examples	`<ushort>0</ushort>`
	`<ushort>+9876</ushort>`
	`<ushort>000023</ushort>`		

unsignedByte

The *unsignedByte* type represents the set of all nonnegative integers that can be stored in an 8-bit field—all integers between 0 and +255.

Base Type	Derived Type	SQL Server Type	.NET Type
unsignedShort	N/A	*TINYINT*	*System.Byte*
Applicable Facets	*enumeration, fractionDigits, maxExclusive, minExclusive, maxInclusive, minInclusive, pattern, totalDigits, whiteSpace*		

Examples	`<ubyte>0</ubyte>`
	`<ubyte>+98</ubyte>`
	`<ubyte>000023</ubyte>`		

Date and Time Types

Figure A-3 shows the date and time types in the XSD type hierarchy. As you can see in the figure, all the date and time types are primitive types. Please note that all dates are expressed as dates in the Gregorian calendar.

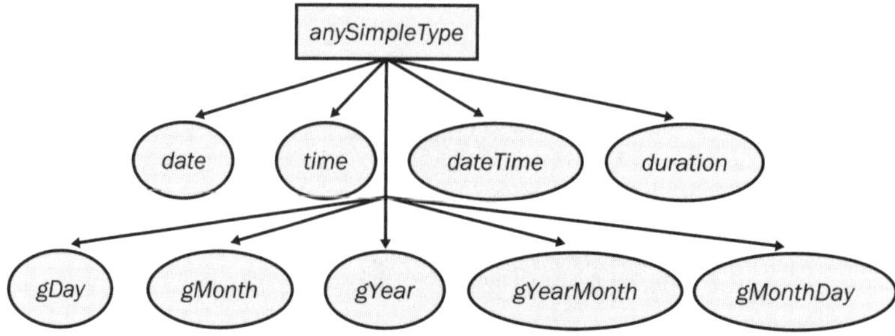

Figure A-3 The date and time type group contains only primitive types.

date

The *date* type represents a calendar date. It takes the form *YYYY-MM-DD*, where *YYYY*, *MM*, and *DD* represent the year, month, and day, respectively, of the date in question. You can add a time zone to the right of the date, expressed as a Z to indicate Coordinated Universal Time (UTC) or as the difference between local time and UTC.

Base Type	Derived Type	SQL Server Type	.NET Type
anySimpleType	N/A	*DATETIME*	*System.DateTime*
Applicable Facets	*enumeration, maxExclusive, minExclusive, maxInclusive, minInclusive, pattern, whiteSpace*		
Examples	`<date>2010-05-25+01:00</date>` `<date>2001-07-14</date>`		

dateTime

The *dateTime* type represents an instant in time given as a concatenation of a date and a time. It takes the form *YYYY-MM-DDThh:mm:ss*, where *T* is the separator between date and time, and *YYYY*, *MM*, *DD*, *hh*, *mm*, and *ss* represent the year, month, day, hour, minute, and second, respectively, of the instant in time. You can express the number of seconds by using a decimal fraction, and you can add a time zone to the right of the time, expressed as a Z to indicate UTC or as the difference between local time and UTC.

Base Type	Derived Type	SQL Server Type	.NET Type
anySimpleType	N/A	*DATETIME*	*System.DateTime*
Applicable Facets	*enumeration, maxExclusive, minExclusive, maxInclusive, minInclusive, pattern, whiteSpace*		
Examples	`<datim>2003-03-10T16:10:06+01:00</datim>` `<datim>1993-06-02T00:00:00</datim>`		

duration

The *duration* type represents a period of time written in accordance with ISO 8601. It takes the form *PnYnMnDTnHnMnS*, where *T* is the separator between date and time, and *nY*, *nM*, *nD*, *nH*, *nM*, and *nS* specify the number of years, months, days, hours, minutes, and seconds, respectively, in the period of time. If $n = 0$ for any of these units, the unit can be omitted as long as *P* and one unit of time are still present. If you're not using hours, minutes, or seconds, you can also omit the separator *T*.

Base Type	Derived Type	SQL Server Type	.NET Type
anySimpleType	N/A	N/A	*System.TimeSpan*
Applicable Facets	*enumeration, maxExclusive, minExclusive, maxInclusive, minInclusive, pattern, whiteSpace*		

Examples	`<dur>P1Y4M15DT9H7M15S/dur>`
	`<dur>P10DT8M</dur>`
	`<dur>P3M</dur>`		

gDay

The *gDay* type represents a specific day of the month. It takes the form ---*DD*. You can add a time zone to the right of the date, expressed as a Z to indicate UTC or as the difference between local time and UTC.

Base Type	Derived Type	SQL Server Type	.NET Type
anySimpleType	N/A	N/A	*System.DateTime*
Applicable Facets	*enumeration, maxExclusive, minExclusive, maxInclusive, minInclusive, pattern, whiteSpace*		
Examples	`<gD>---17</gD>` `<gD>---01Z</gD>`		

gMonth

The *gMonth* type represents a specific month of the year. The type's value takes the form --*MM*--. You can add a time zone to the right of the date, expressed as a Z to indicate UTC or as the difference between local time and UTC.

Base Type	Derived Type	SQL Server Type	.NET Type
anySimpleType	N/A	N/A	*System.DateTime*
Applicable Facets	*enumeration, maxExclusive, minExclusive, maxInclusive, minInclusive, pattern, whiteSpace*		
Examples	`<gM>--02--</gM>` `<gM>--01--+10:00</gM>`		

gMonthDay

The *gMonthDay* type represents a specific day in a specific month (that recurs annually). It takes the form --*MM-DD*, where *MM* and *DD* represent the month and day, respectively. You can add a time zone to the right of the date, expressed as a Z to indicate UTC or as the difference between local time and UTC.

Base Type	Derived Type	SQL Server Type	.NET Type
anySimpleType	N/A	N/A	*System.DateTime*
Applicable Facets	*enumeration, maxExclusive, minExclusive, maxInclusive, minInclusive, pattern, whiteSpace*		
Examples	`<gMD>--02-28</gMD>` `<gMD>--08-12-07:00</gMD>`		

gYearMonth

The *gYearMonth* type represents a specific month in a specific year. It takes the form *YYYY-MM*, where *YYYY* and *MM* represent the year and month in question, respectively. You can add a time zone to the right of the date, expressed as a Z to indicate UTC or as the difference between local time and UTC.

Base Type	Derived Type	SQL Server Type	.NET Type
anySimpleType	N/A	N/A	*System.DateTime*
Applicable Facets	*enumeration, maxExclusive, minExclusive, maxInclusive, minInclusive, pattern, whiteSpace*		
Examples	`<gYM>1976-06</gYM>` `<gYM>3001-09-13:00</gYM>`		

gYear

The *gYear* type represents a specific year. It takes the form *YYYY*, where *YYYY* represents the year in question. You can add a time zone to the right of the date, expressed as a Z to indicate UTC or as the difference between local time and UTC.

Base Type	Derived Type	SQL Server Type	.NET Type
anySimpleType	N/A	N/A	*System.DateTime*
Applicable Facets	*enumeration, maxExclusive, minExclusive, maxInclusive, minInclusive, pattern, whiteSpace*		
Examples	`<gYr>1876</gYr>` `<gYr>2061-07:00</gYM>`		

time

The *time* type represents a time of the day. It takes the form *hh:mm:ss*, where *hh*, *mm*, and *ss* represent the hour, minute and second, respectively, of the instant in time. You can express the number of milliseconds by adding a decimal fraction to the right of the time value, and you can add a time zone to the right of the time, expressed as a Z to indicate UTC or as the difference between local time and UTC.

Base Type	Derived Type	SQL Server Type	.NET Type
anySimpleType	N/A	N/A	*System.DateTime*
Applicable Facets	*enumeration, maxExclusive, minExclusive, maxInclusive, minInclusive, pattern, whiteSpace*		

Examples	`<time>12:00:00.00+03:00</time>`
	`<time>18:59:31.436-07:00</time>`
	`<time>09:30:42Z</time>`		

XML Types

The XML types group includes primitive and derived types that relate to XML document processing. Figure A-4 shows the XSD type hierarchy for this group. As you can see in the figure, all the primitive types appear in ovals.

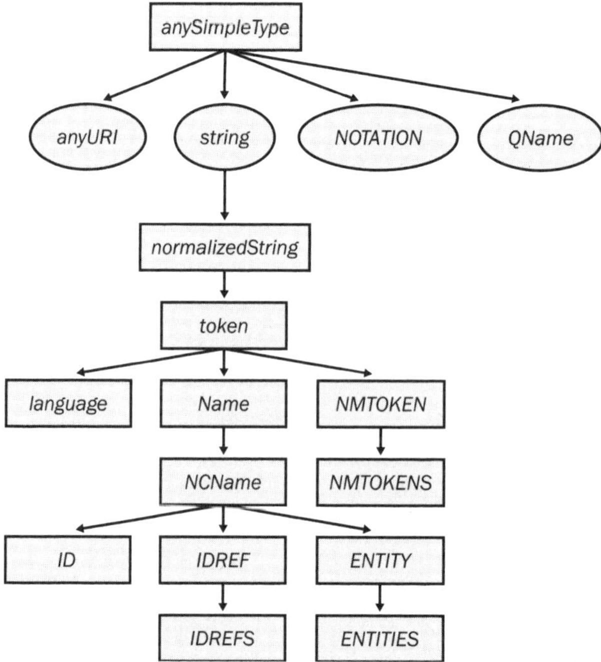

Figure A-4 The XML type group

Primitive XML Types

The primitive XML types are *anyURI*, *NOTATION*, *QName*, and *string*.

anyURI

The *anyURI* type represents the set of all URIs (which is the set of all URLs and URNs) written in accordance with RFCs 2396 and 2732. These can be relative or absolute and include a fragment identifier.

Base Type	Derived Type	SQL Server Type	.NET Type
anySimpleType	N/A	*VARCHAR*, *TEXT*, *NVARCHAR*, or *NTEXT*	*System.String*
Applicable Facets	*length*, *minLength*, *maxLength*, *pattern*, *enumeration*, *whiteSpace*		

Examples	`<uri>http://www.microsoft.com</uri>`
	`<uri>urn:uuid:4D36E96A-E325-11CE-BFC1-08002BE10318</uri>`
	`<uri>urn:notashop/wscr:AppA</uri>`		

NOTATION

The *NOTATION* type represents the XML 1.0 NOTATION type, which is used to identify the format of non-XML data. Note that the *NOTATION* type cannot be used directly in a schema. You must first derive a type from it using the enumeration facet and then use it only for attributes.

Base Type	Derived Type	SQL Server Type	.NET Type
anySimpleType	N/A	*VARCHAR*, *TEXT*, *NVARCHAR*, or *NTEXT*	*System.String*
Applicable Facets	*length*, *minLength*, *maxLength*, *pattern*, *enumeration*, *whiteSpace*		
Examples	See below		

```
<xs:simpleType name='mediaPlayers'>
  <xs:restriction base='xs:NOTATION'>
    <xs:enumeration value='wmp' />
    <xs:enumeration value='real' />
    <xs:enumeration value='qcd' />
  </xs:restriction>
</xs:simpleType>
```

QName

The *QName* type represents the set of all fully qualified names that comply with the Namespaces In XML specification. That is, they contain a namespace URI and a local name (an NCName), separated by a colon.

Base Type	Derived Type	SQL Server Type	.NET Type
anySimpleType	N/A	*VARCHAR*, *TEXT*, *NVARCHAR*, or *NTEXT*	*System.Xml. Xml-QualifiedName*
Applicable Facets	*length*, *minLength*, *maxLength*, *pattern*, *enumeration*, *whiteSpace*		
Examples	<QN>xsd:element</QN> <QN>wscr:alongunwieldyQName</QN>		

string

The *string* type represents all finite-length strings of Unicode characters (ISO-10646) that comply with the Char production in XML 1.0.

Base Type	Derived Type	SQL Server Type	.NET Type
anySimpleType	*normalizedString*	*VARCHAR*, *TEXT*, *NVARCHAR*, or *NTEXT*	*System.String*
Applicable Facets	*length*, *minLength*, *maxLength*, *pattern*, *enumeration*, *whiteSpace*		
Examples	<str>String</str> <str>99 Pink Elephants</str> <str>Wo ist Himbeerstraße?</str>		

Derived XML Types

normalizedString

The *normalizedString* type represents the set of all white space–normalized characters—that is, all strings that do not contain the carriage return (#xD), line feed (#xA), or tab (#x9) character. To normalize a string containing those characters, you replace those characters with spaces.

Base Type	Derived Type	SQL Server Type	.NET Type
string	*token*	*VARCHAR*, *TEXT*, *NVARCHAR*, or *NTEXT*	*System.String*
Applicable Facets	*enumeration*, *length*, *maxLength*, *minLength*, *pattern*, *whiteSpace*		
Examples	<nStr>no line feeds here</nStr> <nStr> pas de weiss spaces </nStr>		

token

The *token* type represents the set of all tokenized strings—all normalized strings (as just described) that have no internal sequence of two or more spaces and no leading or trailing spaces.

Base Type	Derived Type	SQL Server Type	.NET Type
normalizedString	*language*, *NMTOKEN*, *Name*	*VARCHAR*, *TEXT*, *NVARCHAR*, or *NTEXT*	*System.String*
Applicable Facets	*enumeration*, *length*, *maxLength*, *minLength*, *pattern*, *whiteSpace*		
Examples	`<tok>no extraneous spaces here</tok>` `<tok>pas de weiss spaces</tok>`		

language

The *language* type represents the set of all valid language identifiers as given in the XML 1.0 specification. This data type is usually used with attributes.

Base Type	Derived Type	SQL Server Type	.NET Type
token	N/A	*VARCHAR*, *TEXT*, *NVARCHAR*, or *NTEXT*	*System.String*
Applicable Facets	*enumeration*, *length*, *maxLength*, *minLength*, *pattern*, *whiteSpace*		
Examples	`<element lang = "en-GB"/>` `<element lang = "es" />`		

NMTOKEN

The *NMTOKEN* type represents the XML 1.0 NMTOKEN type—all literal values containing one or more of the following characters: a letter, digit, period, comma, underscore, or colon. *NMTOKEN* should be used only on attributes.

Base Type	Derived Type	SQL Server Type	.NET Type
token	*NMTOKENS*	*VARCHAR*, *TEXT*, *NVARCHAR*, or *NTEXT*	*System.String*
Applicable Facets	*enumeration*, *length*, *maxLength*, *minLength*, *pattern*, *whiteSpace*		
Examples	`<element NMT="token_of_some_sort" />` `<element NMT="but,with,no,spaces" />`		

NMTOKENS

The *NMTOKENS* type represents the XML 1.0 NMTOKENS type—all white space–separated lists of *NMTOKEN* values. *NMTOKENS* should be used only on attributes.

Base Type	Derived Type	SQL Server Type	.NET Type
NMTOKEN	N/A	N/A	*System.String[]*
Applicable Facets	*enumeration, length, maxLength, minLength, whiteSpace*		
Examples	<element NMTS="token of some sort" /> <element NMTS="nmtoken1 nmtoken2 nmtoken3" />		

Name

The *Name* type represents the set of all valid XML 1.0 Names.

Base Type	Derived Type	SQL Server Type	.NET Type
token	*NCName*	*VARCHAR, TEXT, NVARCHAR,* or *NTEXT*	*System.String*
Applicable Facets	*enumeration, length, maxLength, minLength, pattern, whiteSpace*		
Examples	<name>Whizzo_Chocolate</name> <name>asd:some.name</name>		

NCName

The *NCName* type represents the set of all valid XML 1.0 Names that do not contain colons. NCNames are most commonly used as local names for XML elements. NCName stands for *noncolonized name.*

Base Type	Derived Type	SQL Server Type	.NET Type
Name	*ID, IDREF, ENTITY*	*VARCHAR, TEXT, NVARCHAR,* or *NTEXT*	*System.String*
Applicable Facets	*enumeration, length, maxLength, minLength, pattern, whiteSpace*		
Examples	<NCN>Crunchy_Frog</NCN> <NCN>no.colons-here</NCN>		

ID

The *ID* type represents the XML *ID* attribute and the set of all strings that can be used as XML element IDs. This is the set of all valid NCNames.

Base Type	Derived Type	SQL Server Type	.NET Type
NCName	N/A	*VARCHAR, TEXT, NVARCHAR,* or *NTEXT*	*System.String*
Applicable Facets	*enumeration, length, maxLength, minLength, pattern, whiteSpace*		
Examples	<ID>Viking-spam</ID> <ID>Calendar_Header_1</ID>		

IDREF

The *IDREF* type represents the XML *IDREF* attribute and the set of all strings that can be used as XML element IDs. An XML *IDREF* must match an ID value elsewhere in the same XML document and should be used only as an attribute value. This schema type set is the set of all valid NCNames.

Base Type	Derived Type	SQL Server Type	.NET Type
NCName	*IDREF*	*VARCHAR*, *TEXT*, *NVARCHAR*, or *NTEXT*	*System.String*
Applicable Facets	*enumeration*, *length*, *maxLength*, *minLength*, *pattern*, *whiteSpace*		
Examples	`<a ref="Viking-spam" />` `<a ref="Calendar_Header_1" />`		

IDREFS

The *IDREFS* type represents the XML *IDREFS* attribute and the set of all finite, nonzero-length space-delimited lists of IDREF strings that can be used as XML element IDs. An XML IDREF must match an ID value elsewhere in the same XML document and should be used only as an attribute value.

Base Type	Derived Type	SQL Server Type	.NET Type
IDREF	N/A	N/A	*System.String[]*
Applicable Facets	*enumeration*, *length*, *maxLength*, *minLength*, *pattern*, *whiteSpace*		
Examples	`<a ref="Viking-spam spam_and_chips spam_sandwich" />` `<a ref="Calendar_Header_1 Calendar_Header_2" />`		

ENTITY

The *ENTITY* type represents the XML *ENTITY* attribute and the set of all strings that can be used as XML entities. The value given must match an unparsed *ENTITY* declared elsewhere in the document and should be used only as an attribute. This schema type set is the set of all valid NCNames.

Base Type	Derived Type	SQL Server Type	.NET Type
Name	*ENTITIES*	*VARCHAR*, *TEXT*, *NVARCHAR*, or *NTEXT*	*System.String*
Applicable Facets	*enumeration*, *length*, *maxLength*, *minLength*, *pattern*, *whiteSpace*		
Examples	`<something id="$Entity_value" />` `<something id="$chutzpah" />`		

ENTITIES

The *ENTITIES* type represents the XML *ENTITIES* attribute and the set of all finite, nonzero-length space-delimited lists of *ENTITY* strings that can be used as XML element IDs. An XML *ENTITY* must match an ID value elsewhere in the same XML document and should be used only as an attribute value.

Base Type	Derived Type	SQL Server Type	.NET Type
ENTITY	N/A	N/A	*System.String[]*
Applicable Facets	*enumeration, length, maxLength, minLength, pattern, whiteSpace*		
Examples	`<something id="$Entity_value margarine butter" />` `<something id="chutzpah bluster luck" />`		

Miscellaneous Types

The miscellaneous types group contains three primitive types: *base64Binary*, *boolean*, and *hexBinary*. Figure A-5 shows the relationship among these types in the XSD types hierarchy.

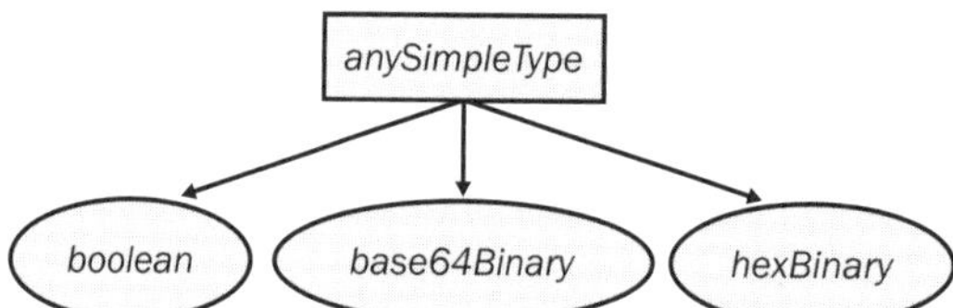

Figure A-5 The remaining three XSD built-in types are all primitive types.

base64Binary

The *base64Binary* type represents the set of all Base64-encoded data of up to infinite length where the entire binary stream must be encoded with Base64 Content-Transfer-Encoding as defined in Section 6.8 of RFC 2045. It lexically covers the set of all finite-length sequences of binary octets.

Base Type	Derived Type	SQL Server Type	.NET Type
anySimpleType	N/A	*BINARY, VARBINARY,* or *IMAGE*	*System.Byte[]*
Applicable Facets	*enumeration, length, maxLength, minLength, pattern, whiteSpace*		
Example	`<b64>0Ae5FTIw</b64>`		

boolean

The *boolean* type represents the set of values 1, 0, true, and false.

Base Type	Derived Type	SQL Server Type	.NET Type
anySimpleType	N/A	*BIT*	*System.Boolean*
Applicable Facets	*pattern, whiteSpace*		
Example	`<bool>true</bool>`		

hexBinary

The *hexBinary* type represents the set of all hex-encoded data of up to infinite length. It lexically covers the set of all finite-length sequences of binary octets. Note that uppercase is preferred when using the hex digits A to F.

Base Type	Derived Type	SQL Server Type	.NET Type
anySimpleType	N/A	*BINARY, VARBINARY*, or *IMAGE*	*System.Byte[]*
Applicable Facets	*enumeration, length, maxLength, minLength, pattern, whiteSpace*		
Example	`<hex>0A2CF9</hex>`		

B

Webliography

This appendix lists useful Web sites that focus on Web services and related issues, and it lists all the Web sites referenced in the book. The entries in the Web Service Development section are listed alphabetically. The entries in the chapter sections are listed in the order in which the links appear in the chapter.

Standards and Standards Bodies

- **World Wide Web Consortium (W3C)**
  http://www.w3.org/
- **W3C Web Services Group**
  http://www.w3.org/2002/ws/
- **Web Service Reference Architecture**
  http://www.w3.org/TR/ws-arch/
- **XML 1.0 specification**
  http://www.w3.org/XML/
- **Annotated XML 1.0 specification**
  http://www.xml.com/axml/testaxml.htm
- **XML Schema 1.0 Primer**
  http://www.w3.org/TR/xmlschema-0/
- **XML Schema 1.0 Structures**
  http://www.w3.org/TR/xmlschema-1/
- **XML Schema 1.0 (XSD) Datatypes**
  http://www.w3.org/TR/xmlschema-2/

- **SOAP 1.1 specification**
  http://www.w3.org/TR/SOAP/
- **SOAP 1.2 / XML Protocol Working Group**
  http://www.w3.org/2000/xp/Group/
- **WSDL 1.1 specification**
  http://www.w3.org/TR/wsdl
- **WSDL 1.2 Working Group**
  http://www.w3.org/2002/ws/desc/
- **W3C Web Services Choreography Group**
  http://www.w3.org/2002/ws/chor/
- **OASIS Open Standards Group**
  http://www.oasis-open.org/
- **UDDI 2.0 and UDDI 3.0 specifications**
  http://www.oasis-open.org/committees/uddi-spec/doc/tcspecs.htm
- **GXA / WS-* Interop specifications**
  http://msdn.microsoft.com/webservices/understanding/gxa/default.aspx

Web Service Development

- **Devx Web services articles**
  http://www.devx.com/dotnet/Door/10588
- **GotDotNet Web Services home page**
  http://www.gotdotnet.com/team/XMLwebservices/default.aspx
- **Hewlett-Packard Web services home page**
  http://devresource.hp.com/drc/topics/web_services.jsp
- **IBM developerWorks Web services zone**
  http://www-106.ibm.com/developerworks/webservices/
- **Microsoft Web Services Developer Center**
  http://msdn. microsoft.com/webservices/
- **O'Reilly Web services center**
  http://webservices.xml.com/
- **Remote Methods Web services directory**
  http://www.remotemethods.com/
- **Sun Java Web services home page**
  http://java.sun.com/webservices/

Sites Referenced in the Book

The following sites are referenced by URL in this book. URLs beginning with *http://localhost* are not included, nor are namespace URLs.

Introduction

- **The first Web service**
  http://philip.greenspun.com/WealthClock
- **Microsoft Web Services Developer Center**
  http://msdn. microsoft.com/webservices/
- **GotDotNet**
  http://www.gotdotnet.com
- **Visual Studio .NET Product trial and product requirements**
  http://msdn.microsoft.com/vstudio/productinfo/trial/default.asp
- **Visual Studio .NET home page**
  http://msdn.microsoft.com/vstudio/
- **ASP.NET Web Matrix development tool**
  http://www.asp.net/webmatrix/
- **Microsoft Press book support**
  http://www.microsoft.com/mspress/support
- **Microsoft Press Knowledge Base support**
  http://www.microsoft.com/mspress/support/search.asp
- **Home page for this book**
  http://www.microsoft.com/MSPress/books/6707.asp
- **Microsoft Support**
  http://support.microsoft.com

Chapter 1

- **XHTML 2.0 specification**
  http://www.w3c.org/TR/xhtml2
- **W3C XML Schema home page**
  http://www.w3.org/XML/Schema
- **ASP.NET home page**
  http://www.asp.net

- **Microsoft UDDI Registry**
  http://uddi.microsoft.com
- **IBM UDDI Registry**
  http://uddi.ibm.com

Chapter 2

- **Namespaces in XML 1.0**
  http://www.w3.org/TR/REC-xml-names/
- **SOAP 1.1 specification**
  http://www.w3.org/tr/soap
- **Latest version of SOAP 1.2**
  http://www.w3.org/2000/xp/Group/#soap12
- **The XML Infoset specification**
  http://www.w3.org/TR/xml-infoset/
- **TcpTrace proxy utility**
  http://www.pocketsoap.com/tcptrace/

Chapter 3

- **WSDL 1.1 specification**
  http://www.w3.org/TR/wsdl
- **W3C Web Services Description Working Group**
  http://www.w3.org/2002/ws/desc/

Chapter 4

- **Amazon Web services**
  http://www.amazon.com/webservices
- **Google Web API**
  http://www.google.com/apis
- **UDDI home site**
  http://www.uddi.org
- **OASIS home site**
  http://www.oasis-open.org
- **UDDI specifications**
  http://www.uddi.org/specification.html

- **Microsoft UDDI Registry**
  http://uddi.microsoft.com (and *http://test.uddi.microsoft.com*)
- **IBM UDDI Registry**
  https://uddi.ibm.com/ubr/registry.html
  (and *https://uddi.ibm.com/testregistry/registry.html*)
- **SAP UDDI Registry**
  http://uddi.sap.com (and *http://udditest. sap.com*)
- **NTT UDDI Registry**
  http://www.ntt.com/uddi
- **Dun & Bradstreet numbers**
  http://www.dnb.com
- **"Using WSDL in a UDDI Registry"**
  http://www.oasis-open.org/committees/uddi-spec/bps.shtml

Chapter 5

- **Soap 1.1 schema**
  http://schemas.xmlsoap.org/soap/envelope

Chapter 6

- **XML Schema 1.0 Structures**
  http://www.w3.org/TR/xmlschema-1/
- **XML Schema 1.0 (XSD) Datatypes**
  http://www.w3.org/TR/xmlschema-2/
- **Schematron .NET**
  http://sourceforge.net/projects/dotnetopensrc
- **"Understanding XML Schema"**
  http://msdn.microsoft.com/library/en-us/dnxml/html/understandxsd.asp

Chapter 7

- **WS-Inspection specification**
  http://msdn.microsoft.com/library/default.asp?url=/library/en-us/dnglobspec/html/ws-inspection.asp

Chapter 8

- **freedb.org**
  http://www.freedb.org
- **IBM's Web services qualification proposal**
  http://www-106.ibm.com/developerworks/webservices/library/ws-qual/?dwzone=webservices
- **Microsoft .NET Alerts**
  http://alerts.microsoft.com/Alerts/
- **Microsoft UDDI Services**
  http://uddi.microsoft.com
- **SOAP Toolkit download area**
  http://msdn.microsoft.com/library/default.asp?URL=/downloads/list/websrv.asp
- **Weather forecasting Web service from WebserviceX.NET**
  http://www.webservicex.net/usweather.asmx
- **WebserviceX.NET**
  http://www.webservicex.net

Chapter 9

- **W3C**
  http://www.w3.org
- **Aaron Skonnard's XML links**
  http://staff.develop.com/aarons/xmllinks.htm

Chapter 10

- **Newtelligence (good source for sample SOAP extensions)**
  http://www.newtelligence.com/
- **Soap Extension Wizard for Visual Studio .NET**
  http://www.newtelligence.com/downloads/SoapExtensionWizard-0-1.zip

Chapter 11

- **aspnet_setreg utility**
  http://download.microsoft.com/download/asp.net/Utility/1.0/WIN98MeXP/EN-US/Aspnet_setreg.exe

Chapter 12

- **Microsoft GXA home page**
  http://msdn.microsoft.com/webservices/understanding/gxa/default.aspx
- **DIME specification**
  http://www.ietf.org/internet-drafts/draft-nielsen-dime-02.txt
- **W3C XML Signature recommendation**
  http://www.w3.org/TR/2002/REC-xmldsig-core-20020212/
- **W3C XML Encryption Syntax and Processing recommendation**
  http://www.w3.org/TR/2002/REC-xmlenc-core-20020210/
- **OASIS WS-Security Technical Committee**
  http://www.oasis-open.org/committees/tc_home.php?wg_abbrev=wss

Chapter 13

- **Microsoft GXA home page**
  http://msdn.microsoft.com/webservices/understanding/gxa/default.aspx
- **Microsoft Web Service Enhancements home page**
  http://msdn.microsoft.com/webservices/building/wse/default.aspx
- **DIME specification**
  http://www.ietf.org/internet-drafts/draft-nielsen-dime-02.txt

Chapter 14

No references to URLs

Chapter 15

- **Platform SDK update (makecert tool)**
  http://www.microsoft.com/msdownload/platformsdk/sdkupdate/update.htm

Chapter 16

- **Web Service Reference Architecture**
  http://www.w3.org/TR/ws-arch/
- **XML 1.1 specification**
  http://www.w3.org/TR/xml11
- **Namespaces in XML 1.1 specification**
  http://www.w3.org/TR/xml-names11/

- **Issues between Unicode and XML**
  http://www.w3.org/TR/unicode-xml
- **HTTP Extension Framework**
  http://www.w3.org/Protocols/HTTP/ietf-http-ext/
- **W3C XML Protocol project (XMLP)**
  http://www.w3.org/2000/xp/Group/
- **Reliable HTTP**
  http://www-106.ibm.com/developerworks/library/ws-phtt
- **XML Infoset specification**
  http://www.w3.org/TR/xml-infoset/
- **"Is the XML Infoset Worth It?"**
  http://www.xml.com/pub/a/2002/11/20/ends.html
- **List of differences between SOAP 1.1 and SOAP 1.2**
  http://www.w3.org/TR/2002/CR-soap12-part0-20021219/#L4697
- **Web Ontology Guide (Semantic Web Activity)**
  http://www.w3.org/TR/2002/WD-owl-guide-20021104/
- **Schematron**
  http://xml.ascc.net/xml/resource/schematron/schematron.html
- **UDDI home site**
  http://www.uddi.org
- **OASIS home site**
  http://www.oasis-open.org
- **WS-Inspection**
  http://msdn.microsoft.com/library/en-us/dnglobspec/html /wsinspecspecindex.asp.
- **Summary of non-Microsoft efforts across the advanced Web service architecture**
  http://www.zapthink.com/reports/poster.html
  or *http://webservices.xml.com/pub/a/ws/2002/01/09/soap.html*
  or *http://www.xml.com/2003/02/12/deviant.html*
- **SOAP over e-mail specification**
  http://www.w3.org/TR/soap12-email
- **SOAP attachments specification**
  http://www.w3.org/TR/SOAP-attachments

- **XLang specification**
  http://www.gotdotnet.com/team/xml_wsspecs/xlang-c/default.htm
- **Web Service Orchestration issues**
  http://www.infoworld.com/article/02/07/05/ 020708plweborch_1.html
- **Implementing the W3C XML Key Management System in ASP.NET**
  http://msdn.microsoft.com/library/en-us/dnaspp/html/implementing xkms.asp
- **OASIS Web Services Reliable Messaging technical committee**
  http://www.oasis-open.org/committees/wsrm/
- **SOAPBuilders community**
  http://www.soapbuilders.org
- **WS-I Basic Profile**
  http://www.ws-i.org/Profiles/Basic/2002-10/BasicProfile-1.0-WGD.htm
- **Linux Standard Base project**
  http://www.linuxbase.org/
- **Web service scenarios**
  http://www-106.ibm.com/developerworks/webservices/library /ws-bestcol.html
- **Water language home page**
  http://www.waterlang.org
- **News of X#**
  http://www.microsoft-watch.com/article2/1,4248,766199,00.asp

C

Glossary

A

ASP.NET pipeline A construct hosted inside Microsoft Internet Information Services (IIS) that receives Web requests (including those for Web services) and returns appropriate responses.

authentication The process of determining who a user is, usually via a username and password combination.

authorization The process of determining whether a user has permission to perform a particular task.

B

Business Process Modeling Language (BPML) A draft standard for collaboration and interaction among Web services.

D

deserialization Conversion of a SOAP message into .NET objects and method calls.

Direct Internet Message Encapsulation (DIME) An Internet draft standard for the creation of multipart (SOAP) messages. DIME builds on the Multipurpose Internet Mail Extensions (MIME) specification.

DISCO *See* Microsoft Discovery (DISCO).

Document Type Definition (DTD) The first type of document to define a grammar for XML documents. DTDs are being made obsolete by XML Schemas.

dynamic discovery A system that allows IIS to find and catalog all the Web services on a server.

E

Enterprise Application Integration (EAI) Catch-all term for the integration of legacy applications, data, and systems into an enterprise's current system.

Enterprise UDDI Services The UDDI server that comes as part of Microsoft Windows Server 2003.

Extensible Markup Language (XML) An extensible markup language that allows you to create documents with structured content. XML is extensible because, unlike the fixed Hypertext Markup Language (HTML), it allows you to extend it to suit a wide variety of needs. Indeed, XML is a metalanguage that allows you to build your own markup languages for communicating structured content. XML is an application profile of the Standard Generalized Markup Language (SGML) defined by ISO 8879, which means, roughly speaking, that XML is a subset of SGML.

G

Global XML Web Services Architecture (GXA) A Microsoft and IBM initiative to create standards that build on the basic Web services architecture. Also known as the WS-* Interop initiative.

H

HTTP handler The endpoint for a request message in the ASP.NET pipeline. It processes the request and returns a response.

HTTP module An intermediary request-and-response processing unit in the ASP.NET pipeline. HTTP modules are the .NET equivalent of ISAPI filters.

Hypertext Markup Language (HTML) An Internet standard for creating Web pages.

Hypertext Transfer Protocol (HTTP) An Internet standard transport protocol. Currently used for sending almost all Web service requests and responses across the Internet.

M

machine.config A systemwide .NET configuration settings file.

metadata In the context of Web services, information about the Web service as a whole (contained in WSDL and UDDI) and the context of a message between service and client (contained in SOAP and HTTP headers).

Microsoft Discovery (DISCO) A Microsoft-only alternative to UDDI.

Multipurpose Internet Mail Extensions (MIME) An Internet standard that defines the format of a message and its contents. The MIME type for SOAP messages is currently *text/xml*, although the SOAP 1.2 standard suggests changing this to *application/soap*.

N

.NET Framework Microsoft's current platform for application development.

.NET My Services Microsoft's first attempt at a commercially available set of consumer-based Web services. It was withdrawn while still in beta in 2002.

R

Reliable HTTP An IBM implementation of HTTP that includes the reliability measures normally associated with messaging systems and some quality-of-service implementations.

remote procedure call (RPC) A call to a method on a different machine as the callee.

S

Schematron An extension for XML schemas that allows the user to create rules for elements in a SOAP message based on the actual contents of the message rather than just structure and type.

Section 5 encoding *See* SOAP encoding.

Security Assertion Markup Language (SAML) An XML-based Internet standard that provides a means of exchanging authentication and authorization information over the wire.

security token A structure that encapsulates the security credentials of a message transmitter. A security token is "signed" if it has been endorsed by a specific authority. (Examples include X509 certificates and Kerberos tickets). It is "unsigned" otherwise.

serialization Conversion of an object into text that is ready for transmission across the Web.

SOAP An Internet standard that describes the standard format of a message between a client and a Web service. Previously an acronym for Simple Object Access Protocol.

SOAP body The element of a SOAP message that contains the payload.

SOAP encoding SOAP's rules for serializing method calls, parameters, and results into text. SOAP encoding was created as a stopgap until XML Schema was completed as a standard. XML Schema is now rendering SOAP encoding obsolete. Also known as Section 5 encoding.

SOAP envelope The root element of a SOAP message.

SOAP extensions (1) SOAP adjunct specifications or Web services advanced architecture specifications that extend the use of the SOAP envelope by defining new SOAP header elements.

SOAP extensions (2) Reusable modules that can be attached to the default ASP.NET Web service handler.

SOAP header The element of a SOAP message that contains information (metadata) about the message.

SQLXML XML extensions for SQL Server. SQLXML is an API that allows you to retrieve XML directly from Microsoft SQL Server.

Standard Generalized Markup Language (SGML) A metalanguage that is used to define XML.

T

tempuri.org The default namespace given to ASP.NET Web services that have not been explicitly given their own namespace.

tModel A structure used in UDDI to create a technical fingerprint for each service entered in a UDDI business registry.

U

UDDI business registries The four root UDDI servers that maintain the worldwide list of Web services that are publicly available for use.

Unicode The universal character set.

Universal Discovery, Description, and Integration (UDDI) An Internet standard for the cataloging of Web services.

Universal Resource Identifier (URI) A short string that identifies a resource on the Web. Takes the forms of a URL or a URN.

V

Visual Studio .NET Microsoft's official development tool for .NET Framework applications.

W

web.config A virtual application–specific .NET configuration settings file.

Web Matrix A free development tool from the ASP.NET development team.

Web service A Web-based interface to some resource.

Web Service Endpoint Language (WSEL) IBM's standard for providing an XML format for handling endpoint management, including quality-of-service, usage, and security characteristics to include in SOAP headers.

Web Service Enhancements (WSE) Kit An add-on pack for .NET developers that provides a first, incomplete implementation of the GXA specifications.

Web Services Architecture (WSA) An Internet draft standard that outlines the (generic) needs of a Web services stack and how to implement them.

Web Services Description Language (WSDL) An Internet standard for describing the public interface of a Web service and its protocol bindings.

Web Services Flow Language (WSFL) An Internet draft standard for the description of Web services composition as part of a business process definition.

Web Services Interoperability Organization (WS-I) An Internet body dedicated to promoting the development of Web services that work on every platform.

World Wide Web Consortium (W3C) The Internet standards body that is responsible for most standards that make up the basic Web services stack.

WS-Addressing A GXA specification that provides a means of specifying endpoints and intermediaries for a SOAP message.

WS-Attachments The GXA name for DIME.

WS-Coordination A GXA specification for a framework in which Web services can work together.

wsdl.exe A command-line tool used to generate .NET classes for a Web service or a service's client, given the WSDL document for the service.

WS-Inspection A GXA specification that governs how Web service–related information should made be available to clients.

WS-* Interop initiative Another name for GXA.

WS-Policy A GXA specification for a framework in which a Web service can make its policies known. Includes WS-PolicyAssertions and WS-PolicyAttachment.

WS-Referral A GXA specification that provides for the redirection of a SOAP message to an endpoint by a third party.

WS-ReliableMessaging A GXA specification for a transport protocol that reliably transports messages between sender and target recipient even in the case of software or hardware failure.

WS-Routing A GXA specification for a SOAP header–based protocol that allows the routing of SOAP messages between client and server via several intermediary points.

WS-Security A GXA specification for securing Web services and the messages transmitted between client and server. Includes WS-Trust, WS-SecureConversation, and WS-SecurityPolicy.

WS-Timestamp A specification that provides for the inclusion of a timestamp in a SOAP message.

WS-Transaction A GXA specification built on the WS-Coordination framework to provide transactional support for Web service exchanges.

X

XHTML HTML rewritten as XML.

XLang A Microsoft XML-based language for orchestrating the interaction between Web services.

XML *See* Extensible Markup Language (XML).

XML DOM API The XML random access API in .NET.

XML Information Set (XML Infoset) An Internet standard containing a consistent set of definitions for use in other specifications that need to reference XML documents. A sort of glossary for referring to pieces of an XML document.

XML Key Management System (XKMS) An XML grammar used to enable public key interchange and thus secure communication between client and Web service.

XML Namespaces An Internet standard that allows you to distinguish your XML elements from other elements.

XML Protocol (XMLP) A prospective standard that defines a purely XML-based transport protocol that would replace HTTP and SOAP.

XML-RPC The original name for SOAP.

XML Schema The successor to DTDs. An Internet standard for defining and strong-typing XML grammars and documents. Contains the XSD type system.

XML Schema definition language (XSD) A language for defining the structure and data types for XML documents.

XML Schema Instance Documents XML documents written according to a given schema or set of schemas.

XML Streaming API The forward-only XML API in .NET.

XPath An Internet standard XML node selection syntax with a path-like structure.

XQuery An Internet standard XML equivalent of the SQL database query language.

xsd.exe A command-line tool used to generate .NET classes for a Web service from its schema, and vice versa.

Index

A

B

C

D

I

S

T

U

V

W

X

Y

Damien Foggon

Damien is a Web developer based in Newcastle (the Upon one not the Under one). After working for BT, he decided that big companies weren't for him and went to work for a dotcom at the end of the boom. After that enterprise went pear-shaped, he mucked around, reviewed a lot of books, cofounded Thing-E Ltd.—a Web development company based in London, and then decided that it was time to get a proper job. After two years of working his own hours, he finds it exceedingly difficult to get out of bed to start work on a morning, but it makes the weekends all the more pleasant.

Damien can be found online at *http://www.littlepond.co.uk*, but watch out for the big fish!

Daniel Maharry

Daniel Maharry is a freelance writer and editor who has, in no particular order, taught English, maths, and guitar; directed, crewed, acted in, and produced a few plays and short films; been a film and music columnist for four years; cofounded two Web sites (COMDeveloper.com and ASPToday.com); rewritten his own Web site several times (HMobius.com); opened an office in India; variously edited, reviewed and written pieces of more than 40 programming books; qualified as a sound engineer; and consumed enough caffeine in his lifetime to keep most of China awake for a week.

Occasionally, he sleeps. Sometimes.

Chris Ullman

Chris Ullman is a freelance Web developer and technical author, who has spent many years stewing in ASP/ASP.NET like a teabag left too long in the pot. Coming from a computer science background, he started as a UNIX/Linux guru, who gravitated toward Microsoft during the summer of ASP (1997). He cut his teeth on Wrox Press ASP guides, and since then he has written more than 20 books, most notably as lead author for Wrox's bestselling Beginning ASP/ASP.NET series. He also has contributed chapters to books on PHP, ColdFusion, JavaScript, Web Services, C#, XML, and other Internet-related technologies too esoteric to mention, now swallowed up in the quicksands of the dotcom boom.

Quitting Wrox in August 2001, he branched out into Visual Basic 6 programming and ASP development, maintaining a multitude of sites from *http://www.cuasp.co.uk*, his "work" site, to *http://www.atomicwise.com*, a selection of his writings on music and art. He now divides his time between being a human punchbag for his 20-month-old son Nye, playing keyboards in a psychedelic band, The Bee Men, and tutoring his cats in the art of peaceful coexistence, wherein they refrain from violently mugging each other on the stairs.

Karli Watson

Karli Watson is a freelance IT specialist, author, developer, and consultant. For the most part, he indulges in .NET and related technologies and has written numerous books about these. Occasionally, though, he has been known to cross the dark divide into the realm of WAP and Flash. In endeavors other than his technical writing, Karli is in the process of trying to get his first novel published, which doesn't have any computers in it at all. Karli is also a snowboarding enthusiast, although a bad landing resulted in ongoing back trouble. He is counting the days until he breaks through the critical fitness barrier and hits the powder once again.

If Karli ever appeared in a "Where's Waldo" picture, he'd be the one wearing brightly coloured clothes and eating a cheese fondue.